CASTE PRIDE

Praise for *Caste Pride*

'Manoj Mitta has written a superb and unsparing account of how the inherent violence of caste has been both perpetuated in new forms and challenged over the last two centuries. Drawing extensively on archival sources, Mitta weaves into one compelling narrative many crucial events during this period, highlighting not only well-known events but also relatively unknown aspects of these events, as well as many that are as yet unstudied or understudied even by scholars—the use of stocks for disprivileged castes, the Caste Disabilities Removal Act of 1850, the passing of the first-ever law against untouchability in 1926 at the initiative of R. Veerian, Ambedkar's crucial but little known role in a 1929 bill that sought to throw temples open to Dalits, the dilution of the 1955 Untouchability Offences Act despite Ambedkar's and Raman Velayudhan's warnings. In the process, he also rescues from obscurity many pivotal but now forgotten moments and actors. What makes Mitta's book all the more topical is that he often traces the unfolding of these events into our present. And while the book is addressed to a general audience, scholars too will find it an extraordinarily generative read, one that opens up new avenues for further exploration. As a narrative of the events that have made caste what it is today, this book is indispensable; there is simply no equivalent to it.'

– Ajay Skaria,
Professor of History, University of Minnesota

'The existing literature on caste scarcely presents the dynamics of caste reforms since early colonial times, and misses out on the contributions of many pioneers to the cause of the depressed classes. Manoj Mitta has focused on this unexplored and grossly understudied material, exploding many myths, restoring credit to some forgotten heroes and pointing out errors of facts and errors of judgements that crept into some hallowed studies on caste. With painstaking research into the debates that took place in courts, legislatures and governments over two centuries, he lucidly presents his observations, making them consumable by ordinary reader as well as sophisticated researcher. The book undoubtedly is an invaluable contribution to understanding the evolution of the Indian society along its defining dimension of caste.'

– Anand Teltumbde,
Scholar, Writer and Civil Rights Activist

'Studies of India's legal history have generally ignored the central aspect of it—caste. Manoj Mitta's book sheds light on the uneasy relationship between caste and law, i.e., how caste was strengthened by law; how constitutional law attempted to dilute the shackles of caste; how the force of caste tends to challenge and overcome legal mechanisms; and how there is a continuous contestation between caste and the constitutional conception of law. The book is also a key reflection on the British colonial administration's dual policy on caste: how it benefited from already entrenched laws of caste and supported the dominance of the oppressor castes, while also indirectly promoting an anti-caste assertion. Mitta also documents stories of several unsung individuals who invoked law to challenge the manifestations of caste, while exposing the adverse attitude of nationalist leaders towards solving the caste problem. He has unmasked how caste has been infiltrating supposedly neutral legal processes and institutions. This book adds to the literature on how India's oppressed castes have used the vocabulary and mechanisms of constitutional State structures in their struggles to annihilate caste.'

– Anurag Bhaskar,
Constitutional Scholar and Commentator

'This truly remarkable book analyses in a very nuanced manner how caste has—and has not—been reformed in India since the British Raj. The ambivalence of the British and of most of the governments which followed till today has resulted in the—reluctant—making of laws which are unevenly enforced, so much so that inter-caste marriages and access to temple remain purely theoretical for many groups, for instance. Even more importantly, Manoj Mitta shows that Dalits are still victims of caste violence and atrocities in spite of very progressive laws. This book, based on the meticulous study of dozens of pieces of legislation and an even larger number of case studies, bears testimony to the gap between the official principles of "the world's largest democracy" and their very limited implementation; a must read!'

– Christophe Jaffrelot,
Author of *Dr Ambedkar and Untouchability: Analysing and Fighting Caste*

'Manoj Mitta has written a fascinating and path-breaking book on caste in India. I urge every Indian to pick this up and read it. In this brilliant treatise, he holds a mirror to history, and we are shamed and shocked in turn at the horrifying violence of this oppressive system and the desperate steps made to maintain the structural status quo. The annihilation of caste is a conversation that all of us should be having, please throw this book at anyone who is not convinced. It is heavy enough to inflict injury, solid enough to precipitate a change of heart.'

– Meena Kandasamy, Poet and Novelist

'With telling detail and incisive argument, Manoj Mitta's *Caste Pride* offers a fresh and penetrating addition to the literature on India's caste system and on the country's remarkable effort to regulate and transform it.'

– Marc Galanter, Author of *Competing Equalities: Law and the Backward Classes in India*

'Manoj Mitta's painstakingly put together compendium of legal cases involving caste is an invaluable treasure trove of unknown and little-known facts. The cumulative impact of two centuries' worth of documentation on the legal life of caste is stunning. Though utterly accessible and fascinating, this is not light reading—it is an unexpectedly moving account that is both profoundly depressing and deeply inspiring. This book is a must read for anyone interested in the social history of caste, the legal system or the State in India. Scholars working in these areas owe Mr Mitta their heartfelt gratitude for the time and effort he has invested in putting it together.'

– Satish Deshpande, Professor,
Department of Sociology, University of Delhi

'This book is breathtaking: in scope, in research and in passion, in telling the story of the battles over thinking about equality and citizenship in a deeply iniquitous society where Manu occupies the streets, the home, the kitchen and the birth of children, and the Constitution is regarded as a document to be combated by the patriarchs of a caste-based Hindu society even today. It tells the story of the unsung men and women who had the courage to stand up to the monstrosity of caste by leading struggles over entry to streets, to temples, to the right to use water, to refuse the strictures on clothing based on caste, and the right to marry above or below the endogamous circles defined by tradition. The battles come alive as does the heartbreak of failed legislative attempts to reform Hindu society and the refusal to give up on the battles for reform. It is a story more than relevant today and is sure to be read and used widely, perhaps even by those who have battled against reform. The book is an archive as much as it is an analysis of the story of social reform and the heartbreak it entailed then as it does now for those who challenge the past. It is an archive that documents the birth pangs of a new order.'

– Uma Chakravarti,
Feminist Historian and Democratic Rights Activist

MANOJ MITTA

CASTE PRIDE

BATTLES FOR EQUALITY IN HINDU INDIA

context

First published by Context, an imprint of Westland Books, a division of Nasadiya Technologies Private Limited, in 2023

No. 269/2B, First Floor, 'Irai Arul', Vimalraj Street, Nethaji Nagar, Alapakkam Main Road, Maduravoyal, Chennai 600095

Westland, the Westland logo, Context and the Context logo are the trademarks of Nasadiya Technologies Private Limited, or its affiliates.

ISBN: 9789357762946

10 9 8 7 6 5 4 3

Typeset by SÜRYA, New Delhi
Printed at Parksons Graphics Pvt. Ltd

For Pragati, my first-born
and
my greatest learning experience

CONTENTS

V. IMPUNITY FOR VIOLENCE

STYLE NOTE

Based on legislative, judicial and government records going back two centuries, this book deals with terms that were constantly evolving, with denotations that were either distinct or interchangeable. Depending on the context, the term 'caste' denoted 'varna', the four-fold hierarchy of the Hindu scriptures, or the more familiar 'jati', which ostensibly came under one or the other of the varnas. In some contexts, 'jati' actually referred to a sub-caste, while 'varna' served as a substitute for caste.

The related concept of 'gotra' works inversely in relation to caste. As the principle of endogamy is central to jati, *inter*-caste marriage is what was—and largely still is—frowned upon. But in the case of gotra, the members of which are believed to have descended from a common male ancestor, it is the *intra*-gotra marriage that was traditionally forbidden.

Though the spellings of the four varnas tended to vary over time and across regions, the book tries to avoid confusion by using a standardised form wherever possible or necessary. Brahman and Brahmin, Rajpoot and Rajput, Sudra and Shudra are some examples. There are also variations in their adjectival form: Brahmanical or Brahminical.

The three elite varnas, Brahmins, Kshatriyas and Vaishyas, which alone had the prerogative to undergo upanayana, or the Hindu rite of passage, were collectively addressed in historical discussions by different terms: Traivarnika, twice-born varnas, Dwijas and regenerate castes. From the vast swathe of castes constituting Shudras, two castes figure repeatedly because of their valiant struggles to overcome social and religious disabilities. They are the Tamil-speaking Shanars or Nadars and the Malayalam-speaking Ezhavas or Thiyyas, both of whom were stigmatised because of their traditional occupation of toddy-tapping.

For all their graded inequalities in relation to each other, the castes of the four varnas are called 'Savarnas', which literally means those belonging to the varna system. The castes that fall below the varna system are called 'Avarnas'. The line between the more backward castes among Shudras and the Avarnas was, and remains, fuzzy. Though they had been treated as Avarna, Ezhavas and Nadars were among the rare castes that raised their status to Savarna, as evident from their current classification as 'Other Backward Classes'. As the most oppressed, Avarnas underwent several name changes and were referred to variously at different times. The more prominent among those terms were Chandala, Achhoot, Antyaj, Panchama, Atishudra, Untouchable, Suppressed Class, Depressed Class, polluting caste, Harijan, Scheduled Caste and Dalit. While the term 'Chandala' is now identified with the section of Avarnas who traditionally dealt with the disposal of corpses, the original scriptural reference was to the broader category of those born of the union between a Shudra male and a Brahmin female. Considered the most repugnant form of varna sankara, or the mixing of castes, such illicit relations were linked to the origins of untouchability.

I use the term 'untouchables' in the matter-of-fact—indeed, insurgent—sense in which B.R. Ambedkar continued to use it even after the formal emancipation of these castes.

The book also broadly reflects the official spellings of the names of people and places in use at the time. For instance, for what's regarded as the holiest of Hindu places, Benaras was its colonial-era spelling, and it became Banaras after Independence. Likewise, the spelling used by the most famous Hindu administrator of the nineteenth century was T. Madava Row, which posthumously became T. Madhava Rao.

LEGAL MILESTONES IN THE BATTLES AGAINST CASTE

- 1795: In a bid to win over upper castes, the East India Company exempts Benaras Brahmins from the death penalty.
- 1816: For dealing with minor offences, the Company imposes on lower castes in Madras a barbaric form of punishment called 'confinement in the stocks'.
- 1817: In a policy change, the Company restores the option of imposing the death penalty on Benaras Brahmins.
- 1829: Defying the clout of upper castes, William Bentinck abolishes Sati, enacting a law to the effect that, whether the sacrifice of a Hindu widow is voluntary or forced, those who abet it shall be deemed guilty of 'culpable homicide'. Aggravated cases involving coercion invoke the death penalty.
- 1850: Protecting the inheritance rights of any Hindu who is 'deprived of caste', Lord Dalhousie enacts the first-ever national law on caste disabilities.
- 1855: The London-based Privy Council upholds the claim of Rajputs to the varna status of Kshatriyas, thereby rejecting the Brahmin theory that they had all been annihilated by Parashurama.
- 1858: The dewan of Travancore, T. Madava Row, forbids low-caste women from covering their breasts in public.
- 1859: Under colonial pressure, Madava Row allows low-caste women to cover their breasts, but with the caveat that they avoid the style of their upper-caste counterparts.
- 1862: Appeasing the sentiments of upper castes, the British Raj reduces the Sati offence to abetment of suicide.

- 1868: Adjudicating the validity of an adoption in a zamindar's family, the Privy Council lays down the far-reaching principle that, for Hindus, local custom would outweigh even the Shastras.
- 1887: Madava Row becomes the founding president of the Indian National Social Conference, which was set up by M.G. Ranade to bring about social reforms.
- 1890: In the context of the reformist Satyashodhak marriage developed by Jotiba Phule, the Bombay High Court rules that the local priest is not entitled to fees if Brahminical rituals have been eschewed.
- 1890: The Allahabad High Court holds that Kayasthas in the Hindi heartland are Kshatriyas, although their counterparts in Bengal are considered Shudras.
- 1898: As a judge of the Bombay High Court, M.G. Ranade rejects the Brahmin claim that Vaishyas are extinct.
- 1908: In a landmark verdict disallowing low-caste members from entering a temple, the Privy Court holds that temple trustees are guilty of a breach of trust if they allow any deviation from the temple's customary restrictions.
- 1913: The Allahabad High Court dismisses Motilal Nehru's defence of the Sati-accused who pleaded spontaneous combustion of the funeral pyre.
- 1916: Maneckji Dadabhoy breaks the silence in the Imperial Legislative Council on untouchability, forcing the Raj to initiate special measures for the amelioration of its victims.
- 1918: In a first, Vithalbhai Patel introduces a bill proposing inter-caste marriage within the Hindu framework.
- 1919: Under pressure from upper-caste legislators, the Raj repeals the special punishment that was in force for over a hundred years in Madras for lower castes in the form of confinement in the stocks.
- 1919: In Madras, M.C. Rajah becomes India's first legislator from among untouchables, and then debates with the governor who appointed him on the need to let his brethren access public amenities.

- 1920: The Mahatma Gandhi-dominated Nagpur session of the Indian National Congress calls upon 'the leading Hindus to settle all disputes between Brahmins and non-Brahmins ... and to make a special effort to rid Hinduism of the reproach of untouchability'.
- 1921: Following the Montagu–Chelmsford reforms, the Raj introduces quotas for non-Brahmins, including untouchables, in provincial legislatures, most generously in Madras.
- 1922: Presenting segregation as an option, the Congress Working Committee resolves that 'where the prejudice against the untouchables is still strong in places ... separate wells must be maintained out of Congress funds'.
- 1923: The Bombay Legislative Council adopts S.K. Bole's resolution to let untouchables access a range of public places, including watering places.
- 1924: The Madras Legislative Council adopts R. Srinivasan's resolution on the access issue, leading to a violent backlash from Palghat Brahmins as low-caste members enter their neighbourhood in Malabar's Kalpathy during a festival.
- 1926: On the bill of R. Veerian, an untouchable, the Madras Legislative Council passes the first-ever legislation in the country against untouchability, although as an amendment to a local-body law. Viceroy Irwin pushes Governor Goschen to give his assent to the enactment.
- 1926: The Bombay Legislative Council comes up with the Joshi Act, disentitling the local priest from claiming fees for a wedding without Brahminical rituals.
- 1927: In line with the Bole Resolution, the newly nominated legislator in Bombay, B.R. Ambedkar, leads the historic Mahad Satyagraha for untouchables to draw water from a public tank.
- 1928: The Bombay High Court rules that Marathas are either Kshatriyas, if they belong to certain elite families, or Shudras, who comprise the majority of that community.
- 1929: Ambedkar drafts what becomes the first national bill against untouchability, seeking to overcome the legal impediment to temple entry posed by the 1908 Privy Council decision.

- 1930: After M.R. Jayakar's abortive attempt, R.K. Shanmukham Chetty introduces the Ambedkar-drafted bill against untouchability in the national legislature.
- 1932: A day after the untouchables give up their right to a separate electorate through the Poona Pact, its caste Hindu signatories make a reciprocal gesture of declaring that the untouchables' right to access public amenities shall have 'statutory recognition at the first opportunity'. But this Gandhi-drafted resolution avoids the term 'right' in regard to temple entry.
- 1933: On the bill of G.A. Gavai, an untouchable, the Central Provinces Legislative Council passes the first stand-alone law in India specifically letting untouchables use public amenities.
- 1933: C.S. Ranga Iyer introduces in the national legislature the Gandhi-promoted temple-entry bill, which was designed to throw open only such temples, case by case, where the majority of local devotees had given their consent through a referendum.
- 1936: In a first anywhere in the country, Travancore Maharaja Chithira Thirunal issues a temple-entry proclamation declaring that there shall be 'no restriction placed on any Hindu, by birth or religion'.
- 1937: On the bill moved by N.B. Khare, India enacts its first inter-caste marriage law within the Hindu framework, though confined to the reformist Arya Samaj sect.
- 1938: On the bill piloted by M.C. Rajah, Madras acquires the second stand-alone law in India against untouchability in secular spaces.
- 1938: In a first in British India, Bombay enacts a temple-entry law, replacing Gandhi's formula of a referendum of local devotees with the opinion of the trustees on whether their temple was ready for the reform.
- 1939: Ambedkar's party blocks the Congress government in Bombay from pushing through a law on access to secular spaces due to the legislation's failure to make untouchability offences cognisable by the police.
- 1939: After trying for a referendum-based temple-entry law for the Malabar district alone, Rajaji encourages low-caste volunteers

to gatecrash the Madurai temple and then pushes through an indemnity law.

- 1946: Elevating untouchability to an offence that the police could book under, Bombay enacts a law on access equality that is more in tune with Ambedkar's approach—despite the rout of his party.
- 1946: On the bill of Gopalrao Deshmukh, India validates intra-gotra marriage under the Hindu law.
- 1947: Breaking new ground on temple entry, Madras enacts a law that replaces the local option with a general rights-based approach and introduces penalties for those blocking untouchables. Bombay follows with more stringent penalties.
- 1948: Amid slogans of 'Mahatma Gandhi ki jai', the Constituent Assembly adopts the clause abolishing untouchability, and this is despite opposition from Dakshayani Velayudhan, the sole female untouchable in that gathering.
- 1948: The intransigence of the trustee of the Jagannath temple at Puri forces Orissa to enact a law that throws open even a temple that is purportedly open only to a section of Hindus.
- 1948: Bombay incorporates the Orissa definition of temple to counter the exemption claimed by the Swaminarayan sect on the ground that their temples are open only to a section of Hindus.
- 1949: On the bill of Thakur Das Bhargava, India validates inter-caste marriage under the Hindu law.
- 1950: The abolition of untouchability comes into force with the constitutional stipulation for a national law defining and penalising various offences relating to the practice of untouchability.
- 1953: The Madras High Court invalidates the non-Brahminical form of Hindu marriage developed by Periyar.
- 1954: Kashi Vishwanath turns into a battleground for temple entry over issues ranging from whether Harijans could be allowed to enter through the main gate to whether they could be allowed, like other devotees, to touch the deity.

- 1955: Five years after the abolition of untouchability, India enacts the law meant to enforce it—without addressing most of the objections to the bill that Ambedkar had raised in Parliament.
- 1956: Bombay enacts a temple-entry law specially to counter the claim of the Swaminarayan Sampraday that, irrespective of caste, they are entitled to close their temples to everyone other than members of their own sect.
- 1959: In an election dispute, the Supreme Court dismisses V.V. Giri's claim that caste identity was no longer dependent on the accident of birth.
- 1966: Upholding the 1956 Bombay law, the Supreme Court rejects the claim of Swaminarayan followers that they are not Hindus, and rules that 'the true teachings of Hindu religion' are consistent with the constitutional object of throwing open temples to Harijans.
- 1967: The Annadurai government incorporates the Suyamariyadai, or self-respect form of marriage, in the Hindu law.
- 1968: In the first recorded instance of mob violence targeting Harijans, forty-two people, mostly women and children, are burnt alive in Kilvenmani in Madras state.
- 1969: In a review of the untouchability law, a parliamentary committee recommends the reforms suggested by Ambedkar in 1954.
- 1973: The Madras High Court exonerates all the accused of all the charges in the Kilvenmani case, saying that most of them are 'rich men', and therefore 'it is difficult to believe that they themselves walked bodily to the scene and set fire to houses'. Curiously, the High Court suppresses the crucial detail that the accused were tried for murder.
- 1976: Revamping the untouchability law, the Indira Gandhi government incorporates the recommendations Ambedkar made in 1954.
- 1977: A mob kills eleven people in Belchhi, including eight Harijans. The Morarji Desai government's attempt to portray it as a gang war rather than a caste atrocity is challenged by a

committee of Harijan MPs that visited Belchhi. The episode rose to prominence after Indira Gandhi's elephant ride to the remote area in pouring rain.

- 1982: In the Belchhi case, the Supreme Court upholds the death penalty for two of the convicted men, including the one found to have killed two Harijans.
- 1983: The hanging of Mahabir Mahto in the Belchhi case marks the first and only recorded instance in India of a killer of Harijans being judicially executed.
- 1987: Responding to the nation-wide outrage triggered by a case among Rajputs, the Rajiv Gandhi government elevates the practice of Sati to the status of murder and reintroduces the death penalty for abettors of the crime.
- 1989: In response to the escalation of untouchability, India enacts a stringent law focused on caste atrocities or violent crimes against Dalits.
- 1990: The Supreme Court upholds the acquittals of all the accused for the 1968 Kilvenmani massacre even as it unwittingly uncovers the High Court's suppression of the murder charge.
- 1991: Eight Dalits are hacked to death in Tsundur, Andhra Pradesh, making it the first case in which a special court is set up under the 1989 caste atrocities law.
- 1992: In its first adjudication under the 1976 untouchability law, the Supreme Court acknowledges impunity and judicial complicity.
- 1996: In the first of a series of mass killings involving it, Ranvir Sena, a Bhumihar outfit in Bihar, kills twenty people in Bathani Tola. The deceased are mostly Dalits and a few Muslims, all but one of whom are women and children.
- 1997: At Lakshmanpur Bathe in Bihar, the Ranvir Sena kills fifty-eight Dalits, the highest death toll for a caste atrocity anywhere in the country, prompting President K.R. Narayanan to term it a 'national shame'.
- 1997: In the first mass killings of Dalits in a big city, the Mumbai police shoots dead ten people in Ramabai Nagar while they are protesting against the desecration of Ambedkar's statue.

- 1998: A judicial inquiry into the Ramabai Nagar incident finds that the firing ordered by Sub-inspector Manohar Kadam was 'without warning, unjustified, unwarranted and indiscriminate'.
- 1999: The Ranvir Sena massacres twenty-three Dalits at Shankarbigha in Bihar and the police names twenty-four accused persons in the FIR.
- 2002: A mob lynches five Dalits on the premises of a police post near Jhajjar in Haryana on the baseless suspicion of cow slaughter. In deference to the Hindu sentiment about cow, the big police force on the spot neither protects the victims nor takes any action against the miscreants.
- 2006: At Khairlanji in Maharashtra, a mob drags out of their hut and clobbers to death four members of a Dalit family, including a mother and her teenage daughter. The first of the bodies fished out from a nearby canal is of the seventeen-year-old Priyanka, bruised and stark naked. An official inquiry finds 'a deep-rooted conspiracy towards suppressing the crime and the evidence'.
- 2009: In the Ramabai Nagar firing case, the trial court gives life sentence to Sub-inspector Kadam for 'culpable homicide not amounting to murder'. He is released immediately on bail by the Bombay High Court.
- 2010: Denying the caste angle to the Jhajjar lynching, the trial court awards life sentence to seven men, including a Dalit. It says the accused were 'not even aware of the caste of the victims'.
- 2012: In the Bathani Tola case, the Patna High Court acquits all twenty-three accused who had been convicted by the trial court, including the three who had been awarded the death penalty.
- 2013: In the Lakshmanpur Bathe case, the Patna High Court acquits all twenty-six convicted persons, including the sixteen who had been awarded capital punishment by the trial court.
- 2014: In the 1991 Tsundur case, the Andhra Pradesh High Court acquits all fifty-three accused who had been convicted by the trial court. Conscious of its controversial decision, the High Court orders the police to 'ensure' that there are 'no celebrations or protests'.

- 2015: As all fifty prosecution witnesses in the Shankarbigha massacre case turned hostile one by one, the trial court acquits the twenty-four accused persons, saying 'the evidence of the prosecution has fallen short'.
- 2018: The Narendra Modi government repeals the 1850 law on 'caste disabilities'.
- 2019: On the Khairlanji caste atrocity, the Supreme Court upholds life sentence for the eight accused, but rules out any caste angle to the massacre of the Dalit family.

PREFACE

Over the last two centuries, many a battle has been fought against caste, a defining feature of India's public life. These battles abound in tragedy and farce, courage and subterfuge, bigotry and humanity. They have been recorded most meticulously in the debates that took place in courts, legislatures and governments. While other communities in India were also infected by caste, the legal battles to reform it were essentially among Hindus, because of its origin in their religion.

In the existing corpus of literature, such duels against a prejudice endemic to India have somehow remained understudied or even unexplored. The omission is curious given the difference that the resultant reforms, however deficient, have made to all castes, for better or for worse, in varying degrees and forms.

Take the vexed issue of inter-caste marriage, which fell foul of the governing principle of endogamy. All that is commonly known is that, in the wake of its decolonisation, India took the long overdue step of legalising inter-caste marriage within the Hindu framework. But the many debates that preceded this enactment over three decades in the national legislature have gone unnoticed. These debates reveal that the ones who blocked the reform for so long were not the colonial rulers but a section of Hindus themselves.

In fact, when the first-ever inter-caste marriage bill was introduced by Vithalbhai Patel in 1918, it triggered a heated discussion in the Imperial Legislative Council on the alleged role of Brahmins in keeping castes apart. In different ways, conservatives like Madan Mohan Malaviya and Surendra Nath Banerjea pushed back against Patel's bid to institute equality and fraternity among Hindus.

The historic 1918 debate fell through the cracks, but it does illuminate why marriage across castes is still not the norm in Indian society even a century later. Neither Patel nor even Thakur Das Bhargava, who was instrumental in pushing though that reform at last in 1949, got the attention they merited. The silence engendered a nationalist myth: that India's political freedom finally empowered Hindus to enact the caste reforms that they could not have carried out earlier.

Underlying the legal debates over attempts to reform caste was a question that challenged the dominant narrative. Was the elaborate system of graded inequality, which orthodox Hindus defended as part of their sacred heritage, actually civilisation or barbarism, dharma or injustice?

The caste-reform debates and the myths surrounding them were, however, far from my own mind at the inception of this book. Having written books on the massacres of Sikhs in 1984 and Muslims in 2002, my original plan was to complete a trilogy on mass violence in India. I intended to focus on the killings of Dalits, and to research why there was such impunity in these killings even though a special law on caste atrocities had been enacted in 1989.

But as I delved deeper into Dalit massacre cases, I began to realise the need to go beyond this manifest violence to understand how different functionaries of the Indian state—investigators, prosecutors, trial judges and appellate judges—could get away with blatant displays of caste prejudice, over and over again. To come to grips with the underpinnings of that prejudice, I looked up the legislative debates on caste-related enactments in independent India, whether civil or criminal, as papers related to the abolition of untouchability in the Constituent Assembly.

That was how I gained the insight that the political change of 1947, however drastic, did not offer a clean slate for the enactment of caste reforms. As I dug further back into corresponding debates during the colonial period, I unearthed a trove of archival material that had been overlooked, if not ignored, by scholars. It dawned on me that the surge in the violence against Dalits, and the general impunity for it despite the caste reforms after Independence, was the result of unresolved battles within the Hindu society of the colonial period.

Thus, I widened the ambit of my project to bring out the nexus between violence and other facets of caste. The archival discoveries were far too many though—and far too significant—for me to pack them all into one book. This is the first of two volumes, which I took seven years in all to deliver. Besides unveiling milestones, the material herein upends smug assumptions about India's progress in combating caste. The caste baggage betrayed by iconic figures belies a great deal of confirmation bias about them.

In the history of caste reforms, M.K. Gandhi—Mahatma Gandhi, as he is better known—often plays a pivotal role. However, in this specific context, he does not always come across as a Mahatma. For the longest period, he lagged behind his followers and other contemporaries, including his adversaries, in recognising the incongruity of not just the four-fold varna system but even untouchability.

His protégé, Jawaharlal Nehru, should have fared better, given that it was during his transitional reign that India crossed milestones such as the abolition of untouchability and the validation of inter-caste marriage. In reality, he neither resisted caste reform nor did he engage much with it. So, where Nehru does appear in stories of caste reform, his role is limited to a cameo.

Freedom fighters were not necessarily equality champions.

Bhimrao Ramji Ambedkar plays a more prominent part, of course, though not one without its share of surprises. This book shines a light on some of his little-known contributions towards setting reform norms at a time when he was neither in the government nor in the Constituent Assembly. Yet, for all his brilliance in challenging caste, Ambedkar also appears to have faltered more than once in his understanding of its legal aspects.

Even as it grappled with the colonial interpretation of uncodified Hindu law, the Indian discourse on caste unravelled various internecine conflicts. One was between the elite 'twice-born' castes and the 'impure majority' of Hindus. Another between the unabashedly orthodox Sanatan Dharma and the relatively progressive Arya Samaj. Yet another was between the original Congress strategy of prioritising political reform over social reform and the liberal constitutionalist approach of preparing for self-rule through social reform. And then came Ambedkar's radical challenge to Gandhi's incremental approach of taking on untouchability.

Over time, these varied strands of legal contestation produced a range of ideas about a discrimination that claimed to derive sanction from Hindu customs or scriptures. The enactment of caste reforms, such as they were, reflected India's chequered history, right from the colonial encounters of the early nineteenth century to the ongoing challenges of this twenty-first century—in living up to its constitutional values.

These revelations from the past underlie many of the fault lines of today's India. Whatever caste reforms India pulled off after its Independence have their origins in the pioneering struggles against Hindu conservatives that had been waged under British rule.

The reformers were mostly unsung heroes. Notable among them were legislators such as Vithalbhai Patel, Maneckji Dadabhoy, B.V. Narasimha Ayyar, Kalicharan Nandagaoli, Hari Singh Gour, M.R. Jayakar, M.C. Rajah, R. Srinivasan, R. Veerian, S.K. Bole, G.A. Gavai and Thakur Das Bhargava. Of the several reasons they did not get their due in history, one was that these caste reformers either did not belong to the Indian National Congress, or if they did, had swum against its mainstream consensus. Besides, some who contributed to caste reform were not Indian (for example, Lord Willingdon and Lord Irwin), or were part of the colonial machinery (Justice Sadasiva Iyer and Justice Shadi Lal), or were British subisidiaries (Chithira Thirunal). This was regardless of the British ambivalence on caste, an attitude driven more by expediency than by principle.

On the other hand, some prominent Congress leaders—such as T. Madava Row, M.G. Ranade, B.G. Tilak, Motilal Nehru, Madan Mohan Malaviya, Surendra Nath Banerjea and C. Rajagopalachari—

pushed back against caste reforms at different times even as they positioned themselves as reformers. Indeed, those who tiptoed around caste or blatantly opposed its reform were not always from overtly Hindu formations.

In spite of all his rhetoric against untouchability since the 1920 Nagpur session of the Congress, Gandhi took another twelve years to engage with legislation on temple entry. It came as a reciprocal gesture to Ambedkar and other untouchables for giving up, under his pressure, their hard-fought, if controversial, right to a separate electorate. Even then, in the wake of the 1932 Poona Pact, all that Gandhi was prepared to support was a law to throw open only such temples, case by case, where a majority of local devotees had given their consent through a referendum. Such grudging concession to caste reform underscores a paradox running through this book—the paradox of a religion that prides itself on offering *liberty* to choose any path to God while denying *equality* in practically every respect, even among its own adherents.

❖

Divided thematically, this book traces the trajectories of socio-legal reforms that were meant to place shared humanity over uncanny notions of purity and pollution. Owing to the odds stacked against them, those measures have had only a limited effect, some have even proved counter-productive. For all the pious rhetoric surrounding it, the abolition of untouchability in 1950, if anything, escalated the violence against the formally emancipated untouchables. One of the new forms of atrocities that followed as a pushback from dominant castes was mass killings.

The first such acknowledged massacre took place in 1968 at Kilvenmani in what was then Madras state. Successive courts acquitted the accused of the charge of homicide, thereby setting a template for impunity. But even where justice was done, as in the case of the 2006 Khairlanji massacre in Maharashtra, courts have betrayed a reluctance to admit the caste angle. If legal safeguards have proved to be dysfunctional, it is evidently because violence has remained intrinsic to the inequality bred by caste. Impunity is but a facet of this structural violence. The world's largest democracy is still mired in caste, whatever its avatar and however much it is camouflaged.

1

EARLY CODES

1

THE PUNISHMENT RESERVED FOR LOWER CASTES

The Old Testament prophet, Jeremiah, concerned about the moral corruption that he believed was spreading through Jerusalem, made prophecies of doom. His warnings incurred the wrath of priests who had him whipped and detained. The manner of his detention was common in the region at the time. For a whole day, he was confined to the stocks—an instrument of punishment made up of a wooden frame with holes for clamping the convicted person's legs.

The Bible says, 'When the priest Pashhur … heard Jeremiah prophesying these things, he had Jeremiah the prophet beaten and put in the stocks.' It was only the next day that 'Pashhur released him from the stocks'.[1]

There is a reference to the stocks in the New Testament too. Two of Jesus's disciples, Paul and Silas, had been detained. A jailer in Philippi, which is in modern-day Greece, locked them up in the stocks for allegedly causing public nuisance. 'Having received such a charge,' the Bible said, 'he put them into the inner prison and fastened their feet in the stocks.'[2]

By the onset of the modern period, this instrument of confinement and punishment was extensively employed in Europe to display its victims as a public spectacle, exposing them to humiliation and ridicule. This was how, in the sixteenth century, the English language saw the entry of the expression 'laughing stock'.

Early in the seventeenth century, in Shakespeare's tragedy *King Lear*, the protagonist's disloyal daughter Regan and her husband confined in the stocks the king's servant, Kent. Act 2 Scene 4: 'Lear spies Kent in the stocks and is shocked that anyone would treat one of his servants so badly.'

That a servant was thrown into the stocks in *King Lear* reflected a class bias that this punishment had acquired by then in Britain. This bias was the result of a medieval law enacted against labourers on the heels of the Black Death, the pandemic in which a third of the European population had perished between 1347 and 1351. In the labour shortage that followed, the Statute of Labourers 1351 was promulgated to penalise those who refused to work for pre-pandemic wages. To ensure compliance, the law required servants to be 'sworn' twice a year before the 'lords, stewards, bailiffs and constables' of the village or town concerned.

In what was probably the earliest statutory reference to this punishment, the 1351 British law mandated that labourers who violated their oaths of good behaviour 'shall be put in the stocks'. Accordingly, it required the local authorities to install stocks in every human settlement. A historical assessment of this unabashedly anti-poor law pointed to evidence that 'employers frequently succeeded in securing this penalty of stocks for labourers unwilling to work'.[3]

❖

It was an obsolete provision meant to deal with 'cases of a trivial nature'. Yet, 138 years after its enactment, B.R. Ambedkar, the prime architect of the Indian Constitution, spoke of it in Parliament in 1954. He was then an Opposition leader and was debating a bill meant to provide teeth to the constitutional proclamation abolishing untouchability.[4] He was discussing the gratuitous caste distinction made by that clause—Section 10 of the Madras Regulation XI of 1816.[5] While vesting 'heads of villages' with punitive powers to deal with cases of a trivial nature, such as 'abusive language and inconsiderable assaults or affrays', the East India Company's regulation prescribed two kinds of punishment, depending on the caste of the offender.

The general penalty was to lock up the offender in the 'village choultry', a makeshift jail, for a maximum period of twelve hours. But if the offender belonged to 'any of the lower castes of the people', they were to be 'put in the stocks' for up to six hours.

The British toolkit had been given an Indian twist. While the 1351 British law targeted lower classes, the 1816 Madras law targeted lower castes. Whether someone deserved to be confined in the stocks depended not on the gravity of the offence but on the caste identity of the offenders; in other words, the accident of their birth.

However, in the absence of any official list of lower castes at the time, there was no objective basis on which village heads could have determined during their summary proceedings whether a certain caste fell in the category reserved for the harsher treatment. The only guidance they had was a crude yardstick supplied by the same Section 10. It simply stated that the stocks were meant for 'the lower castes of the people on whom it may not be improper to inflict so degrading a punishment'. This was statutory recognition of caste prejudice, validating the notion that it might not be improper to inflict a degrading punishment on people belonging to lower castes.

Ambedkar referred to it as 'a discriminatory regulation' while speaking in the Rajya Sabha on the Untouchability (Offences) Bill—postcolonial India's first attempt to enact a national legislation on untouchability. It was no surprise that this little-known instance of the codification of caste prejudice caught his notice. Apart from being inequitable, it also allowed for subjectivity in the village head's decision-making.

The two safeguards built into Section 10 were purely cosmetic. One was a duty cast on the village heads to report to the police officer of the district 'all cases in which they shall have exercised the power of punishment granted to them'. The other formality was that the carnum (traditional record-keeper) of each village was required to register—and transmit every month to the magistrate—the names of all persons convicted by the village head, their offences and the punishment meted out to them.

The prescribed register did not, however, contain any column to record the castes of the persons confined in the stocks, although that was the basis for inflicting this corporal punishment. Besides, according a preeminent status to Brahmins, the colonial administration at the time had but a broad sense of upper and lower castes. It was yet to enumerate castes falling under either of those categories. Therefore, the administration was yet to recognise the nuance that the most marginalised of the lower castes were untouchables. The distinction between Shudras, the lowest of the four varnas and the largest in terms of population, and untouchables, who were branded in Madras as Panchamas (the non-existent fifth varna), gained currency decades later with the introduction of the caste-based census.

The idea of extending caste discrimination to sentencing had been introduced on the recommendation of the highly esteemed British administrator, Thomas Munro, whose equestrian statue still stands at a prominent junction in Chennai.[6] Consider the testimonial offered by C. Rajagopalachari, who ruled the Madras province both before and after Independence: 'Whenever any young civil servant came to me for blessings or when I spoke to them in their training school, I advised them to read about Sir Thomas Munro, who was the ideal administrator.'[7]

When he came up with this idea of applying confinement in the stocks to lower castes, Munro was president of the Judicial Commission tasked with drafting regulations for the Madras province on a wide range of subjects. In the retrospective view of the Madras High Court, Regulation XI of 1816 signalled a reversion to 'the indigenous police system of the country', under which police and revenue functions were conferred on the village headman.[8] Munro went on to become governor of the Madras province in 1820. Within a year, he came up with another law, Regulation IV of 1821, extending the ambit of Section 10, Regulation XI of 1816 to 'petty thefts'.

There was, of course, more to Munro than this instrumental use of caste in criminal justice. Among the far-reaching reforms he instituted in his seven-year tenure as governor was the introduction of a land revenue system called 'ryotwari'. A departure from the zamindari system in the Bengal province, ryotwari proved to be an early version of land reforms as it transferred ownership rights to cultivators, opening up opportunities for, among other things, the more advanced of the Shudra castes in the Madras province.

Why did such an administrator draft a regulation that legitimised caste prejudice? A letter of his, reproduced in a posthumous biography, offers some clues. The letter enumerates three principles on which the 1816 regulations had been framed, one of which might explain the induction of village heads into the criminal justice administration. Based on the principle of horses for courses, Munro advocated 'the improvement of our internal administration by employing Europeans and natives in those duties for which they are respectively best suited'.[9] He also indicated winning over dominant sections of the Hindus by institutionalising their disdain for lower castes in the penal policy. Or, as he put it, 'the strengthening of the attachment of the natives to our government by maintaining their ancient institutions and usages'.[10]

Caste prejudice was integral to the 'ancient institutions and usages' that Munro had sought to maintain as part of a cynical strategy to co-opt local leaders into the colonial machinery. Since Manusmriti had been translated by then, he was likely to have been aware of its strictures imposing corporal punishment on Shudras. Even so, the internalisation of the native mindset in their policies led to a degree of discomfort among some British officers, as is evident from a communication written in a different but related context in the Madras administration. In 1828, a revenue functionary called N.W. Kindersley wrote: 'Slavery and the degradation of the lower castes are undoubtedly contrary to the abstract principles of justice, yet both are tolerated by our government in deference to the customs of the country.'[11]

To be fair, though, Munro wasn't the first colonial administrator who thought that deference to caste inequalities would capture the hearts and minds of privileged sections of the Hindus. Take the Bengal Regulation XVI of 1795 enacted by Governor General John

Shore, which recognised the claim of Benaras Brahmins to immunity from capital punishment,[12] reinforcing the graded inequality of caste, in this instance, from the upper end of the hierarchy.

Given the opacity of the process in Section 10, Regulation XI of 1816, little is known about the background of those who suffered the punishment imposed in the name of caste. The victims of it were unlikely to have had the resources to place their grievances before higher judicial forums. Unsurprisingly, the four reported judgments of the Madras High Court on the matter, delivered between 1883 and 1915, were about convicts whose main grievance was that they had been subjected to the stocks despite not belonging to any of the lower castes. Two of those cases, in fact, involved the further issue of whether people belonging to other religions, regardless of their social status, were exempt from this degrading punishment as caste was essentially a Hindu custom.

The 1883 case, *The Queen v. Nabi Saheb*,[13] raised this question in the context of a Muslim who had been put in the stocks for three hours on the charge of stealing 'an iron measure and eight annas' worth of copper coin' by the village munsif of Anjulipatti in Dindigul Taluk. The district magistrate of Madura referred the case to the High Court on the question of whether confining a Muslim in the stocks was contrary to the (possibly unreported) rulings of the High Court in two cases in 1878 and 1879.

According to the 1883 verdict, the earlier rulings had introduced an element of class in the enforcement of Section 10. Those precedents had laid down two conditions for imposing the special punishment: 'the one having relation to the position of the caste to which an offender belongs, and the other to the social status of the person himself'.

In other words, Section 10 could not be interpreted to mean that all lower-caste offenders could be, as a matter of course, put in the stocks. Rather, it was meant only for those among them whose social status too was demonstrably such that it would not be degrading for them to suffer that punishment. Since colonial courts were not empowered to strike down unfair laws, the best that the

Madras High Court could do was to come up with an interpretation aimed at containing the damage.

In the 1883 case, the High Court was inconclusive about the class stipulation. It held that as a 'dealer in petty wares', Nabi 'may or may not be a person on whom the infliction of the punishment may be degrading'. Insofar as the condition relating to caste was concerned, the judgment delivered by Chief Justice Charles Turner agreed with the magistrate that 'a Muhammadan cannot be said to belong to the lower castes of the people'. In a tacit reference to the many Muslim rulers in Indian history, Turner added: 'It is probable the framers of the regulation had in view those castes who, prior to the introduction of British rule, were regarded as servile.' Though Nabi had already served out three hours in the stocks, the High Court quashed the sentence in a symbolic vindication of his protest.

In the second reported case, *Rattigadu v. Konda Reddi,*[14] the aggrieved person was a Christian who had earlier been a Hindu of the untouchable Mala caste. This Telugu-speaking caste was generically referred to in the judgment as 'pariah', the term then in currency in the Madras province for all untouchables, despite the existence of a specific caste by that name among Tamil speakers. The reference from the district magistrate of Kistna (now Krishna, in Andhra Pradesh) was on the issue of whether Rattigadu, despite his conversion to Christianity, was still liable to be confined in the stocks. A 'cooly' (unskilled labourer), Rattigadu had been put in the stocks for two hours by the village munsif for using abusive language with the complainant. Though the two were indeed found to have had an altercation when the complainant had 'pastured his cattle in a burying ground', District Magistrate R. Morris was 'doubtful' whether the accused had actually used abusive language.

In any case, his reference to the High Court was on the legality not of the conviction but of the sentence. While Muslims had been spared by the verdict in the Nabi Saheb case from the stigma of belonging to lower castes, 'conversions to Islam from the low caste Cherumurs of Malabar are of daily occurrence'. And if Muslims 'by reason of their creed' could still be generally exempt from confinement in the stocks, 'so ought converts to Christianity to be exempt, even though born in one of the lower castes of the people'.

In his verdict delivered in 1900, Justice Benson pointed out that there was nothing in the Nabi Saheb case to suggest that the offender had converted from Hinduism, let alone from one of its lower castes. It could, therefore, not be regarded as 'an authority for holding that every professor of the creed of Islam, whatever caste he may have belonged to before conversion or after it, is outside the purview of the regulation'. The focus of the regulation was taken to be not on the creed but on the caste of the offender.

The court was clearly of the view that a change of creed would not make a difference if the offender could be shown to have clung to his caste. This was a remarkable interpretation for a British judge to have made. Had he instead accepted the prayer to save all Christian convicts from the stocks, it could well have served to encourage further conversions from lower castes.

Benson's test to determine whether Rattigadu could be considered a lower-caste individual despite his conversion to Christianity was as follows: 'If he continues to accept the rules of the caste in social and moral matters, acknowledges the authority of the headmen, takes part in caste meetings and ceremonies, and, in fact, generally continues to belong to the caste, then in my judgment, he would be within the purview of the regulation.'

Whether Rattigadu had actually abandoned his caste after converting to Christianity was, therefore, 'a question of fact' determined by his post-conversion conduct. Since this required verification on the ground by the district magistrate, the High Court verdict was inconclusive on whether Rattigadu fulfilled the first of the two judicially inferred conditions of Section 10, namely, whether he belonged to any of the lower castes. However, Benson categorically ruled that Rattigadu, being merely a cooly, was not exempt under the second condition, namely, whether his social standing rendered it improper to inflict so degrading a punishment on him. In other words, if it was found that his conversion had not rid him of his old Hindu baggage, then the double whammy of low caste and low class would mean that confinement in the stocks could not have been degrading to Rattigadu.

The other two reported cases on the issue were decided in 1915. *Uppala Kotayya Nagaram, In re,*[15] was an instance where, on an appeal, the sub-divisional magistrate (SDM) noticed that the accused was 'not a pariah but a govandla ryot owning some lands'. The SDM, therefore, held that, for Nagaram, 'imprisonment in stocks is a great disgrace' and 'reduced the sentence'. Nagaram still took the matter to the Madras High Court as he was aggrieved with the SDM's failure to consider whether, in view of his caste identity and his social status, he was at all 'liable to the punishment of confinement in the stocks'. This question in turn determined whether he was guilty of the more serious charge of resisting apprehension when he was to be put in the stocks. As the High Court said, 'If on this ground the sentence of confinement in the stocks was illegal, accused cannot be convicted of an offence under S. 224, Indian Penal Code [IPC], in escaping from it.'

On this additional charge, Nagaram was liable to be imprisoned up to two years. But he obtained relief from the High Court. Justice William Ayling set aside the SDM's order and directed him to restore Nagaram's appeal against the village authority's decision to impose the penalty of stocks. Thanks to his relatively superior caste and landed property, Nagaram was spared not only the disgrace of being locked in the stocks but also the risk of being imprisoned for defying that unlawful order.

The last reported case, *Madasamy Nadan, In re,*[16] involved a Hindu from an upwardly mobile caste called Shanar, who have since come to be known as Nadar. Madasamy Nadan had been convicted by the village magistrate for 'insult and assault'. The Madras High Court was to decide the validity of the sentence from the viewpoint of caste. In his verdict, Justice Abdur Rahim drew on the Rattigadu precedent that had held that an untouchable-turned-Christian was exempt from the stocks if he had 'adopted also the Christian moral and social standards instead of those of his caste'.

In the case of Nadan, the judge felt no need to verify the

offender's moral and social standards before pronouncing that confinement in the stocks was 'not warranted by law' in his case. Justice Rahim made his decision on the basis of the advancements displayed by the collective of Nadan's caste: 'In the case of Shanars, we would not be far wrong in saying that they would, at least at the present day, regard themselves degraded by the infliction of such punishment.' Following the precedents that had considered both caste and class, he laid down that the self-perception of the Nadar community was 'one important test for determining the question whether the second condition applies'. He cited an array of reasons for acknowledging the confidence developed by the Nadars on the strength of the battles they fought to overcome caste disabilities. 'Many members of that community have now taken to trade and business or are landowners and farmers and with improved material prosperity, a greater sense of self-respect has come to them.'

Another significant factor cited by Rahim was that a considerable number of Nadars had adopted Christianity, 'in many cases perhaps as a protest against the rigidity of the ancient caste system'. Though they were considered to be less than a Shudra caste due to their traditional occupation of toddy-tapping, the Nadars themselves claimed to be Kshatriyas. 'Whether that claim be well founded or not, the fact that it is made,' the High Court said, 'is evidence to show that Shanars as a community would regard being put into stocks as a degrading form of punishment'.

Despite the differences in their approach, these four Madras High Court judgments displayed an anxiety to reduce the ambit of the draconian clause. All the same, they ended up echoing the suggestion implicit in the clause that the tradition of caste had so dehumanised a section of Hindus that what could be degrading to others was not so to them.

Just a few months before *Uppala Kotayya Nagaram* and *Madasamy Nadan* in 1915, the Madras province legislature had begun to show signs of redressing this statutory discrimination, which had by then been in force for almost a century. Madras was at the time a huge province that included, in today's terms, almost the whole of Tamil

Nadu and Andhra Pradesh, besides parts of Odisha, Karnataka and Kerala. The legislative rethink on confinement in the stocks was the result of an incremental gain in representation for Indian legislators in provincial Councils, thanks to the Morley–Minto reforms of 1909. As it happened, *Mahratta*, the Poona-based publication brought out by the redoubtable freedom fighter Bal Gangadhar Tilak, covered these developments.

Tilak's own reference to the punishment of stocks was in the context of his ongoing Home Rule campaign.[17] The issue of the 1816 regulation was raised for the first time in the Madras Legislative Council in 1913 in the form of a question by Kesava Pillai. A member of the dominant Vellalar caste from the Shudra category and a Congress party leader of long standing, Pillai was from a town called Gooty in Ananthapur district, now in Andhra Pradesh. Gooty was, in fact, where Munro, the author of the 1816 law, was first buried in 1827 after he had suddenly died of cholera while on a farewell tour. Though the government's response to Pillai's initiative had apparently been 'sympathetic', *Mahratta* underscored the lack of any follow-up action in the four years since then. It quipped, 'There was never any lack of sympathy in Government utterances.'

In February 1915, another progressive legislator, B.V. Narasimha Ayyar, came up with a fresh question about why Section 10 continued to persist. Three months later, on 25 May 1915, Ayyar upped the ante by introducing an amendment bill, saying 'a degraded form of punishment [was] no longer to be continued in these times of civilization'.[18] All it sought to do, in technical terms, was to delete the last forty-five words of the first clause of Section 10, zeroing in on the egregious portion of the provision.

Executive Council Member Harold Stewart, however, urged Ayyar to withdraw his bill, claiming that the government was going to introduce legislation 'on a more comprehensive basis very soon'. Far from satisfied, Ayyar requested that pending such a legislation, the government gave a preview of its will 'by an executive order to put an end to such punishment'. A contemporaneous report in the *Times of India* went on to say, 'The government promised to consider this request and Mr Narasimha Ayyar withdrew his motion.'[19]

No executive order followed, but the government did initiate the process of drafting a larger bill to which it tagged the proposal of repealing the 1816 regulation, as suggested by Ayyar, to the extent that it authorised confinement in the stocks. The twenty-seven sections of the draft bill were otherwise focused on revamping the Madras Village Courts Act, 1888. On 28 September 1916, more than a year after Stewart's assurance, the secretary to the Home (Judicial) Department in the Madras government, P. Rajagopala Achariyar, wrote to his counterpart in the Government of India, James DuBoulay, to consult him on the draft bill. Outlining the provisions of the draft bill, Achariyar said: 'The antiquated penalty of confinement in stocks, authorised by Regulation XI of 1816, is abolished, as public feeling is *now* [emphasis added] against this form of punishment.'[20]

Thus, in an internal communication and through an official of Indian origin, the colonial administration acknowledged in the hundredth year of this codified caste prejudice that public feeling had by then turned against it. The provocation for its admission was the demand for abolition not only from legislators like Pillai and Ayyar but also from untouchables themselves, although they were yet to gain access to Legislative Councils anywhere in the country. On 21 April 1916, the Depressed Classes Society of South India addressed memorials to the viceroy of India, Lord Chelmsford and the London-based secretary of state for India, Austen Chamberlain, listing the 'abolition of punishment as a stock' among its ten demands.[21]

Responding to Achariyar's letter, the Central government on 23 February 1917 suggested four changes to the draft bill, none of which affected the proposed amendment to the 1816 law.[22] DuBoulay's letter also pointed out that the draft bill required the formal sanction of the Central government under the Government of India Act, 1915. But before the Madras government could take the next step in this ponderous law-making process, Ayyar struck again.

On 2 April 1917, Ayyar made a renewed attempt to introduce his bill.[23] Executive Council member H.F.W. Gillman responded by updating the Madras Legislative Council on the government's ongoing efforts to fulfil its promise of abolishing confinement in the stocks. Gillman also assured Ayyar that the bill was likely to be introduced in the next session of the Madras Legislative Council due in November. Given the delay thus far, Ayyar was not willing to withdraw his bill again. This was how, much to the government's discomfort, the motion to introduce Ayyar's bill came to be voted and defeated.

Referring to Ayyar's valiant efforts, an article in the *Mahratta* on 8 April 1917 said that 'a popular representative of the Madras Legislative Council has brought to the notice of the public, not for the first time' this discriminatory clause.[24] Disregarding the indigenous origins of caste prejudice, it blamed Section 10 entirely on colonialism. 'The punishment of stocks especially reserved for lower castes by the Madras statute is an indication,' it said sarcastically, 'of the special solicitude for the lower orders which, we are asked to believe, the foreign bureaucrat possesses in abundance!' At the same time, in a bid to assuage non-Brahmin fears about the Home Rule campaign, the *Mahratta* specially mentioned that Ayyar, an associate of Tilak, was a Brahmin. 'Thoughtful non-Brahmins will find herein an argument for blessing the Home Rule movement.'

Stressing the need to repeal the archaic clause, the article cited an estimate that the number of people who had been put in the stocks across the Madras province over the previous three years was still as high as 2,000. It added that, following the rejection of Ayyar's motion, 'we have no hopes of getting a bill passed in the near future'.

Despite all the pressure, the Madras government took another three months to get back to the Central government with the changes that had been suggested by it. In a letter dated 5 July 1917, it also sought statutory sanction for introducing the bill. The otherwise detailed Statement of Objects and Reasons (SOR) attached to the bill was laconic on the provision dealing with caste prejudice. It just said: 'Opportunity is also taken to abolish punishment by confinement in stocks authorized by Regulation XI of 1816.'[25] No explanation was offered for the proposed abolition. The colonial government was perhaps loath to admit the moral wrong that had been committed in the first place by legitimising caste prejudice.

So, when he finally introduced what was formally called the Madras Village Courts Bill in the legislature on 20 November 1917, all that Gillman said in passing was this: '… we have incidentally introduced a clause in regard to the promised abolition of punishment by stocks'.[26] At the end of a debate that was preoccupied with other clauses of the bill, the Legislative Council referred it to a Select Committee. Two years later, on 19 November 1919, Gillman's successor A.R. Knapp presented the Select Committee's report, which made no change in the clause abolishing the punishment by stocks.

By this time, the Madras Legislative Council had acquired the distinction of having the first-ever lawmaker from among the untouchables anywhere in the country: M.C. Rajah. He did not, however, participate in the brief debate that followed the presentation of the Select Committee's report.

Ayyar did get a chance to speak, recalling that he was the person who had asked for 'the deletion of one provision five years ago about Panchamas being put in stocks'.[27] The House, at last, passed the bill into law that day. The governor of Madras, Lord Willingdon, gave his assent on 1 December 1919. The viceroy of India, Lord Chelmsford, followed on 24 December 1919. It was in such circumstances that the degrading punishment Thomas Munro had reserved for lower castes was repealed, a full 103 years later.

The earlier law of 1795, exempting Benaras Brahmins from the death penalty, did not last so long. In fact, just a year after Munro's law came into force, Bengal Regulation XVII of 1817 rescinded the 1795 law and called for magistrates 'to execute all sentences of death against Brahmins', provided the execution did not take place on a 'spot of ground held sacred by the Hindoos'.[28] The special dispensation to members of the highest caste, inspired by the concept of Brahmahatya, the scriptural injunction against killing Brahmins under any circumstances, was reduced to a symbolic privilege in a matter of twenty-two years.

The 1816 provision remained in force almost five times longer perhaps because, unlike the Benaras law, the stocks were essentially a colonial device. Britain had a history of importing the penal method of confinement in the stocks to its colonies, including America. As for its anti-labour law of 1351, which was the first to confer statutory status on this form of punishment, the British Parliament repealed it altogether in 1863.

Although the 1919 repeal in Madras was followed by a surge in assertiveness by untouchable castes across the country, Ambedkar got that piece of history wrong when he spoke in Parliament in 1954. He listed the 1816 regulation among the laws that were 'absolutely essential to modify in order to bring them in conformity with the Constitution'.[29] Addressing the presiding officer of the Rajya Sabha, Ambedkar said, 'There can be no question, sir, that this regulation is a discriminatory regulation, and should be repealed.' Further, he said that he had drawn a list of such laws before he resigned as law minister in 1951. Clearly, he was unaware that the problematic part of Section 10, which he specifically mentioned in his speech, had long been repealed.

Such an uncharacteristic mistake on the part of Ambedkar underlines a basic premise of this book, that several legal milestones in combating caste have gone unnoticed. One reason that even the greatest legal mind on caste issues did not know about this could have been Ayyar's exit from the legislature shortly after the reform. Following a tragedy in his family, Ayyar devoted the remaining three decades of his life to spiritual pursuits.[30]

But the main factor, perhaps, was the low-key manner in which the reform was carried out, with the British administration anxious to avoid drawing attention to its original sin. The quiet burial was an opportunity loss for equality champions. For reforms are known to have a cascading effect—and the impact of this reform could have propelled others to follow. As it was, the story remained untold.

2

THE PREROGATIVE TO COVER BREASTS

On 1 November 1858, shortly after the British Crown had taken over from the East India Company, Queen Victoria made a proclamation. Disclaiming any intention 'to impose our convictions on any of our subjects', Victoria affirmed that 'none [shall] be in any wise favoured, none molested or disquieted by reason of their religious faith or observance', and that all shall enjoy 'equal and impartial protection of the law'. A restatement of the colonial relationship, it was meant to provide a healing touch to a country recovering from the great uprising.

But the proclamation had a curious effect in Travancore—a princely state on the southwestern tip of peninsular India that had little to do with the 1857 revolt. Like other princely states, it was ruled indirectly by the British under a subsidiary alliance.

The proclamation led to an escalation of caste tensions in Travancore. The Malayalam translation of it apparently intensified a local skirmish in which men of the dominant Nair caste assaulted both men and women of the Nadar caste. Their objective was violent—they wanted Nadar women to uncover their breasts.

The assailants converted Victoria's proclamation into a licence to revive a misogynous practice: that lower-caste women should be, as a token of their inferiority, bare-breasted in public. This caste restriction was enforced particularly against Nadars, who were known then as Shanars. They were an assertive lot for a variety of reasons, including conversions to Christianity, exposure to education, increase in economic strength, abolition of slavery in India in 1843 and the relatively greater freedom enjoyed by their caste counterparts in the contiguous areas of the Madras Presidency.

The prohibition on lower-caste women covering any part of the body above the waist and below the knee was part of an elaborate set of caste restrictions that were peculiar to Travancore and its vicinity in the nineteenth century. Another aspect of such restrictions was the notion of graded distance pollution. The greater the difference in caste status, the larger the physical distance that a lower-caste member was required to maintain from an upper-caste member.

Accordingly, a Nadar had to keep away by as much as thirty-six paces from a Nambudiri, who, as a Malayalam-speaking Brahmin, embodied the apex of the caste hierarchy in the Kerala region. In keeping with the logic of these varying levels of purity and pollution, the distance that a Nadar was ordained to maintain from a Nair was only twelve paces.

Though the Nambudiris and Nairs comprised the landed aristocracy in Travancore, the Nambudiris, who were the arbiters on caste matters, relegated the Nairs to the status of Shudras, the lowest in the four-tier varna system. Therefore—despite the fact that the Nairs constituted the bulk of Travancore's military—they were alternatively referred to as 'Soodras' in contemporaneous official documents and press reports.

On the other hand, the Nadars were stigmatised for their traditional occupation of toddy-tapping—although they too claimed to be Shudras, even if only at the bottom of that category. Since they were considered beneath the varna hierarchy, the Nadars were subjected to the disabilities of untouchability, including restrictions on carrying an umbrella and wearing shoes or gold ornaments. It was because untouchability was practised most egregiously in the Kerala region that it saw the highest percentage of conversions to Christianity, especially from the Nadar community.

In deference to the Nairs, the Hindu rulers of Travancore did precious little to protect Nadar women from being stripped and shamed. Instead, on 27 December 1858, the Travancore administration came out with an order that blamed the violence on the victims for covering their bosoms with what was called the shoulder cloth. Indeed, all that was in dispute in tangible terms was an unstitched garment that was used to cover the breasts and therefore referred to variously as the shoulder cloth or breast cloth or upper cloth. At the time, even the higher-caste women in Travancore did not wear a stitched garment, such as a jacket or a blouse.

Therefore, the wearing of that unstitched garment by Nadar women was deemed an infringement on the prerogative of the higher castes. The upper-caste sentiment was offended even though the alleged caste marker was worn by the Nairs and Nadars in their own different ways. As a contemporaneous news report put it, 'while the Soodra woman wears a distinct small cloth over one shoulder, crossing the breast, and brought down to the waist on the opposite side, the Shanar woman wears a continuation of the body cloth itself brought up over one shoulder in a similar style'.[1]

In the legalistic approach adopted by the government, the Nadars fell foul of the law by their mere act of wearing the shoulder cloth. Though discriminatory, the existing usage was deemed sacrosanct. Calling out the troops, the government ordered that Nadar women who persisted in wearing the shoulder cloth were liable to face strict action.

> Whereas some Shanar women, contrary to the usage which has prevailed up to this time, are now wearing the shoulder cloth, in consequence of which disturbances are taking place between Shanars and the higher castes, and whereas, if it were thought desirable to set aside a usage of such antiquity, the proper way would be to make a representation on the subject to government and act according to the orders that government might issue, whilst it is clearly wrong to violate ancient usage without authority, it is therefore hereby announced, that whoever does so in future, shall be severely punished. Shanars are to hear this and act accordingly.[2]

The authority issuing this regressive order was ironically the very dewan or prime minister who reputedly modernised Travancore and developed it into a 'model state' in the nineteenth century. That dewan was Tanjore Madava Row, whose statue is a landmark in Thiruvananthapuram, standing right in front of the Kerala Secretariat. In fact, the seat of the state government is known as Statue Junction. In the crucial phase of reconstruction that followed the 1857 revolt, Madava Row was an inspirational figure across India. He demonstrated successively, in Travancore and two more princely states, that Indians were capable of governing themselves.

For all his contributions, though, Madava Row, a Marathi-speaking Brahmin from the Madras Presidency, was a laggard in the sphere of social reform. Anticipating Justice K.T. Telang's approach to social reform of taking 'the line of least resistance', he advocated his own brand of pragmatism, as evident from a posthumously published compilation of his opinions. 'Do not attempt to abolish all caste distinctions ... Every social reformer discards judicious judgment and wants to assert intellectual excellence or independence by rushing to extremes and wants to display a heroic spirit by attempting present impossibilities; the consequence being that little or nothing is actually achieved.'[3]

Madava Row's rejection of the Nadar women's right to wear the shoulder cloth lay in his theory of unalterability, that is, 'The quantity, quality and style of dress must generally remain unalterable.' Alluding to the violence over the Nadar women altering their dress, Madava Row said: 'I know that European missionaries have attempted a change in some places, but have failed except in a few individuals and in their presence. The impossibility of altering costume or dress must be particularly recognized in the case of women.'[4] He drew on precedents to maintain the status quo forbidding Nadar women to cover their breasts with the shoulder cloth.

About three decades earlier, on 3 February 1829, the government had passed an order on the same subject, proclaiming that 'Shanar women have no right whatever to wear the shoulder cloth'.[5] Then too there had been social unrest that was strikingly similar to what was happening in 1858. Consider the introductory part of the 1829 order: 'Whereas Shanar women in opposition to orders and ancient propriety are wearing their cloth over their shoulders, in consequence of which there are many disturbances in the country …'

But the 1829 order was relatively liberal as it made a concession to those of the low-caste women who had converted to Christianity. Passed under pressure from the colonial regime, which had been lobbied by missionaries, the 1829 order of Travancore allowed Christian Shanars to cover their bosom, provided they did so by wearing a jacket rather than the shoulder cloth. The reasoning was that the short, tight-fitting jacket called 'kuppoiam' was commonly worn by Syrian Christians and Moplah Muslims, while the shoulder cloth apparently rendered Nadar women indistinguishable from their higher-caste counterparts.

The idea of legally barring low-caste women from wearing the shoulder cloth actually went back to an order issued in 1814. It was conceived then as a hurried rollback of an initiative taken by Col. John Munro who was, quite unusually, both the dewan and British resident of Travancore. Like Thomas Munro, his namesake in the Madras presidency, Col. Munro was a popular administrator. Munroe Island, a popular tourist destination in Kerala, is named after him for the difference he had made by integrating backwater regions through a network of canals.

Among the reforms Munro introduced was the short-lived order of 1812 that provided relief to Christian converts: 'Women who become Christians, may wear the shoulder cloth, in accordance with the decency which is befitting the Christian religion and in accordance with the custom prevailing in Christian countries, and we hereby order that no opposition be shown by anyone to Christian women who thus wear their cloth.'.[6] Munro's radical measure of exempting a section of low-caste women from the shoulder-cloth prohibition, on account of their conversion to Christianity, set off reverberations that lasted for decades.

Munro himself was forced to modify his order in 1814 following protests from dominant-caste members of an official Council, who argued that it would erase caste distinctions and cause everything to become polluted.[7] The 1814 order thus restricted the Christian converts to wearing jackets, so that the upper cloth remained the preserve of the dominant castes.

Yet, the principle underlying Munro's original 1812 reform was upheld in 1823 by a court, thanks to an early display of judicial activism. A complaint had been lodged against some Christian Nadars for allegedly violating the 1814 order by wearing the upper cloth instead of a jacket. Disregarding the express purpose of the 1814 order, the Padmanabapuram district court put a leading question to a missionary. It asked whether Christians were allowed by their religion to wear the upper cloth. On receiving an affirmative reply, the court decided in favour of the accused on that point.[8]

The 1829 government order was specially meant to override the precedent set in the context of Christian Nadars. It gave an expansive interpretation to the judgment to avoid singling out Christians: 'we hereby annul a decision of the Padmanabapuram Zillah Court allowing Shanar women to wear the shoulder cloth'.

Against this backdrop, and amid the caste violence that followed Victoria's proclamation, the Travancore government reiterated its shoulder-cloth policy in the 1858 order. Despite the professed commitment to secularism and equality in Victoria's proclamation, the ruling elite of Travancore read an ambiguity in it. Nairs and state officials interpreted her stated deference to 'ancient rights, usages and customs of India' to mean that Queen Victoria not only prohibited all future interference with caste, 'but annulled all previous interventions'.[9]

Travancore was one of the tributary states of the Madras Presidency. In his first report on the caste violence to the Madras government, dated 13 January 1859, the British resident of Travancore, Lt Gen. William Cullen, wrote that 'the wearing of the cloth by Shanar women, like that of the Sudras [Nairs], had led gradually to violent outrages and quarrels and almost to an insurrection'.[10] But Cullen's superiors in Madras were equally concerned about his own accountability—especially since he was found to have taken no step to prevent the Travancore government from reacting intolerantly to the Nadars' legitimate aspirations. The

Nadar inhabitants of Travancore flagged their misgivings about Cullen's role in representations to the Madras government.

One such representation[11] recalled, for instance, the pioneering contribution of Col. Munro in 1812 in seeking to relax the ban on the shoulder cloth for at least a section of Nadar women. Referring to the otherwise mixed record of British residents in dealing with this form of caste prejudice, the petition said that, 'while it has always been the custom of the higher castes to oppress your petitioners, the position taken by the Travancore government … has been different at different times in accordance with the recommendations of different Residents'.

The petition lamented that the British resident's influence had been exerted 'on the side of the worst abuses of caste'. It alleged that Cullen had 'adopted and sanctioned the idea that to do honour to the higher castes, it is necessary to do dishonour to the lower'. The petitioners said that they had been 'rarely molested at all and never seriously molested … right up to date of the publication of Her Gracious Majesty's proclamation'. Their charge was that the proclamation had been 'grossly and maliciously misinterpreted' by the higher castes and officers of Travancore.

This representation also explained why the Nadar women persisted in wearing the shoulder cloth despite the compromise attempted by the Travancore government since 1814, permitting the Christian converts among them to cover their breasts by wearing the jacket. To begin with, the permission had a limited ambit, as Christian converts apparently formed 'only about a fifth' of the Nadar community. Besides, the great majority of Nadar women, 'like other Hindoo women', were 'unable to sew, and therefore unable to make those jackets'. Thus, the jacket, 'an article of dress peculiar to the Moplahs', was regarded as 'a sign of foreign manners' by the petitioners, who were 'as certainly Hindoos as the higher castes themselves'.

In the light of such petitions, as also reports regarding the ongoing violence in Travancore, the governor of the Madras Presidency, George Harris, held a meeting with his officials on the matter on 26 January 1859. The day after these proceedings of the Governor in Council (the formal designation for the governor and his cabinet), the chief secretary to the Madras government, Thomas Pycroft, wrote a sharply worded letter to Cullen, instructing him 'to be careful to give no countenance to the idea that the British government recognises any exclusive distinctions, or the right of any set of men to prevent others from following, in all matters of social or domestic life, such course as they may see fit, provided it be not repugnant to public decency and morals'.[12]

As a corollary, Pycroft urged Cullen to impress upon the Travancore rajah that prohibitions, such as those contained in the 1814 and 1829 orders, were 'unsuited to the present age and unworthy of an enlightened prince, and that he is not to look for the support of the British government in any attempts to maintain them, as respects any class of his subjects'. This stinging note led to a prolonged and telling correspondence between Madras and Travancore on the unlikely subject of whether—or how—certain women could cover their breasts.

The stern warning from Madras on 27 January 1859 seemed to have had a salutary effect on the Travancore administration. It conceded the need to amend its anti-Nadar proclamation, which had been issued less than two months earlier.

On 12 February 1859, Madava Row wrote to Cullen, saying, 'The authority of the Sirkar having been vindicated, it may be desirable to take an early opportunity to consider that modification should be made in the proclamation of 1004 [1004 M.E. is the Malayalam calendar equivalent of 1829], so as to suit the requirements of altered times and circumstances, and satisfy parties as far as it may be possible to do so; from which I infer that His Highness the Maha Rajah is sensible that the conduct of a portion of his subjects towards the Shanar women belongs to an age of barbarism, utterly unsuited to the present advanced stage of civilisation in this country.'[13]

This was quite a comedown for the dewan of Travancore who had started with a public declaration that Nadar women 'wearing the shoulder cloth' would be 'severely punished'. However, it was more a tactical retreat than a change of heart, given that Madava Row showed no sign of taking, as promised, 'an early opportunity' to modify his order.

In its reminder a month later on 12 March 1859, the Madras government conveyed to Cullen his colonial responsibility to undo the damage done by a native authority: 'The degree of interference which for many years past has been exercised by the representative of the British government in the affairs of Travancore, is so large, and his intervention so general, that the credit or discredit of the administration greatly rests with the British government, and it has thereby become their duty to insist upon the observance of a system of toleration in a more decided manner than they would be at liberty to adopt if they had merely to bring their influence to bear on an independent state.'[14]

Pycroft's tutorial on what might seem to be the 'white man's burden' failed to dent Cullen's indifference to the plight of the Nadar women. The matter was escalated to the new governor of Madras, Charles Trevelyan, who had succeeded Harris. On 6 May 1859, Trevelyan wrote to Cullen a note that was more stirring than his predecessor's.

> I have seldom met with a case, in which not only truth and justice, but every feeling of our common humanity are so entirely on one side. The whole civilised world would cry shame upon us, if we do not make a firm stand on such an occasion. If anything could make this line of conduct more incumbent on us, it would be the extraordinary fact that persecution of a singularly personal and delicate kind is attempted to be justified by a Royal Proclamation, the special object of which was to assure to Her Majesty's Indian subjects liberty of thought and action, so long as they did not interfere with the just rights of others. I should fail in respect to Her Majesty if I attempted to describe the feelings with which she must regard the use made against her own sex, of the promises of protection so graciously accorded by her.[15]

Trevelyan also referred to the 'numerous petitions' that had been presented to the Madras government in the wake of the Travancore order of December 1858, complaining of 'the ill-usage and indignities to which the Shanar women are exposed'. The operative part of Trevelyan's mail was his direction to Cullen that he should 'without further delay, yield obedience to the repeated orders' that had been conveyed to him from Madras since 27 January 1859, and report what the maharajah had done in consequence.

As the new governor tightened the screws on him, the dewan of Travancore was left with no option but to take the next step towards complying with the instructions from Madras. Reporting that he had a detailed discussion with Maharajah Uthram Thirunal, Madava Row wrote to Cullen on 17 May 1859, saying, 'His Highness certainly feels that the provisions of the Proclamation of 1004 M.E. on the subject of the dress of the inferior castes require to be greatly modified.' The operative part of the letter was: 'His Highness now proposes to abolish all rules prohibiting the covering of the upper parts of the persons of Shanar women and to grant them perfect liberty to meet the requirements of decency any way they may deem proper'.[16] Even so, this perfect liberty would be conferred on the Nadar women 'with the simple restrictions', he clarified, 'that they do not imitate the same mode of dress that appertains to the higher castes'.

In other words, even as it was finally prepared to let all Nadar women cover their breasts, the Travancore government was still unrelenting on reserving the shoulder cloth strictly for their higher-caste counterparts. Madava Row explained that the maharajah 'would not have made even this small reservation were it not for the fear that sudden and total abolition of all distinctions of dress which have from time immemorial distinguished one caste from another may produce most undesirable impressions on the minds of the larger portion of his subjects and cause their serious discontent'. All the same, he added that 'by the present concession, the demands of decency have been fully answered without needlessly offending the feelings peculiar to the other castes'. Having agreed to this compromise under colonial pressure, Madava Row ended his letter to Cullen expressing hope that the proposed via media 'would meet with your approval and that of the Madras government'.

Madava Row also claimed that Travancore was less conducive than British India to social reform: 'It is of course needless to remind you of those many circumstances which would make the introduction of decisive reforms, especially in matters of caste and religion, much more difficult in Travancore than in Her Majesty's Territories.' He offered no explanation for this claim.

Cullen, who had been serving as resident in Travancore since 1840, remained complicit in denying freedom to Nadar women. He gave his approval to Madava Row's half measure even before seeking the Madras government's feedback on it. Worse, when he forwarded Madava Row's report to Pycroft on 21 May 1859, Cullen glossed over the compromise involved in the proposal of retaining the ban on the breast cloth. In spite of the reprimand he had already received from Madras, Cullen decided to brazen it out, writing that Madava Row's proposed order might be considered by the Governor in Council as 'satisfactory'. He also made it clear that he was presenting his superiors with a fait accompli. 'I have replied to the Dewan, that I see no objection to the immediate issue of a corresponding proclamation.'[17]

In the event, the Governor in Council gave a tentative approval. Trevelyan reiterated his abhorrence for the system that had been previously put in place by Madava Row with Cullen's blessings. In his minute dated 30 May, Trevelyan said: 'This concession must, I think, be accepted as a practical earnest on the part of the Raja of a desire to put an end to the barbarous and indecent restriction previously existing upon the dress of the Shanar women, but we cannot pronounce a final opinion until we see the working of the new regulation.'[18] A week later, Trevelyan's minute assumed the form of an order to Cullen, and in turn to Madava Row.

On 7 June 1859, the Madras government sent a copy of the order, along with an update to the secretary of state for India in London, an office that had taken over from the Court of Directors of East India Company the previous year. On 19 August 1859, Secretary of State for India Charles Wood gave Madras a cautious go-ahead. 'From the enclosures to your letter of the 7th June, I learn that the Rajah proposes to abolish all rules prohibiting the covering of the upper parts of the persons of Shanar women and to grant them perfect liberty to meet the requirements of decency in any way they may deem proper with the simple restriction that they do not imitate the same mode of dress that appertains to the higher castes.'[19]

As the highest colonial authority, Wood acknowledged the limitations of Trevelyan's options. 'With this concession, though it seems short of what you originally contemplated, you deem it expedient, under the circumstances stated, to be satisfied, and I am of opinion that you are right in accepting the proposed concession and earnestly hope that it will have the desired effect.'

Even after this, the Travancore administration dragged its feet for another couple of months before enacting its compromise formula. In the intervening period, it inserted an alternative, besides the jacket for the Nadar women to cover their breasts without violating the shoulder-cloth restriction. Given the complaints that the jacket was infeasible for the Hindu community, the new option that the legislation proposed had the advantage of being an unstitched garment. It was a mode of dress borrowed from the Mookoovar, the fisherfolk spread across Hindu, Muslim and Christian communities in Kerala. In a manner unique to them, the Mookoovar women wrapped a coarse cloth around the torso as high as the armpits and tied it in front, leaving the upper part of the bosom and shoulders bare.[20]

The royal proclamation issued under the name of Maha Rajah Uthram Thirunal on 26 July 1859 was as follows:

> Whereas we are given to understand that the rules of dress of Shanar females, enacted by the Proclamation of the 23rd Magarom 1004 [the Malayalam version of 3 February 1829] are felt to be a hardship, and whereas it is our earnest desire to satisfy all parties as far practicable, it is hereby proclaimed, that there is no objection to the rest of the Shanar females wearing the Cooppayom, in the same manner as Christian Shanar women, nor to Shanar females of all sects wearing a thick cloth in the way the Mookoovar women do, or covering their bosom in any other manner, provided they

> avoid adopting the dress used by the women of the higher castes.
> All persons should know the above and act accordingly.[21]

The message was loud and clear: caste distinction that was visible on the person remained an inviolable condition of the manner in which Nadar women were allowed to attire themselves. Though the dewan had consulted the Madras government through its resident on the efficacy of this principle, it was kept out of the loop on the actual drafting of the proclamation. In fact, Cullen did not send Pycroft a copy even after the publication of the proclamation. It took two further petitions from the Nadars and the Madras government's response to them before the colonial administration received a copy of the proclamation from Travancore.

Meanwhile, the Nadars objected to the proclamation because of, among other things, the introduction of the Mookoovar garb as an option. They said that this mode of dress was followed 'by only the very poorest' among the fisherwomen, and that 'only when they are at work and when they carry baskets of fish on their heads to the market'. The Nadar women, on the other hand, 'have never been known to wear the cloth in this manner out of doors, and the government in prescribing this mode of dress for them is acting in a most arbitrary manner'.[22]

In two identically worded petitions submitted to the governor of Madras towards the end of August 1859, Nadar inhabitants of Travancore said that the proclamation of the rajah regarding the women of their caste was 'unjust and useless', and that, in a potential re-run of what had happened a few months earlier, 'the Soodras, taking advantage of it, are beginning to abuse and harass them'. So, the petitioners urged Trevelyan to 'reverse' the proclamation and 'publish a better one in its stead authorizing them to enjoy the same freedom and choice as regards dress, jewels, etc as their brethren' in the Madras province.[23]

Since it had no clue about the contents of the proclamation, the Madras government asked Cullen on 20 September 1859 'to procure and submit, for the information of Government, a copy of the proclamation issued by His Highness the Rajah in accordance with the view expressed in the Dewan's letter dated 17th May, 1859'. Ten days later, Cullen's deputy, Major Heber Drury, finally sent to Madras the Malayalam and English versions of the proclamation 'upon the future regulations of dress for the Shanar women in Travancore'.[24]

Only as late as October 1859 did Madras discover that the punitive policy on the crime of covering breasts had eased up. Even as it maintained the ban on the shoulder cloth for the Nadar women, the new proclamation had mercifully done away with the threat issued by its predecessor of 'severely punishing' the violators. The change was relevant to an inquiry Madras had made on 29 August 1859 about the jailing of some Nadar women earlier that year. The district court of Palpanabapuram in Nagercoil, which was then in Travancore, had sentenced them to four months' imprisonment 'for no other alleged crime', as Madras put it, 'than that of wearing a cloth over the upper part of their bodies'.[25] Adding that the women were serving their sentence in 'Trevandrum Jail', the Madras government asked its Travancore resident to explain the circumstances of the case and confirm whether any of them were still in confinement.

On 28 September 1859, Drury did confirm that 'by a report received from the Appeal Court of Travancore, it would appear that two Shanar women were sentenced to four months' imprisonment by the Criminal Court of Palpanabapuram for having worn cloth over the upper part of their persons, contrary to custom and the provisions of the [Travancore] Proclamation'.[26] In India's gallery of shame, this was perhaps the last recorded instance of women being punished with imprisonment for covering their breasts, or rather for the manner in which they had chosen to cover them.

The sentence of imprisonment was commuted to a fine at the appellate stage. As Drury put it, 'The Appeal Court having considered that a fine would have been a more appropriate punishment for the offence committed, immediately ordered their release, on hearing of the sentence that had been awarded. They had then been one month in imprisonment.' He added that there were no Nadar women 'now imprisoned on conviction of wearing the upper cloth'.

The commutation of the sentence evoked appreciation from the Madras government. On 12 November 1859, Pycroft signed an order on behalf of the Governor in Council approving the proceedings of the Appeal Court. 'It is presumed that their ruling has been made generally known for the guidance of all the lower courts,' the Madras order said, adding, 'If it has not, it should be.' Looking ahead, it observed, 'The Honourable Governor in Council, however, hopes that the time is not far distant when His Highness the Rajah will abolish all legal restrictions upon female dress in his dominions.'[27]

The hope expressed by Trevelyan's Council proved to be over-optimistic. The time when all legal restrictions upon female dress in Travancore disappeared was far distant and most gradual. The battles against such restrictions spilt over well into the twentieth century. And those restrictions were by no means limited to Nadars. It took even longer for the more oppressed Pulayas, who were the largest untouchable caste in Travancore, to secure similar rights for their women. In 1915, Pulaya leader Ayyankali launched an agitation that was instrumental in saving female untouchables from wearing bead necklaces as a caste marker and in allowing them to wear blouses.

That such a hope of early reform was expressed at all by Trevelyan's Council in 1859 belied the rift within the colonial structure over the breast-cloth controversy. While one section saw it for what it was—an issue of decency, freedom and equality—the other had internalised the mindset of the dominant castes in deferring to the primacy and inviolability of custom.

Among Indians, the one person most responsible for pushing back against any reform to liberate Nadar women was Madava Row. That he was none the worse for it was a reflection of the times. Having served as dewan in Travancore from 1857 to 1872, he went on to hold the same office successively in Indore and Baroda, reinforcing his image as an astute administrator.

During his Baroda stint, Madava Row is credited with having written the first-ever treatise on statecraft in modern India, *Hints on the Art and Science of Government*. In that book, amid the homilies he delivered to an Indian prince ruling as an ally of the British Raj, Madava Row underscored the sanctity he attached to custom: 'The evil which is sought to be corrected must be clearly shown; what is the evil exactly; what is its magnitude; how many persons does it affect; do the people themselves complain of the evil; does the evil really diminish the happiness of the people, which is the great object of good government? In short, unless the evil is so material that the people themselves or an intelligent portion of them would wish it to be remedied, leave the long established customary law as it is.'[28]

In May 1887, about five years after he had retired from Baroda, Madava Row was appointed chairman of the reception committee for the upcoming Madras session of the Congress. He was a prize catch for the nascent Congress, as evident from the official report of what was its third annual session, the one that took place in Madras in December 1887. 'Independent of Sir Madava Row's great and just reputation as an experienced statesman, the prominent part he took in the proceedings is interesting, because it has been the habit of the opponents of the Congress to declare that the older and abler leaders of the Indian community held aloof from it.'[29] The Congress report boasted that this 'assertion received a strong contradiction' with the participation in Madras of Madava Row, whom it described as 'the foremost of Indian statesmen'.

The Congress's unqualified adulation of Madava Row translated into another great honour. He became the founding president of the first-ever national forum for social reform—ironic, in view of his record of resisting caste and gender reform in Travancore. The Indian National Social Conference came into being in 1887 in Madras as a non-political offshoot of the Indian National Congress.

The moving force behind the Social Conference, M.G. Ranade, invited Madava Row to preside over its inaugural session, betraying the extent to which it was captive to upper-caste interests. The kind of causes the conference espoused in its initial years makes this doubly evident—only issues that affected dominant castes, such as the disabilities attendant on distant sea voyages, ruinous expenses of weddings and child marriages, made it to their table of concerns. Since iniquities affecting lower castes were not on its radar, the Social Conference had no qualms about installing as its first president the man who had once forbidden Nadar women to cover their breasts.

3

THE FIGHT TO BURN WOMEN ALIVE

In the early decades of the nineteenth century, the East India Company promulgated at least two enactments that struck a blow against Hindu orthodoxy. The first was the 1817 regulation which restored the death penalty for Benaras Brahmins. The other, bigger knock came a dozen years later when the Bengal Regulation XVII of 1829 abolished Sati. Invested with religious sanctity, the practice was rampant among Brahmins and other high castes.[1]

A succession of Bengal's governors general, who were effectively the rulers of British India, were confronted with this custom of burning alive a widow on her husband's funeral pyre. In 1813, Lord Minto took the first reform measure by issuing 'circular instructions' that were more incremental than radical. He hoped to keep widows alive without offending Hindu sentiment. Quoting the more progressive 'Pundits', or Brahmin scholars, the instructions declared that Sati was legal but subject to a caveat: it should be performed in consonance with the 'Shasters', or scriptures, of Hinduism.

The repercussions of Minto's instructions can be seen in a case of 1821, *Government v. Bhurachee,* where a Brahmin widow was burnt alive without the presence of the police and, strangely, without even the corpse of her husband. The verdict delivered in the matter by Judge C. Smith expressed concern about the anarchy that had been caused by Minto's instructions. 'Our government by modifying the thing and issuing orders about it have thrown the ideas of the Hindoos on the subject into a complete case of confusion.

They know not what is allowed and what is interdicted; but upon the whole they have a persuasion that our government are rather favourable to Sati than otherwise.'[2] Displaying an activist streak, Smith suggested that the confusion could be dispelled only through legislation. 'They will then believe that we disallow the usage when we prohibit in toto by an absolute and peremptory law.'

However, Lord Hastings, who was governor general at the time, was wary of legislating on Sati, let alone 'an absolute and peremptory' law, for fear of offending upper-caste soldiers. 'I was aware how much danger might attend the endeavouring to suppress, forcibly, a practice so rooted in the religious belief of the natives,' he wrote. 'No men of low caste are admitted into the ranks of the Bengal army. Therefore, the whole of that formidable body must be regarded as blindly partial to a custom which they consider equally referable to family honour and to points of faith. To attempt the extinction of the horrid superstition, without being supported in the procedure by a real concurrence on the part of the army, would be distinctly perilous.'[3]

Thus, the practice of Sati continued with 'unabated vigour', as did the attendant abuses.[4] Hastings's successor, Lord Amherst, too stayed clear of the issue. In a minute written in March 1827, when his five-year tenure was drawing to a close, Amherst declared: 'I am not prepared to recommend an enactment prohibiting Sati altogether.'[5] He argued that Sati could be banned only when the people were ready for it. 'I must frankly confess, though at the risk of being considered insensible to the enormity of the evil, that I am inclined to recommend to our trusting to the progress now making in the diffusion of knowledge among the natives for the gradual suppression of this detestable superstition. I cannot believe it possible that the burning or burying alive of widows will long survive the advancement which every year brings with it in useful and rational learning.'

This was where things stood when William Bentinck succeeded Amherst in July 1828. He did finally venture to outlaw Sati in December 1829, in large part because of the reassuring feedback he had obtained, as detailed in his minute written a month earlier. He had sought the opinions of forty-nine army officers holding key positions, and of the five judges of the Nizamat Adawlat, then the highest criminal court. The feedback convinced him that the time for legislative intervention had come, and it would 'wash out a foul stain upon British rule'.[6]

Bentinck's minute of November 1829 pointed to the 1817 regulation, the very existence of which proved 'the general existence of the exception' that had been made for Brahmins. He said that it was 'impossible to conceive a more direct and open violation of the shasters, or one more at variance with the general feelings of the Hindu population' than the 1817 regulation. For good measure, he added: 'To this day, in all Hindoo states, the life of Brahmins is, I believe, still held sacred.' Yet, the British administration had chosen to legislate equality across castes in respect of the death penalty.

Bentinck's regulation, passed in December 1829, began with a culture-neutral declaration that the practice of Sati was 'revolting to the feelings of human nature'. He followed this up by challenging a culture-specific stereotype: 'It is nowhere enjoined by the religion of the Hindoos as an imperative duty'. Given that widow marriage was still nowhere close to being legalised among upper castes, Bentinck held that 'a life of purity and retirement on the part of the widow is more especially and preferably inculcated'.

He pointed out that, in many instances of Sati, 'acts of atrocity have been perpetrated which have been shocking to the Hindoos themselves, and in their eyes unlawful and wicked'. Discarding Minto's approach of running with the hares and hunting with the hounds, Bentinck's regulation displayed his own 'conviction that the abuses in question cannot be effectually put an end to without abolishing the practice altogether'.

Dispensing with the distinction between lawful and unlawful Sati, the regulation treated it as an offence in all circumstances. It clarified that those who were convicted of 'aiding and abetting' in the sacrifice of a Hindu widow, 'whether the sacrifice be voluntary on her part or not', shall be deemed guilty of 'culpable homicide'.[7]

A provision this stringent was more than what even Rammohan Roy, the progressive Brahmin who led the Indian campaign against Sati, had bargained for. Rather than 'any public engagement' that might 'give rise to general apprehension', all that Roy advocated in a conversation with Bentinck, according to the latter's minute, was that the practice be 'suppressed, quietly and unobservedly, by increasing the difficulties, and by the indirect agency of the police'.

Roy's biographer, historian Amiya P. Sen, acknowledged this, noting that, when compared with Bentinck, the social reformer was on the side of 'restraint and caution'.[8] That said, once the regulation had been enacted, Roy presented Bentinck with a 'congratulatory address' signed by about 300 eminent Hindus, thanking him for 'rescuing us forever from the gross stigma hitherto attached to our character as wilful murderers of females'.[9]

Most radically, for aggravated forms of Sati, the regulation empowered the Nizamat Adawlat to impose no less than the death penalty. This ultimate punishment was prescribed for persons convicted of using 'violence or compulsion' or of having assisted in burning alive a widow who was or had been put under 'a state of intoxication or stupefaction or other cause impeding the exercise of free will'.[10]

The unapologetic combativeness of the 1829 regulation was perhaps the only instance throughout 190 years of colonial rule where a social legislation was enacted without offering any concession to orthodox sentiments. This was all the more remarkable for the fact that, in legal terms, the East India Company was still primarily a commercial enterprise. It was not until the British Parliament passed the Charter Act in 1833 that the company formally became a governing body. That was when Bentinck was upgraded from the governor general of Bengal to the first-ever governor general of India.

By then, through a fresh enactment in 1830, his ban on Sati the previous year in Bengal had been extended in substance to the rest of British India.[11] It took another twenty years for most of the princely states to outlaw the practice.[12] Thus, long before

Mahatma Gandhi famously deployed moral pressure against the British Empire, Bentinck had pitted the same force against the caste and gender prejudices intrinsic to Sati. By criminalising this one native custom that had so corroded the colonised, the coloniser scored a moral point.

Unfazed, orthodox Hindus, led by scholar Radhakanta Deb, filed a petition challenging Bentinck's premise that Sati was not an imperative duty under their religion. The petition quoted the opinions of pundits and extracts from Hindu scriptures to make an elaborate case for revoking the ban on Sati. When Bentinck showed no sign of relenting, the petitioners went all the way to London to appeal before the Privy Council, the court of last resort for the British colonies. This unusual development was noticed by the British media in 1831: 'The British public will learn with amazement ... that an English lawyer has come to this country from India to prosecute an appeal before the Privy Council, made by a few Brahmins in Bengal, against Lord William Bentinck's prohibition of suttees.'[13]

The following year, it was reported that the Privy Council hearings were attended by Rammohan Roy,[14] who had filed a counter-petition. His participation in the proceedings helped ensure that the Privy Council upheld the Sati regulation in 1832. Ruling that the regulation 'cannot properly be regarded as a departure from the just and established principles of religious toleration', the Privy Council said that 'the rite is not prohibited as a religious act, but as a flagrant offence against society'.[15]

On the question of whether 'the rite is sanctified by the religious institutes of the Hindoos', it pointed out that 'by many of the most learned Hindoos of the present day it is regarded as absolutely sinful'. Echoing Bentinck's argument that Sati was 'revolting to the feelings of human nature', the Privy Council said that it was the duty of the government 'to prohibit a practice which so powerfully tended to deprave the national feeling and character, and which taught perverted religion to predominate over the best feelings of the heart'.

Bentinck's redesignation as governor general of India in 1833 by the Charter Act was accompanied by the creation of the post of law member, which was meant to enhance the quality of legislative drafting. The first incumbent of this crucial office was Thomas Macaulay. More than any legislative work, though, Macaulay is best known for his controversial minute on education. Making disparaging remarks about Indian literature, Macaulay proposed in 1835 a Western curriculum in Indian schools with English as the medium of instruction.

But his most significant assignment was the drafting of a consolidated law of penal offences—a global first. In his parallel capacity as chairman of the first Law Commission of India, Macaulay helmed the drafting of the IPC from 1835 to 1837. This elaborate exercise of drafting the IPC had begun just as Bentinck's term in India was ending.

On 14 October 1837, Macaulay submitted the Law Commission's final report on the IPC to Bentinck's successor, Lord George Auckland. The draft IPC, it turned out, diluted the Sati law. Macaulay conceived of a homicide that was qualified thrice over: 'voluntary culpable homicide by consent'. It was defined as a crime that occurred 'when the person whose death is caused, being above 12 years of age, suffers death, or takes the risk of death, by his own choice'.

That this offence was linked to Sati became clearer from an illustration cited in the provision: 'Z, a Hindoo Widow, consents to be burned with the corpse of her husband. A kindles pile. Here A has committed voluntary culpable homicide by consent.'[16] In other words, if someone could claim with supporting testimonies to have lit the pyre at the instance of the widow concerned, it was proposed that he be let off lightly. Eroding the advancement made by Bentinck's 1829 regulation, Macaulay's report in effect revived the 1813 concession of treating the widow's consent to her immolation as an extenuating circumstance.

A note that Macaulay appended to an interim draft of the IPC in 1836 explains why: 'In the first place, the motives which prompt men to the commission of this offence are generally far more respectable than those which prompt men to the commission of murder. Sometimes it is the effect of a strong sense of religious duty, sometimes of a strong sense of honour ...'[17] Such killers, Macaulay held, 'would, except in Christian societies, scarcely be thought culpable, and even in Christian societies would not be regarded by the public, and ought not to be treated by the law, as assassins'.

Macaulay's sympathetic position on Sati found resonance with the British government two decades later when his draft of the IPC was dusted off in the wake of the great revolt of 1857. While several revisions were made to the original draft before it was enacted in 1860, Macaulay's loophole for the perpetrators of Sati made it to the statute book, at least in principle. It fit the colonial strategy of appeasing the high-caste Hindus who had played a leading role in the 1857 violence.

In the IPC enacted in 1860, Lord Canning's Legislative Council dropped both the unwieldy nomenclature and the Sati-specific illustration that Macaulay had suggested. Instead, the loophole for Sati perpetrators appeared as Exception 5 to the definition of murder in Section 300 of the IPC. The wording of the exception, which still exists in the IPC, is deceptively innocuous: 'Culpable homicide is not murder when the person whose death is caused, being above the age of eighteen years, suffers death or takes the risk of death with his own consent.'

Exception 5 made no distinction between Sati and any other death caused with the consent of the person concerned. This anodyne exception took Sati out of the peculiar religious and caste contexts in which widows were conditioned or pressured by their relatives to submit to the supposed glory of immolation.

The IPC's dilution of the Sati provision was a response to the simmering grievances against social legislation, be it the 1829 Sati regulation, the 1850 law empowering outcasted and apostate Hindus to inherit family property or the 1856 law allowing widow remarriage among upper-caste Hindus too.

In fact, offended religious feelings were the larger political context in which violence had broken out in 1857, even if the precipitating factor was unrelated to social reform. The immediate trigger was the outrage among upper-caste soldiers in the Bengal army's base in Meerut. A predominant section of the Bengal army, those Hindu soldiers—most famously, Mangal Pandey—were incensed over reports that the cartridges that they were required to tear open with their teeth had been greased with fat derived from the holy cow. Their Muslim counterparts were likewise indignant over reports that the cartridges were greased with pig fat.

If there was any doubt about whether the IPC had eroded the Sati law, it was dispelled by an amendment to Bentinck's regulation itself. Enacted in May 1862, Act XVII was an omnibus law meant to weed out penal provisions that were overlapping or inconsistent with the IPC.[18] Though it consisted of only seven sections, it had a 'Schedule of Regulations and Acts Repealed' running into thirty pages. The last column in that table was headlined 'Extent of Repeal'. Where the Schedule referred to the Sati law, Regulation XVII of 1829, the last column specified that the repeal was to the extent of 'Sections IV and V'. The amendment to the 1829 regulation essentially repealed both its penal provisions: one stipulating that Sati shall be punished as culpable homicide and the other imposing the death penalty in aggravated cases.

The new law also specified that the 'Regulations and Acts set forth in the Schedule ... shall be held to have been and are hereby repealed from the 1st day of January 1862'. The retrospective application ensured that the amendment repealing the penal clauses of the Sati regulation and the IPC's lenient alternative to consensual homicide was deemed to have come into effect the same day.

The repeal of the provision penalising aggravated cases also meant that the law thereafter presumed that Sati could only be voluntary. This allowed the accused to claim that the victim had consented to her life being terminated at her husband's funeral; that it was a case of suicide rather than homicide. Sure enough, Sati accused began to be tried and convicted only on the charge of abetting suicide under Section 306 of IPC. In its legislative journey from 1829 to 1862, the crime of Sati had diminished from culpable homicide to abetment to suicide.

❖

Motilal Nehru is best known in history as the founder patriarch of the Nehru-Gandhi dynasty, which ruled India for decades in the immediate aftermath of decolonisation. A two-time president of the Congress party, he led the eponymous committee that came up in 1928 with what was formally the earliest draft of fundamental rights for Indians. His son, Jawaharlal Nehru, is credited with having laid, as India's first prime minister, the foundations for the country's diverse achievements in science and technology. And his granddaughter, Indira Gandhi, another long-reigning prime minister, inserted in the Constitution a fundamental duty enjoining every citizen to 'develop the scientific temper, humanism and the spirit of inquiry and reform'.

But in the context of Sati, Motilal Nehru himself displayed greater fidelity to his Brahmin background than the values of scientific temper and humanism and spirit of inquiry and reform. In 1913, at the height of his legal practice before the Allahabad High Court, Nehru appeared for the accused, all Brahmins, in a Sati case. He was already active in politics by this time, and had presided over a provincial conference of the Indian National Congress in Allahabad six years ago. And about six years later, he would go on to become the national president of Congress in the wake of the Jallianwala Bagh massacre.

In between those two milestones, he became a member of the United Provinces Legislative Council following the Morley–Minto constitutional reforms of 1909. So it was that a very politically engaged Motilal Nehru's defence of the Sati accused came about eight decades after that custom had been abolished—by the very colonial power that he was fighting against. The Sati case he represented became a landmark for the audacity of the defence.

Thanks to the erasure of Bentinck's penal provisions, Motilal Nehru had only to establish that his clients were innocent of even the lesser charge of abetment of suicide. His clients claimed that the pyre had ignited miraculously through the sheer piety of the widow. Nehru argued on their behalf that, since nobody had lit the fire, there was no question of suicide, much less so of abetting it. He was putting forward the blatantly unscientific 'theory of spontaneous combustion'.[19]

Motilial Nehru's Sati case was centred on the death of a Brahmin called Ram Lal in village Jarauli in the Mainpuri district of what was called the United Provinces of Agra and Oudh. He died of an illness on the morning of 27 June 1913. Despite having an infant child, his widow, Jai Debi, apparently expressed an intention to commit Sati. Based on this alleged desire, she was hurriedly burnt alive the same morning, amid much excitement and religious fervour, in front of a crowd estimated to have been 1,500- to 2,000-strong. Jai Debi had been reduced to ashes before a messenger could walk eight miles to the nearest police station and the policemen could in turn walk the same distance to reach the spot.

Under the circumstances, the police had no option but to depend on the reverent onlookers to the crime to reconstruct the role played by each of the accused persons. The narrative as summarised by the High Court was as follows:

> Jai Debi then, after walking round it seven times, mounted the pyre, sat down and placed the head of the corpse on her lap. She stripped off her ornaments and threw them into a cloth held by Chote and Dodraj.
>
> She then demanded Ghi. Dodraj handed her a lota full. She poured it over the pyre and her own person. She demanded more and Ram Dayal gave it to her. This also she poured over herself and the pyre. Then Ram Dayal also poured some over her and the pyre. The pyre was then fired, but the witnesses refused to state by whose hand this was done.
>
> In a short time the woman and the corpse were both consumed. When the police arrived at about 3 pm, they found a heap of smouldering ashes and burnt bones ...

Though less commonly practised since 1829, Sati continued to be valourised and revered in certain parts of India, especially among higher castes. Its undiminished allure in 1913 in the Mainpuri district did not deter the rule of law.

Within twenty days of Jai Debi's unnatural death, the sessions judge of Mainpuri, E.O. Allen, convicted five men, all Brahmins, on the charge of abetment of suicide. Though the IPC provided imprisonment of up to ten years for this offence, Allen awarded lenient sentences: two years' imprisonment for two of them, even less for the other three.

During the appeal proceedings before the Allahabad High Court, Motilal Nehru argued that the prosecution witnesses had conceded three 'facts' in favour of the accused:

- That the accused tried to dissuade her from immolating herself and sent information to the police.
- That they resolutely refused to burn the funeral pyre.
- That they carried out certain details under her orders, such as preparing the pyre and supplying her with ghi etc., but they knew that these would be infructuous without the final act of setting fire, which they never did.

In Motilal Nehru's narrative, these facts established 'all reasonable precautions against the actual act of suicide being committed' on the part of the accused, and so he argued that the trial court's finding of their aiding in the act was 'wrong'. As to the tasks they had carried out to assist the widow, Nehru claimed that they had all been done 'under her orders ... on account of fear'. At the same time, the accused, 'had done all they could to prevent her from immolating herself and had refused to light the pyre'. He added for further clarity, 'They were not bound to drag her off the funeral pyre.'

Motilal Nehru took care to enter an alternative plea in the event the High Court too upheld the charge of abetment of suicide. 'Assuming what the accused did was technically an offence,' he said, 'a light sentence would meet the ends of justice.'

The two British judges of the High Court bench were so unconvinced by Nehru's arguments that they did not even wait to hear the government advocate on behalf of the prosecution. On 1 November 1913, they went on to deliver their judgment on Jai Debi's Sati. *Emperor v. Ram Dayal* was the first case where a High Court ruled on the legality of the defence claim that the funeral pyre had spontaneously combusted.

The main judgment, delivered by Justice William Tudball, addressed Nehru's claim that the accused had tried to dissuade her from committing Sati: 'The appellants themselves did not deny the parts they respectively took in the matter, except that Ram Dayal did not admit that he poured ghi over the woman, though the evidence proves that he did so.'

The tricky part was to demystify the supernatural angle that had been attributed to the crime, even by the prosecution witnesses. As Tudball put it, 'Both the witnesses and the accused stated that when all was ready and the widow demanded fire, Ram Dayal and Dodraj refused to give it to her, telling her that if there were any virtue in her she could produce it for herself whereupon she whispered into the ear of the corpse and raising her arms aloft prayed to God, and shortly after the pyre burst into flame.'[20]

In a bid to lend their story a semblance of plausibility, the participants and onlookers claimed that Jai Debi had performed miraculous deeds earlier in the morning too. The main accused further stated that the widow 'threatened to curse them both and cause them to be burnt up if they did not allow her to be Sati'.

None of this washed with Justice Tudball. 'It is clear that the sympathies of the witnesses are naturally with the accused and that there is a conspiracy of silence as to who actually fired the funeral pyre,' he ruled. 'It is equally clear that the miraculous stories have been invented for this purpose. The theory of spontaneous combustion put forward is equally unworthy of belief as the alleged miracles and I have no doubt in the circumstances that the pyre was fired either by the widow or one or both of the accused Ram Dayal and Dodraj.'

Since Nehru's entire defence was based on this tale of divine intervention, Tudball made short work of his related claim that the accused had nothing to do with the ignition. 'To plead that they did everything necessary except the very last act without the intention of assisting her to commit suicide is to ignore facts and to put aside all experience of human nature,' Tudball reasoned. Holding that 'no really effective steps were taken to prevent the suicide', he said, 'A very little force would have been necessary to prevent the woman ascending the pyre. Moreover, it was not absolutely necessary to burn the corpse at so early an hour.'

He also made light of Nehru's diversionary argument that it was 'a gross negligence of the police not to have arrived in time'. Tudball said: 'Though information had been sent to the police, no serious attempt was made to await their arrival on the scene. Sixteen miles had to be walked before they could arrive and the accused must have known that no police officer could possibly arrive until after midday.'

In his concurring verdict, the other judge on the bench, Justice Alfred Edward Ryves, extended the courtesy of saying that the appeal had been 'very ably argued by Pandit Motilal'. At the same time, he deplored the cover-up in which 'the firing of the pyre was attributed to supernatural agency'.

Finding that they had 'intentionally aided the doing of the deed', the Allahabad High Court rejected Motilal Nehru's contention that, in the absence of any eyewitnesses testifying to instigation, the accused could not be held guilty of abetting suicide. The judgment not only upheld the convictions on the charge of abetment of suicide, they enhanced the penalties for the two main accused, Ram Dayal and Dodraj, doubling their prison terms from two years to four years.

In June 1928, just around the time the Motilal Nehru Committee came up with its historic draft of fundamental rights, the Patna High Court happened to refer to this Sati precedent. It was judging a Sati case that had taken place at Barh in Bihar in a Brahmin family, and the accused had in this instance too sought refuge in a miracle story. They even admitted that they were 'expecting a miracle' and that the pyre had caught fire when they were in 'that state of mind'.

The Patna High Court ruled that, for a finding on abetment, 'the method of ignition of the fire, whether miraculous, whether self-applied or whether applied by others, is totally immaterial'.[21] It cited the 1913 Allahabad High Court decision which, having dismissed a similar miracle story, was held to be 'conclusive on this point'.

Later, in a 1932 case of Sati among Rajputs in the Kanpur district, it was claimed that the pyre had caught fire on its own the moment the widow shouted 'Satnam'. Invoking the law that had been laid down on the spontaneous-combustion theory in the 1913 precedent, the Allahabad High Court said that it agreed with 'everything that is said in that case'.[22]

Whatever might have prompted Motilal Nehru to appear in 1913 for those miracle-claiming Sati perpetrators, it is a matter of some irony that, forty years after Indian independence, a government led by his great-grandson Rajiv Gandhi enacted a law that criminalised for the first time the 'glorification of Sati'.

The Commission of Sati (Prevention) Act, 1987 defined glorification as including 'the supporting, justifying or propagating the practice of Sati in any manner'. And for such glorification of Sati, whether committed 'before or after the commencement of this Act', the punishment prescribed by the 1987 law was imprisonment of up to seven years. So anyone who propagated the spontaneous combustion theory, such as in Motilal Nehru's 1913 case, was liable to be punished under Rajiv Gandhi's stringent new law. Regardless of whether the accused were alleged to have abetted the crime or just witnessed the immolation, indeed, even if they were not present at the site, they could be held liable for glorifying Sati.

The enactment of such a law, more than 150 years after the abolition of Sati, indicates the grip that this custom has continued to have over higher-caste citizens. What provoked Rajiv Gandhi to come up with a sanction against glorification was the most notorious Sati in recent decades, involving an eighteen-year-old Rajput widow called Roop Kanwar in village Deorala of Sikar district, Rajasthan.[23] Though it was officially acknowledged as the forty-first case of Sati booked in India since Independence,[24] this 1987 immolation provoked outrage like never before. The unabashed deification of Roop Kanwar by a vocal and conservative section of Rajputs and the magnitude of protests by feminist groups that it provoked were what triggered the legislation.

Besides penalising the glorification of Sati, the Commission of

Sati (Prevention) Act elevated it to the status of murder and re-introduced the death penalty for its abettors in aggravated instances. Thus, in the formulation of its approach to Sati, the 1987 law preferred Bentinck over Macaulay.

The force of Bentinck's influence was evident even in the preamble of Rajiv Gandhi's law. It reproduced verbatim Bentinck's culture-neutral declaration that Sati was 'revolting to the feelings of human nature'. The preamble also borrowed from his contention that Sati was 'nowhere enjoined by the religion of Hindus as an imperative duty'. Except that the 1987 law replaced 'the religion of Hindus' with 'any of the religions of India', as though the problem applied to other religions as well.[25]

Notwithstanding this little change, the incorporation of Bentinck's opening lines in the 1987 law was a tribute paid, even if unwittingly, by a decolonised country to its erstwhile coloniser. Equally, it was a tacit acknowledgement that, in sheer moral and religious terms, a long-liberated India could still do no better than to echo the early British conception of Sati. It is another matter that, in the course of the legislative debates in the two houses of Parliament in December 1987, the Rajiv Gandhi government did not acknowledge these borrowings from Bentinck, despite repeated references to his 1829 regulation. The incongruity of it all was lost on a society that was perhaps as blinded by caste prejudice as it was in Bentinck's days.

4

THE EPIPHANY BEHIND THE FIRST LAW AGAINST CASTE

A group of leading residents of Calcutta—European and Hindu—held a series of meetings in 1816. The venue of those meetings added to their significance: the house of Sir Edward Hyde East, chief justice of the Supreme Court. They had gathered to discuss the ambitious project of establishing what would be India's first institution of higher learning, at least in the modern sense.

The confabulations of that mixed group were what led to the founding of the Hindoo College in Calcutta in 1817. The Hindu attendees would be in charge of managing the institution. Their collective wisdom was to set up a college 'for the tuition of sons of *respectable* Hindoos' (emphasis added).[1] This qualification meant that the college was open only to upper-caste folks, those who came to be known in Bengal as 'Bhadralok'.

The Hindoo College was rechristened 'Presidency College' in 1855 when the East India Company took over its management and opened admissions to male students from all castes and communities. The next big leap came almost a century later, in 1944, when the institution opened its portals to women students. In deference to its special place in India's history and its high academic standards, the college was conferred the status of a university in 2010.

As for Justice East, he returned to London in 1822 after an eight-year stint as chief justice in Calcutta. The following year, he was elected to the House of Commons as a legislator who had a lengthy experience of working in India. It was in this capacity that, on 9 March 1830, East appeared before a Select Committee of the House of Lords, which was tasked with enquiring into the affairs of the East India Company.[2]

Besides answering questions verbally, East submitted five papers offering his analysis and recommendations on a range of subjects pertaining to India. In his paper on 'the state and condition of the native population ... in respect of laws and usages', East dwelt on, among other things, the anomalies relating to those who had converted from Hinduism to Christianity.

In a sardonic tone, East cited the example of an unnamed Brahmin who, even after he had declared himself a Unitarian, would still 'not do anything willingly to forfeit his caste, considering it probably as the nobility of his country, which he is desirous to preserve'. As a corollary, in deference to the customary bar on dining with people from outside his caste, he 'declines eating with us, though he invites company to his house and sits at the table with them'. Referring to the custom of upper-caste males wearing a sacred thread, East said that the Brahmin, despite changing his religion, regarded his string as 'a mark of high descent to which he naturally clings'.

The distinction sought to be maintained by such a professed convert to Christianity seemed, he said, 'to leave him essentially Hindoo as to customs and laws'. Did that ambiguity mean that he could, like any Hindu male of the time, 'maintain a lawful plurality of wives, on which the legality of his issue, on a question of inheritance, must depend'? East asked, 'Is such a person to be deemed a Hindoo in point of law for one purpose and not for another? ... Or is he to lose the benefit of the one code without acquiring that of the other?'

East went on to make a seminal recommendation: a statutory provision stipulating that 'no native of India shall forfeit any rights of property or personal benefit, on account of his profession of any particular faith or doctrine'. Thus, while seeking to protect the inheritance rights and other civil rights of converts, East proposed that Indians be provided the right to freedom of religion and liberty of conscience.

The idea appealed to the court of directors of the East India Company, especially in the context of British missionary activity in the country. In a letter to Governor General William Bentinck on 2 February 1831 on the disabilities faced by native Christians, the court of directors made a guarded reference to the proposal that East had placed before the Select Committee.

The directors began by admitting that 'it is impossible for us to prescribe to you the adoption of Sir E. Hyde East's suggestion without being more completely informed than we are at present, how far it is necessary or would be advisable'. So, they asked Bentinck to inquire and report to them 'in what manner and to what extent conversion to Christianity exposes the convert or his descendants to the loss of property or other civil rights, and what means, in your opinion, can be taken to relieve them from such disadvantage'.[3]

Eleven months later, on 3 January 1832, Calcutta got back to London with a draft of the regulation that proposed to address the issue that East had flagged. It said that, though Bentinck was 'not aware that any practical injury has been sustained by native converts in consequence of the existing laws', he believed that 'the possibility of such an occurrence should be guarded against by an express enactment'.[4] The accompanying draft provision was subsequently enacted as Section 9 of the Bengal Regulation VII of 1832.

> Whenever in any civil suit the parties to such suit may be of different persuasions ... or when one or more of the parties to the suit shall not be either of the Mahomedan or Hindoo persuasion, the laws of those religions shall not be permitted to operate to deprive such party or parties of any property to which but for the operation of such laws, they would have been entitled.

Though it was couched in general terms, Section 9 aimed to ensure that a convert would not be deprived of his inheritance. This secular law superseded the religious law. Although it was in response to East's proposal to protect converts to Christianity, the colonial administration brought into Bengal the concept of liberty of conscience. Bentinck enacted this radical provision just three years after his famous Sati regulation. Both enactments impinged on the religious domain and, albeit in different ways, drastically affected property claims within families.

Yet, the provision protecting the interests of Hindu apostates provoked no reaction from orthodox Hindus. While the 1829 Sati regulation was a standalone law, the 1832 provision on the rights of converts was tucked away in a larger regulation dealing with the powers of judicial officers in adjudicating civil suits. Coincidentally, the 1832 provision was enacted the very year in which the Privy Council delivered its landmark verdict upholding the Sati regulation.

Among the lawyers who appeared before the Privy Council for the opponents of the Sati regulation was John Eliot Drinkwater Bethune. A contemporaneous news report in Britain confirms this young man's participation in the proceedings that took place on 23 June 1832.[5] Less than twenty years later, the same Bethune went on to play a crucial role in expanding the ambit of the freedom of religion provision of 1832.

This reform began with a Law Commission proposal in 1841 to turn the 1832 Bengal regulation into a national law. The draft published by the Law Commission in 1841 said:

> So much of the Hindoo and Mahommedan law as inflicts forfeiture of property or rights upon any party renouncing either of those religions, is abrogated.[6]

Departing radically from the language of the 1832 Bengal regulation, the first draft of the national law remained focused on conversions. Governor General Lord Auckland ordered the circulation of this draft bill among administrators across British India.

In the course of this process, H.T. Prinsep, a senior functionary in Calcutta, took the opportunity in 1842 to suggest a change that was more deferential to religious sentiments. Since the draft expressly referred to Hindu and Mahomedan laws, he said, 'We cannot pretend to abrogate what is a matter of religious belief, and supposed to have revelation for its origin.' So he suggested that the word 'abrogated' be changed for 'shall not be enforced by any court'.

In 1843, the Council of Madras Governor George Hay made a more significant suggestion. It pointed out that the 1841 draft protected only such a person as had renounced his religion 'as his own act'. In the best tradition of liberalism, the Madras government argued that the object should rather be to uphold the personal rights of individuals, 'whether they voluntarily renounce their own creed or are ejected from its communion by others'.

But then, was there anything really like a communion—a unity based on religious beliefs—in a community that was deeply segregated by caste? Acknowledging the uncanny subtext of caste, the Madras government added that its proposal to deal with involuntary exit too would 'afford a remedy in all cases against those provisions of Hindoo law which deprive the outcast of his civil rights'.

This passing reference to the complexity of caste did not seem to have registered with the Council of Governor General Henry Hardinge. In the draft of the Liberty of Conscience Bill published by it in 1845, Hardinge's Council did incorporate Princep's concern about making the text more respectful to religious sentiments as also Hay's stress on protecting those expelled from community. The draft bill took no cognisance, however, of caste.

> So much of the Hindoo and Mahomedan law as inflicts forfeiture of rights or property upon any party renouncing or who has been excluded from the communion of either of those religions, shall cease to be enforced as law in the Courts of the East India Company.

The 1845 draft failed to recognise that the exclusion of a Hindu who had converted to Christianity was more likely to be from his caste fraternity than any communion of his religion as a whole. This deficiency was redressed rather dramatically only days before the bill was enacted in 1850.

❖

Even as modernity began to percolate through British India in the first half of the nineteenth century, patriarchy continued to maintain a vice-like grip on women and girls. This was especially true of those from the upper castes who were burdened with maintaining the 'purity' of their lineage, and for whom even stepping out of their homes was discouraged. These women were in no position to avail the schooling opportunities that had now opened up for them.

Their counterparts from the lower castes faced fewer constraints. Some of them joined the schools launched by Christian missionaries. Evidently, lower castes were less worried—or perhaps had less reason to worry—about their girls being exposed to missionaries, despite their notoriety for engaging in religious conversions under the guise of imparting education.

It was, therefore, no coincidence that the Indian social reformers who famously broke the taboo on the education of women and girls were from a backward caste. And from a city that was steeped in Brahminism—a legacy of the Peshwa reign which had ended in 1818. Early in their lifelong crusade against Brahminism and the misogyny inherent in it, Jotirao Phule and his wife Savitribai Phule, who belonged to the lowly Mali caste, started a pioneering school for girls in Poona on 1 January 1848.

That same year, in the imperial capital of Calcutta, John Elliot Drinkwater Bethune, one of the lawyers who had appeared before the Privy Council for Sati proponents, arrived from London. He was to assume the high office of law member in the Council of Governor General Lord Dalhousie. His attitude to social reform had changed drastically by this time, and Bethune now displayed unusual sensitivity in taking on social inequities in India.

Like Edward East, he came up with a radical initiative in the field of education and executed it in his personal capacity. On 7 May 1849, within a year of his arrival, Bethune set up out of his own pocket a first-of-its-kind school in Calcutta. It was a non-missionary school designed to attract upper-caste girls.

Meanwhile, Jotirao's father, unable to bear the pressure exerted by upper castes to force the closure of the Poona school, expelled the rebellious couple from his home. Given that the Phule school's students were mostly from the inferior castes, it violated customary restrictions in respect of not only women but also low castes.

While Jotirao was a product of missionary education, Savitribai had been educated at home by her husband. And it was she who most offended the gentry—for she dared to serve, in a first for the country, as a teacher in the school. As Jotirao's biographer Dhananjay Keer put it, 'They threw mud, dirt, stones at her when she was on her way to the school.'[7]

Though Bethune would hardly have been subjected to such humiliation, the environment in Calcutta, too, was far from conducive to educating girls. Despite all the trappings of his colonial authority, he needed to tread cautiously. When he started running what was variously referred to as the Native Female School or Hindu Balika Vidyalaya, Bethune took care to avoid drawing any funds for it from the East India Company. He was wary of associating the government with the establishment of the school, although he was also president of British India's Council of Education.

Bethune's reason for making 'this experiment on my own responsibility',[8] as he explained later to Dalhousie, in a letter dated 29 March 1850, was to shield the government from any social repercussions. 'I considered that my station in the Council of India and as President of the Council of Education afforded me peculiar advantages in endeavouring to discover whether my belief was well founded that the time has come when this important step in the system of education of the natives can be taken with a reasonable hope of success,' Bethune wrote. 'I wished the discredit of failure to rest with myself alone, if my expectation had proved abortive, and that the credit of the Government should not be pledged to the measure until its success was assured.'

Bethune's experiment was to increase the school's acceptability by 'excluding from it all religious teaching' and, contrary to Macaulay's controversial Minute on Education, to have Bengali as the medium of instruction, while teaching English only to those 'whose parents wished it'. For all his strategic moves to woo upper castes, Bethune's school started with 'only 11 pupils' as it was 'vehemently opposed by many of the most influential natives of Calcutta'.

He recorded his gratitude to three upper-caste collaborators who helped him in various ways: Ram Gopal Ghose for being his 'principal adviser in the first instance' and for procuring his early pupils, Dakshinaranjan Mukherjee for donating land for the school without any previous acquaintance with Bethune, and Madan Mohan Tarkalankar for sending his two daughters to the school and compiling a series of elementary Bengali books for it. But then, 'every kind of annoyance and persecution was set on foot to deter my friends from continuing to support the school', thereby causing the number of enrolled students to 'dwindle to seven'.

One mitigation measure that was proposed to him during that phase of struggle was that he offer a stipend of five or six rupees a month to each student. This was so that 'I might count on immediately recruiting the school to any extent that I might think desirable from Brahminical families of unquestionable caste and respectability.' He turned down this proposal, however, as he was 'anxious to ascertain whether any real desire for the education of their daughters exist in any respectable class of the community'.

Instead, Bethune provided non-monetary incentives. 'The only allowances which I have made have been for carriage hire for those who required it and occasional presents of dresses, when any of the little girls appeared in rather too primitive a state to correspond with any notions of decency.' According to the historian Sumit Sarkar, 'What was striking about Bethune's endeavour in 1849 was that daughters of respectable families were now being encouraged to go out to a school.'[9] The carriage provided by him to transport those girls was emblazoned with a Sanskrit verse declaring that 'a daughter's education was a father's religious duty'.[10]

Bethune's experiment in Calcutta emboldened a few upper-caste social reformers to start similar schools elsewhere in the Bengal presidency. Since they too faced opposition, it was but natural for those schools to approach Bethune for help in his official capacity. As Bethune put it in his March 1850 letter to Dalhousie,[11] 'Wherever a school has been established, there has been a repetition of the same system of persecution and attempts at intimidation which we have had to contend with in Calcutta, and frequent applications are made to me for support and encouragement, as the position I have assumed naturally marks me out as the patron of all such undertakings.'

Towards the end of his eleven-page letter, Bethune urged Dalhousie that the time had come for him to declare, at the risk of incurring the wrath of conservative Indians, that the government looked on all those girls' schools 'with a favourable eye'. Regarding his own school, Bethune said that he would continue to defray its expenses 'so long as I remain in this country, and when I leave it, I have little doubt of being able to interest others to supply place'.

In his minute written on 1 April 1850, Dalhousie appreciated Bethune's 'labours for the foundation of a female school' as also his proposal of sending out a signal meant to deter attacks on such undertakings.[12] And so, the Bengal government was instructed to undertake 'the superintendence of native female education and that wherever any disposition is shewn by a native gentleman to establish female schools, they should give them all possible encouragement'. He also noted that Bethune's 'determination to make the experiment as an individual and not first to engage the government in it seemed to me to be most judicious'.

The government did get involved with Bethune's school barely a year later, and it was for a tragic reason. On 12 August 1851, Bethune passed away. He was fifty. Shortly before his death, he had transferred all his rights in the school property to the East India Company, 'with an expression of his hope that the institution would be endowed in perpetuity by the government'.[13]

Since the necessary clearance for such an endowment from the company's Court of Directors in London was bound to take a while, Dalhousie immediately stepped into Bethune's shoes, meeting the school's expenses from his own funds. This was how Dalhousie recorded his decision on 20 September 1851, a month after Bethune's death. 'Having undertaken on my own part and on that of Lady Dalhousie, as private persons, to provide for the maintenance of the Native Female School founded by Mr Bethune so long as we may remain in India, the question of its endowment by the Hon'ble Court does not press for immediate decision.'[14]

The decision from London finally came in early 1854. It was a qualified approval, subject to the condition that a fee shall be charged from those able to pay. While acknowledging the sanction to grant a monthly allowance to Bethune's school, the Supreme Council of India recorded as follows on 3 February 1854: 'Their orders be carried into immediate effect in order that the Marquis of Dalhousie may be relieved of the expense he so liberally undertook.'[15] The governor general, however, continued to patronise the school until 1856, consistent with his personal resolve to provide for its maintenance so long as he remained in India.

Slowly and steadily, the school gained acceptance. Following the takeover of its management by the government, the school was officially renamed after Bethune. Iconic social reformer Iswar Chandra Vidyasagar served as secretary of Bethune School. Years later, in 1879, as its students completed schooling, Bethune organically developed into India's first women's college. Besides producing the country's earliest female graduates, Bethune College was for many years the only institution in India offering higher education to women.

❖

In the relatively brief period of three years that they worked together, from 1848 to 1851, Dalhousie and Bethune were also instrumental in enacting the first-ever national legislation touching upon caste disabilities. Act XXI of 1850 was an unforeseen outcome of what began as an attempt to go national with the 1932 Bengal regulation on the freedom of religion. What emerged was the first enactment to take on the nexus between religion and caste.

As it happened, both the 1832 provincial and 1850 national enactments had been propelled by education pioneers: Edward East and John Bethune.

The historical incongruity of Bethune—a British lawyer who had represented the orthodoxy in the Sati battle and then went on to break with tradition and set up the first girls' school in Calcutta—has long been part of Bengali folklore. Sunil Gangopadhyay's *Sei Samay* (*Those Days*), the 1985 Sahitya Akademi-winning historical novel in Bengali, too explores this unusual course of Bethune's career.[16] Less known is the fact that this storied colonial administrator was also the moving spirit behind the very first legislative measure at the national level to combat caste disabilities.

While the preamble of the 1850 Act claimed that it was meant only to 'extend the principle' of the Bengal regulation to the rest of British India, the duo of Dalhousie and Bethune went beyond that remit. They widened the ambit of the law to protect the inheritance rights of not just converts to Christianity but also of those who had been excommunicated from their castes for any reason whatsoever. The latter category was potentially larger.

The draft first published by the Dalhousie administration in October 1849 made no reference to caste. The only change that was made was to replace the specific reference to religious laws with a generic one: 'So much of the Hindoo and Mahomedan law' in the 1845 draft became 'so much of any law or usage now in force' in the 1849 draft. This modest change followed a cautious minute that Bethune had written on the proposed law on 31 May 1849.[17] (Incidentally, this was the very month in which Bethune had been devoting a great deal of his time, energy and money to setting up his non-missionary girls' school.)

The minute was a response to a letter he had received the same month from the bishop of Bombay calling upon the Dalhousie administration to enact the law without any further delay. In his letter, dated 14 May 1849, the bishop said that there were several cases in which the converts had been deprived 'not only of property but some of wives and children'. This was the first indication Bethune received, even if not in so many words, that the freedom of religion could not be seen in isolation from caste disabilities.

Yet, in the minute he wrote a fortnight later, the law member, who had just set up a girls' school in his personal capacity, sounded wary of joining another social reform battle in his official capacity. Even as he admitted to 'some lingering doubt of the justice of the measure' contained in the 1845 draft, Bethune aired his anxiety to give the law 'the slightest possible appearance of interfering with the religious notions of the natives'.

The notion he found most challenging was the one prevalent among Bengali Hindus that, in keeping with their Dayabhaga school of law, the son's right to succeed to his father's property was 'commensurate with his obligation to perform his funeral from which the outcaste is necessarily excluded'. Bethune came to grips with the complication that a Hindu apostate was liable to be reduced to an outcaste and therefore religiously divested of his succession rights. Even as he refrained from taking any view on this religious sensitivity in his 1849 minute, it prompted him to rid his draft of any express reference to 'Hindoo and Mahomedan law'.

The cosmetic change did little to allay the fears of orthodox Hindus, as driven home by the two memorials sent by them. While the first memorial was from inhabitants of 'Bengal, Behar and Orissa', the second was from inhabitants of Madras. The first was led by Raja Radhakanta Deb who was associated with the founding of the Hindoo College and had spearheaded the campaign against the ban on Sati. Thus, in the legal proceedings challenging the Sati regulation before the Privy Council in London in 1831–32, Bethune was among the lawyers representing Deb's side. In another curious coincidence, Deb was among the Indians who had, emulating Bethune's example, started schools for girls in Bengal. In fact, Deb's school in Calcutta was set up barely a fortnight after the launch of Bethune's.

All the same, the memorial organised by Deb was an exemplar of the anxiety that Bethune's minute had expressed. The memorialists took umbrage at what they saw as interference with their religious notion of confining inheritance rights to those who were qualified to perform the last rites of the property owner. As the memorial put it, '(I)f you quit your father's religion you must quit your father's property ... You are civilly dead, and the property which you inherited from your father must go to your father's nearest heir, capable of fulfilling those duties, for which the Hindoo law gave it to you, to insure his and his ancestors' eternal bliss in that future world to which we all journey.'

Claiming the authority to declare civil death for the apostate, the memorialists intended to enforce it through the rigours of caste. 'His family and Hindoo friends would be unable [any] longer to associate or eat with him without becoming out-casts,' they said, adding without any sense of irony, 'but in no other way would he be persecuted.'

In that disclaimer was the unabashed admission that the apostate would indeed be persecuted through excommunication. As if that was not bad enough, the memorialists asserted that even those who associated with the apostate were liable to suffer similar caste disabilities. 'To eat or consort with him in any way would necessarily create a loss of caste in those who remained true to the religion of their ancestors.'

The memorialists thus asserted that caste associations were empowered to deprive the apostate of not only his caste but also his inheritance rights. And that they could deprive a person of inheritance rights not only for apostasy but also for any other caste violation. Their audacious foray into the domain of the courts to adjudicate civil rights seemed to have jolted Bethune out of the tentative position he took in his May 1849 minute. By the time he wrote his second minute on the bill ten months later, Bethune had shed all his squeamishness about appearing to interfere with the religious notions of the natives.

His minute dated 26 March 1850 noted: 'The whole argument of the memorialists turns on the fact ... that according to Hindoo law, a man who becomes an outcaste, either by change of religion or in any other way, is liable to be deprived of the share of his patrimonial inheritance which would otherwise belong to him.'

Consequently, what was originally meant to be no more than a general enactment on the freedom of religion became the first social reform of the Hindu law after the Sati regulation. It also contained an unprecedented reference to caste in a national enactment.

Bethune made this breakthrough through the carefully placed insertion of five words—'or being deprived of caste'—into the legislation. Since it was moot whether the term 'communion' could apply to Hindus in general, the insertion was made right after that portion. The final draft protected the inheritance rights of not only those who had been 'excluded from the communion of any religion' but also those who had been, presumably in the case of Hindus, 'deprived of caste'.

Significantly, Muslims voiced no objection to either draft of the bill, published four years apart. Their religion, like Christianity, was also a proselytising one. Since Bethune had to deal only with the religious arguments advanced by Hindu memorialists, his second minute was mostly devoted to debunking the 'fallacy in the statement that the right of inheritance depends on the obligation to perform the funeral rites'.

This led him to introspect in his second minute on the interplay between excommunication and inheritance rights, drawing a parallel with the history of Christians in England. He said that it was 'a mistake to suppose that the incapacity to inherit arising out of excommunication is peculiar to the Hindu religion'. Having critiqued the record of his own community, Bethune said: 'It is the policy of professors of every claimant religion to convert as much as possible their spiritual armoury into a storehouse of weapons of offence for securing objects of earthly advantage; in this respect the Christian and the Hindu histories shew the same kind of device.'

That he likened Hindus to Christians was a remarkable display of self-deprecating candour on the part of a colonial administrator. And a far cry it was from how Bentinck, for instance, could score a moral point in the context of Sati, a practice peculiar to Hindus.

However, insofar as the authority to enact religious reforms was concerned, Bethune was better placed in 1850 than Bentinck had been in 1829. The 1833 Charter Act had strengthened the structure of India's governance. As Bethune put it in his minute, 'There was more room of doubting [prior to the Charter Act 1933] whether it was within the power of the local legislature to make any regulation in any way affecting the laws of inheritance of Hindoos but there is now no such restriction on the power of the Governor General in Council.'

The law member of Dalhousie's Council also laid down a principle separating the spiritual from the temporal: 'I take the high ground of inherent and inalienable right of every Government to regulate the law of property, and to deprive any claim of its subjects of the power of securing conformity to their own opinions by the infliction of penalties which it belongs to the Government only to impose.' Having rejected the 'expedient' of the memorialists to connect 'the possession of property with the performance of religious duties', Bethune said that it was 'a sufficient recognition of the liberty of conscience if they are left undisturbed in the performance of their ceremonies'.

Two weeks later, on 9 April 1850, Governor General Dalhousie recorded his minute endorsing Bethune's proposal to build further on Bentinck's 1832 initiative: 'I entirely agree with Mr Bethune in the principle he lays down that it is the duty of the state to keep in its own hand the right of regulating succession to property.' He sought to clarify, however, that the principle enunciated by Bethune in his second minute regarding the duty of the State was not inconsistent with the assurance held out by the same councillor in his first minute to honour the religious notions of the natives. 'In now acting on this principle,' Dalhousie said, 'I can see no semblance of interference with the religion of the Hindoos, nor any unauthorized interference with rights secured to them.'

He added that the rights secured to the Hindus could not, under any circumstances, extend to denying a family member of their legal entitlement to inheritance. The government would be failing in its duty, 'if it leaves unchanged any portion of that law which inflicts personal injury on any one by reason of his religious belief'.

Once Dalhousie decided to bite the bullet, the enactment of this change in law was but a formality. On 11 April 1850, two days after

Dalhousie's minute and less than a fortnight after Bethune's spirited reaction to the memorialists, the Governor General in Council passed Act XXI of 1850.

Incidentally, the discussion between Bethune and Dalhousie leading to this landmark legislation overlapped with their correspondence on the incipient trend of girls' schools being set up. Barely three days after his 1850 minute on protecting apostates and outcasted Hindus, Bethune wrote to Dalhousie about his engagement with girls' education. And about a week before his go-ahead to Bethune's legislative proposal on religious and caste disabilities, Dalhousie had written his minute on 1 April 1850, endorsing his law member's suggestion that girls' schools needed to be protected from attacks.

After all its iterations over the years, the section enacted in the single-clause 1850 legislation read as follows:

> So much of any law or usage now in force within the territories subject to the Government of the East India Company as inflicts on any person forfeiture of rights or property, or may be held in any way to impair or affect any right of inheritance, by reason of his or her renouncing, or having been excluded from the communion of, any religion, or being deprived of caste, shall cease to be enforced as law in the Courts of the East India Company and in the Courts established by Royal Charter within the said territories.

Of all the laws enacted during his eight-year tenure as governor general, Act XXI of 1850, according to one of his biographies, 'was always regarded by Lord Dalhousie as the most important of those passed by him'.[18] To be sure, he is remembered more for introducing railways, telegraph and uniform postal service in India, and for pursuing the doctrine of lapse and expanding the domain of British India in the lead-up to the 1857 uprising. Dalhousie gets little credit in popular history for being instrumental in striking a blow against caste—however nominally—for the first time ever in a national legislation. More than a century after its enactment, an American scholar of social justice in India, Marc Galanter, wrote that the 1850 law was the 'only legislation during the British period bearing directly on caste autonomy'.[19]

So much so that, in 1897, when the legislature conferred 'short titles' on several old laws, Act XXI of 1850 came to be formally named as the Caste Disabilities Removal Act, 1850. The rationale behind the Short Titles Act, 1897 was to follow in India what had by then become a practice in England, that 'every Act should be capable of being cited by means of a short title'. Given that the original intent behind the enactment of the 1850 law was only to protect the inheritance rights of apostates, Lord Elgin, who was the viceroy of India in 1897, could well have named it the Freedom of Religion Act or the Religious Disabilities Removal Act. After all, there was just a passing reference to caste in that single-clause law.

That Elgin's Legislative Council chose to highlight the caste angle in the short title was perhaps a sign of the growing colonial understanding of the dynamics peculiar to Hindu society. Or the choice might have been made with a political intent, to put the emerging band of Hindu nationalists on the defensive by drawing attention to the caste divisions inherent to their community.

The title was misleading though. Far from the impression conveyed by its overbroad title, the 1850 law was limited to protecting the civil rights of those who had, for whatever reason, been 'deprived of caste'. Everyday issues of caste prejudice—such as restrictions on members of lower castes from accessing public spaces and on members of any caste from dining with, let alone marrying, members of other castes on pain of excommunication—fell outside the scope of this law.

But then, before the law even had a name, conservative Hindus already saw it as loaded against them. Consider this file noting by a Fort William official in 1893: 'It is easy to see why a Hindu should object to Act XXI of 1850. Practically there are no converts to Hinduism except from aboriginal tribes, who scarcely come before the courts, whilst converts are made from Hinduism.'[20]

❖

That the 1850 law facilitated a one-way street out of their fold rankled Hindu nationalists for decades. In 1927, a legislative proposal was made by N.C. Kelkar, who was the late Bal Gangadhar Tilak's political follower, journalistic successor and biographer. He was also a leader of the Hindu Mahasabha and a member of the Central Legislative Assembly, the forerunner of the Lok Sabha. In December 1927, Kelkar introduced a bill that sought to repeal the Caste Disabilities Removal Act, 1850.

It was not the first time that a native legislator had moved to get rid of a national law enacted by the colonial masters. The 1816 Madras regulation prescribing confinement in the stocks for lower-caste offenders had been repealed in 1919 due to similar attempts by Indian legislators.

The difference, however, was that Kelkar's 1927 bill sought to undo what was a social reform, at least in the eyes of progressive Hindus. To discredit the 1850 law, he stressed on the absence of any Indian lawmaker's involvement in its enactment. As his formal SOR put it, 'The Caste Disabilities Removal Act was purely a Government measure and does not represent the will of the people.'[21]

In the event, Kelkar's bill served as an opportunity for rival Hindu voices to be heard for the first time in the national legislature. It led to a counterblast from fellow legislator Hari Singh Gour who saw the 1850 law as a social reform that needed to remain in the statute book. In social terms, it was a debate between a conservative Brahmin from Poona and a progressive Kshatriya from Sagar, in what was then called the Central Provinces.

Like East and Bethune, Gour too was associated with the founding of educational institutions. A jurist who had a doctorate in law from Cambridge and post-doctorate from Dublin, he was the first vice chancellor of Delhi University when it was established in 1922. It was an exceptional honour for an Indian to be the first head of a university that the British had opened in their new capital. Subsequent to his term in Delhi, Gour served twice as vice chancellor of Nagpur University. His crowning glory though was a university he set up in Sagar, his home town, in 1946, with the money he had made as a leading lawyer. Until his death three years later, Gour served as the first vice chancellor of Sagar University, the oldest institute of higher learning in what is today Madhya Pradesh. It has since been renamed Dr Hari Singh Gour University. His seminal books on law included *The Hindu Code*, which was published in 1919.[22]

In his parallel avatar as a national legislator from 1921 to 1934, Gour served as the moving force behind a range of social reforms, including one that he believed complemented the 1850 law. The scriptural basis on which Hindus had traditionally denied inheritance rights to an excommunicated family member was an injunction from Manu, that most controversial of law-givers of antiquity. Chapter IX, Section 201 of the Manusmriti denied inheritance rights even to Hindus suffering from other disabilities. As the authoritative translation of the time put it, 'Eunuchs and outcastes, persons born blind or deaf, madmen, idiots, the dumb, and such as have lost the use of a limb, are excluded from a share of the heritage.'[23]

It was in defiance of this injunction that Gour introduced a bill in October 1927, stipulating that other than a born lunatic, no Hindu shall be excluded from inheritance 'by reason only of any disease, deformity, or physical or mental defect'. He also cited judgments that had, on the strength of the Shastric or classical Hindu law, discriminated against vulnerable people. The Central Legislative Assembly passed the Hindu Inheritance (Removal of Disabilities) Bill on 22 March 1928. Four days later, there was a heated exchange between Gour and Kelkar when the latter's bill to repeal the 1850 law came up for discussion in the same House.

The reasons Gour cited in support of the 1850 law were mainly about caste, vindicating thereby the short title that had been given to it in 1897. While Kelkar projected the law as a colonial ploy to encourage Hindus to convert to Christianity, Gour saw it as a social reform protecting the legal rights of outcasted Hindus. Addressing other Hindu legislators as well as the government, Gour urged them to help retain the law 'if only on the short ground that it has been on the statute book for 78 years and there is no prima facie case for reconsidering it'.

His historical narrative of the 1850 enactment was somewhat questionable, though. Gour made out that it was the outcome of 'a reforming movement' in which both 'orthodox and heterodox Hindus' had clamoured for the 'freedom of conscience'. In reality—unlike the 1829 Sati regulation or the 1856 Widow Remarriage Act—the 1850 law was not linked with the campaign of any Hindu social reformer.

East had come up with the idea in London in 1830. The only Hindus who sent memorials to Fort William in 1845 and 1849, when successive drafts of the bill had been published, were those who wanted to deny apostates any inheritance rights. Only Bethune's last-minute move had extended the protection to all outcasted Hindus. But maybe Gour did not have access to the relevant archival information. Or, following the rupture brought about by the Jallianwala Bagh episode of 1919, he was possibly being tactical in 1928 in crediting the 1850 law to a Hindu reforming movement rather than the colonial machinery.

Regardless of the reason for his imaginative reconstruction of this history, Gour was well qualified to speak on the working of the law. Having 'read all the cases' decided under the Caste Disabilities Removal Act, Gour appreciated the salutary effect of the secular law in circumscribing the domain of caste. He said: 'If you have any social opinion, if you can organise social ostracism, social persecution of the man who transgresses the caste law, you are entitled to do so. But so far as the courts are concerned, they will not enforce the penalty, which the shastras enjoin upon a person who forfeits his caste.'

Recalling the bill that the House had passed four days earlier at his instance, Gour said that the need for it had arisen because, as suggested by courts in some cases, the 1850 law was only a 'half measure'. For loss of property ensued from not only loss of caste but also loss of a limb or organ.

Having addressed this inequity in the Shastric law with his recent bill, he was poised to drive home the incongruity of simultaneously repealing the reform that had been made in 1850. 'If you are to take that away you will have once more placed upon us the shackles of caste. You will have once more thrown us into the cage of the Hindu caste-ridden religion; you will have completely destroyed that emancipating and reforming movement which is purifying and purging Hinduism and Hindu society.'

In his response, Kelkar barely touched upon this scathing critique of the caste system. Instead, he only echoed a key argument of the 1849 memorial of conservative Hindus led by Radhakanta Deb. 'What is the use of succeeding to your father's property and claiming a share therein if you do not take your father's religion also?' Kelkar asked, adding, 'If you want to change your religion, by all means do so, but have the ambition to prove yourself a fresh stock of descent both for property as well as for religion.'

Further, rejecting Gour's description of the 1850 law as a 'refreshing breeze from the West', Kelkar said that it had been enacted when the legislature was 'not representative'. Glossing over the tyranny of the caste hierarchy as a possible cause for conversions, he said, 'Other religions at present benefit by apostasy but the Hindu religion on the contrary suffers.'

Kelkar responded to only one of Gour's contentions on caste: the frivolous grounds on which Hindus could be expelled from their castes under the Shastric law. As a possible illustration, Gour said that the Shastric law would have penalised Kelkar for 'coming to the tiffin room and receiving our hospitality or taking a cup of tea in that tiffin room. The moment he does that he would be deprived of his caste.' Though Kelkar interrupted him with a 'No', Gour went on to say: 'And the moment he is deprived of his caste, he is deprived of all his heritage; that is the Shastric law. The Shastric law is rigid, inflexible, remorseless, in excluding all persons who transgress in the slightest degree the requirements of caste.' Gour was pointing to the fact that Kelkar, being a Brahmin, was liable to transgress the caste restriction on dining with non-Brahmins like him.

An angry Kelkar responded, 'My friend Dr Gour's ideas are very queer about the causes of a man going out of caste ... But I challenge him to prove that any man is outcasted except for very reprehensible reasons. It is absolutely ridiculous that I should be outcasted simply on account of taking a cup of tea ... He does not simply know that it is not for such small matters that persons are outcasted.'

Not for such small matters? Not for sharing a cup of tea? Not for anything but very reprehensible reasons? These claims were astounding, given that Kelkar's biography of Tilak, first published in 1923, had dwelt on an episode in which this conservative Brahmin had been excommunicated for the very same crime of having tea with non-Brahmins.[24]

The controversy acquired notoriety as the 'Panch Howd Mission Tea Party', and landed Tilak in the dock alongside the renowned champion of social reforms, Mahadev Govind Ranade, who was also a Brahmin. They happened to be among the invitees to a lecture in a Christian mission school in Poona in October 1890. The event was organised by another social reformer, Gopal Joshi, who had helped his wife, Anandi Joshi, become the first Indian female physician. Joshi and Ranade were ideological adversaries of Tilak's. As Kelkar put it in his biography, 'Tilak did certainly ridicule over-education of girls and its frivolous effects on their behaviour.'

The outrage caused by the event was not because of the lecture but the refreshments that followed. Tilak and Ranade apparently had tea and biscuits with the other guests. This would have been no more than a matter of course, but for one detail of immense significance to Hindu society. Namely, the hosts and guests were from diverse castes and communities—a violation of the strict prohibition on what is called 'inter-dining'.

Joshi made this caste transgression public, even if unwittingly, by writing about the lecture and the after-party in a local newspaper, naming the prominent guests in attendance. The ensuing outrage translated into a social boycott by the caste members of the unlikely duo of Tilak and Ranade, which ended only after they had submitted to the prescribed rituals of expiation.

Over three decades later, in a chapter titled 'Tilak and Social Reform', Kelkar portrayed the tea party as a 'trap' that Joshi had laid. It is clear that he did not then see it as a 'small matter'. Kelkar alleged that Joshi saw religion as 'a plaything', and that 'he would condemn without compunction Hinduism as heartily as he would condemn Christianity to which he was converted'.

On the other hand, Tilak underwent penance despite his conviction that 'the merest sipping of tea … called for no such purification'. The principle underlying this apparent contradiction between Tilak's belief and conduct was complex. It was 'to take a leap forward in social reform', as Kelkar put it, 'without forsaking the people far behind and at the same time without bringing the religion of the forefathers into contempt or even into slight disrespect'.

This was how Tilak, in Kelkar's narrative, lived up to his principle when he was tested by the tea-party controversy. 'Public opinion in Poona was whipped up into condemning the supposed rebels and excommunication was the busy topic of the day … As, however, the pangs of social boycott were experienced by the offenders, one after another, they scrapped the whole question by subjecting themselves to the punishment of penance under one pretext or another. On certain occasions, Tilak too felt the inconveniences, if not agonies, of such boycott and he cut the Gordian knot by doing the penance when he had gone to Benares.' Kelkar's book made clear that even Ranade was forced 'by domestic circumstances to eat the humble-pie'.

Their atonement for 'the merest sipping of tea' vindicated Gour's contention that, under the customary law of Hindus, Kelkar could be excommunicated for receiving such hospitality from him. While social rebels could thus be persecuted with impunity within the caste domain, their inheritance rights were safeguarded by the very law that Kelkar sought to repeal.

The government of Lord Irwin, for its part, declared that it would go by the consensus in the House on whether the bill should be circulated for soliciting public opinion. The government's neutrality spelt doom for the bill, especially in view of Kelkar's cursory response to the legal arguments that Gour had advanced. Besides, 'the personal opinion' expressed by Home Member J. Crerar during the debate was that the bill was 'extremely reactionary'. The motion to circulate the bill was defeated twenty-nine to nine, thereby ending its journey.

Kelkar's bill was clearly out of sync with the political mainstream of the time. In that very year, 1928, a committee of the All Parties' Conference chaired by Motilal Nehru came up with a liberal vision in what was the first draft by Indians of their constitution. The fundamental rights listed in that draft expressly guaranteed the 'freedom of conscience', the principle underlying the 1850 law.

However, before the collapse of his bill, Kelkar had the consolation of mentioning that the 1850 law suffered from a 'want of reciprocity with regard to the inheritance by apostates'. In other words, if a Hindu converted to Islam, he could inherit from, say, his Hindu brother but the latter could not in turn inherit from the former, as that would be forbidden by Islamic law.

So, he threw down a challenge to his interlocutor: 'I do ask Dr Gour—are there no anomalies in regard to the inheritance by apostates?'

Gour's unhesitating reply was: 'There are anomalies to improve [the law] and not to repeal it.'

Two years later, in 1930, the Privy Council dealt with another anomaly in the law. It resolved a confusion caused by 'two conflicting lines of decisions' on whether, after the apostate or outcasted Hindu had benefited from it, the 1850 law could still be invoked later by their descendants.[25]

The Allahabad High Court took a 'wide view' on that question in 1888, ruling that, if a Hindu became a Mahomedan, then the descendants of that Mahomedan 'throughout the ensuing generations, without any limit', could keep claiming inheritance from the Hindu family.

The other line of decisions exemplified by the Madras High Court in 1917 took a 'narrower view', which the Privy Council held was the 'correct' one. Namely, that the 1850 law 'only applies to protect the actual person who either renounces his religion or has been excluded from the communion of any religion or has been deprived of caste'. The property inherited by such a person under the 1850 law could be passed on to his descendants, but they in turn were barred from claiming any further inheritance from the ancestral family whose religion or caste had been abandoned. The Privy Council said that this was 'the only reasonable construction that can be put upon it'.

During decolonisation, India had occasion to review the 1850 law, as well as the Privy Council's interpretation of it, as part of an ambitious exercise to codify Hindu personal laws. The official committee entrusted with this task was confronted with a renewed demand for the repeal of the 1850 law. Not satisfied with the Privy Council's narrow interpretation, the Hindu right wanted that 'not only the convert's descendants but the convert himself should be disqualified from inheriting the property of his Hindu relatives'.

The Hindu Law Committee, headed by jurist B.N. Rau, upheld the protection given to converts. However, the committee took a somewhat different view from that of the Privy Council on the descendants' inheritance rights. Descendants were offered inheritance rights as an incentive if they were to return to the Hindu fold before the succession opened. This formulation first appeared in the Hindu Code Bill published in February 1947.[26]

After Independence, Law Minister B.R. Ambedkar undertook the enactment of the Hindu Code Bill on a priority basis. But the Jawaharlal Nehru government abandoned the plan in 1951 in the face of resistance from the Hindu right, leading to Ambedkar's resignation. Subsequent to the 1952 general election, the government made the strategic decision to take up first the less sensitive task of updating the civil marriage law. The resultant Special Marriage Act, 1954 made a direct reference to the 1850 law.

Under Section 20 of the Special Marriage Act, 'any person whose marriage is solemnized under this Act shall have the same rights and shall be subject to the same disabilities in regard to the right of succession to any property as a person to whom the Caste Disabilities Removal Act, 1850 (21 of 1850), applies'.

The legislation's incongruous suggestion that a law meant to remove caste disabilities had resulted in disabilities as well was an acknowledgement of the restriction imposed by the Privy Council in 1930 on the right of succession.

The passage of the Special Marriage Act paved the way for the enactment of Hindu personal laws in a piecemeal manner over the next two years. The provision relating to the 1850 law, as drafted by the Rau Committee, came to be enacted as Section 26 of the Hindu Succession Act, 1956. It specified that, where a Hindu had converted to another religion, 'children born to him or her after such conversion and their descendants shall be disqualified from inheriting the property of any of their Hindu relatives, unless such children or descendants are Hindus at the time when the succession opens'.

Section 4 of the same 1956 Act stipulated that any previous enactment that was 'inconsistent' with its provisions shall 'cease to apply to Hindus'. Yet, the 1850 law was conspicuous by its absence from the scheduled list of enactments that had been superseded. That the 1850 and 1956 laws were meant to coalesce was also evident from the wording of Section 26. By barring heirs born after conversion from inheriting the property of any of their Hindu relatives, Section 26 tacitly acknowledged that the inheritance rights of the apostate himself or herself were already protected by the 1850 law.

When Section 26 was being discussed in Parliament, the focus was entirely on religious conversions with no reference to the benefit that had also been conferred by the 1850 law on outcasted Hindus. It was as if the allusion to caste disabilities in the nomenclature of the old law was taken to be a colonial euphemism for religious conversions.

While introducing the Hindu Succession Bill in the Lok Sabha on 8 May 1956, Law Minister Hari Vinayak Pataskar was asked why a convert from Hinduism should be allowed to retain his inheritance rights. Pataskar put a counter question: 'Is it desirable, is it just that simply because a man in these days chooses to change his faith, he should be deprived of his right in the property itself?' That the

Nehru government's law minister could come up with such an impassioned defence of the principle in 1956 was a testament to the farsightedness of his distant predecessor, the law member of the Dalhousie government in 1850.

Pataskar went on to assert that, if the protection offered by the 1850 law to the apostate were to be scrapped, it would be 'entirely [the] wrong thing, not consistent with the principles which we have decided to follow'. As for the restriction that was being introduced by Section 26, he said it was designed to deal with the scenarios in which a convert 'gets children after his change of religion or by marriage with a woman of a different religion'. Echoing the 1930 Privy Council verdict on such children, Pataskar said, 'It is thought that unless they are Hindus, they should not be made sharers or inheritors on the basis of a law which is made applicable only so far as Hindus are concerned.'

Subject to this caveat, the nineteenth-century law continued to be invoked in several cases even in the twenty-first century. Little wonder then that each time the Law Commission of independent India drew up a list of obsolete laws that needed to be repealed, the Caste Disabilities Removal Act, 1850 never figured in it.

The first time the Law Commission published a list of obsolete laws was in 1984. The next list came in 1993 and the third in 1998. And then, in 2014, the newly elected Narendra Modi government requested the Law Commission to make a fresh survey of obsolete laws. The Law Commission was then chaired by Justice A.P. Shah, who is best known for his 2009 judgment from the Delhi High Court on the controversial 1860 provision, Section 377 of the IPC. A bench headed by Shah had ruled that Section 377 could no longer criminalise consensual sex between adults of the same gender.

It was, therefore, fortuitous that, when the Law Commission received the Modi government's communication, it was led by someone with Shah's track record. Responding with due urgency, the Law Commission came up with as many as four reports on obsolete laws. In the first of those reports published in September 2014, it mentioned the 1850 law in the 'list of statutes for further study with a view to assess suitability for repeal'.[27] At the end of publishing the four reports, once again, the Law Commission refrained from recommending that the 1850 law be repealed.

But that did not matter. The Modi government had already put in place a fallback option. On 1 September 2014, the Prime Minister's Office (PMO) appointed a committee consisting of bureaucrats R. Ramanujam and V.K. Bhasin, 'to identify the Central Acts which are not relevant or no longer needed or require repeal/re-enactment in the present socio-economic context'. Just two months later, on 5 November 2014, the PMO's committee recommended that the 1850 law was 'obsolete and can be repealed'.[28]

This drastic recommendation was made without any admission that, unlike the other laws identified by it, the 1850 law had never ceased to figure in litigations across the country. The only substantive reason the committee gave was that the Legislative Department headed by Law Minister Ravi Shankar Prasad had written to it that the 1850 law was 'required to be repealed in the light of changing socio-economic environment'. There was no explanation of what these socio-economic changes were and how they rendered obsolete a law that was still in currency.

There was, of course, a major change that year, and it was on the political front: the avowedly Hindu nationalist Bharatiya Janata Party (BJP) had formed the government for the first time with a majority of its own in the Lok Sabha. That a party committed to toughening the anti-conversion regime in the country would disapprove of the 1850 law protecting the inheritance rights of outcasted and converted Hindus—as also the Nehru government's position on it in 1956—was no surprise.

What was remarkable, though, was that the Modi government could push through the repeal proposal in both Houses of Parliament in 2017 without triggering any political or ideological controversy. And thus it came to be that the first-ever legislation on caste disabilities died a quiet death, with little clarity on the implications of the void left in its wake.

Though Kelkar had lost the vote in 1928, his view prevailed

ninety years later when the repeal of the 1850 law came into effect on 8 January 2018. The complement authored by Gour to the 1850 law, the Hindu Inheritance (Removal of Disabilities) Act, 1928, too had been repealed three days earlier. However, the repeal of Gour's law was in line with the Law Commission's recommendation, which said in 2014 that its purpose had been 'subsumed' by Section 28 of the Hindu Succession Act, 1956.[29] And Section 28 did indeed provide that no person shall be disqualified from succeeding to any property on the ground of any disease, defect or deformity.

Thus, the 1956 law superseded Manu's injunction to deny inheritance to persons with special needs. As for Manu's caste prejudice, the legislative exertions to overcome it had all started, at least in name, with Bethune's epiphany in 1850.

2

IMPURE MAJORITY

5

THREE SHADES OF TWICE-BORN

In the course of their colonial encounter, Hindu nationalists began portraying the Bhagavad Gita as their equivalent of the Bible or the Quran. Yet, in their religious tradition, the four Vedas were the more exalted scriptures—so much so that these texts had no parallel in other communities. So lofty and exclusive were they that most Hindus were forbidden to have anything to do with the Vedas.

Access to them was determined by varna, the social hierarchy sanctified by Hindu scriptures. It was only the Brahmins, Kshatriyas and Vaishyas, the elite varnas, who were allowed to chant—or even hear—verses from the Vedas. Shudras, the last of the four varnas, alongside untouchables, constituted the impure majority, all of them cast out of knowledge of the Vedas. While each of the top three varnas typically comprised a handful of jatis, or castes, in any given region, Shudras consisted of numerous castes.

At the root of this religious discrimination was the Vedic rite of passage, the upanayana ceremony: the investiture of the sacerdotal cord, or sacred thread, that symbolised a second birth in a purer state. The rite, accompanied by the chanting of the Gayatri Mantra, was meant only for young male members of the elite varnas. Hence, the varnas in which men wore the jeneu, or the sacred thread, were called 'Dwija', commonly translated as the twice-born or regenerate castes.

Dwija varnas were the traditionally privileged among the Savarna jatis or 'caste Hindus', a category that included all castes belonging to any of the four varnas. Untouchables, who were of castes that did not belong to any of the varnas, were called Avarnas or those without a varna. Though Avarna has become virtually obsolete, Savarna is increasingly used as a pejorative reference to the exploitative alliance of Dwijas and upper Shudras, or the 'intermediate castes'.

Among the three Dwija varnas, Brahmins were the most privileged, for they alone could perform Vedic ceremonies, whether for themselves or others. This meant that Brahmins held the key to the twice-born status of the other two elite varnas. Over a period, this monopoly emboldened the priestly class to eject Kshatriyas and Vaishyas from the Dwija rank. In the early decades of the nineteenth century, the social and religious tussles that ensued from this ousting took, for the first time, the form of a legal dispute in colonial courts.

What triggered this suit in 1817 was the denial by Brahmins of the very existence of Vaishyas. Originating in the port town of Masulipatnam, in the Andhra part of the Madras Presidency, the litigation began when members of a Telugu-speaking caste called Comati, claiming to be Vaishyas, filed a suit in the district court. The suit was against members of the Mantri-maha-nad, which was a 'secret assembly' of Brahmins set up for 'avenging encroachments on the rites and rules of caste'. The litigation dragged on for almost three decades, ending with a judgment from the Privy Council in 1845.[1]

The issue was whether Brahmins were justified in refusing to perform religious ceremonies for Comaties in the coveted 'language of the Vedas'. Since the Vedas were the preserve of the twice-born, the message of their refusal was clear: that Brahmins were repudiating the claim of the Comaties that they were Vaishyas, the scripturally recognised trading class. Having been designated Shudra, the servile class, the Comaties were forced to settle for ceremonies that were performed in the language of the Puranas rather than the Vedas.

After two layers of courts had decided the question in favour of the Comaties, the Sudder Adawlat, then the highest court in the

Madras Presidency, reversed the decree in 1833, vindicating the Brahmins. The Comaties filed an appeal before the Privy Council, which led, twelve years later, to an unforeseen consequence. At that advanced stage of litigation, the Privy Council raised a preliminary issue that had evidently been thus far overlooked. Could the refusal by Brahmins to chant from the Vedas be legally regarded as a 'case of injury' done to them? In other words, what civil right had the Comaties been denied?

Answering in the negative, the Privy Council said in 1845 that 'no question remained but of a mere declaration of a right to perform certain religious ceremonies'. But then, even if the courts below were assumed to have 'jurisdiction to proceed to the determination of that question in this suit', it found that 'the Plaintiffs have not produced sufficient evidence to establish such a right'. Accordingly, the Privy Council dismissed the plaint, holding that the entire proceedings stretching over twenty-eight years were, as summarised by a law journal at the time, 'irregular'.[2]

Having dismissed the suit 'without prejudice to the existence or non-existence of the right claimed by the Appellants', the Privy Council left open critical questions which both sides had raised. The Comaties received no response on whether they could compel Brahmins to chant Vedic mantras at their ceremonies. Likewise, the Brahmins got no answer on whether the third varna had either 'ceased to exist' or degraded to the status of Shudras 'by the adoption of impure customs'.

The peculiar contention that an entire community had 'ceased to exist' was even more charged in a similar dispute over the second varna, Kshatriyas. In fact, the long-running dispute between Brahmins and those claiming the status of the warrior class had first manifested in the pre-colonial era, most famously in the context of Shivaji, the iconic founder of the Maratha Empire in the seventeenth century.

Born into the Bhonsle clan, Shivaji was condemned by Marathi-speaking Brahmins to the status of a Shudra—a varna category that served as an impediment to Shivaji's growth. When he had wished to be elevated as Chhatrapati, or Emperor, the Brahmins of his domain refused to perform the 'abhisheka', the necessary Vedic rite, because of his alleged lack of standing. Ambiguities in the scriptures, which they were in charge of deciphering, allowed them to determine the caste identity even of their ruler. Despite his exceptional record of military conquests and leadership qualities, those Brahmins, including Shivaji's own prime minister Moro Pant Pingle, denied his claim to being a Kshatriya.

Moreover, they asserted that not a single Kshatriya existed in Kali Yug, the current Hindu epoch. The basis of their assertion was the Puranic legend of Parashurama, an avatar of the main Hindu god, Vishnu. In the aeons preceding Kali Yug, Parashurama was believed to have annihilated all Kshatriyas for the abuse of their caste privileges. Therefore, the Brahmins argued, the kings in Kali Yug were all of the Shudra stock. They could only be rulers in fact, not by right, and so the question of Shudras being formally honoured with an abhisheka did not arise.

Yet, Shivaji secured the title of Chhatrapati on 6 June 1674 due to a fortuitous circumstance. In the lore of the Rajputana region, far beyond his territory, Kshatriyas were believed to exist despite the Parashurama legend. Among these Kshatriyas was a Rajput clan, Sisodiyas of Mewar, the most famous ruler of which was Maharana Pratap, renowned for his valiant battles against the Mughal emperor Akbar. Displaying remarkable ingenuity, Shivaji, a contemporary of Akbar's great-grandson, Aurangzeb, procured a genealogy that claimed descent from the Sisodiyas of Mewar. His newfound genealogy, however, failed to impress the Brahmins in his court. In the face of their continuing resistance, Shivaji procured the endorsement of a Brahmin all the way from Benaras.

In this cross-continent operation, Gagabhat, the Brahmin from Benaras, validated the Maratha Bhonsle's attempt in the Deccan to trace his roots to the Sisodiyas of Mewar. He also reconciled the existence of Kshatriya pockets with the Parashurama legend. His alternative theory was that a section of Kshatriyas had indeed survived Parashurama's purges, and still existed in Kali Yug. However, they were in a degraded state that had reduced them to Shudra-like status due to the non-performance of upanayana over generations. So, the remedy Gagabhat reportedly applied in Shivaji's case was a purificatory ceremony called 'vratyastoma', which restored him to the status of Kshatriya. In turn, this made Shivaji eligible for the Vedic rites of upanayana and abhisheka, in that order.

Gagabhat's compromise did not endure. Within three generations, Shivaji's descendants were reduced to Shudra status once again because the Peshwas, their own prime ministers, who were Chitpavaṇ Brahmins, had assumed the levers of powers in the Maratha Confederacy by then. The Peshwas portrayed Shivaji's legacy as that of a Go-Brahman Pratipalak, or the protector of cows and Brahmins.

In order to tighten their political control, the Peshwas adopted the simple expedient of denying Shivaji's descendants the privilege of Vedic rites. 'This could happen only because the Brahmins claimed the power to do and undo the status of any Hindu at any time,' B.R. Ambedkar observed. 'Shivaji's case proves that their sovereignty in this matter is without limit and without challenge.'[3]

Their sovereignty continued well into the colonial period, even after the Peshwa rule had ended in 1818 following the Battle of Bhima Koregaon. However, in colonial courts, 'Brahmin Pundits' who were formally engaged as 'law officers', were reduced to giving non-binding advice on matters of religion, caste and family—a check on their previously untrammelled powers.[4]

The Brahminical thesis that there were no Kshatriyas in Kali Yuga resurfaced in a dispute from the Bengal Presidency. In 1857, the Privy Council in London was called upon to deal with this peculiar confluence of Hindu mythology and caste prejudice.[5] The inheritance of a feudal estate in the case hinged on varna identity, which was one step removed for most Hindus from their immediate caste identity.

Varna was the frame of reference for all Hindus, including those who were considered to be in the vast and amorphous category of the impure. While untouchables were 'Avarna' (without varna), the more numerous Shudras were technically 'Savarna' (belonging to varna). The bother about fixing varna status was, however, not only about social standing, it had legal implications too.

Owing to the burden placed upon the regenerate varnas to maintain their purity, the personal law that applied to them was different from the one that applied to those in the Shudra category. Varna status determined, among other things, the legitimacy of a son and his inheritance rights. Shudras were more liberal than regenerate classes in their treatment of illegitimate offspring.

The Parashurama legend had been invoked before the Privy Council in 1857 to determine whether 'Rajpoots' were Kshatriyas or Shudras. Their varna status in turn determined whether the appellant, the only son of a deceased aristocrat, was entitled to inherit 'the Rajdom and Zemindary of Ramnuggur', which was in 'the District of Sarun', near Patna in the Bengal Presidency. The inter-related questions of varna and property entitlement had to be addressed, as the Privy Council put it, 'according to the Hindoo law and right of caste'.

The appellant, Chouturya Run Murdun Syn, produced various depositions and extensive documentary evidence to establish his right to succeed his father as the next rajah.

- When his father, the late Rajah Umur Purtub Syn, had married the appellant's mother, it was according to the custom of his family.
- The appellant was a Rajput.
- The Rajdom was duly conferred upon him by his father by the ceremony of investing him with the sacerdotal cord, and by placing him on the guddee or throne.
- The title of Chouturya was conferred on him by his father.
- In conformity with the custom of the family, the title could be assumed only by the heir apparent of the Rajdom.
- He was in the habit of eating and drinking with the two previous rajahs: his father, and before that, his uncle.
- He had duly performed the funeral rites of his father.
- He was married to the daughter of a Rajpoot.

- He was in the habit of eating and drinking with his father-in-law.
- Five years before his death, Umur Purtab Syn had purchased an estate in the appellant's name as his acknowledged son.
- Such an intimate relationship was substantiated by the fact that the appellant had been described as the son of the late rajah in the receipt and bill of the sale of the estate.

Given such detailed evidence of having been groomed as the successor, combined with the fact that he was the only child of a father who had three wives, Run Murdun should have been regarded as the obvious inheritor. On the other hand, the respondent, Sahub Purhulad Syn, had first claimed the estate on behalf of his infant son on the basis of what was found to be a fabricated will. Instead of withdrawing in disgrace, Sahub Purhulad came up with a fresh claim, this time in his own name: on the ground that he was related to the late rajah, howsoever distantly, through a common male ancestor.

Run Murdun had lost the case in Indian courts because of a deficiency that was taken to override all the factors in his favour as well as all the factors against the respondent. That deficiency was caste.

The appellant's mother was apparently of an inferior caste. On account of the bar on inter-caste marriage, her caste antecedents were why the respondent questioned the legitimacy of the appellant. Sahub Purhulad even produced evidence from a previous judicial proceeding in which Run Murdun's mother had been reviled as 'bhutranee', or concubine.

The son of a Rajput father was forced to take refuge in the debasing Parashurama legend, seeking to downgrade the varna of the Rajput caste from Kshatriya to Shudra. Claiming that his father, being a Rajput, was a Shudra, the appellant contended that, even if his parents had not been legally married, his entitlement was unaffected. The strategic shift embroiled him in a contradiction, though. Despite admitting to having been invested with the sacred thread that was reserved for Dwija varnas, the appellant claimed that his parents were married under Shudra custom.

Ironically, Chouturya Run Murdun Syn was invoking the very legend that Brahmins had used to dispute Shivaji's claim of being a Kshatriya. As the Privy Council put it, 'It was contended on the part of the Appellant, that the Khatri and Vaisya classes have ceased to exist, and were sunk into the Soodra class, and that there are now two classes only, namely, the Brahmin and the Soodra.' And in order to show that 'the proper genuine Khatri are extinct', the appellant cited several 'authorities', which were largely translations of Indian books and colonial attempts to understand native legal systems.

One of these books was Arthur Steele's *Summary of the Law and Customs of Hindoo Castes*. The Privy Court verdict quoted this 1827 book as saying: 'The Brahmuns assert that Persuram destroyed the whole of the Kshutiryas ... The Rajpoots, Maratha chiefs of the Sattara or Bhonsle, and Kolapoor families, &c., and other houses, lay claim to the title of Kshutriya, and wear the Jenwa. But they are considered Soodras by the Brahmuns.'

One of the two Brahmin pundits consulted by the Indian courts in this Bengal Presidency case confirmed this thesis too. The bywasta, or opinion, given by the Brahmin pundit of the Sudder Dewanny Court, was that 'among Hindoos of the Rajpoot caste, a son who is not born from a woman of equal rank and caste, can be reckoned as son, and will be entitled to the estate of his deceased father'. The pundit's reasoning was that 'a Rajpoot is of the Soodra caste, and a son born to an individual of the Soodra caste, even from the womb of a slave, is reckoned his son by the Shaster laws'.

Like the courts below, the Privy Council disagreed with this opinion of the pundit as well as the authorities cited by the appellant. Its estimation of the status of Rajputs in the face of the Parashurama legend was, if anything, reminiscent of Gagabhat's intervention in the Shivaji episode in accepting the survival of Kshatriyas. 'Whatever weight may be due to these authorities in support of a speculative opinion, entertained perhaps, by learned Brahmins and others, their Lordships have, nevertheless, no doubt that the existence of the Khatri class, as one of the regenerate tribes, is fully recognised throughout India, and also that Rajpoots in Central India and in this district are considered to be of that class.'

Accordingly, the Privy Council held that the real issue before it was 'not whether the illegitimate son of a Soodra man by a Soodra woman can inherit', as made out by the appellant, but 'whether the illegitimate son of a Khatri can in any event inherit, whether his mother be a Soodra or any other caste'. Relying on the counter-authorities cited by the respondent, it ruled that 'the illegitimate son of one of the three regenerate or twice-born races cannot succeed to the inheritance of his father'.

The only consolation to Run Murdun was that, despite the rejection of his inheritance claim, he was granted maintenance. The Privy Council concluded, 'The right of an illegitimate child of one of the three regenerate classes to maintenance out of the estate of his father, is recognized by all the authorities on Hindoo law relating to this subject.' While Brahmins were not a party to this case, the Privy Council's decision of 1857 was a setback for them. Even if it did not lay down any test for distinguishing a Kshatriya from a Shudra, it was now clear that, despite the Parashurama legend, Brahmins could no longer claim to be the only surviving regenerate class in Kali Yug.

❖

Read together, the two Privy Council decisions of 1845 and 1857 thwarted the designs of Brahmins to replace the old Chaturvarna, or four-tier hierarchy, with a two-tier one, in which Kshatriyas and Vaishyas were reduced to—and clubbed with—Shudras. Once the existence of Kshatriyas had been judicially confirmed in 1857, the same logic was bound to apply to Vaishyas, although the question about their survival had been left open-ended in 1845.

Take this 1889 case[6] in which the Madras High Court invalidated an adoption by a Komati (as Comati came to be spelt by then) because the adopter had omitted to perform the Vedic fire ceremony of homam. The Vedic procedure was deemed indispensable in this case because the Komati was 'a Vaisya by caste and belonged to the third of the regenerate classes'.

Thus, by enabling Kshatriyas and Vaishyas to return to the company of the Brahmins, the Privy Council was instrumental in reviving the original fault line that had divided Hindu society into the three Dwija varnas and the rest. This led to a slew of cases in which various castes claimed to belong to one or the other of the three regenerate varnas. Litigation around it resulted in a substantial case law that grappled with the interplay between varna and caste in a hierarchy that was believed to be of divine origin.

Divesting Brahmins of their decision-making authority, these cases evolved elaborate criteria for distinguishing regenerate varnas from Shudras or determining a varna upgrade claimed by a certain caste. In the churn that followed, those criteria were sometimes revised in other cases or the same caste found itself placed in different varnas in different provinces, occasionally even in the same province.

The rash of legal tussles over varna status involved some of the most influential castes from across the country. The sections below discuss some milestones from the case law around varna determination.

1878

One of the early milestones pertained to Lingayats. Despite their origins in the twelfth century as an anti-caste sect, by the nineteenth century, the Lingayats had turned into a caste. They were spread across the Bombay Presidency and neighbouring princely states. A dispute concerning the varna status of the Lingayats arose in one of the smaller states, Akalkot, which was ruled by a branch of Shivaji's Bhonsle clan.

In the curious arrangement that existed between the imperial power and its subsidiary states, a judicial decision made by the political superintendent of Akalkot, a colonial official, came to be appealed before the Governor in Council of the Bombay Presidency. Like Run Murdun's case from the Bengal Presidency, this one raised the question of whether the illegitimate son of a Lingayat could inherit his estate. The answer, as in the Rajput case, depended on whether Lingayats belonged to a regenerate varna.

In this case, Nagamabai, one of the two widows of the deceased Lingayat, was contesting the illegitimate son's inheritance right. Her main ground was that Lingayats 'belonged to one of the regenerate classes, and were not Sudras'. Finding merit in the varna claim, the political superintendent of Akalkot, Major Baumgartner, refused 'the certificate of heirship' to the illegitimate son, Khanderav.

On Khanderav's appeal, the Governor in Council of Bombay remitted the case for further evidence to the collector of Sholapur, a district in the Bombay Presidency adjoining the Akalkot state. On the basis of further evidence recorded by him, Collector Crawford reckoned that, if Baumgartner's decision was confirmed, 'the general effect will be good'. This was because Crawford felt that the practice of allowing a 'dasiputra', or illegitimate son, to share inheritance with a son born in wedlock was 'degrading for the women', and that 'educated and leading men' among Lingayats 'disapprove of it'.

Recommending a departure from the colonial policy of deferring to custom, Crawford wrote, 'If they are willing to get rid of a demoralizing custom, I do not think that Government should confirm it, even if it were shown to be practised by a part of the community or in a particular locality.' Since the plaintiff was an affected widow, rather than a distant male relative, Crawford may have felt justified in suggesting that a harsher policy for those who had the misfortune of being born illegitimate would better serve the cause of justice.

On 18 November 1878, however, the Governor in Council rejected Crawford's recommendation as it felt that its position on the occasion was 'judicial, and not political or legislative'. Reversing Baumgartner's decision, the Council, chaired by Bombay Governor Richard Temple, held itself bound by an 1827 judicial precedent from Poona, in which an illegitimate son of a Lingayat had been found to be entitled as an heir.

In disposing of the case, the government resolution said: 'The main question is, are the Lingayets, Vaishyas or Sudras? They now call themselves Vaishyas, but there are points among their customs, such as the adoption of a sister's son, which indicate a Sudra origin.'

It added though that, in the fifty years that had elapsed since the 1827 case, Lingayats 'began to rise in social position and acquired the desire to assume a higher caste status than was probably their due'.

Treading a fine line, the Bombay government observed: 'Cases of this kind cannot be decided on sentimental grounds; and much as it might be for such reasons desirable to give a decision which might tend to raise Lingayats in the social scale, Government is bound to decide this case strictly in accordance with the Hindu law, or of a custom contrary to that if it can be clearly proved.' It added that, in the matter on hand, 'Government do not think that it has been proved that a customary deviation from the general law has been accepted by the caste generally.' Lingayats were thus held to be Shudras.

This was an unusual instance, where the executive arm of the colonial state had pronounced on the varna status of a caste in a princely state. But the case was quoted extensively in a Bombay High Court judgment that came soon after.[7] The later judgment, delivered by Chief Justice M.R. Westropp on 14 March 1879, was on an adoption dispute in a Brahmin family from the presidency's Satara district.

A Brahmin man had adopted his daughter's son. On his death, the man's brother and nephew challenged the validity of the adoption. The High Court rejected his widow's plea to declare that her biological grandson was her legally recognised adopted son. It was held that, barring evidence of a special custom to the contrary, Brahmins, Kshatriyas and Vaishyas were 'absolutely prohibited from, and incapable of, adopting a daughter's or sister's son or son of any other woman whom they could not marry by reason of propinquity'. Quoting a jurist, the High Court said that the prohibition on an 'adoptee' from being 'the son of one whom the adopter could not have married' was a rule that 'applies only to the three superior classes, and does not extend to Sudras'.

It was to underline this point—the application of separate laws for twice-born varnas and Shudras—that the High Court judgment digressed into the Lingayat case, which had been decided just a few months earlier by the Governor in Council of Bombay. From that precedent, the Bombay High Court inferred that the succession right enjoyed by an illegitimate son, the admission of such a son 'to dine with and marry in the caste' and the prevalence of '*pat* marriages', or abridged weddings (for widows, for instance), were 'so many badges of the Sudra tribe'.

1884

Some of Bengal's greatest icons during the colonial era were Kayasthas, including eminences such as Swami Vivekananda, Aurobindo Ghosh, Jagadish Chandra Bose and Subhash Chandra Bose. Though Kayasthas were part of the Bhadralok, or refined folk, their varna status was low as they had long been considered Shudras in Bengal. The question of their varna status came under judicial scrutiny in an adoption case involving a Kayastha from the 'Behar' region of the Bengal Presidency.[8]

The propinquity principle surfaced in this case too. Chandan Lall had adopted one of his sister's sons, Bissessur Dyal, in preference to his brother's sons. If Kayasthas were taken to be Kshatriyas, as claimed by the plaintiffs, then Chandan Lall could have adopted his brother's son but not his sister's because the propinquity test would then have applied. Further, the plaintiffs claimed that there was a regional variation in the varna status of Kayasthas between Behar and the rest of Bengal Presidency. Their attempt was to dissociate Kayasthas in Behar from the settled law that their counterparts in the Bengali-speaking region were Shudras.

The Calcutta High Court sought to put the matter in perspective by quoting a jurist named Shamachurn Sircar who had made two broad points. First, the Kayasthas, 'whether of Bengal or of any other country', were all originally Kshatriyas. Second, for several centuries, 'the Kayasthas (at least those of Bengal) have been degenerated and degraded to Sudradom'.

Sircar mentioned two broad ways in which Kayasthas came to

be degraded. One was by using after their proper names the surname 'Dasa' peculiar to the Sudras, and giving up their own, which is Varma. The other and more important way—or 'principally'—was by omitting to perform 'the regenerating ceremony Upanayana hallowed by the Gayatri'.[9]

In its verdict delivered on 4 March 1884, the Calcutta High Court examined four practices, other than that of adoption, to determine whether Kayasthas in Behar, unlike their counterparts in Bengal proper, were still Kshatriyas. The four particulars identified by the two-judge bench were: one, wearing the sacred thread; two, ability to perform the homa or Vedic fire ritual; three, the rule as to the period of impurity in relation to bereavement; and, four, the rule as to the incompetence of illegitimate sons to succeed.

Taking all such evidence into account, the verdict authored by Justice Field said that 'it fails to establish that the Kayasthas of Behar, as a class, have observed the four rules relied upon so uniformly and so regularly that they are entitled to say that upon the basis of these observances they must rank among the three superior classes'. Since the Kayasthas of Behar were thus found to be Shudras, the High Court upheld the adoption that was contrary to the propinquity principle.

1890

The argument that there was regional variation in the status of Kayasthas had failed before the Calcutta High Court in 1884, but proved effective before the Allahabad High Court six years later.[10] This case required the Allahabad High Court to establish whether a widowed Kayastha, Musammat Larei, could adopt a male heir without the prior permission of her deceased husband ('Musammat' is a precolonial term that remained in currency as a title for women in official documents).

Doubting the correctness of the 1884 ruling of the Calcutta High Court, a three-judge bench of the Allahabad High Court held that the practices of the Bengali Kayastha were 'separate and distinct from the 12 Chitraguptavanshi sub-branches' living in North-Western Provinces and Oudh, which broadly correspond with today's Uttar Pradesh. Based on a Puranic legend, these sub-branches of Kayasthas claimed descent from Chitragupta who was the scribe of Yama, the Lord of Death.

The judgment was authored by Justice Syed Mahmood, the first Indian judge of the Allahabad High Court and son of Sir Syed Ahmed Khan, founder of the Aligarh Muslim University. Disagreeing with the Calcutta High Court verdict, Justice Mahmood said, 'I entertain considerable doubts as to the soundness of the view … that the literary caste of Kayasthas in this part of the country … falls under the category of Sudras.'

The very reference to them as a 'literary caste', in part at least on the basis of their mythological link with Chitragupta, meant that the Kayasthas living in the jurisdiction of the Allahabad High Court were allowed to claim Dwija status. Accordingly, the widow was not allowed to adopt an heir owing to the absence of the deceased husband's prior permission. Based on this judgment, while the Kayasthas living in the Bengal Presidency remained Shudras, their counterparts in the Hindi heartland came to be recognised as Kshatriyas.

1898

F.C.O. Beaman, the district judge of Belgaum in the Bombay Presidency, displayed greater deference to Brahminical propaganda than the 1857 Privy Council ruling on the caste of Rajputs had done.

In a dispute between a widow and the illegitimate sons of her deceased husband, Beaman ruled that the latter were entitled to inheritance on the ground that the late 'Bapuchand was certainly a Shudra, no pretence being made that he was a Brahmin'. His reason for rejecting the widow's claim that the family belonged to the Vaishya varna was as follows: 'In this Kaliyug there are according to the authorities only two classes among the Hindus, the regenerate Brahmanas and the unregenerate Shudras.'

On the widow's appeal to the Bombay High Court, it fell to Justice M.G. Ranade, a Brahmin himself and a renowned social reformer, to apply the corrective on the state of the varna system.[11] Ranade authored the judgment delivered by a two-judge bench of the High Court on 12 April 1898. 'It appears to us that the District Judge was in error in the cardinal assumption that there are now only two principal castes, and that if a man is not shown to be a Brahmin, he must belong to the Shudra caste, as pure Kshatriyas and pure Vaishyas are now not recognized.'

As for the two works of British scholars that Beaman had cited, Ranade said that they were actually 'compilers' who did not state any such conclusion as their own, 'but only represent the opinion which Brahmin Shastris and pandits hold on the point'. He added, 'These latter opinions have no juridical value.' If anything, in those two scholarly works, he said, 'elaborate lists of numerous castes are given which claim to be Kshatriyas or Vaishyas'.

Pointing out that the courts had 'always recognized the fourfold division', Ranade said that the 'leading case' on the subject was the 1857 Privy Council judgment, 'where the opinion of the pandits, that Kshatriyas and Vaishyas have become extinct as castes, was discussed and negatived, and the existence of Rajputs as Kshatriyas was affirmed in the most positive manner'. Underlining the relevance of this precedent to the case on hand, Ranade said, 'This ruling is of special importance, for the dispute in that case related to the claims of illegitimate sons.' Moreover, it made 'perfectly clear that there is no foundation for the supposition that there are now only two principal caste divisions'.

Since the widow's claim to inheritance in this case hinged on her assertion of Dwija status, Ranade took pains to bring out the dodgy basis on which the existence of Kshatriyas and Vaishyas had been denied by the pandit lobby. 'The Kshatriyas were, according to this view of the pandits, exterminated by Parshuram … There is no such mythical explanation even suggested for the extinction of the Vaishyas. We cannot, therefore, accept the correctness of this myth; and it must be discarded in a judicial settlement of questions relating to caste and status.'

For all his myth-busting zeal, Ranade unquestioningly accepted the elitist assumption that 'the ordinary Hindu law' meant 'the law of the three regenerate castes'—although they were a minority within the Hindu community. He betrayed this bias while dealing with the complexity that the parties to the case were Jains. Ranade began on an unexceptionable note, 'The Jains are dissenters, and purely orthodox traditions about caste status can have no place when they are applied to Jains.' But then, he added, 'As the Jains are mostly Vaishyas, it is plain that the *exceptional rules laid down for Shudras* can have no place in matters relating to Jains' (emphasis added). Thus, to Ranade, the law applicable to the elite varnas was the norm, while the one governing the majority of Hindus was the exception.

1919

This was again a case of a regional variation claimed in the varna status of a caste between two regions of the same province. A Shudra from the Marathi-speaking area of Dhulia in the Bombay Presidency wanted to avoid sharing inheritance with his father's illegitimate sons. To this end, he claimed that he belonged to the Leva Kunbi caste, which was originally from Gujarat, where it had Dwija status.[12] He said that, back in Gujarat, his caste was also called Leva Patidar, and was considered to be either Kshatriya or Vaishya. On that basis, he said, the illegitimate sons of his deceased father would not be entitled to a share in the family estate.

The Bombay High Court, however, ruled that it was 'needless' to express any opinion on 'the status of the Leva Patidars or Kunbis in Gujarat'. Its 18 August 1919 judgment said that, even if it was assumed for the sake of argument that the community to which the parties belonged had migrated from Gujarat and that the Leva Kunbis of Gujarat were not Shudras, 'it does not necessarily follow that they have retained in modern times the same customs and status as the Leva Kunbis in Gujarat may have retained'.

Justice Lallubhai Shah, who authored the High Court verdict, wrote: 'The recent history of the caste, as disclosed in the evidence, shows the adoption of customs, which are indicative of their present status as Sudras, and that, in my opinion, is sufficient for the purpose of this case.' Shah's stress on going by 'the present status' for fixing their varna was reminiscent of the Calcutta High Court's 1884 ruling that the Kayasthas of Bengal had over the centuries 'degenerated and degraded to Sudradom'.

The customs that indicated the Shudra status of the parties in Maharashtra included the absence of the propinquity rule. 'The fact that the adoption of a daughter's son or a sister's son is prevalent in this community shows that parties are Sudras,' Shah said. The Bombay High Court also took into account the practice of divorce and widow remarriage as evidence suggesting that the illegitimate sons were also entitled to inherit. The High Court held: 'It is clear that that the caste, in which these customs are proved to obtain, can reasonably and properly be treated as Sudras.'

Further, it was found that the caste to which the parties belonged had originally been called 'Pajne Kunbis' and had been changed to 'Leva Kunbis' only 'during the last twenty years'. Shah read the change in nomenclature as an attempt by the legitimate son 'to show, if possible, a higher status with a view to escape the liability in the present suit'. The judge was clear, however, that, in view of their customs, the parties would be considered Shudras 'whatever may have been the real status of the ancestors who migrated from Gujarat'. In a word, the varna status of a caste could change over a period based on the customs it practised.

1924

In a later inheritance case, a two-judge bench of the Madras High Court delivered two concurring judgments, together running into 229 pages.[13] Both these judgments of 1924, one by the British acting chief justice and the other by an Indian High Court judge, extensively discussed the varying accounts of the circumstances in which Shivaji had undergone the upanayana ceremony at the age of forty-seven through Gagabhat's intercession.

This unlikely foray into the medieval history of another region was triggered by an inheritance case relating to a Maratha kingdom that had existed deep inside the Madras Presidency in Tanjore until 1855.

Founded independently of Chhatrapati Shivaji in the seventeenth century by his estranged half-brother Ekoji alias Venkaji, the Maratha reign over Tanjore ended in 1855, when the last ruler, also named Shivaji, died 'without leaving a son by birth or adoption'. In 1862, after annexing Tanjore, the colonial administration made over the last ruler's private estate to his widows at their request.

Subsequently, the estate came to be disputed for various reasons, beginning with the decision of the senior widow to adopt the Tanjore Maharaja Shivaji's sister's grandson and transfer all the properties to him. The descendants of the last ruler's 'sword wives', or permanent concubines, whom he could not marry as they were from other castes, also made claims to the property. The descendants of Chhatrapati Shivaji, from the Kolhapur and Satara branches of the family, were also drawn into the litigation.

Unsurprisingly, the inheritance issue was, in large part, dependent on whether the late Tanjore ruler belonged to a family of Kshatriyas or Shudras. The sons from his sword marriages would be legally entitled to inherit only if he was found to be a Shudra. On the other hand, the very recourse to sword marriage was cited as 'a token of Kshatriyaship'.

That his descendants from Kolhapur and Satara were among the potential stakeholders was an additional reason for the Madras High Court to examine different scholarly interpretations regarding the coronation of Chhatrapati Shivaji. At the end of the exercise, Acting Chief Justice Charles Gordon Spencer, in his judgment delivered on 21 January 1924, came to a guarded conclusion. 'It is unnecessary to express any opinion on this much vexed question whether Sivaji represented a fallen Kshatriya restored after penance or a good Sudra king elevated to Kshatriya rank by bribing the Brahmins, upon which historians have been at controversy.' Even if it was assumed that Chhatrapati Shivaji and his descendants were

Kshatriyas, Spencer said, 'it does not follow that Ekoji, his half-brother, who did not go through the ceremonies of purification and coronation, as Sivaji did, and his descendants are anything more than Sudras, seeing that the two brothers separated before the date of Sivaji's coronation'.

Instead, adopting the principle that 'the consciousness of a community is a good test of Varna', he examined a wide range of evidence to see if the Tanjore branch satisfied this test. Since the ceremonies they performed were a key element of the community's consciousness, it was but natural to look for evidence relating to the sacred thread investiture. As it turned out, Spencer found them wanting in what he called 'the chief distinguishing mark of the twice born'. He said, 'There is evidence that some of the members of this family put on poonul or thread, but there is very little evidence that before doing so they went through the ceremony of Upanayanam.' After considering several such strands of evidence on the consciousness of the community, Spencer ruled that the claim of the Tanjore royal family 'to be classed as Kshatriyas has failed'.

In his separate but concurring verdict, the other judge on the High Court bench, Justice C.V. Kumaraswami Sastri, came up with more reasons for rejecting the Tanjore family's claim to Dwija status. Sastri referred to 'a dispute in Kolhapur as to whether the rulers were Kshatriyas or Sudras and whether they were entitled to the performance of ceremonies with Vedic rites like Kshatriyas or with Puranic rites like Sudras'.

In fact, this very 'Vedokta controversy' was what propelled Shahu Maharaj of Kolhapur to the ranks of India's great social reformers. As he was taking a holy dip in Panchganga in his territory in 1899, Shahu Maharaj noticed that the priest chanted mantras from the Puranas rather than the Vedas. He realised that, while the more auspicious 'Vedokta mantras' were reserved for Dwija varnas, the Shudras had to make do with 'Puranokta mantras'. Aghast that even a ruler was not spared such caste discrimination, Shahu Maharaj took on the priestly class, beginning with the appointment of a non-Brahmin as the religious head. Without naming the late Shahu

Maharaj, the High Court judge said that 'recourse had to be had to dismiss the priests and resume their jaghirs and otherwise coerce them to submission'.

The upshot of the Tanjore case was that, in keeping with the liberal dispensation of the Shudras, the last raja's estate was divided between the descendants of the posthumously adopted son and the descendants of the sword wives' sons. In terms of principle, this case signified that the criterion of 'the consciousness of the community' did not rely upon the caste's self-projection when its claim to Dwija status was being tested.

1926

About forty-two years after they had been declared Shudras, the status of Bihari Kayasthas came under fresh scrutiny. By this time, Bihar was no longer part of the Bengal Presidency. A separate province called 'Bihar and Orissa' had been carved out in 1912, and a High Court was established for it in Patna in 1916.

The 1884 verdict of the Calcutta High Court, holding that Kayasthas, whether from Bengal or Bihar, were Shudras, had been reinforced by subsequent judgments. In the recast province of Bengal, the Calcutta High Court had, in two cases in 1921 and 1924, gone so far as to legalise intermarriages between Kayasthas and artisan communities called Tantis and Doms on the ground that both were 'sub-castes of Shudras'.[14]

The Patna High Court, while deciding an adoption case on 23 February 1926, disagreed with the Calcutta High Court's comparison of Bihari Kayasthas to their counterparts in Bengal rather than those in the renamed province in the west, United Provinces and Oudh.[15] 'The social position, religious observances, customs and manners of the Kayasthas of Bihar are the same as those of the United Provinces and Oudh.' The judgment authored by Justice Jwala Prasad observed, 'Their marriages take place in the Kayastha families of the United Provinces and they dine with each other.' It was apparently just the opposite with their counterparts in the east. 'They do not marry in the Kayastha families of Bengal and in fact have no concern with the Kayasthas of Bengal in matters social or religious.'

Given its disagreement with the 1884 Calcutta verdict, it was no surprise that the Patna High Court commended the 1890 Allahabad verdict that had 'doubted' the correctness of equating Bihari and Bengali Kayasthas. Prasad rejected the inference that Kayasthas had 'degraded to Sudradom' due to factors like non-observance of upanayana, as the Calcutta High Court had said. He asserted that such lapses 'would not cause any actual degradation or the loss of rights of the Kayasthas in matters of inheritance, marriage and adoption'.

Bringing in another nuance on the working of caste, Prasad said that if any twice-born failed to comply with the prescribed practices, 'he can purify himself by the rules of expiation'. But if he failed to exercise the option of purifying himself, it held that 'he may only be looked down upon but cannot be degraded to Sudradom or the status of a Sudra so far as his civil rights are concerned'.

Having upheld the notion of purity, the Patna High Court coolly postulated: 'His caste for civil matters is that which he acquires by birth.' Harking back to Gagabhat's remedy, Justice Prasad said that omitting to wear the sacred thread would 'only deprive a twice-born of his sacramental rights and he can regain that by performing the Vratyastoma ceremony'. And thus, Prasad asserted that 'in any case the Bihari Kayasthas are not Sudra'.

1928

If the status of Kayasthas was subject to regional variations, the status of Marathas varied even within the Bombay Presidency. The Bombay High Court ruled on 26 January 1928 that the Marathas falling in its jurisdiction could be either Kshatriyas or Shudras.[16] The ruling drew upon the tests that had been laid down by various High Courts, such as the consciousness of the community and the customs followed by it.

The Bombay High Court found that the label of 'Maratha' was

used by three classes. The first two classes, which were called 'the five families' and 'the ninety-six families', were held to be Kshatriyas. The third class covering 'the rest' of the Marathas, the majority, were declared Shudras.

Though the line between the second and third classes 'may not always be clear', Justice Govind Madgavkar of the High Court said, 'Many in the third class have not in the reported cases in the Courts set up a claim to be Kshatriyas but are, apparently and for the most part, content to be governed by the rules applying to Shudras.'

Of the first two classes, Madgavkar said that their claim to Kshatriya status 'dates from centuries' and also 'satisfied' the tests he had formulated. They were found to have adopted 'the custom of the twice-born castes', such as the wearing of the sacred thread. Accordingly, Madgavkar held that 'it would be a retrograde step for the Courts to deny them their claim and to insist against their will that the law should include them in the other category'.

The High Court was deciding the validity of an adoption by a widow of her deceased husband's sister's son. Since the late Hambirrao Patil was found to belong to the second class of ninety-six families, Madgavkar concluded that he was 'a Kshatriya and not a Shudra, and the appellant's adoption is invalid'. The judge ignored a claim by the appellant that his community followed a special custom permitting such an adoption against the propinquity rule mandated for Dwijas. The other member of the High Court bench, Justice S.S. Patkar rejected the special custom claim, as the precedents cited by the appellant were 'recent ones', no more than ten years old.

1935

In accordance with the more broadminded mores of the Shudras, the illegitimacy of a son was never held against him, as evident from the recognition of his inheritance right. However, in a bid to assuage the fears of upper castes, the Shudras were allowed to be so generous only to the kind of illegitimate son who could be called a 'dasiputra', literally, the son of a female slave. The subtext to this term was that the permanently kept concubine, to whom the illegitimate son was born, would have to be of an inferior caste for her to be branded as a 'dasi'.

So, what if a Shudra happened to have a concubine from a Dwija caste? Would the son born to such a mistress not be entitled to inherit from his father? Would the recognition of such an inheritance right encourage more twice-born women to enter into such familial arrangements with Shudra men?

The Bombay High Court addressed one such fraught situation in an inheritance case from Dharwar on 27 June 1935.[17] The legitimate son and nephews of a deceased Shudra, Doddappa Naik, filed a suit against the illegitimate son, Ramchandra. In a bid to deny him any share in the family property, the plaintiffs sought a declaration that Ramchandra was 'neither a legitimate nor an illegitimate son' of Doddappa Naik. It meant that he could not be called a dasiputra as Gangawa, Ramchandra's mother and Doddappa Naik's mistress, was a Brahmin.

The assistant judge at Dharwar, G.H. Guggali, held that Ramchandra was entitled to inherit as a dasiputra because Gangawa had become a Shudra by living with a Shudra. Guggali based his ruling on a scripture called 'Apastambha Smriti', which said, 'Brahmins who eat the food of a Shudra for a month will become Shudras for ever in this life and after death they will be born as dogs.' Thus, for Ramchandra, the trial court's invocation of a scriptural penalty for a Brahmin who mixed with a Shudra served as a blessing.

The High Court in its turn drew on another scriptural penalty, which had no such redeeming side to it. The verdict authored by Justice Harsidhbhai Divatia held that the late Doddappa Naik's relationship with Gangawa was 'of the most degraded character'. He quoted this stricture of the ancient lawgiver Yajnyavalkya: 'A son begotten by a Shudra on a Brahmin woman becomes a Chandala, the most degraded of human beings, and therefore outcaste to all religion.'

Divatia said: 'Thus the view of the Shastras is that any relationship between a Shudra male and a Brahmin female, whether it purports to be a relationship by so-called marriage or a state of concubinage, is not recognized by Hindu law … If, therefore, such children are regarded as chandalas and outcastes, it clearly follows that they cannot claim any right to a share in the property of their father.'

As to the anomaly caused by such a confluence of patriarchy and caste prejudice, Divatia said, 'At first sight it may seem strange that the son of a Shudra by a Shudra mistress can inherit to him while his son by a Brahmin mistress cannot, but the origin of this view is to be found in a sense of abhorrence towards any sort of connection between a Shudra man and a Brahmin woman leading to degeneration of the race, and it is in order to discourage such connections that the texts expressly enjoin that the children should be regarded as outcastes and therefore not entitled to any share in the property.'

Disagreeing with the trial judge's reading of the scriptures that a Brahmin mistress cohabiting with a Shudra would herself become a Shudra, Divatia said that that was 'not the general trend of the authoritative ancient texts'. A worse fate awaited her. 'Such a woman does not become a Shudra but becomes patita, that is to say, a degraded woman, and hence an outcaste.' And thus, Divatia ruled that Ramchandra was 'not a Dasiputra who alone among the class of illegitimate sons would be entitled to a share in the inheritance'.

1955

Six years after the Indian republic had been founded on lofty constitutional guarantees regarding the right against discrimination 'on grounds only of' caste, there was little change as yet in practice. This was borne out by a case decided by the Nagpur High Court on 13 October 1955, displaying the persistence of the varna framework.[18]

A Komati tenant farmer called Ramulu had died in 1945, leaving behind a concubine who belonged to the Gond tribe and the three sons he had with her. The suit filed by the landlord to recover the land from Ramulu's survivors was premised on a varna argument: since Komati had long been judicially accepted as a Vaishya caste, his concubine and illegitimate sons were alleged to have no right to inheritance. The defendants in turn denied that Ramulu was a Dwija at all as he had never worn the sacred thread.

Though it was supposed to have been operating in terms of the egalitarian scheme of the 1950 Constitution, the High Court took pains to determine the varna of the deceased person. As Ramulu had never married, the High Court said, 'The fact that Upanayanam does not take place among the Komatis until marriage is not a point against their claim to be Vaishyas.' Decoding the complexities of varna, it said: 'The non-performance of Upanayanam is a very important piece of evidence to show that the person belonged to the Shudra caste and not to the higher caste. But the converse case of the non-performance of the Upanayanam by the twice-born does not necessarily show that the person belongs to the lower caste.'

As for the other omissions on Ramulu's part in adhering to custom, the High Court said, 'Lapses from the highest orthodox standards or practices as in the offering of oblations or performing other religious rites do not necessarily mean that the caste is not regenerate.' Accordingly, it held that Ramulu was 'a Vaishya and of the regenerate caste', and his mistress and illegitimate sons were therefore not entitled to inherit his property. Thus, the notion of the regenerate caste was recognised in independent India too, without any pretence on the part of the court of reconciling it with the Constitution.

1959, Case 1

About five years after the promulgation of the Constitution, the gap between its egalitarian values and Hindu personal law decreased dramatically with the enactment of four caste-neutral Hindu laws. These hard-fought enactments meant that Hindus finally had a uniform dispensation in matters such as marriage, succession, adoption and guardianship, overriding various varna-specific customs.

Thus it was that, in the Hindu Adoptions and Maintenance Act, 1956, none of the newly prescribed 'requisites of a valid adoption' had anything to do with either jati or varna. On the contrary, it said that 'any text, rule or interpretation of Hindu law or any custom or usage as part of that law in force immediately before the commencement of this Act shall cease to have effect with respect to any matter for which provision is made in this Act.' This meant that the interplay of varna and caste, which continued to manifest in social life, no longer had any legal basis.

Yet, in 1959, the Mysore High Court decided an adoption case on the basis of varna rather than the 1956 Act.[19] The dispute had predated the reform introduced by the Nehru government, but the judgment came three years after the enactment. It made no attempt at all to examine whether the 1956 law applied retrospectively to the present case. Instead, contrary to the letter and spirit of that law, and certainly of the Constitution, the High Court contemplated the possibility of Parliament actually upgrading the varna status of the caste concerned.

The High Court's apparent disconnect with the historic codification and reform of Hindu laws could have been partly due to the manner in which the appeal had been framed before it. The challenge to the adoption itself was stated unabashedly in terms of caste and varna, which in turn was due to the fact that this adoption suit had been originally instituted during that unsettled period between the enforcement of the Constitution in 1950 and the enactment of the 1956 law.

A Lingayat man's adoption of his wife's brother was the cause of action. The suit challenged the adoption using an odd combination of egalitarian constitutional provisions and varna-based distinctions from the then uncodified Hindu law. As a result, it invoked the principle of propinquity in relation to Lingayats, although that rule applied only to twice-born varnas. The suit argued that viruddhasambandha, as the propinquity rule was termed, should be extended to Shudras too.

Although the case reached the High Court after the enactment of the 1956 adoption law, the appellant remained focused on varna. He contended that the 'dubbing of Lingayat community as Sudras contravenes the provisions of the Constitution'. The exemption of Shudras from viruddhasambandha would violate, he said, some of the fundamental rights enshrined in the Constitution: the right to equality, the right against discrimination and even the abolition of untouchability.

Couched in the language of equality, the appeal in effect sought to impose a Dwija restriction on Lingayats. Here, the condition of propinquity meant that, as the biological mother of the adoptee was the mother-in-law of the adoptive father, the adoption was not legal.

Logically, the High Court ought to have rejected the attempt to apply viruddhasambandha to Lingayats, given that it had ceased to hold even for twice-born varnas. Instead, the verdict authored by Justice Iqbal Husain held that the classification of Lingayats as Shudras was 'no discrimination' against them. It added that, if anything, in the absence of the viruddhasambandha restriction, Lingayats enjoyed 'an enlarged right' in the matter of adoptions. Besides this suggestion that the adoption right depended on varna, the High Court's notion that 'the general Hindu law' still 'classifies Hindus into four classes' betrayed the fact that the High Court had not recovered from its colonial hangover.

Having ruled that 'the restricted scope' of the case was 'whether the adoption of a wife's brother by a Lingayat is valid in law or not', the Mysore High Court sympathised with the appellant's 'grievance' about the placement of 'the Lingayat community under the last class'. The grievance, it said, 'has much to be said in its favour in the sense that the term "sudra" has gathered round it certain uncomplimentary connotation'.

But it pleaded its inability to relieve them of the Shudra tag. Responding to the question of why Lingayats 'with a culture and a philosophy of their own should be dubbed as Sudras', the Mysore High Court said that 'it is for the Legislatures to change the nomenclatures'. This judgment showed up the fact that the judiciary, like the rest of Indian society, was struggling to adjust to the paradigm shift represented by the caste-neutral Hindu personal laws that had been enacted in the early years of the republic.

1959, Case 2

About a century after all doubts about the existence of Kshatriyas had been dispelled by the Privy Council in London, the newly founded Republic of India was grappling with another question concerning this varna. Could the Kshatriya status be conferred on someone born outside the varna? This was part of a larger theological debate on whether someone's caste was determined purely by the accident of their birth or by their own actions and qualities. There were scriptural authorities supporting both views.

The debate arose from an election petition filed after the second Lok Sabha poll held in March 1957 regarding what was then a two-member constituency in Parvatipuram, Andhra Pradesh. Such constituencies were designed to ensure that at least one of the two members elected from them belonged either to a Scheduled Caste or a Scheduled Tribe.[20] The reservation in Parvatipuram was for Scheduled Tribes. But as the two candidates who had won the most number of votes turned out to be from the reserved category, the general seat in Parvatipuram was also filled by one of them.

The reserved candidate who bagged the general seat in this unusual result was Dippala Suri Dora, who had been fielded by the Socialist Party. The general candidate who lost out to him was V.V. Giri, a prominent Congress leader who had been minister for Labour in the Nehru government. Giri filed the election petition in April 1957 contending, among other things, that Dora should not have been allowed in the first place to contest in the reserved category. Giri sought Dora's disqualification as a reserved candidate on the ground that he had 'ceased to be member of the Scheduled Tribe at the material time because he had become a Kshatriya'.[21]

In other words, Giri espoused the liberal interpretation that, far from being trapped by birth for life, Hindu scriptures allowed an individual to rise to a higher caste. Driven perhaps by this religious conviction, Giri persisted with the litigation even after he had been appointed governor of Uttar Pradesh within three months of that electoral defeat. So, even as he held that high constitutional office, Giri challenged the validity of Dora's election, first before the Election Tribunal in Hyderabad and then before the Andhra Pradesh High Court and finally before the Supreme Court.

Giri won the first round of litigation, but the High Court reversed that verdict, prompting him to take his case to the Supreme Court. Justice Jivan Lal Kapur, from the five-judge Constitution bench that heard his appeal, expounded on Giri's thesis that caste identity was fluid. He framed the question thus: 'whether a member of Scheduled Caste or Scheduled Tribe can by his own act transform himself into different and higher caste'. That is, 'whether caste is dependent upon birth or it varies as a consequence of Guna, Karma and Subhavana, that is merit on qualities, actions and character'.

In his answer to those questions, Kapur divided the trajectory of caste into three stages: 'In Hinduism, caste had its origin in vocation and was not dependent upon birth. Birth as the sole criterion of caste is a much later development, and caste became rigid and hereditary when vocations became hereditary.'

But before mentioning the third stage, Kapur dwelt further on the first stage saying, 'Caste was nothing but division of labour.' Wittingly or otherwise, this assertion of Kapur's was at odds with Ambedkar's interpretation of caste. In his famous tract, *Annihilation of Caste*, Ambedkar said: '(T)he Caste System is not merely a division of labour. *It is also a division of labourers* [emphasis in original]. Civilized society undoubtedly needs division of labour. But in no civilized society is division of labour accompanied by this unnatural division of labourers into watertight compartments.'[22]

In the same work, Ambedkar blamed this immutability on the scriptures that gave caste 'a perpetual lease of life'. In contrast, Kapur held that there was 'a high authority to support the view that, in Hinduism, caste was dependent upon actions and not on birth'. His judgment cited the following scriptural sources to support his reading:

- The oft-quoted sloka from the Bhagavad Gita in which Krishna declares, 'The four castes were created by me in accordance with their aptitude and actions; know me the author of these castes, though I am actionless and inexhaustible.'
- In another part of the Mahabharata, Yudhishtira says: 'Truth, charity, fortitude, good conduct, gentleness, austerity and compassion—he in whom these are observed is a Brahmana. If these marks exist in a Shudra and are not found in a twice-born, the Shudra is not a Shudra nor the Brahmana a Brahmana.'
- According to Bhagavata Purana, 'One becomes a Brahmana by his deeds and not by his family or birth; even a Chandala is a Brahmana, if he is of pure character.'
- In a Chandogya Upanishad parable, when Satyakama asked his mother, Jabala, about the identity of his father, she pleaded helplessness, saying that she had been with several men in her youth. His candid admission of his uncertain parentage so impressed Sage Gautama that he considered Satyakama a Brahmin and accepted him as his student. Kapur remarked: 'Thus, it was his character and not his birth which determined his caste.'
- Among others who 'raised themselves to the position of Brahmana by their good qualities' were Sage Matanga who was a Chandala and Sage Vishwamitra who was a Kshatriya.

In his zeal to make out that the original conception of caste was totally benign, Kapur glossed over all scriptural evidence to the contrary. That is, the evidence on which Sanatanist, or orthodox, Hindus unabashedly defended descent-based discrimination.

No less selective was Kapur's depiction of the third and current stage of caste. 'Hinduism might have become static at one stage but its modern history shows that this is not so now and it would not be wrong to say that caste in Hinduism is not dependent upon birth but on actions. The whole theory of Karma is destructive of the claim of caste being dependent upon birth.' He gave no example of how caste had, in modern times, reverted to what was allegedly its original conception. Kapur's sanitised assessment of the state of play was shared by none of the other four judges on the Supreme Court bench. They spoke instead through a radically differing judgment authored by Justice P.B. Gajendragadkar, who was himself a Brahmin and a reputed scholar of Hinduism.

To begin with, Gajendragadkar made clear that caste was still captive to birth. He said, 'Whatever may have been the origin of Hindu castes and tribes in ancient times, gradually castes came to be based on birth alone. It is well-known that a person who belongs by birth to a Depressed Class or Tribe would find it very difficult, if not impossible, to attain the status of a higher caste among the Hindus by virtue of his volition, education, culture, status.'

Unlike Kapur's dissent, Gajendragadkar's majority verdict was rooted in history. 'The history of social reform for the last century or more has shown how difficult it is to break or even relax the rigour of the inflexible and exclusive character of the caste system.' An example of this was the fact that, after decades of struggle waged by social reformers, it was only around the time of Independence that India enacted laws permitting inter-caste marriage, or indeed temple entry for stigmatised castes.

Acknowledging that little had changed on the ground towards overcoming this deeply entrenched prejudice, Gajendragadkar expressed hope that 'the cherished ideal of casteless society truly based on social equality will be attained under the powerful impact of the doctrine of social justice and equality proclaimed by the Constitution'. In a tacit criticism of Kapur's assertion that caste had already been unshackled from descent, Gajendragadkar said that 'at present it would be unrealistic and utopian to ignore the difficulties that a member of the Depressed Tribe or Caste has to face in claiming a higher status amongst his co-religionists'.

The proclivity of a lower-caste person to seek a higher status was no doubt borne out by the evidence that Giri had produced in Dora's context. Giri unearthed documents showing that, though born into a Scheduled Tribe family, Dora had, for almost three decades and in different ways, proclaimed himself to be a Kshatriya.

Dippala Suri Dora did betray signs of 'Sanskritisation', as sociologist M.N. Srinivas described the susceptibility of a lower-caste person seeking upward mobility through emulation. He had allegedly adopted the customs and rituals of Kshatriyas, including the sacred thread. But the court held that, even if the evidence adduced by Giri was accepted at face value, 'it falls far short of establishing' his plea that Dora had turned into a Kshatriya.

The majority judgment of the Supreme Court accepted the High Court view that whether a person had succeeded in changing his varna status should be determined 'in the light of the recognition received by him from the members of the caste into which he seeks an entry'. The evidence produced by Giri was instead found to have shown only that Dora intended to assert a higher status. 'But unilateral acts of this character cannot be easily taken to prove that the claim for the higher status which the said acts purport to make is established.'

Thus, in a four-to-one verdict on 20 May 1959, the Supreme Court dismissed Governor V.V. Giri's two-year-long personal crusade to establish that the caste identity of a Hindu, at the individual level, was no longer trapped in the accident of birth. As it happened, a decade after he had suffered this blow, Giri became the president of India in an extraordinary election that led to a split of the Congress Party. On completing his five-year term as head of state, Giri was awarded the Bharat Ratna in 1975. In all this time, it had not become any easier for a tribal or lower-caste person, however accomplished, to gain admission into the exclusive club of the twice-born.

1965

Thirty years after the Bombay High Court had disqualified the son of a Shudra's Brahmin concubine from the succession rights due to a dasiputra, the Supreme Court of India dealt with a similar challenge from Andhra Pradesh. Once again, a Brahmin concubine and her sons were claiming a share in the estate of the Shudra father.

Lingayya and Sitharamamma had three illegitimate sons, who

staked their claim to inherit as dasiputras. During the time that she lived with—and 'preserved sexual fidelity' to—Lingayya, from 1938 till his death in 1948, Sitharamamma was married to one Ramakrishnayya. She did not have the option of ending that marriage as the concept of divorce was not available to her until the enactment of the Hindu Marriage Act, 1955.

In their suit against Lingayya's brothers and nephews, Sitharamamma and her three illegitimate sons claimed that they were 'exclusively entitled' to Lingayya's estate. They faced two legal hurdles: that the concubine of the Shudra was a Brahmin and that she was a married woman. The trial court dismissed the suit, saying that 'she was not the lawfully wedded wife of Lingayya and the children born of the union were not his legitimate sons, nor were they Dasiputras and as such entitled to his properties'. This was in line with the 1935 Bombay decision, which held that a Shudra's Brahmin concubine did not fit the definition of dasiputra.[23]

Although it endorsed the trial court's decision, the High Court gave Sitharamamma and her sons some reprieve, permitting them to file a fresh plaint, this time seeking maintenance in place of inheritance. The lowering of ambition paid off, and the subordinate judge, at the end of the second trial in 1954, awarded them maintenance out of Lingayya's estate. After the High Court reaffirmed the quantum of the maintenance, the matter reached the Supreme Court on an appeal filed by Lingayya's brothers and nephews.

Meanwhile, in 1956, Parliament passed the Hindu Adoptions and Maintenance Act, which had the effect of complicating this case. One of the main questions before the Supreme Court was whether the new law came in the way of the maintenance that had been awarded under the old Hindu law. The new law excluded a concubine from among the 'dependants' who were entitled to maintenance from the estate of a deceased man. And though it did include an illegitimate son, the 1956 Act entered a caveat, saying that he could be maintained only 'so long as he remains a minor'. (The corresponding restriction in the case of an illegitimate daughter was 'so long as she remains unmarried'.)

In its judgment delivered on 18 February 1965,[24] a five-judge bench of the Supreme Court made a distinction between the provisions that operated prospectively and those that operated retrospectively. What was found to operate retrospectively was, for instance, the provision for the maintenance of a Hindu wife by her husband. This was because it expressly stated that the wife was entitled to maintenance 'whether married before or after the commencement of the Act'.

There was, however, no such time stipulation in Sections 21 and 22 of the Act, the provisions that excluded the concubine and the adult illegitimate son from among the dependants entitled to maintenance. Accordingly, the Supreme Court ruled that these sections operated prospectively and the maintenance that had previously been awarded to Sitharamamma and her illegitimate sons would not be affected by the restrictions imposed by the 1956 law. The verdict, authored by Justice R.S. Bachawat, said: 'The continuing claim of the respondents during their lifetime springs out of the original right vested in them on the death of Lingayya and is not founded on any right arising after the commencement of the Act.'

But there was still a question mark over Sitharamamma, given the High Court's ruling that she could not be regarded as a dasi since she belonged to a higher varna, besides her being married to another man. This prompted the Supreme Court to explore an alternative traditional concept, 'avaruddhastree', which meant a woman subjected to control or restraint. This euphemism was first employed by the Mitakshara, an influential legal commentary from the twelfth century, for a woman permanently kept in concubinage and living in the house of her paramour.

The Supreme Court relied upon a 1944 Bombay High Court judgment that had, in a radical interpretation, extended the concept of avaruddhastree to a married concubine.[25] That court had held that the married woman was 'entitled to maintenance from the estate of the paramour so long as she preserved her sexual fidelity to him'. Agreeing with this reasoning, the Supreme Court held that 'the Bombay decision lays down the correct law'. As for the sons of an avaruddhastree, they were, unlike dasiputras, entitled only to maintenance and not inheritance. Justice Bachawat concluded, therefore, that the maintenance claim of Sitharamamma and her sons 'cannot be defeated on the ground that the first respondent was a Brahmin and her paramour was a Shudra'.

1968

A temple located in Ayodhya and dedicated to the deity Thakur Anand Behari ji had a qualification in its trust deed for the position of mahant, or chief priest: that the man should be a 'Vaishnava Virakt Ramanandi Brahman'. When the incumbent died in 1959 without appointing a successor, the claimants to the mahantship were Ram Dulari Saran, a Brahmin, and Mahabir Das, a member of the Bhumihar caste, a dominant community in Bihar and eastern Uttar Pradesh.

What emerged from their conflicting suits were allegations that each had failed to fulfil at least one of the two basic qualifications for the successor. Saran was said to be ineligible as, contrary to the condition of being 'virakt', or unattached, he was a householder with a wife and children. Likewise, Das was allegedly ineligible because, contrary to its claims, his Bhumihar caste did not belong to the Brahmin varna.

In his judgment on 30 May 1966, the additional civil judge of Faizabad dismissed the Bhumihar claimant's suit and decreed that of the Brahmin claimant to be valid. The trial court's reasoning was that, at the time of his mentor's death, Saran had 'renounced his Grihasth life', or worldly connections, and 'thus he had become Virakt Ramanandi Brahman'. As for Das, the trial court held that he was 'not a Brahman', and therefore 'not qualified for appointment as Mahant'. As the trial court put it, 'the Bhumihars may call themselves Bhumihar Brahmans but it is nowhere established that they are really Brahmans'.

While the appeal filed by Das against this judgment was

pending before the district judge of Faizabad, a Hindi weekly called *Virakt* published articles in August 1966 attacking the trial court for preferring Saran over Das. It argued that putting 'a particular community in the category of Ṣhudras and non-Brahmans and holding them incompetent to perform the Puja of the Supreme Being was beyond the powers of the court'.

This prompted Saran to file a contempt of court application against Das and the three men connected with the offending publication. The matter was heard by Justice Shiva Nath Katju who had been in the thick of the larger changes that unfolded in independent India.

A Hindu nationalist under the big tent that the Congress party was, Shiva Nath Katju was a legislator in Uttar Pradesh for a decade. His father, Kailash Nath Katju, was successively minister for Home and Defence in the Nehru government. After retiring from the High Court, Shiva Nath Katju went on to become president of the Vishwa Hindu Parishad and campaigned for the controversial Ramjanmabhoomi temple in Ayodhya. His son, Markandey Katju, would go on to become a judge of the Supreme Court.

The contempt petition proved to be a showcase for the evolution in judicial understanding of the varna–caste nexus. In view of the egalitarian provisions of the 1950 Constitution, Justice Katju did not feel bound to the criteria evolved by colonial courts to determine the varna status of a given caste. In fact, his judgment, delivered on behalf of the Allahabad High Court on 17 January 1968,[26] also deviated from the law laid down by the Supreme Court in the V.V. Giri case.[27]

Though Gajendragadkar had ruled that varna status depended on whether the individual concerned had been accepted by the caste to which they wished to belong, Katju made out that the choice rested with the caste seeking such recognition. 'Whether the Bhumihars are Brahmans or not is a question which has to be determined primarily by the Bhumihars themselves and relatively by the other sections of the Hindu society.'

Without any reference to the case law, Katju portrayed a utopia that overlooked the prolonged and irreconcilable dispute between Brahmins and Bhumihars. 'The question of caste, in the Hindu society, has always been a matter primarily for the caste itself and for the Hindu society. All that a Court could do is to recognise what has been declared and decided by the people themselves on the evidence before it.' He gave no indication of how the people themselves would decide and declare the varna status of a caste.

Since it was in the limited context of contempt of court, Katju washed his hands of the matter saying, 'A court could neither take upon itself the task of finally and conclusively declaring for all times the status of a particular caste or section of the Hindu Society nor could it expect that its verdict would be the last word on the subject.'

Insofar as the contempt case before him was concerned, Katju said, 'I am not prepared to take a harsh notice of the comments made by the respondents that the Bhumihars are Brahmans and that the court had erred in deciding otherwise.' While Mahabir Das was exonerated on the charge of complicity, the three men accountable for the articles were held guilty, but let off with a token penalty of Rs 40 each as they had tendered apologies.

'Considering the nature of the controversy and the importance of the question to the Bhumihars in general who form a large section of the people of Uttar Pradesh and Bihar,' Katju said, 'I cannot overlook the agitation which must have been caused in their minds in consequence of the decision of the Court.'

1979

In January 1886, less than two years after the Calcutta High Court's ruling that Bengali Kayasthas were Shudras,[28] a twenty-three-year-old member of that caste, Narendranath Datta, became a sanyasi. Swami Vivekananda, as he was then renamed, went on to become the most celebrated sanyasi in modern India. However, his renunciation of worldly life challenged the orthodox view that only Brahmins—or at a stretch, members of the twice-born varnas—were eligible to join the ranks of sanyasis.

There was a pointed reference to this issue in a judgment of the Allahabad High Court in 1971.[29] In his verdict, Justice A.K. Kirty recalled that Ramakrishna Paramahamsa, the legendary Brahmin mystic, had nominated Vivekananda as his chief disciple, despite his Shudra status. 'It would be preposterous to say, in my opinion, that Swami Vivekanand having been born as a Sudra was inherently disqualified from entering the order of Sanyasam.'

This endorsement of heresy was a clear setting aside of colonial-era precedents, a string of which, in deference to scriptural authorities, had ruled that a Shudra could not be a sanyasi. The first such judgment came from the Madras High Court in 1899, by when, unconnected to the case, Vivekananda had already established his pioneering monastery, the Ramakrishna Math.

The 1899 Madras ruling was that, as a Shudra was incompetent to enter the order of yathi or sanyasi, his property could not devolve to his monastery.[30] After his death, the property should instead be regulated by the ordinary law of inheritance. Consequently, the Madras High Court decreed the saffron-robed Shudra's property to 'the secular heir, the brother of the deceased as against the members of the Mutt into which the deceased had been admitted'.

The case in which Justice Kirty made a reference to Swami Vivekananda, almost seven decades after his death, had also thrown up a question about varna vis-à-vis monasteries. Could a monastery in the holy city of Varanasi be headed by a Shudra, given that courts had long held in other cases that members of that varna could not even become a sanyasi?

The dispute was over a property purchased from the offerings of devotees by the earlier mahant of the Garwaghat Math, Baikunth Singh alias Swami Atma Vivekanand. After his passing, his Shudra successor, Mathura Ahir alias Swami Harswanand, filed a suit on behalf of the monastery for declaration of title to that property. But Baikunth Singh's son, Krishna Singh, contended that he was entitled to succeed to that property despite his father's renunciation of familial attachments. Krishna Singh's main ground for claiming inheritance was that his father's successor 'being a Sudra could not be ordained to a religious order and become a Sanyasi or Yati and therefore [be] installed a Mahant of the Garwaghat Math'.

The Allahabad High Court cited the example of Swami Vivekananda to respond to this assertion. Whether it was due to 'custom, usage or practice or of sacramental precept', Justice Kirty said that 'Sudras might have been considered to be incapable of entering into the order of Sanyasam at one time', but that 'such disqualification ceased to exist long ago and can no longer be held to exist now'.

Among the reasons he cited for this change was that, after Independence, India had been relieved of the colonial burden of pandering to orthodoxy. Referring to the pre-Independence judgments that had de-recognised sanyasis from Shudra castes, Kirty said that 'the authoritative force or the persuasive value of such rulings no longer subsists'. He added that 'the discriminatory ban on or bar against Sudras, even if enjoined by Hindu Law, stands abrogated'. This was, he said, because 'the strict rule enjoined by the Smriti writers' on who could become sanyasis had 'ceased to be valid because of the fundamental rights guaranteed under Part III of the Constitution'.

When the sanyasi case came up before it in appeal, the Supreme Court, however, rejected the idea that fundamental rights, a secular source, would have a bearing on a religious restriction on Shudras.[31] Taking a conservative view, Justice Ananda Prakash Sen's judgment said, 'Part III of the Constitution does not touch upon the personal laws of the parties.'

Sen's proposition that Part III had nothing to do with personal laws was at variance with Kirty's interpretation that at least nine provisions from it aided Shudras in combating caste disabilities. Besides the fundamental rights to equality and non-discrimination, Kirty referred to the freedom of religion provision, which contained a clause specifically to reform the Hindu personal law.

Despite disagreeing with it, the Supreme Court did not actually overturn the High Court verdict. Instead, in its judgment delivered on 21 December 1979, the Supreme Court found a remedy right within the Hindu law in regard to sanyasis, even though it had admitted that 'according to the orthodox Smriti writers, a Sudra cannot legitimately enter into a religious order' and that they did not 'sanction or tolerate ascetic life of the Sudras'.

Paradoxically, to overcome colonial rulings on the subject, the Supreme Court relied upon a principle of the Hindu law that had been laid down by the Privy Council in 1868:[32] that clear proof of usage would outweigh the scriptures or written text. As Justice Sen put it, 'It cannot be denied that the existing practice all over India is quite contrary to such orthodox view. In cases, therefore, where the usage is established, according to which a Sudra can enter into a religious order in the same way as in the case of the twice-born classes, such usage should be given effect to.'

Thus, the Supreme Court threw open to Shudras only such monasteries as did not have a usage of barring them, and not as a fundamental right. By upholding the conclusion of the Allahabad High Court in such a qualified manner, the Supreme Court protected the right of the twice-born classes to keep out Shudras. That such a judgment came from the highest court of the land more than three decades after the enforcement of the Constitution was, to say the least, a reflection on the persistence of the larger dynamics of caste and varna.

6

A WEDDING WITHOUT A BRAHMIN

While it was common practice that a priest was always a Brahmin, western India had a peculiar custom that privileged a set of Brahmins. It elevated the priest to a watandar joshi, or hereditary office-holder, who had monopoly on the exercise and benefits of that office in his assigned locality. In other words, for all the social or religious events in his family, the choice before the layman was reduced to one particular priest, the local watandar joshi. And since the designation was purely hereditary, the people had no say in the selection of their assigned priest. They had to put up with him regardless of his merits. A legacy of the Peshwa reign that had ended in 1818, the custom remained legally enforceable under colonial rule.

This retrograde institution was reinforced in 1874 by no less an authority than the Bombay High Court. The watandar joshi of village Rede in the Solapur district, Vithal Krishna Joshi, filed a suit against another priest, Anant Ramchandra. The grievance was that Ramchandra had received a fee for performing a ceremony, thus violating Vithal Joshi's monopoly. Though the subordinate judge had partially upheld Joshi's plea, the first appellate court threw out his claim for his failure to show that Ramchandra was 'under any obligation not to officiate as a priest in the village of Rede'.

However, on a second appeal, heard by Chief Justice Michael Roberts Westropp and Justice Raymond West of the Bombay High Court, that decision was reversed. The verdict was written by West, considered an expert on the subject, given that he had co-authored *Digest of Hindu Law*. West ruled that the watandar joshi was entitled to claim damages from any intruder who 'assumes to act in the office and receives the fees'.[1] So, if any other priest had performed the ceremony and earned remuneration for it, he was liable to 'refund' it to the watandar joshi of that area.

Emboldened by this recognition, a group of four watandar joshis in Poona, led by Dinanath Abaji, filed a fresh suit. They wanted to extend the liability to the layman, who was formally referred to as 'yajman', or ritual patron. The suit sought a decree declaring that the designated priest alone was 'entitled to perform' ceremonies such as weddings and 'receive fees for the same'. This plea ran contrary to rulings by the courts of other provinces that 'a man might select his own priest'.

The plaintiffs cited a ruling that predated the establishment, in 1862, of the Bombay High Court. Its predecessor, the Sudder Dewanny Adawlat, deferring to customary law in some cases, had ordered the yajman to compensate the watandar joshi for failing to employ him. In one such case of 1857, the court held that the watandar joshi could exact payment irrespective of who had done the work or what the work was: 'If the ceremonies, whether optional or obligatory, have been performed, the person entitled by hereditary right to perform is entitled to his fee.'[2] Dinanath Abaji's suit sought a reaffirmation of this principle two decades later, even though much had changed after 1857, including the upgradation of the judiciary.

The first class subordinate judge of Poona adjudicating the case in the first instance was none other than Mahadev Govind Ranade, who went on to become a leading social reformer of India. Yet, while dealing with this challenging suit early in his judicial career, Ranade displayed little reformatory zeal. He passed a decree that rendered the layman vulnerable to pre-emptive action by the watandar joshis: 'the plaintiffs are entitled to perform the ceremonies irrespective of yajman's wishes, as well as to receive the fees'.[3]

Ranade's British superior felt compelled to mitigate his

illiberal interpretation of the customary law. On an appeal filed by the yajmans named in the suit, the district judge of Poona, W.H. Newnham, said that he was 'very strongly of opinion' that the duty of a Hindu to employ 'a particular joshi' in the performance of religious duty 'might very well be left to be enforced by religious sanctions and not by legal means'. As Newnham put it, the use of legal means for such a purpose was 'opposed to the spirit of our law and to public policy', adding that 'the civil courts do enough if they protect joshis against pecuniary loss'.

Newnham's toned-down decree no longer empowered the joshis to 'obtain injunctions restraining the yajmans from having the ceremony performed by anyone but themselves'. But if they had not been employed, the joshis were still entitled 'to receive on each occasion a fee equal in amount' to that paid by the yajmans to the other priests. This was an improvement on Ranade's judgment in that it restored to the Hindu his freedom to employ any priest, subject to the liability forced by the Bombay custom that he must pay an equivalent fee to his watandar joshi.

Aggrieved at this attempt to balance the conflicting rights of the joshi and the yajman, the plaintiffs decided to appeal the decision. Like in the *Vithal Joshi* case, the *Dinanath Abaji* appeal went before a Bombay High Court bench headed by Chief Justice Westropp. And this time, Westropp himself authored the judgment delivered in 1878. While conceding that 'we are bound by authority to hold this suit to be maintainable', Westropp said, 'We, however, approve of the variation made by the District Judge [Newnham] by his decree in that of the Subordinate Judge [Ranade].'

The High Court added that it was 'somewhat surprised that the plaintiffs should have thought it worth their while to appeal against it in consequence of the slight variation made by the District Judge'. Indeed, for the watandar joshi continued to enjoy the monetary benefits of his special status. If anyone had cause to be aggrieved, it was the layman, for he had been penalised with the burden of paying the uninvited joshi as well.

Against this backdrop, a radical form of wedding took shape in the Bombay Presidency, doing away with not just the watandar joshi but any kind of Brahmin priest. It took on Brahminical hegemony head-on.

The Satyashodhak Samaj, or the Truth-Seeking Society, established by social reformer Jotirao Phule in Poona in 1873, was the moving force behind this reform. The aims of the society, enumerated in its first report, published in 1877, said: 'Some wise gentlemen founded this Samaj on the 24 September 1873, in order to free the Shudra people from slavery to Brahmans, Bhats, Joshis, priests and others. For thousands of years, these people have heedlessly despised and exploited the Shudras, with the aid of their cunningly-devised books.'[4]

In a bid to mobilise the multitude that formed the lower castes, the Satyashodhak Samaj came up with an alternative, egalitarian conception of God. As the scholar Rosalind O'Hanlon put it, 'The decision to dispense with Brahmin priests struck, as the leaders of the society intended, at the very heart of existing Hindu ideas about the proper means of access to divine power. By insisting that God was available to all his human creatures, that no intermediary was necessary for the invocation of divine power, the society attempted to remove any justification for the special sanctity of Brahmins.'[5]

Nowhere was the 'special sanctity' more evident than in the presumption that they were indispensable to the solemnisation of marriages. In a revolutionary move, Phule introduced an extra-legal social reform under which a member of the same caste as the bridal couple would perform the wedding ceremony, a simple rite that consciously diverged from the traditional rituals. The gradual spread of the Satyashodhak form of wedding led to another round of litigation in the Bombay Presidency some fifteen years later, drawing once again on the institution of the watandar joshi.

The hereditary priests of village Otur in Poona district, led by Waman Jagannath Joshi, filed a suit against Balaji Kusaji Patil, a close associate of Jotirao Phule, for eliminating their role in the weddings of his two daughters. Seeking damages from Patil, the plaintiffs complained that 'their services were not employed although as such joshis they had a right to officiate on such occasions and were ready and willing to conduct the ceremonies'.[6] Their claim for damages was based on the decree passed in the context of a regular Hindu wedding in the Dinanath Abaji case.

Patil agreed that he had employed a fellow Kunbi to perform the weddings of his daughters in the Satyashodhak style. The question, therefore, was whether the custom of watandar joshi could apply to this new form of wedding that expressly intended to do away with Brahminism. The court of first instance held that, despite the departures made by Patil, the hereditary joshi was still 'entitled to be employed in the performance of such ceremonies and functions of his office as are usual amongst Sudras'.

The judge was pointing to the fact that the mantras chanted at weddings tended to vary based on the varna status of the parties concerned. So, the mantras that were 'usual among Sudras' were not from the Vedas, which were reserved for the superior varnas. The Shudras had to make do with mantras from the less sacrosanct Puranas. This was why Phule's Satyashodhak form of marriage got rid of both the Brahmin priest and his discriminatory rituals. Yet, the judge believed that Patil owed the watandar joshi his dues.

The first appellate court reversed the trial court judge's decree. On Balaji Patil's appeal, judge M.N. Nanavati held that the watandar priests were not entitled to any payment unless the wedding had been performed in 'any of the modes known to the Hindu law'. The manner in which he framed his judgment exposed, perhaps inadvertently, an opportunity to raise a more fundamental question that the priests had missed, one that could have gone in their favour. Namely, if a wedding between Hindus did not comply with any of the modes known to the Hindu law, could that marriage be considered valid at all?

Insofar as the limited issue of entitlement was concerned, Nanavati said that, for the priests to receive their sum, they would have to show that the mode of the wedding was specifically as described for Shudras in an authoritative book on Hindu law written by the foremost expert of the time, Vishvanath Narayan Mandlik.

Published in 1880, Mandlik's book said, 'The ceremonies of the Sudras are to be performed with Puranik texts.'[7] Whether such ceremonies had been observed in the Patil weddings was thus a point of fact that could not be determined without reference to evidence and inference. However, on the evidence that the trial court itself had recorded, Nanavati concluded that 'the marriages in dispute being not performed in any such way', the watandar joshis were not entitled to recover fees 'in virtue of any right'.

Waman Joshi and his cohorts took the matter before the Bombay High Court. Thus ensued a historic contestation in 1888 on the reform of Hindu marriage before a bench of Chief Justice Charles Sargent and Justice E.T. Candy. The chief question before the two judges was whether the weddings of Balaji Patil's daughters had deviated from the Brahminical practice for Sudras.

The counsel for the priests, Mahadev Chimnaji Apte, insisted that the only deviation in those weddings from the Hindu norm was the engagement of a non-Brahmin priest. 'There was an invasion of their [his clients'] privilege by the person who performed the ceremonies.' So, the Brahmin priests were entitled to 'whatever was paid to the Kunbi priest' by Patil.

On the other hand, the counsel for the lower-caste rebel, Ghanasham Nilkanth Nadkarni, sought to reinforce the first appellate court's finding: 'The marriages were performed without any prescribed ceremonies, and no priest, as such, was employed.' Nadkarni cited at least four grounds to establish this claim. One: 'There was no Ganesh pujan', the necessary preliminary of every Hindu marriage. Two: 'There was nothing beyond the placing of garlands on the necks of the bride and the bridegroom.' Thus, there was no tying of the mangalsutra around the neck of the bride, a feature representative of the Hindu conception of marriage as kanyadaan, or the gift of the bride. Three: 'There was no distribution of fees (dakshana); therefore, the village joshis cannot claim any fees.' This means that the Kunbi who had performed the weddings was not treated as an alternative priest. Four: 'There is a separate ritual for the Sudras of the defendant's caste. That ritual was not performed.' No Puranic mantras had been chanted.

In her book, *The Caste Question*, historian Anupama Rao wrote, 'The 1888 judgment by Justices Sargent and Candy supported the Satyashodhak's argument that because the wedding of Patil's daughter was not performed as a (legally) recognizable non-Brahmin or Shudra marriage, the Joshi was ineligible for fees.'[8] Though the Bombay High Court did eventually decide in favour of Patil, the operative part of the 1888 judgment was far from what Rao suggests.

To their credit, Justices Sargent and Candy took pains to avoid the lack of rigour that the lower courts had betrayed in arriving at conflicting findings on the mode of the weddings. The Sargent–Candy bench ordered a probe to unearth what had transpired.

The judgment, authored by Sargent, pointed out the procedural deficiency in Nanavati's finding: 'But no issue was expressly raised as to the manner in which the marriages in question were performed; and although in the course of the hearing some evidence was given on the subject, neither party, we think, clearly understood what was the real issue between them on that part of the case.'

Accordingly, the Sargent–Candy bench sent down the following issue 'for a finding' by the District Court: 'What ceremonies were performed on the occasions of the marriages, or either of them, and by whom?' Permitting the parties to give 'fresh evidence', the order dated 30 July 1888 set a two-month deadline for the District Court to submit its findings. The paper trail of a case that centred on a major social reform, however, ends at this tantalising point. The Bombay High Court's order, consequent to the Poona District Court's finding on the mode of the weddings, went unreported somehow. This uncharacteristic omission on the part of the law journals of the time raises a doubt about whether the case's religious or social sensitivities had anything to do with it.

Caste, Conflict and Ideology, the most authoritative book on Jotirao Phule, written by historian Rosalind O'Hanlon, dwelt on this case and even quoted at length a proclamation that had been issued as part of the 'Satyashodhak propaganda' in 1888 just before the appeal proceedings began in the High Court. Yet, she does not refer to the dramatic nature of the case in the High Court, much less so the fresh evidence recorded on the nature of the two Satyashodhak ceremonies. Like Rao, all that O'Hanlon disclosed about the appeal proceedings was, 'The High Court returned the verdict in favour of Phule's side.'[9]

Another biography of Phule, written by Dhananjay Keer, contains a more detailed account of these legal developments. Keer not only mentioned the reference to the District Court in 1888, but also disclosed that the final judgment, in light of the fresh evidence, was a victory for Patil. He wrote that it was a bench comprising Chief Justice Sargent and Justice K.T. Telang that delivered this final verdict on 8 January 1890, about ten months before Phule's death.[10] 'The first month of the year 1890 brought a great triumph to Jotirao who was ailing.' But he indicated neither the source of his information nor the oddity that so important a judgment had remained unreported.

While the date of the judgment and the composition of the bench is still unclear, there is thankfully an unimpeachable source on the substance of the final judgment in the Otur case. And that is another Bombay High Court judgment delivered about twenty-five years later. The 1915 verdict too involved a question about the watandar joshi's entitlement to wedding fees; this time, it was in the context of the Lingayat community. Concentrated in the Kannada-speaking areas of the Bombay Presidency, the Lingayats had an eight-century-old history of resisting Brahminism. The dispute between watandar joshis and Lingayats prompted the bench comprising Chief Justice Basil Scott and Justice Stanley Batchelor to look up the Satyashodhak precedent.

While referring to the outcome in the Otur case, the Scott–Batchelor bench was not able to just quote from a law journal and provide the citation (as the reference is called in legal parlance). Since the final order had not been reported anywhere, the bench was forced to retrieve the papers of the Satyashodhak Samaj case from the court archives.

Their efforts revealed that, on the basis of the evidentiary inputs from Poona's District Court on the Otur weddings, the Satyashodhak innovation had been adjudged a mode of marriage unknown to Hindu law, and therefore beyond the coercive reach of the watandar joshi. 'We have referred to the record in that case, and we find that the learned District Judge after stating what ceremonies were, on the evidence taken on remand, performed, stated his opinion that "the ceremonial enumerated by the late V N Mandlik in his Hindu law as observed by lower castes, was not followed on these occasions".'[11]

From the sequence of events as reconstructed by the 1915 judgment, the Bombay High Court took that finding of the Poona District Judge as confirmation of 'the inference' that had been drawn by Nanavati, and thereby upheld his decree in favour of Balaji Kusaji Patil. Since the matter had attained finality, Scott, who authored the 1915 judgment, took the Otur case as 'an authority' on the proposition that 'if the ceremony performed is not a Hindu marriage ceremony as a whole, the Joshi has no right to demand the fees'. In other words, whether one was a member of the Satyashodhak Samaj or the Lingayat community, Brahmin priests had no entitlement outside their domain of the prescribed Hindu ceremonies.

In a bid to plug this loophole, the watandar joshi of village Bhavdi in Poona upped the ante in another Satyashodhak case, which came up before the Bombay High Court three years later. In this 1918 case relating to last rites, he claimed that he was entitled to his fees 'even though no Brahminical ceremony is employed, and all that happens is that a simple lay rite carried out by the villager himself'.[12] A bench headed by Justice Batchelor ruled that 'where these ceremonies are deliberately avoided, it would be difficult to find a ground upon which the joshi could lawfully exact the payment of the fees'.

While these were incremental reforms, the Bombay High Court bore the odium of keeping alive an unconscionable practice in the Hindu mainstream. Thanks to the half measures contained in its decrees, the watandar joshi was still entitled to demand payments from anyone who chose Brahminical ceremonies, as was the norm. To remove this anomaly, a bill was introduced in March 1921 in the recently created bicameral legislature formed in Delhi following the Montagu–Chelmsford Reforms.

The Hindu Ceremonial Emoluments Bill, as it was called, was the first-ever initiative by an Indian legislator to launch a frontal attack on a Brahminical prerogative. Anna Babaji Latthe, the member who piloted it through the Legislative Assembly was, not surprisingly, from the Bombay Presidency. A Jain, he was a close associate (and later, a biographer) of Shahu Maharaj of Kolhapur, who had emerged, after Phule's death, as the tallest leader of non-Brahmins in the region.

In Latthe's three-clause bill, the key provision said, 'No person shall be entitled to claim, as a matter of right, any ceremonial emoluments from any Hindu who does not call in the services of the person claiming those emoluments.' The bill protected the laity by stripping the archaic watandar joshi institution of its coercive powers.

After the bill had been circulated in all the provinces of British India and their responses had been received, Latthe proposed in the Assembly on 27 September 1921 that it be referred to a Select Committee as a prelude to its enactment. He pointed out that, in the Bombay Presidency and Marathi-speaking districts of Central Provinces, the courts had taken the 'misguided' view that 'the hereditary priests have a right to claim emoluments from Hindus who do not even ask those priests to officiate at their ceremonies'. In contrast, the High Courts of Calcutta, Madras, Allahabad and the Punjab, he said, had 'held consistently that no such right exists and nobody can force himself as a priest against the wishes of the laymen'.

The colonial government, on its part, said that since the bill 'really affects only Hindus', it would adopt 'a neutral and impartial attitude in the matter'. Giving an overview of the feedback received, Home Member William Vincent said that, among the provinces that were not affected by the custom of watandar joshi, there was 'a general feeling in support of the Bill'. Despite its professed neutrality, the government singled out—and described as 'sound'—a suggestion from Madras that the bill should be applicable only to the Bombay Presidency and those parts of the Central Provinces where 'the evil is said to exist'. Vincent maintained that the bill could go before a Select Committee if 'the Hindu members of this Assembly think that this is a just measure, that this is a measure demanded by fairness and equity to non-Brahmins, and that it is not inequitable or unfair to Brahmins'.

In the event, the majority of the Hindu members did endorse Latthe's motion to refer his bill to a Select Committee. In its turn, the committee took the view that the ambit of the legislation should be limited to the Bombay Presidency and parts of the Central Provinces. The bill incorporating this amendment was passed by the Legislative Assembly on 28 March 1922, barely two months before the death of Latthe's mentor, Shahu Maharaj.

The bill—reviled as an anti-Brahmin machination of the Satyashodhak Samaj—was introduced in the Council of State by a Brahmin legislator from the Bombay Presidency, V.G. Kale. Referring to its alleged anti-Brahmin character, Kale said, 'It so happens that I myself am a Brahmin, but I do not want to look at this question from the narrow point of view of caste. I want to take my stand upon principle.'

Yet, on 27 February 1923, the bill went on to earn the dubious distinction of being the first in India to be rejected by the Upper House after it had been passed by the Lower House.

This setback was the result of an objection raised by an unlikely source: Leslie Miller, a British 'Nominated Non-Official' member from the Madras Presidency, who was a former judge of the Madras High Court and a former chief judge of the Chief Court of the Mysore princely state. Interestingly, the 1919 report of a committee headed by him had led Mysore to pioneer the concept of job reservations for non-Brahmins. And still, Miller opposed this social-reform bill. His long and impassioned intervention strengthened the partisan opponents to the bill in the Council, led by G.S. Khaparde, a Brahmin legislator from the Central Provinces.

Miller's critique was oddly selective in its treatment of the issues involved. The bill was a 'measure of confiscation', he asserted, as it swept away 'a customary monopoly without making compensation to the holder'. Likening the privilege to recover customary emoluments to 'civil rights to property', Miller said that the bill was 'simply a negation of the right to proceed to the civil court', without providing any alternative remedy. He could not, therefore, 'help thinking' that the bill would add to the crimes that had been 'committed in the name of liberty'. Although he contended that the bill should have a provision for compensation, Miller sidestepped the central issue of whether the priest should have, as he himself put it, 'the right to sue for unperformed services'.

The shadow of Miller's dissent in the Council of State dogged the footsteps of the bill even three years later when it was resurrected in the Bombay Legislative Council. Reproducing Latthe's clause verbatim, the mover of the bill in the state legislature, social reformer and non-Brahmin leader, Sitaram Keshav Bole, tweaked its title to 'Invalidation of Hindu Ceremonial Emoluments Bill'. At the first discussion on it on 19 March 1926, Bole countered Miller by quoting judgments delivered by Brahmin judges from the very same High Court of Madras where Miller had served. In one instance, Justice Sadasiva Iyer said that he was 'strongly against the recognition of the office which could give rise to an exclusive right to officiate as purohit ... especially a right which can be enforced in a court of law'. In another instance, Justice Seshagiri Iyer held that 'such a monopoly to officiate as priests should not be recognised by law'.

However, the June 1926 report of the Select Committee set up by the Bombay Legislative Council contained a dissenting note. R.P. Paranjpye, a Brahmin legislator who had been a minister in the Bombay Presidency, said that it would have been fitting if this bill had contained 'some provision for granting compensation' to the priests who would be affected by it. He even quoted an authority: 'This point was made by Sir Leslie Miller, a retired judge of the Madras High Court in the Council of State, when a similar Bill came up for discussion there and it is unfortunate that such a provision has not been introduced in this Bill.'

The majority in the Bombay Legislative Council disagreed with Miller's opinion, though. After five days of intense debate, the law, unprecedented in its breaking of the nexus between caste and priesthood, was passed in the Bombay Presidency on 3 August 1926. Thanks to Bole's tenacity, the crucial clause that had been framed by Latthe remained unchanged in what gained currency as the Joshi Act.

❖

Almost three decades later, in its post-colonial avatar as a nascent republic, India was still grappling with the validity of a wedding without a Brahmin officiating at it. Only, the battlefield had shifted from Bombay to Madras. The Madras term for 'joshi', the priest who performed nuptial rites, was 'purohit'. And the catalyst for social change in Madras was the Self-Respect Movement led by Dravidian icon Erode Venkata Ramasamy or, as he was better known, Periyar.

The question of whether a Hindu wedding could be valid without a purohit and his Brahminical rituals was addressed for the first time by the Madras High Court in 1953. This was more radical than the reform in the Bombay Presidency, which had essentially dealt with the peculiar entitlement of watandar joshis and their claim for damages. Unlike the Satyashodhak Samaj, the Self-Respect Movement launched in 1925 was not content with mobilising non-Brahmins against Brahminical hegemony. It was an atheistic ideology that revolted against religious sanction for caste. In fact, Periyar's formula for abolishing caste was 'the abolition of God, religion, the Shastras and Brahmins'.[13]

Yet, while it did away with all the sacral elements, including purohits and religious vows, the self-respect wedding, or 'suyamariyadai', still presented itself as being within the framework of the Hindu law. In their submissions before the Madras High Court, Self-Respecters claimed that suyamariyadai was nothing but the old Gandharva-style marriage, which was one of the eight modes of Hindu marriage recognised by the Shastras. It was a deliciously subversive act—digging up an argument from Hinduism's own diverse heritage. The Gandharva wedding was, as the High Court acknowledged, the one mode of marriage among Hindus that was based on 'the mutual agreement of the maiden with her lover'.[14] That this form of marriage was so predicated on the bride's consent in a notoriously patriarchal context was, for Periyar's followers, in keeping with their professed commitment to self-respect and the rights of women.

In its judgment delivered on 26 August 1953, the Madras High Court quoted scriptures to confirm that the Gandharva form of marriage was the exception that proved the rule. In fact, it defied the common practice of kanyadaan, under which, as the High Court put it, 'the essence of the marriage is transfer of dominion by gift'. However, this valiant attempt by Self-Respecters to elevate the bride from a gift to a consenting equal within the framework of a Hindu marriage did not find favour with the bench comprising Justices Prattipati Satyanarayana Rao and Pundi Rajagopalan.

'Assuming that the Gandharva form of marriage was intended', they held that the self-respect wedding was still not valid, 'in the absence of the performance of any religious rites'. In fact, the general principle laid down by Justices Rao and Rajagopalan was that 'ceremonies are essential in the case of all the eight forms of marriage and that the said rule applies even to Sudras'. At the same time, they conceded that the differences in the rites for the Shudras and the twice-born varnas had been judicially recognised since the colonial period. The overall signal was that the Shudras were required to maintain the semblance of a Hindu wedding even if only as a poor imitation of the ways of their social superiors.

One obvious element of imitation was the vivahika, or sacred fire, around which the bridal couple of a regenerate varna would perform saptapadi, or ceremonially take seven steps amid Vedic chants. Wading into the ambiguities in the scriptures and their commentaries and judicial interpretations, the High Court said, 'Of course, a Sudra may not be entitled to kindle the vivahika fire at the time of the saptapadi, but there is no objection for kindling a fire.' Adding insult to injury, the High Court left open the question whether the fire lit at a Shudra wedding could be considered sacred. 'Though some commentators permitted the vivahika fire i.e. the fire kindled at the time of marriage, Medatithi and other commentators say that the Sudra would offer oblations in the ordinary fire and that there is no vivahika fire for the Sudra.'

On the related issue of chants or mantras, the High Court ruled that the Shudras would have to settle for an inferior version while performing any of their samskaras, or religious rites. It approvingly quoted scriptural authorities on the matter. Yama: 'The Sudra also must be similarly sanctified by the performance of the above rites but without the utterances of the sacred formulae.' Vyasa: 'Sudras though being the fourth varna, they too are included among the varnas. So they are entitled to Dharma, except uttering the Vedic mantras and the words "svadha", "svaha" and "vashat".' Marichi was interpreted as saying, 'This applies to all Sudradharmas. The mantras that are chanted should be only puranic and not vedic.'

Although the traditional format denied equality to the Shudras, the High Court faulted the Self-Respecters for claiming that 'in the case of a non-regenerate class (Sudras) all that is necessary to constitute a valid marriage is proof of an agreement between the spouses to enter into marital union and the expression of such an intention in some unequivocal and definite form'. It held, 'There is no authority of any kind to support the extreme contention that a mere agreement followed by a declaration and living together as husband and wife with the exchange of garlands and rings are sufficient to constitute a valid marriage under Hindu law.'

Since a suyamariyadai wedding was being invalidated in the context of a property dispute in a joint family, the High Court spelt out a cruel implication of its ruling: 'the issues of such a union would have to be treated as illegitimate children'.

The judgment would have the sweeping effect of turning many marriages, conducted over three decades, into illicit relationships, thereby stripping their offspring of legitimacy as well as inheritance rights. Naturally, it caused much consternation among the Shudras in the Madras state. This feeling gained piquancy because the judgment came at a time when the chief minister of Madras, Chakravarti Rajagopalachari alias Rajaji, was already embroiled in a caste controversy.

Despite his long record of engaging with caste prejudice, Rajaji, a Brahmin, had been under attack from two major groups championing Shudra interests. One was Periyar's Dravida Kazhagam (DK), the driver of the Self-Respect Movement, and the other was the Dravida Munnetra Kazhagam (DMK), the political party led by Periyar's estranged protégé, Conjeevaram Natarajan Annadurai alias Anna. Rajaji had recently introduced an education reform scheme under which the hours of elementary schooling were reduced from five to three, so that children could spend the other two hours at home learning the occupations of their parents. Critics saw it as a Brahminical conspiracy to confine the children from lower castes to menial occupations.[15]

In this fraught environment, about three months after the High Court judgment on suyamariyadai, Rajaji's government drafted a bill in response to the concerns of the affected people. To the disappointment of the Self-Respecters, though, the bill did not refer to their form of marriage by the name they had given it. Instead, it cast suyamariyadai in negative terms, defining it as a 'non-conforming marriage'. The government's nomenclature was further reinforcing the High Court judgment's premise that every Hindu marriage should conform to the norm of Brahminical ceremonies and values.

Given this meeting of minds between the government and the High Court, the bill displayed no inclination towards eroding the centrality of Brahminical ceremonies, let alone validating the self-respect form of marriage. All it offered was a one-time amnesty scheme to those who had committed the folly of marrying in that non-conforming style. Those who wanted their self-respect marriages to be legalised would be allowed to register them with retrospective effect. And they needed to do this within two years. Hence the title of the bill was the 'Hindu Non-Conforming Marriages (Registration) Bill'.

The registration option applied only to those who had married *prior* to the enforcement of the proposed law. If anyone ventured to marry in the suyamariyadai style *after* the enforcement of the proposed law, their marriage was condemned to invalidity. Candid as it was about conceding only what was politically unavoidable, Rajaji's bill was designed to discourage Self-Respecters from persisting with their style of weddings.

The Jawaharlal Nehru government noticed these deficiencies when the state referred the bill to it on 12 December 1953 for its sanction, as per procedure. The Centre wrote back saying that, while it agreed that 'legislation of the kind envisaged is necessary', it suggested, in effect, an overhaul of the bill. For the self-respect marriages that had been held in the past, the Centre proposed that they be 'validated directly without the further formality of registration'. In another sharp deviation from Rajaji's plan, the Centre suggested 'limiting the application of that formality to marriages which take place in the future'.[16] It also specified that the Madras state should 'in part follow the model' of the colonial Arya Marriage Validation Act, 1937, which had breached the customary restrictions on inter-caste marriage for the Arya Samaj sect. In conclusion, it said that, after the incorporation of those changes, a copy of 'the final draft may kindly be supplied to this Ministry before its introduction in the State Legislature'.

However, instead of making the proposed changes, Rajaji escalated the matter by writing a letter himself, addressed to Home Minister K.N. Katju, who was incidentally his successor in that post. Since he was actually responding to a letter signed by a junior officer in the Home Ministry, Rajaji began his own on a note that was rather unusual for a chief minister, especially one who had been the governor general of India before the promulgation of the Constitution. This was how Rajaji's letter, dated 31 December 1953, opened: 'My dear Katju, Referring to your Deputy Secretary's (Sri N. Sahgal's) letter ...'

The manner in which he dismissed the Centre's forward-looking ideas suggested that Rajaji, a lawyer himself, was counting on the weight of his personality to enforce his will. On the Centre's reservations about the linking of validation with registration, Rajaji's response smacked of orthodoxy. 'A number of such marriages have taken place in the past and they are not recorded anywhere. No priests officiated and the usual accompaniments of a marriage according to custom were not present. It has, therefore, become necessary to provide for the parties to such marriages or their children to come forward to record these marriages. With this aim, the most easy form of procedure, namely, registration, has been provided in the proposed Bill.'

In much the same manner, he dismissed the relevance of the Arya Samaj legislation, which the Home Ministry had cited on the advice of the Law Ministry. The Arya Samaj law, he wrote, related to 'the personal qualification of the parties to form a union' across caste barriers. On the other hand, his concern about suyamariyadai was on 'the adequacy of the form of marriage to give rise to the status of a lawfully wedded husband and wife'. Rajaji gave no indication why suyamariyadai could not be, like the Arya marriage, legislatively recognised on its own terms.

Instead, he spoke patronisingly about the ignorance of the lower castes in attempting such a reform. 'The intention is not to create a new form of marriage in addition to the forms prescribed by religion or sanctioned by custom, but only to secure legal recognition for the parties who, under a mistaken notion that they had married, had lived together as husband and wife, and also to prevent their offspring being regarded as illegitimate. In this perspective, registration of such marriages that have taken place already is not an imposition but only a necessary safety device to avoid disputes of far-reaching consequences.'

Rajaji also smugly assumed that the Self-Respecters had now been forced to give up their social reform: 'As the Madras High Court recently declared such a "self-respect" marriage to be of no legal effect, and the public are now aware that such a form of marriage is not binding on the parties, it is not likely that there will be such marriages in the future. Hence it does not appear necessary to provide for the registration of such marriages.'

In reality, Rajaji underestimated the reformist zeal of his lower-caste detractors. Whether it was despite, or because of, the sanctions imposed by the High Court, the Self-Respecters continued to find takers for their non-Brahminical wedding.

While the Centre reviewed the bill in the light of Rajaji's letter, the file came up before a joint secretary in the Law Ministry, B.G. Murdeshwar, on whose advice those radical changes had been recommended in the earlier round of consultation. In the cryptic note that he wrote on 8 January 1954, Murdeshwar seemed unimpressed by Rajaji's arguments for rejecting the Centre's amendments: 'The difficulties mentioned by the Madras Government are not such as cannot be got over by careful drafting.' That said, the legal expert yielded to Rajaji's insistence on retaining the draft in its original form. Accordingly, the Centre conveyed its go-ahead the very next day, as Rajaji had wanted to introduce the bill urgently.

For all this drama, however, the bill did not pass into law. After it was cleared by the Madras Legislative Council, the bill remained stuck in the other House, the Legislative Assembly, where it was introduced on 7 May 1954. The official explanation for the stalemate was that 'the Government did not proceed with the further stages of the Bill'.[17] The real reason was that Rajaji had by then resigned. His sudden exit was because of growing opposition, even within the Congress party, to his education scheme and the fear that it was casteist in nature. His successor, K. Kamaraj, from the Nadar caste, abandoned not only Rajaji's education scheme but also his bill to register non-conforming marriages.

The bill became redundant that year in any case because the Nehru government promulgated the Special Marriage Act, 1954. This replaced the 1872 law that had, in a limited sense, introduced the concept of civil marriage. Besides extending that concept to marriages across all castes and religions, the new law enabled post-facto registration of other forms of marriage. This meant that Self-Respecters could now register their marriages, at least in theory, under the Central enactment.

In practice, however, the registration option did not catch on.

One reason was that families in villages would have to travel long distances to access the registration offices. Another inhibiting factor was the ideological objection that the Self-Respecters had raised. Their demand was that, just as weddings conducted by Brahmin priests did not need registration, self-respect marriages should be subject to no further condition.

However, the codification of Hindu marriage the following year brought another blow to the Self-Respecters. While this milestone legislation had made a number of advances—abolishing polygamy and introducing a provision for divorce, for instance—the Hindu Marriage Act, 1955 appeared to have compromised with orthodoxy in other respects. The first clause of Section 7 of the 1955 law did recognise diverse forms of marriage, but only within the range of 'customary', or traditional, rituals. It required the Hindu marriage to be 'solemnized in accordance with the customary rites and ceremonies of either party thereto'. In a further nod to the preserve of the Brahmin priest, the second clause of Section 7 specified: 'Where such rites and ceremonies include the Saptapadi (that is, the taking of seven steps by the bridegroom and the bride jointly before the sacred fire), the marriage becomes complete and binding when the seventh step is taken.'

In the second general elections that followed in 1957, the DMK, led by Annadurai, made its electoral debut. Its election manifesto promised to enact a law that would define and validate self-respect marriages. The promise remained on paper so long as the regional party was in the Opposition. In 1966, the Madras High Court provided further impetus for legislative intervention when it refused once again to recognise a self-respect marriage. It was ruling on a plea for restitution of conjugal rights by an abandoned woman, Rajathi.

The verdict went against the Self-Respecters even though Periyar himself had appeared in the case as a witness, testifying on the procedure of Rajathi's wedding with K. Selliah. Periyar deposed that his paper, *Viduthalai*, had published an advance notice of the wedding, which took place in 1958 at Tiruchirapalli. And then, according to the High Court's summary of Periyar's testimony, 'The actual ceremony was conducted by him and in his presence. The parties were seated on a platform before a Kuthuvilakku or lighted lamp. They made a declaration that they were taking each other as husband and wife. Then they exchanged garlands and went round the platform where the Kuthuvilakku was placed. They were declared as husband and wife by E. V. Ramaswami Naicker.'[18]

Justice Tiruvannamalai Venkatadri's verdict disparaged the Self-Respecters: 'No useful purpose would be served by reformers by merely presiding over such marriages and conducting the ceremony according to their own ideas, knowing full well that such marriages are not valid in law. No useful purpose would be served by mere exchange of garlands and making declarations that they would live as husband and wife on equal terms.' The High Court said that the reformers should instead 'mobilise public opinion so as to bring the necessary legislation which would declare that such marriages are valid in law'.

In a remarkable turn of events, that is exactly what happened the very next year. In the elections held in 1967, the DMK stormed to power in Madras state. Reading its maiden victory as a mandate to legalise self-respect marriages, the Anna government lost no time in initiating the legislative process. Soon after being sworn in on 6 March, it shared a draft bill with the Indira Gandhi government for clearance. This process was necessary because the bill proposed a state amendment to the centrally enacted Hindu Marriage Act, 1955.

On 17 July 1967, Law Minister S. Madhavan introduced the bill in the Madras Legislative Assembly. The following day, the Legislative Assembly, in consultation with the Legislative Council, referred the bill to a Joint Select Committee. The Government of India's suggestions were also placed before the committee. From its scrutiny emerged a slightly revised version of the bill. Madhavan presented the new draft to the Assembly on 28 November. The discussion that followed showed that, despite some misgivings and suggestions expressed by Opposition legislators, there was an all-party consensus in favour of the bill. The Assembly passed the bill the same day. The Council followed suit and the bill passed into law when the president of India gave his assent on 17 January 1968. The Hindu Marriage (Madras Amendment) Act, 1967 came into effect three days later. Consequent to the renaming of the state in 1969, 'Madras' was replaced by 'Tamil Nadu' in the title of the law.

The 1967 amendment carved out an exception in Tamil Nadu in the 'ceremonies for a Hindu marriage' prescribed by Section 7 of the Hindu Marriage Act, 1955. Inserted as Section 7A in the 1955 Act, the social reform served to 'render valid' a non-Brahminical form of marriage within the framework of Hindu personal law. This section was, in effect, a negation of Rajaji's outlook that self-respect marriages were non-conforming and so could not be integrated into the Hindu fold. Anna's Act referred to self-respect marriage as 'suyamariyathai marriage'. In fact, it embraced yet another name that self-respect marriage was known by: seerthiruththa marriage (social-reform marriage or reformed marriage). Moreover, the Act proclaimed that every self-respect marriage that had taken place before its commencement in 1968 'shall be deemed to have been', from the date of its solemnisation and without any further formality, 'good and valid in law'.[19]

As for the weddings that were to take place in the future, the Joint Select Committee was instrumental in incorporating a suggestion from the Central government to ensure 'adequate proof of marriage'. The suggestion had stressed the need 'to ensure wider publicity for the marriage and to prevent the solemnisation of the marriage in secluded places'. As a result, Section 7A stipulated that the self-respect marriage would have to be solemnised 'in the presence of relatives, friends or other persons'. Barring this minimal requirement of informal witnesses, without specifying any number, Section 7A offered free choice to the individuals concerned in determining the method of solemnisation. It said that the wedding could be solemnised 'between any two Hindus' in any—or all—of these three broad and simple ways.

- One, 'by each party to the marriage declaring in any language understood by the parties that each takes the other to be his wife or, as the case may be, her husband'. In other words, Sanskrit, the language of the wedding mantras, whether from the Vedas or Puranas, was replaced by colloquial Tamil. Yet, the idea was not to translate the mantras into a language understood by the parties but to discard them altogether. Besides, there was to be no intercession by a Brahmin priest. The solemnisation of a wedding only took the secular declaration by the bridal couple that they were thereby marrying each other in the presence of (an unspecified number of) guests.

- Two, 'by each party to the marriage garlanding the other or putting a ring upon any finger of the other'. The two classic elements of garlands and rings, taken singly or together, had been a common feature of self-respect marriages too. They met the test of reciprocity—both partners could exchange rings or garlands as a token of the solemnisation of their marriage. And these mutual gestures could be in addition to a verbal declaration of their union or entirely an alternative to it.
- Three, 'by the tying of the thali'. This third option did not begin with the expression 'by each party to the marriage', for, the thali, the Tamil word for mangalsutra or auspicious thread, is conceptually one-sided. The most potent symbol of the patriarchy of kanyadaan, the thali was tied by the bridegroom around the neck of the bride. The method was offered as a compromise to ensure that even those who were not inclined to dispense with the thali were able to embrace other non-Brahminical aspects of this mode of Hindu marriage. The tying of the thali, without the usual accompaniment of the purohit and his mantras, was considered radical in itself.

Anna gave an explanation along these lines in the Legislative Assembly on 28 November 1967 before the passage of the bill. The discussion had been triggered by an amendment to the thali clause moved by a Congress legislator, B. Mahadevan. He did not seek to delete the clause altogether; rather, the amendment sought to substitute the word 'tying' with either 'wearing' or 'adorning'. As Mahadevan put it, 'The expression "the tying of the thali" sounds like you are going to buy a bull and tie it with a rope. This is disrespectful to women and so the word "tying" should be removed. It is contrary to the spirit of self-respect.'[20] But then, this was a case of calling a spade a spade. The tying of thali was indeed what transpired in the ritual.

Appreciating the spirit behind the proposed amendment, Anna said,[21] 'I am happy that such a concern has been raised.' Nonetheless, taking the argument to its logical conclusion, he pointed out that 'even the wearing of the thali would be damaging the self-respect of women'. Making a case for retaining the clause in its existing form, Anna explained, 'This law does not make it mandatory to wear thali. It is just one of the three options. They can opt for any of them or all of them. If someone like my friend wants to marry without tying a thali, this law will make their marriage legal.'

Anna then quipped that he hoped 'people from [Mahadevan's] party will hereafter marry without a thali' after hearing the Congress leader's views. Mahadevan in turn withdrew his amendment while maintaining his reservation about the terminology. No legislator in the Assembly objected, even rhetorically, to such a one-sided concept figuring in a law professing to uphold the self-respect of both spouses.

The audacity of a wedding without a Brahmin is what dominated the discussion. The related issue of what impact this social reform would have on the privileged caste came up as well. Would it not affect the livelihood of priests? This question had been hotly contested during the colonial period in the context of the joshi reform in Bombay. The leader of the Opposition, P.G. Karuthiruman of the Congress party, raised it again in 1967, although the purohits of Madras had no watandar joshi-style entitlement. Again, Anna came up with a breezy response, suggesting how those who continued to patronise purohits could compensate them. 'If the Leader of the Opposition is so concerned about their livelihood being affected, then in those weddings where purohits are called, let four or five of them be engaged for each of them.'

In his prolonged exchanges with the Congress leader, a Brahmin, Anna took the opportunity to drive home the difference between

Hindu priests and their counterparts in other religions. While anyone from among Muslims and Christians could be trained to perform priestly functions, it was only 'people like Karuthiruman's ancestors' who were allowed to play that role among Hindus. Referring to the vast segment of non-Brahmins, Anna said, 'There is no class among us that can take to priesthood.'

Deploying a mix of disarming tactics and home truths, Anna pulled off a legislation targeting what was traditionally a source of influence and livelihood for Brahmins across the country. Yet, neither the Centre nor any other state ever attempted to emulate Tamil Nadu's example of providing a non-Brahminical wedding option within the Hindu law. When Anna passed away barely a year later, on 3 February 1969, his mentor, Periyar, paid tribute, saying that 'the most important of his feats is the "Self-Respect Marriages Legalisation Act"', which was 'daring' not just for Tamil Nadu 'but for the entire world'.

Though the suyamariyathai marriage did not catch on in Tamil Nadu as much as Periyar and Anna might have hoped it would, the legal provision that had facilitated it remained a sore point for its detractors. In 2015, a lawyer called A. Asuvathaman filed a writ petition before the Madras High Court challenging the constitutionality of the 1967 enactment. The petitioner's contention was that, as it dispensed with customary rites, Section 7A conflicted with the nationally applicable Section 7 and was 'contrary to the very tenets of Hinduism'. And that it violated the fundamental right to equality for being discriminatory.

On 30 October 2015, a bench comprising Chief Justice Sanjay Kishan Kaul and Justice T.S. Sivagnanam dismissed the petition, saying there was 'no case of discrimination since option is available to any of the parties who want to enter a matrimony to proceed in accordance with the original Section 7 or as per Section 7-A'.[22]

As for the contention that suyamariyathai offended religious tenets, the judgment, authored by Kaul, indicated that the Madras High Court itself had come a long way since its 1953 position, even prior to the enactment of Section 7, that no Hindu marriage could be valid without the backing of Brahminical ceremonies. 'The Hindu religion by itself is pluralism in character and thus, various forms of marriages have traditionally existed depending on the area and the custom prevalent therein. Section 7-A provides for particular kind of marriages i.e. suyamariyathai marriages among two Hindus. It has also stood the test of time now for half a century.'

This measure to emancipate Hindu marriage from the thrall of the Brahmin and his mantras has indeed stood the test of time, although more as a token of pluralism than as common practice.

7

BREAKING THE SILENCE ON UNTOUCHABILITY

For over eight years, from 1836 to 1844, there was a gag on discussing anti-slavery petitions in the United States House of Representatives. Though such petitions continued to be tabled, the House was barred from taking any further action on them, thanks to the white supremacist view that the issue of slavery was unworthy of discussion.

It took a relentless crusade by an exceptional member of the House to have that racist gag rule repealed. John Quincy Adams had already served as the sixth president of the United States. Rather than retiring from public service after his stint in the White House, Adams returned as a lawmaker—the only instance of a former president doing so. He served as a member of the House for seventeen years until his death in 1848.

Despite his campaign against the gag as a restriction on the free speech guaranteed by the First Amendment, successive Congresses reintroduced the rule until Adams mustered enough votes to have it repealed in 1844. The restoration of anti-slavery debates in the legislature paved the way for Abraham Lincoln's Emancipation Proclamation in 1863 and the Thirteenth Amendment in 1865, which abolished slavery.

On the other side of the globe, in colonial India, there was never any official gag on the corresponding practice of untouchability. Even so, its legislature was silent about a form of discrimination that affected about one-fifth of the majority community of Hindus.

This silence was partly because of a reaffirmation of the colonial commitment, in the wake of the 1857 revolt, 'to abstain from all interference with the religious belief' of the natives. But equally, it was because of a lack of remorse about untouchability on the part of the dominant sections of Hindus.

Though Indians had begun to be represented in the legislature since 1861, none of them sought any reform of the caste system, whether for the benefit of Hindus generally or to ameliorate the lot of untouchables, the worst affected. One reason for this omission was that the Indian legislators who had been nominated in the first three decades were zamindars, the feudal class that had a vested interest in perpetuating caste inequities.

However, even after the constitutional reforms of 1892 and 1909 had enhanced the quality and quantity of Indian legislators, the silence persisted. The progressive elements among them were held back from discussing caste on account of a strategic decision announced by the Indian National Congress in 1886.

In his presidential address at the second Congress session, Dadabhai Naoroji laid down the party line that it must 'confine itself to questions in which the entire nation has a direct participation'. He admitted to disquiet over the omission of social reforms: 'It has been asserted that this Congress ought to take up questions of social reform and our failure to do this has been urged as a reproach against us.' While claiming that 'no member of this National Congress is more alive to the necessity of social reforms than I am', Naoroji explained that 'we are met together as a political body to represent to our rulers our political aspirations, not to discuss social reforms'.[1]

Drawing a parallel with the remit of the legislature, Naoroji said that 'if you blame us for ignoring these, you should equally blame the House of Commons [in London] for not discussing the abstruser problems on mathematics and metaphysics'. Having blithely compared social reforms to such improbable subjects, Naoroji made an uneasy reference to caste too. He said that 'there are here Hindus of every caste, amongst whom, even in the same province, customs and social arrangements differ widely'. These caste differences prompted him to counsel restraint: 'What do any of us know of the internal home life, customs, traditions, feelings, prejudices of any class but our own?'

The Indian National Congress's hands-off policy led to the formation in 1887 of the Indian National Social Conference, a non-political offshoot of the organisation. Gradually, it was at this smaller forum that stalwart reformers from the Congress, such as M.G. Ranade, R. Raghunath Rao, R.G. Bhandarkar, N.G. Chandavarkar and G.K. Gokhale, gave vent to their concerns on caste and untouchability. However, their engagement with social reform was confined to the Social Conference, in spite of the fact that two of them, Chandavarkar and Gokhale, went on to become Congress presidents.

The decision to keep social reforms out of the Congress agenda shaped the conduct of its members even when they acted as legislators. Gokhale was no exception to this pattern, despite his richly deserved reputation as the earliest of India's great lawmakers. He set high standards of rigour with his speeches in the legislature analysing the annual budget, and with his vigilance against excessive tax burden and other coercive measures. For all his accomplishments in the Imperial Legislative Council from 1901 till his death in 1915, G.K. Gokhale never directly raised the issue of caste or untouchability in the one forum where he could at least have attempted to bring about legal and administrative changes. The closest he came to dealing with caste in the legislature was in the context of his prolonged campaign seeking elementary education for all.

In the midst of this apathy, suddenly, on 16 March 1916, India found its own John Quincy Adams, someone who broke the silence in the legislature on untouchability. Maneckji Byramji Dadabhoy was an unlikely candidate to have ended Dadabhai Naoroji's virtual embargo of three decades ago. A Bombay-born barrister and industrialist and a councillor for the Central Provinces, Dadabhoy was a Parsi. So, like fellow Parsi Dadabhai Naoroji, he too might have had little exposure to caste prejudice, a deficiency that the Grand Old Man of India had cited to avoid the subject.

Still, not being a Congress member, Dadabhoy had little reason to defer to Naoroji's policy. Maneckji Dadabhoy moved a resolution in the Imperial Legislative Council on 'Depressed Classes', the official term at the time for untouchables. It made two recommendations to the administration of Viceroy Lord Hardinge. One was that a committee of officials and non-officials be appointed to come up with measures for 'amelioration' in the condition of the Depressed Classes. Two, that, as 'a preliminary step', the provincial governments be invited to 'formulate schemes with due regard to local conditions'.

Dadabhoy's resolution led to the first-ever discussion in the national legislature on untouchability.[2] The discussion took place in the chamber that now serves as the Delhi Legislative Assembly, located in Civil Lines, which is to the north of the subsequently built New Delhi.

Though the government declined to appoint the proposed committee, it expressed sympathy for the object of the resolution and promised to write to provincial governments as requested. The fact that the government had committed to such an unprecedented initiative persuaded Dadabhoy to comply with its suggestion that he withdraw the resolution. And as the Centre did make the promised beginning, Dadabhoy's initiative led to data collection throughout British India on a hitherto unexplored subject.

Dadabhoy's attempt to shine a light on the bottom layer of the Hindu hierarchy had met with resistance from two eminent Indian councillors, which explained why the government had declined to set up the committee that he had proposed. Surendra Nath Banerjea and Madan Mohan Malaviya had been presidents of the Indian National Congress. While Banerjea had held that post twice, in 1895 and 1902, Malaviya had held it once, in 1909, and went on to do so again two years later, in 1918, and for the last time in 1932. These Congress stalwarts took umbrage not so much at the substance of the resolution as to what they believed was Dadabhoy's unwarranted attack on their religious community.

Dadabhoy had drawn parallels between blacks in the United States and untouchables in India. Though the southern states of the US were still steeped in lynching and segregation (Jim Crow laws), Dadabhoy commended the progress otherwise made by that country 'since the abolition of the slave trade'. Putting the colonial government in the dock, he sought to establish that the Americans had fared better than the British rulers in India, and detailed the initiatives undertaken in the US to educate and empower blacks.

Given the magnitude of the neglect suffered by the Depressed Classes, he alleged that the colonial policy had been to feign 'helplessness', thereby leaving these communities at the mercy of their traditional oppressors. By way of example, Dadabhoy quoted from a press release that had been recently issued by the Bombay government: 'The position of these castes and tribes in the future depends partly on their own selves, and partly on those more favoured Indian communities, which by extending the hand of human comradeship or hardening their hearts and averting their faces, have it in their power to elevate or to degrade them.'

Given how little had been achieved by the few reformers from 'those more favoured Indian communities', Dadabhoy said caustically of the government's attitude: 'There ends the responsibility of the State and indeed, the shortest way to progress has been shown. People sunk in ignorance, despised, degraded and persecuted must look to themselves and to their persecutors for their elevation! Could there be a greater lack of imagination or appreciation of their duty in an enlightened Government?'

Having torn into the indifference of the colonial rulers, Dadabhoy dwelt on the root of untouchability, namely, the socio-religious conditioning of the Hindus. 'That any man made after the image of god, endowed with brains and a moral sense, should pollute his fellow being with his touch, is incredible. The very idea is revolting and is enough to shock humanity. But despite of our vaunted civilisation, despite of our progress and enlightenment, large bodies, nay millions, of men have been relegated to that infamous position for centuries through Brahmanical persecution.'

With these outspoken remarks, Dadabhoy not only brought untouchability sharply into focus but also laid bare its link to

'Brahmanical persecution'. Though Indians had been members of the Legislative Councils since 1861, it took fifty-five years for any legislator to talk about, let alone excoriate, this rampant social evil. It was the first time that the provision for moving resolutions, which had been introduced in 1909 as part of the Morley–Minto reforms, was deployed against untouchability.

Giving an overview of how untouchability took different forms of varying intensity across India, Dadabhoy cited its aggravated avatar of unapproachability in the Madras Presidency. 'The pariah, under the penalty of severe punishment, must call out from a long distance on the public way to warn high-caste Hindus of his presence. The touch of the filthiest vermin does not offend so much as that of the untouchable man.'

His moral indignation came through in his words. 'Could human perversity go further? Could hatred brutalise humanity more?' he asked, adding, 'It is, Sir, a shame to Hindu society, it is a shame to Hindu culture, it is a shame to India.' The naming and shaming of Hindu society and culture for practising untouchability added to the significance of Dadabhoy's speech in the Legislative Council.

As the government could not 'really sit idle in the face of such enormities', Dadabhoy aired an idea that would evolve over time and eventually come into effect at the founding of the Indian republic in 1950: a constitutional measure abolishing untouchability. Framed as a question, the proposition was whether a colonial regime could lift the 'social ban' on untouchables. On the one hand, 'it may be argued the problem is more social than anything with which Government are directly concerned. Government must be powerless to remove the social ban. It is for the society itself to apply the corrective.' On the other hand, he said, 'it has been pointed out by more than one earnest worker in the cause that, without the removal of the ban, no real improvement in the condition of the Depressed Classes is possible'.

For the colonial administration, the latter option was fraught with risks. Had the government indeed abolished the social ban on untouchables, it would have been more radical than any previous social reform. In all of those reforms, dominant castes had been the direct—if not the main or only—beneficiaries. Consider the stake they had in the reforms relating to Sati, outcasted Hindus, widow remarriage, civil marriage or age of consent. The abolition of confinement in the stocks, the first reform directly benefiting lower castes, was still three years away.

Recognising the odds stacked against the possibility of any coercive action against untouchability, Dadabhoy suggested 'putting aside for the moment this problem of social reform'. The government could instead 'do much', he said, to improve the lot of the Depressed Classes by means of 'well-devised schemes of educational, industrial and political advancement'. And it was for the adoption of such welfare measures that his resolution prayed for the appointment of the special committee and for consultation with the provinces.

Equally significant was the response this speech evoked from other councillors. The first to speak after Dadabhoy was another councillor from the Central Provinces, Gangadhar Chitnavis. He did not 'wholly agree with the somewhat exaggerated picture' that Dadabhoy had given of the treatment suffered by Depressed Classes. As Mahars and Mangs, the two big untouchable castes in his province, were 'freely receiving education in Government and missionary schools', he said that 'the social disabilities of the more thriving amongst them are gradually becoming less oppressive'.

All the same, Chitnavis supported Dadabhoy's resolution for 'a thorough investigation'. He said, 'I share his earnest desire that the elevation of the Depressed Classes should be systematised'. Five years later, when he became the presiding officer of the Central Provinces Legislative Council, Chitnavis did his bit to systematise the elevation of the Depressed Classes as he oversaw the adoption of a series of resolutions concerning untouchability.

The next participant in the debate was Panaganti Rama Rayaningar, better known as the Raja of Panagal, who would go on to lead the Justice Party government in Madras in 1921. In a move unprecedented in British India, Rayaningar provided reservations in government jobs and educational institutions in the Madras Presidency for all non-Brahmins, including the Depressed Classes.

In fact, even while responding to Dadabhoy's resolution in 1916, Rayaningar made a case for reservations. 'Sir, it will not do to consider their claims to educational facilities and to public appointments along with those of the other sections of the community. Regard for the special needs of minorities is one of the accepted principles of this Government. The special treatment of the Depressed Classes will not therefore involve any serious violation of policy.'

Claiming that 'I wanted to move a Resolution about it myself', Rayaningar recalled that when he had raised a question about the Depressed Classes in the Council in 1913, the government's reply was 'disappointing'. Reason: 'They refused to show the members of the Depressed Classes any special consideration in the matter, even of appointment to the low paid public offices. If that attitude continues, there is little hope of progress, but I hope in the interest of the country better counsels now prevail.'

As for the state of Depressed Classes in his own province, Rayaningar reinforced Dadabhoy's point about unapproachability. 'Some of them are not even allowed to enter public places. Their movements on the public way are not free and unrestricted.' The 'social rigours' were so harsh that, to escape them, some oppressed people were driven to embracing other religions, he said.

Rayaningar then made a distinction between the theory and practice of Hinduism. 'Are we Hindus so dead even to our own interests, that we are not prepared to entertain kindlier feelings towards Depressed Classes, and would much rather lose than keep them among us by humane treatment? Can it be believed that the elevation of the Depressed Classes is repugnant to the sublime principles of the Hindu religion, or it was the intention of the ancient lawgivers that they should be permanently kept out of the common rights of humanity?'

Rayaningar's lofty appeal to Hindus to act in their own enlightened self-interest seemed to have resonated with the next speaker: the redoubtable Congress leader, Surendra Nath Banerjea. He began by saying that 'every member of this Council ... will sympathise with the object of this Resolution', and added that 'we all welcome the discussion that this Resolution has given rise to in this Council'. Like several leaders of those times, Banerjea was an educationist. In 1884, he had founded a college in Calcutta named after Viceroy Lord Ripon, who was popular among Indians for his liberal dispensation. Shortly after Independence, Ripon College was renamed Surendranath College after the deceased nationalist, who had founded and run the institution, and had also taught there for a number of years.

Reacting to Dadabhoy's criticism of Hindus, Banerjea cited his own efforts in Ripon College to uplift untouchables. 'We make it a point, when a poor member of the Depressed Classes applies for admission, either to admit him free or to charge him half fees.' With no apparent sense of irony, he added though that there was a 'difficulty' in accommodating them in the hostels of Ripon College: 'while our students will perhaps live with them in the same hostel, they will not dine with them'. The bar on inter-dining applied most stringently in relation to the untouchables, after all.

On the heels of admitting to this glaring lack of fraternal spirit, Banerjea asserted that the ancient Hindu civilisation was 'the guarantee for law and order and social stability'. His explanation was: 'We are trying to evolve a national system in conformity to our present environments, but we cannot push aside all those things which have come down to us in the past … We notice the defects, and we are anxious to get rid of them gradually and steadily … My friend must have a little sympathy for us; he must extend to us the hand of generosity in our efforts to deal with these problems.'

Banerjea's discomfort was in keeping with the Congress party's reluctance till then to engage with untouchability. In fact, Banerjea himself echoed Naoroji in 1895, when it was his turn to deliver a presidential address: 'We cannot afford to have a schism in our camp … It is the Congress of United India … of those who would reform their social customs and those who would not.'[3] However, he concluded: 'Ours is a political and not a social movement; and it cannot be made a matter of complaint against us that we are not a social organization any more than it can be urged against any of my lawyer friends that they are not doctors.'

As it happened, the Congress did abandon its silence on social reforms shortly after—though only because Maneckji Dadabhoy had belled the cat in the Imperial Legislative Council. In December 1917, thirty-two years after it was founded, the Congress finally adopted a resolution on untouchability. However, the resolution moved by Madras-based publisher G.A. Natesan was addressed not to the government (for any legal measures) but to fellow Indians (to be more compassionate). 'The Congress urges upon the people of India the necessity, justice and righteousness of removing all disabilities imposed by custom upon the Depressed Classes, the disabilities being of a most vexatious and oppressive character, subjecting those classes to considerable hardship and inconvenience.'

In retrospect, Banerjea's response to Dadabhoy's resolution was a preview of the party line: that the social disabilities suffered by the untouchables should be remedied by the people themselves, rather than the government. Even though, as Banerjea put it, the government could do 'a great deal by way of education, a great deal by helping forward the industrial movement among the Depressed Classes'. He said he would 'welcome the action of Government in a matter of this kind', but there was a problem with going further. '[I]f you analyse the situation, it is a social problem, and the British Government, very properly, as I think, in conformity with its ancient traditions, holds aloof from all interference with social questions.'

The loose reference to 'ancient traditions' was a disingenuous attempt to perpetuate the colonial myth that it did not interfere with India's social questions. An erudite leader like Banerjea would have been well aware of the many social reforms enacted by the British administration, beginning with the Sati regulation, which happened in his own home town, Calcutta, when it was the imperial capital. Then again, it was a strategy Tilak had employed during the age-of-consent controversy—of holding the colonial regime to its overhyped policy of non-interference. Banerjea said that 'the vital problem, the problem of problems, is one of social uplifting, and there the Government can only afford to be a benevolent spectator. It may sympathise with our efforts but it cannot actively participate.'

This argument resonated with his distinguished party colleague, Madan Mohan Malaviya, prompting the latter to recall that the British Parliament had struggled to enact 'an absolutely harmless' law in 1907, allowing a widower to marry his deceased wife's sister. Malaviya claimed he mentioned this 'only as an instance to show that prejudices die hard' even in Britain. Pointedly, he added, 'We Hindus have got some much worse prejudices to fight against, I acknowledge, I own it. But I do not think it is within the province of a member of this Council either to lecture to the Hindus present here or to those outside as to socio-religious disabilities among themselves which they might fight against and remove.'

Both Banerjea and Malaviya took swipes at Dadabhoy. Banerjea said that, even if he had done it 'unintentionally', Dadabhoy had gone 'somewhat out of his way to level an attack against the Hindu community'. More bluntly, Malaviya said Dadabhoy had gone 'out of his way to make remarks against the Hindu community which, I think, he ought to have avoided'.

Likewise, while Banerjea sought 'sympathy' from Dadabhoy for the efforts that were already being made by Hindus, Malaviya questioned the propriety of raising the issue of untouchability at all. 'I think the province of members of this Council is limited to dealing with matters of legislation or other administrative matters which may properly be taken up by the Government.' Like Banerjea before him, Malaviya based his objection on the government's 'wise and liberal policy' that 'they shall not interfere in matters of religious or socio-religious character'. And that being the case, 'So far as the elevation or depression of that status rests upon social or socio-religious causes, the Government would rightly abstain from making any attempt in that direction. But I submit that it depends largely, almost wholly—nay, I say it depends wholly—upon education. That is the one solvent which will solve this problem.'

Accusing Dadabhoy of doing 'little justice to the Government', Malaviya said that it had been for decades 'endeavouring to promote in a special degree the education of the backward classes'. Given that the government was already 'very much alive' to untouchability, he was anxious that Dadabhoy's resolution should not give the impression that 'we are starting a new campaign'.

It was not surprising that he would frame the issue of education in this manner. Barely a month earlier, on 4 February 1916, the Benaras Hindu University (BHU) had been founded mainly due to his exertions. It was inaugurated by Viceroy Lord Hardinge after the Imperial Legislative Council passed the BHU bill on 1 October 1915. As a member of the Select Committee constituted for it, Malaviya had been instrumental in shaping the legislation. Since it was government-sponsored, Education Member Harcourt Butler in the Viceroy's Executive Council piloted the BHU bill. In the debate leading to its passage, Malaviya defended the clauses under which BHU was designed to be governed entirely by Hindus and have compulsory religious instruction.

Denying the charge that it was a 'sectarian university', Malaviya said it was rather a 'denominational institution' inculcating a 'religious spirit which will promote brotherly feeling between man and man'.[4] Though the university was statutorily open to persons of 'all classes, castes and creeds', the bill contained no provision to integrate the Depressed Classes. While playing a prominent part in political and social activities at the national level, Malaviya went on to serve as BHU's vice chancellor for nineteen years, earning him the epithet 'Mahamana', or the lofty-minded. 'Once you educate the humblest men, once they begin to lead a life of cleanliness, once they wean themselves effectively, extricate themselves from the bondage of the customs and habits and surroundings which have for a long time been associated, unfortunately associated, with their position, there will be absolutely no bar to their being admitted to society, no bar to their being treated as educated brethren.'

In other words, the customs and habits that needed to be corrected were, in his opinion, that of the untouchables—not of the upper castes, nor of the Brahminical persecution that Dadabhoy had attacked.

Significantly, Malaviya, who was Congress president on multiple occasions over two decades, was also a pillar of the Hindu Mahasabha in its early years. He was the president of the Hindu Mahasabha in 1923 and 1924. Even today, Malaviya is held in such high esteem by the Hindu right that, both in 2014 and 2019, Prime Minister Narendra Modi launched the election campaign in his constituency, Varanasi, by garlanding Mahamana's statue in front of BHU's main gate. At the first opportunity in 2014, the Modi government posthumously conferred Bharat Ratna, the nation's highest award, on him. Two years later, Modi flagged off a superfast train between Varanasi and New Delhi named Mahamana Express.

Back in 1916, speaking on Dadabhoy's resolution, Malaviya cited an anecdote from his early years in Allahabad. He had a friend, he said, 'who belonged to the Chamar class'. Yet, Malaviya greeted him, an MA from the same university, 'just as cordially as any other man; and I would in similar circumstances greet any Chamar or any Chandal as cordially'. Was the reference to 'similar circumstances' an admission that, unless an untouchable was educated, this stalwart would not greet him cordially? This literal interpretation of his words might not be misplaced, given a startling revelation in a commemorative volume published by BHU to mark Malaviya's birth centenary in 1961.

One of the tributes carried in it was by Rajkumari Amrit Kaur, who had been a key participant in the Constituent Assembly debates and a minister in the Jawaharlal Nehru government. Though she had found him 'most progressive' in 'all other matters of social reform', Amrit Kaur said that it was a different story when it came to caste prejudice. 'Malaviyaji remained orthodox to the end inasmuch as he would never take food or drink from the hands of anybody other than a Brahmin of his caste. I often asked him why, when he was so liberal-minded in everything else, he could not get over this self-imposed disability. He never argued his point of view with me but I realized that it was part and parcel of his very being and that it would have been quite wrong for anybody to try to dissuade him from following an age-long Hindu tradition.'[5]

Once the Indian councillors and British representatives of provinces had their say on Dadabhoy's resolution, the Hardinge administration responded through Home Member Reginald Craddock. Better known in history as the colonial authority to whom Vinayak Savarkar had personally submitted one of his mercy petitions in Cellular Jail in 1913, Craddock reacted gleefully to the reservations expressed by Banerjea and Malaviya as also their unusual compliments to the government on the floor of the Council.

Though he was aggrieved that Dadabhoy had 'accused the Government of apathy and of merely following a negative policy of drift', Craddock said that his 'task in defending the Government from this charge has been considerably lightened'. Reason: 'Not only have representatives of two [provincial] Governments got up to protest against the accusation, but I find myself in the pleasant position of having two Hon'ble Members, with whom I often have to disagree, as the staunchest supporters of Government of any who have risen to speak. I refer to the Hon'ble Mr Surendra Nath Banerjea and the Hon'ble Pandit Malaviya. I welcome their support.'

It was as close an admission as there could have been of the convergence of colonial and upper-caste interests. Indeed, because Malaviya and Banerjea insisted that the government had only a limited role to play in this matter, Craddock was able to shrug off the principle that Dadabhoy had enunciated: that the responsibility of combating the socio-religious disabilities suffered by the untouchables could not be left to their persecutors.

Indeed, Craddock wholly embraced the narrative of the Congress duo. 'My Hon'ble friends Pandit Madan Mohan Malaviya and Mr Surendra Nath Banerjea have both stated that the educated Hindu of today is prepared to receive his educated brother, whatever be his class or origin,' Craddock said, adding, 'I have no doubt whatever that that statement is correct, and that the educated community are prepared to do all that these Hon'ble members claim for it.'

Still, Craddock could not help striking a note of realism. 'But you must remember that these people live mostly in villages and very often in the back lanes of towns, and that their nearer neighbours have not yet come under these broad and liberal-minded influences.' All the same, he agreed with Banerjea and Malaviya that 'the problem in dealing with this question is more social and religious than purely administrative'. Ergo, the government could do little to stop the discrimination.

Having said this, Craddock rejected Dadabhoy's plea for the appointment of a Central Committee for the Amelioration of the Depressed Classes. Instead, he said that, if Dadabhoy agreed to withdraw his resolution, the government, acting on his other plea, was 'willing to go so far as to ask local governments to put on record what they have done, are doing, and what further they can do, to improve the conditions of these people'.

In contrast to 'the pleasant position' in which Craddock found himself, Dadabhoy found himself 'in a very peculiar and unfortunate position'. Referring to the colonial and upper-caste interests ranged against his proposal, Dadabhoy said there were 'two parties in this Council and they are both on their defensive on this occasion'. His 'justification' for proposing this resolution lay in 'the unenthusiastic and half-hearted support' that he had received from non-official councillors like Banerjea and Malaviya. As regards the charge that he had exceeded his remit by raising the issue of untouchability, Dadabhoy said, 'If I could possibly have avoided it, I would have very cheerfully and willingly done so.'

Dadabhoy pointed out that it was the sixth year of 'the reformed Council', which had been set up under the Government of India Act, 1909, allowing greater Indian participation, and he had himself been on it for five years. While the second of the three-year terms of the Council was 'approaching expiration', Dadabhoy said, tongue firmly in cheek, 'I anticipated that the champions of public liberty, public spirit and public enterprise and culture—men like my friends the Hon'ble Mr Surendra Nath Banerjea or the Hon'ble Pandit Madan Mohan Malaviya—would take the trouble of moving a Resolution to this effect.'

Further, 'I waited all this time to see if one of these enthusiastic members would bring in a Resolution for the amelioration of the

Depressed Classes; but when I found that none of them had taken up the matter—though at times this matter is discussed even in the Congress pandal in a certain manner;[6] when I found that it was not taken up in this Council—I thought it my duty to do so—'

Banerjea interrupted him at this point, 'I must make a correction. We have taken up the matter and we are doing our best in Bengal. It is therefore not a correct statement, so far as I am concerned, to say that we have not been doing anything in connection with the elevation of the Depressed Classes. I hope my Hon'ble friend will make that correction.'

Far from making any correction, Dadabhoy responded tartly, 'My Hon'ble friend has entirely misunderstood me. I said that he had failed to take any action in this Council. I expected him to take this action, and as he had failed to do so, I, as a Parsi, representing a Hindu constituency, thought it my duty to bring this matter for public discussion in this Council.' It was a biting retort to the accusation that he had no locus standi on the matter. 'My friends, the Hon'ble Mr Banerjea and the Hon'ble and learned Pandit, have said that I made certain statements in disparagement of the community to which they have the honour to belong. I entirely repudiate that. I have the greatest respect for the community to which my Hon'ble friends belong.'

But Dadabhoy pulled no punches while discussing the conduct of Hindus towards untouchables. 'In the course of my speech, I first pointed out the history of these Depressed Classes, and showed how Hindu society in the past had neglected its duty in the matter. It is only latterly that enthusiasm has, to a certain extent, been awakened and something done for these unfortunate classes.'

Likewise, on the colonial rulers' approach to untouchability, Dadabhoy alleged that 'theirs was a policy of benevolent indifference', consistent with their understanding that 'this was a social question, more or less'. Since it had rejected his proposal to set up a committee, the government had showed that, even on non-social aspects like education, the government was willing to take 'no special remedial measures of any tangible or appreciable character'. It was clear now that there was little chance of his resolution being adopted by the Council. So, he withdrew it in exchange for Craddock's offer to gather information on the state of Depressed Classes from all the provinces.

As he did so, Dadabhoy expressed confidence that the discussion triggered by his resolution would not be in vain. 'This debate will stimulate our countrymen to further action; it will stimulate our friends, Messrs Banerjea and Malaviya, to take up this cause with greater energy; it will stimulate Government to further beneficent action. I have no doubt the Government will take steps in the near future for giving special facilities for the advancement of these unhappy and wretched classes.'

Whether his friends and countrymen lived up to his expectations or not, the colonial administration did keep its side of the bargain. Although Viceroy Lord Hardinge retired soon after, on 12 May 1916, his successor Lord Chelmsford's administration wrote to the twelve provinces of the time about the assurance given to Dadabhoy, annexing a copy of the twenty-three-page debate proceedings. 'The resolution was ultimately withdrawn but, as will be observed from the proceedings, the Government of India expressed their willingness to consult local Governments as to what has been done and what further can be done to improve the condition of these people.'[7]

At the same time, the letter cautioned the provinces to steer clear of the 'social question', which was defined as 'the relations of one caste to another', and instead focus on 'such disabilities' as were 'within the power of Government to remove'. Reflecting the consensus in the Council between the colonial rulers and the upper castes, the letter said, 'The rest [meaning, the socio-religious disabilities] must be left to the good sense of the community and to the gradual disappearance of the ancient habits of thought.'

This was also the line that the press coverage took. The *Times of India*, for instance, said that, though his speech was 'full of interesting information' on the disabilities suffered by the Depressed Classes, 'unfortunately he allowed himself to be carried away by his feeling and made use of some expressions which were understood as reflecting on the Hindu religion and civilisation, on the one hand, and on the earnestness of Government in desiring the amelioration of the condition of those classes, on the other. The result was that, to use his own words, he found himself in the unfortunate position of being left in the lurch by many of the Hindu members as well as by the official members.'[8] Appreciating the government's letter to the provinces, the *Times* said, 'Mr Dadabhoy's valiant effort in the Legislative Council has not been infructuous.'

Indeed, as the provinces responded to Delhi's letter, some after repeated reminders, Dadabhoy's 'valiant effort' marked the beginning of a centralised compilation of official data on untouchables.[9] This exercise extended to 'aboriginal and hill tribes', or Adivasis, as well, because Dadabhoy had, in his speech in the Council, sought to widen the definition of Depressed Classes beyond untouchables. It took almost four years for the compilation to be ready, due to the special effort some governments had to make to put together information on the Depressed Classes in their territories. This elaborate exercise carried on even after Craddock had left Delhi in February 1918 to become the governor of Burma.

Of all the provinces, Madras was the last to comply, sending in its report only in December 1919. The delay was redeemed by the fact that it had gone further than other provinces in addressing the concerns Dadabhoy raised. In March 1919, Madras had, in a path-breaking decision, appointed a special officer with a suitable staff 'to study the economic conditions of the Depressed Classes and to device means for the amelioration of their condition'.[10]

Recognising that there was 'generally indifference and often hostility to measures calculated to uplift the Depressed Classes', Madras appointed senior bureaucrat George Frederick Paddison to the office of 'Protector of the Depressed Classes'. This heralded the creation of a network of institutions in the future Indian republic tailored to safeguard untouchables and other historically discriminated groups in keeping with its constitutional and statutory provisions.

The corresponding report sent by United Provinces in November 1918 referred to a resolution that Malaviya would have entirely approved of. This resolution was moved by C.Y. Chintamani, a member of the Legislative Council of United Provinces since 1916, and editor of *The Leader*, a newspaper co-founded by Malaviya. Since education was the one issue on which the differing voices on Dadabhoy's resolution in the Imperial Legislative Council had been unanimous, Chintamani moved a resolution in the Legislative Council of United Provinces focused entirely on that point of convergence. His strategic approach paid off, earning him the distinction of moving the first untouchable-specific resolution to have been adopted by a legislature anywhere in the country. The resolution, adopted in Allahabad on 18 July 1917, simply recommended 'a policy of active encouragement of education among the Depressed Classes'.

These developments in the Madras Presidency and United Provinces were only the more striking aspects of the Government of India's consolidated note, recorded on 7 February 1920, based on the provincial reports. After circulating the file among senior officers, the Government of India wrote a letter to Dadabhoy on 28 May 1920, reminding him about the promise Craddock had made on his resolution four years earlier. It updated him on the letter that had been written to the provinces 'in fulfilment of this promise' and the replies that had been received on it. Those reports constituted the earliest compilation of official information at the national level on the constituencies that are now called Dalits and Adivasis.

Mindful of the significance of this exercise, the colonial regime exhibited a measure of transparency and participatory governance. Claiming that the replies 'show that the Local Governments are alive to the importance of the question', it enquired whether Dadabhoy would 'like to see copies of the correspondence' and whether he would 'wish to suggest any further action, and, if so, in what direction'.[11]

The following month, on 4 June 1920, Dadabhoy replied to the home secretary saying that, when he next visited Shimla, the summer capital, 'I shall be glad to call at your office and peruse the correspondence. You need not therefore trouble to send me copies of the correspondence.'

Irrespective of whether he actually visited the Home Department to look at that correspondence and recommended any further action, there is no denying the salutary effect that Dadabhoy already had on the functioning of governments and legislatures in regard to untouchability. The acknowledgement of caste prejudice that he had forced upon them cleared the way for the legal reforms that followed, however haltingly.

Yet, unlike the place accorded to John Quincy Adams in the history of the American legislature, the dramatic debate between Dadabhoy, Banerjea, Malaviya and Craddock received only cursory attention, whether from their contemporaries or subsequent writers.

Take the tributes paid to Dadabhoy in the Council of State on 16 February 1933, when he became its 'first non-official President' in the bicameral legislature. On that 'epoch-making event', his colleagues lauded him for the 'versatility' of his 'genius', referring to his 'remarkable' achievements in a range of fields: law, politics, legislation, industry, finance. (He was, for instance, appointed in 1920 as the governor of the Imperial Bank of India, the precursor to both the Reserve Bank of India and the State Bank of India.) In the long listing of his accomplishments, there was no mention of his equally remarkable achievement in the field of social justice.

It is a pity indeed for, as his contemporaries would have known all too well, Dadabhoy had to pay a price for speaking out on untouchability. Ambedkar pointed to this in a written statement he submitted in January 1919 before the Southborough Committee, which had been set up to determine the franchise for the elections to be held under the Montagu–Chelmsford reforms. In what was his first foray into public life, twenty-seven-year-old Ambedkar made a strong plea for the representation of untouchables in legislative bodies. To underline the need for such representation, he cited the defeat that Dadabhoy had suffered in the election subsequent to his resolution initiative.

'The high caste men in the Council do not like any social question being brought before the legislature, as may be seen from the fact of the Resolution introduced by the Honourable Mr. Dadabhoy in 1916 in the Imperial Legislative Council. That it was adversely criticized by many who claimed to evince some interest in the untouchables is too well known to need repetition.'[12] Ambedkar did not mince his words, even though Surendra Nath Banerjea was a member of the Southborough Committee as well.

'But what is not well known,' Ambedkar said, 'is that though the Resolution was lost, the mover was not pardoned; for the very moving of such a nasty Resolution was regarded as a sin. At a subsequent election, the mover had to make room for the Honourable Mr [G.S.] Khaparde, who once wrote in an article: "Those who work for the elevation of the untouchables are themselves degraded."' Ambedkar asked, 'Isn't this sympathy of the higher castes for the untouchables, sympathy with a vengeance?'

Khaparde's own diary bears out the fact that there was a concerted effort in 1917 to replace Dadabhoy for alienating orthodox Hindus.[13] On 7 May 1917, Khaparde, the leader of Bal Gangadhar Tilak's followers in Nagpur, wrote about Dadabhoy's visit to his home and the strained conversation that had followed: 'He is anxious about his election. I told him our people were in quest for a person of our way of thinking. He admitted the justice of our people voting for one of themselves. He wished to know a good deal but I was sorry I could not tell it to him.' That quest ended with Khaparde himself being fielded as a candidate, with members of the local legislature comprising the voters.

On 7 November 1917, Khaparde noted that his opponents had approached another Parsi politician, S.R. Bomanji, to 'use his influence with Lokmanya Tilak to dissuade me from standing for the Imperial Council. Lokmanya told him that could not be done.' Four days later, on the eve of the election, Khaparde mentioned that his growing circle of campaigners included Hindu Mahasabha leader, B.S. Moonje. 'They have put me forward and are trying their best to get me in.' On 12 November 1917, he wrote that he had been elected by eight votes against six. 'As a party we should stand higher now for this victory practically against the Bureaucracy which helped Dadabhoy with all their followers.' From the tenor of Khaparde's diary entries, it is evident that Dadabhoy's raising of the untouchability issue was seen as another instance of the British ploy of divide and rule.

Almost three decades later, on 26 March 1946, Ambedkar once again referred to the issue of Dadabhoy's resolution, this time as labour member of the Viceroy's Executive Council, speaking in the Central Legislative Assembly. Govind Malaviya, legislator and son of Madan Mohan Malaviya, had raised an objection to a proposal for financial support to a college Ambedkar had founded. He argued that because Siddharth College in Bombay had been launched specifically for the benefit of Scheduled Castes—the official name for untouchables since 1935—it had introduced a 'sectarian spirit' in the educational field. Ambedkar was 'astonished' at Malaviya's allegation.[14]

Pointing to Benaras Hindu University, with which Govind Malaviya was 'a great deal concerned', Ambedkar said that it has had a rule since its inception expressly barring a non-Brahmin, however highly qualified, from becoming a 'Professor of Hindu Religion'. He asked, 'If that is not sectarianism, I would like to know what it is.' Denouncing the tendency of 'talking of nationalism' while 'practicing sectarianism', he said that his college, which gave preferential treatment to untouchables, had no community-based restrictions with regard to teachers or students.

Despite the 'many atrocities, tyrannies and oppression' suffered by untouchables, Ambedkar said, 'I have never seen any Honourable Member moving a Resolution that certain things might be done for the uplift of the community.' This was how he came to recall that there were only two occasions in the past when such a thing had happened, the first one of course being the 1916 initiative of Dadabhoy, 'now the President of the other House'. Not one to let go of an opportunity to embarrass Govind Malaviya, Ambedkar added that 'if my Honourable friend opposite who started this debate were to browse into the proceedings of that debate, he will find that it was his father who turned out to be the most vehement opponent of that Resolution'.

Based on his reference to the 1916 resolution in at least two highly significant forums, it is clear that Ambedkar regarded Dadabhoy's effort as a milestone in the evolution of civil rights in a caste-ridden country. Yet, the many books written on Ambedkar and untouchability have either missed it altogether or treated it perfunctorily.

In fact, a book by the renowned scholar Gail Omvedt actually attributed the abortive resolution to 'Dadabhoy Naoroji'[15] rather than the less-known Maneckji Dadabhoy. Why, even the first volume of *Dr Babasaheb Ambedkar: Writings and Speeches,* considered the most authoritative collection of Ambedkar's works, contains the same mistaken identity. Ambedkar's reference to 'the Honourable Mr Dadabhoy in 1916 in the Imperial Legislative Council' is indexed by the editors of that collection as 'Dadabhoy Naoroji'.[16] Ironically, far from moving any resolution on untouchables, Dadabhai Naoroji had been instrumental in holding the Congress back for three decades from raising social issues for fear of diverting attention from the more pressing political challenges.

For all the heightened awareness of Dalit struggles in recent decades, the first full-blown discussion on untouchability in the national legislature—marked by the selfless courage of Maneckji Dadabhoy in shaming Hindu society, and the betrayal of Brahminical discomfiture by Malaviya and Banerjea—has still not got its due in history.

8

THE OUTRAGE OF MARRYING UP

His more famous younger brother, Vallabhbhai Patel, India's first deputy prime minister, has been posthumously appropriated by Hindu nationalists. Vithalbhai Patel was, however, in the crosshairs of their precursors, including some leaders from the Indian National Congress. They were outraged by the audacity he had displayed in the second decade of the twentieth century in introducing a bill that challenged a non-negotiable part of the Hindu personal law.

Tabled in the Imperial Legislative Council on 5 September 1918, the bill boldly went where no one had gone before, the final frontier of social reform for Hindus. A barrister, Vithalbhai Patel proposed that the age-old ban on inter-caste marriage be lifted, transgressing the custom of endogamy within the Hindu framework itself.

The bill came on the heels of Maneckji Dadabhoy's abortive resolution of 1916. Potentially more disruptive of the social order of Hindus, Patel's bill was based on the premise that the long-term objective of abolishing untouchability could not be realised unless the ban on inter-caste marriage was removed.

Dadabhoy's resolution was relatively modest as it had only tried to make Hindus more compassionate to untouchables. While the 1916 resolution had aimed at making public life more inclusive, the 1918 bill strove to reconfigure the intimate aspect of family life, placing the individual autonomy of Hindus over caste constraint.

The timing of the bill, too, was remarkable.[1] Patel introduced the bill just a day after he had been sworn in as a member of the

Central legislature. He could hit the ground running, so to speak, thanks to a fortuitous time lag of almost six months between his election on 19 March 1918 and his induction in the subsequent session of the Council.

Patel's egalitarian credentials were already established in the Bombay legislature, well before his election to the Imperial Legislative Council. He had piloted a seminal, norm-setting legislation that made primary education free and compulsory, at least in theory, in the urban areas of the Bombay Presidency.[2] Patel pulled this off about five years after Gopal Krishna Gokhale had failed to muster support from the colonial regime for his own pioneering bill of the same nature in the Central legislature.

During his long waiting period as an elected member, Patel gave a notice for the introduction of his bill 'to validate marriages between Hindus of different castes'. The key expression was 'between Hindus'. For it was already possible for members of different castes to inter-marry under the Civil Marriage Act of 1872, subject to two conditions. The first was that such a marriage would have to be solemnised in a secular or non-religious way through the process of registration before a State authority. The second condition was that both parties would have to disclaim Hinduism and thereby suffer its worldly repercussions, whether social (in terms of fraternising) or economic (in terms of inheriting family property). In other words, apostasy was a precondition to inter-caste marriage.

Designed to appease the Hindu orthodoxy, this was the compromise on which the civil marriage law had been enacted at the instance of a radical section of the reformist Brahmo Samaj led by Keshab Chandra Sen. Thus, only those minuscule number of Hindus who had no inhibition in disavowing their religion could avail themselves of the option of civil marriage.

In a logical next step, there was an attempt in 1911 to amend the 1872 law so that Hindus would not have to give up their religion to marry across castes in the secular manner. But when Congress leader Bhupendra Nath Basu had introduced this amendment bill, Hindu conservatives opposed it firmly enough to thwart the reform.

This prompted the Arya Samaj, a larger reformist sect that also had a revivalist agenda, to come up with an even more ambitious proposal. Taking the bull by its horns, the Arya Samaj proposed that inter-caste marriage be legal even when performed with Hindu rituals. Indeed, whether out of love or otherwise, such marriages continued to take place among Hindus in defiance of this unnatural caste restriction and its legal and social repercussions.

In March 1916, the Aryan Brotherhood Conference of Bombay requested the Government of India to take up its draft as a government measure. The colonial administration intimated its willingness to consider the proposal of allowing inter-caste marriage, provided the bill was introduced by a non-official member. This was how Patel, around the age of forty-five, came to be associated with it.

Vithalbhai Patel, long an implacable foe of caste, espoused the cause with conviction. He had, for instance, stopped visiting his ancestral home at Karamsad and renounced all claim over it because his elder brother, Narsinbhai Patel, had insisted on following the tradition of holding a 'caste dinner' on their father's death. The eldest sibling had even rejected the offer made by Vithalbhai—and also by Vallabhbhai—to pay for any charitable activity in place of the caste dinner.[3]

Mahatma Gandhi testified to the ease with which Vithalbhai Patel mingled with untouchables. In an obituary published in the *Harijan* on 3 November 1933, Gandhi recalled a 1916 episode. He had, on the spur of the moment, shifted a conference dedicated to Harijans to a ghetto of that community in Godhra. Though his visit was unscheduled, a surprise awaited Gandhi. 'Whom should I see there if not Vithalbhai Patel, who was then a member of the [Bombay] Legislative Council dressed in the peasant garb with a Sadhu's topee on his head? He mixed with the Harijans with the greatest freedom, and I know that he evinced the greatest interest in the Harijan cause. With him the sweeper was as good as any other person, no matter what his caste might be. He never concealed his opinion or practice in order to please the orthodox.'[4]

In lauding his courage, Gandhi might well have had Patel's

inter-caste marriage bill in mind. The bill contained two provisions, the operative portion of which was blunt and unambiguous: 'No marriage among Hindus shall be invalid by reason that the parties thereto do not belong to the same caste, any custom or any interpretation of Hindu law to the contrary notwithstanding.'[5]

For this short but radical bill, Patel received the sanction of Governor General Lord Chelmsford on 10 August 1918. This paved the way for the introduction of what was titled the Hindu Marriages Validity Bill. After the historic widow-remarriage legislation of 1856, enacted on the eve of the great revolt, this was the first attempt in British India to reform the otherwise uncodified Hindu marriage law.[6]

The bill was also the first caste-related legislative proposal to be introduced since the 1850 law protecting the inheritance rights of a Hindu who had been deprived of his caste. Both the 1850 and 1856 reforms were the work of British legislators. Indians began gaining entry into law-making bodies in an incremental manner only since 1861.

In the SOR attached to his bill, Patel pointed out that, under 'the Hindu law as interpreted' by the courts, marriages between Hindus of different castes had been declared 'illegal'. 'This interpretation, besides being open to question, has caused serious hardship in individual cases and is calculated to retard the progress of the community.'

Detailing the scheme of the bill in the Council meeting in Shimla on 5 September 1918,[7] Patel cited two cases, both from his native region of Gujarat, which fell under the jurisdiction of the Bombay High Court. He chose the cases strategically, in order to draw support from the influential sections of Hindus. In both the cases, a girl from the highest caste, Brahmin, had been married to someone from a lower caste; in one, the husband was a Kshatriya, and in the other, a Shudra.

Such marriages between a superior-caste female and an inferior-caste male were classified under the traditional Hindu law as 'pratiloma', or hypogamy. (While 'loma' means hair in Sanskrit, 'pratiloma' loosely translates to going against the grain.) Given the Hindu patriarchal conception of the daughter as the 'property' of the father, pratiloma marriages were strictly forbidden. So much so that the offspring of marriages between a Brahmin female and a Shudra male, coming as they did from the opposite ends of the varna hierarchy, were said to have originated untouchability.

The restriction was less severe in the case of 'anuloma', or hypergamy, where an inferior-caste female was married to a superior-caste male. (The loose meaning of this Sanskrit term is to go with the grain.) Accordingly, scriptures indicated more tolerance to anuloma than pratiloma marriages. This meeting of patriarchy and caste prejudice resulted in a proclivity to condone anuloma marriages as a 'transgression' of a lower-caste female by an upper-caste male. Likewise, the institutionalised revulsion to pratiloma was comparable to the heightened anger that religious bigots displayed in the case of inter-faith marriages where the wife was from their community.

The repugnance at pratiloma had a long history. Take a twelfth-century instance of such a marriage from Kalyan, now called Basavakalyan, in the Bidar district of Karnataka. The marriage was between Sharanas who were followers of Basava, the founder of the egalitarian Lingayat movement. The groom was the son of an untouchable cobbler, and the bride was the daughter of a Brahmin. Although the Sharanas married with the blessings of Basava, also an influential minister and the brother-in-law of King Bijjala, the marriage provoked a violent backlash from the deeply entrenched Brahminical forces.

Bijjala forced Basava to quit his office as well as Kalyan. In the wave of violence that followed his departure, the fathers of the bridal couple were executed and the couple themselves blinded. Then, in the insurrection mounted by the Sharanas, Bijjala was assassinated for his complicity in the brutal reaction to the pratiloma marriage. Bijjala's son and successor in turn inflicted further atrocities on the Sharanas. Basava's distress over the tragic fallout of the marriage soon drove him to his death.

The Hindu notion of marriage was antithetical to the idea of a contract, and was not conceived of as a union between two equals. It was a sacrament—not only was it legally indissoluble, but it also appointed the groom as the subject, or the doer, while the bride was the object, or the acted upon. At the heart of the sacrament was 'kanyadaan', literally the gift of the bride, which made no bones about marriage as a transfer of the ownership of the bride from her father to her husband. All of which goes some way to explaining why anuloma was less frowned upon than pratiloma.

The first of the two pratiloma cases adduced by Vithalbhai Patel in support of his bill demonstrated that even Brahmins were not spared the rigours of this discrimination. In the case decided by the Bombay High Court in 1912,[8] the Brahmin wife, Bai Kashi, was discarded by her Shudra husband, Mansukh, after they had lived together for twenty-five years and had had eight children. For nine years after her abandonment, she had not sought any legal remedy until finally old age and penury forced her to file a suit for maintenance.

Bai Kashi was denied maintenance on the ground that, due to the intermixing of castes, her marriage itself was illegal. Thanks to her Brahmin antecedents, she had to bear an additional burden of purity. Therefore, she was not even eligible to claim the latitude offered to a dasi, generally a mistress belonging to a lower caste, and seek maintenance on that basis. Likewise, she could not be maintained as a 'concubine' because, as Patel put it, 'with the modesty of a Hindu lady, she had refrained from going to court for nine years'.

The author of that High Court verdict was Justice Narayan Ganesh Chandavarkar, who had been the president of the Indian National Congress in 1900 shortly before his appointment to the bench. Following the precedent set by Justice M.G. Ranade, of combining judgeship with social activism, Chandavarkar led a social reform organisation called the Depressed Classes Mission, which was involved in the struggle against untouchability. Yet, while dealing with Bai Kashi's appeal, the same social reformer, himself a Brahmin, upheld the scriptural restrictions on mixed marriages.

His judgment invoked, among other things, the stipulation of Yajnvalkya Smriti that 'one begotten on a Brahmin woman by a Shudra becomes a Chandala'. Theirs was the most extreme form of pratiloma within the varna hierarchy, and so their offspring was, as Chandavarkar explained impassively, 'the most degraded of human beings' and 'outcaste to all religion, law and customary observance'.

On the distinction between anuloma and pratiloma, Chandavarkar quoted an ancient commentator of Manusmriti, saying that, merely because 'a Brahmin may marry a woman of the Shudra caste ... it does not follow that a woman belonging to higher caste can be married by a Shudra'. Chandavarkar's judgment widened the choice for upper-caste men—they had the option of marrying lower-caste women. It displayed no compunctions in denying a corresponding right to lower-caste men. Cleaving to the Shastric law, the judgment typecast upper-caste female bodies as repositories of the purity of their bloodline.

In the other case cited by Vithalbai Patel, of a pratiloma marriage between the top two varnas,[9] the case was decided in 1900 against the Rajput husband, Kaliansing. The Bombay High Court rejected his plea for 'restitution of conjugal rights'. Though 'his alleged wife', Bai Lakshmi, was actually a ten-year-old Brahmin child, the brief judgment was framed only in terms of caste. It made no reference to the possible violation of the 1891 criminal law reform that had increased the age of consent from ten to twelve.[10]

The High Court bench, headed by Chief Justice Lawrence Jenkins, limited itself to ruling that 'a marriage between a Rajput and a Brahmin girl is not allowed by Hindu law'. In his summary of the 1900 judgment, Patel said that 'although there was a marriage in fact, there was no marriage in law, as the parties did not belong to the same caste'.

Patel also produced an array of social, economic, scientific and moral arguments, contending that Hindu society was ripe for the reform proposed by him. His optimistic summation was that 'education, travel, contact in cities with people of other castes and other such causes have widened the outlook of the younger generations'. He pointed out that his bill also sought to spare Hindus the harsh precondition imposed by the secular alternative for solemnising an inter-caste marriage. 'It will obviate the necessity of Hindus declaring as required by the Civil Marriage Act that they are not Hindus.'

Patel's opening remarks led to an extraordinary debate in the Council. Two colonial officials, in keeping with the administration's assurance to the Arya Samaj, supported the introduction of the bill, while seven of the twelve Indian legislators who spoke opposed it. Two other Indians said grudgingly that they would support the bill if Patel persisted with it despite their reservations about its timing. Only three Indians unreservedly supported its introduction.

Adding fuel to the fire was the government's willingness, expressed through Home Member William Vincent, to let Patel introduce the bill so that it could be circulated across the country to elicit public opinion. The debate intensified, despite a clarification from Vincent that until such opinion had been received, 'it was obviously premature for us to tie our hands in any way'.

The colonial administration also clarified that it would not necessarily defer to majority opinion. Instead, it would be 'largely guided', as Vincent explained, by 'the opinions of those primarily affected by the measure in dealing with it at a subsequent stage'. In effect, the government promised that it would, irrespective of the majority view, place the individual over the collective in formulating its stand on Patel's bill. This stated position was a marked advancement in the colonial administration's inclination to engage with social reforms. Only six years earlier, it had baulked at Basu's bill on civil marriage in the absence of backing by a clear majority.

Having heard two Indian councillors attacking Patel's bill, Vincent appealed to 'those of conservative instincts' to allow their fellow countrymen and co-religionists to examine the bill and express their views on it. 'If then, as is maintained, this Bill strikes at the very root principles of Hindu society, surely the objections which they make now will be more than justified by the opinions which are received.' Vincent also sent them a reassuring signal: 'I am well aware that the Bill involves a change of the Hindu law, and for that reason the Government are rightly cautious in their attitude towards it.'

Madan Mohan Malaviya, former Congress president and all set to resume that post by the end of the year, was among the legislators who addressed the Council subsequent to Vincent's intervention. Sure enough, he was as hostile to the present bill as he was to Dadabhoy's resolution. Malaviya set much store by the fact that barely six years had lapsed since the dropping of Basu's bill due to 'a tremendous volume of opinion' against it. He asked, 'Is it right, then, is it wise, will it serve any good purpose, to agitate the public mind over it again and to ask the Local Governments to reconsider this matter and to express their opinions about it?'

The vehemence of Malaviya's opposition belied the benign assumption laid out in the SOR to Patel's bill that the main hurdle to inter-caste marriage was the judicial interpretation of the Hindu law. In Malaviya's view, the courts only reflected an unchanged consensus in the community: 'I do not wish to go into the merits of the question, except to say that the general sense of the Hindu community will be entirely opposed to this Bill.'

As for the tribulations of Hindus of mixed marriages that Patel had highlighted, Malaviya stopped short of saying, tough luck. 'Individuals and groups of individuals who belong to a large community have to put up with hardships and inconvenience so long as the dominant sense in the community is opposed to the views which they entertain or want to promote.'

Former Congress president Surendra Nath Banerjea shared Malaviya's apprehensions. They had joined forces in 1916 to thwart the untouchability resolution too. But Banerjea's reservations were that the next round of constitutional reforms after the Montagu–Chelmsford Report were building up. He wanted Patel's bill to be shelved while this exercise was in process. It was a throwback to Dadabhai Naoroji's policy for the Congress thirty years earlier: prioritise political struggle over social issues.

'We have enough problems over the Reform Scheme,' Banerjea said. 'The atmosphere is almost electric: why throw an apple of discord into our midst? We want a little peace ... for the consideration of the grave issues involved in the Reform Scheme. And now here is another contentious, controversial Bill introduced which will appeal to the deepest of our sentiments, the sentiment of religion.'

Although he claimed to have 'very deep sympathy' with its objects, Banerjea found the bill 'most inopportune' and therefore felt constrained to 'beg' Patel to withdraw it. Banerjea also taunted Vincent in stilted language: 'Does he lay the flattering unction to his soul that the circulation of the Bill will not cause agitation?'

The next person to take the floor was from among the three non-official councillors who unreservedly supported the introduction of the bill. As a member of both the Congress and the Muslim League, M.A. Jinnah was also the only non-Hindu Indian legislator to participate in this debate. When he was earlier only with the Congress, Jinnah had likewise supported Basu's attempt in 1912 to enable inter-caste marriages through the secular route.

Jinnah found it 'certainly an irony of fate' that Banerjea, who had been 'agitating for the last 40 years', should suddenly be 'so much afraid of agitation and unrest' on account of Patel's bill. He added that though his own community had no direct stake in this bill, 'I am as much interested in coming to the rescue of the Hindu minority suffering today because of this law as anybody else would be interested in coming to the rescue of a Musalman minority if it was suffering.'

Jinnah asserted that it was 'absolutely obligatory' on the part of the government to grant 'liberty of conscience to individuals' so that Hindus could contract marriages 'unfettered by the shackles of caste'. Despite the government's assurance that it would not blindly go by whatever was the majority view on this reform measure, Jinnah seemed to have misheard Vincent, as evident from a torrent of questions he unleashed about the support that the besieged minority among Hindus deserved from the government.

'I ask the Government face to face, if you are going to be guided in the matter only when you get a majority, how many years will you have to wait for it? And is the Government going to stand by and allow the majority to oppress the minority? And remember that this minority is the creation more of the Western education for which you yourselves are responsible. Are you going to deny liberty to those whom you have educated? Are you going to deny liberty to those whom you have trained up in Western ideas, and are they to remain the victims of this caste shackle?'

Jinnah's barrage of questions advancing his liberal viewpoint prompted Law Member George Lowndes to restate the government's position. Lowndes clarified that his colleague Vincent 'did not say that the fate of the Bill would depend upon the majority of the opinions received'. His disclaimer was noncommittal, though: 'All that my Hon'ble Colleague said was that Government would be guided by the opinions they received.'

The law member also sought to allay the apprehensions of 'orthodox members' that the bill would disturb 'the foundations of their religion'. One such member, K.V. Rangaswamy Ayyangar, had cited verses from Manu to say, 'Though Anuloma marriages were allowed, yet they were condemned.' Lowndes agreed that anuloma marriages had been 'allowed by the Shastras in India during the whole of the best period of Hindu history', but disputed Ayyangar's suggestion that they had been condemned: 'They were not only legal but they were recognised as such by every great writer on the subject.'

At this, Malaviya interjected, saying, 'That is not correct.'

Lowndes stood his ground: 'I believe it is quite correct.'

Malaviya did not back down: 'For 3,000 years it has not been so.'

A former judge of the Bombay High Court, Lowndes did not allow Malaviya to get away with this unfounded assertion. He scoffed: 'My Hon'ble friend is very brave, and my Hon'ble friend Mr Ayyangar was braver still, though I fancy with a very slight knowledge of the subject.' It was an extraordinary exchange, not least because this early leader of the Hindu Mahasabha was renowned for his expertise on Hindu legal texts.

Elaborating on the scriptural status of anuloma marriages, Lowndes said, 'I can point out to my Hon'ble friend Mr. Ayyangar and to the Hon'ble Pandit passages in Manu which directly recognise the legality of such marriages.' He admitted that Manu also had passages 'disapproving' of anuloma marriages. In view of such contradictory passages, Lowndes said, the Manusmriti was 'probably a conglomeration of texts belonging to a great number of different periods'. In any event, it was, he asserted, 'hardly an authority as the work contains texts both ways'.

The medieval commentaries that the British had adopted as legal authorities, Mitakshara and Dayabhaga, were more coherent, Lowndes said, and both these schools recognised the legality of anuloma marriages. The evidence served to counter Malaviya's suggestion that there had been a blanket ban on mixed marriages among Hindus for 3,000 years. Questioning the antiquity of the prevailing restrictions, Lowndes urged the Council to appreciate that 'when we hear talk of the foundations of the Hindu religion being disturbed, it is not the foundations of the old Hindu religion, but the foundations of modern custom which has supplanted the old religion since the 16th century'.

Even as he debunked Malaviya's claim, Lowndes ended up conceding, by default, that Patel's proposal of validating pratiloma marriages (and not only anuloma) flew in the face of the Shastras. When Patel spoke next, to make his final pitch for the introduction of the bill, he refrained from addressing this quandary. Instead, he pointed to the incipient trend in princely states of enabling inter-caste marriage, thus stealing a march over British India. For instance, in 1908, under Maharaja Sayajirao Gaekwad, Baroda allowed Hindus of different castes to marry without loss of faith through the civil marriage route.

Patel said that the ruler Shahu Maharaj, a reputed champion of social justice, had done just this in Kolhapur. His enactment was a testament to the fact that inter-caste marriages would not in any way 'interfere with old Hindu religion or Hindu custom', as Lowndes had said too.

Like Patel's bill, the Kolhapur law made no distinction between anuloma and pratiloma marriages. What was innovative though was the tantalising option opened up by a requirement in the Kolhapur law of giving a notice of fourteen days to the registrar. 'That being so, any two persons of different castes residing in British India might go to the Kolhapur State and stay there for 14 days and marry.'

The irony of British India lagging behind a princely state in enabling social reforms—or, more precisely, a Hindu ruler allowing inter-caste marriage—was one of the factors that helped Vithalbhai Patel win the voice vote for the preliminary step of introducing his bill on 5 September 1918. Shortly thereafter, on 14 September 1918, the Chelmsford administration sent copies of the bill to all the provinces of British India.

The ensuing turbulence polarised Hindu society, inducing some of the tallest leaders of the time to weigh in on the bill.[11] On 19 December 1918, Rabindranath Tagore extended his 'heartiest support' to Patel's initiative saying, 'It is humiliating to find that some of our countrymen are opposing this bill under the notion that it will injure Hindu society if it is passed.' Calling such reaction 'a libel against the spirit of Hinduism', Tagore said that the religion had actually been 'allowing mixture of castes and making new social adjustments from the time of the Mahabharat'.

To Tagore's mind, the resistance to inter-caste marriage laid bare a contradiction in the freedom struggle. 'Where society is terribly effective in its weapons of persecution, it is shameful to appeal to a foreign Government to stiffen by its sanction a social tyranny, to rob people of their right to the freedom of conscience, and in the next moment to ask from the same Government a wider political emancipation.'

Lala Lajpat Rai wrote in much the same vein, all the way from New York. 'It will be a great blow to our prestige and good name abroad if this extremely small measure of reform based on actual legal necessity is defeated on foolish sentimental grounds.' A leader of the Arya Samaj as well as the Congress, Lajpat Rai observed that while 'the authors of the Shastras have made a liberal provision for necessary changes in social life and customs', it was 'the rigidity and absurdity of the judge-made law of the British courts that has brought about the existing impasse in the marriage laws of the Hindus'.

Aurobindo Ghose's support was, however, a qualified one: 'I should have preferred a change from within the society rather than one brought about by legislation.' At the same time, 'it would appear', he said, that 'the difficulty created by the imposition of the rigid and mechanical notions of European jurisprudence on the old Hindu Law' could only be 'removed by a resort to legislation'.

Gandhi's reaction to the bill was unmistakably tepid and had more in common with the reservations expressed by Malaviya and Banerjea than with Tagore's emphatic support. To begin with, on 28 January 1919, he asked Patel a loaded question. 'Considering all this commotion among the Hindus, do you still think that your Bill will be useful to the country?'[12]

A month later, according to a report published in the *Indian Social Reformer* on 23 February 1919, Gandhi suggested a milder reform, which did not permit even anuloma marriages. His proposal was that mixed marriages be confined to what he described as 'sub-castes'. This was another way of saying that he was open to mixed marriages if they were not inter-caste marriages but intra-varna marriages. Using the terms varna and caste interchangeably, Gandhi saw 'no objection in inter-caste marriages among the sub-castes of the Brahmin, Kshatriya, Vaishya and Sudra communities', and added that 'on no account should the existing four-fold division be broken through'.[13]

Gandhi also disclosed that Malaviya had 'promised his whole-hearted support' should such a modification be made to the bill on being referred to a Select Committee. Gandhi's avowed commitment for the better part of his life to varna segregations was evident in this telling line in the journal's report: 'In conclusion, Mahatma Gandhi pointed out how a wide chasm yawned between the Brahmin and the Dhed [an untouchable caste] and warned the ardent advocates of marriage reform against short cuts to progress.'

Responding to this report three days later with a guarded disclaimer, Gandhi wrote to the *Indian Social Reformer* on 26 February 1919 stating that 'the views attributed to me represent but a partial truth'. All the same, he reaffirmed his belief in the traditional varna system as opposed to the more fragmentary caste system. He used that distinction to justify his stated anxiety about keeping Brahmins, the purest of varnas, from marrying Dheds, who were beneath the lowest varna.

'Dheds stand in the same relation to Brahmins as Kshatriyas, Vaishyas or Shoodras,' Gandhi said, adding, 'Their peculiar disability is not affected either one way or the other by the Bill. If the Bill constitutes an attack upon Varnashram, as a believer in Varnashram-dharma, I should oppose it.'

He was told by 'orthodox friends that it does constitute such an attack', Gandhi said, and 'the supporters of the Bill' claimed that 'not only does it not interfere with the Varnashram, but it merely seeks to restore the pre-British state of Hindu law, which was wrongly interpreted by judges, who being ignorant of it, were guided by biased or corrupt Pandits'.

Seeking to take a conciliatory approach to the two sides represented by 'very able lawyers', Gandhi said, 'Without deciding one way or the other, I have suggested that the effect of the Bill should be restricted to inter-marriages among sub-castes. This might satisfy the most ardent reformer at least as a first step, and would enable men like Hon. Pandit Malaviya to support it.' It was a tactical concession to Malaviya that he could exercise a veto on behalf of conservatives on the timing and extent of caste reform.

In this letter, Gandhi also admitted his unfamiliarity with the legalities of inter-caste marriage. Though Patel had sent him 'a long and exhaustive memorandum on the subject', Gandhi said that 'with the present programme of work before me, I do not know when I shall be able to study the memorandum which requires looking up old law cases'. Perhaps he never did get around to doing that because of an eruption of far-reaching events, including the Jallianwala Bagh massacre, that catapulted him to unchallenged leadership of the freedom struggle for the next three decades.

These events were set in motion on 18 March 1919 with the enactment of the draconian Criminal Law (Emergency Powers) Bill, also known as the Rowlatt Bill, by the Imperial Legislative Council. As it happened, Vincent and Lowndes, the very officials who had been instrumental in eliciting public opinion on the inter-caste marriage bill, were also responsible for ramming through the Rowlatt legislation. In the united resistance put up by Indian legislators, Vithalbhai Patel played a crucial role, forcing the British-dominated Council to deal first with a motion he had moved to thwart the Rowlatt enactment. Malaviya and Banerjea were among those who rallied behind him.

Even in these fraught circumstances, Vincent oversaw the follow-up action on Patel's bill. The feedback from the public reflected the differences that had emerged during the Council debate on inter-caste marriage. In its cover letter, dated 9 June 1919, the Bombay government concluded that 'the opposition roughly consists of the religious leaders and their following and the more orthodox sections of the Brahmin community; the supporters are mostly "reformers", a few Brahmins and educated non-Brahmins generally'.[14]

The most notable of the reformers who wrote in support of the bill from Bombay was Chandavarkar, whose 1912 judgment invalidating a pratiloma marriage had been cited by Patel to establish the need for legislative intervention. Having ended his judicial career about a year after that verdict, Chandavarkar responded to Patel's bill in his subsequent avatar as president of an egalitarian body, the Social Service League.

Chandavarkar no longer considered pratiloma marriages illegal. He changed his position by the simple expedient of changing the authority he was relying on. In his 1912 verdict, he had quoted the 1880 book of V.N. Mandlik, but in his 1919 opinion, he relied on the fourth edition published in 1910 of a book by Golapchandra Sarkar Sastri.

Chandavarkar's justification for turning to Sastri was that his work on the Hindu law was 'accepted by our Courts as an authority on the subject'. He made no reference to his own 1912 verdict, and thereby avoided explaining why he had, despite Sastri, ruled against pratiloma marriage.

Whatever the reason for his belated wisdom, Chandavarkar quoted Sastri as saying that Hindu texts 'recognise marriage between a woman of an inferior caste and a man of a superior caste to be valid but they do not say anything about the marriage between an inferior man and superior woman'. Sastri was quoted further as saying that, despite the passages in the Smritis, which 'by implication prohibit' pratiloma, it should be observed that 'these prohibitions appear to be of moral obligation only'. The implication, in Sastri's own words, was that although pratiloma 'may be disapproved and condemned still, if such a marriage does in fact take place, the same must be regarded valid as between the parties to it, and the issue legitimate'.

The prolonged disquiet over Patel's bill among Hindus raised concerns about it in the British Parliament. On 6 August 1919, Conservative Member of Parliament (MP) Col. Charles Yate asked Secretary of State for India Edwin Montagu whether he was aware that the introduction and circulation of what he called the 'Patel Hindu Inter Caste Marriage Bill' had caused 'great alarm amongst orthodox Hindus'.[15] Yate, who had been a colonial administrator in India, said that the bill had been seen by such Hindus as 'an interference with their most sacred religious and social usages which it has been the policy of the British Government hitherto never to interfere with'.

Montagu played it safe by saying that Yate's question was based on 'some misapprehension', clarifying: 'The Government of India is not responsible for the Bill, which was introduced by an elected member of the Legislative Council. The Government are in no way committed to support it, but as it received a certain amount of support from the unofficial members, they have taken steps to obtain the full opinion of the Hindu community before the Bill is further proceeded with.'

Though 'the full opinion of the Hindu community' was received by then, it took another six months for the bill to be discussed before the Imperial Legislative Council. The discussion[16] happened on 25 February 1920, following a motion moved by Patel to refer the bill to a Select Committee as the next step in the legislative process. The government had by then prepared a thirty-five-page 'Precis of Opinions on the Hindu Marriages Validity Bill'.

That a substantial section of opinions, including that of Chandavarkar, turned out to be favourable to the bill gave Patel the confidence to address the issue of pratiloma marriages, which he had sidestepped in the previous round of discussion. He readily conceded that the scriptures disapproved of it. Though anuloma marriages were 'admittedly permitted', Patel said that pratiloma marriages were 'condemned by the Hindu Shastras'. But, echoing Chandavarkar's revised view, he clarified that 'such condemnation was, according to the best authorities, merely moral'.

On the strength of this fine distinction between what was considered merely immoral and what was legally invalidated, Patel asserted, 'There is no text on Hindu law which can be cited to prove that Pratiloma marriages were illegal and the issues of such marriages illegitimate.' Based on this reading of the Shastras, he claimed reassuringly that his bill followed 'the line of least resistance' as it retained the sacramental character of the Hindu marriage and did not engraft 'any new principle not sanctioned by Hindus'.

But more than his interpretation of the Shastras, it was Patel's analysis of public opinion on the bill that proved contentious. Though the proportion of adverse opinions was greater, Patel claimed that 'a great majority of the Hindu community, numerically speaking, is in my favour'. The basis of his claim was that most Hindus were Shudras.

Given that his own caste of Leuva Patel Patidars had Shudra status, it was not unnatural for him to break down the feedback from the perspective of the varna that was stigmatised, despite being numerically the largest by a long margin. Patel began by saying, 'I may say at once that the whole community of my Sudra brothers and sisters is entirely in favour of this Bill.' On second thoughts, he claimed that the support base of his bill extended to 'the entire non-Brahmin community', which included Kshatriyas and Vaishyas.

As for the varna that was meant to be protected the most from mixed marriages, Patel agreed that 'the majority of the Brahmins is against my Bill'. Despite his disclaimer that he did not 'wish to lead any attack on any particular community', he said: 'I quite realise that it is only human nature that one who is in possession of power does not like to part with it so easily.'

Presenting a province-wise breakdown of the feedback from Brahmins, Patel said, 'When I say that the opposition mainly comes from one community, I am bound to give this Council some proof in support of this sweeping statement.' Though the bulk of his speech had been devoted to substantiating that claim, Patel concluded, 'I trust my Brahmin friends will excuse me if I have said anything to offend them. I have said what I have felt.'

Before any of them could respond to Patel's unusual attack on their community, Home Member William Vincent contested his claim that the opinions on the bill were polarised between Brahmins and non-Brahmins. Vincent denied that Patel was 'correct in his attack on Brahmins as the real opponents of this measure'. He said the Council was being asked 'to neglect public opinion as voiced by Brahmins', and instead 'be guided by the opinions of the silent millions'. Vincent found that Patel's attitude departed from the default position of Indian leaders that 'there is one opinion in India and that is the vocal opinion of the educated classes'.

Even apart from 'the justice of this attack on the Brahmins', Vincent counselled that Patel should have 'avoided it as a matter of tactics'. For, in his experience of the Council, 'many of the acutest Indian intellects have always been Brahmins'. Vincent recalled that when he had once 'said a word about Brahmins' in the Council, it 'brought a storm about my ears' and he 'avoided doing so again'. Vincent warned Patel that his attack on Brahmins was 'the most dangerous hornet's nest he has ever disturbed'. It was an astute portrayal of the Brahmanical grip over the Indian elite. 'If there is one thing which Hindu members in this Council will not bear, it is any suspicion of what they think is an unfair attack upon the Brahmin community.'

Whatever other Hindu members of the Council might have thought about it, Brahmin legislators certainly showed signs of resenting Patel's attack on their community. One of them was Surendra Nath Banerjea, who spoke at length on the Brahmin issue when the discussion on the bill resumed the following day, on 26 February 1920.[17]

Echoing Vincent's reaction, Banerjea affirmed that 'apart from the inaccuracy of his statements', Patel was 'guilty of a gigantic blunder', for his speech which was 'so full of anti-Brahmanical spirit'. Referring to the history of Brahmins propelling social reforms, Banerjea said, 'It serves no useful purpose to alienate the sympathies of the intellectual leaders of India.'

Banerjea's reaction prompted George Lowndes—now vice president of the Council, presiding over the proceedings in the absence of Viceroy Chelmsford—to intervene: 'I had hoped that after the adjournment yesterday the Council would have agreed to bury the Brahmin question; sufficient has already been said on both sides, and the matter is really quite irrelevant. The motion before the Council is whether the Bill should be referred to a Select Committee or not, and I propose to rule in future that all references to the Brahmin question are out of order.'

The embargo was tested more than once in the course of the debate that day. When Rangaswamy Ayyangar, for instance, faulted Patel for construing the feedback as though 'Brahmins alone' had opposed the bill, Lowndes cut in, 'Order, order, I will not allow the Hon'ble Member to go into the Brahmin question.' Ayyangar protested that, since Patel had 'based his arguments on this point that the majority of the non-Brahmins support his Bill', he should be allowed 'to meet them'. Lowndes, however, did not relent: 'The Hon'ble Member must obey my ruling; he must either obey my ruling or resume his seat.'

Patel himself returned to the Brahmin question, obliquely this time, when he made his closing remarks. He said, 'My Hon'ble friend Mr Banerjea thinks that I made a tactical blunder … in criticising a certain section of the community. Well, I plead guilty to the charge. Perhaps I did make a tactical blunder.'

However, he was 'not prepared under any circumstances' to accept Banerjea's proposition that 'the great majority of Hindus are not in favour of the Bill'. He reaffirmed the three conclusions that he drew 'from the heap of materials placed before this Council': that most Shudras supported his bill, that most non-Brahmins (the larger category that included Shudras) too supported it and that most Brahmins (the smallest category) were against it.

Placing his bill in the larger scheme of things, Patel recalled the 1918 Montagu–Chelmsford Report, which had laid out the road map to 'the attainment of responsible government'. Since caste had been adduced by the report as 'one of the obstacles' to that goal, Patel urged the Chelmsford administration to shed its neutral attitude in the little time that was left of the existing legislature's tenure. 'Is it really not your duty to help those of us who want gradually to get rid of these obstacles?'

In a marked departure from how Basu's bill had been dropped by the colonial administration due to similar adverse feedback, Patel's bill was allowed to go to the next stage of law-making: reference to a Select Committee. Remarkably, this progression occurred despite the difficulty caused by Patel's excoriation of Brahmins.

The composition of the Select Committee was propitious. Its chairman, as per rules, was Lowndes, who had already ventured to say that the Shastras condoned anuloma. The other sixteen members were all Hindu legislators, including Patel. The committee displayed due urgency. Within twenty days of its appointment, on 17 March 1920, the Select Committee submitted its report.[18]

However, the report proved to be disappointing for Patel. It began with the disclosure that the committee, rather than upholding the bill in its proposed form, considered whether it was 'desirable' to reduce its ambit in two possible ways.

One, a tacit tribute to Gandhi's view, was to consider limiting the bill 'to the case of marriages between sub-castes only'. This meant that the committee was mulling the time-tested option of taking an incremental approach to social reform.

Two, the committee considered adopting a watered-down

version of Patel's radical scheme of doing away with all restrictions on mixed marriages. Its proposal was that such reform be made applicable only to a section of Hindus. Could inter-caste marriage be allowed, it pondered, only to 'members of recognised societies who have declared in favour of marriage reform'? Clearly, the committee was alluding to the Arya Samaj, the reformist sect that had mooted the idea of updating the Hindu law to validate inter-caste marriage. This, too, was an incremental approach to reform, in which the freedom conferred on the members of the Arya Samaj was expected to have a demonstration effect on the Hindu mainstream.

After considering these two modest ways of allowing mixed marriages, the Select Committee backed out of recommending either. Its excuse was that, on second thoughts, most members felt that they should either go the whole distance or not do anything at all. 'Some of us would have preferred one or other of these alternatives, but the majority consider that such amendments would not afford an adequate solution of the problem before us and that it is necessary to legalise marriage between all castes.'

Its 'main recommendation', however, betrayed the real reason for its reluctance to propose any reform that could have been immediately enacted. The Select Committee suggested postponing the issue till the bicameral legislature under the Government of India Act of 1919 came into existence in 1921. 'Though the majority of us are in favour of legislation at the earliest possible moment, we recommend that in view of the fact that the Reformed Councils are so shortly to be constituted, the further consideration of this Bill should be deferred till the new Legislative Assembly meets in 1921.'

Thus, it returned the bill to the Council without proposing any changes. The committee said that it did not think 'anything would be gained by formulating specific amendments at this stage'.

On what was effectively a burial of his bill, Patel wrote a note of dissent: 'I regret I cannot accept the majority view that further consideration of the Bill should be deferred till the new Legislative Assembly meets in 1921.' Arguing for immediate enactment, he made two remarkably prescient points.

Firstly, pointing to the inherently uncertain outcome of an election, he said, 'It is possible that the mover of the Bill may not be a member of the new Legislative Assembly.' As it happened, Patel was indeed not a member of the expanded and more representative Assembly that took over in 1921. As part of Gandhi's Non-Cooperation Movement, the Congress party decided to boycott the election. In Patel's absence, no legislator took the risk of reintroducing the lapsed bill, belying the Select Committee's presumption that it would be taken up in the next Assembly.

Only after he had helped found the Congress-breakaway Swaraj Party did Patel contest and win the next election held towards the end of 1923. But when he joined the Central Legislative Assembly in 1924, Patel refrained from reviving his mixed-marriage proposal. In any case, he soon lost the capacity to introduce legislation. In 1925, Vithalbhai Patel became president of the Central Legislative Assembly, earning him the distinction of emerging as the first elected presiding officer of any legislative body at the national level. In the hierarchy created by the 1950 Constitution, the president of the Central Legislative Assembly became the speaker of the Lok Sabha.

Patel's dissent note in the 1920 Select Committee report proved equally prophetic in its despairing observation that 'it will be some years before a similar attempt may be made'—no attempt was made by any legislator in his lifetime. The next attempt to validate mixed marriages in the Hindu mainstream came only in 1935, two years after his death.

Interestingly, the only aspect on which Patel mustered majority support in the Select Committee, even if only in principle, was for his insistence that no distinction ought to be made between anuloma and pratiloma marriages. Those who wanted only anuloma marriages to be recognised, that too in terms of the Shastras, were in a minority. 'Some of us are of opinion,' as the Select Committee report put it, 'that the rights of all children by a wife of a lower caste should be left to be governed by the ancient provisions of Hindu law.' It clarified though that 'the majority of us feel that there should be no differentiation in this respect and that all children, whatever the caste of their mother may have been, should share equally both upon partition and upon intestate succession.' This was the closest the Select Committee came to endorsing Patel's bid to validate pratiloma marriage—the ultimate heresy for Hindus of the time.

On 22 March 1920, Patel went through the motions of presenting the report of the Select Committee at what was the last sitting of the pre-reform Council. The *Times of India* reported that it would be the last time Lord Chelmsford—or any viceroy for that matter—presided over legislative proceedings. The story said, 'His Excellency the Viceroy, winding up the session, regretted that ... he would be deprived of personal touch with the Council, except on formal occasions.'[19]

In his hour of defeat in this caste battle, Patel could not have foreseen that, just five years later, he would become the first Indian to take over the highest legislative office, which had till 1920 been reserved for viceroys.

❖

Fifteen years later, Vithalbhai Patel's daring attempt to enable Hindus to marry without caste restrictions under their personal law would take the form of two bills. While one was a verbatim reproduction of his bill, the other, following one of the two options the 1920 Select Committee had considered, sought to initiate the reform with the Arya Samaj.

Both bills happened to be introduced on the same day, 26 September 1935. The Hindu Marriage Validation Bill was moved by Bhagavan Das,[20] a Sanskrit scholar, educationist and Congress leader from Benaras, who would go on to be one of the earliest recipients of the Bharat Ratna, free India's highest award. The main sponsor of the Arya Marriage Validation Bill was Narayan Bhaskar Khare, a Congress leader who went on to become the first premier of the Central Provinces in 1937, only to leave the government and party a year later to join the Hindu Mahasabha.

The legal landscape in which these two bills were introduced in 1935 was a far cry from the one in which Patel had introduced his in 1918. Despite the Congress boycott, the enlarged legislatures offering greater representation to Indians under the Montagu–Chelmsford reforms proved to be more conducive to social reform. The change triggered a fresh assault on the Hindu conservative restrictions on the civil marriage option. Bouncing back from the defeat they had suffered in 1912 in the context of Basu's bill, Hindu reformists mustered enough strength this time to push through an amendment. The breakthrough came in 1923 with the enactment of a bill that had been piloted by Hari Singh Gour, bringing Hindus under the ambit of the fifty-year-old civil marriage law. Consequent to this reform of the secular option, Hindus could finally enter into an inter-caste marriage without disavowing their religion. The reform came at a price, though. Hard-fought negotiations with conservatives led to the imposition of a statutory penalty on Hindus who chose to have a civil marriage—the couple would be disinherited.

Despite this built-in disincentive, the 1923 Gour amendment to the 1872 Special Marriage Act was a milestone in the history of mixed marriages. It opened up the possibility of inter-caste marriage being legalised within Hindu personal law, that too without the penalty of disinheritance. Such a reform would mean that there would be no discrimination between intra-caste and inter-caste marriages as both would have been solemnised under the same law.

However, disregarding the opportunities thrown up by the changed circumstances, Bhagavan Das took the lazy option of replicating Patel's Bill, which only declared the basic right to marry across caste barriers. In his address to the Assembly on 28 January 1937, Das admitted that he was counting on a Select Committee to make up for any deficiencies of the bill. He said that 'consequential provisions will presumably have to be added by the Select Committee'.[21]

One such provision could well specify, Das added, that, for the purposes of inheritance, 'the Varna or caste of the wife and the children in the case of such marriages shall be regarded as the same as that of the husband and the father'. Since it was not possible to conceive of a Hindu without a caste identity, Das was understandably concerned about the uncertainty that a mixed marriage could create for the wife and children involved.

His attempt to piggyback on Patel's bill failed, though, as the colonial regime came out against Das's motion for the Select Committee reference. One reason was that Lowndes, who had taken on Malaviya during the debate on Patel's bill, was succeeded in the office of law member by an Indian, Nripendra Sircar. So, if Das's motion had been adopted, the Select Committee would have been chaired by Sircar, a direct stakeholder in the proposed reform of the Hindu law.

That would not necessarily have made things any easier for Das. Among Sircar's objections was an allegation that, by simply copying Patel's bill, Das was trying to get the bulk of the legislative drafting done by the Select Committee. 'He has really presented half an anna of his Bill,' Sircar said caustically, 'and he wants the remaining 15 ½ annas to be added by the Select Committee.'

Bhagavan Das responded defensively. Since he did not have 'any legal training worth mentioning', he contented himself with 'copying the Bill brought in by the late Mr. Vithalbhai Patel word for word, out of faith in his legal acumen and patriotism'. As his bill admittedly 'needs additions', Das said that it was 'in guileless simplicity of mind' that he had sought the advice of the Select Committee.

In any case, Sircar was of the view that the bill was a 'retrograde measure'. Far from sharing the in-principle endorsement that had been given by Vincent and Lowndes to Patel's bill, Sircar's assessment betrayed caste prejudice. He alleged that the bill would lead to 'compulsion' even in an anuloma marriage, citing a hypothetical case of 'the daughter of a Mochi [cobbler] marrying in a Brahmin family'. Sircar said, 'It is the idea of Dr Bhagavan Das that this couple will have the right of succession and adoption and the Mochi-Brahmin combination will lead to an issue whom the other coparceners will be bound to recognise for purposes of partition and succession.'

So, this time, both government and Hindu conservatives opposed the bill. In fact, Babu Baijnath Bajoria, representing the Marwari Association: Indian Commerce, went on to repeat Sircar's hypothetical example, only in more demeaning language. 'Suppose a Brahmin marries a Chamari girl ... Will the other members of the family be bound to accept that Chamari into their family?'

Just as Malaviya had led the charge against Patel's bill, another leader of the Hindu Mahasabha, Bhai Parmanand, set upon Das's bill. He began by referring to Ambedkar's famous 1935 declaration that he could not any longer 'tolerate to remain in the Hindu fold'. Parmanand expressed alarm at what he saw as a warning that 'as long as caste Hindus were not prepared to inter-marry with the depressed classes, the depressed classes would never take themselves to be Hindus'. Though he called it 'one great reason' for Hindu leaders to support the bill, Parmanand said: 'The proper way would be to create a desire among the people first; otherwise, this legislation would amount to forcing a reform on the people and would mean putting the cart before the horse.'

Bhagavan Das, however, showed no sign of yielding. If anything, in a tacit counter to the hypothetical anuloma scenarios conjured up by Sircar and Bajoria, he cited the real-life example of a pratiloma marriage that had been caused by love. Mahatma Gandhi's son, Devdas Gandhi, and C. Rajagopalachari's daughter, Lakshmi, had been forced to adopt a circuitous procedure in 1933 to have their inter-caste marriage performed according to their wishes. Though they had wanted to do it with Hindu rituals, they had no choice but to get their marriage solemnised in the first instance under the 1923 amendment to the civil marriage law.

This precaution was imperative because, with the groom being a Vaishya and the bride a Brahmin, their marriage was in the stigmatised pratiloma category. So, they had married twice over—first, the legal way (by compulsion), and then, the traditional way (by choice). This was how Bhagavan Das described it: 'As there was no such provision in the Statute book as my Bill endeavours to place upon it, these two young people, the son of Mahatma Gandhi and the daughter of Sri Rajagopalachari, were compelled to perform a civil marriage first before a Registrar; but they were not satisfied. They took the sacramental view of marriage, and therefore they were married again according to the old Vedic Hindu rites.'

The invocation of such a high-profile example made little difference to the fate of his bill. Undeterred by the odds, Das insisted on a division on 4 February 1937. The bill crashed; his motion for Select Committee reference secured fourteen Ayes as opposed to thirty-eight Nays.

❖

In contrast, the Linlithgow government responded positively to N.B. Khare's Arya Marriage Validation Bill, although it had been introduced on the same day as Das's bill.[22] The difference was mainly because of the pragmatism of Khare's bill, in restricting its ambit to the relatively small reformist section, which was clamouring for inter-caste marriage, rather than the entire Hindu community, which was sharply divided over it.

Apart from turning its back on idol worship and the notion that God would take a human avatar, such as Rama or Krishna, the Arya Samaj's essential deviation from the Hindu mainstream lay in its understanding of caste. While orthodox Sanatanists asserted that it was fixed on the basis of janma or birth (which in their conception was no accident), Arya Samajists saw caste as a fluid identity determined by karma or actions (owing to their interpretation of the Vedas, which they saw as 'the supreme authority').

While suggesting that caste could have the mobility of class, Swami Dayanand, the founder of Arya Samaj, did not dwell on how a Hindu might be promoted or demoted in that rigid hierarchy. 'All individuals should be placed in different Classes according to their qualifications, accomplishments and character. By adopting this system all will advance in every respect, because the higher

Classes will be in constant fear of their children being degraded to the Shudra Class, if they are not properly educated.'[23]

The SOR of Khare's bill stated that the Arya Samajists 'conscientiously believe that the present caste system is not in accordance with their scriptures, the Vedas and the sacred Shastras'.[24] In the prevalent system, marriages between parties 'belonging by birth to different castes or sub-castes are considered invalid and there is a fear of the issue of such marriages being declared illegitimate'. And 'as quite a large number of such marriages have taken place and more would have taken place had there been no such obstacle, it is necessary to have a law which would give relief to the Arya Samajists'.

Khare's bill thus sought to introduce the concept of 'sub-caste' in the statute book. And in keeping with the Arya Samaj's Shuddhi Movement to reconvert Hindus who had embraced Islam or Christianity, the bill included such members too in the ambit of the mixed marriages that were sought to be validated. It applied to parties belonging to 'different castes or sub-castes of Hindus or to different religions'. Equally striking was its consequential provision for 'purposes of succession'. It said that all intermarriages among Arya Samajis shall be deemed to be between persons of 'the same caste of (Dwijas) the twice born Hindus'. This was also the first attempt to confer statutory status on the notion of 'Dwija' or twice-born.

In its report dated 5 August 1936, the Select Committee that had been constituted by the Assembly recast the clause on the validation of mixed marriages 'in a clearer and more comprehensive form', even as it retained the principle of covering those who had been from different castes, sub-castes and religions.[25] But the committee, headed by Sircar, replaced the succession clause with a fresh one that dispensed with the proposal of treating every Arya Samaj marriage as that between twice-born Hindus.

Thanks to the 'considerable diversity of opinion' among its members, the Select Committee 'decided by a majority' to provide that 'questions of succession shall be determined according to the

Indian Succession Act, 1925', which had no reference to caste as it was originally meant for Christians and those who had taken the civil marriage option. In a dissent note, four of the Hindu members of the committee, including Khare and Bhagavan Das, took exception to the amendment, even though they were mostly reconciled to deletion of the 'Dwijas' reference. The alternative they proposed was that 'the Hindu Personal Law of the husband, where he was a Hindu before the marriage, and the Succession Act in other cases, shall govern the case'.

They advocated the application of Hindu personal law in view of the Arya Samaj's foundational belief 'in the Vedas and the sacred Shastras and also in the Varna-Ashrama Dharma'. Its commitment to varna, according to the dissenters, was not inconsistent with inter-caste marriage because unlike the common notion of 'Varna by Janma or birth alone', the Arya Samajists believed in 'Varna by Karma i.e., vocation or occupation'. Hence this corollary: 'To ask them to take to the Succession Act, in cases where the Shastras can apply, is to ask them to forsake their faith.'

Even so, the four dissenters in the Select Committee had differences among themselves on the centrality of Dwijas in the Arya Samaj perspective. This was evident from an additional note from one of the dissenters, Ghanshiam Singh Gupta, a member of the Arya Samaj. It served as an advance warning that he would move for the restoration of the original clause conferring Dwija status on all the marriages solemnised under the proposed law.

Sircar, in turn, warned his colleagues in the government that if any such amendment was moved for restoring the lost provision, 'it should be opposed as it really involves adding by Statute casteless persons to certain castes who are opposed to such inclusion'. In a note to Home Member Henry Craik on 21 August 1936, Sircar wrote, 'The idea of the community which wants to abolish caste as an evil asking for Arya Samajists to be deemed as belonging to the Dwija caste is on the face of it so absurd that it was turned down by the Select Committee, though the majority of the Committee were either Arya Samajists or their supporters.'

Gupta, however, did not stop at seeking an amendment to restore the clause on Dwija status. He also proposed an alternative in which the intermarriage would be deemed to be between 'Sudras in the case of the husband or the wife having belonged to a religion other than Hinduism'. Thus, contrary to the Arya Samaj principle of karma-determined varna, the one who claimed to be the only legislator from that community proposed that all who had reconverted to Hinduism through shuddhi should, for purposes of succession, be treated as Shudras.

By the time the Act was passed on 20 March 1937, though, Gupta had withdrawn his varna-oriented amendments.[26] Instead, as part of a settlement in the Assembly, Gupta proposed that the clause on the application of the Indian Succession Act be omitted. Once this motion of his was adopted, the bill was passed with just the clause on the validation of intermarriages among Arya Samajists. On 7 April 1937, the Council of State, the other House in the bicameral legislature, passed the bill in one day.

Many went on to marry under this law in Arya Samaj temples, both before and after Independence. For decades, it served as a liberal option for runaway couples who wanted sacramental marriage or did not want to forsake their inheritance and succession rights. That first law allowing inter-caste marriage among Hindus, even if it was formally confined to a 'class of Hindus known as Arya Samajists', still stands exactly the way it was enacted in 1937.

Mixed though its motives might have been, the British regime did itself credit at that juncture by blocking all proposals by Hindu nationalists to link succession to varna. The intransigence was, in retrospect, an atonement for the insidious ways in which its courts had reinforced caste prejudice. By rejecting the formulations that had been suggested by Khare and Gupta, the colonial government saved India the ignominy of giving statutory recognition to the scriptural classification of twice-born Hindus.

❖

Musammat Jaggo was by birth an Agrahari, a caste belonging to the Vaishya varna, or in the legal parlance that was emerging then, a sub-caste belonging to the Vaishya caste. As was common for a Hindu woman in the early decades of the twentieth century, Jaggo was married as a minor. And then, when she became a widow, she was married to the younger brother of her deceased husband, in keeping with the custom of levirate. Her second husband, already married, soon abandoned her.

So, Jaggo married for the third time. Subsequently, when she became a widow again, the validity of her third marriage and the legitimacy of her son from it came to be questioned in a property dispute.[27] The challenge was mainly on the ground that her third husband was by birth a Kasaudhan, a sub-caste belonging to the caste of Vaishyas. And though she belonged to a different sub-caste of the same caste, it was contended that such a mixed marriage was forbidden among twice-born Hindus.

Regardless of how prevalent the practice was, the question was whether marriages across sub-castes were as valid among Dwijas as they were among Shudras. In 1936, around the time the legislature was in the process of making a breakthrough for Arya Samajists, Jaggo's case from Gorakhpur in the United Provinces resulted in a landmark decision from the Privy Council in London.

The judgment was authored by Shadi Lal, who, as chief justice of the Lahore High Court from 1920 to 1934, had the distinction of being the first native ever to hold such a high judicial office anywhere in British India. In the even higher position he had acquired since then, Shadi Lal's ruling on behalf of the Privy Council upheld the validity of Jaggo's mixed marriage.

Delivered on 28 April 1936, this verdict was a quantum leap for twice-born Hindus, even if it opened up mixed marriages only within their own varnas. The judgment came the very year in which Ambedkar excoriated them in his most famous tract, *Annihilation of Caste*. The decision was also, on the face of it, a vindication of the watered-down version of the Patel bill that Gandhi had mooted in 1919. However, in making this proposal from his privileged position as a Vaishya, Gandhi was apparently oblivious to the fact that marriages across sub-castes were already prevalent among the Shudras. It took a Privy Council verdict seventeen years later, in a case involving Gandhi's own varna, to dispel that rather Dwija-centric view of the Hindu community.

Rejecting the contention that endogamy barred even intra-varna marriages, the Privy Council said that it was 'not aware of any rule of Hindu law, and certainly none has been cited, which would prevent a marriage between persons belonging to two different divisions of the same caste'.[28] It refused to treat the prevalent practice among the Dwija varnas as customary law. 'There exists no doubt a disinclination to marry outside the sub-caste, inspired probably by a social prejudice; but it cannot be seriously maintained that there is any custom which has acquired the force of law.' The judgment broke new ground as evident from its acknowledgement that the two previous occasions on which the Privy Council had upheld intra-varna mixed marriages in the nineteenth century were in relation to Shudras.

After decades of deference to the Hindu right, colonial India finally established the principle of parity between twice-born Hindus and Shudras, at least on the question of marrying across sub-castes within their own castes or varnas. The following year, this Privy Council judgment paved the way for the marriage law that allowed Arya Samajists to jump the barriers of not only sub-castes but also castes or varnas.

Around the time that Khare achieved his Arya Samaj breakthrough, another legislator from the Central Provinces, Govind Deshmukh, representing Nagpur, pulled off a gender reform.

But this pioneering law, the Hindu Women's Right to Property Act, 1937, proved to be a problematic one. Its limited grant of property rights to women upset both conservative and liberal sections of Hindus. As it disrupted a complex web of privileges rooted in patriarchy, the law ended up being amended the very next year. Even so, Hindus from both camps came up with five more bills to make further changes to Deshmukh's law.

The prolonged uncertainty about the legislative reform of empowering Hindu women to inherit property forced the government on 25 January 1941 to set up an expert committee in which, in a first, the members were all Indians, that too Hindus. Chaired by B.N. Rau, a judge of the Calcutta High Court, the Hindu Law Committee was tasked to examine the 1937 Act 'with particular reference to' the five pending amendment bills. The Rau Committee's mandate was to 'clarify the nature of the right conferred by the Act upon the widow and remove any injustice that may have been [done] by the Act to the daughters'.[29]

Deshmukh decided to take another shot at piecemeal legislation. On 13 February 1941, he introduced in the Legislative Assembly what was titled the Hindu Marriage Disabilities Removal Bill. It sought to provide statutory footing to the Privy Council verdict validating marriages across sub-castes within each caste or varna. Since matrimony between sub-castes was already settled law, the more controversial part of Deshmukh's bill dealt with another restriction on marriage. Gotra, or pravara, was the Brahminical notion of a vastly extended family that had allegedly descended in the male line from an ancient rishi after whom it was named.

While 'gotra' was a reference to this imagined family, 'pravara' pertained to the sages that each gotra was supposed to have descended from. If the sub-caste restriction was about excluding all those who did not belong to one's sub-caste, the gotra restriction was about excluding those who were sagotra, the numerous people who were believed to have hoary family links with the person concerned.

Thus, Deshmukh's bill said that a marriage between Hindus, 'which is otherwise valid', shall not be invalid because the parties belonged to 'the same gotra or pravara' or to 'different sub-divisions of the same caste'. The expression he used for what Gandhi had referred to as 'sub-castes' was borrowed straight from the Privy Council verdict.

This bill highlighted the intricate ways in which freedom of choice was traditionally curtailed in matrimonial alliances among

Hindus. In seeking to bring out its Brahminical origins in the SOR of his bill, Deshmukh underestimated the reach of the gotra custom. He was oblivious to the fact that, like other Brahminical influences, the notion of gotra had trickled down to the lowest and largest varna. His SOR asserted, 'It does not prevail among the Sudras.'[30]

As for marriages between sub-divisions of a given caste, the SOR made a case for reinforcing the Privy Council judgment with a statutory provision. Despite the judicial clarification that there was never actually any legal prohibition, 'the general belief prevails that such marriages, which are rare, are not lawful'.

The introduction of Deshmukh's bill on 13 February 1941 marked the beginning of what turned out to be an unusually long journey for any single legislative proposal—facilitated in part by the unusually long term of the Fifth Legislative Assembly. Though the election to this Central legislature had been held in 1934, the next one could not be conducted until 1945 due to the tumult of the Second World War and the Quit India Movement.

The first sign that Deshmukh's bill was in for a long journey ahead came on 21 March 1941, when he moved a motion for referring it to a Select Committee. The government, true to form, threw a spanner in the works, suggesting that it be first circulated to elicit public opinion.

In a bid to turn the adversity into an opportunity, Deshmukh requested that the bill might also be referred to the Rau Committee. Home Member Reginald Maxwell expressed reservations on a technicality, pointing out that the remit of the Rau Committee was to examine the effect of the bills that made 'a definite modification of the statutory Hindu law', which was of course Deshmukh's own enactment on gender and property. On the other hand, his current bill on gotras and sub-castes, Maxwell said, 'goes entirely outside the statutory Hindu law and introduces a new principle altogether'.[31] The upshot of this discussion was that the bill was circulated for nationwide consultation.

Three months later, on 19 June 1941, the Rau Committee came up with a proposal that had a bearing on this pending bill.

It recommended the expansion of its terms of reference so that it could codify Hindu law in stages, beginning with the law of succession and the law of marriage. The government, upping the ante, gave it the go-ahead.

Following this fortuitous development, Deshmukh sought to espouse his cause by raising a question in the Legislative Assembly about the Rau Committee. Referring to the answers that the committee had received from the public to its questionnaire, Deshmukh asked what percentage of those were in favour of inter-caste and sagotra marriage. The reply given on 28 October 1941 by Law Member Sultan Ahmed, a barrister from Patna, was that '58 per cent were in favour of validating all inter-caste marriages, 70 per cent were in favour of validating all Anuloma marriages and 81 per cent in favour of validating Sagotra marriages'.[32]

Thus it turned out that Sagotra marriage, the only real change in legal position that his bill had proposed, was exactly what enjoyed the most popularity. If anything, public opinion was ahead of his bill, given that it refrained from venturing into inter-varna alliances although a majority of Hindus approved of that too. Leveraging this official data, Deshmukh made a renewed attempt that very day to have his bill referred to a Select Committee.

He wanted to expedite his relatively modest package of Sagotra and sub-caste reforms either through his own bill or as part of the bill that was being drafted by the Rau Committee. The strategy had the intended effect of forcing the government to refer Deshmukh's bill to the Rau Committee. He withdrew his motion for appointing a Select Committee following Ahmed's assurance that the Rau Committee would give his bill 'their fullest consideration'.

On 30 May 1942, the government published the two bills that had been drafted by the Rau Committee. They were titled the Hindu Code, Part I (Intestate Succession) and the Hindu Code, Part II (Marriage). The latter bill disregarded the positive feedback that the Rau Committee had received on inter-caste marriages, particularly the Anuloma variety. Despite the 81 per cent support it had received on Sagotra marriages, the Rau Committee did not dare break this barrier either. The only consolation for Deshmukh was that it endorsed the Privy Council's validation of marriages across sub-castes. While prescribing conditions for the sacramental form of marriage, the committee's bill reiterated the traditional restrictions pertaining to caste, gotra and pravara.[33]

Having left untouched the sacramental form of marriage, the Rau Committee offered a novel compromise: a hybrid option allowing Hindus to conduct a civil marriage within the framework of the Hindu law. For those willing to forsake sacramental rites, this option was meant to facilitate inter-caste and intra-gotra marriages without losing the tag of a 'Hindu marriage' and without suffering the penalty of severance from the family estate imposed by the existing civil marriage law.

As for those who were willing to abide by the traditional restrictions, the separate provision in the Rau Committee's bill for sacramental marriage complied with its pristine purity. Accordingly, one of the conditions laid down in clause 4 for the solemnisation of a sacramental marriage was that 'both the parties must belong to the same caste'.

The intent to accommodate marriages across sub-castes within the sacramental format was made clear by a definition in clause 2 which equated caste with varna. At the same time, the bill maintained the traditional curbs relating to gotra and pravara through another provision. Clause 4 circumscribed the sacramental marriage with the condition that 'if the parties are members of a caste having gotras and pravaras, they must not belong to the same gotra or have a common pravara'.

However, recognising the growing incidence of marriages across varnas or within the same gotra, the Rau Committee's bill granted them legitimacy by adopting the doctrine of *factum valet*. Clause 7 began with the words, 'No sacramental marriage solemnised after the commencement of this Act shall, after it has been completed, be deemed to be, or ever to have been, invalid merely by reason of one or more of the following causes: …' Among the causes that would not invalidate a sacramental marriage was 'that the parties to the marriage do not, or did not, belong to the same caste'. Another such cause was 'that the parties belonged to the same Gotra or had a common Pravara.'

While the norms set in clause 4 signalled the Rau Committee's deference to the Hindu orthodoxy, the exemptions provided in clause 7 were a concession to the growing demand for reform. About a year later, Deshmukh came across further evidence of public support for reform when he received feedback on the circulation of his bill across British India. Speaking in the Legislative Assembly on 26 March 1943, he gloated that 110 opinions were 'strongly in favour of the whole Bill', and that out of the fifty-four opposing it, twenty-six were in fact branches of the same body, the Varnashrama Swaraj Sangh, which 'should therefore be considered as one vote'.

That the proposed codification of the Hindu law had resonated so widely encouraged the government to revive the Rau Committee. On 20 January 1944, the government announced that the committee in its second avatar would 'formulate the remaining parts of the projected Code'. On 5 August that year, the Rau Committee came up with a draft bill encompassing all the branches of the Hindu law. In the accompanying explanatory note, it said: 'It is generally felt that the evils of piecemeal legislation on this subject should be avoided and that an entire Hindu Code acceptable to the general Hindu public should be in operation at an early date.'

This meant that the two pending bills seeking piecemeal legislation on marriage lost their utility. The government did not, therefore, proceed any further with Select Committee scrutiny of the bill that was based on the Rau Committee's earlier draft. Despite the government's resistance, Deshmukh insisted that his bill be referred to a Select Committee. On 1 March 1945, his motion was carried by a margin of one vote. The Select Committee never met, though, because the Assembly was in the process of being wound up. Its unscheduled term of ten years ended barely a month later.

Like Vithalbhai Patel before him, Govind Deshmukh failed to make it to the Assembly in the next election. But his younger brother, Gopalrao Deshmukh, representing Bombay city, was re-elected. Having participated fervently in the debates on his brother's bill during its four-year journey, Gopalrao Deshmukh was well equipped to revive it in the newly constituted Sixth Legislative Assembly.

A general surgeon, Gopalrao Deshmukh had the distinction of being the founding president of the Indian Medical Association, the largest voluntary association of doctors in the country. While the elder brother was from the relatively small Liberal Party, the younger one was from the Congress, which was in a majority in the new Assembly. It was a happy augury for Dr Deshmukh's caste-reform bill, which was reintroduced on 12 February 1946.

When he moved a motion on 6 March 1946 for referring it to a Select Committee, the response it evoked was the very inverse of the previous Assembly's apathy. Though there were still some naysayers, the motion was adopted the same day. Further, the Select Committee report presented by Dr Deshmukh on 30 March 1946 was also unanimously in favour of his bill.

By the time the bill 'as reported by the Select Committee' came up for discussion on 7 November 1946, the interim government of Jawaharlal Nehru had been appointed as part of the process of transfer of power. This proved to be another propitious development for the bill. Instead of a colonial appointee, it was Chakravarti Rajagopalachari, an eminent freedom fighter, who spoke on behalf of the government. This threw up an unusual situation in which Rajaji, speaking as a minister in the Central Legislative Assembly, blamed colonial rule—which had not yet officially ended—for the restrictions that the bill sought to remove.

The marriages were 'illegal according to the orthodox interpretation of the Hindu texts today', Rajaji said. 'Had British courts not been instituted in India and things had been left to the people themselves, the Bill would not have been necessary.' When he blamed the British for 'the petrification so to say of Hindu texts', his own difficult experience of performing his daughter's pratiloma marriage with Gandhi's son must have been on his mind.

Perhaps it was the weight of Rajaji's intervention on 7 November

1946, but the Assembly took only a day to pass the Hindu Marriage Disabilities Removal Bill. The Council of State followed suit on 19 November 1946, again passing the bill in just a day.

It was no coincidence that these events unfolded around the time that the much-awaited Constituent Assembly was to be convened for the first time on 9 December 1946. In the excitement of the political transition, the grip of the orthodox elements over the colonial machinery had weakened, and some reforms got past them. After trying his luck with more such bills, Gopalrao Deshmukh went on to become the first post-Independence mayor of Bombay.

❖

Not long after this unusual surgeon had introduced his bill, a freedom fighter tabled what was by far the most elaborate legislative proposal to reform caste in the context of marriage. Sri Prakasa was among the Congress legislators who had been jailed for their participation in the Gandhi-led Quit India Movement. When he introduced his bill on 6 March 1946,[34] Sri Prakasa was, much like Dr Deshmukh, taking forward a battle that had been initiated by a family member.

His father, Bhagavan Das, had tried a decade earlier to enact the Patel bill. Now titled the Hindu Inter-Caste Marriage Regulating and Validating Bill, Sri Prakasa's bill went further in providing safeguards such as inheritance rights, registration of marriage, raising the marriageable age and the stipulation of monogamy.

The progressive features of his bill found an echo in the report, and the accompanying draft, of the Hindu Code Bill that the revived Rau Committee submitted on 21 January 1947. Reversing its own position on inter-caste marriage that had been taken in 1942, the Rau Committee framed the reform as a return to the forgotten ways of Hindu society. Vindicating the stand that Lowndes had taken during the debate on Patel's bill, the Rau Committee said, 'It is indisputable that marriages between persons of different castes were prevalent in the ancient days, and there is no reason why those who want to revive the old practices should be denied freedom to do so.'[35] This bode well for Sri Prakasa's bill, especially because Rau was now the constitutional advisor to the Constituent Assembly.

On 6 February 1947, Sri Prakasa moved a motion, as was customary, for circulating his bill to elicit public opinion.[36] However, as India had entered the cusp of decolonisation, the sitting of the Central Legislative Assembly on 12 April 1947 turned out to be its last. Sri Prakasa's bill was a casualty of at least two unforeseen circumstances. One, that the British Parliament, while passing the Independence of India Bill in July 1947, fixed a date as early as 15 August 1947 for the transfer of power. Two, consequent to the partition of the country, Sri Prakasa himself was appointed India's first high commissioner to Pakistan.

Meanwhile, a Muslim League member from the untouchable community, Jogendranath Mandal, introduced the Hindu Code Bill as drafted by the Rau Committee on 11 April 1947.[37] He was law minister in the interim government, which had representation from both the Congress and the Muslim League.

Some months later, on 14 August 1947, the Central Legislative Assembly and Council of State ceased to exist as per the terms of the Independence of India Act. Their role was taken over by the Constituent Assembly, which met for the first time on the legislative side on 17 November 1947, with G.V. Mavalankar as its presiding officer.

From then onwards, the Constituent Assembly functioned in two separate capacities. When it was engaged in Constitution-making, it was presided over by Rajendra Prasad. And in its legislative capacity, dealing with issues like the Hindu law reform, it was presided over by Mavalankar. The need for separate presiding officers for the two roles arose because Prasad was also part of the government as minister for Food and Agriculture.

In the very first sitting of the Constituent Assembly in its legislative capacity, Mandal's successor, Law Minister B.R. Ambedkar, moved a motion saying that the consideration of the Hindu Code Bill 'be continued'.[38] A member from the United Provinces, R.V. Dhulekar, raised an objection saying, 'In the new set up we should have no Hindu law and no Muslim law.' He was cut short by Mavalankar, who said that the member could not already be 'speaking on the merits'. Though Ambedkar's motion was adopted without further ado, Dhulekar's objection was a forewarning.

In the aftermath of the violence of Partition, reactionary forces became more vocal than ever before. But then, with Nehru as prime minister and Ambedkar as law minister, Hindu nationalists were unlikely to have the sort of influence over the government that they did thirty years earlier when Vithalbhai Patel's proposal had been defeated.

Even as the Nehru government was pondering reference of the Hindu Code Bill to a Select Committee, a member of the Constituent Assembly from East Punjab, Thakur Das Bhargava, introduced a piecemeal marriage bill. He was the fourth legislator to attempt a reform that validated both Anuloma and Pratiloma marriages, and the first Brahmin to do so—Patel was a Shudra, while Bhagavan Das and Sri Prakasa were both Vaishyas. Though the Deshmukh brothers too were Brahmins, their exertions had been limited to facilitating intra-varna marriages.

On 26 February 1948, barely a month since Gandhi's assassination, Bhargava introduced a bill with the same title as Patel's, the Hindu Marriages Validity Bill.[39] But Bhargava widened the ambit of the bill to cover marriages between 'Hindus, Sikhs, Jains and their different castes and sub-castes'.

Shortly after, the Hindu Code Bill resurfaced. On 9 April 1948, almost a year after Mandal had introduced it, Ambedkar succeeded in referring the bill to a Select Committee, which he would be heading.[40] Four months later, on 12 August 1948, Ambedkar presented the Select Committee report with substantial improvements in the Hindu Code Bill.[41]

Two weeks later, on 25 August 1948, Bhargava deferred the scheduled motion for referring his Hindu Marriages Validity Bill to a Select Committee.[42] He was tied up that day with a prolonged debate over another social reform bill, which proposed tightening the Child Marriage Restraint Act, 1929. Despite expressing his reservations, Ambedkar had supported Bhargava's motion for pushing his child marriage amendments to the Select Committee stage.

At that time, the two were also parallelly engaged in intense backroom negotiations related to the drafting of the Constitution—in particular, the peculiarly Hindu but Gandhi-backed abhorrence of cow slaughter, arguably the most controversial provision in the Constitution. As a result of those negotiations with Ambedkar, on 24 November 1948, Bhargava moved an amendment to shift the restrictions on cow slaughter from the Fundamental Rights section to the non-binding Directive Principles of State Policy. Calling his text 'an agreed amendment' and Ambedkar's 'manufacture', Bhargava disclosed that it was 'the desire of Ambedkar that this matter, instead of being included in fundamental rights should be incorporated in the directive principles'.[43]

On 11 February 1949, the Constituent Assembly, in its legislative capacity, took up, at last, Bhargava's motion on referring his bill to a Select Committee.[44] It was the first time since Independence that the highest legislature in the country discussed the vexed issue of inter-caste marriage. More significantly, in the recurring debates on it since 1918, it was the first time that none of the legislators raised a single objection to the idea of allowing marriages across caste lines.

That the legislators this time happened to be India's founding fathers and mothers couldn't be the only reason that caste purity was no longer touted as a nationalist cause. In the face of the other radical changes that the Hindu Code Bill threatened to bring about (such as divorce and equal share to daughters), even the Hindu nationalists had ceded the battle against this unnatural restriction on inter-caste marriage. They also found Bhargava's proposal of legalising marriages of Hindus with Sikhs and Jains compliant with their strategic object of consolidating the majority community.

In his appeal to the Assembly, Thakur Das Bhargava drew examples from the ground, bearing out the need to bring Sikhs and Jains under the umbrella of the Hindu law. A native of Hissar, now in Haryana, Bhargava said that, in Punjab, 'marriages between Sikhs and Hindus have been held to be valid not by courts but by society in general'. Likewise, there were matrimonial alliances between Jains and Hindus, 'especially Jain Aggarwals and Hindu Aggarwals, but it is doubtful', he said, 'if a Jain Aggarwal could marry validly a Shudra or a Brahmin'.

Among the legislators who unanimously spoke in favour of the bill were K.M. Munshi, Kengal Hanumanthaiah, Bakshi Tek Chand and Mahavir Tyagi. The one note of dissonance came, surprisingly, from Ambedkar, whose own Hindu Code Bill had been pending before the Assembly for six months after its revision by the Select Committee. Ambedkar's 'only objection' to Bhargava's bill was on a principle invoked by his colonial predecessors too: when the larger codification was on the anvil, 'it is wrong now to proceed piecemeal with the legislation'.

Bhargava countered principle with pragmatism. Presciently, he said, 'It is doubtful if it will be passed in this session, next session or some other session.' On the other hand, if his relatively modest bill was passed, it might 'pave the way' for the enactment of the larger one and would serve to validate the inter-caste marriages that took place meanwhile.

He also referred to the pratiloma marriage that Ambedkar himself had conducted, through the secular route, about ten months earlier with a Brahmin doctor who had been taking care of him. 'I am only helping Dr. Ambedkar whose marriage also will be legalized by this Bill.' Ambedkar probably reacted with amusement to the reference to his personal life, as Bhargava went on to say, 'Why should he laugh at this? This may or may not be applicable to him, yet the disabilities if any will be removed.'

When the Hindu Code Bill came up for discussion a fortnight later, on 25 February, Bhargava took pains to 'congratulate Dr. Ambedkar for his accepting in this Bill the principle of the abolition of caste in marriages and adoption'.[45] He framed it as an existential issue: 'If anything has ruined India, marred her progress and became an instrument in creating Pakistan, it is this caste system ... As far as the question of inter-marriages is concerned, till this question is not resolved, the problem of nation-building in India cannot be solved.'

Bhargava's crusade against caste paid off a month later. The only significant change that the Select Committee had made to the Bhargava bill was the addition of the term 'sect' to the categories that could intermarry. So, his bill was now about allowing mixed marriages between parties belonging to 'different religions, castes, sub-castes or sects'. The bill came up again before the Constituent Assembly on 4 April 1949.[46] Speaking through Minister of Works, Mining and Power N.V. Gadgil, the government declared its support for Bhargava's bill without making an issue about the pending Hindu Code Bill.

In his concluding remarks, Bhargava recalled Vithalbhai Patel's pioneering role in this regard. 'He is the original mover of this Bill and if tradition allows, I would like to call this Bill the Patel Hindu Marriages Validity Bill.' It was a fitting tribute to the lesser-known Patel brother that, for once, India's national legislature had denounced the caste system without any qualification or dissenting voice. And, matching words with action, it passed the bill that struck at the sanctity of endogamy, validating even pratiloma marriages.

The greatest repudiation yet of Manu and other ancient law givers, the Hindu Marriages Validity Act, 1949 was possibly the most progressive legislation enacted in the half-light phase between India's political emancipation and the enforcement of its Constitution. The magnitude of this achievement became clearer two years later when the Nehru government, under pressure from the orthodox sections, shelved its Hindu Code project. The setback caused Ambedkar to resign in a huff.

Ironically enough, the only way that the government could revive the process of reforming Hindu law was by reverting to piecemeal legislation. And even that it was emboldened to do only after securing a popular mandate in the first general election held in 1951–52.

As the first of four such piecemeal legislations, Section 30 of the Hindu Marriage Act, 1955 repealed the pathbreaking 1946 and 1949 enactments as well as a clutch of state laws. Section 29(1) of the 1955 Act provided protection to all those who had taken advantage of these laws in the early years of the decolonised country or were entitled to benefit from them. It said: 'A marriage solemnised between Hindus before the commencement of this Act, which is otherwise valid, shall not be deemed to be invalid or ever to have been invalid by reason only of the fact that the parties thereto belonged to the same Gotra or Pravara or belonged to different religions, castes or sub-divisions of the same caste.' This is all that remains on the statute book of the many stirring battles fought from 1918 to 1949 to validate inter-caste marriage.

The impact of the 1949 enactment can be gauged from the judgments that continued to be delivered under it well after it had been repealed. In 1963, the Supreme Court upheld retrospective application of the law to validate a marriage between a Brahmin woman and a Shudra in the Madras state.[47] In the context of a property dispute, it confirmed the legitimacy of the children from such a marriage, although there was no reference to this vital aspect in the 1949 law.

In the judgment authored by Justice K.C. Das Gupta, the Supreme Court ruled that it 'validated marriages that had taken place before the Act between parties belonging to different castes, sub-castes and sects'. Further, 'It is idle to contend that the object of the legislature was only to regularise the status of the husband and the wife. That certainly was part of the object. But equally important, or perhaps more important object was that the children of the marriages would become legitimate.'

For the licence acquired by Hindus to marry across castes, none of the legislators who had fought long and hard battles, from Patel to Bhargava, got their due in history. In the dominant narrative, it is only one more of the reforms introduced by the Nehru government through its comprehensive law on Hindu marriage.

3

ACCESS BARRIERS

9

THE EXCLUSIVITY OF PUBLIC PLACES

Two dramatic and far-reaching exchanges, each between an Indian and a colonial administrator, took place in 1919 on two successive days over 2,000 km apart, in Lahore and Madras. In different ways, the two conversations set benchmarks for governance.

The first, in Lahore on 19 November 1919, followed the Jallianwala Bagh massacre in the neighbouring city of Amritsar seven months earlier. The massacre of an assembly of peaceful and unarmed persons, protesting a wave of repressive measures in the wake of the Rowlatt legislation, had dealt a blow to the moral pretensions of the colonial government.

Given the rage across Punjab and beyond, Secretary of State for India Edwin Montagu pressured Viceroy Lord Chelmsford to institute an inquiry. More remarkably, Montagu insisted that the inquiry committee consist of both European and Indian members. With the object of restoring confidence, the committee, headed by a former solicitor general of Scotland, Lord William Hunter, examined most of its witnesses in the open.

Among the few exceptions to this policy was Lieutenant Governor Michael O'Dwyer, the highest colonial authority in Punjab. Though it had not baulked at summoning him, the Hunter Committee examined O'Dwyer in-camera. This veil of secrecy was not extended to Brigadier-General Reginald Dyer, the officer who had ordered the firing in which about 400 Indians, by the official count, had been killed at Jallianwala Bagh. During his testimony, each of the eight committee members, including three Indians, took turns to interrogate Dyer. Since his evidence had been recorded entirely in public, there was little scope to conceal any information that could shame the British Raj. The colonial administration had set a standard of accountability for State actors in the context of mass violence.

That standard proved too exacting for post-colonial India, however. Take the two inquiries instituted in the wake of the massacres of minorities in Delhi in 1984 and in Gujarat in 2002. Each of those inquiries conducted by a Supreme Court judge dealt with allegations against the leader on whose watch the massacre in question had taken place, Rajiv Gandhi and Narendra Modi, respectively. Yet, the two commissions, one headed by Justice Ranganath Misra and the other by Justice G.T. Nanavati, exonerated the political leader concerned without even summoning him, let alone questioning him in public.[1]

Post-colonial rulers have generally been shielded by judicial inquiries into their culpability, a tendency that involves a complex web of reasons. Perhaps one reason is the institutional memory, even if subconscious, of the political damage that the British Raj suffered because Dyer had been subjected to such unsparing scrutiny.

The combativeness of Chimanlal Setalvad,[2] one of the Indian members of the Hunter Committee, was pivotal to unravelling the corrosive truth of Jallianwala Bagh as he examined Dyer in the witness box. The remarkable exchange[3] between Setalvad and Dyer took place on 19 November 1919 after Dyer had already conceded, in response to questions from Lord Hunter, that 'a good many' in the crowd might not have heard of his ban on the meeting and that he could have 'dispersed them perhaps even without firing'.

Drawing on these disclosures, Setalvad baited him, causing him to testify more recklessly. He asked Dyer if the casualties would not have been higher had the passage leading to Jallianwala Bagh been broad enough to let Dyer take inside the two armoured cars mounted with machine guns that had accompanied him to the venue. Unaccustomed to having a native call him out, the arch imperialist ended up responding to what he could well have shrugged off as a hypothetical line of questioning. Dyer affirmed that he 'probably' would have used those deadlier weapons too had the passage been wider. 'Call it what you like, I was going to punish them. My idea from the military point of view was to make a wide impression.'

Though the peaceful crowd at Jallianwala Bagh had violated no more than a curfew order, Dyer gloated that 'throughout the Punjab, I wanted to reduce their morale; the morale of the rebels'.

This prompted Setalvad to ask, 'Did it occur to you that by adopting this method of "frightfulness"—excuse the term—you were really doing a great disservice to the British Raj by driving discontent deep?'

The question unhinged Dyer further. Portraying his firing as 'a merciful though horrible act', he said, 'I thought I would be doing a jolly lot of good and they would realise that they were not to be wicked.'

On 20 November 1919, just a day after Setalvad had put paid to Dyer, legally as well as morally, there was an equally significant exchange in Madras between an Indian legislator and a colonial administrator. But the honours were even this time, allowing the British to regain some moral ground and to set another benchmark in governance. The argument[4] was about a longstanding inequity of Hindu society: untouchability.

The Indian interlocutor, Mylai Chinna Thambi Rajah, better known as M.C. Rajah, was himself an untouchable and the first-ever legislator in British India from those who were officially labelled the Depressed Classes. Given that upper castes had no role in his elevation to the Madras Legislative Council, Rajah had little reason to tip-toe around untouchability. He lost no time in proposing a resolution on untouchability, probably inspired by the precedent that had been set by Maneckji Dadabhoy in 1916 in the Central legislature.

Rajah initiated the debate on the heels of his nomination to the Madras Legislative Council, which had been reconstituted on 5 August 1919. His main respondent in that chamber was the governor of the Madras Presidency, Lord Willingdon, the very dignitary who had nominated him. Willingdon responded in his ex-officio capacity as the president of the Madras Legislative Council. Before the 1919 Montagu–Chelmsford reforms, the governor of the province, who was its executive head, was also the presiding officer of its legislature. The principle of 'separation of powers' was as yet at a rudimentary stage in India.

The very idea of a debate in a legislature between an untouchable, the lowest of the low among natives, and a colonial ruler, the head of a large province, was hitherto inconceivable. If this still happened, it was because of a promise that had been made three years earlier in the Imperial Legislative Council, persuading Maneckji Dadabhoy to withdraw his resolution. Among all the British provinces, the follow-up to that promise—to undertake measures ameliorating the condition of the Depressed Classes—was most perceptible in the Madras Presidency.

The highlight of these measures was Rajah's nomination. At the time, conferring on an untouchable the honour of serving as a lawmaker was a revolutionary move. Caste Hindus, accustomed to treating untouchables as less than human, were not exempt from addressing him with the honorific 'the Honourable Mr Rajah'. When Willingdon made this civilisational breakthrough, it went beyond the object of the Madras-based Justice Party, which had been founded in 1916 for 'securing to the Non-Brahmins adequate representation' in the legislatures and other public bodies.[5] Focused as they were on countering Brahmin hegemony, non-Brahmins were yet to recognise that, in their own category, untouchables were the most deserving of special care.

Willingdon was ahead of the Indian National Congress too as it had been reluctant to place the issue of untouchability on the agenda of its negotiations with the government. It had taken a position on untouchables only once, at its 1917 annual session in Calcutta. And even that 1917 resolution was addressed not to the government, but to 'the people of India', casting on them the onus of 'removing all disabilities imposed by custom upon the Depressed Classes'.

The Madras governor's radical step might have been inspired by the buzz around the Montagu–Chelmsford reforms, which the British Parliament was in the process of enacting as the Government of India Act, 1919. One of the big leaps it made, while providing greater representation to Indians, was the introduction of statutory quotas for untouchables and other marginalised sections in provincial legislatures. Willingdon's nomination of Rajah in 1919 anticipated this constitutional reform that would manifest two years later, with the launch of the enlarged Legislative Councils.

Besides being a leading member at the time of the Justice Party, Rajah was a Paraiyan, a member of the untouchable community that the British were most familiar with as it was concentrated in districts close to the Madras city. So much so that this Tamil-speaking community had by then entered the English lexicon: pariah, an outcast.

In any case, Rajah was no token diversity nominee. His worthiness was evident from the way he launched his legislative career by proposing a pair of ambitious resolutions concerning the untouchables. Rajah's resolutions were following the precedents set in July that year by two upper-caste legislators from the Bombay Presidency.

On 8 July 1919, D.V. Belvi, a Congress member from Belgaum, moved a resolution[6] which, going beyond the party line, urged the Bombay government to 'make it compulsory' for all municipalities and local bodies to take up measures to address untouchability. Belvi's resolution called upon those public institutions 'either to throw open the existing wells and dharmashalas owned by them to members of the untouchable classes, or to maintain separate wells and dharmashalas for their use'.

If his resolution envisaged maintenance of separate amenities for untouchables as an alternative to equal access, Belvi was perhaps influenced by a corresponding practice in the US. Under the so-called Jim Crow laws enacted in reaction to the abolition of slavery, the southern states in the US institutionalised racial segregation in almost every sphere of life.

In its ambit, Rajah's resolution was much like Belvi's—it too sought the opening up only of secular spaces, given that temple-entry would be an even more sensitive issue. However, he made a couple of changes, one terminological and the other substantive. Rajah replaced 'dharmashalas' with 'choultries', the Madras equivalent of what served then as an inn. More vitally, in the light of his own lived experience as an outcast, Rajah could not accept Belvi's compromise alternative of maintaining separate facilities for untouchables. Instead, in a bid to mitigate access inequality without acquiescing to segregation, he suggested that wells could be more strategically located.

Rajah's resolution was as follows: 'This Council recommends to His Excellency the Governor in Council to make it compulsory on all municipalities and local boards in this Presidency to remove all restrictions which prevent the use of public wells and choultries by the members of the Depressed Classes, and to construct more wells in places adjacent to their dwellings.'[7]

The other Bombay precedent that Rajah followed had been set by R.P. Paranjpye, an educationist and rationalist born in a Brahmin family in Ratnagiri.[8] He moved a resolution for providing due representation to untouchables through nominations to local bodies governing cities and villages. Unlike Belvi's initiative on the access issue, Paranjpye's resolution was adopted by the Bombay Legislative Council—only the second untouchability-related resolution to have been carried by a legislature anywhere in the country.[9] The first, in 1917, was moved by a Telugu-speaking lawmaker in the United Provinces, C.Y. Chintamani, regarding 'a policy of active encouragement of education among the Depressed Classes'.

Rajah was, in fact, not the only Madras legislator to have been inspired by the Bombay precedents. Around the same time, a caste Hindu councillor too proposed two resolutions on the lines of those moved by Belvi and Paranjpye. A member of the reformist Brahmo Samaj, Mahipati Surya Rao shared Rajah's concerns. He was the raja of Pithapuram, a zamindar belonging to the dominant Velama caste near Cocanada (now Kakinada) in the Telugu-speaking part of the Madras Presidency.

So, Willingdon, in his capacity as president of the Madras Legislative Council, needed to allocate time for four untouchability-related resolutions on 20 November 1919. He proposed that similar resolutions be clubbed in what he considered 'a fairer way of dealing with the business before us', that is, to have only one discussion on each of the two subjects. Accordingly, he asked Surya Rao to move the resolution on the representation issue and Rajah on the access issue. The one on representation was taken up first.[10]

While seconding it, Rajah said, 'My task is lightened by one not belonging to my community, undertaking out of purely disinterested motives, to plead for justice to my community.' Referring to Surya Rao's social privilege, Rajah said: '(W)hen that person happens to be a cultured member of the landed aristocracy, I feel that the day is not far off when justice will be done to my community even though difficulties confronting us at the present moment may seem insuperable.'

There was no dissenting voice in the Legislative Council. But Muhammad Habibullah, a member of Willingdon's Executive Council, sprang a surprise, saying that the government preferred Rajah's phraseology on the matter. 'I think it will please the Hon'ble Mr Rajah if I tell him that Government are quite prepared to accept the Resolution that stands in his name,' Habibullah said. He added that, since 'the intention of the Government in this matter is known, the Hon'ble Raja of Pithapuram will have no hesitation in withdrawing his Resolution'. He explained 'the impracticality of giving effect to' Surya Rao's suggestion that the government should 'ensure the adequate representation of Depressed Classes'. Rajah's resolution was less categorical, merely urging the government to 'issue instructions to District Collectors asking them to nominate suitable men from the Depressed Classes'.

Based on practicability in a caste-ridden society, it was Rajah's resolution on representation that was carried by the Madras Legislative Council. This made it the first resolution ever to be adopted by any legislature in India at the instance of a lawmaker from among the untouchables.

Next, as scheduled, Rajah moved his resolution on access inequality. This one proved to be contentious, though. The confrontation over it between Rajah and Willingdon showcased the difficulties that the colonial administration faced in taking on caste prejudice.

In his opening remarks on the denial of access to space as a facet of untouchability, Rajah's ire was directed at not just caste Hindus but also Willingdon. This was because in the run-up to the discussion in the Council, Willingdon had aired misgivings about Rajah's resolution at a public meeting. His misgivings evidently arose from file notings on the subject, particularly an adverse note by Charles Todhunter, the home member in his Executive Council. 'Caste cannot be abolished in a day and any attempt to go too far in advance of public opinion,' Todhunter had cautioned, 'may well do more harm than good.'[11]

Rajah said it was 'very unfortunate' that Willingdon should have referred to his resolution in terms that had been construed as 'unsympathetic' and 'indications of Government's sense of its own helplessness'. As a result, 'I am left to argue before a Government which has made up its mind before it has heard me speak on this Resolution'. Likewise, referring to caste Hindu councillors, Rajah added that it was his lot 'to plead before opponents and critics who would only be too glad to take the cue on this matter from Your Excellency's words'.[12]

Making a case for British support, Rajah remarked acidly, 'While the higher castes are indulging in transcendental politics and nation-building, we are denied the elementary rights of citizenship [such as walking on] the king's highway and drawing water from public wells, places to which every man and woman ought to have free access [by] virtue of their citizenship.'

Countering untouchability with the Western notion of citizenship, he pointed out that there was no policy of discrimination, at least overtly, in colonial institutions such as 'public schools, post offices and courts'. Rajah was aggrieved that, despite such 'precedents and analogous cases', Willingdon had surrendered to 'public opinion' when it came to other public places. He quoted the president of the Council as saying ahead of this debate that, 'on all these questions the Government could pass orders but it is quite impossible for Government to absolutely enforce these orders; that must be subject to the public opinion right throughout the Presidency'.

Accusing the government of abandoning the lower castes to the tender mercies of the upper castes, Rajah thundered: 'Are our rights to be sacrificed simply because a silly people priding themselves on their imaginary religious superiority are to be humoured and their so-called religious scruples which are really the fetters with which they seek to enslave others to be left undisturbed? Is caste-arrogance not only to have its way but also to receive Government recognition?'

Rajah recalled that the same colonial rule had 'abolished Sati' and, in a less-touted reform milestone achieved through the IPC, 'made the Brahmin subject to the penalties of the criminal laws equally with the Panchama'. The point of referring to those old achievements was to raise a sharp question: 'How often has this public opinion not been ignored, if not set at defiance, when the Government was anxious to pass a Bill on which it has set its heart?'

Although he remained a staunch Hindu all his life, Rajah tactically extolled the virtues of Christianity. 'We have hitherto looked upon the British Government with its Christian ideals as our saviours; is that Government now going to hand us over to those who have oppressed us in the past and will do so again if they get the opportunity?' He was referring to the democratic half-measure under the Montagu–Chelmsford reforms that would place a part of the provincial government in the hands of elected Indians, i.e., caste Hindus.

Since the Panchamas had been counselled to 'put up with their exclusion from the use of public wells until a remote date', Rajah dismissed the ongoing exercise of constitutional reforms as 'a big political reconstruction calculated to appease the high caste Hindus'. He concluded by challenging the nationalist approach of steering clear of social reform until the attainment of political freedom. 'If public opinion has not advanced far enough to allow the Panchama his elementary rights of citizenship, is India, I ask, fit for any scheme of representative Government?'

About a dozen councillors, British and Indian, participated in the debate that followed. Every one of them began by piously expressing sympathy for the humanitarian spirit underlying Rajah's resolution. But on the issue of voting, which was what mattered, the pattern was rather different. Only one of those who spoke, a Christian missionary called E.M. Macphail, said that he would vote in favour of the resolution. The predominant view, expressed in different ways, reflected the spirit of the 1917 Congress Resolution: that it was for caste Hindus themselves, rather than the colonial government, to grapple with untouchability.

Todhunter, unsurprisingly, was among those who publicly urged Rajah to withdraw his resolution. Tracing the evolution of the Hindu social-reform movement in Madras over twenty-five years, Todhunter said that there was a common thread running through all the changes—the insistence of caste Hindus 'that they do not want Government help and that the reform is one that must come from within the community'.

Willingdon's advance comments on Rajah's resolution had reaffirmed, in Todhunter's interpretation, that 'we all want to see India [as] a nation, and the first step in national efficiency is the fusion of the classes and the removal of the distinction between touchables and untouchables'. But the question was, he added rhetorically, 'can Government really do any good towards this end?'

His own answer was that the government had no role unless it was a colonial enactment that was found to be discriminatory. By way of an example, Todhunter cited a bill that had been passed the previous day by the same Legislative Council, to remove a form of punishment that discriminated against the lower castes. Conceding that 'if there are any statutory disabilities, they should be removed', Todhunter said, 'The only thing I can think of is the punishment in the stocks which we have just abolished.'

On the other hand, to justify the government's inaction on disabilities arising from custom, Todhunter referred to a letter published in a newspaper two days earlier. It was from Kesava Pillai, a former legislator who was the first to have sought the repeal of punishment by confinement in the stocks. Todhunter quoted Pillai as saying, 'No resolution and no law can easily be enforced in villages in the interior to make the public wells common to all as against the traditional prejudices of ages.'

Drawing legitimacy from such caste Hindu social reformers, Todhunter cautioned, 'If we are to support the low caste man in breaking caste rules by police action, and as it were to enforce pollution, we shall be laying up a very great deal of trouble for everybody concerned.' Having argued that for 'the removal of the bar imposed by caste ... the main action lies with the social reformers', Todhunter said that it was 'doubtful if Government interference would really help forward a movement which has travelled so far under its own impetus'.

Todhunter was followed by B.V. Narasimha Ayyar, who had, picking up the baton from Pillai, forced the government to repeal the punishment of lower castes by confinement in the stocks. He was, however, sceptical about Rajah's demand because he believed that caste restrictions in public spaces did not affect untouchables alone: 'The restrictions exist between caste Hindus themselves.' A choultry built for the benefit of one caste was, he argued, unlikely to be open to those from other castes. So 'the effect of removing the restrictions' in the manner proposed by Rajah 'means that wells and choultries will be used by the Panchamas only'. Warning against the perils of unintended consequences, Ayyar asked, 'Is it our object to penalise all those people who have got this prejudice unfortunately and is that feasible or reasonable?'

Having anticipated such reservations from caste Hindus, Lord Willingdon weighed in, this time formally, on Rajah's resolution. Pointing out that 'there is such a thing in this country as custom and caste', he said that 'until those two things are diminished, it is quite impossible for my Honourable friend to get the equality which I think his community should get at the earliest opportunity'. Willingdon was signalling that he was on the side of untouchables even as he pleaded helplessness in the face of caste Hindu intransigence.

It was in this spirit that he made a qualified admission of the colonial regime's duty towards untouchables. 'We will do everything in our power to see that equality is brought about.' In the same breath, he entered a caveat, saying that 'we are not going to interfere with anything that tends in any way to any interference with the religious scruples of any community'.

The colonial administrator was aggrieved that Rajah did not appreciate the fine line he was treading to uplift untouchables without hurting Hindu sentiment. 'I am pained that my Honourable friend in his opening speech rather suggested all the time that Government were a wicked body; they were not paying attention to his community; they were even antagonistic.' Alluding to the irony of his own nominee from the untouchable community making such allegations, Willingdon said, 'I would ask him whether his presence here is not evidence of a contrary feeling on the part of Government. It is a little hard that he should have taken up this attitude in regard to this Government.'

Further, he said that, unless Rajah's compatriots appreciated 'the desirability of India becoming a nation and of every community being on equal terms, it is extremely difficult for Government to do anything of a serious nature.' Willingdon doubted whether even the resolution that had just been adopted on representation for untouchables in local bodies was feasible. To elucidate, he referred to two councillors, T. Desikachari and N. Subba Rao, who had participated in the debate on access and were also presidents of District Boards. On the one hand, he said charitably, 'I am perfectly sure that they are absolutely sincere and they have done a great deal for the benefit of this particular community.' On the other, he pointed out: 'But have they done the most important thing? Have they got a member of the Depressed Classes into the District Board?'

Revelling in the moral authority he had acquired by nominating an untouchable to a high forum, Willingdon lectured caste Hindu councillors. 'Those are the sort of things which I wish Honourable Members to do. Let them not make any speeches, but let them show that they are anxious about this particular matter; but far more if they will show by action that they are anxious, then we shall get on very much faster.'

The irony of a colonial ruler berating the Indian elite for being trapped in prejudice was not lost on Rajah. But deferring to Willingdon's assurance that the government would do 'everything in their power to further the community in future', Rajah withdrew his resolution. It stood little chance of being adopted anyway, as almost all the councillors who participated in the debate, whether Indian or British, indicated that their sympathy would not translate into votes.

Thus ended the second of the two far-reaching exchanges of 1919. If the first involving Setalvad and Dyer had set a benchmark for transparency and accountability, the second between Rajah and Willingdon set one for inclusive governance and social justice. This paved the way for incrementally providing access to untouchables to a range of public places.

❖

In their separate reports, the European and Indian members of the Hunter Committee indicted Dyer in varying degrees, leading to his disgraceful exit from the Army as well as India. The support he received in London within the House of Lords sparked further outrage across the colony. It was one of the factors that prompted Mahatma Gandhi to launch the Non-Cooperation Movement in a special session of the Congress held in Calcutta on 4 September 1920. The most controversial aspect of his call was to boycott the upcoming national and provincial elections that were to be held under the Montagu–Chelmsford reforms. The elections went ahead as scheduled in November 1920 despite the boycott by India's largest political party.

At its annual session held in the last week of 1920 in Nagpur, the Congress retaliated by extending the boycott call to schools, courts and foreign trade. Integral to this first-ever attempt at mass mobilisation across the country was a belated admission of the nexus between Hinduism and untouchability. It was a departure from the Congress's 1917 resolution, which had made out that the source of untouchability was merely 'disabilities imposed by custom'. The 1920 resolution was more forthright about the role of religion—it began by addressing 'the people of India' generally but concluded with a special appeal from Hindus to Hindus regarding caste and untouchability. Such a gesture of inclusivity within the Hindu community, along with a call for Hindu–Muslim unity, was also a political compulsion at a time when the Congress under Gandhi was exhorting all sections of the population to join the Non-Cooperation Movement.

Moved by Chitta Ranjan Das and seconded by Gandhi, the resolution said that 'the Hindu delegates of this Congress call upon the leading Hindus to settle all disputes between Brahmins and non-Brahmins, wherever they may be existing, and to make a special effort to rid Hinduism of the reproach of untouchability'. In a further admission that the problem had a religious origin, the resolution adopted on 30 December 1920 said that the Congress 'respectfully urges the religious heads to help the growing desire to reform Hinduism in the matter of its treatment of the suppressed classes'.

However, the Congress party lagged behind the non-Brahmin-driven Justice Party and even the British Raj on the issue of social justice, especially diversity in representation. After nominating M.C. Rajah to the Madras Legislative Council, the government was working on reserving constituencies for non-Brahmins and a separate quota for nominating untouchables to provincial legislatures. These quotas reflected demographic variations and were specified in the separate rules that were framed for each province under the Government of India Act, 1919. Rules thus framed for Madras in regard to the quota for untouchables encompassed those living in four linguistic regions: Tamil, Telugu, Kannada and Malayalam. The

Madras rules stipulated that five untouchables would be nominated from the following communities: Paraiyans, Pallans, Valluvans, Malas, Madigas, Chakkiliyans, Tottiyans, Cherumans and Holeyas.[13]

Nominations were made for the first time under these statutory quotas in January 1921 when the enlarged Legislative Councils came into existence. In this set-up, the first legislator to raise the issue of access inequality was not one of the five untouchable legislators, but a Nadar. A beneficiary of the reserved constituencies for non-Brahmins, W.P.A. Soundarapandian Nadar hailed from a lower Shudra caste that had suffered some of the disabilities of untouchability on account of its traditional occupation of toddy-tapping. On 4 August 1921, Nadar moved a resolution in the Madras Legislative Council.[14]

It was more ambitious than the one Rajah had moved earlier. Nadar, who was also a member of the Justice Party, proposed a law penalising those who obstructed untouchables. In another first, Nadar included roads in his list of public places, thereby recognising unapproachability as an element of the untouchability practised in south India.

Nadar's resolution said: 'That this Council recommends to the Government to bring in legislation in the near future, penalising any kind of obstruction, in using public roads, public chatrams, wells, schools, etc., by people irrespective of caste and creed.'

In view of the relative deepening of democracy since Rajah's abortive resolution a year and a half ago, Nadar was optimistic that the situation was now 'ripe' for legislating on the issue of access. This was because, he said, 'the nation has during these days grown much older and much wiser than by a year and a half'.

Nominated afresh, Rajah was among the councillors who spoke in favour of Nadar's resolution. As before, there were dissenting voices. The difference this time was that, under the new dyarchy system, the Cabinet of each provincial governor comprised a mix of 'members' and 'ministers'. While members were, as before, colonial nominees from among Britons and even Indians, ministers were appointed from among the Indians who had been elected to the

Legislative Council. Further, while members dealt with 'reserved subjects' (such as police, finance, revenue and irrigation), ministers dealt with 'transferred subjects' (such as local self-government, public health and education).

In the Madras Presidency, the Justice Party had won the election, a foregone conclusion in the absence of Congress participation. Panaganti Rama Rayaningar—also called the Raja of Panagal, a zamindar from the temple town of Srikalahasti in the Telugu-speaking district of Chittoor—was the chief minister of the Madras Presidency, the head of the 'popularly responsible', or elected, section of the dyarchy. As he held the portfolio of local self-government, the chief minister was the government's voice in the debate. In his earlier avatar as a member of the Imperial Legislative Council, Rayaningar had backed Maneckji Dadabhoy's abortive 1916 resolution on untouchability.

Having since acquired State authority, Rayaningar now appeared a touch wary of Nadar's resolution. In fact, he echoed Todhunter's stand on Rajah's 1919 resolution. Affirming that 'those who obstruct the Depressed Classes from using public roads, wells, etc. will come within the purview of the Penal Code', Rayaningar said that 'any new legislation does not therefore appear to be necessary to penalise the obstruction'. Much like his British predecessor, Rayaningar said, 'The real bar is the bar of social tyranny and that must be broken by social reform.'

Accordingly, he declined Nadar's plea to the government to enact a law on the matter. Passing the buck to private members, Rayaningar said: 'If however new legislation is found necessary to remove the disabilities of the Depressed Classes, I assure the House that the Government have no objection to any member introducing a Bill.'

In other words, Nadar had wrested an admission from the dyarchy that the resolution was not without merit. Yet, he was prepared to push a chief minister from his own party only so far. Just as Rajah had withdrawn his resolution on the basis of Willingdon's assurance, Nadar withdrew his on the basis of Rayaningar's assurance.

About four months later, on 28 November 1921, a legislator from Central Provinces and Berar, Kalicharan Nandagaoli, an untouchable himself, moved a resolution on access equality.[15] He had already succeeded in getting a couple of his untouchability-related resolutions adopted. And the one he moved on the access issue was relatively modest in that it did not ask for any legislative backup.

All that Nandagaoli sought was a proclamation of equality. 'This Council is of opinion that the Depressed Classes should enjoy the same privileges as other communities do, in making use of wells, dharamshalas (serais), ghats on tanks and water pipes already built or which may be built in future at the expense of the public funds in the Central Provinces and Berar.'

Deviating from the Madras precedent of that same year, the provincial government in Nagpur responded through not a minister but a member of the Executive Council. So, rather than an elected Indian representative, A.E. Nelson, a British nominee, replied in the Legislative Council. Unlike Willingdon in the Rajah debate and Rayaningar in the Nadar debate, Nelson did not hold out any assurance of the government's intentions nor did he ask Nandagaoli to withdraw his resolution.

Instead, he left it entirely to Indian legislators to decide the fate of Nandagaoli's resolution. 'Government desires on this occasion to leave the decision of this question to the vote of the non-official members of this Council, on whom it will rest to decide what opinion should be recorded as the opinion of this Council.' So, the motion was put to vote. As only ten Indian members voted in favour of it and twenty-three against it, the motion was lost.

❖

Although the Congress had sat out these debates, it joined them belatedly through its party forum. Its fresh resolution on untouchability followed an announcement that the Non-Cooperation Movement had been withdrawn. Gandhi had insisted on suddenly withdrawing the movement on 12 February 1922 in response to the mass murder of policemen at Chauri Chaura in the Gorakhpur district of the United Provinces. After calling off the movement at its meeting at Bardoli in the Gujarat region, the Congress Working Committee (CWC) resolved to provide untouchables 'the ordinary facilities which the other citizens enjoy'.

Where such basic equality was still unthinkable, it envisaged segregation as an alternative. The CWC Resolution said that 'where the prejudice against the untouchables is still strong in places ... separate wells must be maintained out of Congress funds'. The redeeming feature to that alternative was the caveat that 'every effort should be made [meanwhile] ... to persuade the people to allow the untouchables to use the common wells'.

Bardoli showed that the political mainstream had finally woken up to the moral imperative of letting untouchables access public places. This augured well for the ongoing attempts in various legislatures against restrictions on access. In the next milestone of this legislative struggle, social reformer S.K. Bole moved a resolution in the Bombay Legislative Council on 4 August 1923.[16]

Bole belonged to the Bhandari community, a Shudra caste that, like the Nadars and Ezhavas in south India, was traditionally associated with toddy-tapping. His proposal stood out for its division into two categories of the places that he wanted untouchables to be 'allowed to use'. The first consisted of 'all public watering places, wells and dharamsalas', and the second of 'public schools, courts, offices and dispensaries'.

His resolution gave no indication of the basis on which he had classified those places. A lawmaker from Bombay city, A.N. Surve, sought to fill that gap by moving an amendment. Surve suggested that the first category of public places—watering places, wells and dharamsalas—should be thrown open to untouchables only if they were 'built and maintained out of public funds' or were 'administered by bodies appointed by Government or created by statute'.

Surve's explanation was that some of those places could have been 'in their inception private, but are public now, in the sense that a particular section of the public has unrestricted use of them, and are not maintained out of the public funds of local bodies'. He spelt out the legal implications of this distinction. 'By custom, some people have obtained exclusive right of easement over them, and in such cases even Government, I am afraid, will have no power to compel them to admit Mahars and other members of the Depressed Classes to them.'

The sprinkling of democracy through dyarchy showed signs, at last, of emboldening the colonial regime to deal with the age-old problem of access denial. Since it covered a wide range of public places, the Bole Resolution called for action by more than one department. Thanks to the dyarchic arrangement, the government's participation in the debate involved two ministers and one member of Governor George Lloyd's Executive Council.

The first to speak on behalf of the government was a Muslim: Minister for Local Self-Government Ghulam Hussain Hidayatullah, who had been elected from Sindh, the northern part of the Bombay Presidency. As the leader of a regional party, he went on to become Sindh's first premier in 1937, following its separation from Bombay the year before. After joining the Muslim League, Hidayatullah also became Sindh's first governor in Pakistan.

Hidayatullah disclosed that the government was prepared to accept Bole's resolution with the changes that Surve had proposed. He rejected outright the counterargument that opening up public places built or supported with public funds would wound 'religious susceptibilities'. Hidayatullah clarified: 'But this is not a question of religion at all. It is a question of the civic rights of certain sections of the people.'

Speaking next on behalf of the government was none other than Education Minister R.P. Paranjpye, a man who had long been engaged in battling untouchability. He recalled that, around the time his motion dealing with another aspect of untouchability had been passed in 1919, there was one by Belvi on the access issue, which had been rejected by twenty-two votes to fourteen. Paranjpye did not merely reaffirm the government's support for Bole's resolution as modified by Surve. He appealed to the Council 'to accept the Resolution wholeheartedly, leaving it to the tact of the Government officers and good sense of local people to give effect as fully as possible'.

The imperial section of the dyarchy in Bombay was represented by Home Member Maurice Hayward. While backing the 'general policy' of allowing equal access to public places, Hayward cautioned that 'we must be very careful ... not to infringe on private properties and local prejudices'.

Surve's amendment was boosted further by the support it received from D.D. Gholap, Bombay's first lawmaker from the untouchable community, and also the only untouchable in the first Bombay Legislative Council under the 1919 Constitution. Though the quota was increased later, the rules framed for Bombay provided at the time for just one nomination from 'classes which, in the opinion of the Governor, are Depressed Classes'. Gholap had also been editor of the first newspaper that Ambedkar published, the *Mooknayak*.

Once Bole too endorsed Surve's amendment, the deck was cleared for the passage of his resolution in the revised form. Thus, four years after it had witnessed the first such attempt in the country, Bombay became the first province where the legislature formally called for throwing open public spaces to untouchables. The following month, the Bombay government issued an order in terms of the Bole Resolution as amended by Surve.

The order, dated 11 September 1923, directed that the heads of all government offices 'should give effect to' the Legislative Council Resolution so far as it related to 'the public places, institutions belonging to and maintained by Government'. The language was milder as regards the obligation of local bodies, in deference to their purported autonomy. The order said that collectors be 'requested to advise' local bodies in their jurisdiction 'to consider the desirability of accepting the recommendations made in the Resolution'.[17]

❖

The term of the legislatures under the Montagu–Chelmford reforms was only three years, and so the next round of elections took place in the last quarter of 1923. In Madras, the fresh crop of nominations made by Willingdon to the second Legislative Council under the quota for untouchables included R. Veerian, a thirty-seven-year-old activist from Coimbatore.

Veerian had figured in a discussion in the first Legislative Council when M.C. Rajah moved a resolution on 20 January 1922, seeking to replace the derogatory terms that were officially used for his community. The resolution recommended that 'the terms "Panchama" or "Paraya" used to designate the ancient Dravidian community in southern India should be deleted from Government records, etc. and the term "Adi Dravida" in the Tamil and "Adi Andhra" in the Telugu districts be substituted instead'.[18]

Asserting that his resolution was 'not an individual fancy', Rajah said, 'I am here as a representative of a large community.' As evidence that he was indeed speaking on behalf of the large community of untouchables across the province, Rajah cited this instance: 'My friend Mr Veerian has been agitating for this name in Coimbatore.' The Legislative Council adopted Rajah's resolution, subject to the caveat that the change in nomenclature would be enforced prospectively.

So, when Veerian was nominated, he was officially classified as Adi Dravida, his self-identification. A day after taking oath as a legislator, Veerian spoke for the first time in the House on 27 November 1923. It was on the formal motion for an address to Governor Willingdon regarding the constitution of a fresh ministry under the leadership of the Raja of Panagal. Calling upon all ministers to respect the sentiments of 'the depressed, oppressed and neglected classes', Veerian said that it was 'for the purpose of voicing' them that he had become a legislator. He added rather dramatically: 'I would be committing a grave sin against Divine Law, and a sin from which there is no escape for me, if I do not press the claims of my community.'[19]

And press he did. The first sign of Veerian's combative spirit came in the wake of the famous Vaikom Satyagraha in the neighbouring princely state of Travancore. The year-long agitation for the right of Ezhavas to walk on the roads leading to a temple began on 30 March 1924. While the satyagraha had been driven mainly by followers of the Ezhava spiritual leader Sree Narayana Guru, its profile was enhanced by Gandhi's support and guidance.

Vaikom was, in fact, the first time that Gandhi's agitation technique of satyagraha was being deployed against a social iniquity in Hindu society. The caste reform in question was also consonant with Gandhi's arc of evolution. He backed the Vaikom stir as it was only about accessing the roads leading to the temple—and not the temple itself. As an avowed votary of varna, Gandhi came to terms with the idea of temple entry only eight years later, in the aftermath of the historic Poona Pact.

Less than a fortnight after the launch of the Vaikom agitation, Veerian made it to the national news. Despite his stature as a legislator, Veerian was blocked from entering a road in his native place of Kamalapuram village, Salem district. Untouchables were disallowed the use of that road as it was located in an agraharam, a generic term for an exclusive Brahmin settlement. Though such discrimination was sanctioned by custom, Veerian refused to take it lying down. He shot off a telegram to the chief secretary to the Madras government, portraying his debarment as a violation of his civil rights.

This simple but unprecedented reaction resonated far and wide. On 16 April 1924, the Bombay-based *Times of India* reproduced the entire text of Veerian's long telegram, under the slug: 'A Madras MLC's Complaint: Intolerable Brahmin Tyranny'.[20]

In Veerian's telling of the incident, he intended merely to pass through the 'Agraharam public pathway' in Kamalapuram 'in order to post letters' at a post office located there and 'see' a school in the same vicinity. But 'owing to Panchama pollution', a Brahmin named Monigar Rungier, the village munsif, blocked Veerian's entry into that street. This was in spite of the fact that there was, as Veerian put it, 'no other way except passing through Agraharam' to reach the post office or the school. In conclusion, he alleged that the attitude of the 'Brahmin oligarchy towards depressed classes' was 'cruel and unbearable'.

Given the sanctity attached by Hindus to agraharams, Veerian's complaint against the subordinate judge put the Madras government in a dilemma. It was torn between the equality principle underpinning its policy of nominating untouchables to the legislature and the commitment to its well-worn policy of non-interference with social and religious practices. The Kamalapuram incident also brought back into focus Soundarapandian Nadar's plea for a special law to ensure equal access to public places, which Chief Minister Rayaningar had made light of.

The government's troubles were compounded by the loss of an old hand in Willingdon who, having served out his five-year term, had left office on 12 April 1924. Around the time Veerian was blocked from entering the Kamalapuram agraharam, Governor George Goschen was taking over. Faced with a fraught situation, the Goschen administration shied away from acting against the munsif or throwing open the agraharam. Instead, it tried to address Veerian's grievance without offending the 'Brahmin oligarchy', as the governor termed it.

The Madras government's middle course was to shift the focus from what had happened to what could be done to prevent a recurrence. It was decided that the post office would be moved from the agraharam to another part of Kamalapuram. The colonial regime was thus accepting the Brahminical notion that agraharams were beyond the pale of caste reform.

As postal services were outside its jurisdiction, the Madras government sought the Central government's intervention in what was framed as a matter of 'inaccessibility of the Kamalapuram branch office to the depressed classes'. In due course, the postmaster-general conveyed directly to the aggrieved legislator that the post office had been 'removed to a suitable locality' on 19 April 1924.

Veerian discovered that this was a misleading claim. The post office was still in its original location, deep inside the agraharam.

In his response, Veerian pointed out that 'it was the letterbox and not the post office that had been removed'. Sharing with the Madras government the substance of Veerian's rejoinder, the postmaster-general wrote, 'I have again caused enquiries to be made and shall see that the office is located in a suitable place if this has not already been done.'[21]

It turned out that the colonial regime, reconciled as it was to the exclusivity of agraharams, already had a pragmatic policy of locating post offices outside the boundaries of these localities in villages. As the postmaster-general admitted, 'It has always been the policy of the Department to locate village post offices in places easily and readily accessible to all classes of the public including the members of the depressed classes.'

This weak-kneed approach was publicly exposed when L.C. Guruswami, another untouchable legislator, asked the government on 18 August 1924 to confirm 'whether it is a fact' that Veerian had been 'prevented by the village munsif ... from getting access to the Government Post Office ... (and) the Board School'. This straightforward question received an evasive written reply. 'The village munsif informed Mr Veerian that Adi Dravidas did not usually go into the Agraharam though the Post Office and the Board School were located there.'[22] Rather than confirming that the munsif had denied Veerian access, the government quoted irrelevantly from the offender's account of what had transpired.

This prompted Guruswami to ask if Adi Dravidas could enter agraharams at least in situations that were beyond their control. His supplementary question, put verbally, was: 'Suppose they wish to go when they find it necessary, will they not be allowed?'

Chief Minister Rayaningar, who held the portfolio of local self-government and was the leader of an avowedly non-Brahmin party, was not the one who responded to Guruswami's query. Instead, Home Member Arthur Knapp rose to answer. With no apparent sense of irony, he said, 'I do not quite see how that arises out of the question.' He was reluctant to concede that, by the logic of the government's written reply, an untouchable could enter an agraharam in the event of a necessity.

In a bid to save the British government from getting further entangled in this intra-Hindu conflict, Knapp taunted Guruswami: 'The hon. Member would have done well if he had interpellated the hon. Member Mr Veerian on this matter. It would be much more to the point to ask him than to ask us.' Knapp was being disingenuous. Veerian could hardly have prophesied, on behalf of either the Brahmins or the government, whether there were any circumstances in which Adi Dravidas like him would be 'allowed' inside an agraharam.

The chain reaction that had been set off by Veerian's challenge to the exclusivity of agraharams next took the form of a resolution. Rettamalai Srinivasan, an untouchable who had been nominated to the Legislative Council at the same time as Veerian, proposed one to throw open public places. Srinivisan would come to be widely known six years later when he, along with Ambedkar, had the honour of representing untouchables at the Round Table Conference held in London for the next round of constitutional reforms.

Srinivasan sent his draft resolution to the office of the Legislative Council on 26 June 1924, about two months after Veerian's complaint. It was the first attempt in Madras to take up the access problem since the adoption of the Bole Resolution in Bombay the year before. However, the Srinivasan Resolution followed the Madras precedent of 1921 when Nadar had cited roads as among the public places meant to be thrown open. In fact, triggered by the location of Veerian's humiliation, the Srinivasan Resolution specifically included streets located in agraharams.

Framed as a proclamation that 'there is no objection' to untouchables accessing a range of public places, the resolution made references to agraharams, first in the preambular part and then again in the substantive part. The preamble urged that the proclamation be made by the 'beat of tom-tom … in every village in the Presidency, including streets in Agraharams'. And the substantive part began with the words: 'That there is no objection to any person belonging to the Depressed Classes walking through any public road, streets in Agraharams …'

The bureaucracy in the Ministry of Local Self Government, while formulating their position on the resolution, questioned the very basis of including roads in the first place. They contended that the problem of unapproachability was not spread across the Madras Presidency but confined to the lone Malayalam-speaking district of Malabar.

In an internal note submitted to Rayaningar on 9 August 1924, the ministry officials said that 'it is well known that in Malabar the depressed classes are not allowed to pass through certain streets'. They warned that the proclamation, which Srinisavan wanted to be read out to the beat of drums across the province, would 'not improve matters at all' and might instead 'be the cause of rousing up depressed classes against other castes'.[23]

The bureaucrats submitted this note of caution on the Srinivasan Resolution to Rayaningar so that his orders 'may be taken' on three procedural issues. The first, 'whether he will reply to the Resolution in the Legislative Council'. Rayaningar wrote, 'Yes'. The next question was 'whether any further information should be collected on the subject'. His answer displayed his confidence in the advice of the officials: 'I do not think any more information is necessary.' Taken together, the two replies indicated that Rayaningar was prepared to oppose, as briefed by the officials, Srinivasan's resolution in the Legislative Council.

His response to the third question suggested that he was looking for validation from his British colleagues. The question was whether he 'wishes the attitude of the Government to be discussed in [the entire] Cabinet or by the Governor sitting with [just] the Ministers'. Rayaningar said that he would like to have 'the matter discussed in the Cabinet'. Thus, on the matter of liberating untouchables from caste restrictions, Rayaningar was instrumental in getting the 'popularly responsible' section of the dyarchy set-up to confabulate with the 'authoritarian' one.

In that discussion, Knapp once again took over the matter from Rayaningar. When Srinivasan moved his resolution in the Legislative Council on 22 August 1924, it was not Rayaningar but Knapp—

and Knapp alone—who spoke on behalf of the government.[24] The official file on the Srinivasan Resolution does not offer any explanation for this curious turn of events.

Rayaningar's hesitation was an indication that the elite non-Brahmins he represented shared with Brahmins an uneasiness about letting untouchables have equal access to public places. Also, it was likely that the Cabinet was not supportive of his position. The authoritarian section, which dominated the Cabinet, turned out to be more receptive to Srinivasan's resolution than the popularly responsible section.

Whatever had transpired during the debate within the Cabinet, its outcome was evident in the Legislative Council. The home member displayed sagacity in recognising that, after the Bole Resolution in Bombay, the Madras government could no longer stonewall a similar motion. But even as he endorsed the principle of Srinivasan's resolution, Knapp tacitly took on board Rayaningar's worry that tom-tomming it might exacerbate caste tensions.

Knapp began his address by staking a claim over the Srinivasan Resolution, since one of the departments under his charge dealt with ameliorating the condition of the untouchables. 'The subject matter of this Resolution lies properly in the portfolio of my hon. Friend, the Minister for Local Self-Government. But as I am officially connected with the department which concerns itself mainly with the Depressed Classes, I feel it is only right that I should say a word or two before this Resolution is put to the House.'

He recalled the measures that had been taken in Madras even before the Montagu–Chelmsford reforms, including the establishment in March 1919 of a special office called the Protector of Depressed Classes. In keeping with its record of such pioneering efforts, Knapp said, he was now 'particularly anxious that the Government should be able to accept this Resolution'.

To make it acceptable to the government, he sought to change only the preambular part of the resolution, without touching its substantive part: an amendment that would do away with Srinivasan's idea of literally dinning the message into the heads of

Brahmins. Putting it as 'a matter of practical politics', Knapp said that it would be 'a little bit unnecessarily provocative to send a talaiyari into every Agraharam in the Presidency to tom-tom this information'.

Knapp proposed replacing references in the preamble to the tom-tom and agraharams with text that he considered 'equally effective'. The revised preamble read: 'That it be definitely accepted and announced as the policy of the Government ...'

He was hopeful that both Srinivasan and Rayaningar would be 'willing to accept' the amended resolution. While the mover of the resolution readily accepted the amendment, the minister concerned remained tight-lipped. At the end of the debate, the House passed the resolution with the amendments moved not only by Knapp but also by A. Chidambara Nadar, a low-caste legislator from the southern part of the presidency.

It was on account of Nadar's intervention that the reference to agraharams was deleted in the substantive part too. In his address to the Council, Nadar specified three districts other than Malabar where unapproachability prevailed, or as he put it, 'the difficulties experienced by the Depressed Classes in walking along the streets'. He estimated that the prevalence varied in severity. 'It will be found in a small measure in the Madura district, in a higher degree in the district of Ramnad and as we go to the extreme southern district of Tinnevelly, it will be found in the highest and in the most acute form possible.' In reality, even the clubbing of these three Tamil-speaking districts did not capture the full extent of unapproachability given that Veerian had been humiliated in Salem, which was yet another district.

After establishing so painstakingly the persistence of unapproachability, Nadar proposed the deletion of, ironically enough, all references to agraharams from the resolution. This unexplained contradiction suggested that he was acting in concert with Knapp, perhaps driven by an anxiety to make the tone of Srinivasan's resolution less provocative.

In its final form, the part of the resolution relating to the freedom of movement read: 'there is no objection to any person or persons belonging to any class or community walking through any public road, street or pathway in any town or village'. The part that threw open other public places said: 'there is no objection to any person belonging to the depressed classes having access to the premises of any public office, well, tank or places of public resort, or to places and buildings where public business is transacted in the same manner and to the same extent as persons belonging to the community of the caste Hindus in the country'.

The most prominent participant in the debate was S. Satyamurti, who formally seconded Srinivasan's resolution. In colonial Madras, he was for long Rajaji's most formidable rival to Congress leadership. For a good part of the 1920s, however, Satyamurti was part of the breakaway Swaraj Party which had been formed to circumvent the Congress boycott of legislatures.

Alluding to his Brahmin roots, Satyamurti said, 'I know there are some men in my community who believe that the approach of certain classes of people will pollute the streets. I am not one of those. I claim to understand Hinduism in its higher aspects and I do claim for my religion that it is the most catholic of all religions.' Those who presumably understood Hinduism in its lower aspects did not take long to push back.

The battle lines were drawn on 25 September 1924, when the Goschen administration issued an order in terms of the Srinivasan Resolution. It was the Madras equivalent of Lincoln's Emancipation Proclamation. Ironically enough, despite his studied silence on the resolution in the Legislative Council, Rayaningar was perforce associated with the order that was passed on it. Because the resolution was related to his portfolio, the order had to be issued by his department.

The promulgation of 'Government Order No. 2660, Local and Municipal, dated 25th September 1924', as it was formally labelled, was reminiscent of the Bombay government's counterpart the previous year on Bole's resolution. The difference was that, instead of referring the G.O. to local bodies as a 'request', as Bombay had done, Madras chose to put it as 'guidance' to all.

Besides reproducing the Srinivasan Resolution, the G.O. said, 'The Resolution has been accepted by the Government and is communicated to all local bodies and heads of departments for information and guidance.' The local bodies it addressed were of two kinds: 'local boards', which pertained to rural areas, and 'municipalities', which administered urban areas.

Thanks to Knapp's amendment, the government was spared the catalytic role that Srinivasan had originally envisaged for this radical reform. There was little by way of an organised civil society to take on the entrenched interests of dominant castes. So, in most parts of the Madras Presidency, the response was slow and muted. But it developed into a volatile situation in Malabar—the district that ministry officials had singled out as being 'well known' for practising unapproachability.

The stirrings of assertion in Malabar were actually concentrated in the city of Palghat (now Palakkad). This was because of the lengths to which a local lawyer, M.P. Raghavan, had gone to spread awareness on the order. Having obtained a copy of G.O. No. 2660 from the Municipal Council of Palghat, he gave it 'the widest publicity' not only 'by handbills' but also 'by tom tom'.[25]

Raghavan's caste identity was crucial here: he was an Ezhava. Though they belonged to the lower layer of the Shudra varna, Ezhavas were counted as a Depressed Class and subjected across Malayalam-speaking areas to disabilities similar to those inflicted on untouchables. At this time, the Ezhavas were also engaged in the Vaikom Satyagraha—another battle for accessing roads.

Raghavan's espousal of G.O. No. 2660 caused concern among the Brahmins in and around Kalpathy, a village within the municipal limits of Palghat. These Brahmins believed that they had migrated to Palghat centuries earlier from the Tamil-speaking region of Tanjore. Their lives traditionally revolved around Kalpathy's Viswanatha Swamy Temple, which was called the Dakshina Kashi, or the Kashi of the South. In 2008, in order to preserve its quaint architecture and quainter mores, Kalpathy—described in a Kerala Tourism newsletter as 'the Brahmin hamlet of Palakkad'—was declared Kerala's first 'Heritage Village'.

Their greatest claim to fame was the annual three-day-long Rathotsavam, or chariot festival. In what was popularly described then as 'car festival', Kalpathy Brahmins would take temple idols in processions through agraharam roads. Though it attracted visitors from far and near, they were all required to be Brahmins or other high castes so as to maintain the sanctity of the agraharams.

The conservative Kalpathy Brahmins feared that Raghavan's campaign for the enforcement of G.O. No. 2660 was aimed at contaminating the car festival that was due to start on 13 November 1924. In the run-up to the festival, the chairman of the Palghat Municipal Council, S.K. Ramaswami Aiyar, sent a complaint to the district magistrate of Malabar, J.A. Thorne. The chairman, himself a Brahmin, alleged that members of 'the polluting castes at Palghat intended to enter the Brahmin streets at the time of the car festival'.

While the unabashed usage of the terms 'polluting castes' and 'Brahmin streets' was normal for that period, Aiyar was also describing the roads of Kalpathy as 'Brahmin streets' with the strategic intent of distinguishing them from the 'public roads' that had been thrown open by the order. Thorne's instinctive response was to accept Aiyar's distinction.

Thorne was also the administrator who had dealt with the Moplah Rebellion in Malabar district in 1921. One historical explanation for the large-scale violence by Muslims against Hindus was the British-supported feudal system run by upper-caste members.

In any case, as district magistrate, Thorne's priority was to maintain peace, even if it meant that the age-old arrangements for the car festival, however discriminatory against lower castes, remained undisturbed in the teeth of the G.O. No. 2660. Since he had been camping at Tellicherry, about 200 kilometres away, Thorne instructed his sub-divisional magistrate in Palghat, D.W. Dodwell, to attend immediately to Aiyar's grievance. Reflecting Thorne's anxiety about safeguarding Brahminical sensitivities, Dodwell characterised Raghavan's zeal to exercise the rights conferred by the order as an 'agitation'. The choice of terminology suggested Dodwell's intention of using coercive action to rein in the Ezhavas.

In his feedback to Thorne on 10 November 1924, Dodwell warned that 'the leaders of the agitation were not likely to give up their intention unless a prohibitory order was issued'. In a meeting with Raghavan, Dodwell had forced the Ezhava leader to submit to certain conditions. Accordingly, he informed Thorne that Raghavan was 'willing to abide by any conditions that should be laid down as to the manner in which the demonstration should be made'. It was clear that he had a preconception of Ezhavas as potential law-breakers, for Dodwell did not feel the need to demand any such undertaking from the Brahmins.

At the same time, he could not brush aside Raghavan's argument that the Kalpathy agraharam should be 'considered a public street as the Municipal Council had recently spent money on its repair'. Persuaded by 'the force of this logic', Dodwell suggested that Ezhavas be allowed to enter the agraharam, although in a regulated manner. He reasoned that it was 'doubtful whether the entry of a few members of the polluting castes would be likely to cause a breach of the peace'.

Dodwell's ambivalence set the tone for the administration's response to the issue. In a wire sent the following day, Thorne agreed with Dodwell that 'it should be possible to arrange for their entry into the Gramam [village] at a time and in a manner that would not provoke opposition'. Likewise, Thorne concurred that 'if violence was apprehended' at any point, prohibitory order under Section 144 of the Criminal Procedure Code was 'desirable'.

On 13 November 1924, the entry of low-caste men into the agraharam provoked both opposition and violence. According to the official narrative, when a 'fairly large party' of low-caste members had entered the Kalpathy street, they were 'chased out by the caste people', and in the ensuing stone-pelting, Raghavan and some of his men 'received injuries'. Yet, no action was taken against the aggressors from the upper castes. Instead, Dodwell issued a prohibitory order under Section 144, targeting the low-caste members for exercising their newly won rights under G.O. No. 2660.

In fact, it imposed a blanket ban on members of four specific castes, including Ezhavas and Paraiyans, from entering Kalpathy and the neighbouring Brahmin settlements. Dodwell's order said, 'I do hereby … strictly warn and enjoin all persons of these classes, not to enter these villages' for the duration of the festival. Emboldened by the administration's complicity, the Brahmins performed 'purification ceremonies to remove the pollution' that had allegedly been caused by the entry of low-caste members into the agraharam.

When the rest of the festival had peacefully concluded, the British officials in Malabar were gripped by mixed feelings, as evident from Thorne's letter on 16 November 1924 to the chief secretary, Madras government. On the one hand, he justified the action that had been taken against the Depressed Classes rather than the Brahmins for breach of the peace. He claimed that the disorder could have been averted if Raghavan and his group 'had adhered to the arrangement they had made with Mr. Dodwell that no crowd would attempt entry and that only two or three persons would go in singly and unostentatiously'. Thorne said that it had also been agreed that those low-caste members would 'retire at once if any objections were raised'.

To his mind, Dodwell was justified in this surrender to Brahminism. He felt he had 'handled the situation prudently' by not issuing the prohibitory order until the situation had escalated. 'Undoubtedly if a preventive order had been issued beforehand, it would have been construed by propagandists of the depressed classes as indicating a repressive attitude on the part of the authorities,' Thorne said, adding that the action was 'as much in the interests of the depressed classes as of any other class'.

On the other hand, on the matter of resolving the dispute, Thorne reverted to the legal argument that Raghavan had made in the first place. In the concluding paragraph of his letter, Thorne wrote, 'I am looking into the question of the claim to treat these streets as public within the meaning of the G.O.' He was in effect examining which of the agraharam streets could be considered public because they were being maintained by the Municipal Council. 'Now that the Government have definitely announced the policy of full rights to all classes in using public roads, it seems to me essential that we should know precisely what places are to be regarded as public and what are not.' He signed off with an assurance that he would report later on this point.

Meanwhile, Veerian was keenly following the developments in Kalpathy. On 16 November 1924, he wrote to Knapp protesting against Dodwell's prohibitory order, which he said was 'quite against the spirit of the G.O. No. 2660'. It would have 'been better' if the prohibitory order had instead been issued to 'the non-depressed classes not to molest or abuse or misbehave towards the depressed classes'. The legislator requested the home member to intervene in the matter and ensure access, as envisaged by the G.O., to 'all classes of people'.

The very next day, the district administration appeared to move in that direction. In a fresh order, dated 17 November 1924, Dodwell declined a petition filed by Kalpathy Brahmins asking for an extension of the prohibitory order beyond the duration of the car festival. He clarified that his fear of a riot due to 'the presence of large crowds of strangers during that festival' did not hold any longer. 'The depressed classes have made no attempt to disobey my order during its continuance and I see no reason to suppose that they contemplate any violent action at present.'

In a tacit vindication of Raghavan's argument, Dodwell said, 'Since public money is spent on the Brahmin streets, I think all classes of the public have a prima facie right to have access to them. If the villagers wish to contest this, their proper course is to seek for an injunction in the Civil Courts.' In a dig at Brahmins for presuming that their roads were exempt from the G.O., Dodwell said, 'Their case would no doubt be stronger if they asked for the expenditure of public money on them to be discontinued and undertook to repair them themselves.'

The lifting of the prohibitory order prompted the Ezhavas to declare that they would make a fresh attempt to exercise their right to enter Kalpathy. Raghavan promptly issued a public statement with his account of the violence at Kalpathy, beginning with the leaflet he had published conveying the gist of the G.O.

'The local Brahmins scented danger to their exclusiveness in their villages and interpreted my leaflet,' he said, 'as an indirect invitation to all the depressed classes' to attend the upcoming car festival. Having promised Dodwell that only a limited number of Ezhavas would enter the agraharam, Raghavan ensured that out of the 500-odd people who had gathered outside the village, 'a small body of about 50 persons without weapons of any sort effected entry' which, as he added, was 'unopposed by anybody'.

It was only when those low-caste visitors were 'about to return' that 'Brahmin mobs' began to hurl stones at them and 'brutally assaulted' some of them. Raghavan said that he had 'attracted the largest attention from those gentry', leaving him 'adorned with two black eyes and a bleeding nose'. True to their promise that they would maintain the peace, 'none of the party of Ezhavas retaliated', he said, adding that 'the cause of Hindu unity is at stake'.

Invoking the Montagu–Chelmsford reforms, Raghavan said, 'I appeal to every public worker in the cause of India's orderly progress towards responsible government, to take up the cause of the depressed classes and bring the Brahmins of Palghat to a sense of reasonableness of which they now seem to be devoid in spite of University degrees and Vedantic culture.'

On 17 November 1924, Srinivasan sent Raghavan a telegram, expressing his solidarity with those who were fighting to enforce his resolution in Kalpathy. A day later, Raghavan responded through a letter, urging Srinivasan, with a touch of humour, to take up the matter in Madras: 'I need not tell you that it is now your lookout to ask the Government if their G.O. accepting your Resolution in the Council has any value or if it is only a piece of paper which affects none.'

Within a week, this letter became a part of the official file on the Kalpathy episode because Srinivasan had forwarded Raghavan's letter to Law Member C.P. Ramaswami Aiyar. In turn, Aiyar had forwarded it to Chief Secretary Norman Marjoribanks.

Meanwhile, officials in Knapp's department prepared a note on the letter that Thorne had sent on 16 November 1924. They were sceptical of Thorne's approach of treating as public all the roads that the Municipal Council of Palghat maintained. Apprehending that this might inflame passions and prove counterproductive, they wrote that Thorne was 'apparently unconscious of the difficulty of the position he has taken up and in which he places Government'.

Responding to their concern, Home Member Knapp directed that District Magistrate Thorne be asked to report urgently 'the result of the inquiries' on the expenditure that had been incurred on the upkeep of the agraharam roads. He feared that the matter was 'sure to come up' in the December session of the Legislative Council.

It turned out that all the roads in the agraharams, without exception, were being maintained by the Municipal Council. Thorne's inquiries, in fact, revealed that 'the Municipal Council has embarked on a policy of increased expenditure on these streets'. This rendered untenable the please-both-sides option of throwing open some of the roads rather than all of them.

The expenditure data even prompted Thorne to make a telling confession in his letter to the chief secretary on 27 November 1924: 'In the recent disturbance at Palghat, the magistracy were forced into the awkward position of preventing members of polluting castes from exercising a right which the Government appear to have encouraged them to claim.' This acknowledgement was a prelude to changing tack from a law-and-order approach to a rights-based one.

Pointing out that even if 'the preservation of public security is paramount', Thorne said that 'members of the depressed classes might contend with some show of reason that public peace should be preserved rather by protecting members of the depressed classes in the exercise of their rights than by inhibiting them from exercising them.' Since Dodwell had done just the opposite by inhibiting Ezhavas from exercising their rights, Thorne said, 'It is not inconceivable that the conduct of an officer might be called in question on the ground of the attitude taken by him in an emergency of this sort.'

Thorne's compromise, however, was an extension of the conditions that Dodwell had imposed on Raghavan. 'My own view is that a distinction should be drawn between the unostentatious use of such streets and places by persons having a legitimate necessity to use them and the ostentatious use of them on occasions when the assertion of the right is bound to lead to excitement and opposition.' Thorne was justifying the administration's decision to thwart the entry of Ezhavas at Kalpathy.

He was also proposing for the first time the criteria of 'unostentatious use' and 'legitimate necessity'. Where the low-caste members did not fulfil both these conditions, Thorne said that he would be 'very reluctant' to place the police at their disposal 'to protect them from the resentment of members of the higher castes'. With that, he asked, 'May I know whether this represents the wishes of the Government?'

Before the government could figure out what exactly represented its wishes, Kalpathy Brahmins queered the pitch by adopting Dodwell's suggestion that they could offer to take over the maintenance of their roads. They did so in a representation addressed to Governor Goschen signed by 702 Brahmins. Submitted to Dodwell on 4 December 1924, the representation made three prayers, each seeking to dilute the G.O. No. 2660 in a different way.

- That in keeping with their 'religious susceptibilities', it prayed for orders declaring that the agraharam streets were inaccessible to 'lower castes whose approach pollutes a Brahmin'.
- If the government was 'unwilling to revise' the G.O. 'generally' for the entire province, it prayed that 'the Gramams of Palghat may be exempted from the operation of the G.O. on account of the peculiar customs and manners followed in Palghat from time immemorial and the policy consistently followed by the Government regarding them'.
- But if neither of the above prayers was acceptable, the representation said that Brahmins 'feel so strongly in the matter that they are quite willing to have these Gramams excluded

from the Municipal area so far as the maintenance of roads is concerned and that they may be allowed to make their own arrangements for the same'.

Twenty-seven years earlier, Swami Vivekananda had famously said about this very district: 'Was there ever a sillier thing before in the world than what I saw in Malabar country? The poor Pariah is not allowed to pass through the same street as the high-caste man, but if he changes his name to a hodge-podge English name, it is all right; or to a Mohammedan name, it is all right ... Shame upon them that such wicked and diabolical customs are allowed.'[26]

With the Brahmins digging their heels in, Knapp was worried about the likelihood of another confrontation in the event that the Ezhavas carried out their threat of attempting a fresh entry. In his negotiations with the government, Raghavan agreed to defer the entry plan by about a month while Knapp sought a solution. On 6 December 1924, Knapp noted: 'I hope and believe it has been arranged that there will be no further public assertion of the Ezhava claims until after the 10th of January before which time I have promised to go to Palghat myself.'

Meanwhile, the Ezhavas made another kind of public assertion, this time in the form of a representation to the governor of Madras as a counter to the one submitted by the Brahmins. On 23 December 1924, Raghavan submitted the representation to Dodwell with 225 signatures.

It appealed to the government that the policy it had declared on the basis of Srinivasan's resolution should 'under no circumstances, be departed from or reduced to nullity by executive action as prayed for by the Brahmins of Kalpathy'. To dispel the uncertainty that had been created by the Brahmins, the Ezhava representation wanted G.O. No. 2660 to be reinforced with a clarification from the government. It asked the government to declare that all public roads were open to all classes of people 'irrespective of caste, notwithstanding any inhuman, unholy and unreasonable customs to the contrary'.

Knapp took due note of the representations from both sides while formulating a fresh policy declaration on the subject. He visited Palghat as promised on the first two days of January 1925 to meet the people involved and see for himself the roads under dispute. Knapp was accompanied by a senior bureaucrat, George Paddison, who had been the Protector of Depressed Classes when that office had been created in 1919. For dispassionate inputs on legal aspects, Knapp depended on the advocate general of Madras, T.R. Venkatarama Sastry.

However, as a Brahmin himself, Sastry tendered advice that was in tune with the claims of the Kalpathy Brahmins. In a note he shared with his Cabinet colleagues on 6 January 1925, Knapp quoted Sastry as saying in his preliminary advice that the government 'ought to maintain the existing usage and leave it to the innovators to make the first move'. It was as good as saying that, despite its adoption of the Srinivasan Resolution, the government ought to pretend that nothing had changed in the legal situation, at least not until an 'innovator' like Raghavan obtained a judicial relief on the basis of the G.O.

This view, according to Knapp's note, was based on the fact that, for a long time, the British government had, by its orders and by the orders of its local officers, 'deliberately recognized that the Kalpathy streets are not open to the Ezhavas and the lower castes'. Even as he recognised 'the force of the Advocate General's view', Knapp said, 'I cannot feel that it satisfactorily meets the difficulty in which we are placed'. As had been the case in his discussions with Chief Minister Rayaningar, this time too, Home Member Knapp found himself more sympathetic than Advocate General Sastry was to the growing clamour for equality from the lower castes.

Pointing to Sastry's scant regard for the G.O. No. 2660, Knapp said that 'we cannot now throw it over and practically declare it to be meaningless'. Further, he said, 'So far as our previous support of the Brahmins is said by the Advocate General to tie our hands, I hold that our recent deliberate declaration of policy makes our previous attitude immaterial.'

In an attempt to find the middle ground, Knapp said, 'I have no desire to force a revolution in the matter of throwing open

Agraharam streets to the lower classes.' Echoing the criterion that Thorne had suggested of 'legitimate necessity', Knapp said that the government policy and 'the efforts of the lower castes themselves' should 'concentrate on removing restrictions which actually cause material detriment'. Conversely, he proposed that the government should not support a movement where the grievance of the lower castes was 'merely academic and abstract'. The example he cited of such an illusory grievance was where 'the Agraharam is not a thoroughfare and a member of the lower castes is not likely to have any business there'.

Even as he repeatedly used the expression 'lower castes', Knapp doubted whether Ezhavas, for all the disabilities suffered by them, were entitled to invoke the G.O. He said that the government had 'a right to complain of the manner in which the Ezhavas are attempting to make use of the G.O.', alluding to the complexity that Ezhavas were considered part of the Shudra category, while the G.O. was meant for Avarnas or outcastes. 'The debates in the Legislative Council had nothing to do with the Ezhavas. They were not in our minds at all. Although they are untouchables from the point of view of the Brahmins, they themselves claim a caste status and are themselves as intolerant of the Cherumas and others as the Brahmins are of them.'

Meanwhile, Sastry, in his final opinion, was again unabashedly intolerant of the Ezhava aspirations. He found no justification for opening up any of the agraharam streets. Even if 'the municipality had assumed control and expended municipal money upon their repair and maintenance', the agraharam streets, Sastry said, 'cannot be treated as having become public highways open to all the King's subjects'.

His opinion arrived on the day Knapp had already dispatched his Cabinet note to meet the agreed deadline. The home member recommended to his colleagues that, as 'the streets are prima facie public, we ought to uphold the right of Ezhavas to use them as a thoroughfare'. At the same time, he cautioned, 'I would stop short of any encouragement to them to parade the streets merely for the purpose of asserting an abstract claim and incidentally causing annoyance to the residents in the locality.'

It was on the basis of this ambivalent Cabinet note that the Madras government finally issued a sequel to the G.O. on the Srinivasan Resolution—the 'Right of entry of Ezhavas into Agraharam streets, Kalpathy, Palghat'. Evidently, the violence at Kalpathy had taken the matter out of the jurisdiction of Rayaningar's Ministry of Local Self Government. The Public Department, which came under Knapp, issued G.O. No. 37, Public, dated 9 January 1925. It bore signs of all the compromises that Knapp had suggested to dilute the import of G.O. No. 2660, which had been issued only about three months earlier.

Take this carefully worded sentence from G.O. No. 37, trying to accommodate the concerns of both upper and lower castes. With an eye on the lower castes, the first half said: 'The Government desire to reiterate that the public have a right of access and use in respect of all public highways …' And then came a restriction on the autonomy of the public to appease the Brahmins: '… but it is not for them finally to decide whether a particular street or road falls within the classification'.

This meant that a road could no longer be classified as public merely because the local body was responsible for its upkeep. The new policy introduced a further layer of discretion, which was applied to Kalpathy. 'In the present case, the Government observe that the Palghat Municipality have maintained the road in question and prima facie this appears to the Government to involve the position that the road is one to which all members of the public have access. This circumstance is not conclusive of the matter as its determination will depend amongst other things on whether the municipality in taking over the control of the road accepted or recognised any limitations on such a right in the public.'

Read in the context of Kalpathy, this meant that Brahmins were justified in barring Ezhavas as the Palghat Municipality could be said to have allowed such a restriction, despite retaining its control over the roads. The principle laid down by G.O. No. 37 was: 'The extent to which in any particular case the claim of individual members of the public to exercise the right of using the street should be supported must depend upon the circumstances of each case.'

Besides recognising the subjectivity of the arrangement with the local body, the G.O. made it clear that low-caste members would be allowed entry if they were otherwise likely to suffer what Knapp had described in his Cabinet note as 'material detriment'. The point was made with illustrations. 'Where Agraharam streets form a natural means of access to a main road or business centre, the Government conceive that persons using the streets as thoroughfares should ordinarily be supported against any attempt to obstruct them.'

But as the Kalpathy controversy was over the desire of low-caste members to witness a religious procession, the G.O. clarified that 'the local officers should not regard themselves as necessarily bound to take action in support of the entry into an Agraharam when the entry is dictated merely by the desire to assert an abstract right and had no basis of business or of practical convenience'. The implication was clear: that Dodwell could not be faulted for issuing the prohibitory order against Ezhavas on the first day of the car festival.

This was a dilution of G.O. No. 2660, which had endorsed Srinivasan's resolution in all its emancipatory possibilities. For the violence they had inflicted on those exercising their rights under this order, the Kalpathy Brahmins were rewarded with exemptions designed to discourage low-caste members from entering their agraharams.

❖

About a week after the G.O. on Kalpathy had been issued, Veerian sent a draft bill to the office of the Madras Legislative Council. It was the first legislative proposal in colonial India to take on untouchability. Having seen the influence wielded by the Kalpathy Brahmins, Veerian made the strategic choice of working to impact rural areas rather than cities like Palghat. In that same spirit of caution, he also decided to legislate reforms through amendments to an existing law rather than pushing for a separate law dealing directly with caste.

The vehicle Veerian chose for this purpose was the Madras Local Boards Act, 1920. The SOR of his bill to amend this law referenced Srinivasan's resolution and the consequent G.O. No. 2660. Dated 17 January 1925, the SOR said: 'Though the Government Order has been communicated to all the Presidents of the local bodies, it does not appear that any good has come out of it. Now by the amendments proposed, it is sought to give effect to the Government Order by placing it on a statutory basis.'[27]

The amendments sought to insert clauses that guaranteed universal access to various public places, with violations being penalised with a maximum fine of Rs 100. The new rights that were sought to be introduced were:

- 'No person shall obstruct any person walking along or using in a lawful manner any public road or street or pathway.'
- Insofar as the springs, tanks, wells and other water bodies meant for the 'convenience of the inhabitants' were concerned, Veerian's bill inserted a clause saying that 'they shall be open for the use and enjoyment of all people irrespective of caste or creed for the purpose mentioned above'.
- Likewise, with regard to 'public markets', the bill inserted a clause saying 'such markets shall be open to all people irrespective of caste or creed'.

The bill was radical in its vision of empowering untouchables to fraternise with others in ways that were then unthinkable, that too in a province that was considered the worst in British India in terms of caste prejudice. To its credit, the Goschen administration allowed Veerian to introduce the bill in the Legislative Council on 31 March 1925. This was on the heels of Gandhi's visit to Travancore, a tributary state of Madras, in connection with the ongoing Vaikom Satyagraha.

In such propitious circumstances, Veerian's bill raised no

eyebrows among the other legislators. As recorded in the proceedings of the House, 'No objection having been taken, leave was declared to have been granted to the hon. Member.' On 9 May 1925, the Madras government forwarded a copy of Veerian's bill to the Government of India for information.

This routine action had an unforeseen repercussion. The Legislative Department at the Centre registered an objection. It believed that the Madras government had committed a procedural error in allowing the Veerian bill to be introduced without first obtaining the viceroy's sanction.

Although it aimed to amend only the Madras law on local bodies, the bill was, in effect, regulating the Central subjects of civil and criminal law. In his internal note, the secretary to the Central Legislative Department, L. Graham, contended that the clause allowing universal access to public roads was a matter of civil law and the one making obstruction an offence pertained to criminal law. He added that while the subject matter of the Madras Local Boards Act was 'local self-government in rural areas', the subject matter of Veerian's amendment bill was 'civil liberty'.

On Graham's reference, an official of the Home Department, U.C. Stuart, agreed with his objection to the bill. But he mooted the idea that the Centre should 'express sympathy with the objects' of the Veerian bill. In a remarkably empathetic remark for a colonial officer, Stuart noted, 'The principle of the Bill—a mere affirmation of the rights and liberty of the subject—is innocuous ... but there would seem to be little hope for democracy in a country in which an executive order and legislation are required to enforce such an elementary principle.'

Home Member A.P. Muddiman, however, overruled Stuart's suggestion of conveying support for the principle of the bill. While recommending refusal of sanction on 'the technical ground' that had been mentioned in Graham's note, Muddiman said, 'It is unnecessary to consider the general principle of the Bill.' Graham's proposal of thwarting the Madras Bill was also endorsed by the Executive Council member in charge of his department, B.N. Sarma.

A Brahmin lawyer from Vizag in the Madras Presidency, Sarma said that he was 'not sure' whether the clause in the bill to penalise those blocking access to public roads was 'really necessary'. He listed out the provisions of the IPC that corresponded to this and other clauses in Veerian's bill.

Having obtained the backing of those two Executive Committee members, Graham placed a note before the viceroy on 3 August 1925, explaining that, despite the Madras government's failure to apply for his sanction, he was empowered to intercept Veerian's bill. Graham reiterated his reasons for why he believed that Lord Irwin should 'refuse the requisite sanction'.

The next day, Irwin sprang a surprise. Graham recorded on 4 August 1925 that the viceroy had rejected his recommendation. 'His Excellency has decided to grant sanction to the Bill on the ground that it introduces no real change in the law but merely affirms an existing right and adds a penalty which also is not necessary having regard to the provisions of the Indian Penal Code referred to by Hon'ble Member.' So, even as he approvingly cited Sarma's view that the bill was redundant, Irwin arrived at just the opposite conclusion on whether it should be granted sanction.

As for the argument that the bill interfered with the Centre's domain, Irwin recommended forbearance, given that the Veerian bill introduced no real change in the law as per the Centre's own reckoning. Irwin was disinclined to let the technicalities that had been flagged by his subordinates get in the way of Veerian's valiant attempt, however disguised or symbolic, to take on untouchability.

Meanwhile, the protracted Vaikom Satyagraha was drawing to a close as the Travancore government had thrown open at least three of the four roads leading to the Shiva temple. But the progress in Vaikom made little difference to the exclusionary traditions of the Shiva temple in Kalpathy. Tensions heightened once again in the run-up to the annual car festival due from 13 to 15 November 1925.

This time, the Arya Samaj, the Hindu reformist sect predominant in northern India, intervened. Its foremost leader, Swami Shraddhanand, who had worked with Gandhi on untouchability, came down to Palghat in a bid to help the Ezhavas watch the car festival on the public roads in the agraharams. Shraddhanand's expression of solidarity proved to be ineffective, though.

The Kalpathy Brahmins repeated their strategy of seeking a prohibitory order, bolstered now by G.O. No. 37, which forbade Ezhavas from entering an agraharam if they were only asserting 'an abstract right'. Sure enough, the district administration invoked Section 144. The prohibitory order was not only against Ezhavas and other low castes but also against the Arya Samajists, although to a lesser extent. As the *Times of India* reported, 'The Arya Samajists, being members of a recognised non-caste organisation, could not be prevented from entering Kalpathy, but they would not be allowed to carry on propaganda work during the car festival.'[28]

About a week later, the Vaikom Satyagraha formally ended on 23 November 1925, with happier consequences for the low castes. This was the backdrop against which the Madras Legislative finally discussed the Veerian bill on 14 December 1925.[29] The discussion was on his motion to refer the bill to a Select Committee.

Veerian's opening remarks were an indication of the precarious situation he found himself in. Though his speech dealt at length with the discrimination suffered by the members of his community, he felt constrained to begin with conciliatory noises. 'I beg to submit that I am not going to bring in the subject of caste nor am I going to raise the problem of untouchability in relation to caste.' That he had to disclaim what was so visibly the point of his initiative was a measure of the pressure he was under.

He was also silent on Kalpathy, the epicentre in the Madras Presidency of the wrangling over access inequality. Anyway, Veerian had a technical reason for steering clear of this newsy conflict: since it was within the city limits of Palghat, Kalpathy was beyond the scope of a bill that was confined to rural areas. Taking a deliberately blinkered view, he said, 'The reason for my attempting to amend the Madras Local Boards Act is that difficulties are being felt by the members of the so-called depressed classes in non-municipal areas.'

The closest he came to admitting that urban areas were also

affected was in his general observation that there would have been 'no necessity' for such amendments in 'any progressive country'. Veerian added that 'in India, notably in the southern part of it, the so-called depressed classes have had to fight perpetually for their elementary rights under very distressing circumstances.'

The chief minister too found himself in a predicament. About sixteen months ago, he had maintained a careful silence when the House debated the politically sensitive Srinivasan Resolution. The Raja of Panagal had since been shamed into speaking because of the unusual circumstances in which the viceroy had granted his sanction to Veerian's bill. So, while he announced that he had 'no objection' to having the bill referred to the Select Committee, Rayaningar could not help airing his old misgivings. Peddling the stock conservative argument that 'social reform should be effected by educating the public mind', the chief minister said that he was 'not sure whether this House was the proper forum for such legislation'.

Satyamurti was relatively more receptive to the possibility that the enactment of the Veerian bill might 'protect the rights' of the untouchables. At the same time, he cautioned against the belief that 'simply because you pass a Bill in this House, the age-long wrongs and grievances of these unfortunate members of communities wrongly called the depressed communities would be removed'. His conception of what those 'wrongs' were proved to be curious. Satyamurti went on to say that, more than any access issue bedevilling them, 'the two great evils from which these depressed classes are suffering are ignorance and drink'. He was drawing on the narrative that untouchables should mend their ways before they could use any public amenity.

Given their non-Brahmin politics, Justice Party legislators could not tolerate that insinuation. Opening a round of Brahmin-bashing, Venkatareddi Nayudu alleged that it was Satyamurti's community that was 'really responsible for this state of affairs'. Satyamurti gave it back saying that 'these high caste non-Brahmins are very much more against the rights of the depressed classes than the much-maligned Brahmins'.

The digression into which of the elite castes was more culpable for the perpetuation of untouchability became more strident with the entry of Natesa Mudaliyar, one of the founding members of the Justice Party. To his mind, Brahmins like Satyamurti had an obligation to 'tell the high caste non-Brahmin that all that is said in the Manu Dharma Shastra is wrong'. For it was the Brahmin who was, he said, 'everywhere a political head, everywhere a religious head and everywhere a social head'. Raising the pitch in the House, Mudaliyar said, 'It is he, it is that cobra that infuses the poison into our veins.'

This last remark prompted the president of the Council, Mariadas Ruthnaswamy, to order corrective action: 'He must really withdraw that expression.' But then, even as he went through the motions of withdrawing the offending term, Mudaliyar took the opportunity to explain why he had resorted to it in the first place. 'I used the word "cobra" in the sense that the poison infused by it could be removed only by its biting again,' adding, 'I do not mean that the Brahmin is a cobra.' The president responded sharply: 'I thought that the hon. Member has withdrawn the word, but I see that he is developing the meaning of it.'

At the conclusion of that heated and meandering discussion, the House referred the bill to a fifteen-member Select Committee headed by the Raja of Panagal and including three untouchables, M.C. Rajah, R. Srinivasan and R. Veerian. In its report, which came six months later, the Select Committee proposed a mixed bag of changes to the Veerian bill.

On the one hand, it introduced an explicit reference to caste in the clause providing universal access to public roads: 'The Committee considered that a substantive provision should be made to declare the right of all members of the public irrespective of caste or creed to the use of public roads …' On the other hand, it deleted altogether the clause empowering all classes to access springs, tanks and wells. This it explained by saying that 'the Committee considered that the Bill should be confined for the present to public roads and markets'.

The Select Committee report was accompanied by a dissenting

note from Srinivasan dated 14 June 1926. Given that his own resolution was the genesis of this exercise, Srinivasan recalled that the object of the Veerian bill was to provide a statutory footing to all the provisions of G.O. No. 2660. He was, therefore, concerned that the deletion made by the Select Committee would 'give an inference to the public that the public springs, tanks and wells are not accessible to any person belonging to the depressed classes'. He feared that the deletion might put a question mark over 'several' water bodies which had already been thrown open on the strength of the G.O.

About a month later, on 17 July 1926, a Christian legislator from Mangalore, J.A. Saldanha, surprised the Council with an unusual attack on the chief minister.[30] He blamed Rayaningar, who was heading the Select Committee on his bill, for 'inordinate and unnecessary delay' in processing the bill on access inequality in urban areas. The Veerian bill, dealing with the corresponding scheme for rural areas, was, in Saldanha's opinion, 'progressing satisfactorily'.

Saldanha was aggrieved that Rayaningar was not paying as much attention to his bill as he was to Veerian's although 'the trouble was greater' in the municipalities. His assessment, he said, would be borne out by the legislator from Malabar, Krishnan Nayar, who had 'experience of the recent trouble at Palghat'. Saldanha made no secret of his dissatisfaction with Rayaningar's laboured explanation for why his bill was still pending with the Select Committee.

Before the Madras Legislative Council could take up the Select Committee report on the Veerian bill, there was a related development in the Bombay Presidency. Since many local bodies across the province had failed to comply with the 1923 Bole Resolution on access, the Bombay Legislative Council passed another one on the subject on 6 August 1926. The second Bole Resolution called upon the government to 'reduce any discretionary grants that are paid to the municipalities and local boards which refuse to give effect' to the first one.[31]

At the end of that month, on 31 August 1926, the Madras

Legislative Council took the battle against access inequality to a different level by actually legislating on it. Sensing the magnitude of the achievement that was within his grasp, Veerian did not waste his breath on the the Select Committee's excision of the clause relating to water bodies, which was the heart of the Bole Resolution. There was still enough content in the bill to make a difference.

Mobilising support for his Bill, Veerian recalled instances when untouchables had been obstructed from using public roads in rural areas. He recalled the Kamalapuram episode in which, despite his privileged status as a legislator, Veerian had been obstructed from going to a post office located in an agraharam. As for the clause throwing open public markets in villages to untouchables, Veerian said that he was anxious 'to give them some status and to make other communities regard them at least as human beings, if not as their own brethren'.

Veerian concluded with an appeal that the bill be passed unanimously. Fittingly, M.C. Rajah, the first-ever legislator from the stigmatised community, formally seconded it. The only legislator other than Veerian to give a speech on that occasion was Saldanha, who spoke more about the promoter than his bill. In a touching display of solidarity, Saldanha congratulated Veerian 'on the crowning glory of his self-sacrificing and noble activities on behalf of the Depressed Classes inside and outside this Council for the last three years'.

As Saldanha held forth on Veerian's crusades against untouchability, Ruthnaswamy cut him short. The president asked sarcastically, 'But how is all this relevant to the point at issue? The question is not that Mr. Veerian be taken into consideration, but that his Bill be taken into consideration.' Wrapping up the discussion immediately, the Madras Legislative Council then passed the bill into law. That red-letter day was 31 August 1926.

About ten days later, the *Times of India* analysed the wider significance of the bill: 'It was a great achievement for Mr. Veerian, one of the most militant of their representatives, that he had been able to get his Bill passed.'[32] Dwelling on the backstory of the legislation, the newspaper said: 'Times without number Mr. Veerian had brought to the notice of the House the social tyranny of the higher castes, who would not permit a member of the depressed classes to go to a Post Office situated in a Brahmin street, or to enter the precincts of a Court of Law.' Holding that the government 'could not do anything in the face of these facts', it said: 'Mr. Veerian deserves credit for drawing public attention to the matter and the legislative enactment, which he has succeeded in piloting through the Council, should go a long way to remove many of the social disabilities of his Adi Dravida brethren.'

Goschen then sat on the bill for three months. Perhaps overcompensating for his failure to seek the viceroy's sanction prior to the introduction of the bill, he reserved the bill for the consideration of the viceroy rather than give his assent.

In his letter to the viceroy on 30 October 1926, Goschen made out that the bill had blurred the line between reserved and transferred powers in the dyarchy. Since the Bill made it an offence to obstruct someone from using a public road, it had the effect of, the governor felt, 'including within a transferred subject matters hitherto classified as reserved'.[33] In other words, a local self-government issue falling in the domain of a transferred subject had been turned by the bill into a criminal law subject falling in the domain of a reserved subject.

Irwin was unflustered. In the response sent on his behalf on 18 November 1926, the viceroy recalled that, before its passage, he had already sanctioned the bill in respect of all its provisions. 'No occasion, therefore, has, in the opinion of the Governor-General, arisen for His Excellency the Governor to reserve the Bill …'

As for the suggestion that the bill conflated a transferred subject with a reserved one, Irwin clarified that, despite the enactment of the bill by a provincial legislature, 'those matters remain central subjects'. Since Central subjects were unaffected by the dyarchy that had been introduced only in provinces, it was 'still open' to the Madras governor to 'grant or withhold his assent to the Bill' on the strength of the viceroy's previous sanction to it.

Goschen then gave his assent to the Veerian bill on 13 December

1926, and forwarded to Irwin for his final assent the Madras Local Boards Amendment Act, 1926. Irwin formally gave his assent on 13 January 1927, and the Act was notified as Act I of 1927. By then, fresh elections to the provincial and Central legislatures had already been held in November 1926. In the crop of nominations made to the third Madras Legislative Council under the 1919 Constitution, Veerian's absence was conspicuous.

Adi Dravidas from across the province gave a representation to the Goschen administration, protesting its failure to give him another term in the Council. His supporters saw the exclusion as the price that Veerian had to pay for his prodigious activism in the second Legislative Council. Whatever might have prompted Willingdon to nominate him in 1923, Veerian proved to be perhaps more than Goschen could take. There was a litany of complaints from officials who had been harried by Veerian inside or outside the Legislative Council on every eruption of untouchability.

No matter what the reason for the denial of a second term to Veerian, the enactment of his bill was a rare moment in India's history that, in retrospect, fits the trope of 'one small step for man, one giant leap for mankind'. The province that had been the first to elevate an untouchable to its legislature fittingly also produced the first-ever law against untouchability anywhere in the country. Adding to its significance was the fact that the bill had been piloted by a member of the victim community.

Even so, historians barely took notice of Veerian, let alone his trailblazing legislation. Rupa Viswanath was a rare exception in that her book, *The Pariah Problem,* examined the range of interventions that Veerian had made during his three-year stint as a legislator.[34] But she made no mention of his bill or its enactment, which Saldanha described as Veerian's 'crowning glory'.

As things came to pass, the enactment of Veerian's bill was followed by a succession of laws, in Madras and elsewhere in colonial and post-colonial India, doing away with caste restrictions on access to public places. In a happy coincidence, the promulgation of the Madras Local Boards Amendment Act was closely followed by the Mahad revolt in the Raigad district of the Bombay Presidency. On 20 March 1927, B.R. Ambedkar, a newly nominated member of the Bombay Legislative Council, mobilised an estimated 5,000 untouchables for a conference at Mahad in connection with a two-acre lake called Chavadar Tank, which had been open only to caste Hindus, Muslims and Christians.

This traditional restriction was in defiance of the Legislative Council's Bole Resolution of 1923 legalising access for untouchables to sources of water that had been built or maintained by bodies like the Mahad Municipality. The taboo persisted at the Chavadar Tank despite a resolution adopted by the Mahad Municipality in 1924 to implement the Bole Resolution.

On the basis of a decision taken at their conference, the untouchables, led by Ambedkar, marched to the Chavadar Tank. And, in a simple but subversive gesture, they drank water from it. Given that the Vaikom stir in a princely state had been propelled by Ezhavas, a borderline caste, Mahad was the first real revolt of the untouchables in British India.

This peaceful protest by the untouchables resulted in retaliatory violence from the caste Hindus of Mahad. Adding insult to injury, those touchable classes performed a purification ceremony in which, amid mantras chanted by Brahmin priests, they poured 108 pots of gomutra (cows's urine) into Chavadar Tank. To prevent any further 'desecration' of the lake by untouchables, they forced the Mahad Municipality to withdraw its 1924 resolution, which it did on 4 August 1927.

The purification ceremony and the rollback of the caste reform in Mahad provoked a spirited response from Ambedkar and his followers. On 11 September 1927, they announced that they would offer satyagraha on Christmas that year to reassert their right to access that water body. A few days before the due date, Mahad's caste Hindus filed a suit and sought a temporary injunction, claiming that a fresh contamination of the water would result in an 'irreparable injury' to them.

On 14 December 1927, sub-judge G.V. Vaidya allowed their

prayer saying, 'I am bound to attach great weight to the sentiment of the applicants.' Vaidya's reasoning was more political than legal. He said he was 'taking into consideration, how sensitive the touchable classes generally are on this point, both on account of their religious susceptibilities as well as the wide gulf which has existed between the two communities from time immemorial.'[35]

Despite the judgment, a huge number of untouchables gathered in Mahad on 25 December, the scheduled day of the satyagraha. Though they were now forbidden to draw water from Chavadar, Ambedkar pulled off an even more audacious protest. At what was the second conference he held that year in Mahad, a Brahmin associate of his, Gangadhar Sahasrabuddhe, proposed a resolution against the Manusmriti, the most notorious legal text of caste Hindus. The resolution attacked its verses that 'undermined the Shudra caste, thwarted their progress and made their social, political and economic slavery permanent'.[36] The sanctions that the Manusmriti imposed on the Shudras applied even more virulently to the untouchables, who were largely beneath the notice of the scriptures.

The operative part of the resolution was that 'this conference is performing the cremation rites of such a religious book which has been divisive of people and destroyer of humanity'. After Sahasrabuddhe had read out a few of its objectionable verses, the conference went on to ceremoniously burn the Manusmriti. This unprecedented assault on the Brahminical text sent shock waves across India.

It so happened that the Congress was meeting in Madras the very next day for its annual session. Having boycotted the Simon Committee that had been appointed to devise the next round of constitutional reforms, the Congress set up an 'All Parties Conference' to draft a constitution for India. Chaired by Motilal Nehru, the All Parties Conference served as an opportunity for Congress to review its 1922 Bardoli Resolution in the wake of the developments in Mahad. The Bardoli Resolution had recognised segregation between touchable and untouchable classes as a compromise wherever caste prejudice was too entrenched.

The Nehru report, submitted on 28 August 1928, abandoned this policy. Its segment on Fundamental Rights included this categorical clause: 'All citizens have an equal right of access to, and use of, public roads, public wells and all other places of public resort.' This was the first sign that the Indians had displayed their potential to draft a constitution that made no concession to caste prejudice.

❖

Meanwhile, the Madras Presidency set another legislative milestone. Saldanha reintroduced the Madras District Municipalities Amendment Bill. Broadly mirroring Veerian's original set of three clauses for rural areas, the Saldanha bill dealt with access to public places in urban areas. In the fresh reference that followed, the Select Committee submitted its report in a vastly changed political scenario in Madras.[37]

The Justice Party was no longer in power, and in fact, no party had obtained a majority in the 1926 election. So, an unaffiliated member called P. Subbarayan came to be chief minister. But neither he nor any of his ministers were part of the Select Committee formed for the Saldanha bill. Chastened perhaps by Mahad, the committee headed by T.C. Srinivasa Ayyangar, a Brahmin lawyer from Ramnad, cleared the bill with minor amendments. Besides, unlike the Rayaningar-led Select Committee on the Veerian bill, this one had no objection to throwing open tanks and wells.

So, when Saldanha had presented the Select Committee report to the House on 7 August 1929, there was an attempt to address the resulting asymmetry between urban and rural areas. Srinivasan and a caste Hindu legislator from Bezawada, A. Kaleswara Rao, moved amendments to add a clause providing universal access to water bodies in rural areas too.

Srinivasan's proposal was the more ambitious one in that it sought to throw open not only water bodies that were 'public' but also those that were 'private'. Chief Minister P. Subbarayan expressed reservations about the proposed parity between public and private water bodies. 'With regard to the use of public wells and tanks, I am quite willing to accept the amendment,' Subbarayan said, 'but with regard to private wells, etc., I am afraid I cannot accept this amendment.'

Yielding to the chief minister's concern, Srinivasan said that he had 'no objection to delete the word "private" from the amendment'. No attempt was made to carry out that deletion from Srinivasan's amendment, though. Thus, his amendment was put to the House in its original form, covering private wells too. The upshot was that the House 'negatived' the amendment.

Rao's amendment, however, was confined to wells that were very much public. It still came under attack from A. Ranganatha Mudaliyar, a former minister in Subbarayan's cabinet. Mudaliyar flagged a caste complexity which he believed Saldanha had overlooked: even when a well was considered public, 'all people may not be entitled or are not permitted to use it'. Mudaliyar said that the use of public wells 'in many villages' was 'restricted to one class, viz, the caste people of the village'. He added that 'it has been the immemorial custom in such villages for the caste people to take out water from these wells and pour it out for the use of the Depressed Classes'.

The idea of letting untouchables draw water from public wells in villages was so discomfiting that an upper-caste legislator from Vizag, P.C. Venkatapathi Raju, proposed that any further consideration of Rao's amendment be adjourned. The president of the Legislative Council, C.V.S. Narasimha Raju, who was the leader of the Swaraj Party, the largest group in the House, put the adjournment proposal to voice vote and declared that it was 'lost'. But the Hindu conservatives demanded a 'poll', and the result turned out to be very different: 'Ayes' 82, 'Noes' one and 'Neutral' nine. 'The motion was carried and the consideration of the business was adjourned.'

When the matter was taken up next on 27 September 1929, the presiding officer, Narasimha Raju, hit back with a technical objection to Rao's amendment. Comparing it with Srinivasan's amendment, he said that the two were 'substantially identical'. Since the only difference was that Srinivasan's amendment was not confined to public wells, Raju argued that, when it was under consideration, 'a motion ought to have made for the omission of the word "private"'. But before ruling Rao's amendment 'out of order', Raju said that he wanted to know what the mover had 'to say on the point'.

Kaleshwara Rao asserted that his amendment had 'nothing to do' with the other, and doubted whether it would be legal to throw open private wells as suggested by Srinivasan. Referring to the statutory powers conferred on a local board president, Rao asked, 'When a president restricts the use of a private well for certain purposes, then how can all persons go and use it?'

Narasimha Raju still ruled out Rao's amendment, scuttling the attempt to do away with water-access restrictions in villages. As far as urban areas were concerned, however, the House went on to pass the Saldanha bill that same day—about three years after the untouchables in rural areas had been empowered to access public roads and markets. Governor N.E. Marjoribanks gave his assent to the Saldanha bill on 24 October 1929, promulgating it as the Madras District Municipalities Amendment Act.

The enactment had an immediate impact on the Kalpathy car festival, which began on 13 November 1929. It was five years since the Ezhavas, led by Raghavan, had made their first attempt to witness the festival, following G.O. No. 2660. They were finally able to enter agraharam streets and witness the car festival without triggering violence or facing legal repercussions. The ground for this change was also prepared by, as the *Times of India* put it, 'the unceasing efforts of the Arya Samaj', which remained engaged with the Kalpathy problem despite Swami Shraddhanand's murder in Delhi in 1926. He had been murdered by a Muslim fanatic in retaliation to his controversial 'shuddhi' campaign, which was meant to 'bring back' those who had left the Hindu fold.

Irwin gave his assent to the Saldanha Act on 15 November 1929, which coincidentally marked the conclusion of the three-day car festival. The new law superseded G.O. No. 37, under which Ezhavas and other low castes could have entered the Kalpathy agraharams only for reasons of 'business' or 'practical convenience'. They were now legally empowered to enter those streets even if only to assert their 'abstract right' to watch the car festival or assert their equality.

In its report, the *Times of India* said, '(The) ban has now been completely removed and in consequence this year a large number of Ezhavas entered the Kalpathy agraharam without let or hindrance and thoroughly enjoyed the "tamasha" as much as the high-born among the Hindus.'[38] Such was the dramatic transformation in the heart of the Malabar district, which had long been a byword for caste bigotry. This legal reform flowed from the principle of inclusive governance that had been upheld a decade earlier with the appointment of the first untouchable to the legislature.

❖

Legislative advancements, such as they were, led to a high-level acknowledgement that untouchability prevailed across British India in varying degrees. The 1930 report of the Simon Commission said: 'The disabilities of the Depressed Classes are undoubtedly most severely felt in Madras, and especially in Malabar. In the latter district is still found the phenomenon—now almost unknown elsewhere—of "unapproachability".' The next in order of severity, according to the Simon Commission, were the neighbouring Bombay and Central Provinces. In those two provinces, 'the position', it said, 'though no doubt less acute, is probably more or less comparable to that in Madras'.[39]

The Simon Commission, otherwise known as the Indian Statutory Commission, was the first official body to recommend that the dyarchy be replaced by provincial autonomy. In November 1930, the British government invited Indian leaders from across the political spectrum to the Round Table Conference in London, where this and other findings of the commission would be discussed.

But Gandhi and his associates were in jail at the time for their participation in the Civil Disobedience Movement, and so, the

Congress boycotted the conference. This resulted in the failure of the First Round Table Conference. The negotiations that followed his release in January 1931 culminated a few weeks later in the famous Gandhi–Irwin pact. The Civil Disobedience Movement was called off, and the prospect of the Congress participating in the Second Round Table Conference opened up.

As part of its preparations, the Congress held a special session from 26 to 31 March 1931 at Karachi, where it adopted a resolution on Fundamental Rights for what it called the 'Swaraj Constitution'. Echoing the Motilal Nehru report of 1928, the Congress Resolution envisaged 'equal rights to all citizens in regard to public roads, wells, schools and other places of public resort'.

The day after the Karachi session had concluded, the Congress Working Committee announced two major decisions. One was to appoint Gandhi as its representative at the next Round Table Conference. The other was to equip Gandhi for his London mission with material elaborating on the Karachi Resolution. To this end, it appointed a Fundamental Rights Committee under C. Rajagopalachari, inviting opinions from provincial units and others.

From this consultative exercise emerged a more nuanced clause on access inequality, enriched by previous debates over the two Madras enactments. On 25 June 1931, the Rajaji committee proposed: 'All citizens have equal rights and duties in regard to wells, roads, schools and places of public resort, maintained out of State or local funds, or dedicated by private persons for the use of the general public.'[40] In doing away with the usual qualification of roads and wells with the term 'public', and in coming up with the deft insertion of the term 'private' in relation to persons, the Rajaji Committee's formulation turned out to be more expansive than those early laws.

Around this time, perhaps driven by the breakthrough in Madras, the Central Provinces saw an attempt to legislate on the access issue. The foremost leader of the untouchables in that province, Ganesh Akaji Gavai, introduced a bill that was more audacious than anything that had been tried in Madras. Departing from the Veerian–Saldanha approach of slipping in access-related provisions in general laws concerning local bodies, Gavai's 1931 bill was a standalone law overtly taking on access restrictions in both rural and urban areas: the Central Provinces Public Places User Bill. The one compromise it made was that the penalty imposed on violators was a maximum fine of Rs 50, half of what was laid down by the Madras laws.[41]

While this bill was still pending, there was a dramatic change in the nation's mood in the wake of the Poona Pact. The Select Committee's report, which Gavai tabled on 21 January 1933, actually strengthened the bill, thereby reflecting the reformist zeal that had momentarily gripped the Hindu community. The Select Committee dropped an exception that Gavai had proposed to the general clause on public places—that they shall be universally accessible 'unless they are lawfully constructed, established, reserved or restricted for the use of any particular class, community or caste of people'.

Further, the Select Committee introduced an explanation enumerating some of the public places that would be thrown open and the list included non-secular spaces too. 'Burial or burning ground' was one such inclusion. The opening up of funeral spaces had first been conceded by conservative Congress leader Madan Mohan Malaviya in the wake of the 1932 Poona Pact.

But then, as the practice of burying the dead was more prevalent among non-Hindus, the House made an improvement in the course of its debate by attaching a condition to that clause. 'Provided that a burial or burning ground reserved for or used by people following a particular religion shall be a public place for such people only.' These tweaks were incorporated on the same day, and the Central Provinces Legislative Council passed what was not only the first law against untouchability in British India outside Madras but also the most advanced of the time.

The Central Provinces legislation set the stage for the next round of reforms, this time at the national level. M.C. Rajah—the first untouchable to make it to a legislature, at the provincial level in 1919 and the national level in 1927—was the initiator. He made two attempts to push through a national enactment against untouchability, failing both times. But when he returned to the Madras legislature in 1937 in a vastly changed constitutional scenario, he finally succeeded in his mission, although it was now only a provincial enactment.

His first attempt was the ambitiously titled Untouchability Abolition Bill, which, as he disclosed later, had been drafted by Rajaji. The collaboration between Rajaji and Rajah followed the promises that caste Hindu leaders had made to the untouchables after the Poona Pact at a meeting chaired by Malaviya in Bombay. One of those promises was to secure statutory recognition for the principle of allowing untouchables 'the same rights as other Hindus' in using public places. For his part, Rajah participated in this reform project despite leaving the Justice Party for the little-known Centre Party, headed by the unabashedly orthodox G. Krishnamachariar.[42]

Since a separate bill had been drafted by then for temple entry, the Rajah bill was taken to be mainly about disabilities in the secular sphere. It said that 'no penalty, disadvantage or disability shall be imposed upon, or any discrimination made or recognized against, any subject of the State on the ground that such person belongs to any untouchable caste or class among Hindus'.

Rajah introduced the bill in the Central Legislative Assembly on 24 March 1933. Though the House was presided over by Justice Party leader Shanmukham Chetty, who had a record of engaging with caste reform, Rajah's bill ran into rough weather. When he moved for a Select Committee reference, there was a protracted debate between progressive and orthodox Hindus on three days spread over five months. Eventually, on an amendment moved by his own party boss, Krishnamachariar, the House decided to circulate Rajah's bill for eliciting public opinion. As things panned out, some provinces delayed sending in their feedback, and the bill lapsed on the expiry of the term of the Assembly in 1934.

The feedback, it turned out, was mostly adverse. So, Rajah returned to the next Assembly with another draft that addressed some of the concerns raised. To begin with, the title of the bill he introduced on 26 September 1935 avoided the term 'untouchability'. It was called the Removal of Civic Disabilities Bill. While his first bill referred only to 'an untouchable caste', his second bill covered 'Harijans, Untouchables, Depressed Class or Backward Class'.

Though Rajah's first bill had made no explicit reference to the access problem, his second bill expanded the public places that would be open to equal access even beyond the Madras example: 'stream, river, public well, tank, pathway, convenience or transport or any other service'. Besides, the ambit of his reform was not limited to public places maintained by government or local-body funds, but to all public places that 'the general public belonging to all other classes of Hindus have a right to enjoy or have access to'.

The government insisted on circulating the second iteration too for eliciting public opinion, rather than referring it to a Select Committee straightaway. On 17 April 1936, the Central Legislative Assembly adopted that motion.

A joint secretary in the Home Department, J.A. Thorne, who had served as district magistrate of Palghat at the time of the 1924 Kalpathy violence, was instrumental in scuttling the Select Committee reference. On the vexed issue of caste, he still betrayed the old colonial ambivalence. In a note on 17 September 1936, after opinions had been received from the provinces on Rajah's second bill, Thorne made out that much had changed since the Kalpathy episode. 'If Mr. Rajah's Bill had been limited to removing disabilities in connection with a place or institution maintained by Government funds, it would have been reasonable but such a disability hardly exists *now*.' (emphasis added) On the other hand, Thorne invoked the majoritarian principle to override social justice. 'The opinions received make it clear that the majority of Hindus are against the Bill; the orthodox rural community is solidly against it and this community much outnumbers the urban classes from which the supporters of the Bill mainly come.'[43]

Deterred by such inputs, the Government of India, now headed by Lord Linlithgow, decided that 'the official bloc should remain neutral' on Rajah's bill. But before it could get an opportunity to express its neutrality in the Central Legislative Assembly, the bill lapsed as it was overtaken by major constitutional changes ensuing from the Government of India Act, 1935.

The new constitution incorporated the reservation of electoral constituencies for Depressed Classes as envisaged in the Poona Pact. The 1935 Act renamed the Depressed Classes as 'Scheduled Castes'. It also replaced the system of dyarchy with the much-touted provincial autonomy. In the larger provinces, the Act also introduced a bicameral legislature entailing a Legislative Assembly and a Legislative Council. The presiding officer of the provincial Assembly was designated as the 'speaker'. Unlike the chief minister under the old system, the premier of each province had jurisdiction over all its departments. In the 1937 elections, the Congress obtained a majority, or close to it, in the larger provinces such as Madras, Bombay and the United Provinces. However, the office of governor had been empowered with veto powers undermining the authority of the elected government. The Congress expressed reservations about assuming office under this constitutional uncertainty.

As the resulting stalemate affected his home province too, Rajah saw an incentive in returning to it. The opportunity came on 1 April 1937, just when Rajah was due to move the next motion on his untouchability bill in the Central Legislative Assembly. On 29 March 1937, which was three days prior to the D-Day, Thorne made a cryptic file noting: 'It is quite possible that Mr Rajah will not be present to move his motion—especially if he has hopes of inclusion in the Madras "interim Ministry".'[44] An interim regime was being cobbled together pending the colonial administration's negotiations with the Congress.

On 31 March 1937, Thorne confirmed that Rajah was being inducted into the Madras government the very day he was due to proceed with his bill in the Central Legislative Assembly. And 'it seems therefore that he will not be present tomorrow to proceed with the Bill, even if that were now possible'. Rajah was indeed inducted as a minister in the interim government headed by Kurma

Venkatareddy Naidu, who was, like him, a former member of the Justice Party. In short, the newly introduced scheme of greater provincial autonomy took Rajah back to Madras and spelt the end of his second national bill on caste disabilities.

It took about three months for the British Raj to convince the Congress party that governors were unlikely to misuse their veto powers. Once Rajaji took over as premier, Rajah was back to playing the role of a legislator. This was how his third legislative bid for throwing open public places turned out to be in Madras. And it was a replica of his second bill, which had been abandoned midway in the Central legislature.

On 30 March 1938, Rajah moved a motion for referring his bill to a Select Committee, which included Rajaji and his Harijan minister, V.I. Muniswami Pillai. In his address to the Madras Legislative Assembly, Rajah traced the genesis of his bill to the earliest untouchability-related bill that had been proposed at the national level by M.R. Jayakar in 1929 (an abortive attempt discussed elsewhere in the book). It was curious that he chose to recall the national precedent rather than the older one set in that very province by Veerian, and which Rajah himself had seconded before its enactment in 1926.[45]

Rajah also acknowledged that his first attempt, the Untouchability Abolition Bill, had been drafted by Rajaji and that he only had 'the honour of introducing' it in the Central legislature. For the drafting of the substantially different second bill, which he had also introduced in the Central legislature, Rajah thanked the secretary of the Madras Legislative Council, R.V. Krishna Ayyar. Rajah explained that on receiving Ayyar's draft, he had 'sent it again to Mr Rajagopalachariar for final touches'.

Reacting petulantly to this disclosure, Rajaji said, 'I think the hon. Member's memory is all wrong. I do not think anybody else drafted the Bill but myself.' Rajah stood his ground, clarifying the confusion in Rajaji's mind. 'Sir, I am the person who gave the Bill to Mr R.V. Krishna Ayyar. I am not talking of the first Bill. I am talking of the second Bill, the Bill which is now [replicated] before the House.' Realising that he did indeed confuse the first bill with the subsequent ones, Rajaji suggested as a face-saver that the entire exchange be expunged from the proceedings. 'Sir, it is very nice to refer to all these things, about the drafters of this Bill and so forth; but I submit it should not go into the proceedings.' The speaker, B. Sambamurti, did not agree to expunge the crosstalk on the drafters. And the Assembly passed Rajah's motion for referring his bill to the Select Committee.

The committee made only minor changes, including the replacement of the word 'civic' in the title with 'civil'. The one substantive amendment it made was to underline the distinctiveness of the bill on access to secular spaces from the parallel one on temple entry. The Select Committee replaced the expression 'other service', used in a residuary sense, with 'secular institution'. The change was meant to make it 'perfectly clear' that it was 'not the intention of the present Bill to affect the usages of temples or religious institutions'.

On 17 August 1938, Rajah presented the Select Committee report to the Legislative Assembly.[46] In the course of the same day, it passed the bill unanimously. Since Rajah, as a private member of the Legislative Assembly, did not have access to the Legislative Council, the Rajaji government assumed the responsibility of piloting it in the latter House. On 12 December 1938, T.S.S. Rajan, a Brahmin minister in the Rajaji government, moved the bill there in the form it had been passed by the Assembly.[47]

The members of the Madras Legislative Council who responded to Rajan's address included Srinivasan and Saldanha, access-equality pioneers from the dyarchy era. Srinivasan began with caustic remarks about the social antecedents of Rajan and Rajaji. 'It is very encouraging to me to find the Mover of the Bill and the Premier are Brahmins and Aryans. Their ancients introduced the caste system and caused all these troubles to the people.'[48]

As the Veerian and Saldanha laws had failed to make much of an impact, Srinivasan harked back to a measure that his 1924 resolution had originally proposed—to spread awareness about the reform by the 'beat of tom-tom'. Had this suggestion been retained when his resolution was passed, the subsequent amendments to the general Acts relating to local boards and municipalities might have had a greater impact. Srinivasan said, 'What the Government should do is to give wide publicity to this Bill after its enactment, together with the amendments to the above Acts, by the beat of drums in every village in the Province.'

Saldanha for his part was more concerned about a substantive issue: the absence of any penalty despite the precedents that Veerian and he had set.[49] In the bill that had been 'brought forward by Mr Veerian', Saldanha pointed to the clause 'prescribing a penalty for the infringement of the rights laid down'. He lamented that, in the Rajah bill, 'there is no provision for punishing a man who prevents the enjoyment of any of these privileges'. As Saldanha explained, 'It is simply stated in the Bill that no civil or criminal or revenue court shall recognize any custom or usage; this will lead to nothing if there is an infringement of the custom.' While it was 'more comprehensive' than the earlier laws in terms of coverage and granted immunity to untouchables against the charge of violating caste restrictions, the Rajah bill did not penalise in any way those who obstructed them. 'I consider this to be a very serious defect,' Saldanha said, framing it as an instance of backsliding.

It was indeed telling that so serious a defect existed in the bill adopted by the Rajaji government, the first Congress dispensation in Madras. It showed that Congress could not muster the courage that the Justice Party had displayed more than a decade earlier by penalising caste Hindus for practising untouchability.

The trajectory of M.C. Rajah's advocacy too is revealing. Even before the introduction of the dyarchy system, he had been the first untouchable to have moved a resolution on the issue in any legislature. Two decades later, he was instrumental in the enactment of what was by far the most sweeping declaration of access rights. To make this advancement, though, he forsook the coercive element—the teeth to bite the offenders—that was at the heart of the earlier access-related legislations.

The Council passed the Rajah bill exactly as it had been received from the Assembly. After the 1933 Central Provinces enactment, the

Madras Removal of Civil Disabilities Act, 1938 was the first law that overtly dealt with access to public places. The gap between its grand title and its limited provisions fuelled further battles for equality during the process of decolonisation.

Though the title of the 1938 Madras law was couched in a non-sectarian language, the deeply Hindu nature of the discrimination it was combating came through in its preamble: 'Whereas it is increasingly felt by the Hindu community that the disabilities, which are imposed by social custom and usage on certain classes of Hindus commonly known as Harijans, Untouchables or Depressed Classes, and which have been in certain matters even legally recognized in the adjudication of rights and duties in civil and criminal proceedings, are repugnant to modern conditions and ideas of justice and social solidarity, and should no longer be recognized by law or otherwise enforced.'

10

THE DRAMA OF ABOLITION

The criminal laws in Britain evolved organically, piece by piece, over the centuries. When it came to India, its largest colony, Britain enacted in the nineteenth century comprehensive criminal codes, procedural and substantive. The IPC of 1860 turned out to be what was, at least until then, the world's largest ever consolidation of substantive criminal provisions. For all its professed Indian orientation, though, the IPC steered clear of untouchability, a rampant form of physical and mental cruelty that was inflicted by one section of Hindus on another. The IPC criminalised homosexuality, adultery and defamation, but not the blatant and very India-specific offence of untouchability.

In 1937, almost eight decades later, the Indian National Congress, the largest political party in the colony, assumed power for the first time. Its maiden stint in office in half a dozen provinces lasted about two years. Yet, on the subject of combating untouchability, the Congress governments made legislative progress that was hardly commensurate with Gandhi's rhetoric. ('I would far rather that Hinduism died than that untouchability lived.')

Though discrimination in secular spaces was the less touchy aspect of caste prejudice, no Congress-ruled province of the time, other than Madras, succeeded in enacting a law in this regard. And even that was thanks to the tenacity displayed by the untouchable legislator, M.C. Rajah, who was not part of Congress. The indifferent performance of these Congress governments was not for want of effort though.

The B.G. Kher government in Bombay, in fact, came up with a more advanced bill than the one that had been enacted in Madras. The Bombay bill provided for penalty, thereby preferring, however unwittingly, the Veerian model over the more recent Rajah–Rajaji approach.

To begin with, Section 4 of the Bombay Harijan (Removal of Disabilities) Bill enlisted an array of public places that 'no Harijan shall on the ground that he is a Harijan' be barred from accessing or using 'notwithstanding any law, custom or usage to the contrary'. As a corollary, Section 7 laid down that whoever contravened Section 4 'shall on conviction be punishable with fine which may extend to Rs 200 and in the case of a continuing offence, with an additional fine which may extend to Rs 20 for every day after the first during which he has persisted in the offence'. The penal clause was modest as, even against a repeat offender, all it provided was a monetary fine.

Its penal scheme was a major talking point when Home Minister K.M. Munshi introduced the bill in the Bombay Legislative Assembly on 19 April 1939.[1] The Independent Labour Party, founded by Ambedkar three years earlier, was critical of the bill for not going far enough. Though Ambedkar was a member of the Assembly, he left it to two of his followers, R.R. Bhole and B.K. Gaikwad, to articulate the party's reservations.

Responding to Munshi's motion that the bill be 'read a first time', Bhole said, 'As a matter of principle for the abolition of untouchability by legislation, I might say that our Party is with the Government, but the ways and the means that are incorporated in the Bill … are such that we beg to differ.'

Bhole's main grievance was that the burden of securing conviction under the bill was placed entirely on untouchables without any intervention from the police. None of the untouchability-related offences covered by the bill were 'cognisable', which meant that an aggrieved untouchable would have to file a complaint before a judicial magistrate and prove his charges by engaging a lawyer.

A future judge of the Bombay High Court, Bhole proposed that the offences in question be made cognisable so that the police could take over the responsibility of initiating action against offenders. Speaking on the vulnerability of untouchables, he said, 'Because these people are not able to complain against the atrocities committed by the villagers on them, the police authorities should take the responsibility on their shoulders to conduct their cases and have them decided by a court of law.'

Gaikwad followed up with several instances of denial of access, bearing out the need for the intervention of the police with their coercive powers. When the speaker, G.V. Mavalankar, sought to cut him short, Bhole reiterated, 'My suggestion is that the offences should be made cognizable.' Mavalankar shot back, 'The honourable Member has stated it more than four times in different forms.'

Premier Kher too took a dig at Gaikwad's elaborate speech, but was cryptic about why he rejected the idea of making the offences cognisable: 'The honourable Member will see that the panacea which he suggests, namely, to make everything a cognizable offence, is not the right remedy. It is a bad remedy, and he will find for himself that that is not a remedy through which he or the members of the Scheduled Castes will benefit.'

The mover of the bill, Home Minister Munshi, was more candid in explaining why the government was disinclined to empower the police to deal with untouchability: 'no Government can say that anybody who does anything to the Harijans must invariably be put in a lockup'. Seeking to pass off this strawman argument as pragmatism, Munshi said, 'When a Bill of this kind is put on the Statute Book, it will be effectively carried out. It is no use putting on the Statute Book a Bill which everybody will conspire to frustrate.' Social legislation, he claimed, could go only 'up to the extent to which public opinion is ready', adding, 'In this matter where the prejudices of centuries are concerned, we can go only a little in advance of the public opinion.'

While acknowledging the odds that had been stacked against them for centuries, Munshi made a virtue out of leaving it entirely to Harijans to assert the right conferred on them by the bill. Calling it a 'direct remedy', he said, 'Here it does not depend upon the police or upon the Government to take the initiative. If there is a breach of the provisions of the bill when it is enacted into law, it will be open to the Harijans concerned to take steps.'

After a debate that left unresolved the issue of cognisability, the Assembly referred Munshi's bill to a Select Committee that included Kher and Munshi. Though Ambedkar had declined the previous year to join the Select Committee on a temple-entry legislation, he allowed two of his party colleagues, Gaikwad and D.G. Jadhav, to join the one dealing with disabilities in the secular domain. Nothing came of this Select Committee for six months, and then the Congress decided that all its governments would step down in protest against Viceroy Linlithgow's decision to drag India into the Second World War.

Suddenly, the Bombay bill acquired urgency. On 9 October 1939, the Rajaji government left office in Madras. The very next day, in the Bombay Legislative Assembly, Munshi tabled the report of the Select Committee.[2]

The Select Committee had made several changes, but the offences were still not rendered cognisable. This had provoked both Gaikwad and Jadhav to attach a 'minute of dissent' to the Select Committee report. Calling the bill 'an eyewash', they wrote, 'If the Bombay Government seriously mean to eradicate the evil of untouchability, they must take courage in both their hands and stand forth for bold changes in the social system, come what may.'

Among the bold changes they sought—but were rejected by the other members of the Select Committee—was to take the reform beyond the public spaces that were owned or maintained by the government or local bodies, which was by now a recurring question. Their dissent note said, 'All shops of all kinds ... in short all institutions owned by any individual or individuals in whatever capacity but catering to public needs and dependent on the public for their conduct and maintenance must be thrown open to the Scheduled Castes along with the other members of the public.' To enforce access equality in those privately-owned public places, the duo suggested a compulsory licence which was liable to be 'withdrawn immediately in case the Scheduled Castes are found to be debarred'.

In regard to criminal liability for the offences, Gaikwad and Jadhav upped the ante by saying that denial of access to any of the public places must be 'suppressed with a ruthless hand'. However, there would be no question of any sort of ruthlessness without the coercive powers of the police. 'All the offences under such an Act,' they said, 'shall have, therefore, to be made cognizable.'

Explaining this need further, the two followers of Ambedkar wrote, 'It is an acknowledged fact that the persons belonging to the Scheduled Castes are indigent, ignorant, downtrodden and cannot fight their cases successfully in the courts of law. It is the Government, therefore, that must fight the battle of these Scheduled Castes in the name of humanity and citizenship.'

Without incorporating either of the amendments suggested by Ambedkar's party, the Kher government placed the bill on the agenda of both the Assembly and the Council on 31 October 1939. It was too little too late, for that was its last day in the legislature.[3]

When the Assembly took up the bill, R.R. Bhole was again the first respondent, and he spoke only to express opposition on behalf of the Independent Labour Party. 'In connection with the Harijan Bill, we would oppose it as it stands at present.' Puckishly, Bhole recalled a Marathi proverb: 'Feeling generous, the king gave us a leaky pumpkin.'

In a swift counter-attack, Munshi said, 'As a matter of fact, this Bill was intended to confer certain rights on the Harijans for which the Independent Labour Party was clamouring for long. As they themselves oppose it, we do not want to take advantage of the fact that we have taken it out of its turn. If they oppose, things will remain the same. We are sorry that they oppose it.'

Gaikwad sprang to the defence of Ambedkar and his followers. 'On behalf of my party, I say that we have not been clamouring for a measure of this type. If we go through the Bill, we will find that no provision is made in the Bill to remove the real disabilities of the Scheduled Castes.'

At this point, Kher brought the curtain down on the debate saying, 'The business for the day is finished.' Speaker Mavalankar followed up with a farewell message and adjourned indefinitely the proceedings of the Assembly.

Addressing the Council that afternoon, Kher gave an account of how the bill had collapsed in the Assembly. He said that, though the representatives of the Independent Labour Party were 'most vitally concerned' with it, 'they did not think the Bill went far enough and therefore they were opposed to it'. He explained that his government did not pursue the bill any further as 'it was not our intention to rush any legislation through if members of the Opposition had any objection to it'.[4]

Six years later, Kher would have another opportunity to enact an equal access law. Throughout those years, due to the Second World War, the post of premier had remained vacant. When the next election was held in 1946, the Congress won a thumping majority and Kher was back as premier of Bombay.

In contrast, Ambedkar's new party, the Scheduled Castes Federation, was routed and left with no presence in the new Assembly. Concurrently, since the Congress party had won big in the reserved seats across Bombay, the caste composition of its legislators changed significantly. The Kher government now included a Harijan in G.D. Tapase as minister for Backward Class Department.

On 25 September 1946, Tapase introduced in the Assembly a fresh version of the bill, renamed as the Harijan (Removal of Social Disabilities) Bill. It incorporated not only the amendments that had been proposed by the Select Committee in 1939 but also the change sought by its two dissenting members, Gaikwad and Jadhav, on the issue of cognisability.[5]

Tapase, in fact, used the word 'bold' while announcing a tacit rethink on something Kher himself had dismissed as a 'bad remedy'. 'I will now refer to the most important clause in this Bill, namely, clause 8, which is the crowning-stone of this Bill. This is a bold step that Government has taken. All offences falling under this Bill are made cognizable.'

In another bold step, the Kher government enhanced the penalty by introducing the option of imprisonment of up to three months. Further, a second conviction would take that up to six months and a third conviction would entail imprisonment of up to one year. It was a dramatic upgradation in the profile of access-related crimes—as non-cognisable offences in the previous bill, they would have been punishable only with monetary fines.

Equally remarkable was the response to it, when decolonisation was in the air. There was no opposition from anyone in the Assembly. If anything, some members wished that the bill were more stringent. S.N. Mane, a Harijan legislator from Belgaum, feared that 'untouchables in the villages will not be in a position to take advantage of this Bill' and would 'not dare to lodge complaints against caste Hindus'. Responding to this apprehension, Tapase said, 'I do admit this, and Government is also aware of this fact; and it is because of this that Government have provided … that all offences under this Bill are cognizable.'

After the Assembly had completed the first reading of the new bill on the day of its introduction, the government chose Gandhi's birthday, 2 October 1946, for its enactment. As Kher put it, 'We thought that a reform that was dear to his heart, because he looks upon all humanity as his kith and kin, could well be initiated on a day like this.'[6]

In this reform credited to Gandhi, the Congress regime incorporated another bold change that the dissent note of Ambedkar's followers had demanded seven years earlier: forbidding untouchability even in privately-owned public places. An amendment to this effect was moved by Congress legislator D.N. Wandrekar, who was a parliamentary secretary, a post junior to that of a minister's. Wandrekar simply said that the amendment he was moving was in response to the suggestion that the bill should provide for 'throwing open all shops to the Harijans'.

Tapase promptly said, 'Sir, I accept the amendment.' The amendment was put to the House and 'agreed to' by a voice vote. The result was a clause saying that 'no Harijan shall merely on the ground that he is a Harijan' be prevented from 'having access to a shop to which the members of all other castes and classes of Hindus are ordinarily admitted'. The manner in which caste Hindus were referred to in this clause was consistent with the language used for them elsewhere in the bill.

The collaboration between Tapase and Wandrekar did not end with that. Having made an addition to the section on 'Rights of Harijans', Wandrekar proposed a corresponding duty on those accountable for the public places concerned. Headlined 'Discrimination against Harijans prohibited', the new section said, 'No person in charge of any of the places referred to ... shall impose any restriction on a Harijan or act in a manner as to result in discrimination against him merely on the ground that he is a Harijan.'

Wandrekar explained why this was necessary: 'Although certain rights are given to the Harijans ... it is likely that they may be discriminated against. It is in order to prevent such discrimination that the new clause has been proposed.' Again, Tapase readily accepted the amendment and the House endorsed it.

Joining the debate after these value additions had been carried out, Kher admitted that the provisions of the 1939 bill were 'not quite so wide as the provisions of this Bill are'. All the same, 'we had hoped to pass it before we resigned our office'. And that hope did not materialise only because 'the group which then represented the Scheduled Classes (sic), led by the hon. Member Dr Ambedkar, opposed it'. He took pride in saying that 'we have now brought a Bill which goes very much further'.

He did not mention that these new measures were the kind of changes that Ambedkar's group had demanded, and were the reason why the previous version of the bill had not been passed. Understandably, Kher was keen to avoid explaining how something that he had believed in 1939 to be a 'bad remedy' was desirable in 1946.

In any event, the incorporation of these twelve words in the Bombay enactment—'an offence punishable under this Act shall be cognizable by the police'—was another breakthrough in the evolution of civil rights in India.

The process of evolution began in Madras in 1926, with the Veerian enactment imposing a criminal sanction on the denial of access to untouchables. It took twenty years via the Mahad Satyagraha for Bombay to take the law against untouchability to the next level, where the State was entrusted with the responsibility of bringing the offenders to book. Underlying it all was the immense churn, from Madras to Bombay, which had challenged caste Hindus to accept that untouchability, even in a non-violent form, was worthy of an FIR. The norms established by the 1946 Act set the tone for the Constituent Assembly which came into existence around the same time. Both Munshi and Ambedkar would play key roles in drafting the untouchability-related constitutional provisions for decolonised India.

As a member of the Sub-Committee on Fundamental Rights, Munshi proposed on 17 March 1947 what became the first draft of the provision abolishing untouchability. Munshi's draft said, 'Untouchability is abolished and the practice thereof is punishable by the law of the land.' It had two distinct elements: one was the declaration of the abolition across the country and two was that untouchability shall be a culpable offence.[7]

At its meeting on 29 March 1947, the sub-committee headed by Congress President J.B. Kripalani adopted Munshi's draft with one significant change. It put the word 'untouchability' within quotation marks, perhaps signifying the cultural specificity of that term.[8] At a subsequent meeting on 14 April 1947, the sub-committee widened the ambit of the clause to say that untouchability was abolished 'in any form'.[9]

These two changes triggered a debate on 21 April 1947 before the larger Advisory Committee chaired by Sardar Patel.[10]

The first salvo was fired by P.R. Thakur, an activist of the Namasudra movement in East Bengal aimed at uplifting a Harijan community that was previously called the Chandalas. Thakur, said: 'This clause is rather very vague. It cannot possibly mean untouchability in any form. I can tell you definitely that to a Hindu, a Mohammedan or Christian is an untouchable and they will remain untouchable till doomsday. I think what is meant is untouchability within the Hindu fold.'

Patel shot back: 'Do you mean to say that untouchability should be restricted?'

That was exactly what Thakur meant. 'The question of untouchability is due to the disabilities of certain sections of the Hindus.'

Patel stood his ground. 'The idea here is that untouchability in any form should be abolished.'

The discussion on the semantics of untouchability went on in this vein until Jagjivan Ram, the most prominent leader from the untouchable community after Ambedkar, weighed in. 'Untouchability in the ordinary sense of the term is untouchability as it prevails in the Hindu society.'

Rajaji found a solution to 'meet all objections' by latching on to a word that Thakur had used: disabilities. Explaining the 'very definite legal meaning' of the abolition clause, Rajaji said that the 'law will not hereafter recognise untouchability in any form as bringing into existence any right or disability'. Accordingly, he suggested that 'the imposition of any disability of any kind of any such custom of untouchability shall be an offence'.

The clause was reframed thus: 'Untouchability in any form is abolished and the imposition of any disability on that account shall be an offence.' This was how it figured in the draft of the fundamental rights submitted by Patel on 23 April 1947 to the president of the Constituent Assembly, Rajendra Prasad. And this was how it was placed before the plenary session of the Constituent Assembly at the end of the month.

When India was formally decolonised on 15 August 1947, one of the highlights of the day was that Ambedkar was sworn in as its first law minister. An extraordinary achievement as much for Ambedkar as it was for a country that had a hoary tradition of denying education—and indeed, humanity—to his community.

Within a fortnight, the law minister was entrusted with a parallel responsibility, one even more significant, historically and symbolically. On 29 August 1947, the Constituent Assembly set up a seven-member Drafting Committee, which included Ambedkar. The next day, the Drafting Committee 'unanimously elected' him its chairman.

The Drafting Committee worked further on the clause it had inherited on the abolition of untouchability. At its meeting held on 30 October 1947, the committee came up with a fresh formulation which, in a bid to make its meaning clearer, described untouchability as a custom. 'The custom of "untouchability" is abolished and its practice in any form is forbidden. The enforcement of any disability arising out of "untouchability" shall be an offence which shall be punishable in accordance with law.'[11]

Testifying to the continuing sensitivity of the subject, the Drafting Committee had a rethink the very next day about referring to untouchability as a matter of custom. The minutes of its meeting held on 31 October 1947 did not, however, disclose why the first three words—'The custom of'—had been excised from the draft agreed upon on the previous day. The minutes just acknowledged 'the changes' that had been made.

On 21 February 1948, shortly after Gandhi's assassination, Ambedkar submitted to Rajendra Prasad the Drafting Committee's Draft Constitution. The clauses on the abolition of untouchability and the right against discrimination in accessing public places figured in the chapter on Fundamental Rights. In his cover letter, Ambedkar underscored the rigour with which that chapter had been drafted. 'The committee has attempted to make these rights … as definite as possible, since the courts may have to pronounce upon them.'[12]

The Constituent Assembly, on its part, was no less rigorous in scrutinising the proposed fundamental rights. It even made changes, where needed, before formally adding each of these clauses to the Constitution. This was how the Assembly, during the final phase of India's Constitution-making, came to discuss the discrimination and abolition clauses on 29 November 1948.[13]

India was finally set to fulfil the promise that had been made through a resolution drafted by Gandhi sixteen years earlier in the wake of the Poona Pact. The promise was that the right of untouchables across the country to access public places 'shall have statutory recognition at the first opportunity and shall be one of the earliest acts of the swaraj Parliament, if it shall not have received such recognition before that time'.

Shibban Lal Saxena, a Congress member from the United Provinces, objected to having such a provision in the Constitution. He argued that, as there would be a separate provision for the abolition of untouchability, 'this particular sub-clause providing for the elimination of disabilities in regard to tanks, wells and roads is unnecessary'.

He was not only worried about overlap between two constitutional provisions, but also convinced that caste discrimination was on its way out. Saxena contended that 'such disabilities as exist are merely transitory and will vanish with time'. He also invoked nationalist pride. 'But if it becomes permanently incorporated in the Constitution, people in other parts of the world will despise us for the existence of such discrimination in the past.' The other participants in the debate shared neither his view nor his fear.

Among the discussants was the chief minister of Bombay, B.G. Kher, whose government had once been forced by Ambedkar's party to abandon a tame bill on caste discrimination. In a role reversal, Kher was now debating a provision that Ambedkar had piloted. His intervention followed Ambedkar's clarification in response to a question from a Harijan member from Madras, S. Nagappa. He had asked whether the term 'shop' included not just sellers of goods but also those that sold services like 'laundry and shaving saloon'. Kher then asked: 'Does it include the offices of a doctor and a lawyer?'

Ambedkar said yes. 'Certainly it will include anybody who offers his services.' For Ambedkar, this extension of the ambit of access equality was only natural. 'I am using it in a generic sense. I should like to point out therefore that the word "shop" used here is not used in the limited sense of permitting entry. It is used in the larger sense of requiring the services if the terms of service are agreed to.'

This was but one of many instances in which Ambedkar clarified the connotations of the provisions in the making to other members of the Constituent Assembly. That he had emerged as the foremost authority on the Constitution in that gathering of India's founding fathers and mothers was a miracle of history. The leader of the 1927 satyagraha, which had sought to throw open the Mahad tank, was now putting in place a constitutional provision empowering untouchables to access the widest range of public amenities.

Nagappa asked another question that underscored this dramatic evolution: whether the term 'tanks' mentioned in the clause included 'ponds'. Answering 'categorically in the affirmative', Ambedkar said, 'A tank is a larger thing which must include a pond.'

Among the minor amendments that Ambedkar accepted—and the Constituent Assembly adopted—was one to insert the expression 'bathing ghats' between the words 'tanks' and 'roads'. This amendment had been moved by a member from Bihar, Guptanath Singh.

The clause against access discrimination came on the back of struggles waged by untouchables and other low castes, most notably since the 1924 conflicts in Vaikom and Kalpathy. There was no parallel, in India or elsewhere, to the nature and scale of caste discrimination. Yet, the Constituent Assembly made the strategic choice of dealing with the discrimination question in general terms, juxtaposing caste with other cleavages.

And so, the clause finalised by the Constituent Assembly as Article 15(2) reads: 'No citizen shall, on grounds only of religion, race, caste, sex, place of birth or any of them, be subject to any disability, liability, restriction or condition with regard to (a) access to shops, public restaurants, hotels and places of public entertainment; or (b) the use of wells, tanks, bathing ghats, roads and places of public resort maintained wholly or partly out of State funds or dedicated to the use of the general public.' Reflecting the leap made by the 1946 Bombay enactment, the Constitution extended the principle of equal access to privately-owned public places too.

The debate that followed the same day on the clause abolishing untouchability was shorter. Of the six Constituent Assembly members who participated in the debate on 29 November 1948, two were from the Scheduled Castes. V.I. Muniswami Pillai had the distinction of being the first from the community to have held the office of a minister: he had joined the Rajaji Cabinet in Madras in 1937. Dakshayani Velayudhan, a native of the state of Cochin, elected to the Constituent Assembly from Madras, was the only woman from the Harijan community in the Constituent Assembly.

While Pillai welcomed the clause as 'a matter of great satisfaction', Velayudhan's stand was counter-intuitive. Her stance was not unlike Saxena's opposition to putting the non-discrimination clause in the Constitution. While Saxena might have betrayed his upper-caste bias, Velayudhan's unease emanated from her ideological preference for Gandhi over Ambedkar.

Take what she wrote in a signed Editor's Note dated 25 November 1946 in the book *Gandhi or Ambedkar*, which was also published by her on behalf of the Madras-based Gandhi Era Publications. 'Dr Ambedkar has distorted everything really pure and sublime in the social attitudes of Gandhi. The magnificent talent of the Doctor is poisoned by the running sores of frustration and defeatism. However, his pseudo-theories have failed to touch the heart of the Harijans. The awakened community knows who is the true comrade and who runs after the sweets of fame and power. The Doctor can only spread despondency and not emancipation.'[14]

In the debate in the Constituent Assembly on the abolition of untouchability, Velayudhan's opening salvo contained an ambivalent reference to Ambedkar. Addressing the chair, Vice President H.C. Mookherjee, she said, 'Sir, we cannot expect a Constitution without a clause relating to untouchability because the Chairman of the Drafting Committee himself belongs to the untouchable community.'

On the principle of criminalising untouchability, she suggested that it was contrary to the Gandhian approach of winning the hearts of the offenders. On the 'vast change in the outlook and attitude of the people today towards the untouchables', as she saw it, Velayudhan said, 'The change of heart that we find in the people today is only due to the work that has been done by Mahatma Gandhi and by him alone.'

Further, 'When this Constitution is put into practice, what we want is not to punish the people for acting against the law, but what is needed is that there should be proper propaganda done by both the Central and Provincial Governments.' Had those governments carried out proper propaganda, she said, 'there would have been no necessity for an article of this kind in this Constitution'.

Even at that late stage, Velayudhan urged the Constituent Assembly to pass a resolution against untouchability rather than insert the proposed provision. 'If a declaration is made by the Assembly here and now, it will have a great effect on the people and there will be no necessity for us to incorporate such a clause in the Constitution.'

Apart from Velayudhan's dissonant note, the mood in the House was so strongly in favour of the abolition clause that it had only one amendment to consider. And even that was only to strengthen the clause. The change suggested by Naziruddin Ahmad, a Congress member from West Bengal, was more radical than the previous attempts to sharpen the clause. He found the existing clause 'a little vague', and so rewrote it completely to foreground the underlying factors of untouchability. Ahmad's alternative was, 'No one shall on account of his religion or caste be treated or regarded as an "untouchable"; and its observance in any form may be made punishable by law.' He reasoned that since untouchability 'on the ground of religion or caste is what is prohibited', there was a need to make it clear that other forms of untouchability, caused by 'an epidemic or contagious disease', for instance, were not punishable.

Ahmad's suggestion was reinforced by Bombay's K.T. Shah, one of the most active members of the Constituent Assembly. Shah came up with more examples of practices that might be misinterpreted and penalised by this clause. 'We all know that at certain periods women are regarded as untouchables,' Shah said, asking rhetorically if that would be 'regarded as an offence under this article'. His apprehension was that 'the lack of any definition of the term "untouchability" makes it open for busy bodies and lawyers to make capital out of a clause like this'.

When it was Ambedkar's turn to respond to the debate on the abolition clause, he chose to be silent on Dakshayani Velayudhan's criticism—an option he could exercise because she had not in fact moved any amendment. As for the one moved by Ahmad, he was perhaps reluctant to consider such a drastic change when the clause was on the verge of being adopted. Without a word of explanation, Ambedkar said: 'I cannot accept the amendment of Mr. Naziruddin Ahmad.'

Trying a different tack, Vice-President Mookerjee enquired: 'Dr. Ambedkar, do you wish to reply to Mr. Shah's suggestion?' Again, Ambedkar was taciturn. He just said, 'No.'

Mookerjee went through the motions of putting Ahmad's amendment to vote. Once the amendment had been 'negatived', the path was clear for approving the clause, which was numbered then as Article 11. Mookerjee solemnly said, 'The question is: "That article 11 stand part of the Constitution."' According to the record of the proceedings, 'The motion was adopted. Article 11 was added to the Constitution.'

The record related to the abolition of untouchability had an extra line at the end. 'Honourable Members: Mahatma Gandhi ki Jai.' This was the only occasion when any such slogan was chanted, given the solemnity of the Constituent Assembly debates. It was a spontaneous gesture which indicated that—unlike Dakshayani Velayudhan's interpretation of it—most members there regarded their decision to criminalise untouchability as a tribute to Gandhi.

In the final form of the Constitution, which the Assembly adopted in its entirety on 26 November 1949, the abolition clause came to be renumbered as Article 17. '"Untouchability" is abolished and its practice in any form is forbidden. The enforcement of any disability arising out of "Untouchability" shall be an offence punishable in accordance with law.'

Article 17 was the Indian equivalent of two American milestones:

Lincoln's Emancipation Proclamation of 1863 and the Thirteenth Amendment to the Constitution abolishing slavery in 1865. However, while the Thirteenth Amendment proclaimed freedom for the Negros who had been 'legally' enslaved, Article 17 had no immediate effect on the lives of untouchables. Combating a prejudice that had derived sanction from not just custom but also religion needed more than a declaration in the Constitution.

In fact, the abolition of untouchability, which came into force on 26 January 1950, was the easier part of the challenge for it was still in the realm of the abstract. The real test was to follow up with an all-India legislation to punish offences as envisaged by Article 17: 'the enforcement of any disability arising out of untouchability'. The Jawaharlal Nehru government was now required to draft a bill that concretely delineated various forms of untouchability and rendered them 'punishable in accordance with law'. It took all of four years for such a bill to materialise.

11

CRIMINALISING A PIOUS CUSTOM

The nascent republic geared up for a legislative follow-through to the constitutional abolition of untouchability. When the Lok Sabha opened for the week on 15 March 1954, the Jawaharlal Nehru government introduced the Untouchability (Offences) Bill through Deputy Minister of Home Affairs B.N. Datar, an MP from Belgaum in the Mysore state.[1] Coincidentally, the first-ever resolution in any legislature seeking to throw open public places to untouchables during the colonial period had also been moved by a legislator from Belgaum: Congress member D.V. Belvi in the Bombay Legislative Council in 1919.

On the face of it, one novel feature of the Nehru government's bill was its clause defining the term 'untouchable'. This amounted to defining the victims afresh, given that the Constitution, despite its failure to explain untouchability, had already defined 'Scheduled Castes' in view of the special provisions made for them.

In the scheme inherited from its colonial precursor of 1935, the Constitution contained two provisions encompassing the definition of Scheduled Castes. Article 341 laid down the formal procedure for specifying Scheduled Castes. Article 366 (24) defined them accordingly as 'such castes, races or tribes or parts of or groups within such castes, races or tribes as are deemed under Article 341 to be Scheduled Castes for the purposes of this Constitution'.

The definition offered by the 1954 bill acknowledged an overlap between the two terms: 'untouchable means a member of a Scheduled

Caste as defined in clause (24) of Article 366 of the Constitution, and includes any other person who by custom or usage is regarded as an untouchable by any community or section thereof'.[2]

While the first part of the definition was no more than a reiteration of technical details from the Constitution, the second part was an advance. It recognised the ground reality that not all Scheduled Castes had been enumerated yet. Some fell outside the official list, and this definition ensured that they too were covered by the bill. It also accounted for the blurred lines between untouchables and the stigmatised castes among Shudras, which had been highlighted by the 1924 conflicts between Brahmins and Ezhavas in Vaikom and Kalpathy.

The definition extended even to those untouchables who had converted to other religions, as made clear by one of the 'Explanations' included in the clause. This expansion signified a daring assertion of secularism on the part of the Nehru government in the early years of the republic. 'A member of a Scheduled Caste who has been converted from the Hindu religion to any other religion shall, notwithstanding such conversion, be deemed to be an "untouchable" for the purposes of this Act.' Thus, a Muslim or Christian, for instance, could also invoke the proposed law if they were formerly untouchables in the Hindu fold.

The other Explanation in the clause clarified that though a Scheduled Caste was notified under Article 341 in relation to a specific locality, its member 'shall not cease' to be one under the proposed law by reason of residence in another locality.

Having defined 'untouchable' so expansively, the bill used that expression throughout in preference to 'Scheduled Castes'. Take the headings of its clauses concerning access to public places in the secular realm: 'Removal of social disabilities on untouchables', 'Prohibition against refusal to admit untouchables to hospitals, etc.' and 'Prohibition against refusal to sell goods or render service to untouchables'. Repealing all provincial enactments, most of which had been passed not long before Independence, this all-India bill dealt with temple-entry restrictions too with the heading 'Right of untouchables to enter places of public worship'.

For the entire range of offences covered by it, the bill imposed penalties involving a fine up to Rs 500 or imprisonment up to six months or both. In the case of offences committed by companies, those in charge of them were rendered liable. Vindicating the 1939 dissent note by Ambedkar's followers in Bombay, the Central bill provided for revocation of licences through a judicial order. More importantly, on the lines of the 1946 Bombay enactment, this bill also stipulated that all offences under it shall be cognisable.

On 26 August 1954, about five months after its introduction, Home Minister Kailash Nath Katju moved for referring the bill to a Joint Committee—a Select Committee consisting of members from both Houses of Parliament. Four days of discussion later, on 31 August 1954, the Lok Sabha appointed thirty-three members to the Joint Committee. The motion left it to the Rajya Sabha to add sixteen from among its members. It was also decided that the proposed forty-nine-member committee would be headed by Lok Sabha member Upendranath Barman, a Harijan Congress leader from West Bengal.

A fortnight later, on 14 September 1954, Katju moved a corresponding motion in the Rajya Sabha listing the sixteen members who had been chosen from that House. Since the House did not have enough time that day, Katju resumed his speech on 16 September. This day saw a sharp exchange between Katju and Ambedkar, who was among the sixteen Rajya Sabha members picked for the Joint Committee.[3]

The clash was triggered by an abnormal conduct on the part of the minister. Though he was supposed to be piloting it, Katju actually damned the bill, over and over again. Dwelling on the apprehensions that the bill had allegedly raised among its intended beneficiaries, Katju made no pretence of putting them at rest. For instance, he spoke of the fear that 'this law, though enacted, may remain a dead letter'. Far from allaying that apprehension, he confirmed that it could well be true and left it at that. 'If you enact a law of this description which does not command widespread support, then enforcement becomes difficult.'

Extrapolating perhaps from the concerns that Dakshayani Velayudhan had expressed during the making of Article 17, Katju made out that untouchables in general were ambivalent about any penalty being imposed for untouchability. In fact, Katju claimed to have 'heard it said often by members of these communities' that 'if you punish a Kshatriya or a Brahmin or anyone of the so-called high caste people … what would be the result?' He claimed to have even heard them answer that question with a sense of foreboding, fearing that imprisonment would make the offender lose all affection for untouchables.

'The result would be that he will go to jail for six months or three months and when he comes out, his heart will not be overflowing with affection for the members of these communities. His heart will be full of bitterness and the result will be that, while the letter of the law may be obeyed, living conditions may become so difficult that we may even have to migrate and leave the village.'

In effect, Katju said that any punishment for untouchability would be in obedience only to the letter of the law and not its spirit. He added, 'That would be, in my opinion, a bad consequence, and most undesirable. I would hate it.'

Invoking 'the great example of Gandhiji', Katju warned the victims of untouchability that they should not 'use the language of bitterness and say, "Look at us: for five thousand years we have suffered those handicaps but we are not prepared to suffer them any longer".' He said that 'if you want to remove those sufferings today, these laws will not enable you to gain your objective'.

To drive home his message, Katju sarcastically said that the law was 'a case of using the rod—use the rod and punish and then you will bring the opponents to their senses'. He stressed, 'My feeling is that that is extremely wrong advice.'

Thus it came to pass that the home minister of decolonised India, while going through the motions of piloting the untouchability legislation, all but promised impunity to its violators. No sooner had he finished his address than Ambedkar, a leading light of the Opposition since his resignation from the government in 1951, challenged Katju. Ambedkar might also have been triggered by the memory of Dakshayani Velayudhan's speech that he had left unchallenged six years earlier. She had not moved an amendment then, and perhaps he also felt constrained by his office as chairperson of the Drafting Committee.

As luck would have it, Ambedkar was faced with a constraint again, this time in the form of a convention. As someone who had already been proposed as a member of the Select Committee, he was barred from participating in a debate on the reference of the bill to that body. 'I think it is impossible for me to remain silent during the discussion on this Bill, but I find that my hon. friend, the Minister-in-charge, has condescended to put me on the Select Committee on this Bill.' He said that he hoped the convention would not come in the way of his speaking in the House: 'I do not know to what extent the rule has been observed in all its strictness.'

The presiding officer, Deputy Chairman S.V. Krishnamoorthy Rao, a Congress leader from the Mysore state, upheld the convention saying, 'It has not been violated.' This forced Ambedkar to make a hard choice, even as he remarked that the convention was 'not strictly observed' in the other House. 'However, if the convention is a rigid one here I beg permission to withdraw my name, and I hope the hon. Minister will concede.'

Ambedkar's decision to forgo his nomination to the Joint Committee rather than let Katju's speech go unchallenged led to a commotion in the Rajya Sabha. Citing previous departures and other arguments, veterans like N.G. Ranga and H.N. Kunzru urged Rao to let Ambedkar speak in the House without depriving the Joint Committee of his acumen.

Rao, however, stuck to his position. 'A convention if departed from will cease to be a convention. So it is for Dr. Ambedkar to choose whether he will speak on the floor of the House or be a Member of the Select Committee.' Rao's ruling led to further commotion, and ended in a walkout by some MPs.

Ambedkar chose to speak. He did far more than express his views as he also surveyed a wide range of legal issues impacting untouchables since the early days of colonial rule. One such issue was the Madras regulation of 1816, confinement in the stocks for low-caste individuals, a measure that he erroneously assumed was still in force.

Ambedkar's critique of the bill itself proved to be seminal, shaping the law incrementally in the years to come. He brought out the 'defective provisions' and 'grave omissions' of the bill, putting Katju's speech in perspective. Ambedkar paraphrased Katju's attempt to water down the penalty clause as follows: 'Let the punishment be very light so that no grievance shall be left in the heart of the offender.' Ambedkar's response was caustic: 'My hon. friend was very eloquent on the question of punishment. He said that the punishment ought to be very very light and I was wondering whether he was pleading for a lighter punishment because he himself wanted to commit these offences.'

In the same vein, Ambedkar added: 'I suppose his primary premise is that the offenders who offend the untouchables are really very kindly people, overwhelming with love and kindness and that this is merely an errant act which really ought to be forgiven. It is a matter of great solace to me that he has not prescribed the punishment of being warned and then discharged ... Yes, that would be the best; if our object is to make the offender a loving person; well, let him be warned and discharged. He will continue to love and no soreness will remain in his heart.'

The surreal quality of this exchange between Katju and Ambedkar in Parliament was a testament to how little India had changed from the time untouchability had been discussed for the first time in 1916 in the colonial precursor to the Parliament. If anything, the post-colonial government betrayed signs of being more deferential than even the colonial government to the sensitivities of upper castes.

Ambedkar's intervention was intended to ensure that the proposed Central law built upon the provisions that had already been enacted by the provinces prior to Independence. He not only questioned the adequacy of the penalties prescribed in Katju's bill on various grounds, but also suggested changes. His main concern in this regard was Katju's failure to prescribe any minimum punishment. '(T)he six months' imprisonment is really the maximum and a magistrate may only inflict one day's imprisonment and let the man be off. There is no minimum fixed.' Ambedkar asserted that 'there ought to have been a minimum punishment below which the magistrate could not go'. He added that the minimum prison term for any untouchability-related offence could be prescribed as three months.

To arrive at this calculation, Ambedkar used the IPC as a frame of reference. In the case of heinous offences, it prescribed a minimum period of imprisonment or specified that the imprisonment would be rigorous. When he cited the minimum term of imprisonment prescribed for Section 397 as a 'precedent' for an untouchability offence, Katju interjected, 'What is 397?' Ambedkar supplied the detail: 'Dacoity.' And then he compared dacoity with untouchability. 'This is worse than dacoity. I think, to starve a man and not allow him to take water, I think, it is almost causing death.'

Ambedkar also bemoaned the perils of conferring such unfettered discretion on a magistrate who could be susceptible to caste prejudice. 'The whole matter is left in the hands of the magistrate. What sort of a magistrate he may be, it may be quite possible and I can quite imagine that he may be a Pandit from Kashi sitting in judgment in the magistrate's chair. What conscience would he have in the matter of administering this law?' He was underscoring the need for a safeguard to minimise judicial discretion in a society loaded against untouchables.

Another cause for concern was that imprisonment was not the only—or even the likely—option in the event of conviction. As Ambedkar put it, 'The magistrate may very well inflict the alternative punishment of fine and there might be an offender who might be prepared even to pay the five hundred rupees in order to escape the clutches of the law. What good can such punishment do?'

In a radical reimagination of the penal clause, Ambedkar suggested doing away with the fine as an alternative penalty. Instead, he proposed that it should always be levied in addition to the penalty of imprisonment. 'The least that one can expect from him [Katju] is to prescribe … a minimum of three months' imprisonment *and* fine'. (emphasis added) Ambedkar was clear: imprisonment should be mandatory; if anything was optional, it was the fine. 'I am not for inflicting a fine because that only benefits the treasury, but if you say that the fine will go to the victim, I am for the fine also.'

He also took exception to the possibility that the accused could escape conviction altogether. The bill was 'completely silent' on whether the offences mentioned in it were 'compoundable'—that is, whether the accused could legally arrive at a financial settlement with the victims to close the case. He pointed to a contemporaneous finding of a constitutional body, the Commissioner for the Scheduled Castes and Scheduled Tribes. In Ambedkar's paraphrasing of its conclusions, 'the untouchables were not able to prosecute their persecutors because of want of economic and financial means and consequently they were ever ready to compromise with the offenders'. Such a situation was 'not to be tolerated', Ambedkar said. 'The offences must not be made compoundable if the offence is to be brought home to the guilty party.'

Ambedkar cited a technical reason too for doing away with the option of compounding offences. Although only forty-four out of the 400 offences in the IPC were compoundable in his estimate, they included crimes like causing hurt, wrongful restraint or wrongful confinement that were likely to arise in the context of untouchability. 'Therefore, it follows that unless you make a specific and express provision in this Bill, all the offences … will become compoundable and the Bill will be reduced to a complete nullity. It would be a farce.'

Ambedkar stressed on the deficiencies in the penalty clause because he felt the bill did not reflect its genesis in Article 17 of the Constitution. 'The Bill seems to give the appearance that it is a Bill of a very minor character, just a dhoby not washing the cloth, just a barber not shaving or just a mithaiwala not selling laddus and things of that sort. People would think that these are trifles and piffles and why has Parliament bothered and wasted its time in dealing with dhobies and barbers and laddu-walas.' In reality, the bill was intended 'to give protection with regard to civil and fundamental rights'. Ambedkar therefore believed that 'a positive clause' to that effect 'ought to have been introduced in this Bill'.

He also suggested alternative titles to the bill, drawing inspiration from the corresponding American discourse on civil rights. The three names he threw up in the course of his speech were: 'Civil Rights (Untouchables) Protection Act', 'Untouchables Civil Rights Protection Bill' and 'Scheduled Castes Civil Rights Protection Bill'. Disagreeing with the Shakespearean dictum that a rose by any other name would smell as sweet, Ambedkar said that 'a good law ought to have a good and succinct name'. It was necessary to highlight the 'civil rights' of untouchables instead of the 'offences' committed against them, he said: 'After all, what you are doing is nothing more than protecting their civil rights.'

Another glaring omission Ambedkar flagged was the absence of a provision on 'social boycott'. He had himself included such a provision in the draft he submitted to the Sub-Committee on Fundamental Rights of the Constituent Assembly in March 1947. Social boycott is, he said, 'the heinous means which the village community applies in order to prevent the Scheduled Castes from exercising these rights'. Drawing on an official report of colonial vintage, Ambedkar said, 'The village communities most often prefer the social boycott, because it is an act behind the curtain and appears to be perfectly in consonance with the law of contracts, to violence which becomes an offence under the Indian Penal Code.'

There were also a couple of provisions from the general criminal laws that he wanted incorporated in this special law on untouchability. One was to empower the magistrate to demand 'security for good behaviour'. Magistrates were able to invoke the relevant provisions of the Criminal Procedure Code to take security for good behaviour from those who did not keep the peace or were vagrants or habitual offenders. Ambedkar said: 'I am not certain that these provisions could be invoked for the purpose of taking security from persons offending against this law.' Hence his plea for the incorporation of a specific provision on security to put the question beyond doubt.

Likewise, he proposed borrowing a law-and-order measure from the Indian Police Act—imposing a collective sanction in a situation where a dominant section of the village disturbed the peace. As Ambedkar put it, 'the Government can quarter upon them additional police and recover the cost of the additional police from the inhabitants of that village'. He believed that 'a specific clause on the lines of section 15 of the Police Act should have found a place in this Bill if outlawing untouchability is intended to be an effective thing'.

Having laid out this ambitious vision for the untouchability law, Ambedkar advocated that it be administered by the Centre rather than the states to insulate it from local pressures. He held that such a provision would be consonant with Article 35 of the Constitution, which made it clear that Parliament alone could pass the law giving teeth to the abolition of untouchability. The last provision in Part III incorporating the abolition of untouchability, Article 35 says: 'Parliament shall have, and the Legislature of a State shall not have, power to make laws ... for prescribing punishment for those acts which are declared to be offences under this Part.'

The mandate of Article 35 was, in Ambedkar's view, distinct from the distribution of legislative powers through the Central, state and concurrent lists in the Seventh Schedule of the Constitution. 'I do not think that this is a concurrent piece of legislation in which the States can claim to have a right to administer,' the principal framer of the Constitution said. 'I claim that this is a Central law although it does not fall in List I of the Seventh Schedule.'

Ambedkar would pay the price for this speech. After the lawmakers had had their say on the reference to the Joint Committee, the government gave its response on 17 September 1954 through B.N. Datar, Katju's junior. Datar had barely begun speaking when he was interrupted by R.U. Agnibhoj, a Harijan legislator from Madhya Pradesh, who wanted to know 'the attitude of the Government' on the Chair's ruling the previous day that Ambedkar could either speak in the House or be on the Joint Committee.[4]

Datar replied that the government's attitude was 'to obey the Chair'. He announced that Ambedkar would be replaced on the Joint Committee by Kaka Kalelkar, a Brahmin representing the state of Bombay in the Rajya Sabha. Kalelkar was at the time heading the first Backward Classes Commission, which was tasked with identifying the sections that could, in addition to Scheduled Castes and Scheduled Tribes, be given special benefits.

Responding to Ambedkar's suggestions, Datar called the one urging the Centre to assume responsibility for administering the proposed law on untouchability 'a very controversial point'. He did admit that 'if Parliament so desires, as an exceptional measure, it is open to the Government of India to extend its executive authority to the implementation' of this legislation.

However, he doubted 'whether it would be feasible for the Central Government to undertake the implementation of the present penal provision on its own shoulders'. Datar said that 'we have to take into account the question whether the Central Government has any machinery' to perform the necessary policing functions across the vast country. The states were already engaged in the uplift of the Harijans and administering the IPC and other Central enactments. Hence, he added, 'there is no reason to suspect that the various State Governments would not carry out the provisions in the spirit in which they have to be duly carried out'.

As for the contention that the provisions were not stringent enough, Datar echoed Katju: 'we have to take into account certain factors with a sense of realism'. The first factor was the Government's professed Gandhian approach of taking on untouchability without offending caste Hindus. 'It is true that the caste Hindus commit this offence, but after all, as Gandhiji said, we should love the offender but hate his offence. Therefore, the various classes of society have to be slowly brought together. They have to be welded together and the process of welding will not be softened by any other approach.' In other words, the rigours of the law were subordinate to the government's ideas about social welding.

Though 'the sanction of law has certain influence', Datar said, 'it cannot by itself eradicate these evils'. But if 'all the caste Hindus were purposely exasperated to an extent beyond what was necessary, then perhaps it would recoil upon the social reformers themselves and that the very object we have in bringing forward this Bill would be defeated'. It was an old and familiar argument: the untouchability law could be enforced only as far as the consensus allowed.

Frankly adopting a 'middle of the road policy', Datar said, 'we have to be very strict so far as the provisions of the law are concerned and at the same time we have also to take into account its possible reactions upon other members of the society'. The Nehru government was essentially admitting that, even seven years after Independence, India was unable to deal with untouchability without being swayed by extraneous factors.

Hence the government's reluctance to specify rigorous imprisonment in the bill, despite Ambedkar's warning about unfettered discretion in the hands of magistrates. With a straight face, Datar said, 'He will kindly note that the word we have used is imprisonment; whether it is to be simple or rigorous is a matter which is to be left entirely to the judicial discretion of the magistrate.'

As for Ambedkar's apprehension that, in the absence of an express provision, the offences related to untouchability would all be considered compoundable, Datar took just the opposite view. In the Criminal Procedure Code, unless stated otherwise, offences were ordinarily 'non-compoundable by nature'—so was it the case, he made out, with the offences in this bill too. 'They have to be made compoundable by a provision of law and therefore,' Datar said, 'I would point out to this House that all the offences are non-compoundable.'

At the end of Datar's speech, the Rajya Sabha gave its concurrence to the Lok Sabha's recommendation that the bill be referred to a Joint Committee. The committee, which included Katju as one of its forty-nine members, began its work without delay and held nine sittings in all. The report, finalised on 27 November 1954, made changes that went beyond Ambedkar's suggestions and not necessarily in the way he intended.

To begin with, the Joint Committee considered conflicting arguments on 'whether the expression "untouchable" used in the Bill should be retained'. It was concerned about 'the legality and propriety of the use of the expression particularly in view of the abolition of "untouchability" under Article 17 of the Constitution'. Conversely, it examined 'the apprehension that deletion of the word might leave loopholes and the purpose of the Bill might be defeated'.[5]

In the end, while Ambedkar had suggested using the term 'untouchable' even in the title, the Joint Committee decided to do away with all references to it throughout the bill. It concluded that 'the deletion of the expression "untouchable" would not stand in the way of attaining the object of the Bill'. Therefore, 'The definition of "untouchable" along with the two "Explanations" thereto has been omitted.' With that, the only attempt ever by any government at providing a statutory definition of untouchable fell through.

On the issue of penalty, though, Ambedkar had the satisfaction of seeing that the Barman committee strengthened the bill, with changes that were innovative for the time. It introduced, for instance, enhanced punishment for repeat offenders. The committee made it 'obligatory upon a court to impose a sentence of both imprisonment and fine in the case of a second or subsequent offence'. In other words, only a first-time offender could get away with a monetary fine.

In another significant vindication for Ambedkar, the Joint Committee inserted a provision penalising social boycott, marking a statutory acknowledgement that this was one of the 'offences arising out of "untouchability"'. (Though it remained undefined, 'untouchability' figured more often in the revised draft, making up in some measure for the erasure of the term 'untouchable', which had been used frequently in the original one.)

The spirit of Ambedkar's intervention was also discernible in what was by far the most radical change the committee recommended. It resulted from the acceptance of a 'Government Amendment' at the committee's sitting on 5 November 1954.

Recognising the precarity of untouchables, the amendment proposed by Katju departed from a basic principle of jurisprudence: namely, the right of the accused to be presumed innocent until proven guilty. The committee decided to 'shift the burden of proof from the prosecution to the accused', so that there was a presumption of guilt which the accused could rebut only during trial.

But then, it also provided a loophole to the accused by qualifying the presumption with the word 'only'. As the newly inserted clause put it, '(T)he court shall presume, unless the contrary is proved, that such an act was committed on the ground only of "untouchability".' This meant that, even if discrimination based on untouchability had been established, the clause let the accused off the hook if he could prove that there were other reasons too for his conduct.

But, for Ambedkar, the report contained a bigger blow still. Not only did the committee not make the offences non-compoundable, it actually inserted a clause saying that 'every such offence may, with the permission of the court, be compounded'. The committee's explanation for downgrading untouchability offences in this manner was: 'It was felt that if the provisions of the Bill are made strict, they may defeat the very object of the Bill.'

The committee's report was not without its share of dissent notes. Some of them felt that the bill had actually become more stringent. Among them was K.M. Munshi's wife, Lilavati Munshi, who was exercised about the overturning of the presumption of innocence. 'I am afraid if this clause is passed, there may be people who may bring frivolous complaints which may prove to be a cause of unnecessary harassment; because even if the case is not proved, the complainant has nothing to lose.'

Kaka Kalelkar, who replaced Ambedkar on the Joint Committee, wrote a dissent note against the quantum of punishment for social boycott. 'Punishment meted out to persons resorting to social boycott should not be so harsh.' His reasoning was familiar. 'It is easy enough for us to whip ourselves into a fury of righteous indignation, but it is always safe to have mild punishments. The ultimate aim is not to punish reactionaries but convert them, with the aid of law, to a new conception of social well-being.'

On the other side was a more detailed dissent by Raman Velayudhan, a Harijan lawmaker from the state of Travancore-Cochin, who was also Dakshayani Velayudhan's husband. They had the honour of being married at Sevagram in Wardha in the presence of Gandhi. Despite working closely with Gandhi, the Velayudhans had opposing viewpoints on whether untouchability should be criminalised. As a member of the Constituent Assembly speaking on Article 17, the wife had made clear her preference for propaganda over penalty. As a member of the Joint Committee on the bill complying with the Article 17 mandate, the husband sought to strengthen the penal aspect.

Raman Velayudhan began his dissent note with the lament that the bill as amended by the Joint Committee 'instead of improving the original one has taken the shape of a half hearted and halting measure'. He felt that instead of deleting the definition of untouchable, the committee should have added one of untouchability too. 'The Constitution itself does not define as to who is an untouchable and what is untouchability,' Velayudhan wrote. 'So it was essential that these terms should be defined in the implementing Act.'

Further, he appreciated the definition in the original bill for its virtue of covering members of a Scheduled Caste who had converted to another religion. Without such a definition, he felt 'the offender could be made to go unpunished by the defence on the plea that the accused was a Hindu and that the accused thought the complainant was not a Hindu at all and hence excluded him'.

As regards the presumption clause, Velayudhan had two objections. The first was about the presumption being made only when the victim was a member of a Scheduled Caste. Therefore, he lamented that the presumption was 'neither a substitute for a definition nor does it cover cases where persons by custom or usage are treated as untouchable and discriminated against'. Velayudhan was also concerned about the qualification of the presumption clause and related provisions with the word 'only'. He contended that it would make the proposed law 'very vague, and ineffective too—especially when the word "untouchability" is not defined at all'.

Similarly, he resented the committee's decision to make untouchability offences compoundable. Fearing that this change would take away 'the whole advantages arising out of the legislation', he said, 'It should be known that the accused in such cases will be always having more influence and social position than the complainant. All kinds of inducement, pull and influence could be brought against the complainant by the accused.'

Adding to the clout of the offenders was their caste affinity with law enforcers. 'As it is, the bulk of the machinery that will prosecute for these offences and are charged with punishing belong to the offending class,' Velayudhan remarked. Echoing the concerns that Ambedkar had expressed in the Rajya Sabha, he said, 'Unless the provisions in the Act are stringent and even arbitrary, if need be, there will not be much deterrent effect. When we are prepared to act radically in other economic and social spheres to achieve progress, the approach must be equally radical in this respect also.'

Velayudhan's dissent did not end with the submission of the Joint Committee report. He was as forceful in fighting against it when the Lok Sabha took up the amended bill. On 27 April 1955, Katju's more distinguished successor, Govind Ballabh Pant, moved that the bill 'as reported by the Joint Committee' be taken into consideration.[6]

The change of guard finally brought with it an acknowledgement that the proposed law should be enforced irrespective of its repercussions for caste Hindus. A former chief minister of Uttar Pradesh, Pant said: 'The mere passing of the law will not be enough. We will have to exert ourselves, every one of us, so that the law may come [in] handy to supplement our widespread activities all over the land. I hope all Members of Parliament will see to it that wherever offences of this type are committed, the offenders do not escape punishment.'

Once the clause-by-clause consideration began, Pant's main challenge was to answer persistent questions from Raman Velayudhan and others about why the definition of—and all the references to—the term 'untouchable' had been deleted from the bill. In fact, an MP from West Bengal, Sadhan Gupta, had even moved an amendment to restore the definition.

Pant resorted to elaborate and circular reasoning in a bid to justify the government's U-turn on defining an untouchable. Since 'the principle of abolition' had been 'laid down in the Constitution', he said, 'it is not open to us to define "untouchability". If you cannot define "untouchability", you cannot certainly define "untouchable". The two are so connected that the one cannot be de-linked from the other.'

Even otherwise, 'it would be hardly proper', Pant argued, 'to brand any class as untouchable'. His contention was, 'If you put any class as untouchable in this Bill, that, I think, goes against the spirit of the times. It goes against the spirit of this very measure.' A Brahmin minister was signalling to his untouchable colleagues, whether in the Lok Sabha (like R. Velayudhan) or outside (like Ambedkar), that they were out of sync with the egalitarian amendments—the situation was rich indeed in irony.

Pant also questioned the merit of going beyond Scheduled Castes to include others who were, by custom or usage, regarded as untouchables. He said that 'if any other persons come forward, it has to be proved first of all that according to usage or custom, those persons are regarded as untouchables'. It was only after this fact had been established, that 'the question whether any offence has been committed or not will arise'. Holding that it would thus 'only multiply the difficulties', Pant asked, 'What do you gain by this definition?'

The Lok Sabha went on reject the motion for restoring the definition of untouchable. When the remaining provisions of the bill were taken up the next day, on 28 April 1955, Velayudhan moved a motion to reverse another change that had been made by the Joint Committee. It was the recurring qualification that the penalties and the presumption of guilt were limited to cases where the discrimination was 'on the ground only of "untouchability"'. His amendment sought to rid all those provisions of the word 'only'.[7]

Much like Ambedkar, he framed his critique in terms of a logical fallacy. Velayudhan pointed out that 'if we are not inclined to define "untouchability"', which he called 'a basic drawback to this Bill', how could it stipulate that untouchability should be the 'only' ground for the alleged discrimination? Thanks to this anomaly, 'the whole effect of the Bill' would be reduced to 'null and void' and 'add insult to injury'.

Velayudhan was unrelenting in questioning the motive behind this change: 'Why should we adopt this kind of sabotage method by using the word "only" here? Everybody knows what is meant by untouchability. Here there was a lot of speech on Gandhiji ... there was sermonising and there was also sentimentalism. What we are concerned with here is not sentimentalism, nor about praising Gandhiji ... but whether the words that we have now used will be effective so far as the legal aspect is concerned.'

His tirade and the support it gathered hit home. Govind Ballabh Pant grudgingly conceded his demand. 'I personally do not see that the deletion or retention of this word makes any real difference. I have no objection to the word "only" being dropped.' The Lok Sabha thus adopted Velayudhan's amendment. Whether or not this change was efficacious, it was no mean achievement for an untouchable to force this rollback.

As for concerns of the touchable classes about the presumption of guilt, Pant explained, 'This presumption shall be made when the offence had been committed. It is necessary for the person who has committed such an act to establish that he has done the act not because the complainant or the person who had suffered from such a deed was a member of the Scheduled Caste but on some other account. In the circumstances, I do not see what objection can people have to this clause. Scheduled Castes need the protection of law and to the extent this clause extends that protection to them; it should be maintained.'

On the controversy over the untouchability offences being made compoundable, Pant pointed out that they could be compounded under the bill 'only with the permission of the court'. To him, this was enough of a safeguard. 'So, where the court finds that an offence is of a petty nature and that it will be in the interests of the complainant himself that the offence should be compounded, it will give him permission.' Thus, for exposing untouchables to the risk of being intimidated by their tormentors into a compromise, Pant had no qualms in suggesting that the judiciary could be trusted to rise above caste prejudice.

In an even more artful move, he raised a conceptual question as to whether the offences described in the bill could be considered criminal at all. 'You will find that ordinarily, if any of the acts were committed with regard to a person who is not an untouchable, it will not be an offence in law at all. Suppose a hotel-keeper does not allow me to enter the hotel, I cannot drive him into the criminal court,' Pant said, adding, 'The only thing that a man can do and that too in very rare cases is to approach the civil court for some sort of remedy.' Although the wrongs in question were 'essentially of a civil nature', Pant said, 'They are being created as offences under the criminal law in order to put an end to the practices that have survived even after the abolition of untouchability.'

Having thus diminished the gravity of untouchability-related offences, Pant took a jibe at those opposing compoundability. 'We should not therefore, go beyond the requirements of the case and get excited over things which will rebound on us and serve as a boomerang and not help the purposes which we have in view.' The boomerang metaphor was in the context of the odd cases in which the offenders too were untouchables.

'If there are offences against members of the Scheduled Castes themselves—there may be offences committed by persons who happen to commit such offences inadvertently, foolishly—how is the cause of social reform to be advanced? Can this be done by being vindictive or by allowing the parties to come to terms to restore goodwill and to proceed in a manner which will help the growth of good feelings between all sections of the community?'

A recurring anxiety of the Nehru government was on display once again—to avoid offending caste Hindus while complying with Article 17. The Lok Sabha passed the bill on 28 April 1955, and the Rajya Sabha followed suit four days later. Once President Rajendra Prasad gave it his assent, the Untouchability (Offences) Act—or UOA in short—came into force on 1 June 1955.

12

THE POSTHUMOUS VINDICATION OF AMBEDKAR

Following Article 17 of the Constitution, the UOA faithfully reproduced the inverted commas enclosing the word 'untouchability'. The lawmakers used those punctuation marks in lieu of a definition to stress the peculiar sense in which it figured over and over again in the UOA. A social reformer tested this formulation soon after the Act had been passed.

Devarajiah, a resident of Bangalore, invoked the UOA in the context of Jainism, although this ancient religion of India had no comparable history of untouchability based on caste. He was complaining about a pamphlet that allegedly had a 'tendency … to promote untouchability in the Jain community'. The pamphlet circulated among Jains demanded that Devarajiah and some others 'should be excluded from worship, religious services, food etc.' because of their unorthodox conduct.

The magistrate dismissed the complaint, saying that the UOA applied only where disabilities had been imposed on a person 'by reason of his birth'. The Devarajiah case reached the Mysore High Court. On 10 September 1957, the court gave an authoritative ruling on the unusual device adopted by the Constitution to abolish untouchability. 'It is to be noticed that that word occurs only in Article 17 and is enclosed in inverted commas. This clearly indicates that the subject matter of that Article is not untouchability in its literal or grammatical sense but the practice as it had developed historically in this country.'[1]

In his verdict, Justice N. Sreenivasa Rau also explored the logic of the Constitution framers in abolishing untouchability without defining it. 'This omission would appear to be deliberate as the intention presumably was to leave no room or scope for the continuance of the practice in any shape or form.'

As for the replication of the inverted commas in the UOA, Rau said, '(I)t can only refer to those regarded as untouchables in the course of historical development. A literal construction of the term would include persons who are treated as untouchables either temporarily or otherwise for various reasons, such as their suffering from an epidemic or contagious disease or on account of social observances such as are associated with birth or death or on account of social boycott resulting from caste or other disputes.'

Reaffirming the magistrate's interpretation, the Mysore High Court said, 'The imposition of untouchability in such circumstances has no relation to the causes which relegated certain classes of people beyond the pale of the caste system. Such relegation has always been based on the ground of birth in certain classes.' In other words, it was caste that separated the 'literal' meaning of untouchability from the 'historically developed' one that fell within the ambit of the UOA.

The enactment of the national legislation against untouchability did serve to increase the profile of this crime. Yet, on the crucial parameter of securing convictions, it proved to be less effective than the state laws that it repealed. The statistics were telling.

- In the period preceding the enactment of the Central law, from January 1952 to May 1955, the conviction rate under the state laws was 70.9 per cent, while the proportion of cases compounded was 11.4 per cent and 17.7 per cent resulted in acquittals.
- But in the period following the enactment of the UOA, from June 1955 to December 1959, the conviction rate dropped to 42.8 per cent, which was a fall of about 28 percentage points from the time of the state laws. The proportion of cases compounded increased to 33.3 per cent and acquittals to 23.9 per cent.

- In the period from January 1960 to December 1963, convictions under the UOA dropped further to 31.1 per cent, while the proportion of compounded cases rose to 37.5 per cent and acquittals to 31.4 per cent.[2]

Did these figures mean that the reformist fervour of the republic's early years had already faded? Or was the steep drop in the conviction rate a result of the mixed signals on enforcement from ministers in the Nehru government? Two comparative findings by the scholar Marc Galanter on the prosecution of untouchability-related offences over a decade throw some light on these questions:

- In areas covered by the state Acts, there were more anti-disabilities prosecutions in the early 1950s than in the early 1960s.
- In the early 1950s, the conviction rate in anti-disabilities cases was close to the average rate of convictions for all criminal trials in India. But by the early 1960s, the convictions in anti-disabilities cases fell to less than half of the former rate.[3]

Eventually, on 27 April 1965, about a decade after the enactment of the law, the Lal Bahadur Shastri government appointed a committee to study 'the various aspects of untouchability, in particular, the working of the Untouchability (Offences) Act, 1955'. It was headed by an untouchable leader from Madras, L. Elayaperumal. As a member of the first Lok Sabha, Elayaperumal had participated in the debate that led to the enactment of the UOA.

In its report submitted on 30 January 1969, the Elayaperumal Committee had unearthed several insidious ways in which the UOA was being subverted. The report vindicated the concerns that Ambedkar had first raised in his 1954 speech in the Rajya Sabha.[4]

Drawing on a sample of seventy cases from the second half of the 1960s, the committee found that 32.8 per cent of them resulted in convictions, 44.3 per cent ended in acquittals and 22.9 per cent were compounded. The committee found that 'on the whole, the caste Hindus have the police and the magistracy on their side'.

This skew was starker still when convictions were studied. The committee discovered that in 73.9 per cent of these cases, the convicted persons were allowed to get away with just a fine. And in 70.6 per cent of the cases where only fines were imposed, the penalty was Rs 25 or less, although the maximum fine prescribed in the UOA is Rs 500. The penalty in some cases was, in fact, no more than a token fine of Re 1 or Rs 3 or Rs 5. Echoing Ambedkar, the Elayaperumal Committee suggested that 'unless a minimum sentence is made mandatory by suitable amendments to the Act, the aims of justice would not be met and the purpose of the social legislation would not be served'.

Ambedkar was also prescient about the provision for compounding cases. The committee discovered that cases had been compounded without the court's permission—an express stipulation in the UOA. The court's permission was meant to ensure that the compromise was in the best interests of both parties, and that the untouchables settled for it of their own volition. But that safeguard proved so ineffective that, in some of those cases, 'the accused were acquitted even without such permission being expressly accorded by the court'.

In one such instance of judicial abdication, the order simply said that 'the offence having been compounded out of court, the accused are acquitted'. In another, the magistrate ordered an acquittal as some of the witnesses had 'turned hostile and effected a compromise with the accused'. In neither case was there a pretence that the magistrate had adhered to the law.

These findings confirmed that untouchability, though formally abolished, had morphed into new forms. But the Elayaperumal report came during a particularly turbulent phase in India's history. It took about three years for the Indira Gandhi government to act on the proposed legislative reforms. A bill seeking to make extensive amendments to the UOA finally came in the twenty-fifth year of Independence.

❖

On 13 April 1972, Minister of Education, Social Welfare and Culture S. Nurul Hasan introduced the Untouchability (Offences) Amendment and Miscellaneous Provision Bill in the Lok Sabha. The move to tighten the law was in effect an acknowledgement that the scourge of untouchability was far from conquered.

When the bill came up next on 23 May 1972, Hasan sought to fast-track the process by skipping the norm of referring the bill to a Select Committee. Instead, he moved a motion that the bill 'be taken into consideration'. He was cryptic though about the inordinate delay in the first place in introducing the amendment bill. Admitting that 'the whole matter has been gone into great detail by the Elayaperumal Committee', Hasan said, 'The report of the Committee was submitted in 1969 and for reasons best known to the House, it has not been possible for Government to bring forward legislation amending this very important Act.'[5]

The highlight of the bill was the incorporation of the committee's recommendation to make 'offences under the Act non-compoundable'. But on the recommendations relating to penalties, the government's response was a mixed bag.

Insofar as imposition of a monetary fine was concerned, the government accepted the recommendation that, rather than being an alternative penalty, it should be a necessary liability in addition to imprisonment. Accordingly, the bill specified a minimum penalty of Rs 50 and a maximum of Rs 200.

As regards the imprisonment clause, the government claimed to have made 'a small change' from what the Elayaperumal Committee had recommended. The committee had prescribed a minimum term of three months' imprisonment for the first offence, which Hasan's bill reduced to one month. He explained that it was a matter of calibration: 'While Government naturally agree that the punishment must be deterrent, it has been felt that if the punishment for the first offence is quite so deterrent, there may be a tendency on the part of courts to acquit the accused on the basis of some doubt or the other.'

But he took pains to clarify that the issue was still open to discussion. 'Government do not wish to adopt any very rigid attitude in the matter and if it is the general feeling of the House that we should accept the Elayaperumal Committee's recommendation *in toto,* I would be prepared to do so.'

The general feeling of the House, in the event, was in favour of enhancing the penalties for untouchability. Even the leader of the Hindu nationalist Bharatiya Jana Sangh, Atal Bihari Vajpayee, who represented Gwalior, expressed this sentiment. In fact, Vajpayee created a stir by alleging that, not very far from Parliament, untouchability was being practised on the premises of the Central Secretariat. He said he had received complaints that a separate surahi, or pot of drinking water, was kept in that government office for Harijans.

And so, Hasan conceded that 'from the speeches I heard here, I gathered that hon Members would prefer that the minimum punishment ... should not be lowered.' He said he would move an amendment. 'I am, therefore, going to crave your indulgence that the minimum punishment recommended by the Elayaperumal Committee, of three months plus Rs. 50 as fine, should be incorporated in this Bill.'

As a prelude to such an amendment being moved, K.N. Tiwari, who was in the chair, put it to the House whether the bill should be taken into consideration as had been introduced. Scarcely had Tiwari asked the question when Hasan's own Cabinet colleague, Minister for Parliamentary Affairs Raj Bahadur, intercepted the bill. Addressing the chair, he pleaded for an adjournment, saying, 'Sir, before you put it to the vote of the House, I want to make one submission. There is a strong feeling in the House and we have to take note of it, that the Bill requires further consideration; there is a suggestion to refer it to the Select Committee. If you could permit us to have some time and postpone this Bill till tomorrow, I shall be grateful.'

Vajpayee demanded to know if the proposed adjournment was meant to refer the bill to a Select Committee. Raj Bahadur responded that the matter deeply affected 'the psychological satisfaction' of the

Scheduled Castes. 'We must not do anything in a hurry which leaves a feeling in their mind that we are rushing with the Bill.' At the chair's prodding that he address Vajpayee's question, Raj Bahadur said, 'The purpose is to consider whether this Bill could not be referred to a Joint Select Committee.'

Tiwari gave the go-ahead saying, 'I think this is the opinion of the House also.' The House adopted the motion for adjournment in circumstances that were anything but routine. Speaker G.S. Dhillon said as much on 30 May 1972 when Nurul Hasan moved a motion to resume the debate on the UOA amendment bill. Dhillon reproached him, 'This is a solitary instance that happened. I don't think any such case happened in the past. It should not be repeated in future. When the Bill was taken up, it was abruptly postponed and then another motion that the discussion be resumed had to be moved. This is very unusual. This should be done very rarely.'[6]

Hasan promptly apologised: 'I express my sincere regret for having—'

Dhillon interrupted him: 'I only wish that you should not do any more.'

Vajpayee pointed out that it was actually Raj Bahadur who was accountable for the abrupt postponement on the previous day of the debate.

This forced Raj Bahadur also to apologise. 'I do express my regret. I was instrumental at the instance of the Members of the House belonging to Scheduled Castes.' Amid interruptions, he added: 'They were all very much agitated about it. I am very sorry about it.'

Eventually, on the same day, Nurul Hasan moved a motion referring the bill to a Joint Committee with thirty members from the Lok Sabha and fifteen from the Rajya Sabha. This layer of parliamentary scrutiny caused further delay. The Joint Committee held twenty-four sittings over the next two years before it submitted its report.

In the meantime, Nurul Hasan ceased to be in charge of the bill as the Department of Social Welfare was shifted to the domain of the Home Ministry. Thereafter, the minister of state in the Ministry of Home Affairs, Ram Niwas Mirdha, a Jat leader from Rajasthan, dealt with the nitty-gritty of the reforms before the Joint Committee.

The chairman of the Joint Committee was also replaced when R.D. Bhandare, an Ambedkarite-turned-Congress member, was appointed governor of Bihar in 1973. Another Congress legislator from the Harijan community, S.M. Siddayya, took over from him. Elected in 1971 from Chamarajanagar in Mysore, Siddayya had translated into Kannada two of Ambedkar's most seminal works, *The Untouchables* and *Annihilation of Caste*.

Indeed, Ambedkar's influence on the report submitted by the Joint Committee on 22 February 1974 was unmistakable. Having been a member of the Elayaperumal Committee, Siddayya was instrumental in incorporating more of the reforms that Ambedkar had propounded in his 1954 Rajya Sabha speech. What was underway was an incremental process of reform. The government had already agreed to do away with both the option of compounding offences and the notion of a fine as an alternative penalty.

This time, without referring to Ambedkar's 1954 Rajya Sabha speech, the Joint Committee adopted his idea of replacing 'offences' with 'civil rights' in the title. The fresh title chosen by it was 'The Protection of Civil Rights Act', or PCRA.[7] The Joint Committee proceeded to insert a provision defining 'civil rights' in the Indian context: 'any right accruing to a person by reason of the abolition of "untouchability" by Article 17 of the Constitution'.

The abolition had put beyond all doubt that an untouchable, like any other citizen, was entitled to the right to equality under Article 14 and the right against discrimination under Article 15. As the Joint Committee put it, 'It has to be particularly noted that Article 17 of the Constitution which abolishes "untouchability" is included in Part III which deals with the Fundamental Rights.' The refocusing of the law on protecting civil rights subsumed the original object of penalising untouchability offences.

The change in nomenclature was one of several changes made in this spirit by Siddayya and his team. For instance, more public places were thrown open by deleting a qualifying expression from the 1955 law. The provision in question penalised refusal of admission on the ground of untouchability to 'any hospital, dispensary, educational institution or any hostel attached thereto'. The committee deleted the words 'attached thereto' so that access equality became obligatory for every hostel, 'whether it is attached to an educational institution or otherwise'.

Another change was along the lines of an intervention by Ambedkar during a Constituent Assembly debate on accessing public places. Ambedkar had interpreted the term 'shop' widely to include petty service providers like laundry and shaving saloons. The Joint Committee tweaked the definition of 'shop' to cover the entire range of petty traders that untouchables were likely to approach as customers: 'The Committee have enlarged the definition of "shop" so as to include places from where goods are sold by a hawker or vendor or from mobile van or cart.'

Also, reacting to the Elayaperumal Committee's findings on the working of the untouchability law, the Joint Committee introduced a provision to render public servants 'punishable as abettors' for 'any negligence in the investigation of any offence under the Act'.

But when it came to prescribing the minimum period of imprisonment, the Joint Committee ignored the Ambedkar-inspired suggestion of the Elayaperumal report that it should be three months. Instead, tacitly acknowledging that some offences might be too petty for a three-month sentence, it retained the original provision in the government bill, fixing the minimum term as one month. Nurul Hasan's assurance in Parliament that the government would raise the minimum term to three months had clearly been set aside.

As for the fine, which was no longer an alternative to imprisonment, the Joint Committee changed both the lower and upper limits of it. The Elayaperumal Committee had reduced the maximum fine from Rs 500 to Rs 200. The Joint Committee restored it to the level of Rs 500, to be levied in addition to imprisonment.

Likewise, on the more sensitive issue of the minimum fine—

which the government, at the instance of the Elayaperumal Committee, had fixed at Rs 50—the Joint Committee increased the levy to Rs 100. Thus, the new range of fines was from Rs 100 to Rs 500 in addition to a prison term.

In fact, the Joint Committee recommended extending Ambedkar's principle of a minimum penalty for discrimination offences to those involving violence as well—even though these offences were punishable under the IPC, irrespective of the caste angle. The Joint Committee's justification was that the general law failed to make allowance for the peculiarity of the violence fuelled by untouchability.

'The Committee feel that where the offences are committed against a person as a reprisal for the exercise by such person of any right accruing to him on account of the abolition of "untouchability", the minimum punishment should be imprisonment for a term which should not be less than two years to which fine should also be added.' The rigour of the minimum two-year sentence, it was clarified, applied only where the offence itself was punishable with imprisonment for a term exceeding two years. (In 1989, this conceptual breakthrough on caste-based violence developed into a full-blown and more stringent law called the Prevention of Atrocities Act.)

In another borrowing from Ambedkar, the Joint Committee introduced the concept of 'collective fine'. It felt the need for such a penalty in cases where untouchability offences were committed 'by the whole community in a particular area'. The provision empowered state governments 'to impose a collective fine on the inhabitants of that area and to apportion the fine so imposed'.

On 6 May 1975, Minister of State for Home Affairs Om Mehta moved, in the Lok Sabha, that the bill to amend the UOA be taken into consideration. Through this junior minister, the Indira Gandhi government declared its acceptance of most of the changes the Joint Committee had made, including the change in the name of the law and the introduction of the concept of collective fines. Mehta said, 'All these suggestions of the Joint Committee are commendable and would lead to a better enforcement of the provisions of the Act.'[8]

Among the few recommendations that the government did not entirely accept was that public servants should be deemed abettors for negligence in the investigation of untouchability offences. Citing jurisprudence principles, Om Mehta argued: '(M)ere negligence cannot be said to be an act of abetment in law in the absence of a criminal intention on the part of a doer.' From the viewpoint of equity, he said, 'Care must also be taken to ensure that police officers are not exposed to frivolous or vexatious criminal proceedings.'

The government, he said, would accept the Joint Committee's recommendation on this clause with a qualification: 'to the extent that only wilful negligence on the part of officers investigating untouchability offences will be deemed to be abetment'. Even this concession came with the caveat that 'prosecution in such cases should be launched only after obtaining the prior permission of Government'. Whatever justification the government provided for thus calibrating the accountability of public servants, it presaged the lack of any will to throw the book at them even when there was evidence of wilful negligence.

The prolonged exercise in fresh norm-setting, initiated by the Shastri government in 1965, was driven by Harijans like Elayaperumal and Siddayya and moderated by ministers like Nurul Hasan and Ram Niwas Mirdha. In 1976, it culminated in the adoption of what came to be renamed as the Protection of Civil Rights Act, 1955. Incidentally, this was at the height of Indira Gandhi's Emergency—a time when Om Mehta had otherwise emerged as one of its villains.

In that dark phase, when Fundamental Rights were suspended and Opposition leaders were in jail, the Lok Sabha finally passed the amendments to the untouchability law on 2 September 1976. The Rajya Sabha did the same the next day. After President Fakhruddin Ali Ahmed had given his assent, the PCRA came into force on 19 November 1976.

In many ways, the Act followed Ambedkar's blueprint of 1954. What was considered audacious at the time was now law. It is another matter that, despite all the rhetoric about making the untouchability law more effective, there was little difference on the ground. If anything, in its new avatar, the law seemed to have made the securing of justice even more elusive.

According to the statistics collated by the Commission for Scheduled Castes and Scheduled Tribes, the conviction rate under UOA had already dropped to 27.2 per cent in 1969–70, the year in which the Elayaperumal report had been submitted. In 1977–78, the year following the enactment of PCRA, the conviction rate under it went further down to 17.1 per cent.[9]

Equally telling was the corresponding increase in acquittal rates. In 1969–70, the acquittal rate under UOA was 23.3 per cent while 49.4 per cent of the cases had been compounded. Since PCRA had no provision for compounding cases, the acquittal rate under it in 1977–78 jumped to 82.8 per cent.

One reason why PCRA proved so ineffective was that it assumed that wilful negligence among public servants would be restricted to police officials. In reality, there were cases where, even after the police had acted diligently, the judiciary betrayed caste prejudice.

Consider a case under the untouchability law—the first to go up before the Supreme Court in the four decades since its enactment. On appeal was an age-old issue: the denial of access to water sources. In 1978, due to the march of technology, the bone of contention was a borewell.

The dispute arose in northern Karnataka's Belgaum district, a place that had repeatedly figured in the evolution of the untouchability law. When Belgaum was part of the Bombay Presidency, its representative, D.V. Belvi, had raised the issue of denial of access to wells way back in 1919, a first in any legislature across British India. Later, another legislator from Belgaum, B.N. Datar, a junior minister in the Nehru government, had introduced the UOA bill in Parliament in 1954, even if that had been more a matter of chance than of personal initiative.

The background to the dispute was that, under the orders of the Karnataka government, two borewells were being drilled in village Malikwadi in Chikodi taluk of Belgaum district. One of these borewells was just 15 feet from a Mahar settlement. This was exactly what M.C. Rajah had proposed sixty years earlier: 'to remove all restrictions which prevent the use of public wells ... by the members of the Depressed Classes, and to construct more wells in places adjacent to their dwellings'.

On the evening of 17 September 1978, residents of Malikwadi, including Mahars, gathered to observe the drilling operation. When water sprouted from the borewell at about 9.30 p.m., caste Hindus immediately laid claim to the borewell. They performed pooja on the spot, and drew water from the borewell to do abhisheka in a nearby temple. At the same time, by 'show of force', they restrained the Mahars from approaching the borewell on account of their caste. The Mahars were forced to return to their homes with empty pots.

One of the affected Mahars filed a complaint. Since the facts fell squarely under PCRA, the police booked five caste Hindus. On 10 April 1980, a judicial magistrate in Chikodi convicted all five accused persons. Exercising its sentencing discretion, the trial court imposed on them the minimum prescribed penalties under PCRA: imprisonment for one month and a fine of Rs 100.

Five months later, on 5 September 1980, an additional sessions judge of Belgaum upheld the conviction of three of the accused persons while acquitting the other two. The three who remained convicted filed a criminal revision petition before the Karnataka High Court. On the other hand, the State did not appeal against the acquittals of the other two.

The case collapsed in the High Court on 1 April 1981, as Justice M.S. Patil found it fit to acquit the remaining convicted persons too. Holding that 'it cannot be said with any amount of certainty which among the accused was guilty of the offence', the Karnataka High Court gave the benefit of the doubt to all the arraigned persons. 'The evidence adduced on behalf of the prosecution was wholly insufficient to establish the charge ... levelled against them.'[10]

Justice Patil admitted that 'ordinarily sitting in revision, the High Court will not interfere with the concurrent finding of the courts below'. However, where the lower courts' conclusions 'cannot be supported by the evidence on record and the appreciation is not proper, the High Court will not hesitate to interfere with the finding of the facts also'.

Put differently, Justice Patil found the appreciation of evidence by the lower courts so improper that it forced him to depart from the principle of not interfering with their concurrent finding. His compulsion apparently was that each of the four Mahars who had testified in the trial court as prosecution witnesses 'gave a different version' of how they were blocked from accessing the borewell. 'Their evidence is not uniform as to what were the actual words uttered and how the accused prevented,' Patil wrote.

While insisting on greater uniformity in their testimonies, Patil glossed over the evidence of how the Mahars had been intimidated into keeping away from the borewell. This was despite his own reference to the prosecution's allegation that one of the accused persons 'told some of his men to bring [a] gun from his house saying that he would see how those Harijans would take water from the well'.

Patil described the discrepancies that he made much of in the testimonies of four prosecution witnesses (PWs) as follows:

- According to PW-1, three of the accused persons said, 'You have come to take water from here. You are Mahars. You have your own well.'
- PW-2, on the other hand, stated that all the five accused objected (to) them collecting water and said, 'You Mahar could not hold water.'
- PW-3, however, stated three of the accused 'came in their way and objected (to) them stating that they were Mahar' and as such they cannot collect water.
- PW-4 stated that one of the accused persons told two others that 'they are "Mahar" and they should not be allowed to take water'.

Though all four PWs had testified broadly on the same lines, the Karnataka High Court found the evidence 'discrepant and not consistent'. This was because, in Justice Patil's view, 'what is not certain from the evidence is as to who among the accused persons obstructed and used those particular words attributed to the accused'. Faulting the lack of granular detail, the High Court said sarcastically, 'It cannot expect that all the accused would use the words simultaneously in a chorus in the manner the witnesses stated before the [trial] court.'

The acquittal of the remaining accused jolted the Karnataka government into appealing against it before the Supreme Court. The appeal was pending in New Delhi for over a decade, in which time one of the three accused persons passed away. The bench that finally heard the case against the two surviving accused comprised Justice Kuldip Singh, a Sikh from Punjab, and Justice K. Ramaswamy, a Dalit from Andhra Pradesh. In their separate but concurring judgments delivered on 1 December 1992, Kuldip Singh and Ramaswamy set aside the High Court's acquittal.

Holding that it 'fell into patent error in rejecting the prosecution evidence', Justice Kuldip Singh said, 'The High Court lost sight of the fact that the social disability of the Harijan community was enforced on a threat of using a gun. It is proved beyond doubt that the complainants were stopped from taking water from the well on the ground that they were untouchables.'[11]

Agreeing with Justice Kuldip Singh's verdict, Justice Ramaswamy underscored the impunity with which untouchability had been practised, despite the checks provided in PCRA. For the acquittal of more than 75 per cent 'at all levels', Ramaswamy acknowledged judicial complicity. 'Apathy and lack of proper perspectives even by the courts in tackling the naughty problem is obvious,' he said. 'For the first time after 42 years of the Constitution came into force, this first case has come up to this Court to consider the problem.'

Insofar as Justice Patil's role in the case on hand was concerned, Justice Ramaswamy said, 'The learned Judge concentrated more on the sequence or absence of parrot-like repetition of ocular words spoken by illiterate persons … The High Court gave the benefit of the doubt when in fact no such benefit does arise from the evidence if considered in a proper perspective.'

The angst expressed by Justice Ramaswamy was but the latest

episode in a struggle that was being waged by untouchables from within the State structure, from the time that M.C. Rajah was first appointed as a legislator in 1919. The battles fought by them and their sympathisers in the legislature, executive and judiciary testified to the resilience of caste prejudice. A civil right as elementary as equal access to public places or amenities for about a fifth of India's population remained, and indeed still remains,[12] an open question—in practice, if not in theory.

4

TEMPLE ENTRY

13

AMBEDKAR'S FORGOTTEN BILL

With his historic address in the Parliament of Religions in Chicago on 11 September 1893, Swami Vivekananda is said to have introduced Hinduism to America. His eloquence apparently made such an impact that he ended up staying on in the West for over three years. When he finally returned from his maiden visit on 16 January 1897, the thirty-four-year-old monk received a hero's welcome near the holy city of Rameswaram in the Madras Presidency. The reception had been organised by a zamindar, the raja of Ramnad in the Madura district, Bhaskara Sethupathi.

In his response to the 'address of welcome', Vivekananda shared with Sethupathi the credit for his spiritual conquest. 'Perhaps most of you are aware that it was the Raja who first put the idea into my mind of going to Chicago, and it was he who all the time supported it with all his heart and influence. A good deal, therefore, of the praise that has been bestowed upon me in this address, ought to go to this noble man of southern India.'[1]

About four months later, that noble man filed a suit against a bunch of lower-caste men who had forcibly entered a temple of which he was the hereditary trustee. Their entry had triggered retaliatory violence. Sethupathi was a Maravar, a dominant caste that, because of its alleged tendency for violence, was classified by the British in 1911 as a 'criminal tribe'. While 'criminal tribe' was a colonial construct, caste was not. In the caste hierarchy, rendered more bewildering by its regional variations, Maravars looked down upon the Shanars or Nadars, who had a major presence in the area.

For all their upward mobility in everyday life, Nadars were considered, much to their umbrage, to be below the Shudra category, largely because of their traditional occupation of toddy-tapping. They were clubbed with untouchables who, being outside the varna hierarchy, were generally the target of temple-entry restrictions.

Fifteen Nadar men had entered the Siva temple on 14 May 1897 in a village called Kamudi in Sethupathi's zamindari. In his plaint, Sethupathi alleged that 'the Shanars, as a caste, were prohibited both by custom and by the Shastras from entering the temple in suit'.[2] Having still entered 'in procession with music and torches and performed acts of worship', they had, as part of a concerted campaign 'polluted the temple and caused obstruction to the lawful worshippers'. Accordingly, Sethupathi prayed for a declaration that Nadars were 'not entitled to enter the temple', and sought a 'perpetual injunction restraining them from so doing' as well as damages.

It was an incongruent plea for someone who had so recently been eulogised by Swami Vivekananda, the exponent of the Advaita Vedanta philosophy that 'each soul is potentially divine'. But then, Vivekananda's outlook too was dichotomous. Even as he denounced untouchability, Vivekananda defended the caste system, at least in what he believed was its original varna form. Even his own experience of caste prejudice was no deterrent to this belief. Before he had left for Chicago, travelling across India as an unknown monk, Vivekananda had himself been a victim of temple-entry restrictions. He waited in vain for three days in 1892 to enter the Kodungallur Bhagavathy temple in the princely state of Cochin. As a Kayastha, a Shudra caste in Bengal, Vivekananda was in fact eligible to enter the temple, but the custom in Kodungallur was to block anyone from a distant land if their caste was hard to determine.

Since Hindu law was yet to undergo modern codification, colonial courts relied upon custom and the Shastras in the adjudication of civil disputes related to it. In the event of a conflict between the two, custom—however local its application—overrode the Shastras, thanks to the law laid down for all of British India, coincidentally, in another Ramnad case. The context of that case was the Madura collector's bid to take over the zamindari of Ramnad by questioning the adoption of Bhaskara Sethupathi's father. Moottoo Ramalinga Sethupathy's adoption was challenged on the grounds that, contrary to the Shastras, it had taken place after the death of the previous zamindar.

In a landmark 1868 ruling against the colonial administrator, the Privy Council upheld the adoption on the basis of the custom that was found to be applicable to Ramnad: 'For under the Hindoo system of law, the clear proof of usage will outweigh the written text of the law.'[3] After this ruling, the colonial courts in India shifted their focus from interpreting the Shastras to determining whether there was any overriding customary rule on the point in dispute.

Sure enough, in the case brought against them by Bhaskara Sethupathi, the Nadars based their defence on custom as well. Rather than invoking the secular principle of equality, they made the strategic choice of coming up with their own interpretation of custom. They took care to yield precedence to Brahmins, who alone had the prerogative of serving as priests in the temple. The Nadars claimed that they had 'a right to use the temple ... in the same manner and to the same extent as any other class in the village except Brahmins'. The implication was that they were caste Hindus or Savarnas, not untouchables or Avarnas.

The Nadars said that they had been 'from time immemorial exercising such right and participating in the puja and worship therein'. This claim of immemorial access was hardly verifiable though, especially for a caste struggling to shake off the disgrace associated with their hereditary occupation of supplying an intoxicant.

In his judgment delivered on 20 July 1899, the subordinate judge in Madura who heard Sethupati's suit laid bare a dilemma. On the one hand, he felt constrained to uphold the customary prohibition: 'The rules of worship in the plaint-temple prohibit the entrance of persons engaged in that occupation.' On the other hand, he could not help admitting uneasiness: 'Courts of law have recognized and enforced customs of this character although they may be repugnant to generally received notions of what is just and proper. It is not for this Court to examine whether the doctrines or usages obtaining in a particular temple are defensible from a logical or equitable standpoint in the light of modern enlightenment and civilization.' This was as far as a colonial court would go in admitting that caste restrictions on temple entry, though binding on it, were archaic.

All that the subordinate judge could do was 'to ascertain correctly ... what the custom and usage is as observed and practiced by the community for whose use and benefit the temple ... is dedicated'. On the basis of the evidence adduced before him, the judge found that 'the custom set up by them in support of the right of entry has not been made out'. The Nadars, he said, belonged to 'a class which, under custom and the Shastras, are precluded from entering the plaint-temple which is governed by the ritual prescribed in the Saiva Agamas adopted as authoritative and current in the Madura district'.

The only consolation he could offer the Nadars, while passing a perpetual injunction against them, was a finding that they were 'not guilty of the special acts of sacrilege they were charged with by the plaintiff'. So, rather than the damages of Rs 2,500 that had been claimed by Sethupathi, the subordinate judge ordered the Nadar defendants to pay Rs 500 for the expense of 'purifying the temple'. Still, the humiliation of their very presence being held to have desecrated the Kamudi temple was a blow to their aspirations to equality.

The aggrieved Nadars filed an appeal before the Madras High Court. Barely had the appeal been filed when the case saw a dramatic twist—Bhaskar Sethupathi had a change of heart. Whether this was due to the pull of his Advaita Vedanta connection or for reasons more mundane was a matter of speculation. Rather than opposing their appeal, as the sole trustee of the Kamudi temple, the raja of Ramnad entered into a 'compromise' with the Nadars. Forsaking the legal gains that had been made by him and his fellow Maravars from the trial court's judgment, Sethupathi took a big leap forward: he recognised the rights of Nadars to worship there.

On 2 May 1901, the Nadars placed the compromise on record and requested the High Court to revise the decree accordingly. However, it soon became apparent that Sethupathi had not bothered to get the other stakeholders on board. Three men, including the officiating priest of the temple, filed applications to be treated as respondents to the appeal. On 18 September 1901, the High Court admitted these men—the priest and two Maravars of Kamudi—as parties to the appeal proceedings.

The developments in Madras caused concern in other parts of British India, given that the temple-entry issue had 'brought about serious riots involving great loss of life and property', as reported by the Bombay-based *Times of India*. According to it, 'Some worshippers, questioning the Rajah's bona fide in entering into a compromise, filed an affidavit in the High Court alleging corrupt motives to the Rajah, and asking to be made parties to a suit to defend the appeal. The High Court today passed orders admitting the petition and expressing inability to reconcile the present attitude of the Rajah with his past strenuous and successful efforts against the Shanars.'[4]

Taken aback by this turn of events, Sethupathi changed his mind once again, dissociating himself from the compromise. The High Court took a serious view of the matter. On 25 September 1901, it passed strictures on him while rejecting the prayer of Nadars for a decree in accordance with the concessions that Sethupathi had made to them in writing. The High Court said 'it was a breach of trust on the part of the trustee of the temple and as such unlawful under the provisions of … the Civil Procedure Code'.[5] By invoking the serious offence of breach of trust, the High Court signalled that, as a trustee, Sethupathi had no option but to keep out any caste that was believed by other Hindus, even if only of that local area, to pollute the temple.

With the compromise out of the way, a bench comprising Justice Ralph Benson and Justice Lewis Moore heard all the parties, old and new, on the merits of the case and agreed with the trial court. In reaffirming that the Nadars were prohibited from entering the temple 'owing to their hereditary caste occupation', the Madras High Court set more store by custom than by the indicators of their upward mobility.

As its judgment dated 4 February 1902 put it: 'No doubt many of the Shanars have abandoned that occupation and have won for themselves, by education, industry and frugality, respectable positions as traders and merchants and even as vakils and clerks; and it is but natural to feel sympathy for their effort to obtain social recognition and to rise to what is regarded as a higher form of religious worship; but such sympathy will not be increased by unreasonable and unfounded pretensions, and in the effort to rise the Shanars must not invade the established rights of other castes.' The Nadars had received little beyond a token of sympathy from the High Court.

Undaunted, they took the matter to the Privy Council in London. It was a measure of the wealth that the Nadars in general had acquired by then that a dispute which pitted them against a dominant caste reached the highest tribunal in the British Empire at their instance. By the time the Kamudi case came up for hearing before a five-judge bench of the Privy Council on 16 June 1908, Bhaskara Sethupathi had been dead for over four years. But, while contesting the findings of the Madras High Court, the counsel for the Nadars brought up his short-lived compromise with them.

'The fact of the compromise itself showed that there was no substantial ground of the kind alleged which prevented the appellants from having the use of the temple; and the feelings the respondent pressed at the time of the compromise were very inconsistent with his former and present attitude towards the appellants,' the counsel argued, using the word 'present' rather loosely for a dead man. Turning the High Court's finding of 'unreasonable' pretensions on its head, the Nadars alleged that the custom itself failed the test of reasonableness: 'Even if proved, the custom prohibiting the appellants from using the temple was invalid in law as being unreasonable.'

Thus, the second Ramnad case, which came some forty years after the first, provided the Privy Council with an opportunity to examine a fresh proposition on custom. The Nadars were asking whether a custom could be binding even when it was so unreasonable as to block the doors of the temple to an entire section of the Hindu community purely on account of the accident of their birth into a certain caste.

So put off were their Lordships by the arguments of the Nadars that they did not even want to hear the other side. In a burst of conservatism, the Privy Council rejected the appeal then and there, saying that its reasons would be given 'on a later day'. While recording that the lawyers for the respondents 'were not heard', the operative part of the order dated 16 June 1908 said that 'their Lordships were agreed ... that the appeal should be dismissed'.

The promised reasons followed on 1 July 1908 in a terse judgment authored by Lord Robertson. The bench included Sir Andrew Scoble, who had, as law member of the Viceroy's Executive Council in India, piloted the 1891 social-reform legislation increasing the age of consent. Yet, the Privy Council verdict displayed none of the discomfort that the two Indian courts had betrayed on the point of social reform. It presented the respondents' version even before—in fact, without ever—laying out the grounds on which the Nadars had filed their appeal. 'It is alleged by the respondents that the presence of persons belonging to the appellants' caste is repugnant to the religious principle of the Hindu worship of Siva and to the sentiments of the caste Hindus who worship in this temple, and that it is contrary to custom in this temple.'

Steering clear of the 'delicate and abstruse questions of Hindu religious doctrine', the Privy Council claimed to have arrived at its decision on two 'palpable and limited' facts. First, the Nadars 'worship by themselves in a temple of their own'. Second, their 'complete failure to prove any resort' by persons of their caste to the Kamudi temple. 'Those two facts,' it held, 'negative the case of the appellants that they "have been from time immemorial ... participating in the puja and worship" in the disputed temple.'

The Privy Council added that those two facts also vindicated the contention of the respondents that 'this separation in worship between the two classes was not accidental or voluntary, but rested on a deeper ground'.

It was plainly reluctant to test custom on the touchstone of reasonableness. 'All this however, as matter of theological argument, is too rationalistic; while, on the other hand, it wanders from the region of fact and custom.' Insofar as the Privy Council was concerned, '[w]hat the respondents have succeeded in proving is that by custom the appellants are not among the people for whose worship this particular temple exists'.

Having reaffirmed the pre-eminence of custom in the Hindu law, the Privy Council was scathing in its remarks against Sethupathi for 'the episode in the proceedings euphemistically described as "the compromise"'. After the subordinate judge had decided against the Nadars, Sethupathi had 'thought fit to profess that he now saw that he and the Judge were wrong; and he asked that the judgment should be altered, so as to defeat his own action'. Further, it said that 'a very sordid motive for this surrender was specifically asserted and has not been disproved'.

Such was its displeasure with Sethupathi that the Privy Council faulted him even for returning to his original position after the Madras High Court had admitted more plaintiffs. In a parenthetical remark, it said acidly that Sethupathi's 'confidence in the justice of his suit had by this time convalesced'. Commending the High Court for its finding against him of a breach of trust, the Privy Council said, 'The principles applicable to the case of a trustee who thus betrays his trust by surrendering a decree have been well stated and applied by the High Court.'

The substance and tone of the Privy Council's 1908 verdict in *Sankaralinga Nadan v. Rajeswara Dorai* had a far-reaching effect. For one, by signalling that trustees could be held guilty of breach of trust for failing to maintain the customary restrictions, it strengthened the grip of a custom that was inconsistent with the notion of equality. And for another, judges in colonial India were stripped of all discretion in determining the reasonableness of a practice that had the aura of custom.

Consider a 1914 judgment of the Madras High Court, which upheld the customary restriction on members of the Elaivaniyar community from proceeding beyond the dhwajastambha, or flag post, of a temple.[6] As the Nadars had done before them, Elaivaniyars contested the reasonableness of the discrimination against them even on the touchstone of caste rules. Claiming that they were a Shudra caste and not untouchables, Elaivaniyars said that their traditional occupation of oil-pressing should by no means have stigmatised them. This dispute was also situated on the blurred line between the lower Shudras and the untouchables in the context of temple-entry restrictions.

Making a frustrated reference to the Privy Council's extension of the stigma to a section of Shudras as well, Justice Sadasiva Iyer of the Madras High Court said:[7] 'Speaking for myself, if I were not bound by authority, I should like to hold that a custom which prohibits one who belongs to a community which is not lower than a Sudra caste from going beyond the Dhwajastambha is an unreasonable custom and ought not to be recognised.' Throwing up his hands, Iyer added: 'But as even such unreasonable customs ... have been held to override the law and Shastras ... I think I am bound to follow such rulings.'

The impact of the 1908 Privy Council judgment was also evident in a specific reference to it, over two decades later, in a legislative proposal at the national level. This was the only judgment that was named in the SOR of the first-ever—but, astonishingly, little known—bill combating the malaise of 'disabilities affecting untouchable castes of the Hindu community'.

❖

The Hindu Untouchable Castes (Removal of Disabilities) Bill was a pioneering attempt to take on untouchability across British India. This bill of 1929 vintage was drafted by none other than Dr Bhimrao

Ramji Ambedkar—one of modern India's most scrutinised and valourised figures.

Yet, none of the books on the principal architect of India's Constitution, including the seventeen-volume *Dr Babasaheb Ambedkar: Writings and Speeches,* make any mention of this crucial achievement. The omission is hard to understand especially because of the excitement that the bill had generated contemporaneously. When its text was published on 7 December 1929, the timing was propitious. The draft appeared amid the first of the two major temple-entry satyagrahas in the Bombay Presidency. Held from October 1929 to January 1930, the agitation demanded for untouchables the right to enter the Peshwa-era Parvati temple on a hilltop in Poona.

One reason for the bill's obscurity could well have been Ambedkar's own silence on it. His politics soon became more radical and he turned his back on the legislative option. Within three months of drafting the bill, he had his first taste of leading a temple-entry satyagraha—this one meant to throw open the Kalaram temple in Nasik. Starting on 2 March 1930, the Kalaram Satyagraha proved to be the longest such agitation anywhere in the country.

About two years later, while the Kalaram agitation was still on, the issue of temple entry took centre stage in national politics as a result of the historic Poona Pact. However, by the time Gandhi finally engaged with the temple-entry cause in the last quarter of 1932, Ambedkar had shifted his own focus to the non-religious grievances of the Depressed Classes. All this culminated in his historic Yeola declaration on 13 October 1935. While calling off the protracted Kalaram temple agitation, Ambedkar announced that he had decided to leave Hinduism, despairing of the possibility that untouchables would ever find an honourable place within its fold.

Ambedkar's growing disengagement with the politics of temple entry did not, however, detract from the contribution he had made to the cause early in his career as a lawmaker. What Ambedkar's bill did was to acknowledge that an untouchable was as much a rights-bearing individual as any other Hindu, whether in secular or religious spheres. In the caste-ridden society and custom-driven jurisprudence of 1929, this was no less than revolutionary. Unlike the Madras amendments that countered untouchability in a covert manner by amending civic laws, this bill took it on squarely, calling out its wide acceptance as a religiously sanctioned practice.

It took more than audacity to imagine such a legislation. In fact, Ambedkar too had his own learning curve as he came to grips with the arcane law on temple entry during the course of the Poona temple-entry agitation. Although the Privy Council verdict in the Kamudi case had been duly reported in law journals, Ambedkar was somehow unaware of that judgment and its adverse effect on untouchables throughout British India.

In his capacity as president of the Depressed Classes Institute, Ambedkar had written to several Bombay temples of the institute's decision to hold a satyagraha if they continued to deny untouchables their right to worship in their premises. The response to his notice and a subsequent conference put him on the track of drafting a legal measure designed to protect trustees from any legal liability were they to allow untouchables into their temples.

That those trustees in Bombay were inclined to provide access to untouchables reflected the extent to which Gandhi had mainstreamed concerns over untouchability. Under his influence, the Congress had been engaged, however haltingly, in a campaign against untouchability since its Nagpur session in 1920. Though Gandhi was still fuzzy about temple entry, some of his followers went ahead of him. Indeed, the catalyst for the legal consultation with Ambedkar was the intervention of the Congress's Anti-Untouchability Sub-Committee, appointed earlier in 1929.

The secretary of that sub-committee, Jamnalal Bajaj, a Marwari industrialist and close associate of Gandhi, had issued a five-page appeal to the 'Trustees, Owners, and Managers of Hindu Temples' on 1 September 1929 in the run-up to the Poona Satyagraha. The gist of the appeal was 'to throw open the temples under your charge to the so-called untouchables'.[8] But it made no mention of, let alone offer a solution to, the legal impediment that the trustees faced. Like Ambedkar, the Congress members were also apparently unaware of the irony of the situation: that law would come in the way of social reform.

Besides providing leadership to the untouchables and practising law, Ambedkar was then a member of the Bombay Legislative Council, to which he had been nominated in February 1927. He was also a member of a committee that had been appointed by the Bombay government in November 1928 to investigate the grievances of the untouchables. This committee, chaired by British administrator O.H.B. Starte, was exactly the kind that Maneckji Dadabhoy had first sought at a national level through his abortive 1916 resolution in the Imperial Legislative Council. The Starte Committee had been set up on a resolution moved by Dr Purushottam Solanki, an untouchable from Gujarat and a physician, who had been nominated along with Ambedkar to the Bombay Legislative Council.

While touring in his capacity as a member of the Starte Committee, Ambedkar had a grave encounter with caste prejudice which landed him in a life-threatening situation and actually broke his foot. On 23 October 1929, he was first forced to wait for an hour at the railway station of village Chalisgaon after he had been received by his untouchable followers. And when he finally sat in a one-horse tonga, the carriage was driven by one of his followers who had no experience in that skilled job. What transpired was that none of the tongawallas at the station had agreed to transport an untouchable. So, the best that his followers could arrange for was a tonga without its driver—a recipe for disaster.

Recalling the accident, Ambedkar said in his brief autobiography: 'To save my dignity, the Mahars of Chalisgaon had put my very life in jeopardy. It is then I learnt that a Hindu tongawalla, no better than a menial, has a dignity by which he can look upon himself as a person who is superior to any untouchable, even though he may be a Barrister-at-Law.'[9] The hurt he suffered was clearly more than physical.

Oblivious perhaps to this traumatic incident, Bajaj visited Ambedkar just two days later, on 25 October 1929, on a matter of urgent business. A notice had been issued on behalf of the untouchables about the initiation of a temple-entry campaign in Bombay city four days later, i.e., 29 October. Bajaj arrived with a plan to issue a fresh appeal, this time to the general Hindu public, to give up untouchability on Kartik Ekadashi, 13 November 1929. Ambedkar was, however, in no condition to receive visitors. He promptly wrote a regret letter to Bajaj. 'I am sorry I could not meet you personally when you came to call upon me this evening ... as I have been disabled by a severe injury to my foot caused by an accident and confined to bed.'[10]

On Bajaj's ambitious plan of celebrating 13 November 1929 as 'a day of the extinction of untouchability', Ambedkar responded sceptically: 'You are the best judge as to whether such an appeal is likely to succeed.' He added that the only way he could help was 'to cause no prejudice to the efforts you are making'. So, Ambedkar assured Bajaj that he would not launch any action on temple entry before the date fixed by Bajaj for Hindus to redeem themselves. The appeal was subsequently issued as a 'manifesto' signed by, according to Bajaj's report before the Lahore session of the Congress at the end of the year, 'almost all the prominent Hindus of Bombay, a large number of them well-known for their orthodox style of living'.[11]

The intimation of the satyagraha that had been sent to Bombay temples, as it happened, had a salutary effect on those run by Gaud Saraswat Brahmins. On 7 November 1929, Congress leader B.G. Kher—a Brahmin who would go on to become the first premier of the Bombay Presidency after the 1937 election—wrote a letter in his capacity as a solicitor representing the trustees of a clutch of temples, including the prominent Bhuleshwar temple in south Bombay.

The missive was addressed to one of the country's leading barristers, M.R. Jayakar, also a member of the Central Legislative Assembly, and notable for his efforts to enact social reforms. Politically, Jayakar had been with the Congress and its offshoot, Swaraj Party, and was one of the non-Brahmin leaders of the Hindu Mahasabha. In the 1925 Bombay conference of the Hindu

Mahasabha, Jayakar had moved a resolution saying: 'Amongst Hindus, nobody, by reason merely of birth, can be untouchable and all Hindus have equal right to use all public places, watering places and places of worship.'[12]

In the surcharged environment of the Poona Satyagraha, Kher's letter to Jayakar said that the Bombay trustees he represented were 'of opinion that untouchables should be allowed to enter all public places, including temples for the purpose of worship'—a course that was reminiscent of Jayakar's 1925 resolution. The desire to open temples to all sections of Hindus was accompanied by a legal concern that the trustees raised: 'their difficulty is that under the decisions of the Bombay High Court and the Privy Council, they think they have no right to admit into the temples people to whom any section of the worshippers can object on the ground of long standing usage'. Accordingly, Kher sought an appointment with Jayakar so that 'the Trustees could see you to discuss this matter with you'.[13]

Whether it was due to Jayakar's advice or otherwise, the trustees came away more convinced than before about the legal constraint. This came through in a letter written by solicitor G.A. Sabnis to Ambedkar on 11 November 1929. Writing in his capacity as chairman of the 'Board of Trustees of the Temples and Charitable Property of the Gaud Saraswat Brahmin Community', he addressed Ambedkar in the latter's capacity as the president of the Depressed Classes Institute. Although it ended up pleading helplessness in the face of the Privy Council decision, the letter was all the same remarkable in that it displayed remorse on the part of the trustees.

Sabnis began his letter on a conciliatory note. 'At the outset, I am to assure you on behalf of the Board that the Trustees fully sympathize with the just aspirations of the Depressed Classes and feel convinced that it is absolutely imperative that the Depressed Classes (untouchables) should be allowed the free use of, and access to, all the temples for the purposes of worship in the same way as the other Hindu communities.'[14] (parenthesis in the original)

This was a far cry from the hostility displayed by their Chitpavan

Brahmin counterparts in Poona's Parvati temple. But then, as Sabnis put it, 'My Board have, however, most carefully and anxiously considered the legal position regarding their ability to permit the Depressed Classes to enter the said temple in their charge, and are forced to come to the conclusion that in view of the present state of the law bearing on the point they are unable to permit such an entry.' Thus, the letter had raised hopes of reform only to dash them.

Two days after this mixed message from Sabnis, the embargo that Ambedkar had promised Bajaj lapsed on the appointed occasion of Kartik Ekadashi. Despite Bajaj's stirring manifesto against untouchability, the collective of caste Hindus showed no inclination of giving it up voluntarily. The following day, on 14 November 1929, Ambedkar held a closed-door meeting with other untouchable leaders, at the end of which he announced the resumption of their plans to offer satyagraha at certain temples. Without going into details, he labelled it ominously as 'direct action'.[15]

Asked by the *Times of India* about his negotiations with temple authorities, Ambedkar disclosed the substance of the letter he had received from the trustees of the Bhuleshwar temple. But he expressed disagreement with their apprehension that the law did not permit them to let in untouchables. As Sabnis had not mentioned any case law in his letter, Ambedkar alluded to a certain decision of the Bombay High Court which he erroneously believed was the cause of the trustees' misunderstanding. He told the newspaper that 'the trustees had not interpreted the decision of the High Court correctly', and added that he was addressing a letter to the trustees explaining 'the real position of the law'.

It was most unusual for Ambedkar to be ignorant of the established law, especially on caste matters.

The next day, on 16 November 1929, he wrote an eight-page letter to Sabnis. At the outset, Ambedkar expressed 'a great relief' at the fact that the trustees running the temples of Gaud Saraswat Brahmins were open to reform. They showed that 'in this morass of religious degradation in which the whole Hindu world has been wallowing, there is at least one leading community of Bombay which is enlightened enough to recognize the humanity in the untouchable and be ready to admit him to the House of God'.[16]

Insofar as his explanation of 'the real position of the law' was concerned, Ambedkar's letter reflected the misimpression he had already conveyed to the press. He dismissed the apprehension of the trustees that they were 'prevented by law from giving effect to their wishes'. The letter divulged the case law he had hinted at in his press interaction. It turned out to be an 1883 judgment of the Bombay High Court, *Anandrav Bhikaji Phadke v. Shankar Daji Charya.*[17] Ambedkar explained that this five-decade-old judgment had 'recently been paraded in the Press and thrown in the faces of all working in support of temple entry for the untouchables'.

But, as he himself admitted, the 1883 verdict pertained to a dispute between two Brahmin castes, Chitpavan and Palshe, over access to the gabhara, or sanctum sanctorum, containing the deity. So, Ambedkar asserted that this case 'cannot fetter the Trustees if they are really desirous of throwing open the Temple to the Depressed Classes'. As he pointed out, 'They are not asking for an entry into the Gabhara.' All that the untouchables wanted was access only to the extent any of the ordinary worshippers were allowed, which was short of the gabhara anyway.

Ambedkar then proceeded to recommend another precedent in its place, *Saklat v. Bella.* This case appeared to him 'to give the best guidance to the Trustees in arriving at their conclusion'. It was a 1925 Privy Council verdict relating to a Parsi temple that was meant only for those Zoroastrians who were Parsis by race. In a progressive verdict, the Privy Council ruled that even a convert to Zoroastrianism could be admitted into the temple without rendering its trustees liable to breach of trust.

Although the Zoroastrians had nothing remotely akin to the Hindu caste system, Ambedkar told Sabnis that the propositions laid down by this case had 'the most direct bearing upon the matter which your Board is now called upon to decide'. And so, he concluded, it was his 'considered view that the Trustees shall have no legal difficulty in giving effect to their wishes'.

Ambedkar added a disclaimer, though: 'I do not wish to dogmatise about the correctness of the legal position I have tried to put before your Board.' It was just 'a possible view', Ambedkar conceded, suggesting that further consultation was needed. Interestingly, he suggested the very expert who had already been approached by Kher on behalf of the trustees. 'It would be better if a conference was arranged with some senior counsel like Mr. M. R. Jayakar to thrash out the question to the satisfaction of the Board.' Ambedkar added graciously that 'if you desired me to attend such a conference, I would always be ready to respond to your invitation'.

Ambedkar's recommendation to involve Jayakar in this conversation might have been not only in deference to his legal acumen but also because of his track record as a member of the Central Legislative Assembly. After Maneckji Dadabhoy, it was Jayakar who, in 1928, had the distinction of moving the next resolution on untouchability at the national level. Ambedkar's suggestion of conferring with Jayakar on temple entry came the year after that resolution had been, in an unprecedented development, adopted by the Central legislature.

Swami Anand—a follower of Gandhi and an associate of Bajaj, in charge of the Anti-Untouchability Sub-Committee's central office in Bombay—grabbed the opportunity to arrange a meeting with Jayakar and the Bhuleshwar trustees. Anand had worked closely with Jayakar to mediate in the Parvati temple stand-off, and was in touch with him on the Bhuleshwar developments as well. On 22 November 1929, Anand wrote to Jayakar at Lonavla, a hill station close to Bombay, where he had gone to recover from an illness. 'I am trying to arrange a meeting of Dr Ambedkar, yourself and trustees during your stay in Bombay and shall fix up the time and place for it on your arrival.'[18]

The legal conference materialised shortly thereafter, on the evening of 25 November 1929 at Jayakar's residence in Bombay. Though the conference had not been minuted, it did serve to enlighten Ambedkar that the inability claimed by the Bhuleshwar trustees was real. In practical terms, the discussion with Jayakar brought him clarity on the need to overcome the liability imposed on trustees by the Privy Council's 1908 ruling in the Kamudi temple case.

Two days later, on 27 November 1929, in a follow-up letter to Jayakar, Anand recorded that the Privy Council verdict in the Kamudi case had been 'read and discussed at the conference' with Ambedkar and the temple trustees.[19] On 6 December 1929, the *Times of India* reported that the trustees of the Bhuleshwar temple were exploring the option of seeking the Bombay High Court's intervention in the temple-entry controversy. It said that this was 'following an informal conference between two members of the Board of Trustees of the temple, Dr. B. R. Ambedkar, the leader of the depressed classes and other of their representatives recently held at the residence of Mr. M. R. Jayakar'. The newspaper added, 'Up to the present, neither party has made any gesture as to what action should be taken.'[20]

However, the very next day, the same newspaper carried a report with a three-deck headline saying, 'Untouchables' Disabilities—Bill to End Them—Assembly to Consider Dr. Ambedkar's Measure'. Though the *Times* made no attempt to provide a historical perspective, the bill was in fact the first to take on untouchability openly. It was fitting then that, in its report published on 7 December 1929, the newspaper reproduced the entire five-clause preamble and three-clause bill as drafted by Ambedkar. While referring to it as Ambedkar's draft, the *Times* also mentioned the curious possibility that it might be considered by the Central Legislative Assembly, even though he was then a member of the Bombay Legislative Council.

The newspaper's brief introduction to the bill failed to make the obvious connection with the 25 November conference on the Bhuleshwar temple. That introduction did, however, disclose an unusual understanding between two of the participants of that conference, Ambedkar and Jayakar, on the next steps that were to be taken. 'The following Bill has been drafted by Dr. B. R. Ambedkar, Bar-at-Law, for the removal of untouchability by law. It will be moved most probably in the next session of the Legislative Assembly by Mr. M. R. Jayakar or by Dr. Ambedkar in the next session of the Bombay Legislative Council with appropriate changes with respect to the definition of the locality of its application.'[21]

That Ambedkar himself was the source of this story, including the hint of a collaboration between lawmakers from two different legislatures, is evident from a letter he wrote to Jayakar a day after the publication of the bill. The letter contains one confirmation and one revelation. It confirmed that Ambedkar had drafted the historic bill following the conference at Jayakar's residence. It also revealed that Ambedkar had not shared the contents of the bill with Jayakar before releasing the draft to the press. This is why the press report was so open-ended about whether the bill would be moved by Jayakar or Ambedkar himself.

Ambedkar began his handwritten letter, dated 8 December 1929, with an apology saying, 'I could not respond to your last letter owing to my foot trouble which is not yet over.' And then he addressed, rather matter-of-factly, the fait accompli he had delivered to Jayakar: 'You must have seen my draft of a Bill for the removal of untouchability which was published both in the Times and the Chronicle of Saturday last. I shall be glad to know what you think of it and whether you like to move it in the Assembly in the form in which it is or whether you like to make any alterations.'[22]

By the time Jayakar received Ambedkar's letter on 9 December 1929, a Monday, the *Times* had published a sequel reproducing the bill's SOR as well, which made explicit the purpose of the bill: to get over the legal ramifications of the Privy Council verdict in the Kamudi temple case.[23] Jayakar evidently thought so highly of Ambedkar's drafting that he immediately initiated the process of introducing the bill in the next session of the Central Legislative Assembly. The very same day, he sent 'a notice of the Bill' to the Legislative Assembly and an application for 'previous sanction' to the government.[24]

A comparison between Ambedkar's draft, as published in the *Times* in two instalments, and the one forwarded by Jayakar for introduction in the national legislature, shows that, from the Preamble to the SOR at the end of the bill, Jayakar did not make the slightest alteration.

Like the British-drafted Caste Disabilities Removal Act, 1850, the somewhat similar-sounding Hindu Untouchable Castes (Removal of Disabilities) Bill, which came up almost eighty years later, consisted essentially of a single clause. While the 1850 law protected inheritance rights in the event of a Hindu being excluded from his caste, the 1929 bill had a far wider ambit:

> No person belonging to the Hindu community shall be deemed to be incapable by reason of his caste, of sharing the benefit of a religious or charitable trust created for the general benefit of persons professing the Hindu religion, or for sharing the benefit of a convenience, utility or service, dedicated to or maintained or licensed for the use of the general public, any custom or interpretation of the law to the contrary notwithstanding.[25]

Though it only mentioned caste in a generic sense, the reform of entitling untouchables to enter temples was inherent in the amalgam of secular and religious rights conferred by this provision. The Preamble stating the grounds for the bill referred obliquely to the Bhuleshwar episode in which, despite their willingness, the tyranny of custom had deterred the trustees from throwing open the temple to untouchables. Referring to the custom that regarded certain castes as 'untouchable and unfit for association', the Preamble said optimistically that 'many Hindus believe that such imputed impurity is not in accordance with the true interpretation of the precepts of Hinduism and desire that the said disabilities should be removed'.

In drafting the Preamble to his anti-untouchability bill, Ambedkar would seem to have anticipated the principle of fraternity that would be enshrined in the Preamble to the Constitution of India. The Preamble to the 1929 bill said that removing caste disabilities might 'tend to the promotion of the public welfare and the solidarity of the Hindu community'. This resonates with Ambedkar's famous words on 25 November 1949 on the eve of the adoption of the Constitution: 'Without fraternity, liberty would produce the supremacy of the few over the many. Without fraternity, liberty and equality could not become a natural course of things.'[26]

To the grounds cited in the Preamble to the 1929 bill, Ambedkar added a 'significant circumstance' through its SOR. It was that 'British Indian adjudication, respectful as it often is of Hindu usages, has tended to confirm the customs, which have had the effect of excluding the untouchable classes from participation in the benefits of endowments in which it is but just, that they, as members of the Hindu community, should participate'.

Having drawn attention to the colonial dispensation's acquiescence to this Hindu tradition of exclusion, Ambedkar discussed the specifics of the Kamudi temple case. 'One ruling of the Privy Council, in Sankaralinga Nadan and others (Appellants) and Raja Rajeswara Dorai and others (Respondents) … has gone the length of laying down, with all the authority of that august tribunal and the eminent judges who formed the Bench on that occasion, a rule, which in effect provides that the duty of the Trustees of the Hindu Religious Endowment is to follow the ancient custom; it is not for them to vary it, however unreasonable or antiquated it may be, and if they endeavour to alter it, they may be guilty of a breach of trust.'

The SOR went on to conclude that, as a result of such rulings, 'it is difficult to obtain, through the medium of adjudication, a variation of the customs which prejudicially affect the untouchable classes … It is therefore thought desirable to have recourse to legislation, and with its aid to abolish all such objectionable customs, to the extent mentioned in the Bill.'[27]

Unsurprisingly, this highly novel bill raised eyebrows. Within three days of its publication in the Indian press, the *Manchester Guardian* carried reactions from Indians living in London. Its appreciative report, appearing on 10 December 1929, began as follows: 'The news that a Bill to remove the disabilities under which the Indian untouchables labour is likely to be introduced next session into the Indian Legislative Assembly has naturally created much interest among Indians resident in London.'[28]

Though it had been launched in the public domain as Ambedkar's bill, Jayakar got all the credit for it in the discourse that followed, as it went by his name in the official records. Within a week of its publication, for instance, the bill was referred to in the Punjab Legislative Council. On 12 December 1929, the Punjab Speaker said, 'Mr. Jayakar had drafted a Bill for the Assembly to abandon the term untouchables and class the latter among touchables.'[29] Again, on 25 December 1929, a Suppressed Classes Conference, presided over by Gandhi at the Lahore session of Congress, commended only Jayakar for the bill against untouchability.[30] At the same Lahore session, Jamnalal Bajaj's report too attributed the bill to Jayakar alone, despite a reference to the conference at his house bringing together 'some of the Bombay temple trustees and the leaders of untouchables'.[31]

Amid the many issues demanding his attention, Gandhi seemed to have registered neither the import of the bill nor the background of its drafting. The espousal of temple entry by the Congress Sub-Committee turned out to be actually an instance of followers going beyond the anti-untouchability agenda of their leader. Steeped as he was in varna, Gandhi was as yet far from ready to have temples thrown open to untouchables. Although the bill was a result of the sub-committee's interaction with Ambedkar, and although he had contemporaneously praised the Mahad Satyagraha, the Mahatma was unaware that the Doctor was an untouchable. (When the two met for the first time in August 1931, Gandhi famously mistook Ambedkar for an upper-caste reformer.)

Despite its obvious threat to the sensitivities of orthodox Hindus, the bill was received well in the corridors of power. Jayakar had sent his sanction application to two key members of the Viceroy's Executive Council, one British and one Indian. While addressing Home Member James Crerar, Jayakar's tone was formal. 'The Bill is a far-reaching and important measure and I do hope that, when the occasion arises, I will have the sympathy and support of the Government of India in my endeavour to remove the cruel disabilities of the untouchable classes.' In his letter to Law Member

Brojendra Mitter, a fellow member of the Indian bar, Jayakar's tone was more personal. 'I am sure that you will be in complete sympathy with my effort. Will you please help me in securing the assent of the Governor-General for the measure, if that is considered necessary?'[32]

Interestingly, eight years later, when the Federal Court had been set up in 1937 as the first tribunal in India with jurisdiction across the Raj, a precursor to today's Supreme Court of India, Mitter found himself addressing Jayakar as 'My Lord'. By then, Mitter had become the first Advocate General of India, while Jayakar earned the distinction of being among the first three judges to be appointed to the Federal Court.[33] Later, in 1947, Jayakar and Mitter were briefly colleagues in the Constituent Assembly. Mitter was even inducted into the Drafting Committee, where he functioned for a while under Ambedkar's chairmanship before resigning from the Constituent Assembly on health grounds.

In 1929, as law member, Mitter had reacted sympathetically to Jayakar's plea. In an internal note, he recommended sanction, although 'without committing the Government in any way' and with the stipulation that, after the introduction of the bill, 'steps should be taken for circulation for eliciting Hindu opinion'. Though it had raised 'the important question of overriding Hindu usage and custom by legislation', Mitter said that 'the Bill is in the main designed to secure justice to a class of people to whom it seems to have been wrongly denied'. As other members of the Executive Council had broadly endorsed Mitter's note, Viceroy Lord Irwin granted his sanction on 30 December 1929 for the introduction of Jayakar's bill.[34]

After such a propitious start, the bill went nowhere. Jayakar never got an opportunity to introduce it in the Assembly, thanks to a succession of hindrances. To begin with, only a limited time was allotted to bills moved by non-official members such as Jayakar. His untouchability bill was finally scheduled to be introduced on 13 February 1930, the last day of that session for non-official Bills. But, as it happened that day, Jayakar first got an opportunity to table another bill, which, following the extension of civil marriage to Hindus in 1923, sought to provide that option to Muslims as well.

Though this bill had originally been drafted by another reformist legislator, Hari Singh Gour, it fell to Jayakar 'by the luck of ballot' to move it. The idea of providing a secular marriage option to Muslims had, however, provoked such hostility from members of that community that the mere introduction of that bill consumed the whole day. So, the other social reform bills scheduled to be introduced that day, including the anti-untouchability bill, only waited in the wings. Listing out these bills in its report, the *Times of India* said, 'But none of these measures was reached, so absorbing was the debate about the marriage law.'[35]

The jinx followed the untouchability bill into the next session, after which the House itself wound up on 15 July 1930. As luck would have it, Jayakar chose to skip the next elections. By then, along with Indian Liberal Party leader Tej Bahadur Sapru, he was absorbed in an officially sanctioned mission to mediate between the two most important men of the day, Irwin and Gandhi. On 5 March 1931, their discussions culminated in the historic Gandh–Irwin Pact, which led to, among other things, the release of all those who had been incarcerated for the Salt March as well as Gandhi's participation in the Second Round Table Conference and his famous clash with Ambedkar in London. Attending the conference as a representative of the Hindu Mahasabha, Jayakar was witness to the clash between Gandhi and Ambedkar on the question of whether untouchables, like Muslims, should be provided a separate electorate.

In the Assembly elected in 1930, the void left by Jayakar's absence was filled by a member from the Madras Presidency. Justice Party leader R.K. Shanmukham Chetty, in a move consistent with his background in non-Brahmin politics, took upon himself the responsibility of reviving Jayakar's bill.[36] Chetty had in fact inherited two social reform bills from Jayakar, the other being the Devadasi Bill, meant to prevent the dedication of low-caste girls for service in Hindu temples.

Theirs was an older association. In May 1930, when the two men were still colleagues in the previous Assembly, Jayakar had accompanied Chetty to Erode in the Madras Presidency to oversee the Self-Respect Conference organised by the Justice Party.

But there was also an irony to Chetty assuming charge of a bill aimed at empowering temple trustees to defy custom. The Justice Party government had introduced a reform to check the domination of Brahmins by bringing temples under the supervision of a State agency. The move had an unintended consequence: a concession it made in this context ended up providing statutory support to the case law from the Kamudi dispute. Section 40 of the Madras Religious Endowments Act 1926 stipulated that 'the trustee of every religious endowment is bound to administer its affairs ... in accordance with the terms of the trust, the usage of the institution ...'

As it turned out, Ambedkar's bill continued to have a rough time. The first glitch was that Chetty had omitted a part of the preamble while copying the bill for his sanction application. So, he had to apply afresh. And then, as deputy president of the Assembly, he was distracted by the duties of his office. The bill was finally introduced on 18 February 1932, more than two years after it had been drafted and published by Ambedkar.

While moving for leave to introduce the Hindu Untouchable Castes (Removal of Disabilities) Bill, Chetty said that some 'friends' had represented to him that 'the Bill does not go far enough'. Exuding optimism, he signalled that the bill could go as far as the House allowed it. 'My object in introducing the Bill is to give an opportunity to this House to rectify a great blot that now rests on Hindu society.' Promising that he would not 'hurry through this measure', Chetty said he would give 'ample opportunity to this House to record its opinion on the subject'.[37]

His assurance did not stop the Sanatanists from lodging a protest through another member from the Madras Presidency. G. Krishnamachariar said, 'I oppose the introduction of the Bill because it is based upon a fundamental misconception of the rights of the so-called untouchable castes.' Luckily for Chetty, the Sanatanist interjection caused no disruption. Once the Assembly adopted the motion to introduce the bill, Chetty completed the formalities.

When this first-ever bill against untouchability was introduced, the national legislature had only one untouchable member: M.C. Rajah, who too was from the Madras Presidency. Though he was not associated with Chetty's bill, Rajah had the distinction of being the first untouchable legislator in the country, first at the provincial level in 1919 and then at the national level in 1927. The Madras governor responsible for nominating him in 1919 was Lord Willingdon, who, in a happy coincidence, was the governor general of India in 1932 when Chetty introduced the trailblazing bill on untouchability.

None of these propitious circumstances made any difference to the fate of the bill. Despite his promise that the Assembly would have ample opportunity to discuss his bill, Chetty failed to move any further motion in the next two sessions. A curious omission, because those two sessions overlapped with feverish political activity on temple entry, which had resulted from a far-reaching agreement negotiated by Gandhi and Ambedkar in Poona on the composition of the electorate for untouchable candidates. By the end of that second session in April 1933, Chetty had lost the capacity to proceed with the bill. He was elevated to the post of president of the Central Legislative Assembly.[38]

Fourteen years later, on 15 August 1947, Chetty became independent India's first finance minister, while Ambedkar became its first law minister. Just the previous month, Ambedkar, who had lost his seat from Bengal due to Partition, was re-elected to the Constituent Assembly, this time from Bombay and with the help of the Congress Party, filling a vacancy caused by Jayakar's resignation.

The careers of Ambedkar, Jayakar and Chetty, who had collaborated on the pioneering but abortive bill against untouchability, remained intertwined, it appears. Their bill died unsung in April 1933 because, in the sudden zeal for reform that had gripped the nation after the Poona Pact, it was overshadowed by an altogether different approach to temple entry.

14

GANDHI'S BALANCING ACT

In the wake of the Poona Pact, the tale of legislative efforts for temple entry wound a twisty—and less radical—path. An altogether new approach gained salience. Espoused by Gandhi, the progenitor of mass politics, this new approach replaced the ongoing efforts to help untouchables enter temples by conferring a range of rights on them. In fact, it repudiated the progressive notion that temple entry was as much their right as that of caste Hindus.

Gandhi advocated instead that untouchables should enter only such temples where the caste Hindus living in the vicinity were agreeable to such a reform. Ever a seeker of conciliation, Gandhi shifted the emphasis to avoiding coercion. He sought to bring about temple entry on a case-by-case basis. The trustees of each temple could let in untouchables after ascertaining the willingness of its regular worshippers.

His scheme of incremental reform on temple entry developed organically in the course of the events triggered by the Poona Pact. On 24 September 1932, even after the much-awaited agreement had been signed at his instance by representatives of caste Hindus and untouchables, Gandhi refused to break his fast. He now laid down two fresh conditions for doing so.

One was London's acceptance of the Poona Pact, which sought to replace the principle of a separate electorate for untouchables with that of reserved constituencies for them. The other condition, however, posed a challenge to the caste Hindus who had gathered around him in Yeravda Prison. He insisted that the caste Hindu signatories of the Poona Pact should make a public vow to get rid of untouchability in all its diverse forms. This sweeping social reform was to be a reciprocal gesture to the Depressed Classes for giving up the separate electorate that the British prime minister had granted them.

The Hindu leaders met in Bombay the next day under the chairmanship of Madan Mohan Malaviya, the first signatory of the Poona Pact on their behalf. The 'conference' held on 25 September 1932 passed a resolution that had been drafted by Gandhi.[1] Of its two paragraphs, the first began with an unqualified promise stating that 'henceforth, amongst Hindus, no one shall be regarded as an untouchable by reason of his birth'. It was an admission that the prejudice was essentially that of Hinduism, whether due to religion or custom or both.

The first paragraph went on to say that those who had been regarded as untouchables would have 'the same right as other Hindus in regard to the use of public wells, public schools, public roads and all other public institutions'. Further, it undertook that the right to the use of those secular amenities 'shall have statutory recognition at the first opportunity'. Alternatively, it shall be 'one of the earliest Acts of the Swaraj Parliament, if it shall not have received such recognition before that time'.

But when it came to the use of temples by untouchables, which was addressed in the second paragraph of the resolution, a similar desire for statutory recognition was made conspicuous by its absence. In the separate paragraph devoted to temple entry, Gandhi in fact refrained from using the word 'right'. This was a big step back from Ambedkar's 1929 bill, which had sought to confer equal rights on untouchables, making no distinction between secular and religious spaces. Gandhi's cautious approach betrayed an anxiety to avoid ruffling feathers while nudging caste Hindus on the temple-entry issue.

The reference to it came unobtrusively at the end of a long-winded sentence: 'It is further agreed that it shall be the duty of all

Hindu leaders to secure, by every legitimate and peaceful means, an early removal of all social disabilities now imposed by caste Hindus upon the so-called untouchable classes, including the bar in respect of admission to temples.' Yet, in the resolution that was actually moved by the chair at the conference, Malaviya tinkered even with this feeble sentence. He replaced the words 'caste Hindus' with 'custom', implying that the the discriminatory practice in temples was not their fault but that of their circumstances.

Whether for a Sanatanist like Malaviya or a reformist Hindu like Gandhi (who called himself a Sanatanist though for strategic reasons), temple entry was the most sensitive aspect of the untouchability challenge. Ironically, by then, Ambedkar himself had all but abandoned temple entry in order to engage more vigorously with the temporal concerns affecting untouchables. So, the former part of the resolution, promising to go all the way with providing access to secular spaces, was more in tune with Ambedkar's priorities at the time. Gandhi finally ended his fast on 26 September 1932 after he had received the resolution of the Hindu leaders as well as London's acceptance of the Poona Pact.

At the 25 September conference, Malaviya had also announced that, following the Poona Pact, a 'committee' would be formed to conduct a campaign against untouchability throughout the country. It turned out to be more than a committee. Five days later, Malaviya chaired a 'public meeting' in Bombay. It resolved that an All-India Anti-Untouchability League be set up with headquarters in Delhi and branches in all the provinces. The meeting appointed Gandhi's close followers, industrialist G.D. Birla and social activist A.V. Thakkar, as the president and general secretary, respectively, of what came to be known subsequently as the Harijan Sevak Sangh. After the Poona Pact, Gandhi popularised the usage of Harijans, or God's People, for untouchables.

Announcing that the mandate of the new organisation was to carry out 'propaganda against untouchability', the 30 September meeting introduced a proviso that backtracked on the resolution of 25 September. The proviso effectively ruled out any legislative intervention to throw open not just religious spaces such as temples and crematoriums but also secular spaces such as wells, roads and schools. It stipulated that 'no compulsion or force shall be used' to open any of those spaces to untouchables, and added for good measure that 'peaceful persuasion will be adopted as the only means'.

Malaviya's dilution of the resolve had an immediate repercussion. He ceased to be part of Gandhi's further work on untouchability, especially temple entry, during a period when it became the Mahatma's main focus, even to the exclusion of the larger political struggle for freedom. Though there was no falling out between them, there was no mistaking the change in Gandhi's attitude. Thus far, Malaviya had been integral to his activities on caste—indeed, he had been the first signatory of the Poona Pact and had chaired the two Bombay meetings convened in its wake. When Gandhi finally reconnected with Malaviya four months later, the proviso to the 30 September resolution became a bone of contention. By then, Gandhi had been espousing a legislative option to throw open temples, and Malaviya was aggrieved.

This was indicative of the change that Gandhi's outlook had undergone—the result of his engagement with a temple-entry agitation in the Malabar district of the Madras Presidency. Before he could recover from his own fast, Gandhi was drawn into dealing with another fast, undertaken by one of his followers to open the ancient Guruvayur temple.

On an appeal from the zamorin of Calicut, Raja Manavedan Raja, who was the trustee of the temple dedicated to Lord Krishna, Gandhi urged K. Kelappan on 29 September 1932 to call off his fast.[2] After Kelappan, a member of the dominant Nair caste, had reluctantly complied with his advice, Gandhi told the zamorin on 3 October that the fast had been suspended for three months on the condition that he threw open the temple within that period. Gandhi also warned that, if the zamorin failed to meet the deadline, he might go to the 'extent of sharing' Kelappan's fast. Since the zamorin had pleaded helplessness, Gandhi added that he should in the given time 'overcome all difficulties, legal or otherwise', in the way of the 'long deferred reform'.[3]

Clearly, Gandhi was clueless about the 1908 Privy Council judgment and its 1926 statutory reinforcement in the Madras Presidency. While this was once true of Ambedkar too, there had since been repeated references to the Jayakar bill in the 1929 Lahore session of the Congress. In fact, the central aim of the bill was to protect the temple trustees who let in untouchables.

There was yet another reason why Gandhi ought to have been aware of the Jayakar bill: it was pending at the time in the Central Legislative Assembly, where Chetty had introduced it in February 1932. That Gandhi had put so little effort into understanding the legal side of the temple-entry problem was likely because he considered it just another spiritual challenge in which he could use his 'soul force' to bring together reformist and Sanatanist Hindus. This is evident, for instance, from his advice to Kelappan in a letter dated 15 October: 'You will move there gently and courteously. There should be no threats and no loud claims made. The real thing is conversion even of the most orthodox.'[4]

From press reports and the feedback he had received in Yeravda Prison through letters and visitors, Gandhi's reading of the Guruvayur situation was that the resistance to temple entry was only from an orthodox section that was in a minority. He sought to demonstrate that most caste Hindus were on his side and thus his fast could not be considered coercive. In his next letter to Kelappan on 23 November 1932, Gandhi explained, 'Our claim is that the proposed fast can never savour of coercion because it is based on the assumption that the vast majority of the temple-going Savarnas are in favour of temple-entry. If this cannot be proved up to the hilt there is no case for fasting by us. Fasting with the knowledge that Savarnas are opposed to temple entry by Harijans would undoubtedly amount to coercion.'[5]

Gandhi hit upon an idea to prove this claim. As he said in the same letter, 'In order to demonstrate to all concerned the fact that we have the majority of temple-goers on our side, there should be a methodical taking of a referendum of temple-goers, say within a ten-mile radius. And in order to have the thing absolutely above the board, signatures should be taken at public meetings in the presence of witnesses known to the signatories with their full names, addresses and occupations, together with age and sex.'

Since his three-month reprieve before the launch of a fresh fast was running out, Gandhi lost no time in implementing the referendum idea. He set up a committee, headed by one of his followers from Kerala, K. Madhavan Nair, to conduct the referendum. And he deployed one of his top lieutenants, Chakravarti Rajagopalachari, who had played a key role in the Poona Pact negotiations, to oversee this delicate and unprecedented operation. The process of the referendum began on 4 December. Besides public meetings, it entailed a door-to-door survey of caste Hindu voters in the Ponnani taluk in which Guravayur was located.

This initiative inspired a member of the Madras Legislative Council, P. Subbarayan, to draft a bill on temple entry based on the referendum principle. Though he had no party affiliation when he was chief minister of the Madras Presidency from 1926 to 1930 in the pre-autonomy phase, Subbarayan later joined the Congress and served as a minister in Rajagopalachari's provincial government from 1937 to 1939 and Jawaharlal Nehru's Central government after Independence. Before he gave a notice of his temple-entry bill, Subbarayan had already moved a resolution in the Madras Legislative Council on 1 November 1932, urging the government to 'bring up legislation setting at rest ... the doubts and disabilities ... which trustees ... of Hindu temples feel in regard to throwing them open to the Depressed Classes'.[6]

Subbarayan's resolution was carried with an amendment proposed by an untouchable legislator, V.I. Muniswami Pillai. Where the resolution urged the government to take advantage of 'the great impetus' given by the Poona Pact, Pillai suggested an addition of the words 'and the Bombay Conference'. His reasoning was that it was 'only at the Bombay Conferences that ... the social side of the problem was discussed'. Subbarayan accepted Pillai's amendment, little realising that both those gatherings had actually been chary of legislative intervention on temple entry. Although the members of the Justice Party government and the official bloc did not vote so they may 'have the view of this House', there was enough support in the council for it to adopt Subbarayan's resolution with fifty-six ayes and nineteen neutral votes.

Having pulled off the first-ever resolution on temple entry, and one that urged the government to come up with a bill on the subject, Subbarayan himself came up with one before long. Embodying Gandhi's case-by-case approach, Subbarayan's bill proposed a referendum as a statutory precondition for every instance of temple entry. As he put it in the preamble to his bill, it was meant to provide 'legal machinery for the ascertainment of the opinion of the Hindu community'.

Informally called the 'local option' bill, it was laden with procedural details for conducting the referendum in the neighbourhood of the temple concerned on whether members of the 'excluded caste' could be let in. It also proposed an amendment to get around the statutory hurdle of Section 40 of the Madras Religious Endowments Act, 1926, which obligated every temple trustee to administer in accordance with 'the usage of the institution'. Subbarayan's bill proposed to make that obligation subject to the outcome of the referendum on temple entry.[7]

Gandhi embraced the bill that fleshed out his referendum idea. It was, in fact, Subbarayan's bill that marked a shift from his own position of legislative intervention only in secular spaces. Having since hit upon a non-coercive method in the referendum option, he was evidently no longer shy of legislation on temple entry.

Subbarayan's bill dovetailed with Gandhi's plan of going on a fast in Kelappan's company from 2 January 1934 should the zamorin fail to throw open Guruvayur even after the referendum had turned out to be in favour of it. In a press interview given on 5 December, Gandhi made it clear that he was so 'satisfied' with Subbarayan's bill that he now linked it to his fast. He was quoted as saying that 'if Dr. Subbarayan was not granted leave to introduce the bill, the fast would commence on 2nd January'.[8]

Madras Governor George Stanley passed the buck to Viceroy Willingdon on sanctioning introduction of the bill. In its letter to the Government of India on 10 December 1932, the Madras government pointed out, 'Mr. Gandhi has threatened to fast if sanction to the introduction of Dr. Subbarayan's Bill is refused.' While recognising 'the undesirability of an appearance of yielding to a threat of this kind', the Madras government said that the real question for consideration was whether a bill that 'regulates civil rights should not be introduced in the Central Legislature'.

Finding merit in the suggestion that Subbarayan's bill had implications for the Hindu community in the rest of the country, the Willingdon administration decided to consult the other provinces of British India. A letter was sent out to all such provinces on 21 December, and it soon became clear that there was little chance that Willingdon would be able to make up his mind on Subbarayan's bill before Gandhi's 2 January deadline for the launch of his fast.

As the deadline neared, Gandhi changed his mind about the fast. In a statement issued on 30 December 1932, he declared that, pending the 'Viceregal decision' on Subbarayan's bill, the fast stood 'indefinitely postponed'. At the time he made this announcement, the referendum had vindicated his claim of local support for temple entry in Guruvayur. Gandhi said that, out of the electorate of 65,000 caste Hindus in the Ponnani taluk, 55 per cent had voted in favour of temple entry, 9 per cent against, 8 per cent neutral and 27 per cent had abstained. Pointing out that the referendum had been held amidst 'adverse influences', including the hostility of the zamorin, Gandhi said, 'The Ponnani Taluk is the stronghold of orthodoxy and yet there was a decisive majority in favour of admission of the untouchables to that shrine.'

Gandhi also reproduced the resolution of the 25 September Bombay conference, saying he was doing so to remind caste Hindus of their 'original vow'. The version he quoted though was his original draft, which asserted that social disabilities had been 'imposed by caste Hindus', rather than the one amended by Malaviya and actually adopted at the conference, with the words 'imposed by custom'.[9] Conveniently, Gandhi's statement also ignored the 30 September resolution that had disclaimed the legislative option on any untouchability-related reform.

On 4 January 1933, M.K. Acharya, the president of the Madras Varnashrama Swarajya Sangha, sent to Willingdon a copy of a memorandum he had submitted the previous day to the Madras governor. Calling upon the viceroy to deny sanction to the temple-entry bill, the body of orthodox Hindus fired a series of questions: 'How far are the Depressed Classes themselves anxious to abandon their own temples and force their way into the Temples of the Caste Hindus? Are not the Depressed Classes more anxious to ameliorate their worldly wants? Is it not the duty of the reformers more to inculcate among these classes higher standards of cleanliness and morality than to force their entry into the Temples of Caste Hindus? Will not such forcible entry embitter the present relations between the Caste Hindus and their Untouchable countrymen?'[10]

Reviling the reformers as 'intellectual slaves of the West', the Madras Varnashrama Swarajya Sangha said: 'All cheap talk of equality and democracy is due to ignorance of the higher laws of life; that is what the modern West is learning at terrible cost.' It added: 'Our modern reformers including Mr. Gandhi are ignorant of these higher laws of evolution; and so they talk glibly of the supposed Right of every born Hindu to enter and worship in every Hindu Temple.'

Unabashedly, it declared: 'There exists no such universal Right in Hinduism, which teaches on the other hand that every Hindu must worship in the specific manner best suited to his birth and environment. Indeed Hinduism teaches that birth and environment are not accidents but the result of the Law of Karma or spiritual causation. "The one goal through many paths"—this is the supreme teaching of the Sanatana Dharma, and the very mark of its superiority over all other religions in the world. It is through ignorance of this law of the One in the Many that modern reformers are blindly sowing strife where they want peace.'

❖

The year 1932 saw Gandhi engaged, uncharacteristically, in lobbying with the imperial power for passing a law. This was the same leader who had electrified the nation with his Non-Cooperation Movement just over a decade ago. The only other time he had thus engaged with the British government was after his first satyagraha in India in Bihar's Champaran in 1917. As Gandhi admitted to legal expert Tej Bahadur Sapru while seeking his advice on temple-entry legislation, 'To be interested in the passage of Bills is an experience I have not had since the passing of the Champaran Ryots' Relief Bill in 1917.' But his task then was easier as it was a government measure, while this time it was a private-member bill seeking a social reform. As Gandhi put it, 'Here the circumstances are quite novel.'[11]

Indeed they were. And a significant part of that novelty was that, with his advocacy of temple-entry legislation, Gandhi set himself on a collision course with Malaviya, who not so long ago had been pivotal to his negotiations on the Poona Pact. More importantly, Malaviya was at the time the president of the Indian National Congress, a post he was holding for the third time. Besides, as a moving force of the Hindu Mahasabha and a long-time vice chancellor of the Benaras Hindu University, Malaviya had deep links with the Sanatanists, the section of Hindus most opposed to temple-entry legislation, if not temple entry itself.

Malaviya queered the pitch for Gandhi by calling another meeting on untouchability, his third. This time, the attendees were only those who considered themselves Sanatanists. The looming threat of a counter-blast from orthodox Hindus prompted Gandhi to write to Malaviya. He made no secret of his anxiety about the Sanatan Dharma Mahasabha due to be held on 25 January 1933.

Having kept Malaviya out of his temple-entry work for almost four months, Gandhi began his letter dated 20 January with an elaborate, if awkward, explanation. 'I had purposely refrained from worrying you over the question of temple entry. Much as it stood in need of your invaluable assistance, I knew that you were preoccupied with matters of the highest moment, and I felt that the least I could do, as also the most that was possible, was deliberately to forego that assistance.' He segued neatly to this: 'But now I see that you have yourself taken the initiative and a tremendous responsibility. I hope and pray that great good will come out of the Conference.'[12]

Wishing that 'it had been possible for us to meet before the Conference or that we had exchanged ideas before you propounded your suggestions about temple entry', Gandhi proceeded to spell out his position. He first tried to make up for his indiscretion in ignoring the 30 September resolution when he had hailed the 25 September resolution as 'the original vow'. The tack Gandhi adopted now was to claim that he had referred to the two resolutions as one because he accorded equal sanctity to both the meetings and their resolutions.

Gandhi said, 'If the Bombay Meeting, during and immediately after the fast week, that passed the resolution was representative of Hindu India, it is up to every Hindu to make good that resolution in its fullness. That resolution, as you know, has definite reference to temple entry. It prescribes no conditions. The whole trend of the resolution is that temple entry and the use of public institutions by Harijans on the same terms as the other Hindus is a debt long overdue by caste Hindus.' His attempt to pass off the reference to temple entry as an unconditional one flew in the face of the caveats adopted in the second resolution.

But in his interpretation of Hindu scriptures, Gandhi was even more provocative. Citing the discussions he had had with shastris, some favourable and others hostile to the temple-entry movement, Gandhi said, 'I have gathered that there is no warrant whatsoever for untouchability as we now know it.' Repudiating the widely held Sanatanist belief that the Chandalas mentioned in the scriptures were untouchables, Gandhi said, 'Untouchability by birth seems to be utterly non-existent. There is no proof whatsoever to show that any single one of the untouchables so classed is the progeny of a Brahmin woman through a Shudra man or that he is a descendant of such a union.'

Having thus rejected the Sanatanist claim of scriptural sanction for untouchability, Gandhi wrote to Malaviya, 'I would therefore beg of you not to surrender on the matter of principle.' He ended on a note that barely concealed his forebodings about the conference. 'I am most anxious that God may make you the instrument of purifying Hinduism and keeping faith with the Harijans.'

But in the short period between Gandhi's letter to Malaviya and the Sanatan Dharma Mahasabha, the long-awaited viceregal decision on Subbarayan's bill finally came in. On 23 January 1933, Willingdon disallowed the plea to introduce the temple-entry bill in the Madras Council. He agreed with the Madras government that the questions thrown up by any temple-entry bill would 'affect the religious beliefs and practices of the Hindu community generally'. Subbarayan's bill for Madras was, therefore, found to be 'essentially of an all-India character and cannot properly be dealt with merely on a provincial basis'.[13]

However, Willingdon's statement also offered reformists some consolation. He had sanctioned the introduction in the Central Legislative Assembly of a bill that was on the lines of the rights-based scheme drafted by Ambedkar in 1929. M.C. Rajah and a south Indian Brahmin representing Rohilkund and the Kumaon Division of the United Provinces, C.S. Ranga Iyer, had separately proposed the Untouchability Abolition Bill. Given the precedent set by similar bills proposed successively by Jayakar and Chetty, the government was quick to give Rajah and Iyer the go-ahead. In due course, it was Rajah who got the opportunity to move his bill (which has been discussed in Chapter 9 in the context of access to public places in the secular sphere).

Meanwhile, Ranga Iyer reacted immediately to the jurisdictional ground on which the temple-entry bill from Madras had been rejected. On that very day, 23 January, he gave a notice of a bill that was a near verbatim reproduction of Subbarayan's. Iyer's bill differed in only one respect: taking a cue from Willingdon's concern that the question of temple-entry affected the entire Hindu community, it extended the jurisdiction to all of British India. An associate of the late Motilal Nehru, Iyer had been elected to the Assembly from the United Provinces, although he was a native of Malabar, the region that had sparked Subbarayan's bill. This instant reincarnation of the Madras bill at the Centre was reminiscent of a similar collaboration in 1929 between Ambedkar and Jayakar.

In a statement on these developments the next day, 24 January 1932, Gandhi said that he regarded the conversion of the Madras initiative into an all-India bill as 'a bigger and graver contingency', adding firmly, 'But now that it comes upon me as an accomplished fact, I dare not flinch.' He asserted that temple entry was 'an indispensable test' of the removal of untouchability. 'It is one thing that alone can give new life and new hope to Harijans, as no mere economic uplift can do ... The message of the temples will penetrate every Harijan hut; the message of economic and educational uplift will touch only those to whom it is personally brought.'[14]

Gandhi's hard sell of temple entry was particularly addressed to Malaviya's Sanatanist conference due the following day. Once again, he reproduced the Bombay Resolution of 25 September 1932, this time taking care to mention that it had been 'adopted under the chairmanship of the revered Pandit Madan Mohan Malaviya'. Besides, he used the version that Malaviya had actually moved from the chair, shifting the blame from 'caste Hindus' to 'custom'. This time as well, Gandhi made no mention of the 30 September resolution—even though his campaign platform, Harijan Sevak Sangh, owed its existence to it. For someone who called his autobiography, *My Experiments with Truth*, Gandhi could tread carefully around an inconvenient truth.

As if to make up for this omission, Gandhi went out of his way to allay the apprehensions of Sanatanists: 'Where the opinion of the temple-going population is not ripe for the reform, naturally Harijans cannot enter the temples. Where the opinion is ripe, the law cannot be invoked by individuals to thwart the will of the majority.' His justification for the proposed regulation of temple entry by 'mutual adjustment' was this. 'It is not necessary that every Harijan should at once enter the temples. It is enough and necessary if he knows that he has acquired that right.' Indirectly, he was reassuring Sanatanists that, in this case-by-case approach to temple-entry reform, the right provided by the bill to Harijans could often prove to be illusory.

For all his exertions, the conference of Sanatanists on 25 January 1933 amplified the proviso that Gandhi had been skirting. Their objections had little effect, though, on Willingdon's attitude to Iyer's application. After all, at the time of rejecting Subbarayan's Madras bill, Willingdon had virtually committed himself to allowing a temple-entry legislation to be considered at the all-India level. Besides, while giving sanction for moving the Untouchability Abolition Bill in the Central legislature, he had imposed the condition that such a bill could not be enacted 'unless the proposals are subjected to the fullest examination in all their aspects not merely in the legislature, but also outside it by all who will be affected by them'. It was on the same terms that, on 28 January 1933, the Willingdon government gave the go-ahead to the Iyer-proposed Hindu Temple Entry Disabilities Removal Bill.[15]

As for the letter that Gandhi had written on 20 January, Malaviya replied to it almost three weeks later, on 8 February. It gave Gandhi a taste of the reactionary side of his long-time associate, just as Maneckji Dadabhoy had had seventeen years earlier. Emboldened by the endorsement he had received at his conference of Sanatanists, Malaviya tore into the Mahatma's interpretation of not just the Bombay Resolutions but also the scriptures.

Malaviya wrote, 'I fear you have been led to form a wrong impression. There is plenty of authority for the view that certain persons are untouchable under certain conditions and that certain other persons are untouchables by reason of their birth and occupation.'[16] Thus, drawing from the theory of karma, which was loaded in favour of upper castes, Malaviya clinically ascribed religious sanctity to discrimination based on birth and occupation, thereby confirming the worst of the allegations made against Hinduism by detractors like Ambedkar.

While Gandhi regarded untouchability as an excrescence of Hinduism, Malaviya insisted it was an integral part of the religion. Likewise, while Gandhi campaigned to cleanse Hinduism of untouchability, Malaviya sought to purify untouchables and Shudras. After inculcating clean habits in these masses, Malaviya's scheme was to offer them diksha, or ceremonial initiation through a mantra, to help them attain the status of Dwijas. He believed that the scriptures 'also proclaim that, though a man may be of very humble birth, he can, by religiously avoiding certain acts and things which are prohibited, and by practicing those that are applauded, rise to the status of a Vaishya, a Kshatriya, and even to that of a Brahmin'.

Typically, for a Sanatanist, Malaviya could not conceive of a Hindu outside of their varna status. He broke down the category of Savarnas, separating the Dwijas from the Shudras—even though Shudras, whatever their other disabilities, generally had no problem entering temples. Malaviya held out the prospect of emancipation for Shudras and Avarnas based on the earning of good karma in accordance with the scriptures. So, the same orthodoxy that discriminated against them would determine whether they had complied with the prescribed dos and don'ts.

Malaviya contested Gandhi's claim that his support for temple-entry legislation flowed from the 30 September resolution as well. Had it been so, he argued, 'we are equally bound to stand by the proviso to that resolution'. Tellingly, he added, 'I hold that this rules out Satyagraha or fasting to have the temples opened to those who are at present not allowed to enter them. I also hold that this rules out, even more clearly, any attempt to seek the help of the legislature to secure such entry into temples.'

Matters had escalated since Gandhi's letter to him, and Malaviya was cognisant of this. He bristled at the introduction of the temple-entry bill and Gandhi's 'appeal to Hindus to see that it is passed as speedily as possible'. Malaviya said, 'I regret to have to say that this attitude of yours seems to me to be inconsistent with the letter and spirit of the proviso to the Bombay Resolution of 30th September.' Malaviya also recalled that Gandhi had displayed no such urgency when they had worked together on the Poona Pact. 'Before Mr. Kelappan started his fast against your advice and mine, you did not think that the solution of the question of the entry of the depressed classes into temples could not brook delay.'

Malaviya's letter arrived close on the heels of a flat turndown from Ambedkar too. Thus, Gandhi suffered the mortification of being pushed back from both ends of the caste spectrum. On Gandhi's invitation, Ambedkar had visited him at Yeravda Prison on 4 February 1933. But he had declined Gandhi's request to come out in support of Iyer's temple-entry bill.

Ten days later, Ambedkar followed up with a statement, laying out the reasons for his disapproval. He began with a disclaimer that 'the controversy regarding the question of temple entry is confined to the Sanatanists and Mahatma Gandhi'.[17] On the proposed referendum, he said, 'Sin and immorality cannot become tolerable because a majority is addicted to them or because the majority chooses to practice them. If untouchability is a sinful and immoral custom, in the view of the Depressed Classes it must be destroyed without any hesitation even if it was acceptable to the majority.'

Disagreeing with Gandhi's suggestion that temple entry deserved precedence over educational or economic uplift of untouchables, Ambedkar said, 'Once they become well placed in the scale of social life, they would become respectable and once they become respectable, the religious outlook of the orthodox towards them is sure to undergo change, and even if this did not happen, it can do no injury to their material interest.'

Ambedkar had come a long way from the spirit in which he had launched the Kalaram temple agitation barely three years earlier. Now he said that the Depressed Classes 'do not care to fight for' temple entry because of 'the argument of self-respect'. He asked angrily, 'Why should an Untouchable beg for admission in a place from which he has been excluded by the arrogance of the Hindus?' Ambedkar added that the untouchable was prepared to say to the Hindus: 'To open or not to open temples is a question for you to consider and not for me to agitate. If you think it is bad manners not to respect the sacredness of human personality, open your temples and be a gentleman. If you rather be a Hindu than be gentleman, then shut the doors and damn yourself for I don't care to come.'

If Hinduism was ever to be 'a religion of social equality', an amendment of its code to provide temple entry was inadequate, he said. 'What is required is to purge it of the doctrine of Chaturvarna. That is the root cause of all inequality and also the parent of the caste system and untouchability.' By regarding untouchability as an integral part of the varna scheme, Ambedkar's statement echoed the view expressed by Malaviya a week earlier in his letter to Gandhi that there was scriptural sanction for untouchability. In a statement that anticipated his famous tract of 1936, *Annihilation of Caste,* Ambedkar added, 'The Depressed Classes can say that they are Hindus only when the theory of Chaturvarna and caste system is abandoned and expunged from the Hindu Shastras.'

Ambedkar ended on a stirring note. He conceded that 'my right to agitate for the abolition of Chaturvarna and Caste System will not be lost if I accept Temple Entry now'. Still, he countered: 'But the question is on what side will Mahatma Gandhi be at the time when the question is put. If he will be in the camp of my opponents, I must tell him that I cannot be in his camp now. If he will be in my camp, he ought to be in it now.' It was a challenge to Gandhi's approach at the time, of dealing with untouchability without touching upon caste.

Gandhi responded to Ambedkar's poser the same day, in a detailed interview to a news agency.[18] 'He has asked me a straight question, and is entitled to an equally straight answer from me.' Calling himself a Hindu not just by birth but 'by conviction and choice', Gandhi said that there was 'no superiority or inferiority in the Hinduism of my conception'. He added that he was prepared to go 'the whole length with Dr Ambedkar in fighting the arrogation of superiority'. In the same breath, he reiterated his allegiance to varna. 'But when Dr Ambedkar wants to fight Varnashrama itself I cannot be in his camp, because I believe Varnashrama to be an integral part of Hinduism.' Gandhi fell short of the universal principles on which Ambedkar had framed his challenge. It would take some more years before Gandhi was able to distance himself from varnashrama.

On the issue of self-respect, Gandhi's response to Ambedkar was, 'I entirely agree with him that Harijans cannot be and must not be beggars for it. It is for the caste Hindus to open temples whole-heartedly or not at all.' Gandhi also gave up his sweeping claim that temple entry 'alone can give new life and new hope to Harijans'. He made a more modest estimate of its impact now. 'But no betterment of those conditions will give religious equality. That can be attained only by admission into temples.' Thus, although he skirted Ambedkar's proposition that material interest mattered more to untouchables, Gandhi conceded that temple entry was only about religious equality.

As for Ambedkar's objection to regulating temple entry on the majority principle, Gandhi argued that morality could not legislated. 'This religious equality cannot be attained even by statute, but only when the heart of the caste Hindu is changed.' Therefore, Iyer's bill was 'not intended to force open the temples to Harijans, but only to make it possible for the caste Hindus to throw them open when the hearts of the majority are changed'.

This intense exchange on temple entry prompted Gandhi to resume his parallel conversation with the Sanatanists on the same day, 14 February 1933. Worried about the growing resistance to the bill from both sides, Gandhi shot off a telegram to Malaviya asking him to visit him in jail. He wished to explain in person why the legislative option was not only consistent but 'absolutely necessary' in terms of the very 'Bombay pledge' that Malaviya thought was being violated.[19] Gandhi was still loath to acknowledge that the 'Bombay pledge' was actually two resolutions that did not necessarily say the same thing on temple entry.

Malaviya sent him a telegram the next day, expressing regret that his health did not permit him to travel to Poona. On Gandhi's fresh attempt to obfuscate the two parts of the Bombay pledge, Malaviya said, 'By contrast with first part evidently second part did not contemplate legislation in this connection.' To drive home the point, Malaviya reproduced the proviso to the 30 September resolution. Therefore, he argued, Iyer's bill relating to temple entry 'should be withdrawn'.

Like Ambedkar, he questioned the 'very wrong principle' of

throwing open temples based on the preference of a 'majority of Hindu voters of the area'. Their reasons had little in common, of course. While Ambedkar held that temple entry should follow an invalidation of untouchability, Malaviya believed that no religious issue could be determined by a referendum. That the majority opinion 'shall be binding on trustees of the temple and all worshippers therein' was unacceptable to Malaviya. 'I consider it absolutely wrong and unjust to decide a question which is one of religion and conscience by vote of majority. This will be nothing but compulsion.' He added that the question should be solved 'by peaceful persuasion only'.[20]

When he responded to Malaviya only on 24 February 1933, Gandhi had already published the entire correspondence between the two, along with an article by him on their differences over legislating temple entry. It was published on 18 February 1933 in the second issue of *Harijan*, the weekly that Gandhi had launched as part of his campaign against untouchability.

Meanwhile, Gandhi had procured vital feedback on the Iyer bill from two legal stalwarts, Jayakar and Sapru, and even a copy of Jayakar's 1929 bill, which he published in full in the same issue of *Harijan*. This provided him a more compelling argument in support of the Iyer bill. Thanks to the law laid down by the Privy Council in 1908, temple trustees were forced to abide by custom, and there was no option for reform but to overcome this legal hurdle through legislation.

Armed with this legal insight, Gandhi found that the only-by-persuasion proviso—his one weak point—was rendered irrelevant. 'Since in the course of complying with those resolutions it has been discovered that there is a legal difficulty which was not foreseen then, that difficulty has got to be removed at the earliest possible moment.' Gandhi added for emphasis, 'A legal bar can only be removed by a legislative act.'[21]

Gandhi cited the 'two eminent lawyers' whom he had consulted. He said that Sapru had 'expressed his opinion in emphatic terms in favour of' the temple-entry bill. And that, contrary to Malaviya's view, 'Dr Sapru sees no compulsion in it.' In the separate page devoted to Jayakar's 1929 bill, Gandhi said that it was 'in substance a combination' of the two new bills relating to untouchability abolition and temple entry. It showed that 'the matter has been before the country for several years and is in no sense new'.[22] Given that Jayakar's bill had come as a revelation to him, Gandhi was hardly likely to have been aware of Ambedkar's authorship of it.

True to his policy of non-cooperation, Gandhi had not kept abreast of activities in the legislative space, even when they related to untouchability. Just four months earlier, he had been dismissive of the zamorin's plea that he was helpless to throw open the Guruvayur temple. Having since read up Jayakar's bill and its SOR, Gandhi belatedly gathered that the decisions of colonial courts had 'acted on the Hindu Society as a deadweight which has stopped its healthy growth'. He added, 'The two Bills, like Sjt. Jayakar's combination, seek merely to remove the deadweight.'

Jayakar's citation of the Kamudi case also opened Gandhi's eyes to the irony of Malaviya accusing him of facilitating legislative intervention in the religious domain. He discovered that such cases, forbidding untouchables from temple entry, had all been filed by Sanatanists, seeking 'the aid of law' very much to 'regulate religious belief'. Turning the tables on Malaviya, he said in his *Harijan* article that 'legal interference' had been invoked by 'the very people who are today stoutly opposing' the introduction of Iyer's bill.

In his subsequent letter to Malaviya, Gandhi was as forthright as he was friendly. Stressing the need to overcome the Sanatanist-inspired law to keep the Bombay pledge, Gandhi said, 'We cannot plead helplessness under cover of this law, of which I knew nothing at the time I drew up the Resolution about temples. I suppose that you know that the original draft was prepared by me.'[23]

Such were the illuminating debates in the first two months of 1933 that Gandhi, who would be called the Father of the Nation, had with Ambedkar and Malaviya, both of whom were posthumously awarded independent India's highest recognition, the Bharat Ratna, in 1990 and 2014, respectively.

The contestation of ideas between Gandhi and Malaviya set the tone for the further debates on temple entry that took place in the legislatures between reformists and Sanatanists. Yet, scholars have generally been cursory in their reading of the differences that surfaced between Gandhi and Malaviya after the Poona Pact.

As for the differences between Gandhi and Ambedkar, which have received rather more attention, there has still been a tendency to underestimate their fundamental variance on caste. Consequently, some of the most renowned scholars mistook the Gandhi-supported Vaikom Satyagraha of 1924–25 for a temple-entry struggle even though he was at the time far from ready for such a reform in view of his avowed commitment to varna.

- While tracing Periyar's evolution as a caste reformer, Nicholas Dirks writes: 'In the spring of 1924, he entered the campaign at Vaikkam, a temple town in the princely state of Travancore. The campaign concerned the issue of temple-entry for the "untouchable" caste of Ezhavas. Temple entry had become an important concern of Gandhi and of Congress, as an extension of reform activities around the plight of untouchable groups'.[24]
- Clubbing Vaikom with the 1929–30 agitations at Parvati temple in Poona and Kalaram temple in Nasik, Susan Bayly says that they 'came to be referred to as temple entry campaigns'. She adds that '[b]eginning with the Vaikam campaign, these battles [were] over access to Hindu temple precincts'.[25]
- Ramachandra Guha writes that when an Ezhava leader had first broached the subject of temple entry with him in 1921, Gandhi suggested that they 'begin with opening wells and schools to "untouchables" rather than roads or temples'. But when the Vaikom Satyagraha was all set to begin in 1924, Gandhi, in Guha's view, turned receptive to temple entry. 'Three years previously, Gandhi had been lukewarm about temple entry. However, now that a movement was actually under way, he supported it, asking only that it be non-violent.'[26]

The fact, however, is that the Vaikom Satyagraha could not have reflected Gandhi's position on temple entry as it was only about throwing open the roads that led to the temple. He made this distinction contemporaneously on 2 April 1925 in his journal *Young India*: 'For the opening of the roads is not the final but the first step in the ladder of reform. Temples in general, public wells, public schools, must be open to the "untouchables" equally with the caste Hindus. But that is not the present goal of the Satyagrahis. We may not force the pace.'

For all the evidence in the form of his own writings, there has not been enough academic clarity on a basic fact about him, namely that Gandhi could not countenance equal access to temples until the 1932 Guruvayur challenge in the aftermath of the Poona Pact. Even then, Gandhi, as a votary of varna, was agreeable to Avarnas entering only such temples where local devotees had given their consent through a referendum.

The conflicts between the two greatest campaigners against untouchability were an augury of India's tortuous journey over the next decade and half, experimenting with Gandhi's 1932 local-option formula before it finally came around to Ambedkar's 1929 rights-based approach to temple entry. It was only in the excitement of the changes surrounding Independence that the outlook of Hindu society turned 'ripe', to use Gandhi's term, for enforcing this reform across the board.

❖

R.K. Shanmukham Chetty, who had once introduced the Ambedkar-drafted bill on untouchability, was in the chair on 24 March 1933 when C.S. Ranga Iyer introduced the Gandhi-promoted temple-entry bill in the Central Legislative Assembly. Gandhi had not succeeded in his efforts to have the bill exempted from circulation for the eliciting of public opinion. So, the best that Iyer could do to save time was to move a motion the same day asking for such circulation.[27]

G. Krishnamachariar, who had objected the previous year to Chetty introducing the untouchability bill, was the most vocal opponent to the temple-entry bill too. He took advantage of the views that had already been expressed against it by Ambedkar and Malaviya. Krishnamachariar quoted Ambedkar as saying that 'the depressed classes do not want it'. More importantly, he asserted that the bar on untouchables from entering temples was more than just a custom. 'This is an injunction based upon religion,' he said. 'It is not a custom which calls these people untouchable but it is a provision in the holy books.'

Alleging that it interfered with religion and was not merely a 'permissive Bill', Krishnamachariar pointed to the Saiva and Vaishnava Agamas, holy books that prescribed the rules for building temples and consecrating idols. It was only after the ceremonies prescribed in the Agamas had been performed that 'Godhead' entered the idol concerned. 'You turn to the next page, it lays down that if an untouchable enters the temple, Godhead disappears.' Krishnamachariar jibed at reformers, 'Well, you believe the first portion of the book which says that Godhead has come, and you disbelieve that portion which says that Godhead has disappeared.'

When the debate resumed on 24 August 1933, another Sanatanist, Satyendra Nath Sen, traced sanction for untouchability to scriptures further up in the Hindu hierarchy: the Upanishads and the Gita. Contending that 'our birth is determined by the acts performed in previous births', Sen said that, according to the Chhandogya Upanishad, 'those who perform lowly acts get low births such as those of dogs, hogs and chandalas'.[28] Drawing on its scriptural definition, he added, 'A Chandala is the issue of a Brahmin woman and a Sudra father, not legally married, because no legal marriage can take place between the two.' Asserting that 'the Gita also refers to these untouchables in unmistakable language', Sen cited its mention of 'papayonis, i.e. those who are of sinful birth'.[29]

By calling attention to the scriptures, these two Sanatanists challenged the colonial assumption that, like the bar on some Shudra castes in some temples, the bar on untouchables was also no more than a matter of local custom. It was not what they set out to do, but the duo vindicated Ambedkar's thesis that Hinduism could not be a religion of equality unless its Shastras were purged of the theory of Chaturvarna.

When the feedback on the bill came in, the majority opinion among caste Hindus turned out to be on the side of Sanatanists, finding justification for the discrimination in religion or custom or both. For a different set of reasons, the depressed classes too were divided: some were with M.C. Rajah in supporting the incremental reform and some with Ambedkar in spurning this half measure that was dependent on the whim of majority.

All of this came as a blow to Gandhi, who had been assiduously pursuing the cause since the Poona Pact. Despite being in jail, he had assumed direct charge of the untouchability campaign, refocusing it on temple entry. As a result, it had ceased to be a subject under the care of the Congress Sub-Committee on Untouchability, which had been set up in March 1929 under the leadership of Malaviya and Bajaj. Gandhi was instrumental in setting up the Harijan Sevak Sangh on 26 October 1932 as a grassroots network of caste Hindus across British India and the princely states. And then, on 11 February 1933, he launched his weekly *Harijan*, which was, at the time, devoted mainly to sensitising the country to temple entry. Soon, he brought out its Hindi and Gujarati editions too.

Gandhi even embarked on a 'Harijan Tour' after his release from Yeravda on 23 August 1933. The tour took him across the length and breadth of the country, from 8 November 1933 to 31 July 1934. Throughout his hectic travel and speaking engagements, Gandhi kept his sights trained on Iyer's bill. He had in C. Rajagopalachari a point person to lobby with members of the Assembly, particularly its Hindu members. This was according to Gandhi's stated policy that the reform of temple entry should emerge from within the Hindu community, as a token of atonement for its sin of untouchability.

Once the responses to the temple-entry bill had been collated from all over British India, it came up for discussion in the Assembly on 23 August 1934. Confirming Gandhi's apprehensions about the efficacy of the circulation process, the date proved to be too late for the bill to make any further progress. It was already the last day for non-official bills in the final session in the term of the Assembly. Even so, the government appeared to rub it in by urging Iyer to withdraw the bill in the light of adverse public opinion. Lending a farcical touch to the proceedings, Iyer still chose to move a motion, as scheduled, referring his bill to a Select Committee.

This was, in fact, a tactic to launch a diatribe against his ally in the cause, the Congress party. He alleged that the Congress had given up on his bill due to the approaching Assembly election. A week earlier, on 16 August, Rajaji had made a public statement in the *Hindu* newspaper in response to a politically loaded question from the Sanatanists. They had asked whether his party candidates would 'give an undertaking that Congress will not support any legislative interference with religious observances'. While saying that 'similar questions may be asked on a variety of topics', Rajaji replied warily, 'Not all of them, however, are made into election issues at any one time.'[30]

Iyer construed Rajaji's statement as a 'betrayal of the cause of the untouchables', saying that 'this Congress leader is afraid of facing the public opinion which he has roused'. He then disclosed the behind-the-scenes role of 'the principal lieutenant of Mahatma Gandhi' in pushing him to initiate this bill on the very day that Subbarayan's identical draft had been turned down. Recalling the drama of January 1933, Iyer said, '[H]ere is a great Congress leader who sat dharna at our houses with his son-in-law [and the Mahatma's son] Devdas Gandhi, who repeatedly called on me at Delhi and said, "We seek joint support for this legislative measure".'

Accusing the Congress of subsequently 'pandering to the prejudice of the masses', Iyer said, 'Had they gone on with the Temple Entry Bill or the untouchability question, they would have lost many votes, for it is not a popular issue.' In short, the mover alleged that a bill that had been conceived in the spirit of a social compromise had become the casualty of political expediency.

In the next issue of *Harijan*, dated 31 August 1934, Gandhi denied the charge in an impassioned article headlined, 'That Ill-Fated Measure'.[31] To begin with, he disputed the ownership claimed by Iyer over the temple-entry bill. Since it was a bill 'promoted by, and on behalf of, the reformers', Gandhi said that the mover should have 'acted under instructions' from them. 'So far as I am aware, there was hardly any occasion for the anger into which he allowed himself to be betrayed or the displeasure which he expressed towards Congressmen,' he added.

Denying Iyer's charge that electoral compulsions had caused the Congress to back out, Gandhi disclosed that the bill had been dropped for lack of support. He said that he had asked Rajagopalachari to ascertain the views of the Hindu members of the Assembly because 'if it was discovered that the majority was opposed to it, steps should be taken to have the Bill withdrawn'. Whatever the reason, the bill in which Gandhi had been so deeply invested came to a rather abrupt and tame end.

❖

The impact of Gandhi's historic fast and the consequent Poona Pact was not limited to British India. The princely state of Travancore was, in fact, first off the blocks in reacting to it. Within two months of Gandhi's fast, it went further than any province of British India in responding to the call for temple entry. On 25 November 1932, Travancore's twenty-year-old maharaja, Sree Chithira Thirunal, appointed a 'Temple Entry Enquiry Committee' to examine the options for Hindu reform.

This bold initiative was partly an effect of Travancore's proximity to Guruvayur, which had plunged Gandhi into his campaign for temple-entry legislation. More importantly, it had roots in the 1924–25 Vaikom Satyagraha, in which Gandhi, along with social reformers Narayana Guru and Periyar E.V. Ramasamy, had played a key role in forcing the Travancore government to let all sections of people use at least three out of the four roads leading to a temple.

The Vaikom Satyagraha had been driven mainly by Ezhavas, who were traditionally stigmatised as toddy tappers, and were thus the Malayalam-speaking counterparts in Travancore of the Tamil-speaking Nadars. By all material yardsticks, Ezhavas were as advanced as Nadars. In terms of social-reform battles, though, Ezhavas were more effective as they had the advantage of being the largest caste in Travancore. Besides, they had long been galvanised by the teachings of Narayana Guru to strive for equality as a collective. His radically inclusive dictum, 'One Caste, One Religion, One God for Humankind', placed Travancore at the vanguard of the temple-entry movement.

For the first time anywhere in the territories of what is now India, the maharaja-appointed committee recorded the testimonies of both Savarnas and Avarnas on the vexed issue of temple entry. Headed by the former dewan of Travancore, V.S. Subramania Aiyar, the committee took a little over a year to submit a 413-page report. Dated 11 January 1934, the report revealed that, contrary to the largely negative feedback received on Ranga Iyer's bill around the same time in British India, the majority of caste Hindus in Travancore was ready for temple entry. 'From the preponderance of oral evidence of the Savarna witnesses … it is clear that there is a strong feeling among Savarnas in favour of temple entry being allowed.'[32]

Finding merit on both sides in the Ambedkar–Gandhi debate on this issue the previous year, the Aiyar Committee said, 'Though it is conceded that temple-entry will not by itself produce social and religious equality, allowing temple-entry will, to that extent, remove the inequality in those respects.' Therefore, the committee recommended that it was 'desirable that whatever steps are possible should be taken to give the Avarnas greater facilities for worshipping at Savarna temples'. In the same breath, however, echoing Malaviya's concern, it cautioned that 'the faith of the orthodox Hindus in temples and in the sanctity of the deity installed in them should not be weakened'.

This self-contradictory desire to accommodate Avarnas without offending the Sanatanist sentiment stemmed from the Aiyar Committee's compulsion to effect temple entry within the framework of the scriptures. It could not wish away the reality that the Agamas regulating worship in Savarna temples did indeed 'prohibit the entry of the Avarnas', as the Sanatanists said. However, the committee chose to rely on a provision in the same 'sastraic texts permitting rules of conduct to be altered on the recommendation of a Parishat'.

Accordingly, the Aiyar Committee suggested 'two middle courses' that could be adopted by making the necessary changes to the rules.

- The first was that instead of being forced to worship from outside the walls of the temple complex, Avarnas be allowed to enter a peripheral area called 'Balivattom', where subsidiary deities were installed. Since 'the intensity of the pollution' would vary according to the distance from the main deity, the committee saw this 'restricted admission' up to the Balivattom as a way of 'satisfying the aspirations of the Avarnas' without 'destroying the faith of the Sanatanists'.
- The other alternative it suggested was that some temples be thrown open to all Hindus irrespective of caste, while others continued to be 'reserved for the exclusive worship of the Savarnas'. In those liberated temples, Avarnas should be allowed access to the same degree as Savarnas. Such 'mingling' could, as some witnesses testified before the committee, 'serve to demonstrate the baselessness of the fears of the Sanatanists that the temples will lose their sanctity and importance if Avarnas are admitted'.

In addition to these two long-term reforms, the committee recommended interim measures 'independently of the temple-entry movement'. It specified that 'distance pollution or theendal should be removed by appropriate legislative measures' in three secular spaces: public tanks, public wells and government satrams (rest houses). But it was public roads that were a more visible site of distance pollution as evident from the 'theendal palakas' that had gained notoriety during the Vaikom agitation. Theendal palakas were signboards prohibiting untouchables from entering the roads that led to temples. Oddly, despite the breakthrough made in the Vaikom episode, the Aiyar Committee did not include roads in the list of public spaces identified for 'prompt action'.

In a further display of his reformist zeal, the maharaja redressed the Aiyar Committee's omission. He incorporated public roads in the interim measures that were by order to be implemented within ten days of the submission of the committee's report. The communiqué came on the eve of Gandhi's visit to Trivandrum on 20 January 1934 as part of his Harijan Tour.

The communiqué began by saying that the government shared the committee's view that 'distance-pollution or theendal must cease' at 'public tanks, public wells, satrams, etc.'. Repeating those instances in its operative part, the communiqué added 'public roads', showing thereby that the government's will to take on untouchability was greater than that of the Enquiry Committee's. 'They have resolved, therefore, that all public roads, public tanks, public wells, satrams, etc., maintained by them out of their general public funds shall be thrown open to all classes of people irrespective of the caste to which they belong.'[33]

It was a creative way of disarming the Mahatma, who was forced to congratulate the maharaja. At the same time, Gandhi asserted that the communiqué 'cannot possibly satisfy me, much less the Harijans'. He displayed impatience about the delay in addressing the greater challenge of temple entry, saying that there could be 'neither satisfaction nor rest until the States refuse to recognise untouchability in any shape or form'.[34] Evidently, in the decade since the Vaikom Satyagraha, the bar had been raised, especially for Travancore. Insofar as British India was concerned, Gandhi had settled for the Iyer bill, which was plainly designed to allow temple entry only where the majority had endorsed it, but that would not do here.

In fact, two of his followers, who were on the ten-member committee set up by the maharaja to enquire into temple entry, had signed the unanimous report subject to a joint 'dissenting minute'.

In that note, retired High Court judge K. Parameswaran Pillai and retired district judge M. Govindan insisted that temple entry be allowed right away and without any restriction. Holding that equality should be 'not only in the eye of law but also in social and religious matters', Pillai and Govindan wrote, 'This can be achieved only by temple entry being given to all classes of Hindus on equal terms without distinction of caste or colour.'[35] While Pillai was the president of the Kerala Harijan Sevak Sangh, Govindan was the head of its Trivandrum district unit, besides being an Ezhava leader.

But the young ruler would need another three years to take any step on temple entry. It was worth the wait—for he did not settle for either of the middle courses suggested by the main report of the Aiyar Committee. Nor did he adopt the relatively safe option of the referendum scheme that Gandhi had promoted in British India. Instead, exceeding all expectations, he walked the more radical path proposed by Pillai and Govindan.

A legal expert from Madras, C.P. Ramaswami Aiyar, or CP as he was popularly called, helped the maharaja arrive at this courageous and historic decision. Having served as law member in the Madras governor's Executive Council in the 1920s, CP had overseen what were the earliest enactments against untouchability anywhere in the country. In the course of his long consultations with CP, the maharaja appointed him dewan of Travancore on 8 October 1936. About a month later, on 12 November 1936, the day he turned twenty-four, Maharaja Sree Chithira Thirunal Balarama Varma issued the Travancore Temple Entry Proclamation.

Swearing by 'the truth and validity of our religion', the Hindu ruler said that 'in its practice it has throughout the centuries adapted itself to the needs of changing times'. The latest such adaptation was that 'none of our Hindu subjects should by reason of birth or caste or community be denied the consolations and the solace of the Hindu faith'. Accordingly, the maharaja ordained that 'there should henceforth be no restriction placed on any Hindu, by birth or religion, on entering or worshipping at temples controlled by us and our Government'.

It was a watershed moment for not just Travancore but Hindus everywhere. Invoking Hinduism's inherent capacity for self-correction, the maharaja ruled out birth as a criterion for determining access to religious spaces. He disregarded the Aiyar Committee's finding that the Agamas did forbid temple entry for those born in the theendal castes. The maharaja also rejected the committee's slippery option that a Parishat be set up for amending the prescribed dos and don'ts.

The announcement of the new law was followed by a notification of the new rules framed under it. Ironically enough, one of the rules regulating worship at temples had a list of the categories of persons who were traditionally forbidden from entering the premises of a temple. They included non-Hindus, those deemed to be temporarily polluted because of a birth or death in their families and women during their periods. The category made conspicuous by its absence was the Avarna communities.

Even then, in the hard-negotiated framing of rules, a gratuitous reference to caste discrimination had slipped in. In the rule pertaining to some of the more orthodox temples that customarily forbade men to enter unless they had taken off garments covering the upper part of their bodies, the old restriction that no man shall enter 'without the customary caste mark' was retained. Govindan, who had been party to the dissenting note in the Aiyar Committee report, reacted adversely to this rule in his capacity as a leader of the Harijan Sevak Sangh. He said that those words 'could have been omitted ... as most classes now admitted to temples did not have any customary caste mark'.[36]

As with the 1934 communiqué, Gandhi's initial reaction to the 1936 proclamation was cautious. About two weeks after the breakthrough, on 18 November 1936, this was what he wrote in the *Harijan*: 'We do not yet know how the orthodoxy of Travancore and the Harijans will react to the proclamation. If it is not followed up by suitable response on the part of the public, it can easily become a dead letter.'[37] His caution gave way to incredulity when he came to know that the proclamation had had a dramatic impact. In an undated but clearly subsequent interview, Gandhi confessed to apprehending that Travancore would 'at least have to post a strong police force at the main temples, and that at least a few heads would be broken'.[38]

He was probably still burdened by the memory of the Vaikom Satyagraha. 'I only knew that ten years ago our volunteers had been severely hammered for even crossing a forbidden road near the temple at Vaikom. Now the humblest of the humble have entered the Vaikom temple without the slightest difficulty.' He could hardly believe the transformation wrought by the young monarch. 'That the orthodoxy, who used to swear by the letter of the ritual and made so much of the efficacy of temple worship being destroyed by even the shadow of a pariah, would fall in with the proclamation, is a thing I was not prepared for, so soon at any rate.'

The authors of the Aiyar Committee's dissenting note, which had evidently led to the proclamation, were themselves Gandhi's main source of information that its 'actual working' across Travancore was 'most successful'. In a telegram sent to him on behalf of the Harijan Sevak Sangh on 3 December 1936, Pillai and Govindan said, 'No part of temple open to any devotee is barred against Ezhavas and Harijans now ... Orthodox people including Namboodiris have as groups or individuals displayed no hostility, most of them expressing themselves in terms of full approval of Proclamation. We see no signs whatever of resentment. Their behaviour is such as if nothing extraordinary had happened, which from what we know of previous orthodoxy is an astonishing achievement. The noble Proclamation has been followed up by thorough execution.'[39]

Gandhi came to grips with the radical change in an article published in the *Harijan* exactly a month later, on 12 December 1936, in which he also quoted from this telegram. 'The enthusiasm of the Harijans, the absence of all opposition to their entrance to the farthest limit permissible to the highest caste, and the willing, nay, the hearty, cooperation of the officiating priests, show the utter genuineness of the great and sweeping reform.' Calling it 'an instance of mass conversion of caste Hindus' in Travancore, Gandhi hoped that it would spread to other parts of the country. 'If we garner the enthusiasm of Travancore, it cannot be long before the whole of India catches the Travancore spirit.'

In reality, it took the rest of the country a very long time to get there. This was also true of its immediate neighbour, the princely state of Cochin, which, along with Travancore and the Malabar district in the Madras Presidency, had been regarded as Kerala long before the state came into existence in 1956. The maharaja of Cochin, Rama Varma XVII, who shared none of Chithira Thirunal's reformist zeal, reacted adversely to the Travancore Proclamation. He ordered that, on account of the entry of Avarnas, any Hindu who had worshipped or officiated as a priest at Travancore temples would be barred from entering Cochin temples to save them from being polluted.

This regressive decision came when Shanmukham Chetty—who had introduced Ambedkar's anti-untouchability bill in the Central Legislative Assembly in 1932—was the dewan of Cochin. Chetty took over as dewan in 1935 after he had chaired the debate on Iyer's temple-entry bill as president of the Central Legislative Assembly. Six years after his tenure in Cochin had ended in 1941, Chetty went on to become independent India's first finance minister.

The flashpoint of the resultant tension between the two princely states was a temple in Cochin called Kudal Manikkam. On 17 April 1937, Chetty wrote a letter on behalf of the maharaja, directing its superintendent that 'proper purificatory ceremonies should be performed in the Kudal Manikkam temple without delay'. Chetty added: 'His Highness considers that the temple has been polluted by the entry into it of, and participation in the ceremonies by, persons who had officiated in other temples, where the entry of Avarnas has been allowed.'[40] The two princely states in Kerala appeared to be worlds apart.

15

CONGRESS EXPERIMENTS UNDER COLONIAL RULE

Despite the excitement surrounding the Travancore breakthrough, British India took another year to make a fresh attempt at temple-entry legislation. By this time, the Government of India Act, 1935, passed by the British Parliament, had replaced the dyarchy with greater provincial autonomy. So, in provincial governments, Indian ministers were no longer confined to less important portfolios. The British governor of the province, however, retained the authority to suspend the elected government.

In another big step towards self-rule, the head of the provincial government, designated as 'premier', was Indian, as were all the ministers. The political reform also provided for direct elections (enlarging the franchise by five times), introduced bicameral legislatures in provinces (Legislative Assembly and Legislative Council) and increased the number of Indian representatives in the Lower House so that they could form provincial governments on their own on the majority principle.

This was how senior Congress leaders came to be elected to power in the provinces in 1937. The premiers of Bombay and Madras—B.G. Kher and Chakravarthi Rajagopalachari, respectively—had links with the temple-entry movement. The 1937 election was also the first one to have seats reserved for Scheduled Castes (as the 1935 Act renamed the Depressed Classes), a political trade-off resulting from the Poona Pact.

Since Indians had been ceded greater authority in the provinces than at the Centre, M.C. Rajah, the lone untouchable member of the Central Legislative Assembly, chose to shift to the Madras Legislative Assembly. Ambedkar too contested an election for the first time in 1937. He had been till then a nominated member of the provincial legislature. Ambedkar's newly floated Independent Labour Party did well in the election to the Bombay Legislative Assembly, winning fourteen of the eighteen seats contested by its candidates.[1]

The devolution of power to the provinces meant that these governments run by Indians were now empowered to enact laws relating to temple entry and untouchability. Bombay took the lead, with Home Minister K.M. Munshi introducing a temple-entry bill in the Assembly on 24 January 1938. This was also the year that Munshi founded the Bharatiya Vidya Bhavan, a conservative institution driven by his credo that 'India will once again be acknowledged as the Vishwa Guru'. Armed with his own perspective on India's spiritual heritage, Munshi, a Brahmin, waded into the debate of the Sanatanists who opposed temple entry.

Picking up the thread of the earlier Sanatanist vs reformist debate in the Central Assembly, Munshi contested the claim that untouchability derived sanctity from the Vedic scriptures, the highest authority for Hindus. Munshi cited a Vedic verse saying that 'Vasishtha, the great sage, was born of a Ganika—a prostitute'. He pointed out that Vasishtha's illustrious descendants, the sages Parasara and Vyasa, were also born of lower-caste women. 'Therefore, to say that Hinduism is based only on the sanctity of caste is to degrade Hinduism.'[2]

It was an interpretation that cherry-picked in order to downplay the scriptural support for caste. Munshi did not address the oft-repeated Sanatanist references to, for instance, Chandalas in the Chandogya Upanishad or Papayonis in the Gita. As for the Sanatanist charge that legislating the matter amounts to religious interference, Munshi reaffirmed the argument that there was a legal imperative to overcome the Kamudi verdict. Echoing Gandhi's defence of Ranga Iyer's bill, Munshi said that his bill actually 'takes away the interference which the Privy Council decision and the judge-made law in modern India imposes'.

Though the Travancore Proclamation had raised the bar, Munshi's bill stuck to Gandhi's via media of the local option. Mercifully, one improvement it made on the Gandhi model was in terms of dispensing with the requirement of holding a referendum of the regular worshippers in the neighbourhood on whether untouchables could be let inside the temple. The local option envisaged by Munshi's bill was to seek the opinion of the small body running the temple: the board of trustees. This change was organic to the history of Bombay's temple-entry movement. In 1929, Premier Kher, in his earlier avatar as solicitor, had sought to throw open the Bhuleshwar temple to untouchables on behalf of its trustees.

Ambedkar was unimpressed, though, as is evident from his uncharacteristic silence throughout the discussion on the bill. One of his party members, R.R. Bhole, did participate in the prolonged debate—mainly to say that their Independent Labour Party does 'not at all believe in the sincerity of the Congress Government, because of past experience'. Bhole justified his scepticism by quoting extensively from the allegations that Iyer had made against the Congress and Rajaji in August 1934 before withdrawing his bill from the Central Assembly. Bhole also questioned Munshi's logic in making 'a trustee a middleman between the public and the Government'.

Unfazed, Munshi congratulated Bhole for providing him with 'a living specimen of the impatient Harijan'. He said, 'I can quite understand his feelings, and we, the higher classes, have no right to complain about them.' Munshi also brushed aside the reference to Iyer's allegations: 'He does not know the circumstances which made the Congress to drop the Bill at that time. It's old history; I need not go into it again.' Claiming that the Congress was the only body that had 'taken this question to heart', he said, 'It is no use blaming us, saying we are trying to redeem a pledge which we had broken yesterday.' Munshi added that the motive of his party was only 'to see that this stain on our religion, our society, our culture, is removed as early, as swiftly, as possible.'

As proof of his urgency, Munshi also moved that the bill be referred to a Select Committee, which was to submit its report in five days. He then began reading out the names of the members he had in mind for that committee. The second name he proposed was that of Ambedkar. On hearing his name, Ambedkar rose to his feet and said, 'I am sorry, Sir, it will not be convenient for me to serve on the Committee.' This cryptic interjection prompted Munshi to ask, 'Will any member of your party, Mr Bhole for instance, serve on the Committee?' In quick succession, two of Ambedkar's party colleagues, Bhole and D.G. Jadhav, said no.

Besides the reservation he had already expressed in 1933 to Gandhi's local option, Ambedkar's antipathy to the 1938 Bombay bill was compounded by another factor. In his Yeola declaration of 1935, Ambedkar had announced his resolve to renounce Hinduism, so disenchanted was he with it. Yet, all that the Congress government offered was the prospect of untouchables being admitted into some of the temples as an act of generosity on the part of their trustees.

In another twist of history, nine years later, in March 1947, Munshi would propose in the Constituent Assembly what served as the original draft of the historic provision abolishing untouchability. And soon after Independence, Munshi found himself working in the crucial Drafting Committee under the chairmanship of Ambedkar.

The Select Committee submitted its report on 31 January 1938, and the Bombay Legislative Assembly passed the revised bill the same day. Four days later, Munshi moved the bill in the Legislative Council. This time, the first member to respond to Munshi's opening remarks was none other than the leader of Ambedkar's party in the Upper House, P.G. Solanki. It was a dramatic moment because, despite Ambedkar's virtual boycott of it in the other House, Solanki began by saying, 'I wholeheartedly congratulate the Honourable Minister in charge of this Bill.'

Solanki and Ambedkar, both erudite leaders of the Depressed Classes, went back a long way. They started their legislative careers on the same day in 1927 and worked together in the Starte Committee, which had been appointed on Solanki's resolution to survey the state of untouchability. But Ambedkar and Solanki clearly diverged on Munshi's bill. 'Though I am likely to be misjudged and criticized by my own party,' Solanki said, 'yet my conscience tells me that I must speak out on this particular legislation.'

Lauding Munshi for his 'extraordinary courage of conviction', Solanki said, 'Ours is the first Government of the Congress in this whole of India which has taken the first opportunity and has fulfilled the pledge which was given to Mahatmaji as well as to the public at large.' Munshi returned the compliment, saying that Solanki, 'even in defiance of the rather unexpected attitude of his party in the Assembly, had the frankness to record his appreciation of the measure'.

The following day, on 5 February 1938, the Council also passed the bill. Consecrating a variant of the Gandhi-authored principle of local option, the Harijan Temple Worship Bill, the earliest of its kind, came to be enacted in Bombay in the face of Ambedkar's studied indifference.

In any event, it was the first legislative counter in the country eroding, though not overturning, the sanctity attached to custom in the law laid down by the Privy Council in the Kamudi case.

❖

There was more than one reason why Madras should have enacted a temple-entry legislation before Bombay did. To begin with, the Congress had won a landslide victory in Madras (winning 74 per cent of the seats) in the 1937 election, while it had actually fallen short of a majority in Bombay (winning 49 per cent of the seats). So, Rajaji could well have read it as a mandate to implement the long-established Congress policy on temple entry.

Besides, his government was the legatee of the statutory breakthroughs that had been made in the 1920s by Madras in relation to untouchability, long before the introduction of provincial autonomy. And on the issue of temple entry in particular, the Madras legislature had played a pioneering role—first by adopting Subbarayan's resolution and then through the bill he had drafted. Gandhi's template for his temple-entry crusade was, in fact, based on that bill.

Besides, on 24 September 1937, in its very first session, the Madras Legislative Assembly had adopted a resolution on the Travancore Temple Entry Proclamation. Premier C. Rajagopalachari had welcomed the resolution, recalling that, on visiting Travancore immediately after the proclamation, he had ranked Chithira Thirunal alongside 'no less historic figures than Akbar and Asoka'. Feeling the same kind of admiration for the maharaja even ten months later, Rajaji said, 'And I repeat it today lest anybody should imagine what I said then was said in a vein of emotion and that it was pitched too high.'[3]

In the same address, however, Rajaji said that, insofar as the Madras Presidency was concerned, 'we have to secure public opinion which would welcome such a proclamation' or legislation. Whatever reform work had been done till then to prepare public opinion in Madras was enough, in his estimation, to throw open only secular spaces, not the religious ones. 'It is quite enough for the opening of all schools, quite enough for the opening of roads and wells, for the giving of all civil rights. It is enough to laugh out all old prejudices. It is enough to sit together and eat and drink, if we like, but it is not enough for this House to clear its way to throw open its temples.'

In listing out the caste reforms that Madras was apparently ready for, Rajaji had included the customary prohibition against inter-dining. This implied, by process of elimination, that for caste Hindus of Madras, temple entry was still as unthinkable as intermarriage, the ultimate caste taboo. Recalling the fate of Iyer's bill—'a humble measure'—before the Central legislature, Rajaji said, 'That kind of measure we can introduce, but it would be a flash in the pan, a damp squib, if public opinion is not ready to utilize that optional legislation.'

Rajaji's scepticism about public opinion in the Madras Presidency was surprising because he said this shortly after an unanimous resolution on 19 January 1938 by the Tamilnad Congress,[4] the provincial unit of his party, calling for the removal of all legal obstacles to temple entry. He showed no sign of taking up the issue even after the Bombay law had been enacted on 5 February 1938. Instead, Rajaji left it to M.C. Rajah, a non-Congress leader of the affected community, to introduce it as a private member's bill on 30 March 1938.

Thus, unlike Bombay, Rajaji decided that his government would not introduce the bill on temple entry. Despite the constitutional progress of provincial autonomy, the Madras government continued to tiptoe around the sentiments of caste Hindus on the issue of temple entry.

In any case, Rajaji was lucky to have found a willing collaborator in Rajah, who also had first-hand knowledge of the fiasco over the Ranga Iyer bill in the Central legislature. The bill that emerged from the Rajah–Rajaji collaboration was almost a copy of the Iyer bill and, therefore, a homecoming for the referendum-based model that had been originally drafted by Subbarayan. Rajah's bill disregarded the improvement made by the Bombay Act, which empowered trustees to decide on temple entry. Further, by having a member of the excluded community pilot a bill that allowed only caste Hindus to participate in the referendum, Rajaji made a travesty of Gandhi's spiritual conception of it as an act of atonement.

And so it was that, on 17 August 1938, when the Assembly was due to refer Rajah's bill to a Select Committee, the country's first untouchable legislator sought support on the basis that it 'puts no compulsion whatsoever on the caste Hindus'.[5]

When Rajaji spoke next, he disclosed that Rajah's bill had been introduced 'not only with my consent, but I may say even at my request'. Recalling that he had also been associated with the Iyer bill, Rajaji said, 'I cannot forget the scenes when I sat on the galleries above the House and tried to pull the strings of central legislation from there.' He said that 'the exigencies of the circumstances prevented that Bill becoming law'. This time, Rajaji himself came up with an exigency to prevent the Rajah bill from becoming law.

Though he and his cabinet had intended to give it their 'fullest support', Rajaji said that they had since 'turned the matter over' in their heads. He proceeded to explain 'what we think now to be the better means to achieve the object which is so dear to us and which is embodied in this Bill'. Referring to the 'revolution' in neighbouring Travancore and the subsequent resolution in the Madras Assembly, Rajaji said, 'It struck me that we would find this great work, this dear work, much simpler than it might be otherwise, if we utilized the change brought about in Travancore effectively a little more than we had done.'

Betraying yet again his misgivings about public opinion in the Madras Presidency, Rajaji said that he wanted the private member's bill for the whole of the province to be replaced by a bill drafted by his government just for the Malabar district, the site of the Kalpathy agitation against Brahminical restrictions. His strategic reasoning for this curious change was that the Travancore Proclamation must have brought about 'automatically a change in the religious psychology of other Kerala people'.

Valourising the people of the Malabar district at the expense of those living in the rest of the Madras Presidency, Rajaji said, 'If what we want is not a Bill on the Statute Book and a struggle later under the optional provisions of this Bill, if what we want is the reality of a united common form of temple worship for all classes of Hindus, it is unwise to follow the more difficult path when the easier path is before us.'

Angry at this sudden change in policy, Rajah said, 'Sir, six years ago the Hon. Mr. C. Rajagopalachari told me that the country from the Himalayas to Cape Comorin was ripe for a Bill like mine. Now the Premier says the time is not ripe and therefore I must withdraw the Bill.' Declining to do so, he said, 'I am very sorry to say that but I feel that I have been deceived in this matter.' So, just as he had been attacked by Iyer in the Central Assembly, Rajaji had a falling out with Rajah in the Madras Assembly in the context of the same temple-entry legislation. The optics were worse this time as it was a spat between a Brahmin premier and an untouchable legislator over the enactment of a caste reform.

On 1 December 1938, Rajaji himself introduced the promised Malabar Temple Entry Bill.[6] Its SOR all but admitted that Rajaji was piggybacking on the ruler of a princely state. 'By reason of common traditions, identity of language, customs, forms of worship and the like prevailing among the Hindus in the Travancore State and in the District of Malabar, it is considered that the removal of the disabilities aforesaid can be brought about in the first instance more easily in that district.'

During the debate in the Madras Assembly on Rajaji's limited proposal, Rajah contended that public opinion against temple entry had grown across the province in the three months since the scuttling of his more ambitious bill.

He also questioned the wisdom of choosing Malabar of all places for initiating the reform. 'Nowhere in the whole Presidency is the stigma of untouchability more perceptible than in Malabar, aggravated as it is by feelings of unapproachability and unseeability.' Rajah recalled that when Swami Vivekananda had visited Malabar in 1892, he had likened it to a 'lunatic asylum' because of its caste practices. Wondering if 'Malabar has outgrown the times in which that description was made', Rajah asked Rajaji why he had selected 'a rocky place to sow his seed'?

Rajaji turned Malabar's notoriety into an argument in favour of his choice. He said that Malabar had, like Travancore, turned untouchability 'to a fine art, as to how far we can stand from another, we can look at another'. And so 'the very absurd length to which the thing has been carried is the cause for a greater revolt against it in Malabar than in a place where it has whittled down'. Responding to the analogy of the place being too rocky to sow the seed of temple entry, Rajaji said that 'the tillers have toiled more industriously in Kerala than in any other part of the country, against this law of untouchability'. Rajaji presumably saw himself as one of the tillers, having supervised the 1932 Guruvayur referendum that had contributed to his optimism about the Malabar district.

Responding to Rajah's sarcastic demand to know 'in what other districts he was going to introduce similar legislation', Rajaji said,

'With regard to what may follow after Malabar, we need not go district by district. If Malabar succeeds, there is no reason to think of districts. We have crossed the Rubicon and it may very well be the conquest of the whole Province.' And so, the Malabar Temple Entry Act came into force on 7 February 1939. But this law failed to throw open any temples in the district, including Guruvayur. Thanks to the pushback from Sanatanists, led by the zamorin of Calicut, Malabar proved to be a rocky place indeed.

This setback caused Rajaji to abandon his plan of extending the referendum-based law to the rest of the province. Instead, he wanted the Harijan Sevak Sangh to lead the way in building public opinion in favour of such a legislation. Consequently, the Tamilnad unit of the Harijan Sevak Sangh, led by its president, Vaidyanatha Iyer, organised a series of meetings, presided over by the vice president of its national unit, Rameshwari Nehru, a relative of Jawaharlal Nehru.

Rameshwari Nehru had presided over similar meetings in Travancore too in the run-up to the proclamation. Her first-hand experience in both places helped her see that Rajaji was being more wary than the maharaja had been. Despite giving 'his wholehearted support to the cause', Rajaji was 'very keen' that temples be thrown open 'without the aid of law' and 'by the voluntary free will of the people'.[7] Her reading was that he desired a situation where trustees, rather than waiting for legislation, brought about temple entry on their own with the assurance that caste Hindus were willing to worship alongside Harijans.

Rajaji said as much at a provincial-level conference organised by the Harijan Sevak Sangh in the temple town of Madura on 13 June 1939. Regarding the legal risk that the trustees and others involved were liable to face, Rajaji said, 'Don't worry about temple entry legislation, but prepare the way and arrange for the opening of temples for untouchables. If the law is resorted to for the purpose of preventing you from achieving your goal, I will give you legislation within eight days.'[8]

It was an extraordinary statement for the premier of a province in colonial India to make, promising a legal cover to those who breached the caste barrier in temples. Clearly stung by the fiasco that his Malabar experiment had proved to be, Rajaji abandoned his play-it-safe approach. It appears he was now willing to use his party's comfortable majority in the legislature.

Rajaji's express promise of indemnity for those attempting or facilitating temple entry served as an impetus for Vaidyanatha Iyer and his team to set their sights on the historic Meenakshi temple of Madura. The team worked to instil confidence among the trustees and priests of that temple, situated about 90 kilometres from Kamudi, the old flashpoint. On the morning of 8 July 1939, Vaidyanatha Iyer marched to the Meenakshi temple in the company of five Harijans and, in a nod to their pioneering struggle, a member of the Nadar community. They were all received at the gate by a delegation of the temple staff, led by its executive officer, R.S. Nayudu. The six members of the excluded classes were allowed to go in as far as any caste Hindu and worship the main deities in that temple complex.

This simple act of subversion in what was arguably the most famous temple in Tamilnad made news across the country. The *Times of India* reported that temple entry had become 'an accomplished fact' in Madura. 'The temple priest officiated at the worship offered by the Harijan party and distributed prasadam,' it said. 'No reactions are visible, though orthodox Brahmins are agitated.'[9]

A follow-up report the next day told a different story. There was a sharp divide among the priests of the temple, as those of the Sanatanist persuasion had locked up the place and insisted on performing a purification ceremony. 'A deadlock was created in the matter of Harijan worship at the Minakshi Temple here by the priests, who locked the inner shrine and refused to continue puja without the samprokshana (purification) of the deities.' The *Times of India* report also mentioned Nayudu's forceful response to the revolt. 'Ten locks were broken under orders of the Executive Officer after midnight, and worship was resumed. Three hereditary priests have been suspended for defying orders and other bhattars (priests) recruited.'[10]

The news of this nasty turn of events was juxtaposed with a rather upbeat reaction from Rajaji: 'The practical unanimity of public opinion behind this departure from custom rendered any disturbance or irritation impossible. The quiet and pious manner of the whole proceeding and freedom from any bravado or spirit of coercion sanctified the achievement and made it fit in beautifully with the genius of the Hindu religion, tradition and practice.'[11] His statement not only seemed outdated but also betrayed his failure to anticipate trouble despite the rumblings of dissent on the very first day.

Sanatanists in Madurai, led by N. Natesa Iyer, president of the Varnashrama Swarajya Sangha, filed a criminal complaint before a magistrate, and announced that they would also institute civil proceedings. The legal liabilities that the participants in the temple entry feared were all coming true. Worse, since the legislature was not in session, Rajaji was in no position to deliver on his promise to have an indemnification law enacted within eight days.

On 11 July 1939, three days after the temple entry, Rajaji published the draft of the bill that he would introduce when the Assembly met the following month.[12] It was all he could do. The imminence of that bar on legal proceedings did not deter the Sanatanists from filing a suit against ten men on 13 July 1939. The defendants were Executive Officer R.S. Nayudu, Vaidyanatha Iyer and L.N. Gopalasamy from the Harijan Sevak Sangh, the six forbidden Hindus who had entered the temple five days earlier and the priest who had performed puja for them.

Claiming that the temple entry had led to desecration of the temple, the plaintiffs asked for four reliefs. One, that, as the trustee of the temple, Nayudu be directed to cause 'purification ceremonies to be carried out'. Two, that Nayudu, Vaidyanatha Iyer and Gopalasamy be restrained by a permanent injunction from taking into the temple the six trespassers or 'any other member of the prohibited or scheduled classes'. Three, that the six trespassers be likewise restrained by a permanent injunction from entering the temple. Four, that all the ten defendants be directed to deposit Rs 3,100 as cost for the performance of purification ceremonies.[13]

Only a day earlier, Gandhi had written an article on the Madura temple entry for *Harijan* from Abbotabad.[14] He appreciated the efforts of his followers Rameshwari Nehru and Vaidyanatha Iyer, clearly unaware of the revolt and legal threat that had followed. There was no reference to the blowback in his article. Instead, he touched on his pet theme of 'purification', little realising that the Sanatanists had weaponised it in Madura. 'Every opening of a temple to Harijans should mark,' Gandhi wrote, 'greater purification inside and outside the temple opened.'

All the same, Gandhi's article was prescient in suggesting that the Madura temple entry had a more far-reaching significance than the Travancore Proclamation. Though the proclamation was, he said, 'no doubt a very big step', it was 'the prerogative of the Maharaja', which was likely to command greater obedience. 'But the opening of the celebrated temple of Madura is a greater event in that it is the popular will that has brought about the happy consummation.'

Meanwhile, on the ground, the retaliatory move of the Sanatanists spurred Rajaji to resort to the extraordinary power of issuing ordinances under the Government of India Act, 1935. This was the first instance of an Indian head of a provincial government exercising his constitutional power to make an interim law—a provision that was meant for just such a situation, that is, to meet a contingency when the legislature was not in session.

But the premier could only recommend the ordinance; it had to be signed by the governor before it could come into force. And as Lord Erskine was at the time camping in Ooty, that was where the ordinance papers had to be sent, all the way from Fort St George in the city of Madras. Fortunately for Rajaji, Lord Erskine obliged him without further ado. So it was that the Madras Temple Entry Indemnity Ordinance came to be promulgated on 17 July 1939.[15]

Just a week later, on 24 July, the ordinance led to the termination of criminal proceedings against the protagonists of the Meenakshi temple entry. Taking cognisance of the change in law, the Madura city magistrate discharged Nayudu and the eight other accused persons. The ordinance had an effect on the civil proceedings too, as

Madura's district judge, S.P. Thompson, dismissed an appeal against the sub-judge's refusal to grant the injunction sought by the suit.[16]

Even as Sanatanists stepped up their campaign for a purification ceremony in the Meenakshi temple, the ordinance served to encourage other major temples in the Madras Presidency to welcome Harijans and Nadars.[17] So, by the time Rajaji was in a position to introduce a bill in the Assembly on 3 August 1939 to replace the ordinance, it was no more a measure for just the Meenakshi temple. A schedule attached to the bill mentioned six other temples, including Tanjore's renowned Brahadeswara temple.[18]

Likewise, the law that came into effect on 11 September 1939, after being passed by both Houses and receiving the governor's assent afresh, was no longer about indemnifying the range of State and non-State actors involved in violating the customary bar on temple entry. The Madras Temple Entry Authorisation and Indemnity Act also provided a mechanism for throwing open temples.

The indemnity provision only covered incidents of temple entry prior to the enactment of the Act—specifying that no person shall be prosecuted or sued vis-à-vis any act of omission or commission at the Meenakshi temple or any other temple in Madras 'on the 8th day of July 1939 or on any subsequent date up to the commencement of this Act'.

For the incidents that took place thereafter, Rajaji incorporated a provision that facilitated temple entry. While the law fulfilled his promise of extending the Malabar law to the whole province, the new Madras law incorporated the incremental improvement made by the Bombay law. The post-Madura reform authorised temple entry if 'in the opinion of the trustee or other authority in charge of any Hindu temple', the worshippers of such temple were 'generally not opposed to' letting in Harijans.

On 18 September 1939, a week after the indemnity provision had come into effect, one of the respondents to the suit that had been filed by Sanatanists raised an objection, saying that that the case was no longer maintainable. The Sanatanists responded by challenging the validity of the Madras temple-entry law. Though he held on 3 April 1940 that the law had been validly enacted, the subordinate judge did not dismiss the suit.[19] Instead, about twenty days later, he declared that he would decide 'from what places within the temple the various sections of the Hindu community could properly worship'.[20]

This gratuitous twist might have come as a consolation to the Sanatanists, as it had the potential of maintaining caste distinctions even in temples where the reform of temple entry had been achieved. The subordinate judge cited a couple of customs supporting his initiative. The first was the custom that excluded non-caste Hindus from entering the temple. The second was one that set caste-based limits on the extent to which worshippers could enter the temple. Brahmin priests alone were permitted to enter the sanctum sanctorum, while other Brahmins could go up to the ante-chamber or ardhamantapam. As for Kshatriyas, Vaishyas and Shudras, they could not go beyond the outer mahamantapam.[21]

This was a throwback to a 1935 Bombay High Court judgment in which a member of the Lingayat community had been directed to pay damages for entering the ardha mandapa reserved for Brahmins. The affected Lingayat was represented by M.R. Jayakar. As his hands were tied by the 1908 Privy Council ruling in the second Ramnad case, Justice S.S. Rangnekar had said, 'Whatever the opinions of modern society may be, and however obnoxious the custom may appear to civilised people at the present day, it seems to us that it is difficult to hold that this custom was unreasonable.'[22]

The subordinate judge dealing with the Madura temple entry had no such misgivings. However, by the time the respondents filed their responses to his suo motu proposal, the subordinate judge had been transferred. As it happened, his successor, R. Rajagopala Ayyar, would have none of it. On 26 January 1942, he dismissed the case in its entirety. Differing with the line of inquiry that had been ordered by his predecessor, Ayyar pointed out: 'on the plaint no question was raised for determination by the Court as to the places within the temple from which different sections of the Hindu community could properly worship'.

The Sanatanists appealed against Ayyar's ruling before three successive appellate courts, all the way up to the Federal Court, the highest tribunal in British India. Their challenge to the law that had been enacted in the wake of the Madura temple entry dragged on till 27 March 1946, when the Federal Court put its final stamp of approval to the reform. About a month earlier, Gandhi, who was not a temple-goer, had paid a symbolic visit to the Madura temple in the company of Harijans. Nayudu had received him at the gate.

The lawyer who had won the case in the Federal Court for the valiant lot of reformers and alleged trespassers involved in the Madura temple entry was Alladi Krishnaswami Ayyar, popularly known as Alladi. About a year later, he joined the Drafting Committee of the Constitution and went on to play a sterling role as one of the founding fathers of the Indian republic. While Rajaji was an Iyengar, or Vaishnavite Brahmin, it is remarkable that so many Iyers (spelt variously), or Shaivite Brahmins, sided with temple entry in different ways and at different points. Though the worst perpetrators of caste discrimination were often from the Brahmin community, the saving grace was that it also produced some of the most valiant caste reformers.

One of the five Harijan protagonists of the Madura temple entry joined the Congress and rose to become a member of the Constituent Assembly. P. Kakkan ended up representing Madurai in the first Lok Sabha, thanks to the incorporation of the Poona Pact in the Constitution of decolonised India too, reserving some constituencies for the erstwhile untouchables. Kakkan would go on to serve as a minister in the Madras state for ten years, holding the key portfolio of Home for five years.

❖

By the end of the 1930s, Bombay and Madras, the two frontline provinces in temple-entry battles, had crossed the psychological barrier of transgressing custom through legislation. But even in those provinces, the traditionally excluded castes could access only such temples where the trustees, exercising their newly acquired legal power, permitted them to.

The temple-entry reform, such as it was, stalled when Congress governments resigned in October–November 1939 protesting Britain's unilateral declaration that India was at war with Germany. In the political uncertainty that persisted for years, the Hindu Mahasabha, which had contested the 1937 provincial elections, came to taste power. Under the enterprising presidency of Vinayak Savarkar, the Hindu Mahasabha joined coalition governments with the Muslim League or its former allies in three Muslim-majority provinces: Bengal, Sindh and the North West Frontier Province. About a year after Fazlul Haq had moved the historic Pakistan Resolution at the Lahore session of the Muslim League, Syama Prasad Mookerjee entered his coalition government in Bengal as finance minister in December 1941.

Savarkar had paved the way for such unlikely coalitions by making common cause with Sanatanists to form 'a strong Hindu front by adjusting and cooperating on all common major points of unity'.[23] Consider the way he made his pitch with the delegation of a Sanatanist organisation called Shri Bharat Dharma Mahamandal, as recorded by him contemporaneously on 1 July 1941. Savarkar began with a telling admission that the 'Hindu Mahasabha and all Sanatan organisations have 95% points in common'. This was to assuage Sanatanist concerns about temple entry, notwithstanding his much-touted engagement with caste reforms. Savarkar even promised that the Hindu Mahasabha would not allow any legislative intervention in the domain of temples. 'So far as the 5% differences of views are concerned, I guarantee that the Hindu Mahasabha shall never force any legislations regarding the entry of untouchables in the ancient temples or compel by law any sacred ancient and moral usage or custom prevailing in those temples.'

In return, he urged the orthodox section to let the reformists strive for equality among Hindus through methods other than legislation. 'In general the Mahasabha will not back up any Legislation to thrust the reforming views on our Sanatani brothers so far as personal law is concerned but the Sanatanis on the contrary should recognise that in public life all Hindus must be looked upon on the basis of equality and should leave the reformists free to bring about their religious reforms, etc by means of persuation (sic) and mental change.' This was more disconnected from the ground reality than Gandhi's erroneous assumption at the time of the Poona Pact that legislation was dispensable in the case of temple entry. By extending the no-legislation principle to all aspects of reforming the Hindu personal law, Savarkar pretended that inter-caste marriage, for instance, could be legalised without superseding the restrictions imposed by custom and scriptures. As if that was not enough, Savarkar boasted about the impact he had made with his pretence. 'This attitude has greatly been appreciated by the Sanatanist leaders and it is receiving their cordial & Sincere Consideration approbation in several leading quarters.'

Meanwhile, the large provinces of Bombay and Madras remained under Governor's Rule throughout the six-year war and beyond. Congress returned to power only after the next election had been held in January 1946. Sure enough, it picked up the threads of temple-entry reform.

On 29 August 1946, shortly after he had resumed office, the prime minister of Bombay, B.G. Kher, made a case for further reform while participating in a temple entry in Poona. According to a news report, 'Mr Kher said it was time that caste Hindus realized that Harijans should also enjoy the same rights and privileges as other Hindus.'[24] Still, it took another year for Madras and Bombay to introduce fresh bills on the touchy subject.

The Federal Court judgment upholding the 1939 temple-entry law was fortuitously timed for the new Madras government, headed by Tanguturi Prakasam, otherwise known as Andhra Kesari or the Lion of Andhra. The judgment helped revive the trend of temples here and there being thrown open to Harijans.[25] In one such instance, on 24 December 1946, the minister for Religious Endowments, K. Koti Reddy, led Harijans inside two temples in Madura, not far from the site of the 1939 breakthrough. On that occasion, he disclosed that the government was planning to remove 'all legal impediments' to temple entry.[26]

Providing an impetus to that plan was a reference to the challenge of caste prejudice in the Objectives Resolution adopted by the Constituent Assembly on 22 January 1947. One of the eight paragraphs of that resolution, which served as a blueprint for the Preamble, promised that the Constitution would provide 'adequate safeguards' for 'depressed and other backward classes'.[27] Two days later, on 24 January, the Constituent Assembly set up an Advisory Committee from among its members to propose, among other things, the fundamental rights of citizens. Chaired by Vallabhbhai Patel, the Advisory Committee of about fifty members included those who had fought against untouchability or for temple entry: B.R. Ambedkar, C. Rajagopalachari, Alladi Krishnaswami Ayyar and K.M. Munshi.[28] (One conspicuous omission was M.R. Jayakar, who had been sidelined for proposing an amendment to the Objectives Resolution and thereby delaying its adoption by over a month.)

Shortly thereafter, on 28 January 1947, the Prakasam government earned the distinction of publishing the first official bill on temple entry that did away with the local-option approach. Though a number of temples had been thrown open under the provisions of the 1939 Act, the SOR of the 1947 bill pointed out that the government was 'helpless wherever a trustee takes up a recalcitrant attitude and refuses to obey the people's will'. For seeking to empower untouchables to enter temples as a matter of right, the SOR claimed that the government was 'fully satisfied that Hindu public opinion demands this reform'.[29]

Further, the SOR made it clear that, in the case of any temple open to the Hindu public generally, untouchables would have a right to offer worship 'in the same manner and to the same extent as other classes of Hindus'. Prakasam, a Brahmin, included a provision to punish anyone who 'prevents a member of the excluded classes from exercising the right conferred by the Bill or who molests or obstructs such a member in the exercise of such right'. If this caste crime was committed for the first time, it was punishable only with fine up to Rs 100. But in the case of a subsequent offence, it was punishable with fine up to Rs 500 or with imprisonment extending to six months or with both. The provision for throwing a caste Hindu in prison for blocking an untouchable from worshipping in a temple was by far the most audacious aspect of Prakasam's Bill.

On 23 March 1947, before it could introduce this paradigm-shifting bill in the legislature, the Prakasam government fell, for reasons unconnected to temple entry. About a week later, on 1 April, the successor Congress government headed by O.P. Ramaswamy Reddiyar introduced the very same bill in the Madras Legislative Assembly. Taking advantage of the fact that it had been in the public domain for over two months, the minister piloting the bill, T.S.S. Rajan, ensured that the Assembly passed it the same day and without any amendment. Two days later, on 3 April, the Madras Legislative Council followed suit. The most notable participant in the Assembly's debate was P. Kakkan, and in the Council, P. Subbarayan. On 11 May 1947, Governor General Lord Mountbatten gave his assent, thereby turning the bill into the Madras Temple Entry Authorisation Act, 1947.

Although the 1947 law was closer in spirit to the bill against untouchability that Ambedkar had drafted, the legislative debate attributed the spadework only to Gandhi's temple-entry campaign. Claiming allegiance to 'the glorious sect of Sri Ramanuja', the medieval saint who had famously led untouchables inside a temple, the mover of the bill, Rajan, said that he was also 'the follower of modern Ramanuja, Mahatma Gandhi'. Gandhi's advocacy in the 1930s of temple entry through the incremental reform of local option was widely perceived as having prepared the ground for the more advanced rights-based approach in 1947.

The quick enactment of such a sensitive caste reform, with each House taking just a day, dispensing with the safeguard of a Select Committee scrutiny and without making the slightest amendment, suggested that caste Hindus in Madras were suddenly overcome with remorse on the eve of India's Independence. It marked the beginning of a trend across the country (Central Provinces and Berar, Bombay and Orissa, among others). Equally, this temple-entry Act reflected a change in India's outlook on secularism towards the end of colonial rule. Recognising the need for State intervention in combating social evils, India did not hold with the Western conception of secularism as the separation of State and Church.

Whether untouchables could be allowed to enter temples was no longer an internal issue of Hinduism, much less a matter of discretion in the hands of trustees. Despite all the pains taken by Gandhi and his followers to escape the odium of religious interference, the half measures enacted in 1938–39 had to overcome stiff resistance from the Sanatanists. Their reaction to this direct foray into the religious domain was relatively muted, at least in Madras, in the vastly different environment of 1947 when thoughts of freedom and religious consolidation were predominant.

Nevertheless, the Sanatanists did cause trouble in the famed Tirupati temple in Madras Province. The Andhra unit of the Harijan Sevak Sangh was planning to hold a temple entry there on 3 January 1947. Their preparations were elaborate as the pilgrims had to cross seven hills from Tirupati to reach the main shrine in Tirumala. But there was a problem that remained unresolved: in the absence of a decision by the trustees to remove the customary bar, the proposed temple entry did not enjoy legal cover under the 1939 Act.[30] Exploiting this legal deficiency, the Sanatanists obtained an injunction from the Madras High Court. However, the 1939 Act also barred any suit from being entertained unless the plaintiff had obtained 'the previous sanction of the Provincial Government'.

Since the Sanatanists had not obtained the necessary sanction, the maintainability of their suit was suspect. As it happened, the High Court heard the suit on merits in the short gap between Mountbatten's assent to the 1947 enactment on temple entry and the time it came into effect. Though Rajaji was then an education minister in the interim government in New Delhi, he continued to be engaged with the cause of temple entry in his home province. He ensured that the Sanatanists in Tirupati who had invoked the law authored by him were countered by the best-known lawyer in Madras, Alladi Krishnaswami Ayyar.

Having argued the case on 16 May 1947, Alladi wrote to Rajaji the next day, worrying that the judge might miss the wood for the trees: 'According to your desire I appeared in the Tirupati temple case but the judge gave much more trouble in the case than I expected.' Apparently, there was a conflict between the Tirumala Tirupati Devasthanam Act of 1932 and Rajaji's temple entry law of 1939. As Alladi put it, the judge was concerned about 'the specious point that some saving of custom in the Tirumalai Act is not affected by the Temple Entry Act of the Madras Legislature'.

Alladi found this point specious because the bar against suits imposed by the 1939 law extended not only to those filed under the general law of Madras Religious Endowments Act, 1926 but also to those filed under 'any other law'. Since this expression had been 'advisedly put in to cover such cases', Alladi reported to Rajaji, 'I had to put up a very big fight out of all proportion to the merits of the point raised in the case.' He expressed his misgivings thus, 'It looked as if towards the end of the case he was all right but no one can be sure of the attitude of this particular judge who is always vacillating and in the land of doubt.'[31]

The injunction in the Tirupati case was still in force when the gazette notification was published on 28 May 1947, stating that the Madras Temple Entry Authorisation Act would come into effect on 2 June 1947. After the notified date of enforcement, 'obstruction to the entry into any of the Hindu temples in the Province and offer of worship therein by the excluded classes (Harijans) will become a punishable offence'. The notification had an effect on the pending proceedings in the Tirupati case. As the *Times of India* put it, 'In view of this notification, it is considered that the interim injunction granted by the Madras High Court restraining the Tirupati temple authorities from throwing open to the excluded classes will cease to have any practical effect.'[32]

Indeed, the 1947 law changed the situation so radically in the Madras province that its premier himself led a temple entry in Tirupati—something that even a non-State actor like Vaidyanatha Iyer could not do with impunity in Madurai in 1939. The richest temple in the country turned inclusive on 15 June, exactly two months before Independence. 'The well-known Tirupati Temple of Sri Venkateshwara was opened to Harijans today when the Premier, Mr. O.P. Ramaswami Reddiar, led a party of Harijans into the temple and worshipped at the shrine.'[33] The report added, 'The Harijan minister in the Madras Cabinet, Mr. Kurmayya, was also present with his family.'

Meanwhile, on 3 April 1947, the very day that the Madras Council passed this law, Bombay's Premier Kher introduced his own upgrade 'to entitle Harijans' to enter temples in his province. The Bombay bill was more stringent than the Madras one, not taking a lenient view of the first offence. Any offence under it was punishable with imprisonment up to six months or with fine of any amount or with both. The Bombay bill also empowered the police to 'arrest without warrant' any person reasonably suspected to have committed an offence under it.

Like in the case of Madras, most voices in the Bombay Legislative Assembly were in favour of switching from the local-option approach to the rights-based one. But there was to be no fast-track enactment in Bombay, at least in part because the Sanatanist protests were louder here. The Bombay bill was discussed for two days before it was referred to a Select Committee on 7 April 1947.

This was how the Bombay Harijan Temple Entry Bill came to be carried over from colonial India to independent India. The decolonised country was not yet a month old when the Sanatanists were up in arms once again about temple entry.

The Select Committee's report was due to be tabled on 11 September 1947. Before presenting that report, Premier Kher made an unscheduled presentation of a petition on behalf of a delegation of Sanatanists who, he said, had met him the previous night in connection with the temple-entry bill. Even after Kher had clarified to them that he 'differed from their views and could not advocate their case', the Sanatanists pressed for his help 'as they had no one to present the petition', which had been signed by about 1,000 people. The speaker asked Kher to give the House an idea about the contents of the petition. The premier responded: 'In short, the request of the petitioners is that the Harijan Temple Entry Bill should not be put on the statute book.'[34]

The reference to the Sanatanist petition did not impede the Assembly from passing the bill the same day, with minor changes. The Sanatanists then turned their attention to the Bombay Legislative Council to which the bill had moved. On 18 October, members of the Varnashrama Swarajya Sangha barged into the Council Hall and demanded that the bill be rejected. 'The leader of the Sanatanis, Pandit Anna Shastri Upadhyay, with his palms joined together, said that the Government in India were treating orthodox Hindus in the same manner as Hindus were being treated in Pakistan,' a report said.[35]

The extremist view was no longer influential enough even to dilute the bill, let alone block it. On 4 November 1947, the Bombay Council passed the bill, and on 16 November 1947, Governor John Colville reserved the bill, as required, for the consideration of the governor general. But Lord Mountbatten was away in London then to attend the wedding of the heir to the British throne, Princess Elizabeth, to his nephew, Philip.

Rajaji, governor of Bengal at the time, had shifted to New Delhi to function as governor general from 10 to 24 November 1947. Thus, thanks to a quirk of fate, it fell to Rajaji, the author of two early temple-entry laws in Madras, to give the go-ahead to this next-generation bill from Bombay. On 21 November 1947, Rajaji signed as governor general on a note saying, 'I assent to the Bill in His Majesty's name.'[36] His Majesty, the monarch of the United Kingdom, King George VI.

Until India officially became a republic on 26 January 1950, the governor general served as a representative of the British Crown under the transitional provisions of the Indian Independence Act, 1947. Therefore, Rajaji, a leading light of the freedom struggle, found himself thus encumbered by colonial baggage.

A day after Rajaji's assent, even as the signed document was ready for dispatch by air mail, a telegram arrived from Bombay. The governor's private secretary wrote saying that he shall be 'grateful' if the governor general dealt 'immediately' with the bill. He said the Kher government was 'anxious that (the) Bill should become operative before November 24th which is Kartik Ekadashi day of special religious significance so that public temples in the Province may be thrown open to Harijans not later than that date.'

It was a throwback to 1929. Back then, when Kher had been the solicitor for the trustees of the Bhuleshwar temple in Bombay, Jamnalal Bajaj had appealed in vain that all temples be thrown open on Kartik Ekadashi. Thanks to the coercive provisions of the 1947 law, the Kalaram temple, where Ambedkar had launched his satyagraha in 1930, was finally thrown open on 8 December 1947.[37]

Only a day before Rajaji signed his assent on the Bombay bill, he had cleared a similar bill from the Central Provinces and Berar. That enactment came into effect on 22 November 1947.[38]

Central Provinces and Berar had emerged as the second province—Madras being the first—to have abolished untouchability in the religious sphere. It was yet another sign that, around the time of Independence, caste Hindus had become more conscious of the incongruity of discrimination in temples. Linked as it was to their religious practice, they could hardly blame untouchability customs on the recently terminated colonial rule.

❖

If Prakasam was called Andhra Kesari, Harekrushna Mahatab of Orissa was Utkal Keshari. Besides serving as prime minister of the composite Madras province before Independence, Prakasam went on to become the first chief minister of the Andhra state that had been carved out of Madras in 1953. Mahatab also became a premier in 1946, but unlike Prakasam, remained in charge of his state until 1950. Mahatab, who was from the Khandayat caste, the largest in the province, ruled Orissa again from 1956 to 1961.

As soon as he assumed office as prime minister of Orissa on 23 April 1946, Mahatab came up with a law that indemnified violators of temple-entry restrictions. This law would operate retrospectively, from the day he had assumed office. The Orissa Temple Entry Authorisation and Indemnity Act, 1947, protected State and non-State actors involved in any temple entry 'on 23rd April 1946 or any subsequent date up to the commencement of this Act'. Following Rajaji's Madras precedent of 1939, the Orissa Act of 1947 also empowered trustees to throw open their temples from the date of its commencement.

Orissa's was, in fact, the first temple-entry law that Mountbatten gave his assent to, on 9 April 1947. But the one from Madras, which he assented to shortly after, on 11 May 1947, was a qualitatively different one—it took a rights-based approach to temple entry.

Having played catch-up in 1947, Orissa made its own legislative innovation in this regard the very next year.

Following Gandhi's assassination on 30 January 1948 by a Hindu fanatic, urns carrying his ashes were sent for immersion to different provincial capitals and holy places. The coastal town of Puri was a natural choice for Orissa. Mahatab came up with an inspired way of paying homage to the Mahatma. He sought to combine the immersion of ashes in the Bay of Bengal at Puri with a temple entry at Jagannath, Orissa's main shrine. He appealed to the raja of Puri, Gajapati Ramchandra Deva IV, who was the trustee of the Jagannath temple, to take advantage of the 1947 law and lift the restriction on Harijans. The raja was, however, disinclined to break from tradition.

As a *Times of India* report datelined 9 February 1948 said, 'Supreme efforts are now being made to get the world-renowned Hindu temple at Puri of Lord Jagannath opened to Harijans and get this function synchronise with the immersion of Orissa's share of Mahatma Gandhi's ashes in Orissa.'[39] The report added, however, that the raja of Puri and a section of pandas, or priests, 'seem to be opposed to the opening of the temple to Harijans'. Therefore, Mahatab left his headquarters in Cuttack for Puri for 'last-minute talks on the subject'.

The matter escalated into a 'crisis', as a subsequent report said, prompting the Mahatab government to warn that it might 'step in'.[40] And step in it did on 13 February 1948, the day on which Gandhi's ashes were immersed across the country. Despite a huge gathering of pilgrims, the raja of Puri and the priests backing him kept the temple closed most of the day in order to thwart the proposed temple entry. It took the intervention of Puri's district magistrate to finally open the temple doors at 5.30 p.m. It was reported that, amidst the stone-pelting that followed, 'some Harijans mixed with the crowd and entered the temple'.[41]

Mahatab was distraught at what he believed was defiance of public opinion by the temple trustee and other Sanatanists. Admitting the Orissa government's failure, he promised corrective action. 'I saw the sense of disappointment on everybody's face, and I took note of the rebuke which the vast concourse of people administered to our Government for their indifference towards the affairs of the Jagannath Temple. No representative Government dare ignore public opinion in order to accommodate a few so-called religious heads.'[42]

On 20 February 1948, less than a week later, the Mahatab government published a fresh bill.[43] On the face of it, this bill was a copy of the temple-entry laws enacted by other provinces the previous year. While Bombay and Madras took almost a decade to graduate from the local-option approach to the rights-based approach, Orissa made the transition in barely a year, precipitated by the ultra-conservative establishment in Puri.

Mahatab went beyond the existing laws in his definition of a temple. The 1947 Bombay law, for instance, threw open temples that had until then been 'used as of right' by caste Hindus. In a bid to preempt any such rights-based reform in Orissa, the raja of Puri had denied any entitlement to caste Hindus as well in the Jagannath temple under his control. This forced Orissa's 1948 law to define the temple more expansively as a space 'used as a place of religious worship by custom, usage or otherwise by the members of the Hindu community or any section thereof'.

This definition extended the scope of the temple-entry legislation to places that were supposedly open only to a section of Hindus. The provision found resonance in Bombay too. The government there was grappling with a suit instituted in Ahmedabad on behalf of the influential Swaminarayan sect on 12 January 1948, less than two months after the promulgation of the rights-based temple-entry law. The followers of this sect, founded in the early nineteenth century by Swaminarayan, were called 'Satsangis'. Their case was that Satsangis represented 'a distinct and separate religion unconnected with the Hindus and Hindu religion', and as such, their temples were outside the purview of the temple-entry law.

The first respondent they named was the president of the Maha Gujarat Dalit Sangh, Muldas Bhudardas Vaishya, who 'intended to assert the rights of the non-Satsangi Harijans to enter the temples of the Swaminarayan sect'. Therefore, the Satsangis sought a declaration to the effect that the Bombay law of 1947 did not apply to their temples.[44]

Gandhi's last article on temple entry was written on 27 January 1948, three days before his murder. He was responding to a letter that had questioned the logic of allowing Harijans into Swaminarayan and Jain temples 'in which they had no faith'. Holding that the distinction made by the letter writer had 'no meaning', Gandhi said, 'Hindus can and do visit Swaminarayan and Jain temples. Harijans should also visit them … Harijans are not a separate community. Enlightened public opinion and the law which embodies that opinion say that they are one of the varnas, be they four or eighteen, comprising Hindu society.'[45] Gandhi's position had evolved considerably from the time that he could conceive of Avarnas entering temples only with the consent of local Savarnas.

While the Swaminarayan suit was pending before the trial court, the Kher government proposed an amendment incorporating the Orissa innovation. The SOR of the amendment bill said that some temples had been 'closed partially or wholly' by their trustees, using 'sectionalism' to claim that they did not come within the purview of the 1947 Act. Remarkably, the SOR acknowledged that Bombay proposed to amend its conception of temple 'on the lines of the definition in the Orissa Temple Entry Authorisation Act, 1948'. It added that the purpose of the proposed amendment was 'to confer on Harijans the same right to worship as is available to the Hindu community or any section thereof'.

On 5 October 1948, while introducing the bill in the Bombay Legislative Assembly, Minister for Backward Classes G.D. Tapase again acknowledged that the revised definition of 'temple' had been 'bodily taken' from the freshly minted Orissa Act. In the course of the debate in the Assembly that day, he accepted a change in the definition of the term 'worship' too. This was at the instance of a legislator from Sholapur district, G.W. Joshi, who cited a bizarre claim made by Sanatanists to block temple entry at Pandarpur's Vithoba temple, one of the most visited shrines in the Bombay province.

Joshi said that the Sanatanists were now questioning the reform on the ground that Vithoba was 'not a deity that has been installed'. They contended that it was 'swayambhu', or self-manifested, and therefore the temple-entry law did not apply to Vithoba. The 1947 law had defined 'worship' in terms of a deity 'installed' in the precincts of a temple. Following the government's acceptance of Joshi's proposal, the Bombay legislature deleted the term 'installed' from the definition of 'worship'.

On 27 December 1948, Governor General Rajaji gave his assent to Bombay's 1948 amendment bill. This time he signed not as Mountbatten's substitute but as his successor. And, as required by the transitional arrangement, he continued to sign in the name of 'His Majesty'.[46]

16

THE CONSTITUTION'S TELL-TALE CLAUSE

The framers of the Indian Constitution believed that an express commitment to the foundational value of secularism was superfluous. To them, the Constitution itself was a repudiation of the two-nation theory that had led to the Partition.

Yet, conceptualising freedom of religion for the most diverse country in the world was a unique challenge, with no parallels to draw from other jurisdictions. The Constitution framers made a telling but unflattering reference to Hindus while defining the right to freedom of religion in Article 25. India's founding fathers and mothers could well have couched it in general terms—indeed, they had begun with such a draft.

The provision, as it still stands, opens with a general reference to freedom of religion, subject to factors such as 'public order, morality and health' and to other Fundamental Rights enshrined in the Constitution. This is followed by what is called a 'non-obstante clause', stating that nothing in that article shall 'affect the operation of any existing law or prevent the State from making any law' related to two broad subjects. One of these allows the State to regulate or restrict activities associated with religious practice. The other one, which allows law-making for 'providing for social welfare and reform', specifically includes 'the throwing open of Hindu religious institutions of a public character to all classes and sections of Hindus'.

The language was clearly chosen to ensure that neither the Sanatanists nor sects that claimed to have broken away from Hinduism could undermine temple-entry laws in the name of freedom of religion. It was meant to prevent the comeback of that discriminatory custom under the cover of the Constitution. Yet, when they had embarked on the exercise of determining fundamental rights, temple-entry laws were far from the minds of the Constitution-makers.

After the adoption on 22 January 1947 of Nehru's Objectives Resolution, the next big step in the making of the Constitution was the setting up of the Patel-led Advisory Committee the following month. At its first meeting on 27 February 1947, the Advisory Committee set up five sub-committees, one of which was the ten-member Fundamental Rights Sub-Committee headed by Acharya J.B. Kripalani, then the president of the Indian National Congress.

This sub-committee held its first meeting on the very day it was formed. Consisting of eminent persons such as Ambedkar, Alladi, Munshi and Rajkumari Amrit Kaur, it hit the ground running. The members were clear from the very outset that they should formulate only such rights as were enforceable in courts. Kripalani asked them to submit their proposals within three weeks.

Only four of them met the deadline: Alladi, Munshi, Harnam Singh and Ambedkar. Despite their references to untouchability, none of the drafts touched upon temple entry. At its second meeting on 24 March 1947, the sub-committee decided to 'take up' Munshi's draft clause-by-clause and examine it 'in conjunction' with other drafts.[1] At its fourth meeting, on 26 March 1947, Munshi's clause on freedom of religion was discussed. Though it was adopted with some changes, there was a note of dissent too.

Amrit Kaur, a long-time associate of Gandhi, an early feminist leader and a Christian of Sikh origin, recorded her dissent. According to the minutes of the meeting, 'Rajkumari Amrit Kaur wanted it to be recorded that the clause is defective inasmuch as it might invalidate legislation against anti-social customs which have the sanction of religion.'[2] They left it at that as she had no ready solution to the alleged defect. Her concern drew support from the only other female member of the sub-committee, Hansa Mehta, who had been added to the original team.

In fact, Amrit Kaur and Hansa Mehta were something of a team, working in tandem in the Constituent Assembly and its committees, raising a range of issues, especially from the viewpoint of gender justice. Five months later, Amrit Kaur became independent India's first health minister and served in that position for ten years, laying the foundations for public health policies and infrastructure and setting up a centre of excellence, the All India Institute of Medical Sciences. Mehta went on to represent India at different forums of the newly founded United Nations (UN). She is best remembered at the UN for changing in 1948 the opening words of the Universal Declaration of Human Rights, from 'all men are created equal' to 'all human beings are created equal'. At its seventieth anniversary in 2018, UN Secretary General Antonio Guterres recalled that, without Hansa Mehta, 'we would likely be speaking of the Universal Declaration of "the Rights of Man" rather than of "Human Rights".'[3]

Similarly, it was the caution sounded on 26 March 1947 by Amrit Kaur and Hansa Mehta that prompted the Constituent Assembly to amend the freedom of religion clause about a month later—a contribution that ought to be better known. The idea evolved quickly through a succession of iterations, leading to the amendment on 1 May 1947.

- 31 March 1947: Five days after she had first raised the issue in the sub-committee, Amrit Kaur took the matter further on behalf of herself and Hansa Mehta in a letter to Benegal Narsing Rau,[4] the constitutional adviser to the Constituent Assembly. Citing 'customs practiced in the name of religion', she listed 'pardah, child marriage, polygamy, unequal laws of inheritance, prevention of inter-caste marriages, dedication of girls to temples'.[5] The point of listing such retrograde customs was to say: 'We are naturally anxious that no clause in any fundamental right shall make impossible future legislation for the purpose of wiping out these evils.' Amrit Kaur added that the clause drafted by Munshi might 'even contradict or conflict with the provision abolishing the practice of untouchability' in the same draft. Or put a question mark over the 'validity of existing laws' against child marriage or for widow remarriage.

The main purpose of the letter was to propose a solution. They feared that social evils were liable to be passed off as religious practice, and so the Kaur–Mehta proposal was to replace Munshi's expression 'free practice of religion' with just 'freedom of religious worship'.

- 3 April 1947: The interim report of the Sub-Committee on Fundamental Rights submitted to Patel disregarded their amendment, retaining Munshi's framing of the clause as 'the right freely to profess and practice religion'.[6]
- 4 April 1947: In a letter to B.N. Rau, Alladi took up the cudgels on behalf of Kaur and Mehta. In view of the 'bearing' of religion on social legislation, 'including the latest enactment relating to temple entry', Alladi said, 'I feel very strongly that there is a good deal to be said in favour of what the lady members have urged and for inserting an explanation to the clause relating to the freedom of religion on the lines indicated by them.' He added that if courts construed 'practice of religion in a wide sense, it may have the effect of invalidating all existing legislation, apart from prohibiting such legislation for the future'.

Alladi also commended the example set by the British Parliament during the passage of the Government of India Act, 1935. When a delegation of orthodox Hindus had pressed upon it 'to safeguard religious institutions from interference of any kind by the Legislature', the British Parliament refused, as such provision might 'stand in the way of social and religious reform'. He requested Rau to consider 'the terms of the exception or the rider that may be inserted to the freedom of the religion clause for being placed before the committee in the next sitting'.[7]

- 14 April 1947: Kaur and Mehta succeeded in having their way at the meeting this time. The sub-committee recast the freedom of religion clause to replace the reference to practice of religion with the more narrowly tailored 'freedom of religious worship'.[8] This was the first official recognition in the course of India's Constitution-making of the need to fetter the practice of religion.

Meanwhile, Alladi placed on record a note reiterating that he was 'for some clause being inserted on the lines suggested by the lady members of the committee'. He also suggested that, rather than tinkering with the main clause, 'an explanation or proviso' could be added to Munshi's draft. The proposed insertion was that the right to profess and practice religion 'shall not preclude the legislature from enacting laws for the social betterment of the people'.[9]

- 16 April 1947: The final report to Patel reflected the sub-committee's acceptance of the Kaur–Mehta proposal replacing the right to practice religion with 'freedom of religious worship'.[10]

On this day, Munshi also wrote to the Sub-Committee on Minorities, which was to meet for the first time the next day to examine the draft clauses that had been recommended by the Sub-Committee on Fundamental Rights. Some members were common to both sub-committees: Amrit Kaur, Ambedkar and Munshi. The Sub-Committee on Minorities was chaired by Harendra Coomar Mookherjee, a Christian Congress leader from Bengal.

In his letter, Munshi listed out seven rights for the protection of minorities, which he personally wanted incorporated through the Sub-Committee on Minorities. Two of those pertained to temple entry, as untouchables were counted among minorities at the time.

One of Munshi's recommendations was that, notwithstanding any custom, 'all Hindus without any distinction of caste or denomination shall have the right of access to and worship in all public Hindu temples'. The other temple-entry–related right he drafted said: 'Rules of personal purity and conduct prescribed for admission to and worship in these religious places shall in no way discriminate against or impose any disability on any person on the ground that he belongs to impure or inferior caste or menial class.'[11]

- 17 April 1947: At the first meeting of the Minorities Sub-Committcc, Munshi explained the recommendations of the Fundamental Rights Sub-Committee. A Christian member from Madras, M. Ruthnaswamy, suggested that, as Christianity and Islam were 'essentially proselytising religions', they should be permitted 'to propagate their faith in accordance with their tenets'.[12]
- 18 April 1947: Reversing the recommendation of Kripalani's sub-committee, Mookherjee's sub-committee decided to suggest that the words 'religious worship' be replaced by 'religious practice'. It also accepted Ruthnaswamy's proposal of permitting propagation. So, the main clause recommended by this sub-committee read as 'the right freely to profess, practice and propagate religion'.[13] This decision was carried by a majority of ten to five. Besides Amrit Kaur and Ambedkar, the dissentients included Jagjivan Ram, Govind Ballabh Pant and P.K. Salve.
- 19 April 1947: In a report to Patel, the Sub-Committee on Minorities recommended its changes to the freedom of religion clause.[14]

In the light of this report, Alladi recorded a note listing the amendments he proposed to move before the larger Advisory Committee. The recommendation to restore the phrasing 'religious practice', Alladi feared, might 'stand in the way of all social legislation and strike at legislation already passed'. He warned that the word 'practice' would be 'wide enough to cover religious processions, cow-killing, music before mosques, etc.'. Alladi added: 'Instead of leaving it to the good sense of the future legislatures and courts, a constitutional guarantee may have the effect of stereotyping and giving rigidity to existing practices.'[15]

- 20 April 1947: Amrit Kaur submitted her 'emphatic opposition' to the revision made by the Sub-Committee on Minorities to the freedom of religion clause. She said: 'To make the "free practice of religion" a justiciable right is, I submit, an error and will defeat not only social progress but will keep alive communal strife.'[16]

- 22 April 1947: The Advisory Committee chaired by Patel had a prolonged discussion on the two versions of the freedom of religion clause. Jagjivan Ram, a Harijan leader from Bihar, who at the end of a long stint in successive Central governments in independent India would go on to become deputy prime minister, proposed that 'the original clause' protecting religious worship rather than religious practice 'may remain as it is'.[17] Amrit Kaur seconded his suggestion.

This was when Syama Prasad Mookerjee of the Hindu Mahasabha came out against the deletion of religious practice, saying that it would 'lead to considerable hardship and difficulties'. Then, echoing Alladi's suggestion, Mookerjee said: 'As regards social reform, I suggest we insert a proviso to cover that.'[18] This attempt at balance was remarkable for a leader who, after serving as a minister in the first Nehru government, founded the Hindu nationalist Bharatiya Jana Sangh, the precursor to the Bharatiya Janata Party, the current ruling party.

When Patel put the issue to the vote, the decision to insert the words 'religious practice' was taken by a majority of two votes.[19] Thus, in the Advisory Committee, the view of the Sub-Committee on Minorities prevailed.

Rajaji intervened at this point to accommodate both viewpoints. Having accepted 'practice' over 'worship', the Advisory Committee, he said, should provide that 'social reforms in the particular community must be permissible with the consent of the legislature'. Rajaji said that it would also have to provide against 'conflicts and mutual difficulties'.[20]

Chairman Sardar Vallabhbhai Patel responded, 'The principle is accepted. You and Dr Syama Prasad may sit together and draft.'[21] Rajaji and Mookerjee were an unlikely combination to be entrusted with such a task, not only because of their diverging political opinions but also because they were both from the Sub-Committee on Minorities. Ideally, someone from the Sub-Committee on Fundamental Rights should have been involved in the drafting, since it was a clash between those two panels. Perhaps Patel chose Rajaji and Mookerjee on the spur of the moment because they were the only ones to have suggested a via media.

The minutes said, 'It was agreed that Messrs Rajagopalachari and S.P. Mookerjee should submit a draft proviso to this clause permitting social legislation which may affect religious practice.'[22] The draft proviso submitted by the two was as follows: 'The freedom of religious practice guaranteed in this clause shall not debar the State from enacting laws for the purpose of social welfare and reform.'[23]

- 23 April 1947: Incorporating the proviso that had been drafted by Rajaji and Mookerjee, Patel submitted the Advisory Committee's report to the president of the Constituent Assembly, Rajendra Prasad.[24] Instead of limiting the right to 'freedom of religious worship', as had been proposed by Amrit Kaur and Mehta, the proviso circumscribed the 'freedom of religious practice' with a constitutional protection to social-reform laws.
- 1 May 1947: After Patel had moved to adopt the freedom of religion clause in the Constituent Assembly, Munshi moved an amendment to its newly inserted proviso. He found the proposed protection for social-reform laws inadequate as it did not specifically cover temple-entry laws. Clearly, both the clause and Munshi had come a long way from his original draft. His belated proposal of adding a reference to temple-entry laws went beyond what Kaur, Mehta and Alladi had suggested. In a way, Munshi had come a full circle, given that he had piloted the first temple-entry law in the country as a minister in the Bombay government in 1938.

In the Constituent Assembly, he proposed adding the following words to the proviso: 'and for throwing open Hindu religious institutions of a public character to any class or section of Hindus'.[25]

Munshi explained that, despite the caveat that the practice of religion should not interfere with social-reform legislation, there was an uncertainty about temple-entry laws. 'The question arose with regard to the throwing open of all temples to all classes of Hindus, whether it would be religious practice. In order to prevent any such construction of clause, it was decided that the throwing open of Hindu religious institutions shall not be held to contravene the practice of Hindu religion.'

Mindful of the sensitivity of his proposal, Munshi couched it as a decision by a third party. It was perhaps a tacit reference to discussions he had on the sidelines of the Assembly. At any rate, none of the Sanatanist voices in the Constituent Assembly objected to the making of a singular reference to Hindu religious institutions in the proviso on social reform.

As if on cue, Sardar Vallabhbhai Patel, speaking on behalf of the Advisory Committee and its sub-committees, came out in support of it: 'I accept Mr. Munshi's amendment and I congratulate the House on agreeing to pass this very controversial matter which has taken several days in the Committees and gone through several Committees. There might be differences of opinion, but on the whole we have tried our best to accommodate all sections of the people. I move that this clause as amended be passed.'[26]

The president of the Constituent Assembly, Rajendra Prasad, first put Munshi's amendment to the vote. It was adopted. Then he said, 'Now I put the clause as amended to the House.' That too was adopted.

This was how the concern for social-reform legislation that had been raised by Amrit Kaur and Hansa Mehta developed over the course of thirty-six days into a remarkably forthright safeguard for temple-entry legislation. Thanks to the intervention of another woman member of the Constituent Assembly, G. Durgabai, Munshi's amendment underwent a further change more than a year later, on 6 December 1948, when the Assembly was debating the draft Constitution that had been moved by Ambedkar on behalf of the Drafting Committee.

Better known in later years as Durgabai Deshmukh (following her marriage in 1953 to Union Finance Minister C.D. Deshmukh) and as a doyen in the field of social welfare, she held that the temple-entry reference was 'restricted in its scope'. The object of her amendment was 'to secure the benefit in a wider way and to make it applicable to all classes and sections'. The change she proposed was that Hindu religious institutions should be thrown open not to 'any class or section of Hindus' but to 'all classes and sections of Hindus'.[27] Her rationale was that replacing 'any' with 'all' would make the protection for temple-entry legislation more unequivocal.

While rejecting the amendments that had been moved by others to the freedom of religion clause, Ambedkar made an exception in Durgabai's case. Without laying out a reason, he simply said that hers was 'the only amendment I am prepared to accept'. And the Assembly went by his discretion. So, what finally came into effect on 26 January 1950 in Article 25(2)(b) was an amalgam of the amendments made by Munshi and Durgabai.

The role Ambedkar played in helping Durgabai tweak Munshi's language turned out to be the one contribution that he made, however indirectly, with regard to temple-entry legislation—an aspect of the untouchability struggle that he had forsaken after the Poona Pact. Such was the course of Ambedkar's political journey after he had authored the first-ever bill dealing with temple entry, way back in 1929.

❖

What difference did this constitutional protection to temple-entry legislation—Article 25(2)(b)—make in the nascent republic? Not much, it would seem, from anecdotal evidence of holdouts across the country, whether in temples or even in courts.

Take the Swaminarayan suit that had worried Gandhi in the days before his assassination in 1948. The case had forced the B.G. Kher government to amend the definition of 'temple' in Bombay's temple-entry law. However, while the trial court in

Ahmedabad rejected the claim that the sect was not connected to the Hindu religion, its verdict on 24 September 1951 endorsed Swaminarayan's exclusionary practice. The trial court found merit in the Swaminarayan claim that entry into its temples was determined not so much by caste as by membership of its satsang. So, the bar on Harijans was found justified on the ground that they were but a part of the larger excluded category of 'non-Satsangi Hindus'.[28]

A similar attitude was displayed when dealing with an eruption of violence at the Baidyanath temple in Deoghar, which was then in Bihar and is now in Jharkhand. The temple is one of the twelve 'Jyotirlingas', the holiest of Shiva shrines across the country. On 19 September 1953, a mob of pandas assaulted Gandhi's spiritual heir, Vinoba Bhave, for seeking to enter the Baidyanath temple with Harijans in tow. It was reported that Bhave received 'one or two blows' and three members of his party were 'injured' at the gates of the temple.[29]

As it happened, Gandhi himself had been physically attacked in this very city during his famous Harijan Tour two decades earlier. On 25 April 1934, as he emerged from a railway station in Deoghar, a hostile crowd greeted him with black flags, protesting his temple-entry campaign. The car in which he travelled was attacked with sticks and, as he put it, 'the pane just fell on my side' and he would 'certainly have been seriously hurt'[30] had it fallen on him.

The recurrence of that violence, despite the enactment of the Bihar Harijan (Removal of Civil Disabilities) Act, 1949 and constitutional protection for that law, triggered public indignation. On 27 September 1953, the chief minister of Bihar, Shri Krishna Sinha, who had been instrumental in the enactment of the 1949 law, led a group of Harijans into the same Baidyanath temple.[31] This was considered a landmark in the life of Shri Krishna Sinha, a member of the dominant Bhumihar caste and a Congress leader who led the Bihar government for close to two decades. But the pandas took revenge in the tradition of Brahminism, by 'washing and fumigating' the temple to clean it of the pollution they believed to have been caused by the erstwhile untouchables.[32]

The most revered of all the Jyotirlingas, the Kashi Vishwanath temple, located in the holy city of Banaras in Uttar Pradesh, also remained in the thrall of this pollution doctrine and continued to be out of bounds for Harijans. Throwing this temple open proved more challenging, in part due to its custom of letting worshippers do 'sparsh darshan', that is, they could enter the sanctum sanctorum and touch the deity. Naturally, the demand of the Harijans who had been mobilising was that they be allowed to worship at the Kashi Vishwanath temple in the same manner as caste Hindus did, including the privilege of touching the deity. It was now their constitutional right.

The Sanatanist resistance in Banaras was spearheaded by Swami Hariharanand Saraswati, who had hit the headlines at the national level as Swami Karpatri Maharaj while leading a political movement against the Ambedkar-piloted Hindu Code Bill. The Ram Rajya Parishad, a far-right Hindu party that had been founded by Karpatri in 1948 went on to win three seats in the first Lok Sabha elections in 1952. In his pushback against temple entry, however, he needed to be subtler. There was already a general enactment against untouchability in the state, the United Provinces Removal of Social Disabilities Act, 1947, which included an express provision for temple entry. According to Section 3(d) of that Act, 'no person could prevent another from having access to any public temple or enjoying the advantages, facilities and privileges of any such temple to the extent the same were available to other Hindus'.[33]

At the Kashi Vishwanath temple, however, all that the Harijans were allowed to do was to see the deity through a tiny aperture on one of the walls, which could be approached by an outer passage avoiding the main gate.

It took almost seven years after the enactment of the 1947 law for Harijans to muster the courage to protest this blatant violation of it. They printed leaflets and posters declaring that they would march in procession to the temple and enter it on the afternoon of 17 February 1954.

Given that it was not legal any longer to block Harijans from entering the temple as such, the alternative that Karpatri came up with was a form of segregation right inside its premises. True to his religious conception of untouchability, his priority was to deny Harijans the option of sparsh darshan, the most palpable feature of Kashi Vishwanath. Karpatri proposed that, unlike caste Hindus, Harijans be prevented from accessing the sanctum sanctorum or garbhagriha.

At a meeting convened for the purpose, the Sanatanists resolved that the aperture through which Harijans were accustomed to having a glimpse of the deity should be 'substantially enlarged in order that the Harijans could have greater facility in having darshan'. To ensure that they did not stray into the garbhagriha, it was further resolved 'to meet the Harijans at the main door, called the "singhadwar", of the temple and to conduct them to the window, now enlarged, and to let them have "darshan" of the sacred deity from that place in accordance with the old custom'.

The discourse on untouchability had travelled a long way from Madura 1939 to Banaras 1954. The range of political, legal and social changes in the intervening period were reflected in the agency acquired by the Harijans. The temple-entry movement in Banaras was led by legislators from their own community.

Sadly, there was no corresponding progress in the thinking of the Sanatanists. They could not come to terms with the idea of parity between caste Hindus and Harijans, or abide the presence of the latter in the sanctum sanctorum of the Banaras temple. But the law was now on the side of the victims, at least in theory. So, unlike in the Madura of 1939, the opponents of temple entry were liable to fall foul of the law in the Banaras of 1954.

As recorded in a High Court judgment related to this temple entry,[34] this is indeed what happened. A batch of Harijans, led by a Congress legislator from the community, Bechan Ram, arrived as scheduled at the main gate on 17 February 1954. Under the gaze of the district and police authorities, the Sanatanists led by Karpatri greeted the procession with garlands and 'invited' them to have darshan of the deity 'from the window or aperture now enlarged for them'. The court attempted to ascertain whether those Harijans were allowed to enter through the main gate to reach that aperture.

While the Sanatanists claimed that the Harijans had not been 'stopped from entering through the main gate', the State asserted that they had been 'refused entrance ... through the singhadwar'. Weighing the conflicting versions that had been given under oath, the High Court found that 'the Harijans could not, uninterrupted, have access ... through the main gate ... because the Sanatanists ... were at the scene to obstruct their entry'. They had not backed down even after the city magistrate warned them on the spot that 'not allowing the Harijans to have access to the temple through the main gate would be an offence'.

The ploy of appearing to comply with the law (greeting Harijans with garlands) without compromising on their pious prejudice (not letting them enter through the main gate) clearly went awry. In a bid to 'smoothen the way of the Harijans', the city magistrate ordered the Sanatanists 'to clear out of the temple' and instructed the police 'to take them in custody' for violating the law. Despite these arrests, the Sanatanists still had their way—not only were the Harijans denied the right to enter alongside other worshippers, once again, they were allowed darshan only through the aperture, which was now mercifully a little bigger than before.

The showdown made front-page news the next day. 'Apprehending breach of peace, the police arrested today 30 persons, including Swami Karpatriji, leader of the Ram Rajya Parishad, who had been blocking the entrance to the temple of Vishwanath to prevent the entry of a batch of Harijans ... The Harijan group however did not enter the temple and viewed the deity through the window of the outer wall.'[35] The law-enforcement machinery, walking a tightrope, did not facilitate temple entry despite the arrests of its opponents.

Meanwhile, Karpatri played the martyr. He and his followers refused to seek bail, even when it was offered to them at the police station. As the High Court put it, 'The petitioners were told that they could be enlarged on bail in the event of their furnishing such bail, but they refused to give bail with the result that they were sent to jail custody by an order of the City Magistrate, sometime on the night of 17th February 1954.'

From their strategic location behind bars, Karpatri Maharaj and his followers challenged the constitutionality of the law under which they had been arrested. The Allahabad High Court ruled on 16 March 1954 that the 1947 UP law was protected by Article 25(2)(b) of the Constitution: 'this law only provided for the removal of these distinctions which caste Hindus enforced on the Harijans in respect of, among other matters, entry of Harijans in temples on the same footing as caste Hindus'.

While it upheld the substantive grounds on which they had been arrested, the High Court ordered the release of Karpatri and his followers from what was by then a month-long detention in jail. The High Court upheld their additional contention that the arrest was illegal due to procedural violations, such as the failure of the police to produce them before a magistrate within twenty-four hours.

Feeling vindicated by his release, the leader of Ram Rajya Parishad resumed his campaign to save Kashi Vishwanath from being polluted by low castes. Karpatri focused once again on preventing them from entering the sanctum sanctorum and touching the Jyotirlinga. On their part, the Harijans were equally determined to assert their right to do everything that other devotees were allowed to do in that temple. Their fresh temple-entry plan was to go in batches for four days, starting on the festival of Ram Navami, due on 11 April.

The negotiations that followed led to a loose understanding between all the stakeholders. On the one hand, it was agreed that 'though the Pandits would not give their formal consent to Harijan entry as it was against the Shastras, they would not obstruct them if they entered the temple'. On the other hand, it was agreed that 'Harijans would go to the temple in an ordinary way without taking out processions'.[36]

But the 'hope of unopposed entry ... died down' two days before the festival. The Harijans expressed misgivings about the proposal of slipping inside the temple unobtrusively. One of their leaders,

Congress legislator Ram Lakhan, declared that 'unless Harijans went to the temple in a procession, their right of entering the temple would not be considered as accepted'. Reviving the original plan of going in batches for four days, starting on Ram Navami, Ram Lakhan and three other Harijan legislators announced that one of them would lead the procession on each of those days.

The next day came a judicial order restraining them, in the teeth of both the law and the Constitution. On a suit filed by a couple of Sanatanists, the city munsif of Banaras, Rajnikant Srivastava, issued an interim injunction on 10 April 1954 restraining 'some Harijan leaders and the Harijan community from entering the Vishwanath Temple and touching the idol of Vishwanath on April 11 and subsequent days'.[37] The plaintiff contended that 'the Shastras did not permit the Antyaj (untouchables) to enter the temple and touch the deity'. On the basis of this contention, Srivastava granted an interim injunction invoking the principle of balance of convenience. 'I think the opposite party will not be put to irreparable loss or inconvenience if they are restrained from entering the temple and touching the idol of Vishwanath.'

Even four years after the formation of the Republic of India, the court appeared to have not realised that the Shastras had been superseded by the Constitution.

Against the background of these vagaries of judicial interpretation, the Nehru government finally woke up to its duty. As Article 17 of the Constitution says, 'The enforcement of any disability arising out of "Untouchability" shall be an offence punishable in accordance with law.' The enactment of such a law was needed to provide teeth to the abolition of untouchability envisaged by this clause.

The Untouchability (Offences) Act, 1955 (UOA) prescribed punishment for a range of such crimes, including those related to 'enforcing religious disabilities'. Even as it repealed the existing state laws on the subject, the UOA drew upon the essence of these enactments.

For instance, Section 3 of UOA laid down imprisonment for up to six months for whoever prevented any person 'from entering any place of public worship which is open to other persons professing the same religion or belonging to the same denomination or any section thereof'. Though the provision did not specify any community, an explanation attached to it said that 'persons professing the Hindu religion in any of its forms or developments including … the Swaminarayan Sampraday shall be deemed to be Hindus'. This inclusion was clearly with an eye to an appeal pending before the Bombay High Court. The appeal was against the trial court's decision upholding the bar on Harijans from entering Swaminarayan temples.

Yet, the Bombay government found this much awaited Central law to be deficient from the viewpoint of overcoming the 1951 trial court verdict. The dispute was no longer only about establishing that members of the Swaminarayan Sampraday were Hindus, and therefore obliged to let in Harijans. Thanks to the trial court verdict, all non-Satsangi Hindus, irrespective of caste, were now forbidden to enter the temple.

The perceived failure of the Central law to address this broader claim evoked a spirited response from the Bombay government headed by Morarji Desai, who would become the prime minister of India two decades later. Though he did not have Kher's long record of engaging with temple entry, Desai was quick to pick up the threads of the issue.

With the enactment of the Central law and the consequent repeal of its own law of 1947, Bombay would have had, in the normal course of things, no scope for coming up with a further enactment on temple entry. However, the Desai government adopted a legal fiction to get around UOA and enact a fresh law. It decided to pretend that temple entry was no more an intersection of the abolition of untouchability and the freedom of religion. Bombay made out that its latest temple-entry law was only about the freedom of religion. So, it dispensed with the term 'Harijan' that had figured in the titles of its two previous temple-entry laws, whether it was the local-option one of 1938 or the rights-based one of 1947.

Instead, the Desai government's law was titled the 'Bombay Hindu Places of Public Worship (Entry Authorization) Act, 1956'. Leveraging the expression that had been introduced by Durgabai Deshmukh in Article 25(2)(b) of the Constitution, the preamble to the 1956 law said that it had been enacted to make better provision for the throwing open of places of public worship to 'all classes and sections of Hindus'. The closest it came to acknowledging the caste dimension of temple entry was in this definitional clause: '"section" or "class" of Hindus includes any division, sub-division, caste, sub-caste, sect or denomination whatsoever of Hindus'.

Since it was specially meant to overcome the 1951 trial court verdict in the Swaminarayan dispute, Section 3 of the 1956 law authorised the throwing open of Hindu temples to all classes and sections of Hindus 'notwithstanding any custom, usage or law for the time being in force, or the decree or order of a court, or anything contained in any instrument, to the contrary'. As a result, this law overrode the permanent injunction that had been granted by the trial court in 1951 barring Harijans from entering Swaminarayan temples.

Treading a fine line, the Bombay Act of 1956 clarified that its provisions 'shall not be taken to be in derogation of any of the provisions of the Untouchability (Offences) Act, 1955'. In its penalties provision, the law added for good measure: 'Nothing in this section shall be taken to relate to offences relating to the practice of "untouchability".'[38] Such was the subterfuge that the most developed state of India had to resort to almost a decade after the country had been decolonised.

This 1956 law is still in force, as it has been successively upheld by the Bombay High Court and the Supreme Court while deciding appeals arising out of the Swaminarayan dispute. The Supreme Court verdict on the law, delivered by a five-judge constitution bench a decade later, is better known for its exposition on Hinduism than as the last word on temple entry. Since the Satsangis had tried to wriggle out of the 1956 law by disclaiming afresh any connection with Hinduism, the apex court felt compelled to define that religion, stepping beyond the conventional limits of judicial inquiry.

The result was an interpretation of Hinduism as a uniquely inclusive religion, which encompassed a diversity of gods, dogmas, rites and philosophies. Authored by Chief Justice of India P.B. Gajendragadkar, the verdict delivered on 14 January 1966 said, 'Unlike other religions in the world, the Hindu religion does not claim any one prophet; it does not worship any one God; it does not subscribe to any one dogma; it does not believe in any one philosophic concept; it does not follow any one set of religious rites or performances; in fact, it does not appear to satisfy the narrow traditional features of any religion or creed.' Drawing inspiration from philosopher Sarvepalli Radhakrishnan, who was then the president of India, Gajendragadkar famously added: 'It may broadly be described as a way of life and nothing more.'[39]

He sought to establish that all the offshoots of Hinduism remained within its fold. In his description of its glories, though, Gajendragadkar, a Deshastha Brahmin from Bombay, said nothing of the orthodox Hindu belief in caste and untouchability, and its link with the doctrine of karma and rebirth. The omission was particularly noticeable in the context of a judgment that was ultimately about the religious disabilities faced by the erstwhile untouchables.

The closest the court came to acknowledging this contradiction in the Hindu way of life was when Gajendragadkar recalled the teachings of religious reformers over the centuries, from Buddha to Vivekananda. He said, 'All of them revolted against the dominance of rituals and the power of the priestly class with which it came to be associated; and all of them proclaimed their teachings not in Sanskrit which was the monopoly of the priestly class, but in the languages spoken by the ordinary mass of people in their respective regions.'

He went on to refer to other caste-related issues in a euphemistic manner as 'elements of corruption and superstition'. Once again, he overlooked the formidable body of evidence that the Sanatanists had produced of scriptural sanction for caste in the course of the larger temple-entry struggle. Gajendragadkar was able to sidestep these issues because the opponents of the Harijans in this case were the Satsangis, not the Sanatanists. Though both groups were opposed to throwing their temples open to Harijans, there was a crucial difference in how they presented their case. Due to their disavowal of Hinduism, the Satsangis were loath to cite any Hindu scriptures, much less the alleged sanctity of any caste, to justify their exclusionary practice.

Instead, they claimed that their 'apprehension' was that, as the judgment put it, 'the proclaimed and publicised entry of the non-Satsangi Harijans would constitute a violent trespass on the religious tenets and beliefs of the Swaminarayan sect'. However, having held that the Swaminarayan followers were also Hindus, the Supreme Court concluded that 'as often happens in these matters, the said apprehension is founded on superstition, ignorance and complete misunderstanding of the true teachings of Hindu religion and of the real significance of the tenets and philosophy taught by Swaminarayan himself'.

While holding that 'the true teachings of Hindu religion' were consistent with the constitutional object of throwing open temples to Harijans, the Supreme Court neglected to take into account a related aspect: its own previous judgment on the subject in 1957. That earlier verdict too was by a five-judge constitution bench in a case where Gowda Saraswath Brahmins from Mangalore had challenged the validity of the Madras temple-entry law of 1947. The challenge was in the light of Article 26(b) of the Constitution conferring freedom on every religious denomination 'to manage its own affairs in matters of religion'.

If the Bombay section of this privileged community had taken a progressive stand on temple entry in Bombay in 1929, its Mangalore section was among the first in the Republic of India to pit the denominational rights under Article 26(b) against the protection conferred on temple-entry laws by Article 25(2)(b). The Gowda Saraswath Brahmins claimed exemption from the statutory obligation of letting Harijans enter their renowned temple of Sri Venkataramana of Moolky Petta in Mangalore on the ground that the temple had been 'founded exclusively' for their denomination.

In its verdict authored by Justice T.L. Venkatarama Aiyyar on 8 November 1957, the Supreme Court struck a balance between the two apparently conflicting rights by resorting to what is known as 'the rule of harmonious construction'. This means that, where an enactment has two provisions that cannot be reconciled with each other, they should be so interpreted that, if possible, effect could be given to both. Applying this rule, Aiyyar held that 'Art. 26(b) must be read subject to Art. 25(2)(b)'.[40] So, on the issue of temple entry, the denominational right of Gowda Saraswath Brahmins under Article 26(b) 'must yield to the overriding right' of the Harijans under Article 25(2)(b).

Unlike the 1966 decision in the Swaminarayan case, this 1957 decision made no bones about the fact that the Constitution overrode custom and scriptures. While discussing the traditional regulations of temples, the Agamas, Venkatarama Aiyyar recalled the 1914 Madras High Court precedent in which these scriptures had tied the hands of Justice Sadasiva Iyer. In the absence of any statutory provision permitting temple entry at the time, all that Sadasiva Iyer could do was to lament these 'unreasonable customs' as he followed the Privy Council ruling in the Kamudi case.

In contrast, four decades later, Venkatarama Aiyyar was able to brush aside religious pieties in recognising the pre-eminence accorded by the Constitution to temple entry. The only concession he made to the denominational right of the Gowda Saraswath Brahmins was that, 'during certain ceremonies and on special occasions', they could exclude from their temple all other persons, including Harijans. Thus, based on the two Supreme Court judgments, separated by almost a decade, the worst that Hindu denominations could do was exclude all other communities in general, but not Harijans in particular.

In spite of all this, Harijans continued to face religious disabilities, especially in temples that considered themselves more sacrosanct than others. One notable example was the Nathdwara temple of Rajasthan, which violated the law in spirit, if not in letter, as late as 1988. Though Harijans were allowed to enter the temple, they could do so only after they had subjected themselves to purification in the prescribed manner. Each was required to be sprinkled with Ganga jal (water ostensibly from the river Ganga) and wear a kanthimala (a Tulsi, or Holy Basil, necklace).[41] The latter served to mark them out as people who would have traditionally been denied entry.

In the run-up to Gandhi Jayanti in 1988, a couple of lawyers, Surya Narayan Choudhary and P.L. Mimroth, sought the help of the Rajasthan High Court so that a batch of Harijans led by social activist Swami Agnivesh could enter the Nathdwara temple without being subjected to those discriminatory rites of purification. The Congress government headed by Shiv Charan Mathur responded ambiguously. While promising to take 'every step' to stop the discrimination, the government was anxious that the proposed march should not lead to 'disturbance of the peace and tranquillity of the locality'.

On 29 September 1988, three days before the scheduled march, a bench headed by Chief Justice J.S. Verma passed a judgment ordering the temple to abandon the purification rites performed for Harijans. More importantly, it directed the state government to take 'strict steps' to ensure that there was 'no further mockery of this constitutional guarantee'.

Although his judgment on Nathdwara was unexceptionable, Verma stirred up a controversy seven years later in another case in which, as a Supreme Court judge, he invoked an older temple-entry verdict. It was alleged that he conflated the religion of Hinduism with the political ideology of Hindutva. On 11 December 1995, he was ruling on the politically fraught issue of appealing for votes on religious grounds. Verma cited the 1966 verdict in the Swaminarayan case to recall that Hinduism had been found by it to be 'a way of life and nothing more'. From that, he made this leap in logic: that Hindutva too was 'a way of life' and could therefore not be equated with 'narrow fundamentalist Hindu religious bigotry'.[42] Verma's judgment took no notice of the definition of Hindutva by its foremost ideologue, Vinayak Damodar Savarkar: that India belonged primarily to those who regarded it as both their Pitrubhoomi (Fatherland) and Punyabhoomi (Holy Land).[43]

Verma's omission of this key aspect in his analysis of Hindutva was not very different from Gajendragadkar's portrayal of Hinduism as an inclusive religion, side-stepping the contradiction presented by caste and untouchability. All in all, even though India has come a long way from the days when it openly placed custom over equality, judicial prevarication over the years has betrayed a larger failure to break out of the prison of ancient bigotry.

5

IMPUNITY FOR VIOLENCE

17

WHEN JUDGES LET OFF MASS KILLERS

Towards the end of 1968, on the holy occasion of Christmas, India recorded its first instance of mass violence targeting those it had ostensibly stopped treating as untouchables. Sometime after 10 p.m., in a remote village called Kilvenmani[1] in the Thanjavur district of the Madras state, a mob burnt alive forty-two Harijans.[2] Mostly women and children.[3]

It was a new species of caste atrocity. For the sheer scale and barbarity of the killings, this atrocity was unprecedented. It stood out even in a state that had, over two months in 1957 in the Ramnad district, experienced the earliest post-Independence caste riots.[4] Never before had there been a situation where so many Harijans were eliminated in a single mob attack and rendered so vulnerable that they could hardly offer resistance or act in self-defence. Dominant castes weaponised a deeply entrenched prejudice to perpetrate mass destruction.

Neither Gandhi nor Ambedkar nor Nehru had ever encountered such an aggravated form of caste prejudice. In this most brutal avatar of untouchability, India had crossed a new threshold of cruelty. Kilvenmani triggered a political, social and economic churn in a province that had a long history of grappling with caste. The rupture inspired literary works, feature films and documentaries.

In retrospect, the massacre was an omen that the abolition of untouchability, far from mitigating the oppression of Harijans, had turned it more violent and destructive. Kilvenmani set the template for similar atrocities across the country.

The pushback from caste supremacists grew in proportion to the assertiveness of the Harijans. Unlike the struggles against caste in the colonial period, which were largely focused on overcoming social barriers—such as intermarriage, access to public amenities or the right to enter temples—the Kilvenmani Harijans were striving for their livelihood and economic rights.

The landless agricultural labourers of Kilvenmani who, fitting the caste stereotype, were entirely Harijans and they had been waging a prolonged agitation for higher wages. The mirasdars, or hereditary landholders, in and around Kilvenmani were entirely from the dominant castes, most of them Naidus. This hierarchy was reflected in residential segregation along caste lines, a characteristic feature of rural India. Naidus and Harijans lived in neighbourhoods that were strictly demarcated from each other.

The flare-up occurred twenty-one months after the Dravida Munnetra Kazhagam (DMK), a party avowedly committed to fighting caste inequities, had stormed to power in Madras under the leadership of C.N. Annadurai. The political change symbolised, among other things, the empowerment of Shudras, who despite all their rhetoric of social justice had displayed little solidarity with the abolition of untouchability. Since they were also numerically the largest, Shudras were statistically more likely to be the oppressors than the traditional upper castes. Against this backdrop, Kilvenmani came as a bloody reminder of the deepening fault lines between Shudras and Harijans.

Since the amorphous category of Shudras included some of the dominant castes of Madras, the DMK had little elbow room to politically mobilise the Harijans in Kilvenmani. The main opposition party in the state, the Congress, was even less likely to have driven this uprising, owing to its old policy of balancing incremental caste reform with protecting upper-caste interests. So, it was the Communist Party of India (Marxist) (CPI(M)), an ally of the DMK with pockets of influence among agricultural labourers in the fertile Thanjavur district, that took up the cudgels for the Harijans.

The CPI(M) helped the workers establish the Agricultural Workers Association (AWA) in Nagapattinam, the largest town in the eastern part of the district.[5] Muthuswami, a Harijan labourer from Kilvenmani, was president of the AWA's local branch. Emboldened by their newly acquired capacity for collective bargaining, the Kilvenmani Harijans refused to work in the fields unless their demand for higher wages was conceded.

This unheard-of challenge to their hegemony prompted the mirasdars to form their own collective, the Paddy Producers' Association (PPA) in Nagapattinam taluk. The president of PPA was P. Gopalakrishna Naidu, who was from Irunjur, a village adjoining Kilvenmani. To get around the boycott by the Kilvenmani workers, PPA made arrangements for its members to import labourers from other villages.

On the morning of 25 December 1968, a group of eighteen labourers from a nearby village called Irukkai arrived to harvest a paddy field belonging to one of the mirasdars, Govindaraju Naidu. On their way home at the end of the day, the Irukkai coolies walked through the Harijan ghetto. Here, they ran into the local labourers who were resentful of the subversion of their boycott.

In the violence that ensued, the Irukkai labourers were chased out of the village and assaulted by the numerically stronger Kilvenmani workers. When some Irukkai labourers took shelter in the house of one of the mirasdars, Pakkiriswami Porayar, even he was not spared.

According to the prosecution,[6] the police got there shortly and took away the injured persons, including Porayar, to the government hospital in Nagapattinam. On their way, they stopped at the Keevalur Police Station to record the injured mirasdar's statement. It was registered as Crime No. 326 under provisions relating to rioting, Sections 147 and 148 of the IPC, and causing hurt by dangerous weapons, Sections 323 and 324 of the IPC.

A little later, at 11.15 p.m., the police received an alert about retaliatory violence by the mirasdars. A Harijan who had been brought to the police station on a bicycle with injuries from pellet shots was the source of that alert. Muniyan's complaint led to the registration of another first information report (FIR), Crime No. 327. In view of the pellet wounds that Muniyan had suffered on his face and neck, this second FIR, in addition to rioting and causing hurt by dangerous weapons, invoked the more serious offence of attempt to murder, Section 307 of the IPC. Significantly, since Muniyan complained that his house had been burnt along with those of other Harijans, the FIR also invoked Section 436 IPC relating to 'mischief by fire' with intent to destroy a building.

After sending Muniyan to the hospital, the police returned to Kilvenmani around midnight, only to find evidence of further escalation. Pakkiriswami Pillai, one of the Irukkai labourers, had been battered to death. His body was found leaning against a coconut tree in a deserted, arson-hit street. Several thatched-roof houses of the Harijans were still burning or emitting smoke.

The crime scene suggested that Pillai's killing had led to a fresh backlash against the Harijans. The police registered a third case: Crime No. 328, pertaining only to Pillai's murder.

On the counter-violence that the Harijans had suffered, the only action that the police took was to record the statements of a couple of people whose groans had led to their discovery and rescue from the burning structures.

The police somehow missed the bodies of the forty-two Harijans who had been burnt alive. It was only at the break of dawn, around 6.30 a.m., that they noticed something unusual about one of the houses near the spot where Pillai's body had been found. The house belonging to Ramayyan was still emitting dense smoke. And the coconut tree against which Pillai's body had been leaning was, in fact, right in front of Ramayyan's house.

Peering in from the outside, they detected charred human bodies in the house. But the police could not enter the smouldering structure, and sent for the fire service.

It took over three hours for a fire tender to arrive. Only after the fire was doused did the police enter Ramayyan's house. Around 10 a.m. on 26 December 1968, they extracted forty-two bodies: mostly women and children, and a few old men.

From the composition of the casualties, it would appear that those people had taken refuge in Ramayyan's house because they could not run fast enough to escape the mob chasing them. Once the house had been set on fire, why had none of them escaped? Were they not allowed to escape? And why, in that two-room house, had so many people been crammed into the smaller room of 9 ½ feet by 8 ½ feet. All the bodies were found in that room which had turned into a fiery death trap.

Though it was the lead story in the region's newspapers the next day, the headlines played down the caste angle. The *Hindu* said, '42 persons burnt alive in Thanjavur village following Kisan clashes'. Despite mentioning in its report the telling fact that all the forty-two killed were Harijans, the newspaper soft-pedalled the contribution of caste prejudice. Likewise, the headline of the *Indian Express* glossed over the caste factor: 'Kisan feud turns violent: 42 burnt alive in Thanjavur village'.

The reason that the Madras-based newspapers highlighted the term 'kisan' was because of its peculiar usage in southern India. Though kisan generally refers to landholding farmers, the term prevalent for them in the Tamil-speaking province was 'mirasdar'. Hence the conflation of labourers, who are generally referred to as 'mazdoor', with kisans in the headlines and reports on a dispute that involved an overlap between caste and class.

If Kilvenmani set the template for mob violence against Harijans, it did so also for the impunity that flowed from the errors of omission or commission on the part of the State machinery. Take the manner in which the police discriminated between the murder of the mirasdar's agent and the murder of forty-two Harijans. In addition to the FIR that had already been booked at the instance of an injured mirasdar, the police registered a fresh case in Pillai's context duly invoking the murder provision, Section 302 IPC. The police, however, did nothing of the sort upon the discovery of so many bodies of Harijans. Instead, they chose to treat it as no more than an extension of the case of mischief by fire that had already been registered at the instance of a Harijan.

From the contents of Crime No. 327, it is clear that the informant Muniyan had no idea that the more vulnerable members of his community had in their desperation taken shelter in Ramayyan's house. All he had reported was this:

> Tonight, at about 10 pm, as I was in our street, Gopalakrishna Naidu and about 20 or 30 persons came from Irunjur. They entered our street, set fire to my house and shot me with a gun. I have sustained pellet injuries on the neck and face. Other houses have also been burnt down. I do not know what happened to the inhabitants of those houses.

Based on this general reference to arson, the police decided against booking a separate case about the burnt pile of bodies. The decision was made in the presence of their highest-ranking officer in the district, the superintendent of police, who had rushed to Kilvenmani in the morning.

Although the FIR booked the previous night, Crime No. 327, had specifically referred to him, the police took more than twelve hours to arrest Gopalakrishna Naidu. Allaying the fears of the CPI(M) that the investigation would be subject to local pressures, the Annadurai government transferred the case a week later, on 1 January 1969, from the district police to the Crime Branch in Madras.

The recorded testimonies of Harijans not only corroborated Muniyan's allegation that Naidu had led the attack, they also supplied the names of twenty-two other men who had allegedly participated in the violence. When the police filed the charge sheet on 26 March 1969 against twenty-three men from the side of the mirasdars, it did invoke the murder provision in proportion to the gravity of the case.

Even so, the Harijans were no better off when the caste atrocity entered the trial stage. The same sessions judge of East Thanjavur Division at Nagapattinam, C.M. Kuppannan, tried the two murder cases from Kilvenmani—the one in which Harijan labourers had been arraigned by the Keevalur Police Station and the other in which the Crime Branch had put the mirasdars in the dock. The parallel proceedings created an unusual situation: prosecution witnesses in one case found themselves being tried as the accused in the other and vice versa.

In the case pertaining to the recovery of forty-two Harijan bodies from his house, Ramayyan, for instance, appeared as a prosecution witness. But in the related case pertaining to Pillai's murder, he appeared in the same court at roughly the same time as one of the twenty-two accused Harijans. Likewise, the leaders of the two rival organisations were implicated in each of the two trials. While the president of AWA's Kilvenmani branch, Muthuswami, was tried for Pillai's murder, PPA President Gopalakrishna Naidu was the main accused for the massacre of Harijans.

Underscoring the reversal of roles in the two cases, the sessions judge delivered judgments for both on the same day, 30 November 1970. In the Pillai murder case, he convicted eight Harijan labourers, including one Gopal for the main charge of murder and Ramayyan on lesser charges. Shockingly, for the massacre of the forty-two Harijans in Ramayyan's house, Kuppannan convicted none of the twenty-three accused, including Gopalakrishna Naidu, on the charge of murder. The convictions that were handed down against eight of the accused persons were all on lesser offences. Thus, in the two Kilvenmani verdicts that the trial court delivered, the number of convicted persons turned out to be the same even as the charges and penalties were strikingly different.

While they were exonerated on the main charge of murder, the trial court found Naidu and seven others guilty of attempt to murder in relation to firing a gun at Muniyan and other injured survivors. Three of the eight convicted persons, including Naidu, got the maximum sentence of ten years. This was not only for being 'armed with guns' but also because there was 'ample evidence' showing that, on account of their firing, 'a number of victims received pellet injuries'. Holding that there could be 'no doubt whatsoever that they used the guns for unlawful purposes', Kuppannan said that it was 'reasonable to infer that their intention was to commit murder'.

At the same time, in relation to the mass killing, the trial court found that the evidence had not been 'substantiated beyond reasonable doubt'. Kuppannan said, 'I am not inclined to accept the prosecution case that the common object of the unlawful assembly would have been to murder those 42 persons by setting fire to the house of PW 11 [Ramayyan].'

He dismissed the likelihood that the murder of the forty-two Harijans was part of the common object despite his finding that the tragedy was the outcome of 'the strained feelings between the Paddy Producers Association and the Left Communist Kisans[7] and the murder of Pakkiriswamy Pillai'. He was unconvinced that the arsonists were even aware that some Harijans had taken shelter in that house. This was because Kuppannan found it 'unsafe to accept the evidence on the side of the prosecution that the accused saw the persons entering into that house'.

As far as he was concerned, the question of prior knowledge hinged on determining whether the front door of Ramayyan's house had been open at the time of ignition. Though the prosecution contended that the front door had been open, this was how Kuppannan deconstructed the claim. 'If it was the common object of the unlawful assembly to murder those persons by setting fire to that house, one would normally expect the accused to shut the door either before setting fire to the house or after it so that the occupants may perish. There is no scintilla of evidence to that effect.'

The moment Ramayyan's house had been set on fire, 'the inmates should have rushed out, even at the risk of attack from outside'. From the absence of such a reaction, Kuppannan inferred that the door, as claimed by the defence, had already been shut. In the narrative of the defence, the Harijans of Kilvenmani had, anticipating retaliation to Pillai's murder and injuries to others, 'evacuated their houses, removed all their possession, gathered in front of PW 11's house and got ready to fight after possibly secreting the weaker sex, infirm and children into the house of PW 11 to be guarded against attack'.

Based on this, Kuppannan saw 'some force' in the defence's contention that the presence of those forty-two Harijans in

Ramayyan's house could 'neither have been anticipated nor known to the accused'. While holding that there was 'no acceptable evidence to show that any particular accused set fire to the house', he said that 'it cannot be ruled out that the house was set fire to by a member of the unlawful assembly'.

Further, the sessions judge referred to the 'mystery' of how so many had squeezed into 'such a small room', whereby 'all the 42 charred bodies were found one over the other in pell-mell in that room'. Although 'a pathetic and unimaginable occurrence had taken place', it was 'quite probable and imaginable that this house was also set fire to as the rest of the houses without any knowledge of its occupants'.

Accordingly, in relation to the forty-two people who had succumbed, Kuppannan convicted Naidu and seven others only on charges excluding homicide: using unlicensed weapons (Section 27 of the Arms Act), causing grievous hurt (Section 326 IPC) and mischief by fire (Section 436 IPC) and for being part of an unlawful assembly in prosecution of a common object (Section 149 IPC).

Sure enough, Naidu and the others appealed to the Madras High Court against the conviction. The government, meanwhile, appealed against, among other things, the acquittal of the mirasdars and their men of the charge of murder. When a bench of the High Court, comprising Justice K. Venkataraman and Justice S. Maharajan, delivered a common order on 6 April 1973, it upheld the mirasdars' appeal and rejected the government's appeal.

Thus, the High Court exonerated even the eight who had been convicted by the trial court on charges other than murder. If the trial court believed that the massacre of Harijans was an unintended consequence of the arson that had been committed by the mirasdars and their accomplices, the High Court held that the landholders were not guilty of even those lesser offences.

In contrast, in the Pillai murder case, another bench of the High Court had dismissed the appeal the previous year of the eight convicted Harijans and confirmed the sentences that were standing against them.

The judgment authored by Justice Maharajan steered clear of what was arguably the most important aspect of the caste atrocity. It was silent about the grounds on which the trial court had ruled that 'killing those innocent persons did not form part of the common object of the riotous crowd'. While listing out all the provisions under which each of the accused persons had either been convicted or acquitted by the Sessions Judge, the Madras High Court in fact skipped the acquittals that had been made under Section 302 IPC. Such was the level of opacity.

Without discussing any of the evidence before it, the High Court simply upheld the trial court's conclusion on the murder charge. 'It is some consolation to learn,' Justice Maharajan wrote, 'that those who set fire to PW 11's house had no knowledge that 42 persons were inside the house and had no intention to burn them to death.' Yet, he disclosed no basis for his consolation—or the reasons for his agreement with the trial court—that the arsonists had neither any knowledge that there were any people hiding in Ramayyan's house nor any intention to kill them. The withholding of this crucial information made it easier for Maharajan to absolve the mirasdars and their men of the lesser charges as well.

In another dubious aspect of his judgment, Maharajan used the location of Pillai's corpse to reject the testimonies of the Harijans. 'Every one of the prosecution witnesses who claims to have seen the occurrences and the houses including Ramayyan's being set on fire,' he said, 'disowns all knowledge of the corpse of Irukkari Pakkiriswami Pillai lying near Ramayyan's house.' He found their claim that they had not seen Pillai's body to be 'most unnatural', besides betraying 'a guilty conscience'. His reason: 'Being accused in the other case, they were naturally interested in distorting the occurrence in this case.'

His reasoning was that, as the Harijan labourers from Kilvenmani had been found to be evasive about the murder of a labourer from outside their village, they could hardly be trusted to be truthful about the burning alive of their own kith and kin. But even as he attached so much significance to the location of Pillai's corpse,

Maharajan glossed over the anomaly of those forty-two ill-fated Harijans hiding in a house that was right next to it. His judgment offered no explanation for—much less raised any question about—why Pillai's battered body and the charred remains of forty-two Harijans were found so close to each other.

The High Court's complicity in the cover-up went unnoticed. What did become a subject of controversy was the court's classist observations against the arraignment of the mirasdars. Justice Maharajan wrote that there was 'something astonishing about the fact that all the 23 accused implicated in this case should be Mirasdars'. He overlooked the fact, brought out by the trial court judgment, that at least seven of the twenty-three were mirasdars only in name. In their depositions during the trial, seven of the accused had disclosed that, as their landholdings were too small to be viable, they also worked as manual labourers in the fields of others. Cherry-picking the evidence, Maharajan said, 'Most of them are rich men owning vast extents of land.' For good measure, he added that Gopalakrishna Naidu even 'owns a car'.

Maharajan also brushed aside the prosecution's narrative that Naidu had walked with the mob from Irunjur, even though it was, by his own admission in the judgment, 'just one furlong off the scene'. He said, 'However much the Mirasdars might have been anxious to wreak vengeance upon the Left Communist Kisans, it is difficult to believe that they themselves walked bodily to the scene and set fire to houses unaided by any of their servants.'

In deference to their social and economic status, Maharajan minimised their role, 'Rich men, who have vast vested interests, are more likely to play for safety than desperate and hungry labourers. One would expect the Mirasdars to have kept themselves in the background and sent their hired henchmen to commit the several offences, which, according to the prosecution, the Mirasdars personally committed by coming directly to the scene.'

That the High Court could make such derisive comments about the underclass was a measure of the widening gulf between rhetoric and reality in Indian democracy a quarter century after

Independence. The judgment was not considered worthy of being published in law journals. So, the cavalier manner in which the High Court had exonerated all the accused in the Kilvenmani case remained unknown.

The only aspect that emerged in the public domain about a month later was Maharajan's incredulous response to the allegations against 'rich men'. The disclosure was made by CPI(M) activist Mythili Sivaraman, who wrote an article in the *Economic and Political Weekly* titled 'Gentlemen Killers of Kilvenmani'.[8] In what became the most widely quoted article on the subject, Sivaraman's sarcastic summation of the High Court's wholesale acquittals was, 'In brief, gentlemen farmers will also be gentlemen killers.'

This belated disclosure induced the *Times of India,* a mainstream daily and a long-time chronicler of caste battles, to analyse the judgment two months after its delivery. In an editorial headlined 'Burning Shame', the newspaper called it 'curious' that the Madras High Court had let off all the accused saying 'rich landlords could not be expected to commit such crimes personally'.[9]

Putting the judgment in perspective, it said: 'Whether the police failed to arrest all the culprits, or the prosecution bungled, deliberately or otherwise, in marshalling the evidence or the court took too technical a view, the fact remains that 42 innocent Harijans were burnt to death and no one was punished.'

Such impunity for the Kilvenmani atrocity in the Madras High Court coincided with—and was contemporaneously linked with—the supersession of judges in the Supreme Court, which became emblematic of the erosion of institutions under the reign of Prime Minister Indira Gandhi. In a question that proved to be prescient, the *Times* asked, 'Why shouldn't crime against the Harijans proliferate in such circumstances?' It added, 'The crowning irony is that there has hardly been any protest against all this, not even from those who have been shouting hoarse against recent supersessions in the Supreme Court or from those Harijan leaders who are entrenched in positions of power in the ruling party.'

Thus, the media commentary and scholarly analysis on

Kilvenmani, whatever little there was of it, was mainly based on the pro-rich bias in the judgment. Based on the discovery of all the judgments that were passed in the Kilvenmani case, this book has captured the full story of the repeated miscarriage of justice from the trial court to the Supreme Court.

So abnormal was the situation that even the obvious remedy of appealing to the Supreme Court did not follow as a matter of course. The Tamil Nadu government under M. Karunanidhi dithered. Though the judgment ought to have been appealed within three months, the DMK government sat on it for over two years.

It took an unforeseen development, the imposition of Emergency in the middle of 1975, for Karunanidhi to dust off the Kilvenmani case. As a leading non-Congress chief minister who had set his face against the Emergency diktats of the Indira Gandhi government, Karunanidhi's position turned precarious. The DMK thus became politically more dependent on its old ally, the CPI(M).

Thanks partly to pressure from the left, Karunanidhi had already introduced a measure of agricultural reforms in the immediate aftermath of the Kilvenmani atrocity. He had, at the time, just taken over as chief minister of the newly renamed state of Tamil Nadu following Annadurai's death on 3 February 1969. The reforms included the raising of agricultural wages and the passage of the Tamil Nadu Agricultural Labourer Fair Wages Act, 1969.

A little before the dismissal of his government in January 1976, Karunanidhi had overseen the reopening of the Kilvenmani case. The state filed its much-delayed appeal towards the end of 1975. While the Supreme Court condoned the delay, it showed little anxiety to hear the appeal on a priority basis.

About five years later, in 1980, while the case was still waiting to be heard by the Supreme Court, the cumulative delay of twelve years led to a grave act of vigilantism. Gopalakrishna Naidu, who had long been on bail, was murdered. The main accused for this murder turned out to be a left extremist. In any event, Naidu's murder ought to have been a wake-up call for the judiciary.

Yet, it took another ten years for the Supreme Court to take up the Tamil Nadu government's appeal, by which time three more of the accused had died, mercifully of natural causes. On 31 October 1990, the matter came up before a bench comprising Justice S. Ranganathan, a Brahmin from Tamil Nadu, and Justice K. Ramaswamy, who was only the third Harijan ever to have been elevated to the Supreme Court.[10]

Though known for his commitment to social justice from his days in Andhra Pradesh, Ramaswamy's presence on the Supreme Court bench proved to be of little avail in the Kilvenmani case. It took just three hours spread over two days for the Supreme Court to dismiss the state's appeal and reaffirm the High Court's acquittal of all the accused.

The minutes of the proceedings, as recorded by the Supreme Court registry, are telling. On the first day, the junior counsel for the state, V. Krishnamurthy, argued for forty-five minutes. The next day, on 1 November 1990, senior counsel for the state, U.R. Lalit, argued for fifteen minutes. And then, once the counsel for the accused, Raj Choudhary, had made his presentation over two hours, the court concluded the hearing and passed the order the same day.

Little wonder then that, when the final judicial order on independent India's first massacre of untouchables came twenty-two years later, it turned out to be no longer than four pages. But at least on the central issue of the murder charge, the Supreme Court judgment was a wee bit more transparent. Unlike the High Court's ninety-five-page judgment, it acknowledged that the accused had been arraigned for murder in the trial court for the burning alive of Harijans.

Even if it was only a passing reference, the Supreme Court order did mention this elementary fact. It quoted Lalit's submission on behalf of Tamil Nadu that 'the trial court's conclusions ought to have been logically carried to the extent of convicting all the accused before the court under Section 302'. Having recorded it, the least that the Supreme Court owed to the families of the forty-two murdered Harijans was an explanation for rejecting the contention that the government had made on their behalf.

But just as the High Court had done earlier, the Supreme Court steered clear of the evidence on which the trial court had exonerated the accused on the charge of murder. The Supreme Court washed its hands of the matter, saying that the two courts below had given 'concurrent findings' for acquitting the accused of the murder charge.

As for the High Court's decision to absolve the accused of even the lesser charges, all that the Supreme Court recorded was that there were 'no grounds to interfere' with it. Although it skirted the evidence concerning the lesser charges too, the Supreme Court pretended to have dealt with it in some measure. 'We do not deal with the evidence *at great length* [emphasis added] because, ultimately, it is a conclusion of fact that is in issue.' Feigning due process, it held, 'After examining the facts carefully, we find it difficult to agree that the acquittal order passed by the High Court was not warranted by the facts on record.'

The Supreme Court was signalling that its claims about the facts on record should be taken at face value, although it did not disclose, let alone discuss, any of the details. Rather than claiming that they 'do not deal with the evidence at great length', the Supreme Court judges might as well have admitted that they had not dealt with it at all. After all, in their four-page order, they devoted only one paragraph to their own analysis. And none of the facts that were said to have been carefully examined were even mentioned in it.

The Supreme Court's opacity in the Kilvenmani case was all the more noticeable for its timing. This category of crime—the massacre of Dalits—had by the 1990s grown to serious proportions in several parts of the country. And in the light of that trend, the Rajiv Gandhi government had just the previous year pushed through a stringent law to deal with crimes targeting Dalits and Adivasis.

❖

One systemic reform brought about by the Scheduled Castes and Scheduled Tribes (Prevention of Atrocities) Act 1989, or PoA Act, was the option of a special court empowered to hear expeditiously cases coming under that law. However, as demonstrated by the very first case in which this provision had been invoked, the setting up of a special court made little difference to the pace of the proceedings.

The case was about the hacking to death of eight Dalits on 6 April 1991 in a village called Tsundur[11] in the fertile Guntur district of Andhra Pradesh. The members of the mob were mainly from the landed caste of Reddys, and the chief minister of the state was also from that community, N. Janardhana Reddy. Though the trial was due to begin in the special court in 1993, it was held up for over eleven years, thanks to a range of dilatory tactics adopted by the influential accused persons.

Even the appointment of the special court and its location in the Dalit part of Tsundur, for instance, became a subject of litigation before the Andhra Pradesh High Court. Thereafter, the appointment of a Dalit judge to hold the trial was challenged on the ground of bias. The controversy led to the transfer of that judge.

When the special court at last commenced trial on 17 November 2004, the accused were still not done. This time, they contended that since half of the deceased had Christian names, the trial could not be held under the PoA Act, and therefore, the special court was also invalid. Their argument was that, as untouchability was peculiar to Hinduism, those who converted out of that religion would be rid of the stigma. This matter too went to the High Court.

The High Court, however, directed the special court to consider this objection as a preliminary issue in the trial. After elaborate arguments, the special court ruled that the deceased and injured did qualify as Scheduled Castes. Only then did it finally get around to conducting the trial. After an inordinate delay that defeated the object of the PoA Act, the trial concluded on 31 July 2007.

Out of the 219 men who had been arraigned for being part of the marauding mob, thirty-three had died by then. Of the remaining accused, the special court convicted fifty-six, awarding life sentences to twenty-one of them. Both the convicted persons as well as the government appealed against the judgment.

It took another seven years for the appeals to come up for hearing. A two-judge bench of the Andhra Pradesh High Court, headed by Justice L. Narasimha Reddy, started hearing the appeals on 21 March 2014. Before long, the case took an ugly turn as the question of impartiality was raised once again. But this time it was by one of the victims, Jaladi Moses, who filed an affidavit saying he had lost faith in the bench 'having regard to the way the proceedings were going on'.

Much to the court's embarrassment, the senior special public prosecutor, Bojja Tharakam, too filed a similar affidavit. This prompted the bench to issue contempt notices not only to Moses but also to Tharakam, a reputed human rights advocate from the Dalit community. Eventually, the High Court dropped its contempt proceedings even though Tharakam had refused to withdraw his affidavit.

When the High Court delivered its judgment on Tsundur on 22 April 2014,[12] it ended up going the way of Kilvenmani. Authored by Justice Reddy, the verdict acquitted all fifty-six convicted by the trial court. While the Madras High Court was opaque in the Kilvenmani case, the Andhra Pradesh High Court gave an array of reasons for exonerating everyone who had been found guilty of murder in the Tsundur case.

Justice Reddy began with acknowledging the special significance of the Tsundur episode: 'The case became sensational, obviously because a large number of Dalits were put to death. The agitation on caste lines has virtually shaken the State.' The judgment even mentioned an unusual caution that Justice Reddy had observed on account of his own caste background. 'Since many of the accused and the appellants herein are from Reddy Community, we verified from the learned Special Public Prosecutors, before the commencement of arguments, as to whether they have any objection for this Bench to hear the appeals. Both of them stated that they have absolutely no objection, and only then, the hearing was commenced.'

Toward the end of his seventy-two-page judgment, Reddy summed up his reasons for rejecting the murder charge. 'The net result is that the prosecution failed to prove the exact time of the death of the deceased and place of occurrence and the identity of the persons who attacked them.' And so, Dalits were denied justice by one arm of the State machinery, the judiciary, which made no allowance for the likely influence of caste on the other arm, the police.

Though witnesses for the massacred Dalits had been forced to depose in the trial after a gap of thirteen years, the High Court was unsparing of the slightest inconsistencies in their testimonies. Its exacting approach flew in the face of a plethora of precedents that required courts to be more pragmatic in their appreciation of evidence in cases of mass violence.

Recognising that 'precious lives of eight innocent persons hailing from Dalit community were lost, and their families were virtually ruined', the High Court issued an unusual direction to contain the repercussions of its own decision. Clamping down on the fundamental right to free speech and expression, the High Court ordered the police to 'ensure' that there were 'no celebrations or protests' in Tsundur and its vicinity 'at least for a period of three months' from the judgment day.

In the nine years that have elapsed since this controversial judgment, a bunch of appeals filed against it by the Andhra Pradesh government and Dalit groups have been pending in the Supreme Court. The paperwork on Tsundur is yet to be squared up, over thirty years after the massacre.

❖

Separated from Kilvenmani by almost three decades, Bathani Tola in the Bhojpur district of Bihar bore an uncanny resemblance to that old horror. Once again, several women and children who were hiding in one house bore the brunt of a mob attack. All but one of the twenty persons killed in the house of Marwari Choudhary on 11 July 1996 were women and children. Among the dead was a three-month-old infant.

Though the deceased at Bathani Tola included six members of a Muslim family, it proved to be the first of a series of mass killings targeting Dalits in the Bihar of the nineties by an upper-caste outfit called the Ranvir Sena. Banned the previous year, this was a private army of Bhumihars, a land-owning caste claiming to belong to the Brahmin varna.

Unlike in Kilvenmani, this massacre was not about the emerging conflicts between Shudras and Dalits, but about maintaining upper-caste hegemony. Bathani Tola had its share of parallels with Kilvenmani in terms of context too. To begin with, it happened on the watch of another leader closely associated with a social-justice platform, Lalu Prasad Yadav, who was in his second term as chief minister of Bihar.

In another parallel with the 1968 episode, the violence at Bathani Tola was a reprisal for the left-wing mobilisation of landless labourers. The left-wing party here was the Communist Party of India (Marxist-Leninist) Liberation, which unlike most other Marxist-Leninist, or ML, groups was a participant in electoral politics. While the deaths in Kilvenmani were caused by arson, those killed in Bathani Tola were either gunned down or hacked to death.

If the Tsundur trial had taken eleven years just to commence, the Bathani Tola trial started earlier but dragged on for over a decade. Though the trial court at Ara had framed the charges on 24 March 2000, it pronounced its judgment only on 5 May 2010. And as far as justice for the victims was concerned, the trajectory of the Bathani Tola case followed the patterns of Kilvenmani and Tsundur.

After the trial court at Ara had convicted twenty-three Ranvir Sena members, the Patna High Court acquitted all of them on 16 April 2012.[13] The twenty-three acquitted by the High Court included even the three who had been sentenced to death by the trial court.

The stark contrast between the two verdicts in the case was due to the High Court's rejection of the testimonies of all the prosecution witnesses. This list included Radhika Devi who, as one of the women hiding in Choudhary's house, had received a gunshot injury to her chest and regained consciousness only the next day. In rejecting

Radhika Devi's testimony, the High Court ignored the settled law which deemed that a witness injured in such an incident came with a 'built-in guarantee' of her presence at the crime scene and was 'unlikely to spare' her actual assailants in order to frame others.[14]

The prosecution witnesses that the High Court refused to believe also included police officials. It relied, however, on one police official who had been produced as a defence witness because of his proximity to the crime scene. In doing so, it ignored the evidence on record that neither the sight of the belligerent mob nor the sound of the firing triggered any intervention from the three police pickets located within the radius of a kilometre or so.

Instead of holding those police pickets accountable for their negligence, the High Court approvingly quoted the testimony of Sub-inspector Raghuraj Tiwary, who was in charge of the picket in Barki Kharaon, the very village from where the mob was found to have originated. Echoing the line of the accused persons, Tiwary claimed that the firing had been from both sides. According to him, 'the cross firing continued about 15-20 minutes and hundreds of rounds were fired by both sides'.

Even as it admitted that Tiwary had been suspended in the wake of the incident, the High Court lent credence to the false equivalence made by him between the residents of Bathani Tola and the aggressors from Barki Kharaon. The court did not even attempt to reconcile Tiwary's allegation of cross-firing with the admitted evidence that women and children were the main casualties and that their bodies were all found inside one house.

As Tiwary had sent in his version before any of the victims could give theirs, the High Court ruled that the police should have immediately lodged an FIR based on the sub-inspector's allegation of cross-firing. It set much store by the fact that the prosecution had been 'unable to explain why the first written statement of the incident' sent by Tiwary 'was not registered as an FIR and not even brought on record', and instead he had been 'immediately suspended'.

On the other hand, the High Court made light of the actual FIR that had been registered on the information of a victim who had lost his wife in the carnage. Kishun Choudhary testified that, after fleeing from the mob, he had helplessly watched the violence unfold from the safety of a ditch. Though 'he was present in the village in hiding till police arrived', the High Court said that, in his deposition during the trial twelve years later, Kishun Choudhary had given 'a fanciful explanation without any corroboration' and was therefore found to be 'untrustworthy'.

The High Court had no qualms about dismissing the testimonies of the prosecution witnesses who had all been injured or/and had lost family members in the massacre. It was a travesty—all the more glaring in regard to the male prosecution witnesses. Just the fact that they had survived the mob attack by fleeing the settlement became a cause for doubting their account of the violence and the identity of the miscreants.

As the verdict authored by Justice Navaniti Prasad Singh put it, 'People who were intent to liquidate everybody, naturally would have seen that there were no male members, they would have searched for male members who were all hiding in very close proximity to the village itself.' Holding that it was 'unnatural' for them to have been hiding in the vicinity, the High Court said that 'the identifications made by the prosecution witnesses [were] not worthy of reliance for the purposes of this extreme punishment of either death or life imprisonment'.

In other words, the prosecution witnesses were disbelieved for no reason other than the fact that they were alive or without injuries. The Bihar government's appeal against the High Court verdict in the Bathani Tola case is still pending in the Supreme Court.

❖

On 1 December 1997, about a year after Bathani Tola, the Ranvir Sena pulled off what was seen as an even bigger 'spectacle'. The venue was a remote village called Lakshmanpur Bathe, then in Jehanabad district and now in Arwal district. The death toll was fifty-eight, by far the highest for any single caste atrocity. President K.R. Narayanan, himself a Dalit, termed the killings a 'national shame'. It was indeed a shameful depth to which India had sunk in the five decades since Independence.

Unlike in Bathani Tola, the mob attack at Lakshmanpur Bathe took place in the dark at 10.30 p.m., which was around the same time as the Kilvenmani arson three decades earlier. The police arrived only the next morning around 8 a.m. They registered a case at the instance of Binod Paswan, who had had a narrow escape as seven members of his family were being shot dead. Thanks to the light of the battery torches they had carried, Paswan could name twenty-six members of the mob who were from either Lakshmanpur Bathe or the neighbouring village, Kamta.

When the police went to arrest them, many of the identified miscreants were found to be absconding. In a breakthrough for the investigation, the first arrest, which took place about forty hours after the incident, was accompanied by the recovery of a double-barrelled gun. About a week later, following more arrests and recoveries, the Bihar government, which Lalu Yadav's wife Rabri Devi had taken over four months earlier, transferred the Lakshmanpur Bathe case from the local police station to the Criminal Investigation Department (CID) in Patna.

The government also appointed a commission headed by former High Court judge Amir Das on 27 December 1997 to inquire into 'the possible nexus of certain political parties and workers with the activities of the banned Ranvir Sena, responsible for the massacre [that]occurred at Lakshmanpur Bathe'.

Insofar as the criminal proceedings were concerned, the charge sheets filed by the police in due course named fifty persons. After the case had been committed to the Sessions Court in Jehanabad in January 1999, the Patna High Court, driven by well-founded apprehensions of local pressures, transferred the trial to Patna nine months later.

But the Patna trial court failed to take the preliminary step of framing charges even nine years later, and so the High Court transferred the case yet again, this time to a particular judge: Vijai Prakash Mishra, Patna's first additional sessions judge. Mishra, who had been given the case on 29 November 2008, began recording the evidence of witnesses on a daily basis from 2 January 2009 onwards. He delivered his verdict on 7 April 2010, more than twelve years after the massacre.

The trial court convicted the twenty-six men named by Binod Paswan in his FIR.[15] And in a first for any kind of mass crime, including communal violence, Mishra sentenced to death as many as sixteen of them. This meant that the sessions judge was convinced that the culpability of those sixteen was not only proved 'beyond reasonable doubt' but grave enough to fall within the exceptional category of the 'rarest of rare' cases.

Even so, three and half years later, on 9 October 2013, the Patna High Court acquitted all twenty-six convicted persons, including the sixteen who had been awarded the death sentence.[16] This startling reversal came only eighteen months after the Bathani Tola precedent had been set by the same High Court.

Among the reasons for disbelieving the prosecution in the Lakshmanpur Bathe case was once again the sweeping assumption that the High Court had made in its Bathani Tola verdict: that eyewitnesses could not have survived the massacre had they really seen any of those miscreants. The High Court disbelieved even Binod Paswan's testimony.

Though the mob had broken into his house and killed seven of his family members, including his mother, the High Court set aside the testimony of twenty-year-old Binod Paswan because it was unconvinced about the hiding place from which he had claimed to have spotted nine of the accused persons. Similarly, it was unconvinced by his claim that he had subsequently witnessed another seventeen accused persons from a neighbour's rooftop in that darkness. The High Court verdict, written by Justice V.N. Sinha, said that it was 'unlikely that (the) informant would leave the place where he concealed himself (at) the risk of being seen by the assailants who were freely moving in the village'.

This kind of specious reasoning marked the acquittal of all twenty-six convicted by the trial court. About two years later, two of those acquitted persons were caught in an undercover media report confessing—or rather bragging—that they had very much participated in the Lakshmanpur Bathe massacre.[17] While Pramod Singh had been awarded the death penalty by the trial court, Chandeshwar Singh had been given a life sentence. In their separate admissions to *Cobrapost*, published on 16 August 2015, both Ranvir Sena men gave detailed accounts before a hidden camera of their direct complicity in the killings.

The High Court's zeal in acquitting the accused in the Lakshmanpur Bathe case was in contrast to the painstaking manner in which successive courts strove to uphold the terror charges that had been brought against members of an underground left outfit, Maoist Communist Centre, for the 1992 slaughter of thirty-five Bhumihars in Bara village in the Gaya district.[18] Both Bara and Lakshmanpur Bathe were part of a long chain of retaliatory killings on behalf of the landed and landless classes across Bihar.

On 15 April 2002, the Supreme Court confirmed the death sentence awarded to four persons in the Bara massacre who had been tried under the draconian Terrorist and Disruptive Activities (Prevention) Act (TADA). These killers of upper-caste people were deemed to be deserving of the death penalty even though the informant in that case had not even been produced during the trial as a prosecution witness. About fifteen years later, the death sentence was commuted to life as President Pranab Mukherjee accepted the mercy petitions of the four convicted Dalits in view of the prolonged delay in the execution of their punishment.

In the Lakshmanpur Bathe case, on the other hand, the Bihar government's appeal to the Supreme Court against the twenty-six acquittals has been pending since November 2013. As for the Amir Das Commission, the coalition government of Janata Dal (United) and Bharatiya Janata Party (BJP), headed by Nitish Kumar, wound it up prematurely on 8 April 2006, about four months after coming to power.

The termination sparked off a controversy because a host of political leaders had by then deposed before the Amir Das Commission, either in person or through their advocates, on their alleged nexus with Ranvir Sena. The list included BJP leaders Murli Manohar Joshi, C.P. Thakur and Sushil Kumar Modi, as also leaders from the Rashtriya Janata Dal, Shivanand Tiwari and Akhilesh Prasad Singh.

❖

After a string of massacres in which the Patna High Court reversed the convictions that had been awarded by the trial court, there came a case in which the illusion of justice for Dalits was shattered right in the court of first instance. Emboldened perhaps by the High Court's example, the trial court itself acquitted the entire lot of accused persons associated with the Ranvir Sena.

The massacre took place on the eve of the fiftieth Republic Day, 25 January 1999, in a Dalit hamlet called Shankarbigha in the then undivided Jehanabad district. At around 8.30 p.m., a mob attacked the hamlet, killing twenty-three men, women and children. The police registered an FIR naming twenty-four persons on the basis of information provided by a survivor, Pragash Rajvanshi, who had lost six members of his family, including his wife.

About two years later, on 18 December 2000, he testified in Patna before the Justice Amir Das Commission. Rajvanshi said that he could easily recognise the accused and name them before the police for two reasons: their faces were lit by the moon and their torches, and the attackers were mostly from a neighbouring Bhumihar village. They were familiar with each other because the residents of Shankarbigha routinely worked as labourers in the fields owned by the Bhumihars.

But the minute details provided by Rajvanshi were not so relevant to the commission whose remit was to probe the wider issue of Ranvir Sena's political connections. His evidence could have been pivotal to the trial of the persons accused of participating in the Shankarbigha massacre. Rajvanshi would get his turn to depose at the trial only fourteen years later, when a fast-track court was finally set up. By then, the delay had taken its toll.

On 12 September 2014, when he was called by the prosecution to testify before the trial court in Jehanabad, Rajvanshi turned hostile. This was the outcome of a pattern of intimidating or wearing down witnesses in the case—a method more blatant than in earlier instances. Unlike their counterparts in Bathani Tola and Lakshmanpur Bathe, the victims in Shankarbigha had little political support, even from the left-wing parties.

All the prosecution witnesses in the case, who were as many as fifty, were declared hostile in the trial court. They denied having identified any of the culprits during the investigation. Rajvanshi even said that he was not present in Shankarbigha at the time of the massacre and that the police had taken his thumb impression on the FIR without reading out its contents to him.

Unfazed, the prosecution quietly went through the motions of producing its witnesses and getting them declared hostile, one by one. It refrained from raising any concern in court about all its witnesses turning hostile, let alone the likelihood that they were being intimidated by the upper-caste accused and the Ranvir Sena network.

At no point during the time that evidence was being recorded in the trial court over four months, from 23 July to 22 November 2014, did Special Public Prosecutor Arvind Kumar ask the judge to provide protection for his witnesses. Only on 14 November did Kumar, himself a Dalit, write to the district magistrate of Arwal[19] about the need for protecting the remaining witnesses. By this time, most of them had already disowned their testimonies. The district magistrate, in turn, forwarded Kumar's letter to the superintendent of police on 9 January 2015, by which time the recording of evidence had long ended and the trial court was just four days away from delivering its verdict.

Thus, the witnesses in the Shankarbigha case were denied protection despite precedents in Bihar and elsewhere. In the

Lakshmanpur Bathe case, for instance, the trial had been transferred to Patna in a bid to insulate the witnesses from intimidation. More famously, in the 2002 Naroda Patiya massacre, a post-Godhra violence case from Gujarat, the Supreme Court ordered the protection of a Central paramilitary force for all prosecution witnesses, thereby emboldening them to depose against a minister, Maya Kodnani.

No such safeguards were applied to Shankarbigha, although at the time that evidence was being recorded, the chief minister of Bihar was a Dalit: Jitan Ram Manjhi. The damage from that systemic failure was what resulted in the contrasting testimonies given by Rajvanshi before the Amir Das Commission in 2000 and the trial court in 2014.

When this author contacted him in 2015 on behalf of the *Times of India*, Rajvanshi admitted to turning hostile in the trial court because of intimidation by culprits living in the vicinity of his village. 'We deposed fearlessly before the Amir Das Commission because the police had then been deployed to make us feel secure, to escort us to Patna and even give us food,' Rajvanshi said. 'But when it came to the trial in Jehanabad, none of the authorities bothered to dispel the feeling that we were entirely at the mercy of the accused persons and their influential backers.'[20]

The judgment was, needless to say, a foregone conclusion. On 13 January 2015, the trial judge, Raghawendra Kumar Singh, acquitted all twenty-four accused, saying tersely that 'the evidence of the prosecution has fallen short'. Though other Ranvir Sena-related massacres had also resulted in acquittals of all the accused, this was the first instance of all the prosecution witnesses turning hostile, resulting in the collapse of the case at the trial stage itself.

A major reason for this was the trial judge's resolve to maintain his neutrality, despite the clear danger of miscarriage of justice. Indeed, his conception of duty was contrary to the law laid down by the Supreme Court in 1981: 'If a criminal court is to be an effective instrument in dispensing justice, the presiding judge must cease to be a spectator and a mere recording machine. He must become a participant in the trial by evincing intelligent active interest *by putting questions to witnesses in order to ascertain the truth* [emphasis added].'[21] The Supreme Court had invoked this principle in the 2002 Best Bakery massacre, another case of post-Godhra violence, to order a retrial in 2004 in view of the evidence that had emerged concerning the intimidation of witnesses.

However, the trial judge dealing with the Shankarbigha massacre evidently believed that it was no part of his duty to check if any extraneous factors had driven witness after witness to make a U-turn. In his fourteen-page verdict, he showed little curiosity about why all fifty prosecution witnesses—without exception—had turned hostile.

Later, another aspect of the cavalier handling of the Shankarbigha case came to light. One of the acquitted persons, Sheodeni Sharma, filed an application before the Jehanabad court in March 2015 seeking the release of a licensed gun that had been seized from him during investigations into the massacre. Sharma's plea betrayed the fact that, although the police had recovered empty cartridges from the scene of the crime, a fact that is recorded in the judgment, it had failed to place on record any ballistic report.

Had any of those cartridges matched the bore of Sharma's rifle, the trial court could not have so easily acquitted him, even in the face of hostile witnesses. The conflicting forensic evidence might have forced the trial court to concede, if nothing else, the possibility of the intimidation of witnesses.

Though the Constitution had abolished untouchability, the caste system has had the last laugh in a slew of cases where it not only devoured the lives of untouchables but also denied them posthumous justice. It did this through an insidious combination of delay, obfuscation and intimidation, in a sense replacing the intricacies of the scriptures with those of the rule of law.

18

THE DENIAL OF THE CASTE ANGLE

The revival of democracy and civil liberties in India in 1977, following the twenty-one-month Emergency, was accompanied by a curious phenomenon. There was a spike in the incidence of violence against Harijans. This paradox manifested most prominently in a Bihar village called Belchhi, which, though hard to access at the time, was barely 60 kilometres from Patna city.

On 27 May 1977, Belchhi witnessed a mob attack in which eleven people, including eight Harijans, were killed. For the extent of attention it received, as also for its political and legal consequences, the Belchhi atrocity is without a parallel in the history of caste killings.

It took place shortly after Assembly elections had been called in Bihar and eight other states. These elections were to follow an unprecedented transfer of power at the Centre, from the Emergency-tainted Congress to the newly formed Janata Party. The Morarji Desai government had imposed President's Rule in the nine states in view of the Congress party's rout in the March Lok Sabha elections despite being in power there at the provincial level.

On 13 June 1977, as a three-phase polling was going on in Bihar over a span of five days, the Lok Sabha discussed a calling-attention motion on Belchhi.[1] The mover of the motion was Parvathi Krishnan, a member of the Communist Party of India (CPI) representing Coimbatore in faraway Tamil Nadu. This was also a reflection of the dramatic reconfiguration of political representation that had taken place after the Emergency. The Congress was left without a single representative from Bihar in the Lok Sabha. However, Krishnan's party had been its ally right through that period.

Her brother, Mohan Kumaramangalam, originally from the CPI, had been an influential minister in the Indira Gandhi government until he died in a plane crash in 1973. Parvathi Krishnan's father, P. Subbarayan, was the chief minister of the Madras Presidency five decades earlier, and her mother, Radhabai Subbarayan, was a member of the Council of State, a precursor to the Rajya Sabha. Both the Subbarayans had been deeply engaged with caste-reform legislation during the colonial period.

Parvathi Krishnan's portrayal of the Belchhi episode as a caste atrocity on the basis of press reports brought forth an outright denial—not of the killings, but of their alleged link with caste. Equating the victims with the perpetrators, Home Minister Charan Singh declared, 'According to the information received from the Government of Bihar, this was a case of a clash between two groups of hardened criminals having long standing rivalry … A number of victims of this incident were involved in murders of members of the rival group.' He added, 'These two groups have been attempting to eliminate one another and gain exclusive control of the area of their operations.'

Besides being second-in-command in the government, Charan Singh was the foremost leader of Jats, an upper Shudra caste dominant in substantial parts of northern India. Reputedly a champion of peasants, Charan Singh ruled out the influence of caste in the Belchhi episode: 'this incident has no caste, communal, agrarian or political overtones and has nothing to do with atrocities on weaker sections of society as reported in certain sections of the press.'

Parvathi Krishnan hit back, alleging that Charan Singh's denial was based on 'cooked up reports' of the government of Bihar, which, thanks to the President's Rule, happened to be under his control. 'This is really amazing because we have a Government which says it has come in order to restore democracy and freedom,' she said caustically. 'Is it the freedom for the Harijans to be harassed and tortured?'

Pointing to the delay on the part of the police in responding to the initial complaint, she questioned, 'Why did they take five to six hours to reach the place where people have been first shot, then kerosene poured on them and then their bodies burnt?' Krishnan demanded that a judicial inquiry be set up 'so that the whole matter is thrashed out and such eyewash reports from the Government side are not put before us'.

Charan Singh ignored this demand.

Not long after, despite the Centre's public endorsement of its stand on Belchhi, the Bihar government appeared to be rethinking its position. Three days after the Lok Sabha discussion, the results of the Assembly elections in Bihar and the other eight states came in. They indicated that the wave that had swept the Janata Party to power three months earlier at the Centre was still as strong. On 16 June 1977, Bihar, still ruled by the Centre, suspended the investigating officer of the Belchhi case, Avadhesh Kumar Misra, on the charge that 'he did not maintain intelligence about his area'.[2]

Misra was responsible for recording all the statements related to the case, making seizures from the crime scene, and was the one who had formally floated the clash-of-gangs theory. The timing of his suspension suggested that his superiors were having second thoughts. They did not think that the Janata Party government, soon to rule Bihar, would stick by this theory. Their caution proved to be well founded. The government that was formed on 24 June 1977 was headed by Karpoori Thakur, a pioneer of social justice in independent India and a member of the lower Shudra caste of Nais, or barbers.

In fact, four days later, on 28 June 1977, even Parliament House witnessed an extraordinary revolt over the official stand on Belchhi. Ruling party MPs from downtrodden communities joined hands with their counterparts in other parties to question Charan Singh's repudiation of any caste angle to the violence. The meeting was of 'the Parliamentary Forum of Scheduled Castes and Scheduled Tribes Members of Parliament'.

Since Charan Singh had disregarded the demand for a judicial inquiry in the Lok Sabha, this special-interest group set up a Fact-finding Committee of MPs. In a bold non-partisan move, the forum chose the general secretary of the Janata Parliamentary Party, Ram Dhan from Uttar Pradesh, to lead the committee. Also in the committee was Janata Party's Ram Vilas Paswan, who was of the same Dusadh caste as the eight Harijans who had been killed.

The eight-MP committee headed by Ram Dhan visited Belchhi on 2 July 1977 and heard witnesses and victims. They discovered the lie of the clash-of-gangs scenario.[3] In its report published on 14 July 1977, the committee said that the bloodshed was entirely one-sided and that the eight murdered Harijans were either landless labourers or share-croppers. The culprits were a gang led by Mahabir Mahto, a local landlord belonging to the Shudra caste of Kurmis, who were described by the committee as 'dominant peasantry' living in pucca houses.

Mahabir Mahto was found to have had 'a long history of criminal activities', which included a two-year-old episode in which a woman was beaten up 'so severely that she became deaf'. She was 'the wife of the only Brahmin' living then in Belchhi, Barho Jha, who was 'compelled' to move out of the village with her, leaving his landed property in the care of a Harijan called Singheshwar Paswan, also known as Sidheshwar Paswan. That this Harijan had dared to defy his supremacy was among the reasons that Mahabir Mahto had been gunning for Singheshwar Paswan.

The Ram Dhan Committee found that while Mahabir Mahto and his associate from a nearby village, Parsuram Dhanuk, were 'well-known hardened criminals', Singheshwar Paswan and the other murdered Harijans were 'oppressed people who were resisting the atrocities and tyranny' of the killer gang. As for the crimes that had been attributed to the Harijans in the official narrative, the committee alleged that Mahabir Mahto 'in league with the police' had 'falsely implicated' them in a couple of cases.

The all-party panel of MPs also found that, just five days before the killings, Mahabir Mahto and his armed gang had raided the houses of the Harijans in search of Singheshwar Paswan—a crucial piece of evidence. While the terrorised Harijans had disappeared into the nearby fields, Sakal Paswan, a relative of Singheshwar Paswan's and oblivious to the threat, entered Belchhi just then. The Mahto gang fired at Sakal Paswan (who, according to the Patna High Court, succumbed later to his bullet injuries[4]).

Despite an FIR lodged against Mahabir Mahto, Parsuram Dhanuk and other gang members for shooting Sakal Paswan, none of the accused persons was arrested. They continued to roam freely in Belchhi. This led the committee to observe that 'the inaction of local police' on 22 May 1977 'encouraged the culprits' to commit even more gruesome crimes five days later.

When the Mahabir Mahto gang had launched their final attack on the morning of 27 May 1977, Singheshwar Paswan and his associates, unarmed and vulnerable as they were, took shelter in the pucca house of one Rohan Mahto. But Mahabir Mahto and his men broke into that house, and hauled the Harijans to a maize field with their hands tied behind their backs. In the maize field, 'women folk of the culprits had already collected cow-dung cakes, wooden planks and other (inflammable) material alongside tins of kerosene'.

According to the Ram Dhan Committee report, 'Culprits sprinkled kerosene on the body of their captives and they were shot at and thrown into the pyre which had already been lit.' And those who 'leaped out half burnt ... were thrown back into the pyre', as part of an obvious design to leave no trace of the crime. It was only when the police arrived much later, around 5.30 p.m., that 'the culprits slowly moved away from the place of burning'.

The police, it was found, had delayed acting on the information of two residents of Belchhi, who had alerted them of the events of the morning. The first was a Kurmi who had no truck with Mahabir Mahto's criminal activities. Around 9 a.m., Sarjo Mahto approached the Saksohra police post which was about five kilometres from Belchhi. Then, the village chowkidar, Ganesh Paswan, travelled over twenty kilometres to reach the Barh Police Station by around 11 a.m.[5] The Ram Dhan Committee thus inferred that the police 'deliberately delayed the arrival to the village so that the culprits may accomplish their misdeed'.

The Ram Dhan Committee went on to debunk every one of Charan Singh's claims in the Lok Sabha. His contention that the killings were due to a clash between two criminal gangs was found to be 'totally false'. Likewise, his allegation that the victims had themselves been involved in murders was 'baseless' and 'nothing but an attempt to hide the nefarious activities of Mahabir Mahto and his gang'. Equally, the home minister's inference that the murders had nothing to do with caste prejudice was dismissed as 'totally incorrect'. It was an unprecedent indictment for a Union home minister.

Importantly, in the twenty-seven years since the abolition of untouchability, this was the most striking demonstration of the constitutional scheme of checks and balances. A little-known offshoot of the legislature, while exercising oversight, laid bare not only the executive's disingenuous bid to suppress the caste angle to the violence but also the police's collusion with the killers.

The Ram Dhan Committee could set this milestone because its members, who were all MPs from the sections most vulnerable to caste prejudice, had transcended their political affiliations. None embodied this non-partisan commitment more than the ruling party MP who helmed the inquiry. The resultant report exposed some of the covert ways in which the State structure was prone to perpetuating untouchability camouflaged by the rhetoric of the rule of law. Likewise, it demonstrated the difference that members of socially excluded communities could make on wresting a share of political power.

The committee's recording of the inconvenient facts that had been left out of the official narrative on Belchhi emboldened the legislature to hold the executive to account. A fresh discussion took place in Parliament in the light of these findings. A member of the Ram Dhan Committee, N.H. Kumbhare, moved a calling-attention motion in the Rajya Sabha on 22 July 1977.[6]

Chastened by the revelations of the Ram Dhan Committee,

Charan Singh's narrative in the Upper House was substantially different from the one he had provided a month earlier in the Lower House. The new one acknowledged that, after the mob had broken into Rohan Mahto's house, 'Sidheshwar Paswan and other seven deceased were brought out on gun-point and shot in cold blood.'

Equally telling in this reappraisal was Charan Singh's admissions about the role of the police. He conceded that there was a delayed response on the part of the Barh Police Station to the information that had been given around noon by the village chowkidar. 'The officer in charge of the police station reached Belchi at about 6 pm when the bodies of the deceased had been practically burnt.' Further, he divulged that disciplinary action had been initiated. 'Four police officers have been suspended for alleged negligence in connection with this incident and departmental proceedings are underway.' The suspended officers included the man who had conducted practically the entire investigation.

And yet Charan Singh was loath to accept any influence of caste on the killings. Drawing from the investigation that had been 'completed' by the same police that he had just indicted, he continued to maintain that 'the incident arose out of long-standing rivalry between two gangs of criminals, who had been making attempts to liquidate each other'. Though he did refer to the Ram Dhan Committee report in his address to the Rajya Sabha, Charan Singh glossed over its contrary finding that the massacre of Harijans had been driven by caste prejudice.

The saving grace was that he had forwarded a copy of the Ram Dhan Committee report to Chief Minister Karpoori Thakur. Charan Singh specified that he had even suggested to Thakur that 'the investigation so far conducted may be reviewed in the light of the facts brought out in the report of the fact-finding committee'. It was perhaps his way of signalling to the Rajya Sabha that Belchhi could not be seen as a black-and-white situation.

Charan Singh's overall position, such as it was, failed to satisfy the mover of the motion, an MP from Maharashtra and a leader of the Ambedkar-conceived Republican Party of India. Kumbhare asserted that, despite his consistency in rejecting the caste angle to the violence, Charan Singh's statement in the Rajya Sabha was 'a glaring contrast to' his earlier one in the Lok Sabha. As he was 'one of the members who had occasion to make an on-the-spot study', Kumbhare said that he was in 'a better position' than others in the House to say that Charan Singh's original statement was 'nothing short of distortion'.

At this, Charan Singh interjected, denying that there was any difference between his two statements on Belchhi. 'About the way these people were murdered in my previous statement I used exactly the same words which I am using today,' he claimed. A claim that was, of course, economical with the truth.

All that Charan Singh had said in the Lok Sabha was that they had been killed in a clash, and that 'the bodies of the dead were burnt by an armed mob of 50 to 60 persons'. His Rajya Sabha statement, on the other hand, forced by the Ram Dhan Committee report, admitted the crucial detail that the Harijans had been taken captive: 'brought out on gun-point and shot in cold blood'. His compulsion for passing off the two demonstrably different statements as 'exactly the same words' was that he was already facing a privilege motion in the Lok Sabha due to the Ram Dhan Committee report.

Kumbhare was unimpressed. Accusing Charan Singh of giving 'a false statement' in the Lok Sabha, he recalled, 'It was said in specific and in very clear terms that the Harijans were killed in a clash.' Stressing the need to examine the cover-up as well, he said, 'It is really a serious matter which has to be gone into in order to find out who is responsible for this event and the distorted version.'

The 'distorted version' was an allusion to Charan Singh rather than the Bihar officers. Kumbhare, in fact, expressed appreciation for the version that Bihar's chief secretary and inspector general of police had given to the Ram Dhan Committee in Patna on 3 July 1977. 'They definitely said that there was no clash,' he said, adding that the officers also conceded that the victims had been 'brought out, shot dead and burnt'. So he demanded that the House get to the bottom of the 'deliberate attempt ... to give a coloured version so as to show to the country and the world at large that this is not a case where Scheduled Castes people were subjected to atrocities'.

Of a piece with this design, he hinted, was Charan Singh's silence about the attempt on Singheshwar Paswan's life less than a week before he had been killed by the same culprit. Kumbhare recalled that, despite the FIR on the collateral damage that had been suffered by another Harijan in that firing incident, the police did not arrest anyone. He added that 'if the police had been alert and vigilant enough to book the culprits, this ghastly incident would not have happened'.

Kumbhare also pointed out that, in his subsequent statement, Charan Singh had 'omitted' the portion alleging that the murdered Harijans had also been part of a gang of hardened criminals. The omission was forced by the Ram Dhan Committee's clear finding that those Harijans were all, as Kumbhare put it, 'landless persons' who were 'actually living hand to mouth'.

Embarrassed by the manner in which his conduct had been called into question, Charan Singh sought to shift the blame to a letter that the Home Ministry had received from the Bihar government on the eve of his Lok Sabha statement. The letter dated 12 June 1977 showed that, anticipating Parvathi Krishnan's demand for a judicial inquiry, Charan Singh had explored that option with the Bihar authorities. He read out in the Rajya Sabha a letter that had apparently been written in response to the Home Ministry's 'telephonic discussion enquiring about the views of the State Government about the suggestion for holding a judicial inquiry'. The Bihar government replied that the police investigations had resulted in the apprehension of twenty-nine accused persons 'including the major culprit, Mahabir Mahto'. Hence, the Bihar government felt that 'no further useful purpose would be served by holding a judicial inquiry'.

Charan Singh quoted this letter in his defence mainly because it served to indicate that the clash-of-gangs theory had originated in Bihar. He sought to establish that he had only repeated, as a matter of course, whatever had been conveyed to him by the Bihar government. The letter did assert that, according to the inquiries made by senior officers in Bihar, the Belchhi incident was 'not in the nature of an atrocity on the Harijans, but was a clash between two fighting criminal gangs who were trying to liquidate one another since long'.

Kumbhare was unfazed by this old letter from Patna. He had seen the same Bihar officers before the Ram Dhan Committee disclaiming the clash-of-gangs theory. In a further display of tenacity, this Harijan MP pointed out that, even if the Bihar government had declined to appoint a commission of inquiry, it was still 'within the competence' of Charan Singh's ministry to do so.

Charan Singh had only a lame excuse to offer: 'It was open to the State Government also to appoint a commission. So it was suggested to them. But they did not do it.'

Then, driven perhaps by the inadequacy of his reply, Charan Singh made a startling admission. Switching abruptly from the options of remedial action to the nature of the carnage, he said, 'My point is that the word clash used in the message was wrong. That is true. I admit it.'

With these three sentences, comprising no more than nineteen words, Charan Singh tacitly acknowledged the caste atrocity, marking a reversal of the Government of India's position. This was the most remarkable outcome of the pushback led by the Harijan MPs. Its value was more than symbolic. The process of truth-telling, which began with the Ram Dhan Committee report, had a salutary effect on the legal process that followed, as will be seen presently.

Charan Singh's admission did not end the parliamentary debate. He found himself facing an even greater political challenge from the Congress MPs, who were in a majority in the Rajya Sabha. Even after his climbdown on the caste angle, they called out Charan Singh for drawing a false equivalence between the culprits and the victims. He was greeted with interruptions when he had shrugged off responsibility saying, 'But the question is whether I have done it deliberately. That is wrong.'

The interruptions prompted Charan Singh to take a good-faith plea: 'All the passion being imported into it meant that I did it deliberately and twisted the version of the incident. I want simply to say that there was nothing of the kind.'

As the discussion dragged on for over three hours and digressed into parliamentary technicalities, two of his Cabinet colleagues, Biju Patnaik and Lal Krishna Advani, made repeated attempts to bail him out. In a last-ditch effort, Charan Singh read out another letter—one that he had written to Karpoori Thakur as a follow-up to the Ram Dhan Committee report. Surprisingly, he was more forthcoming about the caste angle in this letter, written three days earlier, on 19 July 1977.

He wrote that 'a number of Members of Parliament were not satisfied with the version of the incident given by our Government'. And the subsequent Ram Dhan Committee report, Charan Singh said, had brought out 'certain facts which differ in vital respects from the report sent to us by the Government of Bihar'.

Further, 'This report seems to indicate that it was not a case of clash between two rival gangs having a long-standing enmity but a case of brutal murder of 11 persons, out of whom eight were Harijans, by influential criminal elements in that area in retaliation to resistance to their unlawful activities. The report also cast serious doubts on the role of the local police and in particular, their failure to take any action after the firing incident on May 22, against the gang of Mahabir Mahto. A perusal of the report would suggest that the incident may have political overtones.'

Charan Singh's letter then urged Thakur to order a review of the police investigations that had been 'completed' by then. 'The report submitted by the Committee of Members of Parliament is likely to cause serious misgivings in the public mind regarding the correctness and impartiality of these investigations.'

The disclosure of this telling letter did serve to put in perspective Charan Singh's rethink on whether Belchhi could be called a clash. But he continued to resist the demand for a judicial inquiry. His main justification for it was that the state legislature had already appointed a committee of legislators to probe Belchhi. 'Later, if the committee recommends it or if the Chief Minister or we feel the need for it, we may consider setting up a commission of inquiry,' he said.

Sensing an opportunity to corner the Morarji Desai government, Congress members, led by Kamalapati Tripathi, staged a walkout over Charan Singh's refusal to announce a judicial inquiry. It was an unfamiliar form of protest for Congress MPs to adopt, given that their party had until recently been uninterruptedly in power at the Centre. The *Times of India,* in fact, reported that the Congress walkout had happened 'for the first time'.[7] The walkout turned out to be a prelude to more political drama over Belchhi, this time outside the Parliament.

❖

Given all the focus on him, Mahabir Mahto stood little chance of being released on bail. Some of his gang members were luckier in this respect. But their release led to the 'terror-struck Harijans' of Belchhi being threatened with 'reprisals', reported the *Times of India* on 6 August 1977.[8] One of the gang members, Tulsi Mahto, even jumped bail and went underground.[9]

As if that was not bad enough, the onset of monsoon aggravated the climate of fear. 'Because of floods,' the news report said, 'the village is accessible only by boat from Barh, the sub-divisional headquarters'.[10]

These adverse conditions, in fact, allowed the next most important accused, Parsuram Dhanuk, to make his escape on 1 August 1977. An absconder carrying a reward of Rs 5,000 on his head, he 'boarded a boat with his gang and exchanged fire with the police patrol in broad daylight at Belchhi … By the time the police could procure a boat, Dhanuk and his associates escaped.' When they caught up with him later in his village, they were better organised. 'The police engaged boats, surrounded his village of Bakra, which is adjacent to Belchhi, and nabbed Dhanuk.'

Meanwhile, the unresolved debate in Parliament on Belchhi

offered fresh political opportunities. On the one hand, the leader of the Opposition in the Lok Sabha, Congress veteran Y.B. Chavan, declared that he would soon visit Belchhi to call on the relatives of the victims. On the other hand, Shyam Sundar Gupta, the Janata Party MP from the Barh constituency, which encompassed Belchhi, reverted to Charan Singh's clash-of-gangs theory. Singh's own retraction did little to deter him. Nor did he seem to be troubled by the Congress's attempt to derive mileage from the Belchhi massacre. Insofar as Gupta was concerned, it was merely a clash in which some Harijans happened to die. Their killing, he asserted, 'does not make it a case of organised terrorisation of the weaker sections nor of caste Hindu oppression against the Harijans'.[11]

Ram Dhan took issue with Gupta, exposing the fault lines within the ruling party on the matter. 'I am sorry that Mr. Gupta neither understands the policy of the Janata Party nor its deep commitment to Harijans and weaker sections for whose uplift and security the JP movement for total revolution was launched.'[12]

Then, on the evening of 11 August 1977, everything changed. Sadaquat Ashram, the headquarters in Patna of the Congress's Bihar unit, received a call.[13] It was from the office of former prime minister Indira Gandhi, who had been lying low since her shock defeat five months earlier. The purpose of her call was no less surprising than the call itself.

Indira Gandhi informed the chief of the party's Bihar unit that she had decided to visit Belchhi. Her decision marked a quantum leap in India's engagement with the post-colonial phenomenon of caste-based massacres. Though she no longer held any formal position, Indira Gandhi was still the pole star around whom Indian politics revolved.

Her gesture was as sensitive as it was opportunistic. The trend of mass violence targeting Harijans had begun early in her tenure as prime minister with the 1968 Kilvenmani massacre. But she was visiting one such site of violence only after she had lost power in 1977. Perhaps it was her way of joining the heated debates in Parliament on Charan Singh's statements. She could no longer participate in them as she was not even an MP at the time.

Since her intention was clearly to pre-empt Chavan's imminent plan to visit the village, Indira Gandhi could give the Congress local office only a two-day notice for hers. Even otherwise, her idea of choosing Belchhi for her first foray out of Delhi was audacious. Hardly five months had elapsed since the people of Bihar, having experienced some of the worst excesses of the Emergency, had wiped out her party in every one of its Lok Sabha constituencies.

Indira Gandhi's strategic move laid bare tensions within the Congress. Within a day of the announcement of her visit, Chavan appointed a four-member study group of the Congress parliamentary party to visit Belchhi and other places in Bihar where atrocities were alleged to have been committed against Harijans.[14]

When Gandhi landed in Patna on the morning of 13 August 1977, hundreds of her supporters had gathered at the airport, braving heavy downpour. It set the tone for her arduous journey to Belchhi, which had been inaccessible for several days. When she reached a stretch that was not motorable, Gandhi ended up travelling atop an elephant. The unusual mode of transportation that this sixty-year-old woman was forced to adopt to reach the violence-hit Harijans of Belchhi captured the popular imagination.

Even if Indira Gandhi had only meant to score a political point, her visit served to raise social consciousness around caste violence. She earned the distinction of being the first—and perhaps the only—national leader to have ever visited a caste-atrocity site. She was none the worse for her effort. For its sheer impact, Gandhi's Belchhi visit marked the beginning of her comeback trail.

It also put the Janata Party on the defensive, especially since its own chief minister had not visited Belchhi. In a petulant reaction, Karpoori Thakur declared that the visit was meant 'to defame the Janata Government and project herself as a messiah of Harijans'.[15]

As for his own responsibility, Thakur could make the face-saving claim that, besides suspending four police officials, he had taken a further confidence-building measure by posting in the troubled area a deputy superintendent of police from the Harijan community. In the ensuing trial, the police investigation, despite all its ambivalence about whether there were caste overtones to the violence, proved to be rigorous enough to secure convictions.

❖

On 19 May 1980, about four months after Indira Gandhi was back in power, a Patna trial court delivered its verdict on the Belchhi massacre. Additional Sessions Judge Om Prakash awarded life imprisonment to seventeen of the accused, and the death penalty to two of the seventeen convicted persons, Mahabir Mahto and Parsuram Dhanuk.[16]

All seventeen were found to have been members of an unlawful assembly that had, in furtherance of its common object, committed eleven murders. They were sentenced under Section 302 read with 149 of the Indian Penal Code, which meant they were found guilty of murder (Section 302, IPC) only due to the joint liability arising from being part of the unlawful assembly (Section 149, IPC).

Over and above this, the trial court convicted Mahto and Dhanuk separately under Section 302 IPC. They were found to have murdered two and three persons, respectively. On this more serious count, the gang leader and his deputy were awarded capital punishment.

While Mahto was found to have shot dead two of the eight Harijans, Singheshwar Paswan and his relative, Nawal Paswan, Dhanuk was found to have killed the three non-Harijans. The three that Dhanuk killed were all Sonars, an artisan community of goldsmiths that was classified under the OBC category in Bihar.

But the Belchhi case ran into turbulence when it went before the Patna High Court for the required confirmation of the death penalty as well as on appeals filed by the convicted persons. The two judges on the bench did not agree on whether this case warranted the death penalty. So, Justice Hari Lal Agrawal and Justice Manoranjan Prasad delivered separate verdicts on 29 April 1981.[17]

Justice Prasad ruled that while Mahto and Dhanuk had been

rightly convicted under Section 302 and 149 of the IPC, the charges against them under Section 302 IPC 'do not appear to have been proved beyond doubt by the evidence on the record'. He reasoned that, to prove that the convict had actually committed murder under Section 302 IPC, the threshold of evidence was higher.

Justice Prasad found 'some contradiction' among the testimonies on 'the sequence in which the eleven deceased were shot dead'. It turned out that the Mahabir Mahto gang had fanned out in two groups. The one led by Dhanuk went after Udai Sonar and his two brothers, while the other led by Mahto hunted down the eight Harijans.

The informant, Shyama Devi, testified that Dhanuk had first taken her husband, Udai Sonar, and his brothers to the maize field and shot them dead. And, 'after a short time', she saw the eight Harijans being taken to the same field and shot dead by the mob. But the evidence of other eyewitnesses was that all eleven victims had been 'taken to the maize field at Bagha Tilla simultaneously and were shot dead simultaneously'.

The sequence in Shyama Devi's 'solitary evidence' was found to be 'at variance with' the depositions of the other eyewitnesses. Justice Prasad found this serious enough to conclude that it would be 'unsafe' to go beyond the general charge of joint liability and convict Dhanuk specifically for murdering the Sonars.

However, Justice Agrawal said that he was 'unable to agree with' Justice Prasad's 'rejection' of Shyama Devi's testimony on the shooting of her husband and his brothers merely because there was 'some deviation in the sequence of the shooting of the other victims'. He said 'the fact remains that all the eleven victims were shot down at the same place'. To Justice Agrawal, the senior judge on the bench, Shyama Devi's evidence proved 'beyond all reasonable suspicion' that it was Dhanuk who had shot dead the three Sonars. His judgment, therefore, ruled that Dhanuk was guilty under Section 302 of the IPC.

As regards Mahabir Mahto, Justice Prasad was again concerned about a discrepancy between two witness testimonies, this time on whether he had shot dead both Singheshwar Paswan and Nawal Paswan or only the first one. While Anup Paswan testified that he saw Mahto shooting both of them, Ram Prasad Paswan deposed that only Singheshwar Paswan had been killed by Mahabir Mahto and that Nawal Paswan had been killed by one of his gang members, Rajendar Mahto.

Though Ram Prasad Paswan's evidence had 'not been relied upon by the trial court in support of the prosecution case', Justice Prasad said that 'the defence is entitled to take advantage of the aforesaid contradiction'. Making much of Ram Prasad Paswan's conflicting testimony on the killing of Nawal Paswan, Justice Prasad said that he was 'not prepared to believe' Anup Paswan's testimony on the killing of Singheshwar Paswan either.

Justice Agrawal made short shrift of the two varying versions on Mahabir Mahto's culpability. He ruled that, as the dispute was confined to the shooting of Nawal Paswan, there was 'in any view of the matter ... no contradiction whatsoever' with respect to the killing of Singheshwar Paswan. So, 'taking the line of least resistance, there can be no justification', he reasoned, 'for not maintaining the conviction of appellant Mahabir Mahto under Section 302 of the Indian Penal Code'.

Having upheld the trial court's conviction of both Mahto and Dhanuk under Section 302, Justice Agrawal said, 'The determination with which they committed the gruesome murders, in my view, exposes them to the award of the maximum sentence of death penalty as rightly done by the trial court.'

Split as the court's verdict was, it still unanimously held Mahto and Dhanuk jointly liable under Section 302 and 149 of the IPC and awarded life sentences to both along with others as members of the unlawful assembly that killed eleven people.

Thanks to the split verdict, the matter was heard afresh by a third judge of the Patna High Court, Justice Uday Sinha.[18] It was clear by then that the capital punishment awarded to Dhanuk and Mahto hinged on the testimonies of Shyama Devi and Anup Paswan, respectively. The defence counsel therefore spared no effort in discrediting those two witnesses—even arguing that neither of them could have seen the crime scene. The counsel alleged that the crime scene was hardly visible from the spots that the witnesses claimed to have discreetly witnessed the murders. The site map drawn by the investigating officer was of little help in verifying this new attack on witness credibility. The mahua tree that had apparently served as a cover for Shyama Devi was, for instance, missing from the map.

This led the defence counsel to make the unusual plea of urging the High Court judge to visit the crime scene for a 'local inspection'. Justice Uday Sinha thus travelled all the way to Belchhi in the company of the counsels for all the parties. In his judgment delivered on 11 January 1982, the judge said that 'in the interest of justice, the Court condescended to hold local inspection'.

That the Belchhi massacre had, as Justice Sinha put it, 'gained countrywide, nay, international notoriety', might have been another factor. Coming as it did after the visit of the All-Party Committee of MPs and then of the former prime minister, the High Court judge's spot verification as part of the appeal proceedings underscored the exceptional treatment that this caste atrocity received.

As it happened, the local inspection rebounded on the defence counsel. It bore out Shyama Devi's claim that, from under the mahua tree, she could see Dhanuk shooting her husband and his brothers in the maize field belonging to Sahdeo Mahto. Justice Sinha wrote, 'Local inspection showed that there was a full grown mahua tree south of the house of Rohan Mahto. The size of the tree was such that it could not have been planted after the date of occurrence. Anything happening in the field of Sahdeo Mahto would be clearly visible, if anybody stood near the mahua tree.'

The defence counsel had also alleged that Anup Paswan could not have seen the crime scene from the terrace of another witness, Janki Paswan, who was also his relative. But Justice Sinha found that there was 'no substance' to this contention made on behalf of Mahabir Mahto. 'Local inspection showed that from the terrace of Janki Paswan everything was visible in the field of Sahdeo Mahto.

The distance was not great. It could not be more than 100-150 yards as the crow flies.'

Having seen for himself that both Shyama Devi and Anup Paswan had had a clear view of the crime scene, Justice Sinha was all the more inclined to agree with Justice Agrawal's endorsement of their testimonies. The first-hand knowledge he had acquired of the crime scene put in perspective for him the alleged contradiction between Shyama Devi's testimony and those of the other witnesses on the sequence of the killings.

'This apparent contradiction is not of much consequence,' Justice Sinha said. 'A short gap, may be of 10 or 15 minutes, between the shooting of Sonars and those of eight Paswans is not of such a consequence as to detract from the weight of her evidence ... Not much can be made of the evidence of some of the witnesses that all the eleven were shot simultaneously. The whole episode may well be described as one transaction.'

Likewise, in weighing Anup Paswan's testimony on the murders that had been committed by Mahabir Mahto, Justice Sinha left 'out of consideration' the partly divergent testimony of Ram Prasad Paswan. He had 'hid himself behind a brick kiln'. It was 'doubtful', Justice Sinha said, if this witness 'saw the mass killings in the field of Sahdeo Mahto'. In contrast, Anup Paswan's testimony was found to have 'remained unshaken' despite being cross-examined the most by the defence counsel.

Once he upheld the conviction of both Dhanuk and Mahto under Section 302 IPC, Justice Sinha addressed the issue of the death penalty that had been imposed by the trial court. Quoting a 1977 Supreme Court judgment of V.R. Krishna Iyer,[19] Justice Uday Sinha referred to 'an unmistakable shift in legislative emphasis on life imprisonment for murder as the rule and the capital punishment, an exception'.

On applying the principles enunciated by the Supreme Court, Sinha ruled: 'I am of the view that the case of Parsuram Dhanuk is one of those rarest of rare cases where infliction of the maximum penalty is called for.' He awarded the same sentence to Mahabir

Mahto, whom he described as 'the leader and the prime mover of the entire ghastly carnage'.

Sinha's ruling tilted the balance of the Patna High Court's judgment in the Belchhi case. The 2:1 decision confirmed the death penalty for two and life sentence for thirteen other convicts. From the original list of fifteen life convicts, two had already been acquitted by Justices Agrawal and Prasad.

However, in view of deficiencies in the prosecution's evidence on the motive, the High Court left open the contentious question as to whether the Belchhi violence had been fuelled by caste prejudice. 'The motive for the occurrence ... is in a maze,' Justice Sinha said, adding, 'The failure on the part of the prosecution to prove the motive ... cannot upset the prosecution case as the evidence in regard to the killings is clear and consistent.'

On 21 July 1982, a special leave petition challenging the capital sentence awarded to Dhanuk and Mahto came up before a Supreme Court bench comprising Justice S. Murtuza Fazal Ali and Justice R.B. Misra.[20] The sensitivity of the case did not hold back the Supreme Court from dismissing it the same day, at the admission stage, without recording any reasons. The one-line order said: 'Special leave petition is dismissed.'

The following month, the Supreme Court registry circulated a review petition in the chambers of Justices Fazal Ali and Misra. On 17 August 1982, the two-judge bench passed a slightly longer order: 'We have gone through the review petition and connected papers and find no merit in the Review Petition which is accordingly dismissed.'[21]

In the lead-up to their hanging in the Bhagalpur Central Jail scheduled for 25 May 1983, Mahto and Dhanuk sent a telegram to the Supreme Court pleading for a stay. Since the apex court was on summer vacation, the telegram was placed before the vacation judge, Justice A. Varadarajan. A native of Tamil Nadu, Varadarajan was the first Harijan judge ever to have been elevated to the Supreme Court. It fell upon him to stay the execution of the culprits of Belchhi. Treating their telegram as a writ petition, Varadarajan passed the stay order on 23 May 1983, two days before they were due to be hanged.[22]

He had little choice, in any case, as Mahto and Dhanuk were among several death row prisoners from across the country who were challenging the constitutional validity of Section 354(5) of the Criminal Procedure Code. The two Belchhi convicts joined the batch of petitioners seeking less painful methods of execution than the hanging stipulated by this provision. As Section 354(5) of the CrPC put it, 'When any person is sentenced to death, the sentence shall direct that he be hanged by the neck till he is dead.'

A three-judge bench headed by Chief Justice of India Y.V. Chandrachud heard the petitions on a priority basis. On 23 September 1983, the Supreme Court ruled that hanging caused 'no greater pain than any other known method of executing the death sentence' and that it involved 'no barbarity, torture or degradation'.[23]

The dismissal of those petitions removed the last of the hurdles to the death penalty awarded to Mahto and Dhanuk. They were hanged in Bhagalpur Central Jail on 9 November 1983. 'Before the hanging, both convicts,' it was reported, 'were offered curd and sweets in deference to their wishes. Their bodies were later handed over to their relatives.'[24]

From a human rights viewpoint, the very idea of the death penalty is repugnant. All the same, the hanging of Mahabir Mahto was a milestone in the history of untouchability. It is still the first and only recorded instance of a killer of untouchables being judicially executed. That he was a Kurmi, a dominant caste of the Shudra stock, was a testament to Ambedkar's formulation of graded inequality. As Ambedkar put it, 'Even the low is a privileged class as compared with the lower.'[25]

Equally remarkable is the relegation of Belchhi to a footnote in India's history. While Indira Gandhi's dramatic elephant ride and its political impact are well known, the no less significant institutional response of the legislature and the judiciary passed unnoticed. This oblivion was at least in part due to the failure of law journals to record the vital decisions of the Patna High Court and the Supreme Court in the Belchhi cases in 1981–82. This chapter thus embodies the first attempt to record the legal history of Belchhi, from the commission of the crime to the execution of the death penalty.

❖

In the years following Belchhi, Dalits increasingly shed the term 'Harijan', which had been bestowed on them by Gandhi. The change to 'Dalit', literally 'oppressed', symbolised a rejection of the patronising 'people of God' tag for the more combative term that made no bones about their downtrodden condition. This term was popularised by the Dalit Panther movement of Maharashtra, which, in turn, had been inspired by the Black Panther movement in the United States.

The execution of two killers for the Belchhi atrocity had little deterrent effect. The rising incidence of violence targeting Dalits pushed the Rajiv Gandhi government to undertake a radical legal reform in the last year of its term. The POA, which it passed in 1989, conferred statutory recognition on the concept of 'atrocity', encompassing a range of hate crimes, including the mass killings of Dalits.

Fortuitously, the legal reform was followed by an explosion of Dalit awareness. During the Ambedkar centenary celebrations in 1990–91, he was, among other things, posthumously awarded Bharat Ratna by the V.P. Singh government. And then the country was rocked by a political conflict between social justice forces (Mandal) and those of Hindu supremacists (Mandir).

The demolition of the Babri Masjid on 6 December 1992, Ambedkar's death anniversary, led to an interplay of communal violence and terrorism in Bombay. This, in turn, yielded for the first time in Maharashtra's history a government avowedly committed to Hindutva. It was a coalition of the Mandir forces: the Shiv Sena and the BJP. Parallelly, the Mandal ferment re-energised Dalit activism in Bombay, which was in keeping with its heritage of being Ambedkar's home base.

Against this backdrop, on 11 July 1997, the police shot dead ten Dalits in Ramabai Nagar, a slum named after Ambedkar's wife in the Bombay suburb of Ghatkopar. The deceased were among the Dalits protesting the desecration of an Ambedkar bust. The colony had woken up that morning to the sight of a garland of sandals round the neck of the statue. Coincidentally or otherwise, it was the first anniversary of the Bathani Tola massacre in Bihar. Closer to the ground, the Maharashtra Legislature was in session those days.

Within an hour of its discovery, by about 7.30 a.m., an assistant commissioner of police called S.N. More arrived and parleyed with the protestors surrounding the statue. The protestors asserted that they would not allow the offending garland to be removed until senior police officers visited the spot and suspended the policemen who had been on duty in the nearby chowki. To ensure proper investigation, they also demanded that the garland should remain untouched till the police drew the panchnama or mapped out the crime scene and called a sniffer-dog squad.

Even as More was negotiating with the protestors, a 'striking force' platoon from the State Reserve Police Force (SRPF) reached the stretch of the highway adjoining the colony. The platoon, headed by Sub-inspector Manohar Kadam, was stopped by the section of protestors that had fanned out and blocked traffic on one side of the highway. These protestors had already forced the passengers out of a bus and set it on fire. They now greeted the SRPF platoon with stone-pelting.

In volatile situations like these, the standard operating procedure is to take a calibrated approach to managing or dispersing the crowd. But Kadam straightaway ordered firing. He dispensed with the prescribed preliminaries of first making a lathi charge or firing teargas shells. Seven SRPF men fired fifty rounds of ammunition near the entrance of Ramabai Nagar. Besides killing ten people, they injured at least twelve.

Dalit politicians and activists raised a storm of protest over this mass killing by an arm of the State. Consequently, five days later, Chief Minister Manohar Joshi announced in the Assembly the appointment of a commission of inquiry into the Ramabai Nagar massacre. The inquiry was entrusted to a sitting judge of the Bombay High Court judge, Justice S.D. Gundewar.[26]

Under its terms of reference, the Justice Gundewar Commission was tasked with determining if the desecration of Ambedkar's statue had been 'pre-planned with a view to cause communal disturbances'. The choice of words was curious given that the expression 'communal disturbances' tended to denote clashes between different religious communities in India. This was the closest that the government ever came to acknowledging that the motivation behind the desecration could have been to inflame the Dalits.

The commission was also mandated to probe whether the police had used 'excessive' force to disperse the crowd, and if so, 'to fix the responsibility for such lapses'. But this question was meant to be determined purely in relation to 'the procedure established for riot control'. The mandate did not make even a pretence of ascertaining whether the police had acted high-handedly *because* those at the receiving end were Dalits.

All the same, during the inquiry proceedings, the caste angle to the violence did surface. Despite taking what the commission described as a 'rather neutral stand', the state government admitted that the location of the incident was no coincidence. 'The miscreants seem to have selected this statue for desecration from amongst many statues in the city particularly because the colony is thickly populated by Dalits.'

Shiv Sena, the dominant partner in the ruling coalition, made much of the fact that an old defector from its ranks to the Congress party, Chhagan Bhujbal, was 'the only leader allowed in the colony by the locals'. From this, the Shiv Sena 'insinuated', or so the commission reported, that 'the desecration may be at the behest of somebody from its political rival party i.e. Congress'.

On the other hand, the Congress's Bombay unit alleged that the 'needle of suspicion' pointed to the Shiv Sena. It was 'the outcome of partisan attitude towards Dalits of the police' and that it had been 'preplanned' in order to 'cow down Dalit community'.

The Gundewar Commission still chose to steer clear of all caste overtones in its analysis and conclusions. Weighing the conflicting testimonies of politicians, activists, policemen and victims, the commission said that it was 'unable to record' any definite finding about the desecration. In its report submitted on 7 August 1998, the commission concluded that there was 'no material on record on the basis of which responsibility of desecration could be fastened on any one'. It was equally non-committal about motive and intent: 'the evidence is too short to hold that the desecration was done with a view to cause communal disturbances'.

On the firing, however, the Gundewar Commission was less inhibited, owing to the surfeit of eyewitnesses. It held Kadam accountable for a series of acts of omission and commission. Besides discovering that the decision to open firing 'straightaway' had been taken 'exclusively' by Kadam, the commission said that the firing was 'without warning, unjustified, unwarranted and indiscriminate'.

On 30 December 1998, Manohar Joshi tabled the Gundewar Commission report in the Assembly. A news report said, 'While tabling the report, Chief Minister Manohar Joshi said the government agreed with the observations and conclusions of the commission and assured the house that action would be taken on the suggestions made by it.'[27] Though the Shiv Sena–BJP coalition remained in office for another ten months (till it lost the Assembly election in October 1999), it took no action against the platoon commander.

Likewise, the successor coalition government of the Congress and its recent breakaway, the Nationalist Congress Party (NCP), was in no hurry to indict Kadam. Ironically, when action was finally taken on 21 August 2001, it was by Chhagan Bhujbal whom the Shiv Sena had accused of complicity in the desecration. In his capacity as home minister representing the NCP in the coalition, Bhujbal issued orders to Mumbai's commissioner of police to book Kadam in a case of 'culpable homicide not amounting to murder' under Section 304 of the IPC.[28] Once again, there was no mention of caste atrocity in the government's announcement, despite the enactment of the 1989 Act.

On 30 August 2001, the Maharashtra government registered an FIR against Manohar Kadam under IPC provisions, not invoking the POA at all. Crime Branch, Mumbai, took over the investigation after the case had been registered at the local police station. Even the registration of the case was a breakthrough, though, for it was the first instance of a police officer being investigated for a mass killing of Dalits.

The next tangible action took over a year to materialise. On 20 December 2002, the police arrested their colleague. Within two weeks, on 3 January 2003, a Mumbai court released Kadam on bail. The justification for releasing him was that the trial of the case based on that much-delayed FIR was likely to involve further delays. Sure enough, it took another six years for the trial to conclude.

When the judgment came on 7 May 2009, it struck a blow for police accountability.[29] Trial judge S.Y. Kulkarni broadly echoed the Gundewar Commission's findings on the bloodshed. While noting that the protesters had 'caused damage to several vehicles' on the highway, including the burning of a luxury bus, the trial court faulted Kadam for not observing the conditions precedent to the option of firing. In an oblique reference to caste prejudice, Kadam was found to have disregarded 'the feelings of those people' which were 'hurt on account of the incident of desecration'.

The judgment pointed out that, while there was stone-pelting, even Kadam's counsel had not alleged that the protesters carried 'deadly weapons in their hands'. The defence, therefore, could not claim that the protesters, bereft of such weapons, were still 'likely to cause death' or that Kadam was 'justified in opening firing'.

On the contrary, an independent witness who had been 'constrained to get down along with his wife' from the ill-fated luxury bus testified that the protesters had 'taken care of the life of the passengers'. The trial court said that it could be 'safely gathered' that, before the police firing, there was no evidence on record that the protesters had 'directly tried to kill any person'.

It concluded, therefore, that Kadam had 'failed to establish his right of private defence'. He was meant to deploy the three layers of his twenty-one-man platoon—consisting of a lathi section, a shield section and a rifle section—in a graded manner, with the rifle section meant to be the 'last resort'. Kadam offered no justification for 'what was going on in his mind before opening firing'. The trial court held that Kadam could be 'attributed' foreknowledge of the fatal consequences of his decision. Almost all the casualties at Ramabai Nagar had, contrary to the law, 'sustained injuries above the waist'.

Considering his failure to prove any 'compelling circumstance which constrained him to open firing', the trial court convicted the platoon commander under Section 304 IPC for causing the death of ten stone-pelters. That they were all Dalits was a dimension that remained unexplored. All the same, Kulkarni awarded Kadam a life sentence, the maximum punishment under Section 304. A landmark verdict it was, not only for police accountability but also caste atrocities—even if the fact of it went unacknowledged.

Kadam, it turned out, did not stay in prison for long. On 22 May 2009, less than a month later, a vacation bench of the Bombay High Court released him on bail on an application that accompanied his appeal against the trial court verdict.[30]

The bench, comprising Justices A.V. Nirgude and R.G. Ketkar, granted bail and suspended the life sentence based on a clause in the SRPF Act providing blanket immunity to policemen for any killing committed in the discharge of their official duties. The authority that had sanctioned Kadam's prosecution—a pre-condition to the trial of a public servant—was found to have overlooked Section 11 of the SRPF Act.

Under this provision, a 'reserve police officer is', as the High Court put it, 'protected for using force', irrespective of the limits placed on the general right of private defence. All he needed to show to claim this additional protection was that he had 'reasonable apprehension of assault on himself or his subordinates or of damage or harm to any property or person which or whom it is his duty to protect'. The High Court said that this aspect of the matter 'deserves due consideration and would afford a strong arguable point to the appellant'.

Given its line of reasoning, the fourteen-page High Court bail order too bore no acknowledgement of a caste angle to the violence. There was at best a passing reference to the desecration of Ambedkar's statue. In their sanitised account, the High Court judges refrained from mentioning that the '10 persons' who had been killed on Kadam's orders were all members of a marginalised community. The Dalit survivors who had participated in the High Court proceedings were referred to in an anodyne manner as 'interveners'.

Institutional impunity triumphed over the imperative to provide justice to Dalits. Having granted interim relief to the convicted police officer in such haste, the High Court made no special effort to adjudicate on the merits of his appeal, although well over a decade has elapsed since.

❖

The year 2002 was a watershed in India's history. The mass violence in Gujarat targeting Muslims displayed the extent of influence that a far-right non-political organisation, Vishva Hindu Parishad (VHP), wielded over the ruling Bharatiya Janata Party.

Besides its campaign to build the Ram Janmabhoomi temple in Ayodhya, the VHP had a long record of vigilantism in the name of checking cow slaughter. Its mission, espousing the post-Vedic Hindu taboo against beef, most affected marginalised communities that had been traditionally engaged in leather processing, specifically Muslims and Dalits.

Close on the heels of its temple-inspired depredations in Gujarat, the VHP grabbed an opportunity to defend and celebrate what was by far the most blatant instance of cow-vigilantism. The opportunity came in Haryana during the Hindu festival of Dussehra on 15 October 2002. Around 6 p.m., a group of fourteen cow vigilantes dragged five Dalits in an injured condition to the police post at Dulina in Jhajjar district, less than two hours from Delhi.

In what turned out to be a rumour, the five men were accused of slaughtering a cow. They were, in fact, ferrying a legally procured carcass along with a consignment of cattle hides in their pick-up van. All the same, on the complaint of the vigilantes, the police took the injured Dalits into their custody and booked them under the Punjab Prohibition of Cow Slaughter Act, 1955.

Far from satisfied with this precipitate action, the vigilantes refused to leave the police premises. They were soon joined by others. As it grew bigger and more restive, the mob laid siege to the police post, demanding instant punishment. In about four hours, the siege culminated in the lynching by the mob of all the five Dalits who were in police custody.

Considering its location, the atrocity in Dulina was more outrageous than anything that came before. The Belchhi atrocity, for instance, had been enabled by the fact that the nearest police post was 5 km away. But the lynching in Dulina was inside the police station premises. The five victims were forcibly pulled out of the police lock-up and clobbered to death with rods and lathis, right under the nose of the State machinery.

About seventy policemen had gathered by then, equipped with rifles and cartridges, but they remained mute witnesses to the lynching. Equally passive were the senior police officers and executive magistrates who had rushed there, ostensibly to meet any contingency. In a display of abject surrender, not a single shot was fired while the five Dalits were battered to death in plain sight of all those who had been entrusted with the duty of upholding the majesty of the law.

Compare this wilful dereliction of duty at Dulina with the trigger-happy policemen at Ramabai Nagar. Clearly, the caste identity of the protestors accounted for the glaring difference in the nature of the police response at Ramabai Nagar and Dulina.

It was not the only travesty of law that day. None of the miscreants were arrested on the spot, even though armed policemen were eyewitnesses to the lynching. This is particularly conspicuous in view of the arrival of reinforcements towards the end of the lynching, more than doubling the police strength from seventy-one to 145.

The ruling party in Haryana was an ally of the BJP: Jat leader Om Prakash Chautala's Indian National Lok Dal, which was an offshoot of Charan Singh's peasant movement. The police were obviously under pressure to be lenient, especially because of the involvement of the VHP in the Dulina episode. The following day, the VHP, in collaboration with the Shiv Sena and other Hindu right-wing groups, organised meetings and took out processions on the streets of Jhajjar town in defence of the lynching.[31]

They also submitted a memorandum to the deputy commissioner of Jhajjar demanding that 'no action should be taken against the persons who have killed the accused of cow slaughters'.[32] This was in keeping with the justification that VHP national leader Giriraj Kishore infamously offered in the context of Jhajjar: '*Puranon mein, insaan se jyada gaay ko mahatva diya jata hai.* [In our scriptures, cows are considered more sacrosanct than human beings.]' Chautala turned a blind eye to these brazen displays of solidarity with the perpetrators of mass murder.

On 17 October 2002, a day after the pro-lynching demonstrations, a joint delegation of the CPI and CPI(M) visited Jhajjar on a fact-finding mission.[33] Besides meeting the family members of two of the murdered Dalits, the delegation visited the crime scene and talked with several police officials, including Jhajjar's superintendent of police, Mohammed Akil.

The delegation's report records a peculiar excuse that the police apparently trotted out for their inability to prevent the murders: that the mob had been confused about the religious identity of the alleged cow slaughterers. In Akil's 'assessment', the Dalits were 'actually presumed to be Muslims and that is why they were attacked'. The delegation found that VHP members had been 'directly involved in the spreading of rumours that a cow had been slaughtered and skinned on the open road by Muslims'. The police, who claimed to have 'told the growing crowd repeatedly that 'the men are not Muslims but Hindus', did not manage to dispel those rumours, he claimed.

This alleged confusion was a recurring theme in the official statements that followed. On 24 October 2002, Chautala declared that Jhajjar was a 'case of mistaken identity', without spelling out whom the Dalits had been mistaken for.[34] 'We will not let anyone communalise the issue,' Chautala said, while disclosing that the post mortem of the animal had anyway established that it was not a case of cow slaughter.

But he was 'non-committal', the *Times of India* reported, 'on the role of VHP and Shiv Sena in spreading the rumour that the cow was alive' when it had come into the possession of the Dalits. As for the demand for a judicial inquiry, Chautala announced that he had instead ordered a probe by a senior Dalit officer, R.R. Banswal, who was commissioner of the Rohtak Division.

Whatever his motive might have been, Chautala's selection of Banswal proved to be an inspired decision. For someone conducting what was in effect an in-house inquiry, this officer was unsparing in holding his colleagues culpable for their lapses in the Dulina episode. It was the kind of commitment to truth that Ram Dhan had displayed while probing the Belchhi atrocity, regardless of the embarrassment caused to his own party's government.

Before Banswal submitted his report, there was further controversy over the mistaken-identity theory, this time stoked by the National Commission for Scheduled Castes and Scheduled Tribes. When the commission had attained constitutional status in 1992, Ram Dhan had been its first chairperson. By the time of the Jhajjar killings, however, the institution was in decline.

Ram Dhan's successor in the commission, Bizay Sonkar Shastri, a Dalit leader (despite his upper-caste surname) and former BJP MP, betrayed the Hindutva subtext to the mistaken-identity theory.[35] Echoing Chautala's claim that the mob had mistaken the identity of the alleged cow slaughterers, Shastri blamed the police rather than the VHP for it: 'The mob was told they were Muslims. The police were part of the conspiracy. They knew throughout that the victims were Dalits…'

Despite all the evidence to the contrary, Shastri asserted that there was 'no preconceived desire on the part of the mob to kill the Dalits'. As the *Times of India* put it, 'Giving a new twist to the incident, he said the mob consisted of Dalits as well.' Shastri also said, 'The mob was confused. It was an accident.'

Had the mob known, he all but said, that the alleged cow slaughterers were not Muslims, they would not have been killed. Thus, in the political climate of 2002, a constitutional office-holder contributed to normalising Islamophobia.

Shastri's mistaken-identity theory fit the pattern of denying the caste angle to the violence against Dalits, overlooking a range of inconvenient facts. One such fact was that a section of the same mob had beaten up the alleged cow slaughterers before they were brought to the police post.

While he did recommend that the Haryana government should punish the police personnel involved in the incident, Shastri had nothing to say about the demonstrations in support of the lynching by the VHP and other Hindutva groups. Nor did he comment on the fact that these marches and meetings continued even after it had been established and announced that the victims were Dalits. He was more concerned about the few conversions that had followed the killings. Calling them 'a shameful act', Shastri demanded action against those instrumental in converting the relatives of the Jhajjar victims to Buddhism.

Shastri's sweeping conclusion that the mob had no idea that they were lynching Dalits was belied by the evidence Banswal recorded. His nuanced report,[36] dated 5 December 2002, documented testimonies on the various attempts that the police claimed to have made to pacify the mob during the prolonged siege. One such attempt was to counter their belligerence with a clarification repeatedly made to the cow vigilantes about the religious identity of the targeted men. Deputy Superintendent of Police (DSP) Narender Singh, who was the senior-most officer on the spot, 'told the mob in loud voice that they are Hindus and not Muslims'.

Banswal's analysis of the atrocity turned the focus on the role of the police, and debunked the dominant narrative that denied the caste angle. Regardless of the mob's perception, his indictment of the police was premised on their admitted knowledge that the men under attack were all Dalits. Piercing their veil of neutrality, Banswal's report laid bare the covert ways in which the police had enabled the violence.

The police were found to have, wilfully or otherwise, underestimated the threat. Though 'the matter related to the sentimental feelings of a particular section of society', Banswal said that the policemen on the spot, disregarding the 'sensitivity' of the situation, had acted in a 'casual manner'. They covered it up with their prolonged charade of negotiating with the mob.

The conduct of Station House Officer (SHO) Rajender Singh, of the Jhajjar Police Station—Dulina police post fell within its jurisdiction—exemplifies how casually the police treated the matter. Though the siege had begun around 6.15 p.m., and he had been informed about it within five minutes, Rajender Singh was found to have taken it 'very lightly', reaching the Dulina police post only at 7 p.m. By then, the mob had swollen to about a hundred persons, though they were still 'sitting peacefully'. He had over twenty policemen and three vehicles at his disposal. At that stage, it would not have been 'difficult for the police to shift the injured persons immediately' to the Jhajjar Police Station or the Civil Hospital 'for medical aid and also to control the mob'. Yet, Banswal found that 'the first message for first aid was not sent until 8.15 pm', although the Dalits had been brought to the police post in a bad shape.

The SHO's superior, DSP Narender Singh, and the two executive magistrates who had arrived around 8.15 p.m. were no less negligent. Although the situation had begun to escalate, these officers were found to have been 'trying to pacify the mob' rather than taking 'stern action'. The number of the police personnel was 'sufficient to handle the situation', Banswal said. 'But the theory propounded by each of the witnesses to the occurrence that the SHO, DSP and the Executive Magistrate tried to make the mob understand that the slaughterers were not Muslims is not understandable.' He also spelt out the stern measures that the police could have taken. 'When the mob was becoming more violent and was not ready to hear any reasoning, they should have taken appropriate decisions like heavy lathi charge or firing, etc to disperse the mob and thwart its attack.'

The police's hesitance in exercising any of their coercive powers emboldened the mob to storm the lock-up around 9.45 p.m. The lynching was said to have taken place between 9.45 p.m. and 10.15 p.m.—by which time the strength of the police on the spot had doubled. Banswal concluded, 'The force of 71 police personnel available at 9.20 pm was sufficient to control the situation even if it is presumed that the rest of the police force had reached the police post after the lynching of the five persons.'

By about 10.15 p.m., with the deed done, the crowd quickly dispersed. With a deployed strength of 145 at the time, the police soon outnumbered the mobsters who were '100 to 150 only at the police post after the incident'. It would not have been 'difficult for the police to lay (their) hands on some of the identified persons from the mob', Banswal observed. Not only did they not face any such action, the cow vigilantes were allowed to cock a snook at the law by blocking the police from shifting the dead bodies for post-mortem examination. Banswal pointed out that they 'could have been arrested' then at least for the lesser offence of 'interfering in the performance of lawful duty', if nothing else.

Because the police were reluctant to act against a mob consisting mostly of Jats, the dominant caste in the region, the FIR registered regarding the lynching on the night of 15 October 2002 blamed 'unknown persons'. Yet, the police's four-hour face-off had largely been with local people, as evident from the names recalled by the policemen in their witness statements in the case. Ten days later, on 25 October 2002, a senior officer supervising the investigation, Inspector General of Police Resham Singh, told the press that the police had identified twenty-eight local residents who had been part of the lynch mob. But not a single one of them had been arrested thus far.[37]

The identification of the accused coincided with the post-mortem report on the cow. Since it reconfirmed that the cow had died long before the alleged cow slaughter, the police finally closed the case they had booked against the Dalits to placate the mob.

In the lynching case, the police at long last mustered the courage to make the first arrests almost a month later. On 13 November 2002, five men from the list of identified accused were arrested in a pre-dawn crackdown designed to avoid clashes. But activists of the VHP and its youth wing, Bajrang Dal, responded swiftly with a bandh in Jhajjar district. This led to fresh violence, in which four policemen were injured and the Dulina police post was set on fire.

Thanks to a settlement with local leaders, the police arrested most of the remaining identified persons as and when they 'voluntarily surrendered' in batches, starting on 23 November 2002. It was around this time that Banswal indicted the police in his report submitted on 5 December 2002.

Four days later, the Vajpayee government broke its silence on the Dulina lynching in a statement in the Lok Sabha on 9 December 2002. The statement was in lieu of a debate that Dalit MPs had been demanding ever since the winter session of Parliament had commenced twenty days earlier.

Perhaps Home Minister L.K. Advani remembered only too well the tough time that one of his predecessors, Charan Singh, had faced twenty-five years earlier during the debate in Rajya Sabha on Belchhi. That might explain the government's refusal to allow a debate on Jhajjar. As Charan Singh's colleague in the Morarji Desai government, Advani himself had participated in the Belchhi debate and attempted to shield him. A vain attempt in the face of the Ram Dhan Committee's report.

Banswal's fact-finding had similarly debunked the claim that there was no caste angle to the lynchings. However, as the submission of the Banswal report to the Haryana government had not been made public, the Vajpayee government was able to sidestep its findings and claim that the report was 'expected shortly'.[38]

There was another reason why the Banswal report discomfited the Vajpayee government. The Dalit MP who had been most vociferously raising the Jhajjar issue was Ram Vilas Paswan, one of the fact-finders on Belchhi. About seven months earlier, Paswan had quit the Vajpayee government over the BJP's refusal to sack Chief Minister Narendra Modi over the Gujarat carnage. Adding to the government's embarrassment, Paswan had resigned right on the eve of a discussion in Parliament on Gujarat.[39]

In the case of Jhajjar, though, the government ensured that there would be no parliamentary debate at all. It strategically chose to make a statement without allowing any follow-up discussion. Home Minister Advani, who had also been appointed deputy prime minister six months earlier, did not himself make that statement. It was left to his junior, Minister of State for Home I.D. Swami, to speak on Jhajjar. That was how the statement pretending that the Banswal report was still awaited came to be made.

Speaking for the Vajpayee government and vouching for its political ally, Swami said: 'If anybody is found guilty in the inquiry report of the Divisional Commissioner, Rohtak, the State Government would not hesitate in taking action against them.'[40] This never happened though. Unlike its Maharashtra counterpart in the Ramabai Nagar case, the Haryana government failed to lodge an FIR against any of the police officials indicted by Banswal.

Swami began his statement with an express reference to Paswan's allegation that the five Dalits in Dulina had been killed by the 'police and some communal elements'. But since he was feigning ignorance about the Banswal report, Swami was able to say, 'The magistrates and the police officers present on the spot decided not to resort to firing as the situation would further worsen.' He claimed 'there was no space left between the mob and the police and they were surrounded by the mob from all sides'.

There was a belated admission of the caste angle. Swami announced that a provision from the POA had been 'added to the case'.

However, in the same breath, he came up with a variant of the mistaken-identity theory. 'In fact, it appears that the incident took place because of the mistaken impression,' Swami claimed, 'that a cow slaughter was being committed openly.' Since this impression 'aroused the passions of the people', the minister asserted that 'it should not be treated as a deliberate atrocity committed on the members of the Scheduled Castes'.

Like Chautala's original theory, the new version peddled by the Vajpayee government too claimed that the lynching had nothing to do with caste prejudice. It was a strategic choice between two forms of bigotry. One was Bizay Sonkar Shastri's Islamophobic twist that the alleged slaughterers were mistaken for Muslims. The other was Giriraj Kishore's interpretation of Hindu scriptures that a cow's life mattered more than that of a human. The latter was politically more tenable as it was not discriminatory against cow slaughterers, real or otherwise, on the basis of religion or caste.

More than fifty years after the Indian Republic had formally abolished untouchability and 'its practice in any form', a BJP-led government offered Hindu passions associated with the sacred cow as a mitigating circumstance for a mass murder of Dalits. The dichotomy between the government's political stance and its invocation of the POA inevitably affected the outcome of the trial that followed years later.

On 7 August 2010, a special judge appointed under the POA, A.K. Jain, convicted seven men, including one Dalit, for the Dulina mass crime. The conviction of that solitary Dalit was crucial for determining whether the caste atrocities law should have been applied at all. The trial court held that there was no cogent evidence proving that the crime in question was motivated by the caste of the victims. 'On the contrary, it is apparent,' Jain said, 'that the accused were not even aware of the caste of the victims. In this background, no offence is made out under the Scheduled Castes and Scheduled Tribes (Prevention of Atrocities) Act against the accused.'[41]

Since the lynching had ostensibly been triggered by the suspicion of cow slaughter, the trial court regarded it purely as a religiously motivated crime. Naturally, it missed the wood for the trees. Depending on the identity of the victims, any lynching in the name of cow slaughter was inherently either a communal crime (if the casualties were Muslims) or a caste atrocity (if the casualties were Dalits, as in Dulina).

Almost eight years had gone by since the imagined cow slaughter, but they did nothing to dim the passions associated with it. The Congress party had replaced the BJP in power, both in Haryana and at the national level, but that too apparently made little difference to the political ecosystem. As *Frontline* reported, 'On the day the judgment was pronounced, a huge crowd gathered outside the Jhajjar court in support of the accused, reminiscent of the huge mobilisation on October 16, 2002, to put pressure on the administration against their arrest. Not a word was uttered in support of the massacre victims either then or now. Slogans were raised in support of the cow.'

Two days later, on 9 August 2010, Jain awarded life sentences to all the seven convicted men. At a protest meeting the next day, it was decided to call a bigger assembly involving representatives of a motley bunch of khaps, gurukuls and gaushalas. The fresh wave of protests glorified, as before, the lynching of Dalits as 'just retribution' for their imagined sin of cow slaughter.

❖

'I solemnly assure you that I will not die a Hindu.' Ambedkar took this famous pledge at Yeola in the Nashik district of Bombay Presidency on 13 October 1935. It took him over two decades, towards the end of his life, to fulfil that vow. The day and place he chose were as subversive as his decision to convert, along with a multitude of his followers, to Buddhism.

The place was Nagpur, which had been a battleground against untouchability since the colonial period when it was the capital of the Central Provinces. Referring to its parallel reputation as the hub of Hindu nationalism, Ambedkar made a tongue-in-cheek clarification: it was not because 'the great battalion of the RSS was here in Nagpur, we took the meeting to this city in order to lay them flat'. Though Buddhism had almost disappeared from India, Ambedkar said that, in the distant past, the people of 'Nagpur and the surrounding country' had been in the forefront of spreading that religion.

The date he chose for his historic repudiation of Hinduism was 14 October 1956, Dussehra day. On the occasion of a festival that commemorated Rama's victory over Ravana, Ambedkar read out a vow that said, 'I shall have no faith in Rama and Krishna … nor shall I worship them.'

Another of the twenty-two vows he took on that occasion scoffed at the Hindu co-option of Buddha as an incarnation of Vishnu, calling it 'sheer madness and false propaganda'. The most telling of his vows revolved around caste: 'I renounce Hinduism which is harmful for humanity … because it is based on inequality.'

Though Ambedkar passed away within two months of his conversion, the new significance he had conferred on Dussehra took the form of an annual gathering at that open space in Nagpur, which came to be sanctified as Deekshabhoomi. Fifty years later, Dussehra happened to fall on 2 October 2006, the birth anniversary of Ambedkar's legendary rival Gandhi. Arrangements were being made to accommodate more people than usual, running into lakhs from all over the country and beyond, for the golden anniversary of Ambedkar's conversion.

But three days before that mega event, disaster struck in a village called Khairlanji, just over 100 km from Nagpur. Around dusk on 29 September 2006, a mob lynched four members of a Dalit family. The Bhotmanges were both Ambedkarites and Buddhists. They were also Mahars, the same caste as Ambedkar's.

The mob dragged the family out of their hut and clobbered them to death with sticks and cycle chains. Forty-year-old Surekha and her seventeen-year-old daughter, Priyanka, a school topper and an NCC cadet, were among the lynched. The mob carried their bodies out of the village in a bullock cart and dumped them in a canal.

Acting on a tip-off, Meshram, a beat constable from the local Andhalgaon Police Station, visited Khairlanji around 8.30 p.m., by when the bodies had been removed. Apparently finding nothing suspicious, Meshram reported that the situation was 'normal'. So, the police station took no action that night.

The next morning, around 8 a.m., Surekha's husband, Bhaiyyalal

Bhotmange, the sole surviving member of the family, approached the police in a distraught state. He had fled from his home on seeing the mob. In the absence of any clarity yet about the status of his family, the police refused to entertain his complaint.

Later that morning, Priyanka's badly bruised body was fished out from the canal. It was stark naked.

Still, the inquest report of the police talked only of murder as the apparent cause of Priyanka's death. That she had been found without a shred of clothing on her failed to arouse any suspicion that the teenager might have also suffered sexual assault.

The inquest report set the tone for the post-mortem examination that followed at the 'rural hospital' in a town called Mohadi, which, like Khairlanji, was located in the Bhandara district of Maharashtra. The post-mortem report recorded the tell-tale detail that Priyanka's thighs had bruises. The condition of her genital area was not set down in the report.

Only after the post-mortem report had been received did the Andhalgaon Police Station register an FIR at about 8 p.m. on 30 September 2006—more than twenty-four hours after the carnage. And although it was about twelve hours after Bhaiyyalal had first complained to them about the mob attack, the police station recorded the FIR as if they had just then received the information from him.

The deliberate delay in recording the FIR served to keep the sexual violence angle out of it. Had it been registered immediately after the discovery of Priyanka's naked body, the police would have been hard-pressed to avoid provisions relating to sexual assault. Instead, fortified by the post-mortem report, the police registered the FIR only under provisions relating to murder, with no hint of rape, or even the quaintly worded lesser offence of 'outraging the modesty' of a woman.

There was, however, a grudging acknowledgement of the caste angle. Besides the relevant IPC provisions, the FIR referred to one from the POA as well. But this provision was not about physical violence, sexual or otherwise. Instead, the milder provision on verbal violence, such as the utterance of a caste slur, was invoked: Section 3(1)(x) of POA penalised anyone who 'insults or intimidates with intent to humiliate' a Dalit 'in any place within public view'.

It so happened that the very next provision in POA, Section 3(1)(xi), penalised any non-Dalit who 'assaults or uses force to any woman belonging to a Scheduled Caste ... with intent to dishonour or outrage her modesty'. The most glaring omission was of Section 3(2)(v) of the POA relating to heinous offences, such as the rape and murder of Dalits.

The next day, the police made further discoveries in the canal: the battered bodies of Surekha and her two sons, Sudhir and Roshan. Around the same time, the superintendent of police of Bhandara district, Suresh Sagar, visited Khairlanji for the first time since the lynching. This visit apparently nudged his subordinates into arresting the culprits who had been moving about freely till then. Thus, two days after the lynching, the police suddenly rounded up as many as twenty-eight people.

However, Khairlanji caused no ripple in the proceedings at Deekshabhoomi the next day. A major reason for this uncharacteristic silence on the part of the Ambedkarites was that, in the immediate aftermath of the Khairlanji massacre, the caste angle had been suppressed in the initial news reports, which in any case had appeared only in the local media.

Take the report published on 2 October 2006 in the leading Nagpur-based newspaper, *Lokmat Times.* Neither the headline nor the story mentioned that the deceased were all Dalits: 'Four of a family murdered, 28 arrested'. Though it mentioned their surname, the story went unnoticed at Deekshabhoomi because Bhotmange was an uncommon name among Dalits. Worse, it indulged in victim-blaming—a pattern common to the initial reports. Consider the way the *Lokmat Times* story began: 'Sensation prevailed after four persons of a family were murdered over illicit relations at Khairlanji village near Mohadi in Bhandara.'[42] The leading newspaper of the region had no qualms in suggesting that Surekha Bhotmange had brought this tragedy upon herself and her children by engaging in an illicit relationship. The *Lokmat Times* alleged that she had committed adultery with Siddharth Gajbhiye, a well-to-do Dalit relative from a nearby village.

This far-fetched suggestion that the lynching had been triggered by the moral outrage of neighbours was designed to divert attention from a long-festering hostility between the assertive Bhotmanges and members of the Shudra castes dominant in Khairlanji: Kunbis and Kalars. Gajbhiye was a pillar of support to the Bhotmanges in those disputes, which were over a range of issues, particularly a legal one pertaining to their small landholding in Khairlanji.

The immediate cause for the lynching was a situation that went against the grain of caste. Despite their relatively high status in the caste hierarchy, some of the Shudras living in Khairlanji used to work as labour on the farm owned by Gajbhiye, a Mahar. As the result of a labour dispute, Gajbhiye was assaulted in Khairlanji on 3 September 2006. The police recorded the testimonies of Surekha and Priyanka as eyewitnesses against the twelve men who were involved in the assault that had landed Gajbhiye in hospital.

Since the assault was by non-Dalits on a Dalit, Gajbhiye pleaded that his complaint be registered under the POA, besides the general IPC provision of assault. However, instead of the 1989 caste atrocities law, the police registered the FIR under the older and milder anti-untouchability law, the Protection of Civil Rights Act, 1955.

As a result, the twelve accused persons who had been implicated by Surekha and Priyanka were arrested and released on bail within minutes. The indignity of being subjected, however mildly, to the criminal law process at the instance of Dalits was evidently intolerable to the accused dominant-caste persons.

They retaliated with another assault that very evening. For the dominant-caste persecutors, the audacity displayed by the Bhotmange women in testifying against them was the last straw. This assault was far more brutal.

The truth about the Khairlanji atrocity came out on 7 October 2006 when the Mumbai-based newspaper *DNA* published a report headlined, 'Killed for speaking up'. Besides bringing out the crucial detail that the murdered persons were from a Dalit family, the *DNA* story by Jaideep Hardikar revealed that Surekha and Priyanka had been 'beaten and gang-raped in full public view'. Besides, it referred to allegations that 'the state administration, police and political class' as also the doctors involved in post-mortem investigations had been engaged in a 'cover-up'.[43]

Exactly a month after the atrocity, on 29 October 2006, the news went national. The *Times of India* woke up to it with a sarcastic headline, 'Just another rape story'.[44] As the counter-narrative to the adultery story had gained traction by then, there was a Dalit uprising across the Vidarbha region and beyond. As if to make up for lost time, the uprising was on a scale unprecedented for any caste atrocity.[45] The protests emboldened a section of the State machinery to break away from the conspiracy that sought to play down the sexual and caste aspects of the Khairlanji episode.

In a rare display of institutional autonomy, Ratnakar Gaikwad, a senior Dalit officer, commissioned a probe into Khairlanji in his capacity as the nodal officer designated to oversee the implementation of POA safeguards in Maharashtra. A team of fact-finders drawn from two government organisations, Babasaheb Ambedkar Research and Training Institute (BARTI) and Yashwantrao Chavan Academy of Development Administration (YASHADA), toured Khairlanji and related places for a week from 3 November 2006.

In its interim report, submitted to the Maharashtra government on 10 November 2006, the BARTI–YASHADA team held that there was 'a deep-rooted conspiracy towards suppressing the crime and the evidence'. It buttressed this finding with examples: 'FIR was not filed immediately, wrong reports were given by the police, post-mortem was not carried out properly, etc.'[46]

Having indicted several officers, including some who were Dalit, for being party to the conspiracy, the BARTI–YASHADA report recommended that further investigation of the Khairlanji case should be handed over to the Central Bureau of Investigation (CBI) in order 'to avoid local or political interference'.

The report came as a blow to the coalition government of

the Congress and Nationalist Congress Party (NCP). Against the backdrop of widespread Dalit protests on the issue, the report forced Chief Minister Vilasrao Deshmukh of the Congress and Deputy Chief Minister R.R. Patil of the NCP to yield to the demand for a CBI probe. On 20 November 2006, the Maharashtra government requested the Congress-led coalition government at the Centre that the Khairlanji case be taken over by the CBI.

The charge sheet filed a month later by the CBI vindicated the contention of the Dalit protesters that the lynching at Khairlanji had been driven by caste prejudice. It rejected the police's curious assumption in the FIR that the only provision of POA that could apply to Khairlanji was the one pertaining to the utterance of caste slurs, disregarding the clauses relating to violence.

The CBI pressed charges based on POA provisions regarding murder and destruction of evidence. Further, it made out a case of outraging modesty, citing provisions from the special atrocities law and the general criminal law. The CBI settled for this lesser sexual offence, constrained by the lack of any indication of rape in the post-mortem reports, such as they were.

A special court, set up under POA at Bhandara, conducted the trial in the Khairlanji case. On 15 September 2008, S.S. Das, the trial judge, convicted eight men for murder. However, he acquitted them of all charges relating to sexual and caste offences.

Nine days later, Das awarded the death penalty to six of the eight convicted men. The recourse to this extreme penalty entailed a determination that the Khairlanji atrocity fell in the category of 'the rarest of rare cases'. This required Das to draw up a balance sheet of aggravating and mitigating circumstances.

One of the aggravating circumstances cited was that Priyanka's body had been found without any clothes. Having rejected the charge of sexual offence, the trial judge referred to her disrobed condition with a caveat. Stretching credulity, the trial court upheld the claim of the accused that they had stripped Priyanka only after killing her. Six of the accused were said to have 'removed clothes of Priyanka before disposing her severely injured dead body and thereby wanted to get satisfaction to their sexual eyes at such extreme circumstances'. Though there was no independent evidence corroborating this self-serving admission of the accused, it was on the basis of the necrophilia scenario that the trial court exonerated them of the charge of molestation or outraging modesty.

Central to the trial court verdict was its insistence on treating Khairlanji as a unidimensional crime. It was as if the trial court found it inconceivable that the impulse to take revenge could have been aggravated by caste prejudice. Its exact words were that 'the whole object of the accused was to take revenge against Surekha and Priyanka because the accused believed that they were falsely implicated in the assault of Siddharth Gajbhiye by them and in the process they committed not only murders of Surekha and Priyanka but of Sudhir and Roshan'.

On the strength of this theory of wreaking revenge without any caste consciousness, Das overlooked the sheer disproportionality of their violence against the Bhotmanges. First of all, the offence in which the accused had been implicated on the testimonies of the Bhotmange women was relatively minor, one that was bailable and punishable with imprisonment up to three years. The revenge that they claimed to have exacted for that had far worse consequences for them.

Yet, in its list of mitigating circumstances in relation to the death sentence, the trial court made this sweeping assumption: 'There was no caste hatred for these killings.' Implicit in it was an admission that had caste been a factor, it would have counted as an aggravating circumstance. The trial court, accordingly, ruled out the application of any of the POA provisions that had been cited by the CBI.

In the end, the trial court concluded that the mitigating circumstances were outweighed by the aggravating circumstances, such as the 'depravity' and 'brutality' shown in killing 'unarmed' people who 'did not cause any provocation at the time of the incident'.

Two years later, the Bombay High Court shifted the balance from the aggravating circumstances to the mitigating ones. On the appeals against the trial court judgment, the Nagpur bench of the High Court upheld the conviction of all the eight accused on the charge of murder. But in regard to the six of them who had been awarded the death penalty, the High Court commuted their sentence to imprisonment for twenty-five years.[47] In effect, it sentenced all eight convicts to life imprisonment.

In its verdict delivered on 14 July 2010, the High Court concluded that the six condemned convicts 'do not deserve death sentence'. The very next line in the judgment was telling: 'The incident had not occurred on account of caste hatred ...' Thus, the High Court differed from the trial court only on the quantum of punishment or the evaluation of mitigating and aggravating circumstances. But on the crucial question of caste, it was entirely in consonance with the trial court.

The High Court also reiterated that 'the accused felt that they were falsely implicated in the crime of beating Siddharth Gajbhiye by Surekha and Priyanka'. Carrying forward the deficiencies in the trial court's reasoning, the High Court too offered no explanation for why the indignation of the accused about two Dalit women testifying against them could not have been laced with caste prejudice.

Authored by Justice A.P. Lavande on behalf of a two-judge bench, the High Court verdict upheld the trial court's view that none of the POA provisions applied to the Khairlanji massacre. Successive courts shared the view that if there was any evidence bearing out an alternative explanation, it precluded the role of caste, even if the reaction of the convicts to the Dalits was extreme. In their imagination, the cause of the lynching could be one or the other and never both.

In rejecting the charge of caste slur, for instance, the High Court asserted that 'the whole object of the accused was to take revenge against Surekha and Priyanka' for implicating them in the assault case. Therefore, 'it is difficult to hold that the accused intended to insult Surekha or other deceased who admittedly were belonging to Scheduled Caste'. The High Court was not convinced beyond reasonable doubt that the accused could have uttered any casteist remarks in the course of killing four members of a Dalit family.

As for the allegation of sexual assault, the High Court cited a technical reason for rejecting it. While appealing against the acquittal under the Section 3(1)(xi) of the POA provision of outraging the modesty of a woman, the CBI had omitted to challenge the acquittal of the accused under the corresponding provision in the general law, Section 354 of the IPC. This omission, the High Court said, 'makes it difficult to uphold the challenge of CBI … inasmuch as the offence under Section 3(1)(xi) (of POA) is an aggravated form of the offence under Section 354 of IPC'.

Understandably, Dalit activists were aggrieved that none of the acquittals under the interconnected provisions relating to sexual and caste offences had been reversed. For several years after that, the Supreme Court did not hear the cross appeals filed against the High Court verdict by the CBI and the convicts. Meanwhile, more than a decade after he had lost his entire family, Bhaiyyalal Bhotmange passed away on 20 January 2017 at the age of sixty-two.

Two years later, in an unrelated development, the president of India elevated Justice Bhushan Ramakrishna Gavai, a Nagpur-based Dalit, to the Supreme Court. As an official communiqué put it, 'On his appointment, the Supreme Court Bench will have a judge belonging to Scheduled Caste category after about a decade.'[48] His father R.S. Gavai was a prominent Ambedkarite and Buddhist leader who had been president of the Dr Babasaheb Ambedkar Smarak Samiti, which runs Deekshabhoomi in Nagpur. At the time of the Khairlanji episode, the senior Gavai was the governor of Bihar, while the junior was a judge in the Bombay High Court.

Justice Gavai's Supreme Court tenure began on a dramatic note. The long-pending Khairlanji case was listed to be heard that day, 24 May 2019, before a three-judge bench that included him. Not only did he hear the Khairlanji appeals on his very first day, they were also disposed of the same day. The author of the eighteen-page judgment was Justice Surya Kant, for whom it too was the first day in the last court of appeal.[49] The Supreme Court, like the two lower courts, betrayed a reluctance to recognise that the Khairlanji killings were a caste atrocity.

While upholding the life sentence for the eight convicted persons on the murder charge, the Supreme Court skirted their acquittals on sexual and caste offences. Though it mentioned Priyanka seven times, not once did it even hint that her body had been found unclothed. Had it taken cognisance of this evidence incriminating the accused, the Supreme Court could not have avoided pronouncing on the improbability of their claim that they had stripped her only after murdering her.

The only reference to caste was in the context of its summary of the High Court judgment. In its retelling, the Supreme Court diluted the High Court's phrase 'caste hatred' to 'caste stature'. But where the High Court had made out that vengeance was 'the whole object of the accused', the Supreme Court reframed it as 'the root cause' of the violence.[50]

The admission that the desire for vengeance was only the root cause of the violence and not the whole object of the accused seemed to be a slight improvement in the quality of reasoning. It created space for accepting that caste prejudice could have been a contributory factor. In the event, the Supreme Court made no such acknowledgement and instead reinforced the myth that the 'caste stature' of the Bhotmanges was entirely incidental to their brutal massacre.

After all the drama involved in timing the long overdue hearing with the rare appointment of a Dalit judge, the Supreme Court judgment turned out to be anti-climactic. Its deafening silence on the discovery of Priyanka's naked body stripped India of the pretence of having robust safeguards against untouchability.

From Belchhi to Khairlanji, the postcolonial State has remained steadfast, across decades and across regions, in denying the caste angle to some of the most blatant caste atrocities.

EPILOGUE

In 1890, when child marriage was the norm, Tilak opposed the modest move to increase the age of consent from ten to twelve years. The practice of marrying off daughters before they attained puberty was integral to Brahminical notions of purity. Tilak's pushback by and by led to a consensus in the Hindu right that no social reform should be undertaken until India was rid of colonial rule. Among the casualties was, of course, the struggle against untouchability. Despite numerous efforts by reformers in the intervening decades, no special provisions were enacted to enumerate and penalise crimes arising from untouchability.

Even so, when caste Hindus assaulted untouchables at Mahad on 20 March 1927 for daring to draw water from a lake, the government of Bombay Presidency promptly initiated action under regular criminal law. Within a few months, a trial court convicted nine caste Hindus and sentenced them to rigorous imprisonment for four months.

Ambedkar highlighted this legal vindication of untouchables in a Marathi pamphlet announcing the Satyagraha that was to be held on 25 December 1927, again at Mahad. 'The assaulters among the touchable people have been sentenced to four months of sakt majuri (forced labour).' He added that the court verdict was 'important for both the parties'.[1]

Its signal to caste Hindus, in his view, was this: 'The notion among the touchable people, that it was their right not to let the Untouchables access the Chavadar Tank, has lost its basis. There is no doubt that if they ventured to oppose us in future like madmen, they will have to see the prison gates again.'

As for the importance of the court verdict for his followers, Ambedkar wrote: 'Likewise there is no hitch in saying that the belief among the Untouchables that they had the right to go to the Chavadar Tank has been established. If it had not been so, instead of sentencing those who had obstructed us from going to the tank, they would have sentenced us for having gone to the tank.'

Ambedkar could not have foreseen then that this salutary precedent would be disregarded in various ways by postcolonial India in dealing with offences against Dalits—offences that were far more serious than the non-fatal violence at Mahad. Much less could he have imagined that, seventy-six years later, a Hindu nationalist government would declare the anniversary of his Mahad breakthrough as 'Social Empowerment Day'. The Vajpayee government made this announcement through a press release on 20 March 2003. The decision to elevate Ambedkar's simple gesture of sipping water at a lake to a national symbol of social empowerment could not have been easy for a government that carried Hindutva baggage.

On the one hand, the government acknowledged that the Mahad incident had impressed upon the depressed sections that 'nothing could be secured without struggle'. On the other hand, it left out the awkward detail that caste Hindus had tried to restore the purity of the lake by pouring cow's urine into the water. Instead, it made out that 'upper caste Hindus "purified" the waters of the tank by pouring 108 pitchers of water into it'.[2]

Similarly, while describing the Satyagraha that had been organised in Mahad in response to that purification rite, the government's statement omitted the highlight of it: the ceremonious burning of Manusmriti by Ambedkar and his followers. All it said was that, since he could not go back to the tank on 25 December 1927 because of a civil court injunction that had been obtained by caste Hindus, Ambedkar 'postponed the Satyagrah in order not to break the law'.

Be that as it may, the commemoration of breaching the access barrier at Mahad as Social Empowerment Day is a posthumous triumph for not just Ambedkar but also the equality champions who never got their due for taking on caste in courts and legislatures. Their struggles made it easier for the generations to come, across all castes. But, as this book shows, the battles for equality are far from over and the pushback has assumed more insidious and brutal forms.

If at all Tilak's premise that politically free Hindus could be trusted to reform caste has come true, it is more in letter than in spirit. The practice of caste is constantly mutating as old crudities give way to more sophisticated forms of prejudice and discrimination. However fashionable (and hopeful) it may be to claim that caste is receding in the face of modernity, the daily news cycle, even as it captures only a part of the reality, belies that sanctimonious assertion. This book tracing the legal history of varna is, unwittingly, very much about the current affairs of Hindus—whether they are based in India or are part of the great Indian diaspora.

NOTES

I. EARLY CODES

1. THE PUNISHMENT RESERVED FOR LOWER CASTES

1 Jeremiah 20:2.
2 Acts 16:24.
3 Bertha Haven Putnam, 'The Enforcement of the Statutes of Labourers', *Studies in History, Economics and Public Law,* edited by the Faculty of Political Science of Columbia University, Vol. XXXII, Longmans, Green and Company, New York, 1908, p. 181.
4 Parliamentary Debates (Rajya Sabha), Vol 7-B (16 September 1954), pp. 2424–66.
5 Statutes, Acts and Regulations in Force in the Madras Presidency, Higginbotham, Madras, 1876, Harvard Law Library; Z211, M16 35659, Tamil Nadu State Archives.
6 On Anna Salai, Triplicane.
7 V. Sriram, 'Unsung hero of Madras', *The Hindu,* 26 July 2010.
8 *The Midnapore Zemindari Company Limited v. Appayasami Naicker,* Madras High Court, (1918) ILR 41 Mad 749, authored by Chief Justice John Wallis.
9 John Bradshaw, *Sir Thomas Munro and the British Settlement of the Madras Presidency,* Clarendon Press, Oxford, 1894, p. 180.
10 Ibid.
11 Nancy Gardner Cassels, *Social Legislation of the East India Company,* Sage, New Delhi, 2010, p. 249.
12 Ibid., p. 113.
13 (1883) ILR 6 Mad. 247.
14 (1901) ILR 24 Mad. 271.

15 *Uppala Kotayya Nagaram v. Unknown*, 1916 Cr. L.J. 672; Madras High Court, 3 September 1915.

16 *Madasamy Nadan vs Unknown*, 1916 Cri. L.J. 4 (1), Madras High Court, 11 November 1915.

17 Bal Gangadhar Tilak, 'Home *Rule or …?*', *Mahratta*, 8 April 1917, pp. 162–3, Nehru Memorial Museum and Library.

18 'Madras Legislative Council', *The Times of India*, 26 May 1915, p. 8.

19 Ibid.

20 Home Department, Judicial, 1917, Proceedings No. 214, National Archives of India.

21 Home, Political, 1922, Proceedings No. 684, National Archives of India.

22 Home, Judicial, 1917, Proceedings No. 214, National Archives of India.

23 'Budget Presented', *The Times of India*, 3 April 1917, p. 8.

24 *Mahratta*, 8 April 1917, pp. 162–3, Nehru Memorial Museum and Library.

25 Home Department, Judicial, 1917, Proceedings No. 214, National Archives of India.

26 Madras Legislative Council Proceedings, 1917, Tamil Nadu State Archives.

27 GOI Legislative Department Proceedings, January 1920, Nos 15–7, National Archives of India.

28 Nancy Gardner Cassels, *Social Legislation of the East India Company*, Sage, New Delhi, 2010, p. 19.

29 Parliamentary Debates (Rajya Sabha), Vol. 7-B (16 September 1954), pp. 2424–66.

30 Narasimha Ayyar became a renunciate called Narasimha Swami. He is best known as an apostle of Shirdi Sai Baba, who, exemplifying India's syncretic culture, remained ambivalent about his religious identity. In his biography of Baba, Narasimha Swami wrote: 'Prejudices die hard and the devotee … wonders how people can believe that Baba was a Brahmin and his parents were Brahmins when he had lived all his life in a mosque and when he was believed to be a Muslim. It was only a few persons … who saw clearly that Baba was neither Hindu nor Muslim, but above all castes, sects and religions.' (Narasimha Swami, *Life of Sai Baba*, All India Sai Samaj, Chennai, 2004, p. 6.)

2. THE PREROGATIVE TO COVER BREASTS

1 'Serious Disturbances in Travancore', *The Times of India*, 23 February 1859, p. 125. (From 1838–59, the publication was actually called *The Bombay Times and Journal of Commerce.*)
2 Documents referred to in the above petition, *The Times of India*, 12 February 1859, p. 102.
3 V. Nagam Aiya, *Raja Sir T Madhava Rao: Part II*, 1915, pp. 90–1, Tamil Nadu State Archives.
4 Ibid., pp. 88–9.
5 Documents referred to in the above petition, *The Times of India*, 12 February 1859, p. 102.
6 Ibid.
7 S. Cohn, *Colonialism and Its Forms of Knowledge*, Princeton University Press, New Jersey, 1996, p. 140.
8 Robert L. Hardgrave, Jr, *The Nadars of Tamilnad*, University of California Press, Berkeley and Los Angeles, 1969, p. 60.
9 Bernard S. Cohn, *Colonialism and Its Forms of Knowledge*, Princeton University Press, New Jersey, 1996, p. 141.
10 Ibid.
11 'Petition from Travancore', *The Times of India*, 12 February 1859, p. 102.
12 'Shanar Women', *The Times of India*, 7 December 1859, p. 781.
13 Ibid.; Also see: V. Nagam Aiya, *Raja Sir T. Madhava Rao: Part I*, 1915, p. 40, Tamil Nadu State Archives.
14 'Shanar Women', *The Times of India*, 7 December 1859, p. 781; Also see V. Nagam Aiya, *Raja Sir T Madhava Rao: Part I*, 1915, p. 41, Tamil Nadu State Archives.
15 'Shanar Women', *The Times of India*, 7 December 1859, p. 781; Also see: V. Nagam Aiya, *Raja Sir T Madhava Rao: Part I*, 1915, pp. 37–38, Tamil Nadu State Archives.
16 'Government Records', *The Times of India*, 25 June 1859, p. 407; Also see V. Nagam Aiya, *Raja Sir T Madhava Rao… Part I*, 1915, pp. 42–43, Tamil Nadu State Archives.
17 'Government Records', *The Times of India*, 25 June 1859, p. 407.
18 Ibid.
19 V. Nagam Aiya, *Raja Sir T Madhava Rao: Part I*, 1915, pp. 43–4, Tamil Nadu State Archives.
20 'Travancore Government and Travancore Shanars', *The Times of India*, 31 August 1859, p. 558.

21 GO No. 666, 12-11-1859, Political Department, Government of Madras, National Archives of India.
22 'Travancore Government and Travancore Shanars', *The Times of India*, 31 August 1859, p. 558.
23 GO No. 666, 1859, Political Department, Government of Madras, National Archives of India.
24 Ibid.
25 Ibid.
26 Ibid.
27 Ibid.
28 Rahul Sagar, The *Progressive Maharaja: Sir Madhava Rao's Hints on the Art and Science of Government*, HarperCollins, Gurugram, 2022, p. 60.
29 Detailed Report of the Proceedings of the Third Indian National Congress, 1887, Tamil Nadu State Archives.

3. THE FIGHT TO BURN WOMEN ALIVE

1 Lata Mani, 'Contentious Traditions: The Debate on Sati in Colonial India', *Cultural Critique*, No. 7, 1987, pp. 119–56, https://doi.org/10.2307/1354153.
2 Quoted in *Emperor v. Ram Dayal*, (1914) ILR 36 All. 26.
3 Andrea Major (ed.), *Sati: A Historical Anthology*, Oxford University Press, New Delhi, 2007, p. 111.
4 Ibid.
5 Proceedings of the Council of the Governor General of India, 19 March 1891, p. 100.
6 Andrea Major (ed.), *Sati: A Historical Anthology*, Oxford University Press, New Delhi, 2007, p. 115.
7 Ibid., p. 118.
8 Amiya P. Sen, *Rammohun Roy: A Critical Biography*, Penguin Viking, New Delhi, 2012, p. 115.
9 Andrea Major (ed.), *Sati: A Historical Anthology*, Oxford University Press, New Delhi, 2007, p. 145.
10 Ibid., p. 118.
11 Ibid., p. 228.
12 Nancy Gardner Cassels, *Social Legislation of the East India Company*, Sage, New Delhi, 2010, p.106.
13 Appeal to the Privy Council for permission to bury or burn Hindoo widows alive, *The Guardian and the Observer*, 2 October 1831, p. 2.

14 'Rite of Suttee in India', *The Guardian and the Observer*, 24 June 1832, p. 4.
15 Abstract of the Proceedings of the Council of the Governor General of India, 19 March 1891, p. 147.
16 A Penal Code prepared by the Indian Law Commissioners and published by command of the Governor General of India in Council, Calcutta, 1837.
17 Ratanlal & Dhirajlal, *The Indian Penal Code*, Wadhwa and Company, Nagpur, 1987, p. 294.
18 Titles of the Acts passed by the Governor General of India in Council in the year 1862, Wikimedia Commons.
19 *Emperor v. Ram Dayal*, (1914) ILR 36 All. 26.
20 *Emperor v. Ram Dayal*, (1914) ILR 36 All. 26.
21 *Emperor v Vidyasagar Pande*, 1928, ILR 8 Pat. 74.
22 *Kinder Singh v. Emperor*, 1933 All. LJ 7.
23 All those implicated in Roop Kanwar's Sati were, however, acquitted by the trial court in 1996. And the eleven who had been tried for glorifying her Sati were acquitted in 2004.
24 Parliamentary Debates, Rajya Sabha, 16 December 1987, p. 151.
25 Post abolition, the most famous Sati was the one that took place in 1839 after the death of the great Sikh ruler, Maharaja Ranjit Singh, when four of his wives and seven of his slave girls burnt themselves on his funeral pyre. Two of those four wives were Hindu Rajputs. That Sati was committed in the face of strictures from Sikh gurus.

4. THE EPIPHANY BEHIND THE FIRST LAW AGAINST CASTE

1 Rajesh Kochhar, 'Hindoo College Calcutta revisited: Its history and the role of Ram Mohan Roy', *Science and Culture*, 78, Proceedings of the Indian History Congress, Vol. 72, Part I (2011), pp. 280–305.
2 Minutes of Evidence taken before the Select Committee of the House of Lords appointed to enquire into the present state of affairs of the East India Company, London, 1830, Bodleian Library.
3 Appendix to the Report from Select Committee of the House of Commons on the Affairs of the East India Company, 16 August 1832, p. 122, New York Public Library.
4 Ibid., p. 124.
5 'Rite of Suttee in India', *The Guardian and The Observer*, 24 June 1832, p. 4.

6 All excerpts on the making of Act XXI of 1850 are from Legislative Consultations, 4 April to 10 May 1850, Nos 57 to 87, India Office Records P/207/59, British Library, London. The corresponding material in the National Archives of India is classified under 'Home, Public'.

7 Dhananjay Keer, *Mahatma Jotirao Phooley*, Popular Prakashan, Mumbai, 2013, p. 25.

8 Home, Public, 11 April 1850, Nos 73–8 KW, National Archives of India.

9 Sumit Sarkar, Tanika Sarkar (eds.), *Women and Social Reform in Modern India*, Permanent Black, Ranikhet, 2017, p. 181.

10 Ibid., p. 88.

11 Home, Public, 11 April 1850, Nos 73–8 KW, National Archives of India.

12 Ibid.

13 Home, Public, 17 October 1851, Nos 4–6, National Archives of India.

14 Ibid.

15 Home, Public, 1854, OC 3 February, No. 3, National Archives of India.

16 Sunil Gangopadhyay (Penguin Classics Edition), *Those Days*, Penguin, New Delhi, 2000.

17 As noted before, all excerpts on the making of Act XXI of 1850 are from Legislative Consultations, 4 April to 10 May 1850, Nos 57 to 87, India Office Records P/207/59, British Library, London. The corresponding material in the National Archives of India is classified under 'Home, Public'.

18 Sir William Lee Warner, *The Life of the Marquis of Dalhousie*, KT: Vol. I, Macmillan, London, 1904, pp. 297–8, Central Secretariat Library.

19 Marc Galanter, *Caste Disabilities and Indian Federalism*, Indian Law Institute, New Delhi, Vol. 3, No. 2 (April–June 1961), pp. 205–34.

20 Home, Judicial, 1894, Proceedings 30–7, National Archives of India.

21 Home, Judicial, 1927, File No. 776/27, National Archives of India.

22 Hari Singh Gour, *The Hindu Code*, Butterworth, Calcutta, 1919.

23 Sir William Jones, *Institutes of Manu or the Ordinances of Manu*, Lawbook Exchange, New Jersey, 2007, Chap. IX. Sec. 201.

24 N.C. Kelkar, *Life and Times of Lokamanya Tilak*, Anupama, Delhi, 1987 reprint, pp. 208–14.

25 *Mitar Sen Singh v. Maqbul Hasan Khan*, Privy Council judgment Appeal No. 123 of 1928 delivered on 30 June 1930, AIR 1930 PC 251.

26 Report of the Hindu Law Committee, 1947, National Archives of India.
27 'Obsolete Laws: Warranting Immediate Repeal', 248th Report of the Law Commission of India, 12 September 2014.
28 Report of the Committee to identify the Central Acts which are not relevant or no longer needed or require repeal/re-enactment in the present socio-economic context, Prime Minister's Office, 5 November 2014.
29 'Obsolete Laws: Warranting Immediate Repeal', 250th Report of the Law Commission of India, 29 October 2014.

II. IMPURE MAJORITY

5. THREE SHADES OF TWICE-BORN

1 *Namboory Setapaty and others v. Kanoo-Colanoo Pullia,* 3 MIA 359 (PC) (Q).
2 Ibid.
3 B.R. Ambedkar, 'Who were the Shudras?', *Dr. Babasaheb Ambedkar: Writings and Speeches,* Vol. 7, Ministry of Social Justice and Empowerment, p. 184.
4 This kind of institutionalised consultation by colonial courts with 'Brahmin Pundits' lasted until an enactment ended it in 1864.
5 *Chouturya Run Murdun Syn v. Sahub Purhulad Syn,* 1 MIA 18:4 WR 132 (PC).
6 *Ranganayakamma v. Alwar Setti,* ILR 13 Mad. 214.
7 *Gopal Narhar Safray v. Hanmant Ganesh Safray,* (1879) ILR 3 Bom. 273.
8 *Raj Coomar Lall and Ors v. Bissessur Dyal and Ors,* (1884) ILR 10 Cal. 688.
9 Shamachurn Sircar, *Vyavasthá-Darpana: A Digest of the Hindu Law as Current in Bengal,* Calcutta, 1867, India Office Library.
10 *Tulsi Ram v. Bihari Lal,* (1890) ILR 12 All. 328 (FB).
11 *Ambabai v. Govind,* (1898) ILR 23 Bom. 257.
12 *Manchharam Bhiku Patil and Anr v. Dattu and Two Ors,* (1920) ILR 64 Bom. 166.
13 *Maharaja of Kolhapur v. S. Sundaram Ayyar,* (1925) ILR 48 Mad. 1.
14 *Bishwanath Gosh v. Srimati Shroshi Bala Dasi,* (1921) ILR 48 Cal. 626 and *Bhola Nath Mitter v. King-Emperor,* (1924) ILR 51 Cal. 788.
15 *Ishwari Prasad v. Rai Hari Prashad Lal,* (1927) ILR 6 Pat. 506.
16 *Subrao Hambirrao Patil v. Radha Hambirrao Patil,* (1928) ILR 52 Bom. 497.

17 *Ramchandra Doddappa Naik v. Hanamnaik Dodnaik Patil*, (1935) 37 Bom. LR 920.
18 *Mt. Nagi v. Rajkunwar Saheba*, 13 October 1955, Nagpur High Court.
19 *Sangannagouda v. Kalkangouda*, AIR 1960 Mys. 147.
20 Parliament abandoned this experiment in 1961 vide the Two-Member Constituencies (Abolition) Act.
21 *V.V. Giri v. Dippala Suri Dora*, 1959 AIR 1318, 1960 SCR (1) 426.
22 B.R. Ambedkar, 'Annihilation of Caste', *Dr. Babasaheb Ambedkar: Writings and Speeches*, Vol. 1, Ministry of Social Justice and Empowerment, p. 47.
23 *Ramchandra Doddappa Naik v. Hanamnaik Dodnaik Patil*, (1935) 37 Bom. LR 920.
24 *Amireddi Rajagopala Rao v. Amireddi Sithramamma*, 1965 SCR (3) 122.
25 *Akku Prahlad Kulkarni v. Ganesh Prahlad Kulkarni*, AIR 1945 Bom. 217.
26 *Ram Dulari Saran v. Sri Yogeshwar Sri Ram Balbhacharya ji*, AIR 1969 All. 68.
27 *V.V. Giri v. Dippala Suri Dora*, 1959 AIR 1318, 1960 SCR (1) 426.
28 *Raj Coomar Lall and Ors v. Bissessur Dyal and Ors*, (1884) ILR 10 Cal. 688.
29 *Krishna Singh v. Mathura Ahir*, AIR 1972 All. 273.
30 *Dharmapuram Pandara Sannadhi v. Virapandiyam Pillai*, (1899) ILR 22 Mad. 302.
31 *Sri Krishna Singh v. Mathura Ahir*, 1980 AIR SC 707, 1980 SCR (2) 660.
32 *Collector of Madura v. Moottoo Ramalinga Sethupathy*, 12 (MIA) 397 (1868).

6. A WEDDING WITHOUT A BRAHMIN

1 *Vithal Krishna Joshi v. Anant Ramchandra*, 11 BHCR 6.
2 *Krishnumbhut v. Anunt Gungadhurbhut*, 4 Morris. 111.
3 *Dinanath Abaji v. Sadashiv Hari Madhave*, (1878) ILR 3 Bom. 9.
4 Rosalind O'Hanlon, *Caste, Conflict and Ideology: Mahatma Jotirao Phule and Low Caste Protest in Nineteenth-Century Western India*, Permanent Black, Ranikhet, 2016, p. 230.
5 Ibid., p. 237.
6 *Waman Jagannath Joshi v. Balaji Kusaji Patil*, (1889) ILR 14 Bom. 167.
7 Vishwanath Narayan Mandlik, *Vyavahara Mayukha or Hindu Law*, Asian Publication Services, New Delhi, 1880, p. 161.
8 Anupama Rao, *The Caste Question*, Permanent Black, Ranikhet, 2019, p. 53.
9 Rosalind O'Hanlon, *Caste, Conflict and Ideology: Mahatma Jotirao Phule and*

Low Caste Protest in Nineteenth-Century Western India, Permanent Black, Ranikhet, 2016, p. 280.

10 Dhananjay Keer, *Mahatma Jotirao Phooley*, Popular Prakashan, Mumbai, 2013, pp. 259–60.

11 *Rangappa Bin Ningappa Immadi v. Venkanbhat Bin Lingabhat Joshi*, (1915) ILR 40 Bom. 112.

12 *Bala Genuji Navale v. Balvant Laxman Ghatpande*, (1918) 20 Bom. LR 454.

13 V. Geetha, 'The Story of a Marriage: Being a Tale of Self Respect Unions and What Happened to Them' in S.V. Rajadurai and V. Geetha (eds), *Themes in Caste, Gender and Religion*, Bharatidasan University, Trichy, 2007, pp. 288–320.

14 *Deivanai Achi v. Chidambaram Chettiar*, AIR 1954 Mad. 657.

15 D. Veeraraghavan, *Half a Day for Caste? Education and Politics in Tamil Nadu: 1952–55*, Leftword, New Delhi, 2020.

16 Home Department, Judicial, 1953, File No. 17/158/53, National Archives of India. The ensuing discussion on the fate of the bill is from this source.

17 A Review of the Madras Legislative Assembly (1952–1957), Legislative Assembly Department, p. 54.

18 *Rajathi v. K. Selliah*, (1966) 2 MLJ 40.

19 Hindu Marriage (Tamil Nadu Amendment) Act, 1967: Tamil Nadu Act No. 21 of 1967.

20 MLA Debates Official Report, November 1967, Vol. 6, No. 4.

21 Ibid.

22 *A. Asuvathaman v. Union of India*, AIR 2016 Mad. 17.

7. BREAKING THE SILENCE ON UNTOUCHABILITY

1 *Congress Presidential Addresses*, G.A. Natesan & Co, Madras, 1935, pp. 10–11.

2 Abstract of the Proceedings of the Council of the Governor General of India, 1916, Vol. LIV, Published by Authority of the Governor General, Parliament of India Library, pp. 1–23. All excerpts quoted in this chapter are from the officially recorded proceedings.

3 *Congress Presidential Addresses*, G.A. Natesan & Co, Madras, 1935, pp. 182–4.

4 Proceedings of the Council of the Governor General of India, 22 March 1915.

5 Amrit Kaur, *Mahamana Malaviyaji Birth Centenary Commemoration Volume*, Banaras Hindu University, 25 December 1961, Call No. 920 M 291M, 1961, National Archives of India.
6 He was clearly referring to the Indian National Social Conference which used to be held at the same venue.
7 Home, Public-A, Proceedings, July 1916, Nos. 130–1, National Archives of India.
8 'The Depressed Classes', *The Times of India*, 26 May 1916, p. 6.
9 Home, Public-A, Proceedings, August 1920, Nos 329-41 & KW, National Archives of India.
10 Ibid., Nos 320–1.
11 Ibid., Nos 329–41 & KW.
12 B.R. Ambedkar, Written statement submitted in January 1919 before the Southborough Committee, *Dr Babasaheb Ambedkar: Writings and Speeches*, Vol. 1, Ambedkar Foundation, New Delhi, 2014, pp. 264.
13 *Correspondence and Diary of G.S. Khaparde: 1897-1934*, Government of Maharashtra.
14 Proceedings of Legislative Assembly, 26 March 1946, Parliament of India Library, New Delhi.
15 Gail Omvedt, *Dalits and the Democratic Revolution: Dr Ambedkar and the Dalit Movement in Colonial India*, Sage, New Delhi, 2013, pp. 146.
16 B.R. Ambedkar, *Dr Babasaheb Ambedkar: Writings and Speeches*, Vol. 1, Ambedkar Foundation, New Delhi, 2014, pp. 264 & 493.

8. THE OUTRAGE OF MARRYING UP

1 GOI Legislative Department, Assembly and Council-A Proceedings, February 1921, Nos 1–20, National Archives of India.
2 Bombay Municipality Primary Education Act, 1918.
3 Gordhanbhai I. Patel, *Vithalbhai Patel: Life and Times*, R.A. Mormakar, Bombay, pp. 290–1.
4 *The Collected Works of Mahatma Gandhi*, Vol. 56, p. 174.
5 Home, Judicial-A Proceedings, 1918, Nos 18–22, National Archives of India.
6 The exception though was the little-utilised Malabar Marriage Act, 1896, passed by the Madras legislature concerning a custom peculiar to the Nairs.
7 Proceedings of the Council of Governor General of India, Vol. LVII, April 1919–March 1920, Parliament of India Library.

8 *Bai Kashi v. Jamnadas Mansukh Raichand*, (1912) 14 Bom. LR 547.
9 *Bai Lakshmi v. Kaliansing Raghunathsing*, (1900) 2 Bom. LR 128.
10 The Age of Consent Act, 1891.
11 Gordhanbhai I. Patel, *Vithalbhai Patel: Life and Times*, R.A. Mormakar, Bombay, pp. 302–5.
12 *The Collected Works of Mahatma Gandhi*, Vol. 15, p. 80.
13 Ibid., pp. 122–3.
14 Legislative Department, Assembly and Council-A Proceedings, February 1921, Nos 1–20, National Archives of India.
15 *Hansard*, HC Deb., 6 August 1919, Vol. 119, c. 332.
16 Proceedings of the Indian Legislative Council, which met at the Council Chamber, Imperial Secretariat, Delhi, on 25 February 1920, *The Indian Legislative Council*, Vol. 58, Book No. 3.
17 Proceedings of the Indian Legislative Council, 26 February 1920, Published by Authority of the Governor General, Delhi, Vol. LVIII.
18 Legislative Department, Assembly and Council-A Proceedings, February 1921, Nos 1–20, National Archives of India.
19 'Imperial Council: Conclusion of Sessions', *The Times of India*, 23 March 1920, p. 9.
20 Home, Judicial, 1935, File No. 36/23/35-Judl., KW, National Archives of India.
21 Legislative Assembly Debates, Vol. I, 1937, pp. 270–320. Parliament of India Library.
22 Home, Judicial, 1935, File No. 36/19/35, Judl & KW, National Archives of India.
23 Swami Dayanand, *Light of Truth* (Translation of *Sathyarth Prakash by Chiranjiva Bharadwaja)*, K.C. Bhalla, Chapter 4, p. 103.
24 Cabinet Secretariat, Executive Council Office, File No. 30-E.C.O/36, National Archives of India.
25 Home, Judicial, 1938, File No. 28/14/38-Judl, National Archives of India.
26 Legislative Assembly Debates, Vol. III, 1937, pp. 2289–95, Parliament of India Library.
27 *Gopi Krishna Kasaudhan v. Jaggo*, AIR 1936 PC 198. (Note: All biographical details of Jaggo's case are gleaned from the Privy Council judgment on it.)
28 Ibid.

29 Chitra Sinha, *Debating Patriarchy: The Hindu Code Bill Controversy in India*, Oxford, New Delhi, 2012, pp. 50–1.
30 Executive Council Office, File No. ECO/18/41, 1941, National Archives of India.
31 The Legislative Assembly Debates, Vol. II, 21 March 1941, pp. 1744–53, Parliament of India Library.
32 The Legislative Assembly Debates, Vol. IV, 28 October 1941, p. 136, Parliament of India Library.
33 The Legislative Assembly Debates, Vol. II, 3 March 1944, pp. 817–33, Parliament of India Library.
34 Legislative Assembly Debates, Vol. III, 1946, Parliament of India Library.
35 Report of the Hindu Law Committee, 1947.
36 Legislative Assembly Debates, Vol. I, 1947, Parliament of India Library.
37 Legislative Assembly Debates, Vol. V, 1947, Parliament of India Library.
38 The Constituent Assembly of India (Legislative) Debates, Vol. I, 1947, Parliament of India Library.
39 Ibid., Vol. II, 1948.
40 Ibid., Vol. V, 1948.
41 Ibid., Vol. VI, 1948.
42 Ibid., Vol. VI, 1948.
43 The Constituent Assembly Debates, Vol. VII, 1948.
44 The Constituent Assembly of India (Legislative) Debates, Vol. I, 1949.
45 Ibid., Vol. I, 1949.
46 Ibid., Vol. III, 1949.
47 *V.R. Sadagopa Naidu v. Bhaktavatsalam*, AIR 1964 SC 1126.

III. ACCESS BARRIERS

9. THE EXCLUSIVITY OF PUBLIC PLACES

1 In 2010, a member of the Supreme Court-appointed special investigation team, A.K. Malhotra, interrogated Modi. However unlikely the claims that Modi had made in his defence, the police officer did not test any of his answers with follow-up questions.
2 When Ambedkar founded Bahishkrit Hitakarini Sabha in 1924 to uplift the untouchables, he chose Chimanlal Setalvad as its president.

3 Evidence taken before the Disorders Inquiry Committee, 1920, Vol. III, pp. 114–39.
4 Proceedings of the Governor of Fort St. George from July 1919 to June 1920, Vol. XLVII, pp. 149–61, Tamil Nadu State Archives.
5 P. Rajaraman, *The Justice Party: A Historical Perspective 1916-37*, Poompozhil Publishers, Madras, 1988, p. 291.
6 'Debates on Resolutions: Rights of Depressed Classes', *The Times of India*, 10 July 1919, p. 9.
7 Proceedings of the Governor of Fort St. George from July 1919 to June 1920, Vol. XLVII, pp. 149–61, Tamil Nadu State Archives.
8 The first Indian to top Cambridge University as a mathematics undergraduate, R.P. Paranjpye was vice chancellor of Bombay University and founding president of the Indian Rationalist Association. The movie director Sai Paranjpye is his granddaughter.
9 'The Bombay Legislative Council Meeting', *The Servant of India*, Poona, 17 July 1919, p. 280.
10 Proceedings of the Governor of Fort St. George from July 1919 to June 1920, Vol. XLVII, pp. 149–61, Tamil Nadu State Archives.
11 This 1919 noting was recalled in file relating to G.O. No. 2660, Local and Municipal, 25 September 1924, Tamil Nadu State Archives.
12 Proceedings of the Governor of Fort St. George from July 1919 to June 1920, Vol. XLVII, pp. 149–61, Tamil Nadu State Archives.
13 The Government of India Act, 1919: Rules thereunder and Govt. Reports 1920, Annual Register Office, Calcutta, 1920, p. 186.
14 Madras Legislative Council, 4 August 1921, pp. 333–9.
15 Proceedings of the Central Provinces Legislative Council, 28 November 1921, pp. 59–68, Central Secretariat Library, New Delhi.
16 Bombay Legislative Council, 4 August 1923, pp. 409–28.
17 Dhananjay Keer, *Dr Ambedkar: Life and Mission*, Popular Prakashan, Mumbai, 2015, p. 53.
18 Proceedings of the Madras Legislative Council, 20 January 1922, pp. 2047–52.
19 Madras Legislative Council, Vol XV, 27 November 1923, pp. 49–50.
20 'The Depressed Classes', *The Times of India*, 16 August 1924, p. 8.
21 G.O. No. 3464, Law (General), 5 December 1924, Tamil Nadu State Archives.
22 Ibid.

23 G.O. No. 2660, Local and Municipal, 25 September 1924, Tamil Nadu State Archives.
24 Madras Legislative Council, 22 August 1924, pp. 822–30.
25 G.O. No. 37, Public, 9 January 1925, Tamil Nadu State Archives. (Note: All the details relating to the Kalpathy episode and its repercussions are from this file.)
26 *Complete Works of Swami Vivekananda*, Vol. 3, p. 294.
27 Home, Judicial, 1925, Judicial File No. 561, National Archives of India.
28 'Car Festival at Kalpathy: Precautionary Measures', *The Times of India*, 13 November 1925, p. 7.
29 Madras Legislative Council, 14 December 1925, pp. 82–97.
30 Madras Legislative Council, 17 July 1926, pp. 624–6.
31 Bombay Legislative Council, 5 August 1926, pp. 716–29, and 6 August 1926, pp. 815–25.
32 'In Aid of the Untouchable: Social Legislation: Bill passed by Madras Council', *The Times of India*, 11 September 1926, p. 7.
33 File No. 109-III/26-G, Notes S Nos. 1-3, National Archives of India, and G.O. No. 531-532 (Mis.), 16 December 1926, Tamil Nadu State Archives.
34 Rupa Viswanath, *The Pariah Problem: Caste, Religion and the Social in Modern India*, Navayana, New Delhi, 2014.
35 Anand Teltumbde, *Mahad: The Making of the First Dalit Revolt*, Aakar, Delhi, 2016, pp. 340–3.
36 Ibid., p. 351.
37 Home, Judicial, 1927, Judicial File No. 1076/27, National Archives of India.
38 'Kalpathy Car Festival: Untouchables Participate', *The Times of India*, 21 November 1929, p. 5.
39 Report of the Indian Statutory Commission, Vol. 1, May 1930, p. 38, National Archives of India.
40 Report of the Fundamental Rights Committee appointed by the Working Committee of the Indian National Congress, 1931, Private papers of C. Rajagopalachari (Lot VI to XI: Printed Material), Nehru Memorial Museum and Library.
41 Central Provinces Legislative Council, 21 January 1933, pp. 142–60, Central Secretariat Library.
42 Home, Political, 1935, File 24/31 35, Political and K.W., National Archives of India.

43 Ibid., pp. 13–115.
44 Ibid., p. 16.
45 Madras Legislative Assembly, 30 March 1938, pp. 1169–85.
46 Extract from the Debates of the Legislative Assembly of the Province of Madras, 17 August 1938, File No. 24/31 35, Political and K.W., 1935, Home—Political, pp. 297–304, National Archives of India.
47 Madras Legislative Council, 12 December 1938, pp. 86–7 (Appendix X).
48 Ibid., pp. 46–56.
49 Ibid.

10. THE DRAMA OF ABOLITION

1 Bombay Legislative Assembly, 19 April 1939, pp. 3161–91. Legislature Library of Maharashtra State, Mumbai.
2 Bombay Legislative Assembly, Vol. 7, Appendix No. 4, pp. 2343–6, Legislature Library of Maharashtra State, Mumbai.
3 Bombay Legislative Assembly, Vol. 7, 31 October 1939, pp. 2333–4, Legislature Library of Maharashtra State, Mumbai.
4 Bombay Legislative Council, 31 October 1939, pp. 429–33, Legislature Library of Maharashtra State, Mumbai.
5 Bombay Legislative Assembly, Vol. 9, Part 30, 25 September 1946, pp. 1202–52, Legislature Library of Maharashtra State, Mumbai.
6 Bombay Legislative Assembly, Vol. 9, Part 36, 2 October 1946, pp. 1533–81.
7 B. Shiva Rao, *The Framing of India's Constitution: Select Documents*, Vol. 2, Universal Law Publishing, New Delhi, 2012, p. 74.
8 Ibid., pp. 129–33.
9 Ibid., pp. 163–5.
10 Ibid., pp. 213–27.
11 Ibid., p. 327–8.
12 Ibid., p. 510.
13 Constituent Assembly Debates, Vol. VII, pp. 650–69.
14 Dakshayani Velayudhan (Ed.), *Gandhi or Ambedkar*, Gandhi Era Publications, Madras, 1946, Nehru Memorial Museum and Library, New Delhi.

11. CRIMINALISING A PIOUS CUSTOM

1 Parliamentary Debates, House of the People, Vol. 1, 1954, p. 2218, 15 March 1954, Parliament of India Library.
2 Bill No. 14 of 1954, The Untouchability (Offences) Bill, 1954, as introduced in the House of People.
3 Rajya Sabha Debates, Vol. VII, No. 18, 16 September 1954, pp. 2410–82, Parliament of India Library.
4 Parliamentary Debates, Rajya Sabha, Vol. VII, No. 19, 17 September 1954, pp. 2483–522, Parliament of India Library.
5 Report of the Joint Committee, The Untouchability (Offences) Bill, 1954, Lok Sabha Secretariat.
6 Lok Sabha Debates, Vol. III, 27 April 1955, pp. 6538–76, Parliament of India Library.
7 Lok Sabha Debates, Vol. III, 28 April 1955, pp. 6679–824, Parliament of India Library.

12. THE POSTHUMOUS VINDICATION OF AMBEDKAR

1 *Devarajiah v. B. Padmanna*, AIR 1959 Mys. 84, 10 September 1957.
2 March Galanter, *Law and Society in Modern India*, Oxford University Press, Delhi, 1989, p. 210.
3 Ibid., pp. 209–10.
4 Report of the Committee on Untouchability, Economic and Educational Development of the Scheduled Castes and Connected Documents, 1969, Department of Social Welfare, Government of India.
5 Lok Sabha Debates, Fifth Series, Vol. XIV, 23 May 1972, pp. 146–244.
6 Lok Sabha Debates, Fifth Series, Vol. XIV, No. 55, 30 May 1972, pp. 176–9.
7 Report of the Joint Committee, The Untouchability (Offences) Amendment and Miscellaneous Provision Bill, 1972, Presented in the Lok Sabha, on 22 February 1974, Parliament of India Library.
8 Lok Sabha Debates, Fifth Series, Vol LII, No. 46, 6 May 1975, pp. 341–4.
9 Marc Galanter, *Law and Society in Modern India*, OUP, New Delhi, 1989, p. 210.
10 *Appa Balu Ingale v. State of Karnataka*, Criminal Revision Petition No. 478 of 1980, Karnataka High Court, 1 April 1981.
11 *State of Karnataka v. Appa Balu Ingale*, AIR 1993 SC 1126.

12 Ambika Aiyadurai, 'Even After a Century, Water Is Still the Marker of India's Caste Society', *TheWire.in*, 23 August 2022, https://thewire.in/caste/even-after-a-century-water-is-still-the-marker-of-indias-caste-society.

IV. TEMPLE ENTRY

13. AMBEDKAR'S FORGOTTEN BILL

1 'Reply to the Address of Welcome at Madura', Lectures from Colombo to Almora, *The Complete Works of Swami Vivekananda*, Vol. 3, Advaita Ashram.

2 *Sankaralinga Nadan v. Rajeswara Dorai*, ILR (1908) 31 Mad. 236, (1907–8) 35 IA 176. All the details given here of this case are from the reported Privy Council judgment and notes.

3 *Collector of Madura v. Moottoo Ramalinga Sethupathy*, 12 MIA 397 (1868).

4 'A Temple Dispute', *The Times of India*, Bombay, 19 September 1901, p. 5.

5 *Sankaralinga Nadan v. Rajeswara Dorai*, ILR (1908) 31 Mad. 236, (1907–8), 35 IA 176.

6 *Gopala Mooppanar v. Dharmakarta Subramania Aiyer*, (1914) 27 MLJ 253, AIR 1915 Mad. 363.

7 He was one of the judges cited by S.K. Bole in the Bombay Legislative Council in 1926, as mentioned in Chapter 6, for rejecting the claim that certain Brahmins had an exclusive right to officiate as purohits at weddings.

8 Jayakar Papers, 1929, Roll 00060, File No. 422, pp. 125–30, National Archives of India.

9 B.R. Ambedkar, 'Waiting for a Visa', circa 1935–36, http://www.columbia.edu/itc/mealac/pritchett/00ambedkar/txt_ambedkar_waiting.html.

10 Jayakar Papers, 1929, Roll 00060, File No. 422, p. 6, National Archives of India.

11 Ibid., pp. 112–23.

12 Namrata R. Ganneri, 'The Hindu Mahasabha in Bombay (1923-1947)', *Proceedings of the Indian History Congress: Platinum Jubilee (75th) Session, Jawaharlal Nehru University, New Delhi, 2014*, Department of History, Aligarh Muslim University, Aligarh, 2015, pp. 771–82.

13 Jayakar Papers, 1929, Roll 00060, File No. 422, p. 33, National Archives of India.
14 'Gaud Saraswat Temples: Legal Difficulty: Trustees' Sympathy with Untouchables' Demand', *The Times of India,* 16 November 1929, p. 15.
15 'Temple Entry in Bombay: Leader's Move: Organizing Forces for Direct Action', *The Times of India,* 15 November 1929, p. 13.
16 Jayakar Papers, 1929, Roll 00060, File No. 422, pp. 91–8, National Archives of India.
17 (1883) ILR 7 Bom. 323.
18 Jayakar Papers, 1929, Roll 00060, File No. 422, pp. 86–7, National Archives of India.
19 Ibid., pp. 100–2.
20 'Temple Entry Dispute: Question of Reference of Controversy to High Court', *The Times of India,* 6 December 1929, p. 13.
21 'Untouchables' Disabilities: Bill to End Them: Assembly to Consider Dr Ambedkar's Measure', *The Times of India,* 7 December 1929, p. 10.
22 Jayakar Papers, 1929, Roll 00060, File No. 422, pp. 104–5, National Archives of India.
23 'The Disabilities of Untouchables: Object of Bill to End Them', *The Times of India,* 9 December 1929, p. 6.
24 Home, Judicial, 1929, File No. 1046/29, National Archives of India.
25 Ibid.
26 Constituent Assembly Debates, Vol. XI, 25 November 1949, Ambedkar's last speech in the Constituent Assembly, titled 'Grammar of Anarchy'.
27 Home, Judicial, 1929, File No. 1046/29, National Archives of India.
28 'Young India and Untouchables: Views on the Proposed Legislation: Growth of Public Opinion', *The Manchester Guardian,* 10 December 1929, p. 18.
29 'Punjab Money Lenders Bill', *The Times of India,* 14 December 1929, p. 19.
30 'The Suppressed Classes: Mr Gandhi's Advice', *The Times of India,* 27 December 1929, p. 10.
31 Jayakar Papers, 1929, Roll 00060, File No. 422, pp. 112–23, National Archives of India.
32 Home, Judicial, 1929, File No. 1046/29, National Archives of India.
33 Proceedings of the Inaugural Sitting of the Federal Court, *The Federal Court Reports,* 6 December 1937.
34 Home, Judicial, 1929, File No. 1046/29, National Archives of India.

35 'Social Reform: Bills in the Assembly', *The Times of India*, 14 February 1930, p. 9.
36 'Social Reform Measures for Discussion in Assembly', *The Times of India*, 21 January 1932, p. 10.
37 Legislative Assembly Debates: 18 February 1932, Vol. II, No. 1.
38 Home, Judicial, 1931, File No. 6/31, National Archives of India.

14. GANDHI'S BALANCING ACT

1 *The Collected Works of Mahatma Gandhi*, Vol. 51, The Publications Division, New Delhi, p. 139.
2 Ibid., p. 150.
3 Ibid., p. 177.
4 Ibid., p. 242.
5 Ibid., Vol. 52, pp. 42–45.
6 Proceedings of the Madras Legislative Council, 1 November 1932, Tamil Nadu State Archives.
7 C. Rajagopalachari, *Plighted Word*, Servants of Untouchables Society, Delhi, 1933, pp. 11–6.
8 *The Collected Works of Mahatma Gandhi*, Vol. 52, The Publications Division, New Delhi, p. 125.
9 *The Collected Works of Mahatma Gandhi*, Vol. 51, The Publications Division, New Delhi, p. 307, Statement on Untouchability–XIII.
10 Home Political, 1933, File No. 50/I/33-Pol. & K.W., National Archives of India.
11 *The Collected Works of Mahatma Gandhi*, Vol. 53, The Publications Division, New Delhi, p. 156, Gandhi's letter to Sapru dated 26 January 1933.
12 Gandhi's letter to M.M. Malaviya, *Harijan*, 18 February 1933, Vol. No. 1, Issue 2, p. 2.
13 Home, Political, 1933, File No. 50/I/33-Pol., & K.W., National Archives of India.
14 Statement on Viceroy's Decision, *The Collected Works of Mahatma Gandhi*, Vol. 53, The Publications Division, New Delhi, p. 128–32.
15 Home, Political, 1933, File No. 50/I/33-Pol., & K.W., National Archives of India.
16 M.M. Malaviya to Gandhi, *Harijan*, 18 February 1933, Vol. No. 1, Issue 2, p. 3.

17 B.R. Ambedkar, 'Statement on Temple Entry Bill: 14th February, 1933', *Dr. Babasaheb Ambedkar: Writings and Speeches*, Vol. 9, Ministry of Social Justice and Empowerment, pp. 108–13.
18 *The Collected Works of Mahatma Gandhi*, Vol. 53, The Publications Division, New Delhi, pp. 305–8.
19 Ibid., p. 298.
20 M.M. Malaviya to Gandhi, *Harijan*, 18 February 1933, Vol. No. 1, Issue 2, pp. 6–7.
21 Gandhi to M.M. Malaviya, *Harijan*, 18 February 1933, Vol. No. 1, Issue 2, p. 7.
22 *Harijan*, 18 February 1933, Vol. 1, Issue 2, p. 2.
23 Gandhi's letter to Malaviya, dated 24 February 1933, *The Collected Works of Mahatma Gandhi*, Vol. 53, The Publications Division, New Delhi, pp. 387.
24 Nicholas B. Dirks, *Castes of Mind*, Princeton University Press, Princeton, 2001, pp. 257–8.
25 Susan Bayly, *Caste, Society and Politics in India: The New Cambridge History of India*, Cambridge University Press, Indian Edition, 2005, p. 248.
26 Ramachandra Guha, *Gandhi: The years that changed the world, 1914–1918*, Penguin Random House, Gurugram, 2018, p. 212.
27 The Legislative Assembly Debates, 24 March 1933, pp. 2525–32, Parliament of India Library.
28 The Legislative Assembly Debates, 24 August 1933, pp. 208–41, Parliament of India Library.
29 The reference is to Bhagavad Gita verse 9.32, which, according to Srila Prabhupada's translation, says: 'O son of Prtha, those who take shelter in Me, though they be of lower birth—women, vaisyas (merchants), as well as sudras (workers)—can approach the supreme destination.'
30 Private Papers, C. Rajagopalachari, (IV) Sub. File 26, Nehru Memorial Museum and Library.
31 *The Collected Works of Mahatma Gandhi*, Vol. 58, The Publications Division, New Delhi, pp. 381–3.
32 *Report of the Temple Entry Enquiry Committee*, Trivandrum Government Press, 1934.
33 *The Collected Works of Mahatma Gandhi*, Vol. 63, The Publications Division, New Delhi, p. 19.
34 Ibid.

35 Report of the Temple Entry Enquiry Committee, Trivandrum Government Press, 1934, p. 413.
36 S.R. Venkatraman, *Temple Entry Legislation*, Bharat Devi Publications, Madras, 1946, p. 42.
37 *The Collected Works of Mahatma Gandhi*, Vol. 64, The Publications Division, New Delhi, p. 83–4.
38 Ibid., p. 27.
39 Ibid., pp. 124–6.
40 'Cochin Temple "Pollution": Ceremonies for Purification', *The Times of India*, 21 April 1937, p. 6.

15. CONGRESS EXPERIMENTS UNDER COLONIAL RULE

1 Eleanor Zelliot, *Ambedkar's World: The Making of Babasaheb and the Dalit Movement*, Navayana, New Delhi, 2013, pp. 180–1.
2 Proceedings of the Bombay Legislative Assembly, 24 January 1938, Maharashtra Legislature Library.
3 Proceedings of the Madras Legislative Assembly, 24 September 1937, Tamil Nadu State Archives.
4 This local entity of the Congress came into being in pursuance of Gandhi's 1920 policy of reorganising the party into twenty-one provincial units on the basis of language in British India. It was part of his strategy to turn the freedom struggle into a mass movement.
5 Proceedings of the Madras Legislative Assembly, 17 August 1938, Tamil Nadu State Archives.
6 Ibid., 1 December 1938.
7 Rameshwari Nehru, *Gandhi Is My Star*, Pustak Bhandar, Patna, 1950, p. 109.
8 *The Mail*, 16 June 1939. The promise of a legislation within eight days is also mentioned in Rajmohan Gandhi, *The Rajaji Story: 1937-1972*, Bharatiya Vidya Bhawan, Bombay, 1984, p. 34.
9 'Harijans worship in Madura Temple: Priest Officiates', *The Times of India*, 10 July 1939, p. 3.
10 'Madura Temple Deadlock: Harijan Worship Trouble', *The Times of India*, 11 July 1939, p. 6.
11 Ibid.
12 'Draft Bill: No Legal Proceedings over Temple Entry', *The Times of India*, 12 July 1939, p. 13.

13 'Madura Temple Suit: Damages claimed for Harijan entry', *The Times of India*, 15 July 1939, p. 9.
14 'Meenakshi Temple Open', *Harijan*, 12 July 1939, *The Collected Works of Mahatma Gandhi*, Vol. 69, The Publications Division, New Delhi, pp. 421–3.
15 'Temple Entry Ordinance: Priests Indemnified: Action by Madras Governor', *The Times of India*, 18 July 1939, p. 9.
16 'Temple Entry in Madura: Ordinance Upheld by District Judge', *The Times of India*, 25 July 1939, p. 8.
17 'Purification Move Fails: Madura Temple Dispute', *The Times of India*, 31 July 1939, p. 12.
18 S.R. Venkatraman, *Temple Entry Legislation*, Bharat Devi Publications, Madras, 1946, pp. XLV–XLIX.
19 His name is not mentioned in the High Court and Federal Court judgments in the case.
20 *Manikkasundara Bhattar and others v. R.S. Nayudu and others*, Federal Court Reports 1946 (67).
21 *Manikkasundara Bhattar and others v. R.S. Nayudu and others*, (1945) I (MLJ) 372.
22 *S.K. Wodeyar v. Ganapati Madhuling Dixit*, AIR 1935 Bom. 371.
23 Vinayak Damodar Savarkar, Whirlwind Propaganda: Statements, Messages and Extracts from the President's Diary of his Propandistic Tours, Interviews from December 1937 to October 1941, A.S. Bhide (Ed.), n.p., Bombay, 1941, pp. 423–26, NMML.
24 'Poona Temple Open to Harijans: No Special Favour, Says Mr Kher', *The Times of India*, 30 August 1946, p. 7.
25 'Many Temples to Allow Harijans: Madras Ministry's Go-Ahead Policy', *The Times of India*, 21 September 1946, p. 8.
26 'Temples Opened to Harijans: Rejoicings in Madura', *The Times of India*, 25 December 1946, p. 5.
27 B. Shiva Rao, *The Framing of India's Constitution: Select Documents*, Vol. 2, Universal Law Publishing, New Delhi, 2012, pp. 3–4.
28 Ibid., pp. 56–7.
29 Secretariat of the Governor General (Public), 1947, File No. 12/53/47-GG (B) & K.W., National Archives of India.
30 'Tirupathi Temple Entry: Demonstration Plan', *The Times of India*, 4 January 1947, p. 5.

31 Private Papers of C. Rajagopalachari, (IV) Sub file-43, Nehru Memorial Museum and Library.
32 'Madras Temple Entry', *The Times of India*, 29 May 1947, p. 7.
33 'Tirupati Temple Entry', *The Times of India*, 17 June 1947, p. 6.
34 Proceedings of the Bombay Legislative Assembly, 11 September 1947, p. 41, Legislature Library of Maharashtra State.
35 'Demonstration before Bombay Council: Hindu Opposition to Temple Entry Bill', *The Times of India*, 19 October 1947, p. 6.
36 MHA, Public (A), Section File No. 38/33/47, Public (A) & KW, 1947, National Archives of India.
37 'Alandi Temple Entry', *The Times of India*, 9 December 1947, p. 7.
38 'Harijan's Temple Entry Right: C.P. & Berar Measure', *The Times of India*, 24 November 1947, p. 7.
39 'Entry of Harijans into Puri Temple: Congress Talks', *The Times of India*, 11 February 1948, p. 9.
40 'Puri Temple Entry Crisis: Official Action Likely', *The Times of India*, 12 February 1948, p. 3.
41 'Orissa Ministry Take Over Puri Temple', *The Times of India*, 14 February 1948, p. 1.
42 Ibid.
43 'New Orissa Temple Entry Bill: Obstruction to be punished', *The Times of India*, 22 Feburary 1948, p. 7.
44 *Sastri Yagnapurushadji v. Muldas Bhudardas Vaishya*, (1966) 3 SCR 242.
45 'Harijans and Temple Entry', *The Collected Works of Mahatma Gandhi*, Vol. 90, The Publications Division, New Delhi, p. 499.
46 GOI, MHA, Judicial Section, 1948, File No. 5/126/48, Judicial, National Archives of India.

16. THE CONSTITUTION'S TELL-TALE CLAUSE

1 B. Shiva Rao, *The Framing of India's Constitution: Select Documents*, Vol. 2, Universal Law Publishing, New Delhi, 2012, p. 116.
2 Ibid., p. 122.
3 'Remarks at opening of exhibit on the 70th Anniversary of the Universal Declaration of Human Rights', https://www.un.org/sg/en/content/sg/speeches/2018-12-06/70th-anniversary-universal-declaration-human-rights-remarks.
4 A key figure in the drafting of the Constitution, Rau went on to become the first judge from India in the International Court of Justice.

5 B. Shiva Rao, *The Framing of India's Constitution: Select Documents*, Vol. 2, Universal Law Publishing, New Delhi, 2012, pp. 146–7.
6 Ibid., p. 140.
7 Ibid., pp. 143–4.
8 Ibid., p. 165.
9 Ibid., p. 160.
10 Ibid., p. 173.
11 Ibid., p. 202.
12 Ibid., p. 201.
13 Ibid., p. 205.
14 Ibid., p. 208.
15 Ibid., p. 211.
16 Ibid., p. 213.
17 Ibid., p. 264.
18 Ibid., p. 265.
19 Ibid., p. 291.
20 Ibid., p. 267.
21 Ibid.
22 Ibid., p. 290.
23 Ibid., p. 291.
24 Ibid., pp. 294–99.
25 Constituent Assembly Debates, Vol. III, 1 May 1947.
26 Ibid.
27 Ibid., Vol. VII, 6 December 1948.
28 *Sastri Yagnapurushadji v. Muldas Bhudardas Vaishya*, (1966) 3 SCR 242.
29 'Acharya Bhave and Party Beaten by Priests at Temple Gates', *The Times of India*, 20 September 1953, p. 1.
30 'Statement to the Press': 25 April 1934, *The Collected Works of Mahatma Gandhi*, Vol. 57, The Publications Division, New Delhi, p. 433.
31 'Harijans Enter Deoghar Shrine: Dr Sinha Leads Big March', *The Times of India*, 28 September 1953, p. 1.
32 'India's Insuperable Problem of Caste: Legislation Nullified by Orthodoxy', *The Manchester Guardian*, 5 October 1953, p. 5.
33 *Swami Hariharanand Saraswati v. Jailor IC Dist. Jail Banaras*, 1954 CriLJ 1317. (Most of the details of the Banaras case are from this Allahabad High Court judgment.)
34 Ibid.

35 'Swami Karpatriji Arrested: Banaras Temple Entry Issue, *The Times of India*, 18 February 1954, p. 1.
36 'Agreement Not Adhered To: Agitation Started', *The Times of India*, 12 April 1954, p. 9.
37 'Harijan Entry into Temple: Restraint Order Issued', *The Times of India*, 12 April 1954, p. 9.
38 The Act is available in full here: https://bombayhighcourt.nic.in/libweb/acts/1956.31.html.
39 *Sastri Yagnapurushadji v. Muldas Bhudardas Vaishya*, (1966) 3 SCR 242.
40 *Sri Venkataramana Devaru v. The State of Mysore*, 1958 SCR 895.
41 *Surya Narayan Choudhary v. State of Rajasthan*, AIR 1989 Raj 99.
42 *Ramesh Yeshwant Prabhoo v. Prabhakar Kashinath Kunte*, 1996 SCC (1) 130.
43 Vinayak Damodar Savarkar, *Essentials of Hindutva*, 1923.

V. IMPUNITY FOR VIOLENCE

17. WHEN JUDGES LET OFF MASS KILLERS

1 Alternatively spelt as Keezha Venmani or Keezhvenmani.
2 The unofficial death toll of forty-four is more popularly accepted.
3 The memorial on the spot commemorates sixteen women, twenty-three children and five men.
4 Triggered by an election dispute, the prolonged riots were between members of the dominant caste, Thevar, who supported an opposition party called the Forward Bloc, and Harijans of the Pallar community, who were on the side of the ruling Congress party. While Thevar casualties were mainly in police firings, Pallars were killed in caste violence.
5 Nagapattinam district has since been carved out of Thanjavur district.
6 *State v P. Gopalakrishna Naidu*, Sessions case No. 80 of 1969 and 26 of 1970, Sessions Judge of Nagapattinam division of Thanjavur district, 30 November 1970; *P. Gopalakrishna Naidu v. State rep. by Inspector of Police, CBCID, Madras*, Madras High Court, 6 April 1973.
7 'Left Communist' was a reference to the CPI(M), which had broken away in 1964 from the CPI, which was called 'Right Communist'.
8 Mythili Sivaraman, 'Gentlemen Killers of Kilvenmani', *Economic and Political Weekly*, Vol. 8, No. 21, 26 May 1973, pp. 926–8.
9 'Burning Shame', *The Times of India*, 14 June 1973, p. 6.

10 *State of Tamil Nadu v. P. Gopalakrishnan Naidu & others*, Supreme Court Criminal Appeal No. 17 of 1976, 1 November 1990.

11 Also spelt as Chunduru.

12 *Chidipudi Srinivasa Reddy and Others v. The State of Andhra Pradesh*, Criminal Appeal Nos. 1021 of 2011 and batch, Andhra Pradesh High Court, 22 April 2014.

13 Death Reference No. 7 of 2010, *State of Bihar v. Ajay Singh and Others*, Patna High Court, March.

14 *Abdul Sayeed v. State of Madhya Pradesh*, (2010) 10 SCC 259.

15 *State v. Girija Singh*, Sessions Case No. 2 of 1999, 1st Additional Sessions Judge, Patna, 7 April 2010.

16 *State v. Girija Singh*, Death Reference No. 5 of 2010, Patna High Court, 9 October 2013.

17 K. Ashish, 'Operation Black Rain: Revisiting the Killings of Dalits of Bihar and Confessions of their Killers', *CobraPost.com*, 16 August 2015, https://www.cobrapost.com/blog/operation-black-rain-revisiting-the-killings-of-dalits-of-bihar-and-confessions-of-their-killers/895.

18 *Krishna Mochi v. State of Bihar*, (2002) 1 SCC 81.

19 After the creation of Arwal district in 2001, Shankarbigha came under its jurisdiction.

20 'How the Shankarbigha massacre became a foregone conclusion', *The Times of India*, 5 April 2015.

21 *Ram Chander v. State of Haryana*, 1981 SCR (3) 12.

18. THE DENIAL OF THE CASTE ANGLE

1 Lok Sabha Debates, 13 June 1977, Vol. II, pp. 238–44, Parliament of India Library.

2 *The State of Bihar v. Mahabir Mahto and Parsuram Dhanuk*, Death Reference No. 1 of 1980 with Criminal Appeal Nos. 154, 155, 215, 217and 218 of 1980, Patna High Court, 29 April 1981, p. 11.

3 *Report of the Fact-Finding Committee: Massacre of Harijans in Belchhi*, Parliamentary Forum of Scheduled Castes and Scheduled Tribes Members of Parliament, Private Papers of Haridev Sharma, Second Lot Other Papers—1, Nehru Memorial Museum and Library.

4 *The State of Bihar v. Mahabir Mahto and Parsuram Dhanuk*, Death Reference No. 1 of 1980 with Criminal Appeal Nos. 154, 155, 215, 217 and 218 of 1980, Patna High Court, 29 April 1981, p. 36.

5 The Barh area, a Kurmi stronghold, produced the future chief minister Nitish Kumar.
6 Rajya Sabha Debates, 22 July 1977, pp. 70–167, Parliament of India Library.
7 'Walk-out by Congress elders', *The Times of India*, 23 July 1977, p. 1.
8 'Reprisal threat to Belchhi Harijans', *The Times of India*, 6 August 1977, p. 10.
9 *Tulsi Mahto v. The State of Bihar*, 1991 (2) PLJR 638.
10 'Reprisal threat to Belchhi Harijans', *The Times of India*, 6 August 1977, p. 10.
11 'The Belchhi Affair', *The Times of India*, 8 August 1977, p. 8.
12 'Janata MPs differ on Belchhi issue', *The Times of India*, 7 August 1977, p. 9.
13 'Indira Gandhi's visit to Belchhi: A well-calculated political move?', *India Today*, 15 September 1977.
14 'Probe into Cong. poll funds sought', *The Times of India*, 13 August 1977, p. 1.
15 'Belchhi visit was to defame Janata: Thakur', *The Times of India*, 20 August 1977, p. 5.
16 'Death sentence for two accused in Belchi case', *The Times of India*, 20 May 1980, p. 1.
17 *The State of Bihar v. Mahabir Mahto and Parsuram Dhanuk*, Death Reference No. 1 of 1980 with Criminal Appeal Nos. 154, 155, 215, 217 and 218 of 1980, Patna High Court, 29 April 1981.
18 Ibid., 11 January 1982.
19 *Joseph Peter v. State of Goa*, Daman and Diu, 1977 AIR 1812.
20 Petition for special leave to appeal (CRL) No. 607 of 1982, Supreme Court, 21 July 1982.
21 Review Petition No. 413/82 (On SLP No. 607/82).
22 'Court stays two more hangings', *The Times of India*, 24 May 1983, p. 5.
23 *Deena v. Union of India*, 1983 AIR 1155.
24 'Convicts hanged', *The Times of India*, 12 November 1983, p. 9.
25 B.R. Ambedkar, 'Untouchables or the Children of India's Ghetto', *Dr Babasaheb Ambedkar: Writings and Speeches*, Dr Ambedkar Foundation, 2014, p. 102.
26 Report of the Justice Gundewar Commission, 1998, Legislature Library of Maharashtra State.

27 'Cops blamed for Ramabai Nagar riots', *Rediff on the Net*, 30 December 1998.
28 'Kadam will be prosecuted in Ramabai Nagar case', *The Times of India*, 24 August 2001.
29 *The State (at the instance of DCBCID) v. Manohar Yashwant Kadam*, Sessions Case No. 22 of 2003, In the Court of Sessions for Gr. Bombay at Sewree.
30 *Manohar Yashwant Kadam v. The State of Maharashtra*, Bail Application No. 548 of 2009 in Criminal Appeal No. 441 of 2009, In the High Court of Judicature at Bombay Criminal Appellate Jurisdiction.
31 T.K. Rajalakshmi, 'Slaughter of Dalits', *Frontline*, 22 November 2002.
32 Inquiry report on the facts and circumstances leading to the incident that occurred at Police Post, Dulina (Distt. Jhajjar), in which five persons were lynched by the mob on 15 October 2002, R.R. Banswal, IAS, Commissioner, Rohtak Division, Haryana Government.
33 Report of the Left Parties' Delegation to Duleena, Jhajjar District, Haryana, on 17 October in protest against Dalit lynching atrocity, 18 October 2002.
34 'Dalit killings a case of "mistaken identity": Chautala', *The Times of India*, 25 October 2002.
35 'Jhajjar lynching was "mistaken identity"', *The Times of India*, 29 November 2002.
36 Inquiry report on the facts and circumstances leading to the incident that occurred at Police Post, Dulina (Distt. Jhajjar), in which five persons were lynched by the mob on 15 October 2002, R.R. Banswal, IAS, Commissioner, Rohtak Division, Haryana Government.
37 *Dalit Lynching at Dulina—Cow Protection, Caste and Communalism*, A report of People's Union for Democratic Rights, Delhi, February 2003, https://pudr.org/sites/default/files/2019-02/jhajhar_dalit_lynching.pdf.
38 Lok Sabha Debates, 11th Session, 13th Lok Sabha, 9 December 2002, pp. 464–69, Parliament of India Library.
39 'Paswan quits Cabinet over Gujarat issue', *The Times of India*, 29 April 2002.
40 Lok Sabha Debates, 11th Session, 13th Lok Sabha, 9 December 2002, pp. 464–69, Parliament of India Library.
41 T.K. Rajalakshmi, 'Justice, at last', *Frontline*, 10 September 2010.
42 'Four of a family murdered, 28 arrested', *Lokmat Times*, Nagpur,

2 October 2006. (Photocopy of the news story is reproduced in 'Caste Atrocity in Khairlanji', a report from the Manuski Advocacy Centre, Pune.)

43 'Killed for Speaking Up', *DNA*, 7 October 2006.

44 'Just another rape story', *The Times of India*, 29 October 2006.

45 For details, see Anand Teltumbde's *The Persistence of Caste: Khairlanji Murders and India's Hidden Apartheid*, Navayana, New Delhi, 2010.

46 *Organised Killings of Dalits in Khairlanji Village, Tal. Mohadi, Dist. Bhandara: A Report under SC-ST (POA) Act, 1989*, Commissioned by Nodal Officer, SC-ST (POA) Act, 1989, November 2006.

47 *Central Bureau of Investigation v. Sakru Mahagu Bijewar*, Bombay High Court, Nagpur Bench, Criminal Confirmation No. 4/2008, 14 July 2010.

48 'Re: Filling up vacancies of Judges in the Supreme Court', The Supreme Court Collegium, https://main.sci.gov.in/pdf/collegium/09-05-2019/2019-May%2008-SC%20Apptt.pdf.

49 The head of the three-judge bench was Justice Arun Mishra, who after his retirement from the Supreme Court went on to become chairperson of the National Human Rights Commission.

50 *Central Bureau of Investigation v. Sakru Mahagu Bijewar*, Supreme Court, Criminal Appeal Nos. 1791–1795 of 2014, 24 May 2019.

EPILOGUE

1 Anand Teltumbde, *Mahad: The Making of the First Dalit Revolt*, Aakar, Delhi, 2016, pp. 344–5.

2 'March 20 Observed as Social Empowerment Day to Commemorate Mahad Satyagrah by Dr. Ambedkar', Ministry of Social Justice & Empowerment, https://archive.pib.gov.in/archive/releases98/lyr2003/rmar2003/20032003/r200320038.html.

what sustained me during that vulnerable period when I repeatedly failed to meet self-imposed deadlines. Citing his own example, Ram assured me that there couldn't be deadlines for an author exploring uncharted territory. Given the volume of new material that had come my way, Ram nudged me in the direction of turning it into more than one book. I can't thank him enough for all the confidence he instilled in me in various ways, beginning with the grant of the fellowship, to pull off this ambitious venture.

The NIF fellowship came with the big bonus of Rivka Israel editing my draft chapters. Given that Rivka was effectively their first reader, her role was not limited to refining the copy. Her comments—especially her assurance that my narrative was lucid despite all the complexities I was attempting to convey—meant the world to me. I also owe NIF my very fruitful association with Abhishek Chaudhary, who is from my cohort of fellows. Our paths often crossed and we bonded with each other, sharing the highs and lows of research. Abhishek cannot imagine though how much I have benefited from his tips on accessing archival resources on the internet and the difference his friend Sana Khan has made to my work.

When I decided to widen the ambit of this book, it was because of the magic that had happened in libraries and archives, bearing out my hypothesis that the legal history of caste in India could be as rich and revealing as that of race in the US. And my sounding board for this critical decision was Akshaya Mukul, an old friend and accomplished author. Sharing the excitement of my initial discoveries, Akshaya encouraged me to venture into the domain of academics. With his experience as a NIF fellow from an earlier cohort, he assuaged my fears that Ram might object to such a radical departure from the original proposal. This was just one of the many ways in which Akshaya's influence has been profound, even if intangible, in the evolution of the book. He also touched me with his generosity of spirit. When I was once struggling to understand the political context of a certain social reform, Akshaya took the risk of sending me a book at the height of the pandemic lockdown.

The National Archives of India (NAI), where I took a picture of myself for this book, is the place that changed the course of my project. I made eye-opening discoveries in the NAI's repositories relating to British India and princely states as also its library of old books and collection of private papers. The archivists at NAI were unfailingly courteous and helpful. The leads provided by Jaya Ravindran have been productive beyond measure. The void left by her retirement is hard to fill. I must also thank Udey Shankar, Hitender Kumar, Rupam Kumari, Sumita Das Majumdar and Fareed Ahmad for their unstinting assistance.

Needless to say, Nehru Memorial Museum and Library (NMML) has been another major source of information, no less for its rare books than for its collection of private papers. While the staff in all the sections have been uniformly friendly, I must thank in particular Jyothi Luthra in the manuscript section for her personal touch. The Parliament Library of India has also been crucial to my research, particularly because of its repository of committee reports. My friend Ronojoy Sen unlocked its potential by introducing me to an official of the Lok Sabha Secretariat, Antony Jacob, who facilitated access to the sections of the library I wanted to consult. I also spent many useful days in the Central Secretariat Library, although the books there could be more organised.

Since the main battlefields for caste reforms during the colonial period were the Madras and Bombay Presidencies and the princely state of Travancore, it was natural for me to draw heavily from the archival resources available in Chennai and Mumbai. Chennai was also my window to Travancore, which was a tributary state of the Madras Presidency. I made multiple visits to the Chennai-based Tamil Nadu State Archives (TNSA) for the sheer volume of caste-related material stored there and the willingness of the staff to dig out colonial records. I should thank in particular E. Jegan Parthiban in the library section of TNSA for going out of his way to help me. When I ran out of time on my last visit to TNSA, my luck extended to finding an exceptionally helpful student. Darshan, as he prefers to be identified, traced the 176-page file relating to the Kalpathy episode and emailed me a scanned copy of it. I can't thank him enough for his kind gesture. I also benefited from the records available at the Connemara Public Library in Chennai. For the access I gained to the Legislature Library of Maharashtra State, I am grateful to my journalism classmate Sudha Iyer Vemuri. And I am thankful to my journalist friend Geeta Seshu and her partner M.J. Pandey for their warm hospitality in Mumbai. Given the nature of my research, I also obtained documents from the India Office Records at the British Library in London. This was facilitated by a London-based student, Tarit Gautham.

The libraries and archives, which are the haunt of historians, have yielded records mainly on the debates in legislatures and governments. Regarding the battles fought in courts, I depended on the generosity of members of the bar and bench to access old judgments and reports. I also picked their brains on the cases, if any, that they had themselves handled. Such contributors included serving judges, Justice V. Ramasubramanian of the Supreme Court and Justice Gautam Patel of the Bombay High Court, and retired judges, Justices K. Ramaswamy (now deceased), A.P. Shah, M.N. Rao, S.G. Gundewar and K. Chandru. I must thank in particular Justice Chandru, an old comrade in arms, for the pains he took to help me get the elusive Supreme Court records in the Kilvenmani and Belchhi cases. Given the value they added to the chapters on violence, I am indeed lucky to have had Chandru in my corner. This was all before a movie based on his life, *Jai Bhim*, became a blockbuster. I may add that long before I started working on this book, Justice J.S. Verma had discussed with me—and given me a typed copy of—his Rajasthan High Court judgment on temple entry.

Among lawyers, the most notable help came from my childhood friend, P.S. Narasimha, who is now a Supreme Court judge. Though I am a little too radical in his perception, it never stopped him from being affectionate with me nor did it ever hold him back from doing whatever he could to aid my research. When I had, for instance, mentioned that the six-volume set of B. Shiva Rao (*The Framing of India's Constitution*) seemed to be out of print, Narasimha immediately bought one set for me from his regular book supplier, but wouldn't hear of letting me reimburse him for it. Encouraging me to stay the course, Narasimha put at my disposal the deep resources of his library, physical and digital. I often used his centrally located Sundar Nagar office as the base for working with my journalist friend Nandita Sengupta to make notes out of my collection of records related to the book.

To me, Nandita has been my closest experience of Paulo Coelho's famous dictum: 'When you want something, all the universe conspires in helping you to achieve it.' Well after I had entered the writing phase and finished some of the chapters, Nandita called me out of the blue and offered her services to me. I could not have imagined then that she was going to be deeply involved with this project and in a sustained manner. She often travelled long distances to visit my home and help me wade through the piles of papers I had amassed. She found nothing strange about my need to make multiple drafts of notes before I could make drafts of chapters. Her spirited engagement with me on the nuances and ironies of caste was one of the factors that got me through this long and uncertain journey. She was patient enough to read and offer suggestions on the drafts of my chapters while they were still far from complete. If Rivka was the first reader of the completed chapters, Nandita was privy to most chapters even as they were being written. She remained closely engaged with the book during the stages of editing and proofreading. And whenever I thanked her for her countless gestures of kindness, she maintained that she felt privileged to participate in the evolution of the book.

In terms of understanding the import of my archival discoveries, social justice scholar V. Geetha has been tremendously helpful because of the insights she shared with me on Ambedkar, Periyar and the Justice Party. In the little time that was available to wind up her affairs after the announcement of the pandemic lockdown, she took the trouble of couriering me a rare book that I had asked for. When the courier reached me several weeks later, it served as another reminder of my good fortune in having such incredible friends.

The breakthrough I made in unearthing the Patna High Court judgments in the Belchhi case was thanks to a stranger—or, more accurately, a friend of a friend of a friend! On one of the rare occasions when I had driven out of the National Archives to have lunch, I fortuitously bumped into the academic Apoorvanand at the popular Triveni Terrace Café. He introduced me to a friend from Patna, Arshad Ajmal, who was with him. Given my state of mind then, I took it as a cue to share with Ajmal that for a long time I had been struggling to locate the Belchhi judgments of the Patna High Court. Ajmal readily offered to help me, saying he had a friend working in the registry of that very court. That was how, after a search that had stretched to a few more months, Vinod Kumar, who is better known as a Hindi theatre director, played a crucial part in unearthing the papers of that historic case. So, for this priceless find, I must record my gratitude to Vinod Kumar, Arshad Ajmal and Apoorvanand, however unwitting the role of the last.

The lawyers to whom I am indebted for sharing their insights included two veterans, who have regrettably passed on by the time this book is ready for publication. One was Bojja Tharakam, who had appeared and even faced contempt proceedings in the Tsundur case, while the other was P.L. Mimroth, who had initiated the Rajasthan temple-entry case leading to Verma's judgment.

For the different legal battles covered by the book, I have a wide range of lawyers to thank. Those who helped me get a grip on the Bihar cases of mass violence included Abhinav Mukherjee and Rahul Singh. Sangharaj Rupwate was of much help in researching the Mumbai case of police firing on Dalits. S. Sathia Chandran shared with me papers related to some of the Tamil Nadu cases of violence. U.D. Jai Bhima Rao and G. Siva Nageswararao were similarly of help with Andhra Pradesh cases. I must make a special mention of Clifton Rozario who obtained a certified copy on my behalf of an unreported judgment of the Karnataka High Court. It was the one that went on to become the subject matter of the first case decided by the Supreme Court under the untouchability law.

The book benefited from the nuggets of information shared with me by eclectic sources: activist Kavita Krishnan on caste massacres in Bihar, author Dhirendra Jha on the Hindu right, activist Subodh More and scholar Shweta Ahire on Ambedkarite struggles in Maharashtra, academic Parimala V. Rao on caste in the colonial period, journalist Kumar Ashish on his undercover Cobrapost story on the Ranvir Sena, journalist Soutik Biswas on his BBC story on caste violence in Tamil Nadu, academic Dinyar Patel on early Congress history, scholar K. Ragupathi on Dalit leaders in the Madras Presidency, author Arvind Jain on Sati. My knowledge of caste has been enriched by the animated conversations I have had on it over the years with diverse thinkers: Bezwada Wilson, Chandra Bhan Prasad, Rama Lakshmi, Amrith Lal, S. Anand, D. Ravikumar, Kancha Ilaiah, Gita Ramaswamy, Vasanta Lakshmi, D. Shyam Babu, Chitrangada Choudhury, Ravi Nair, Nupur Basu, T.K. Rajalakshmi, Sudipto Mondal, Paul Divakar, Sirivella Prasad, Varun Kumar 'Samantara', Suhas Palshikar, Biju Mathew, Sangeeta Kamat, Mukund Jha. It pains me that three eminent civil servants, P.S. Krishnan, S.R. Sankaran and S. Guhan, who had shaped my outlook on social justice challenges in a caste-ridden society, are not around to see this book.

At the sites of violence that I managed to visit, I have had stirring interactions with some of the victims: Janki Paswan at Belchhi, Naeemuddin Ansari at Bathani Tola, Binod Paswan at Lakshmanpur Bathe, Pragash Rajvanshi at Shankarbigha, Jaladi Moses at Tsundur. Activist Mannam Brahmaiah accompanied me to Tsundur to meet several Dalit victims who spared the time and the emotional labour of speaking to me of their first-hand experience of the dysfunctions of the atrocities law. I regret that due to the space constraints of what is already a long book, I had to leave out the learnings from some of the other atrocity sites that I had visited. None of the considerable research I did, for instance, on Kambalapalli with the help of activist N. Venkatesh and lawyer Manoranjini Kundal is reflected in the book.

I am happy to thank Nirupama Subramanian, author and my journalism classmate, for helping me locate R.R. Banswal, the officer who had long retired since his inquiry into the Jhajjar atrocity. I am also thankful to a journalist friend, the author Moupia Bose, for the trouble she took to pick up for me Justice Gundewar's report on the Ramabai Nagar episode from his house in Pune. It was typically thoughtful of another journalist friend and author, M. Rajshekhar, to lend me books that really came in handy. A friend and former colleague Praveen Dass scoured several libraries in Chennai before he could locate an old book on untouchability which I badly wanted to consult. My close relative Rajini Ravi helped out in translating the Tamil part of the proceedings in the Madras Legislature. Likewise, journalist Akshay Deshmane assisted me in understanding the Marathi parts of documents from Bombay.

A special word of thanks to the political scientist Himadeep Muppidi, one of my oldest and closest friends, for ungrudgingly responding to the many demands I made on him in the course of this book saga. I never hesitated to reach out to him for any help as he has endured right from our school days my unquenchable curiosity about caste and its attendant notions of purity and superiority.

My immersion in this project has served to put in perspective a 1934 framed photograph I have of my maternal grandfather, Erram Satyanarayana, a Gandhi follower in the Nizam's territory. The caption in the frame describes him as 'Treasurer' of the 'Hyderabad Deccan' branch of the Harijan Sevak Sangh. I have come to see this family heirloom as a testament to the unfulfilled potential of solidarity between Shudras and Ati-Shudras that had been envisioned by Phule and Ambedkar to annihilate caste. The serendipity of my personal history coming alive has pushed me to explore the legal history of caste with a renewed sense of mission.

The miracles did not end with the research and writing part. After the manuscript of the book had been completed by the end of 2021, a new set of people joined its journey. The first was Shruti Debi as my literary agent. She took a while to read my manuscript as she was distracted by the repercussions of the sudden closure of a leading publisher called Westland. When her feedback came, Shruti floored me with her perceptive reading of the manuscript and the suggestions that emanated from it. Her structural editing done with a light touch enhanced the readability of my manuscript without detracting from my writing style. It was touching to see the conviction with which she pitched my book to publishers. One of them was Westland, which was reemerging by then in a purely Indian avatar. I was delighted that Westland went on to acquire my book for their Context imprint, thereby fulfilling a long-standing desire for an opportunity to work with the dream team of publisher Karthika V.K. and editor Ajitha G.S.

Given that she is a product of a top law school, I couldn't have asked for an editor better suited than Ajitha to deal with the interface of law and caste central to my book. The experience of working with Ajitha on her edits drove home the blessing of working with someone relating deeply to all the dimensions of the book. I owe thanks to Sanjana Tiwari for a fine job of proofreading. My compatibility with Westland has extended to its design team headed by Saurabh Garge. The very first cover design proposed by Zainul Abid has turned out to be this brilliant one that is so evocative of the theme of the book. I am also looking forward to working with the ever-ebullient Amrita Talwar on the publicity and marketing aspects. Thanks are also due to CEO Gautam Padmanabhan for the confidence with which Westland has invested in this book.

Needless to say, while all the above-mentioned people have contributed variously to the research and writing as also editing and production of the book, any errors of omission and commission are solely mine. Regarding the endorsements carried with the book, I must say that the response from the outstanding experts whom I approached has exceeded my expectations. I am honoured by the kind words of Marc Galanter, Uma Chakravarti, Anand Teltumbde, Satish Deshpande, Ajay Skaria, Christophe Jaffrelot, Meena Kandasamy and Anurag Bhaskar. It was fascinating and instructive to see how each of them connected with the book.

Here's wishing that the goodwill of the people associated with *Caste Pride* will, at the least, translate into a wide readership. And I hope that the kind of support I got while working on this book, institutional and otherwise, will extend to the companion volume that will bring out new material on further elements of the legal history of caste.

INDEX

O

P

STOP